Constitutional Domains

Constitutional Domains

Democracy, Community, Management

Robert C. Post

Harvard University Press
Cambridge, Massachusetts
London, England
1995

LIBRARY OF CONGRESS CATALOGING-IN-PUBLICATION DATA

Post, Robert, 1947–
    Constitutional domains : democracy, community, management /
Robert C. Post.
        p.   cm.
    Includes bibliographical references and index.
    ISBN 0-674-16545-4 (cloth)
    1. United States—Constitutional law—Social aspects.
2. Sociological jurisprudence.   I. Title.
KF4552.P67   1995
342.73—dc20
[347.302]   94-29882
                    CIP

*To my loving parents, Ted and Thelma
and to my beloved family, Fran, Sasha, and Amelia
and to the future I hope they may inhabit*

Contents

Acknowledgments   ix

Introduction: The Social Domains of Constitutional Law   1

  I Community and Human Dignity
- 1 Theories of Constitutional Interpretation   23
- 2 The Social Foundations of Privacy: Community and Self in the Common Law Tort   51
- 3 Cultural Heterogeneity and Law: Pornography, Blasphemy, and the First Amendment   89

  II Democracy and Human Freedom
- 4 The Constitutional Concept of Public Discourse: Outrageous Opinion, Democratic Deliberation, and Hustler Magazine v. Falwell   119
- 5 Between Democracy and Community: The Legal Constitution of Social Form   179

  III Management and Instrumental Reason
- 6 Between Governance and Management: The History and Theory of the Public Forum   199
- 7 Meiklejohn's Mistake: Individual Autonomy and the Reform of Public Discourse   268

Reprise: The Racist Speech Problem   291

Notes   333
Sources   451
Index   453

Acknowledgments

I am blessed with many generous friends and colleagues who have given me the benefit of their time and advice. The essays in this volume have benefited immeasurably from their influence and insights. I would especially like to thank Alexander Aleinikoff, Ed Baker, Vincent Blasi, Jesse Choper, Meir Dan-Cohen, Melvin Eisenberg, Cynthia Fuchs Epstein, Julian Eule, Daniel Farber, Owen Fiss, Merrick Garland, Angela Harris, Don Herzog, Sanford Kadish, Kenneth Karst, Seth Kreimer, Sanford Levinson, Kristen Luker, Michael McConnell, Shelly Messinger, Frank Michelman, Martha Minow, Paul Mishkin, Rachel Moran, Hanna Pitkin, Scott Powe, Eric Rakowski, Terrance Sandalow, Joseph Sax, Frederick Schauer, Ferdinand Schoeman, Philip Selznick, Martin Shapiro, Reva Siegel, Jerome Skolnick, Michael Smith, Geoffrey Stone, Cass Sunstein, Jan Vetter, Jeremy Waldron, James Weinstein, Bernard Williams, and Franklin Zimring. Kristin Largent-Moyes performed heroic and utterly indispensable service in preparing this manuscript for publication; without her unselfish dedication I doubt this book would ever have been produced. My copyeditor, Katarina Rice, was inspirational in her relentless push toward grace and precision. And certainly the essays in this book would not have been written without the loving support of my wife, Fran Layton, to whom I am profoundly grateful.

Constitutional Domains

Introduction

The Social Domains of
Constitutional Law

American constitutional scholars of my generation inhabit the aftermath of legal realism. No longer for us can the law glow with an innocent and pristine autonomy; no longer can it be seen to subsist in elegant and evolving patterns of doctrinal rules. Instead we naturally and inevitably read legal standards as pragmatic instruments of policy. We seek to use the law as a tool to accomplish social ends, and the essence of our scholarly debate revolves around the question of what those ends ought to be.

This orientation has carried with it the unfortunate tendency to separate social ends from the concrete legal arrangements in which they must necessarily find their ultimate fulfillment. Many years ago Lon Fuller identified this tendency and subjected it to a searching critique. He observed that "any social goal, to be meaningful, must be conceived in structural terms, not simply as something that happens to people when their social ordering is rightly directed."[1]

The implication of Fuller's point is that constitutional values often subsist in the very legal structures in which they find their actual embodiment. These structures frequently involve patterns of rules that establish recognizable forms of "social ordering." Constitutional values inseparably inhere both in these forms of social ordering and in the experience these forms facilitate and make possible. For this reason the realization of constitutional principles requires careful attention to the relationship between constitutional law and systemic forms of social order.

The essays in this volume represent an effort to reinterpret constitutional law in the light of this insight. The essays seek to demonstrate the pervasively important ways in which essential constitutional principles are embodied in specific forms of social order that carry their own internal logic and integrity. Three distinct forms of social order are especially relevant to understanding our constitutional law. I call these community,

1

management, and democracy. To put the matter briefly and aphoristically, one might say that law creates community when it seeks authoritatively to interpret and enforce shared mores and norms; it is managerial when it organizes social life instrumentally to achieve specific objectives; and it fosters democracy by establishing the social arrangements that carry for us the meaning of collective self-determination.

Each of the three forms of social order—community, management, and democracy—embodies a different social goal that requires for its fulfillment a distinct kind of internal logic and coherence. The three are for this reason in tension with one another in significant respects. And yet, as the essays in this volume argue in detail, these three forms of social order also presuppose and depend upon one another in ways that are fundamental and essential. We might say that community, management, and democracy are simultaneously complementary and contradictory.

This paradoxical relationship leads me in the essays that follow to use a characteristic metaphor of "domains" and "boundaries." Within a given domain the logic of a specific form of social order will hold sway, excluding its competitors. But because these forms of social order are ultimately interdependent, the excluded logics cannot be suppressed. They are instead displaced, so that constitutional law can usefully be conceptualized as a process of establishing boundaries between differing and incompatible social domains.

I have selected the essays in this volume with particular attention to making historically and sociologically visible the efforts of American constitutional law to establish a distinctive and bounded domain of democracy. I have tried to illustrate the many subtle ways in which this democratic domain has required for its full realization the maintenance of the complementary but incongruous domains of community and management, and I have attempted to make salient the elemental but largely unappreciated struggles within our constitutional tradition about how the boundaries between these distinct realms are to be fixed.

In thus partitioning the social world among different forms of social order, American constitutional law has not itself functioned as a transparent instrument. We must understand the law generally as a social system that impinges upon the behavior of those it seeks to regulate. By varying the quality of its rules, the complexion of its reasoning, or the allocation of power within its organization, the law can alter its own institutional characteristics so as to make them more or less compatible with distinct kinds of social orders. Like a chameleon, the law transforms itself to mimic and enhance the social domains it establishes and sustains.

The essays in this volume use First Amendment doctrine to illustrate these complex dynamics. First Amendment jurisprudence provides many occasions to observe how constitutional law divides social life into the discrete domains of community, management, and democracy, and also how constitutional law itself changes in the process.

In the remainder of this introduction I offer an outline of this general approach to legal analysis. First I sketch the defining characteristics of community, management, and democracy; then I discuss the ways in which the law itself varies in these different domains; and finally I offer a broad overview of the mutual interdependence among these three important forms of social order.

Community

Community, as Philip Selznick writes in *The Moral Commonwealth*, turns on "a framework of shared beliefs, interests, and commitments" that "establish a common faith or fate, a personal identity, a sense of belonging, and a supportive structure of activities and relationships."[2] Laws instantiating community seek to reinforce this shared world of common faith and fate. They characteristically articulate and enforce norms that they take to define both individual and social identity.

Chapter 2 offers an extended account of the common law tort of invasion of privacy, which is an exemplary instance of the law organizing itself to instantiate the social order of community. Some have contended that the very existence of legal rights is incompatible with the ability of law to serve this function, because legal rights necessarily imply "an image of the rights-bearer as a self-determining, unencumbered, individual, a being connected to others only by choice."[3] But, in Chapter 2, I argue that this contention is inaccurate, for the rights created by the tort of invasion of privacy explicitly serve to define and defend social norms, which the tort conceptualizes as essential for maintaining the stable identity of individuals. Like other legal actions redressing "dignitary harms,"[4] the tort conceives personal dignity as subsisting in socially defined forms of respect.[5] The tort protects these forms of respect and thereby safeguards the particular community that makes this dignity possible.

Legal attempts to instantiate community always rest on claims that are essentially normative. For this reason the empirical fact of a common cultural identity must be distinguished from the continual effort of the law to articulate and enforce such an identity. The former exists in the realm of descriptive phenomena, perhaps to be ascertained by the investigations of competent social scientists. The latter is a normative orientation adopted by the law whenever it seeks to speak for a particular vision of community. The purpose of using law to instantiate community is to realize a form of social life in which we may share common "commitments and identifications" that will enable us "to determine from case to case what is good, or valuable, or what ought to be done."[6] The extent to which such a common culture already actually exists might be highly relevant to this purpose, but it is not by itself determinative.[7]

Because the purpose of using law to establish community is essentially normative, legal attempts to accomplish this purpose are intrinsically contestable. The normative force of community mores is neither given nor fixed, but always the result of interpretation and critique. Contingent historical circumstances will affect whether legal efforts to articulate and enforce cultural values will be received as integrative and harmonious or whether they will provoke bitter controversy. The former is likely when law seeks to uphold values that are in fact widely shared, the latter when law is perceived as taking sides in divisive cultural disputes. Where the formal jurisdiction of the law is defined geographically and spans a diversity of cultures, legal endeavors to assert the values of a single dominant culture may also be attacked as hegemonic. Such disagreements are more or less endemic to the underlying effort to fuse culture and the state by having the law articulate and enforce a common cultural identity.

Legal attempts to establish the social order of community are also subject to a different and more fundamental challenge. Such attempts must ultimately be justified on the grounds that the conduct regulated by the law ought to be governed by shared social norms. But this justification may be resisted. It may be argued that the law ought to structure its interventions according to the principles of a different form of social order altogether.

Management

An increasingly common alternative is for law to structure its interventions according to the form of social order I call management. Management, as Philip Selznick writes, "suggests rational, efficiency-minded, goal-driven organization."[8] Management arranges social life for the achievement of given objectives. It ignores the independent requirements of community values or identity, following instead the logic of instrumental rationality.

The distinction between community and management can be seen in the contrast between a criminal law that seeks to predicate punishment on a moral allocation of blame and responsibility, and a criminal law that attempts instead narrowly and strictly to fulfill the goal of preventing harmful forms of behavior. By seeking to align criminal punishment with relevant cultural norms, the former displays the authority of community; by seeking instead instrumentally to achieve an explicit objective, the latter regulates conduct with the authority of management.

In general the twentieth century has witnessed a significant shift from the former to the latter. This may be seen in the striking transformation of older forms of duty-based tort law, which attempted to use the normative construction of the reasonable person to infuse legal rules with the values of the ambient community, into the more modern forms of strict and efficiency-based liability rules, which seek to use tort law as a means of engineering the accomplishment of discrete objectives, such as the achievement of efficient allocations of risk.

The triumph of the progressive vision of the administrative state has ensured the increased prominence of management in modern law. This is because management is necessary whenever the state, in Walter Lippmann's prescient words, wishes to exercise "mastery" over the "drift" of society, and so "to deal with it deliberately, devise its social organization, alter its tools, formulate its method, educate and control it."[9] The trend toward management compounds itself, because the growing rationalization of society undermines cultural norms that might otherwise sustain the alternative authority of community.

Laws establishing the social order of management can be controversial in a variety of ways. The goals that they seek to achieve may be challenged. In the concluding chapter, for example, I discuss how disputes over hate speech regulation in universities can most profitably be understood as disagreements over the underlying mission of educational institutions. Managerial laws may also be challenged because they do not actually achieve their goals. An important strand of the contemporary debate concerning public regulation of the media turns on whether such regulation in fact achieves its objective of establishing a fairer and more informative press. Controversies of this kind are implied by and internal to the logic of management.

A more fundamental challenge to managerial laws involves the repu-

diation of managerial authority itself. This kind of challenge can be illustrated by Justice Goldberg's famous query in Griswold v. Connecticut.
Appealing to "the traditional relation of the family—a relation as old and
as fundamental as our entire civilization," Goldberg asked whether the
Constitution could possibly permit, in the absence of "a showing of a
compelling subordinating state interest," a law requiring "that all hus-
bands and wives must be sterilized after two children have been born to
them."[10] The point of Goldberg's question was to reveal our reluctance
to find such a statute constitutional merely upon a showing that it bears
some instrumental connection to a legitimate end. Goldberg suggested
that the constitutionality of the statute ought instead to be assessed by
reference to the "traditions and [collective] conscience of our people."[11]
In essence, therefore, Goldberg was advocating that the constitutionality
of regulations of procreation within the family ought in most instances to
be determined by reference to community norms rather than by reference
to the instrumental logic of management.[12]

Democracy

In contemporary constitutional adjudication, it is most common to find
both community and management challenged by the claims of yet a third
form of social order, which I call democracy. In the succinct words of Karl
Marx, democracy entails "a self-determination of the people."[13] Democracy carries this same specific meaning within the American constitutional
tradition: "Democracy promises collective self-determination."[14] Collective self-determination, like any other value, requires particular social
arrangements for its realization. In this volume I shall speak of constitutional law as seeking to establish democracy when it promulgates the rules
necessary for these arrangements.

This formulation is meant to break fundamentally with the approach of
a previous generation of constitutional scholarship, which conflated self-
determination with "majoritarian democracy," which is to say with a
"commitment to control by a majority of the governed."[15] This approach
is subject to the same critique that Habermas so tellingly makes of Schumpeter. It "defines democracy by procedures" rather than by the underlying values that the procedures are meant to embody.[16] The significance
of majority rule lies in its function as a mechanism to realize the value of
collective self-determination. Viewing majoritarianism as an end in itself
leads to difficulties that are plain in John Hart Ely's work. He recognizes

that simple majoritarian processes can through prejudice turn oppressive and antidemocratic, but he nevertheless struggles to present a purely procedural account, which is inherently incapable of offering a convincing explanation of this phenomenon.[17]

Rousseau saw early on that the question of collective self-determination was theoretically inseparable from the question of individual self-determination. Democracy locates agency in the people collectively, who are authorized to govern themselves. But we could not plausibly characterize as democratic a society in which "the people" were given the power to determine the nature of their government, but in which the individuals who made up "the people" did not experience themselves as free to choose their own political fate. Imagine a society, for example, in which every detail of daily life was fixed by continual votes, so that the collective will of the society was unrestrained, but in which the individuals composing the society felt continuously oppressed.[18] We would most likely reject such a society as fascist or totalitarian. Jean Piaget had it exactly right, therefore, when he observed that democracy requires us "to replace the unilateral respect of authority by the mutual respect of autonomous wills."[19] The essential problematic of democracy thus lies in the reconciliation of individual and collective autonomy.

The American constitutional tradition understands this reconciliation to take place within an open structure of communication. I call this structure "public discourse." If public discourse is kept free for the autonomous participation of individual citizens, and if government decision-making is subordinated to the public opinion produced by public discourse, there is the possibility that citizens will come to identify with the state as representative of their own collective self-determination. Protecting freedom of public discourse thus satisfies a necessary (although not sufficient) condition for the realization of democratic self-government. That is why our constitutional tradition regards the First Amendment as "the guardian of our democracy,"[20] even though the Amendment is itself frankly anti-majoritarian in purpose and effect.

The reconciliation of individual and collective self-determination entails a serious internal tension. On the one hand, a democratic social structure must provide an appropriate space for individual autonomy. Within that space democracy must function negatively; it must refuse to foreclose the possibility of individual choice and self-development by imposing preexisting community norms or given managerial ends. On the other hand, a democratic social structure must also function positively, to foster an identification with the processes that enable the collective experience of self-determination. I argue in Chapters 4 and 7 that these processes presuppose forms of social cohesion that depend upon community norms and that these processes also often require strategic managerial intervention.

There is thus a paradox at the center of democracy. Democratic theorists tend to finesse this contradiction by conceptualizing the community and managerial structures necessary for democratic social cohesion as voluntary—hence Brandeis' famous observation that democracy "substitutes self-restraint for external restraint."[21] But in point of fact enforceable legal obligations are sometimes required, and for this reason laws attempting to establish democracy are intrinsically contestable. It can always be maintained either that they have overly stressed the preconditions of social cohesion and hence have impaired the individual autonomy necessary for democratic legitimacy, or, conversely, that they have overly stressed individual autonomy and hence have impaired the social cohesion that is equally necessary for democratic legitimacy. This tension is internal to the domain of democracy.

It is also possible, however, to transcend that domain and to argue that particular aspects of social life ought not to be organized according to a democratic logic. Democratic forms of social ordering have a particular and bounded sphere of appropriate application, which is defined by reference either to those aspects of persons deemed morally necessary for the participation of autonomous citizens or to those aspects of society deemed necessary for the success of collective processes of self-determination. It is always open to contention whether specific behavior regulated by the law ought to lie outside the boundaries of this sphere and be ordered instead according to the logic of community or management.

During the era of Lochner v. New York,[22] for example, the sphere of democratic authority was delineated by reference to the will of the individual citizen, as concretely expressed in the institution of private property. It was believed that depriving a citizen of his "property, which is the fruit and badge of his liberty, is to . . . leave him a slave."[23] Hence "due protection for the rights of property" was "regarded as a vital principle of republican institutions."[24] Accordingly, property rights were strictly enforced as a bulwark of the struggle of democracy against socialism. But this underlying concept of the person crumbled during the triumph of the New Deal, and a different moral image of the autonomous citizen emerged that focused on the independence of reason rather than of will.

As a consequence the First Amendment was fundamentally reinterpreted along democratic lines, and regulations of property were largely relegated to the managerial authority of the state.

Analogous debates about the proper scope of democratic authority are reflected in contemporary disputes over the application of substantive due process principles that seek to safeguard from state control the capacity "to define one's identity that is central to any concept of liberty."[25] When Justice Brennan interpreted Griswold in Eisenstadt v. Baird as protecting "the right of the individual, married or single, to be free from unwarranted governmental intrusion into matters so fundamentally affecting a person as the decision to bear or beget a child,"[26] he was in essence repudiating the logic of community evoked by Justice Goldberg. Brennan was seeking instead to bring the domain of childbearing and its attendant sexuality within the logic of democratic authority. Brennan's implicit claim was that this domain was so essential to the autonomy of the individual citizen that its routine subjection to either managerial imperatives or community norms would be inconsistent with the requirements of a democratic social structure.[27]

American constitutional law is exceptional in the intensity of its commitment to the social order of democracy. This is most plainly visible in our First Amendment jurisprudence, which is demonstrably idiosyncratic among national legal systems because of its ambition to maintain public discourse free from the control of community norms. Recent Canadian decisions upholding regulations of public discourse prohibiting pornography and hate speech are typical of the tendency of other nations legally to subordinate public discourse to fundamental community values of respect and civility.[28] American constitutional law generally condemns such efforts as impermissibly paternalistic.

Although the American position follows from the internal logic of democracy, it is not required by that logic. It could be said either that Canadians experience the withdrawal of legal support from fundamental community values as compromising the social cohesion necessary for collective self-determination, or, conversely, that Americans experience legal enforcement of such values as compromising the individual autonomy necessary for self-government. How a national legal system negotiates between these dialectically opposing positions is a matter of contingent historical and cultural circumstance.

In this regard, the American position has no doubt been deeply influenced by our classic commitment to individualism—to that "calm considered feeling which disposes each citizen to isolate himself from the mass of his fellows."[29] Without question this individualism has sensitized us to the personal autonomy side of the democratic equation. And, more subtly, it has transformed our sense of community identity into something that is experienced as voluntaristic, provisional, and negotiated. This means that we understand the diverse and antagonistic communities within American life to perpetuate themselves by competing for the allegiance of individuals.

The American effort to exempt public discourse from the legal imposition of community norms might in fact be analogized to the truce among hostile religious groups created by the Establishment Clause. Just as the Clause ended competition among religious groups for domination of the nascent American state by placing government altogether off-limits to religious control, so the First Amendment has since the New Deal enforced a similar neutrality within the sphere of public discourse. That sphere has been placed off-limits to the control of all community norms, and hence all communities are free to use public discourse as a "marketplace of communities" to compete on equal terms in the search for new adherents.

Social Orders and the Concept of the Person

Management, community, and democracy each assume a different image of the person. Within management, persons are objectified. They are relevant only as facts of nature to be arranged for the achievement of the state's purposes. Within community, persons are normalized. They are conceived as thickly embedded within a constitutive skein of social norms that simultaneously defines their identity and invests them with dignity. Within democracy, persons are represented as autonomous. They are imagined as beings who seek to determine their own fate and who are consequently able to transcend both the constitutive norms that happen to define them and the managerial purposes that constrict them.

These differences may perhaps be made more concrete by considering the distinct ways in which the law is required to organize itself to fulfill the different prerequisites of management, community, and democracy. Consider regulations of the theater. A legislature concerned with the dangers of fire might pass a statute, call it statute M, which bans all theatrical costumes made from flammable material. The purpose of statute M is to control the behavior of actors so as to achieve the end of safety. A system is thus created in which the legislature directs and the actors obey. In this system agency is transferred from the actors to the legislature. The actors exist only as counters in the comprehensive scheme of the legislature.

Compare statute M to a different statute, call it statute C, in which actors are charged with the duty of taking all "reasonable" safety precautions. Because the measure of "reasonableness" is "the normal standard of community behavior,"[30] statute C necessarily assumes that actors can understand and apply community standards. It assumes that actors possess this knowledge and capacity because they are competent and appropriately socialized members of the community.

Statute C thus seeks to enforce standards that are conceived as internal to the very identity of the actors. Statute M, in contrast, imposes standards that are externally dictated. Thus while statute M objectifies actors, statute C understands itself as requiring actors to behave in ways that they themselves would regard as responsible. In this way statute C restores to the actors a normalized form of agency.

Statute C also demands that actors exercise complex forms of judgment, far more complex than those required by statute M. This is because community standards are characteristically "flexible, substantive, and circumstantial" in nature.[31] Managerial legislation like statute M, on the other hand, typically strives to sweep with scythe-like precision and indifference through the entangled fields of such contextualized community norms. From the perspective of statute M, community norms can only interfere with the clear line of command emanating from the legislature.

Suppose now these statutes were challenged under the First Amendment as inconsistent with our system of freedom of expression. Because the theater is undoubtedly included within public discourse, a court would analyze the constitutional issues according to the logic of democracy. It would ask whether the statutes unacceptably compromise the ability of those engaged in theatrical productions to participate in the communicative processes necessary for democratic self-determination.

Presupposed by this question is the notion that actors can make original contributions to public discourse. This is a very different representation of the actor than that projected by either statute C or statute M. The actor is envisioned as an autonomous subject rather than as an object or as a normalized agent. The actor is deemed capable of transcending the internalized norms that, from the perspective of community, create individual identity. The actor is also deemed capable of resisting managerial regulation by seizing the power to determine his own ends.

The Law as a Form of Social Order

These examples serve to illustrate the ways in which management, community, and democracy each imply distinct configurations of persons and of the social worlds those persons inhabit. They also illustrate the ways in which the law can modify its own institutional interventions so as to become consistent with these different configurations. The law can vary its image of the "legal subject" so as to match that image with the form of social order that the law seeks to establish. It is not useful to ask which of these different images is more "real," for reality here is a function of the social order itself.[32]

It is important to note that the legal system can transform itself in other, equally important ways when it attempts to establish social domains. When the law seeks to make itself compatible with the social order of community, it characteristically defers to lay decision-makers, like juries, who are instructed to apply the extralegal standards of the ambient culture. When the law seeks to pattern itself on a managerial social order, it most often follows classic Weberian models of instrumental rationality by concentrating decision-making power in legal professionals who promulgate rules that are more or less impervious to traditional community norms. When the law seeks to render itself compatible with democracy, it tends to stress judicial explanation and justification. Just as democracy envisions collective self-determination as occurring through processes of deliberative exchange, so the law itself embodies these communicative processes when it carefully assesses the quality and significance of regulatory concerns and measures them against competing commitments to self-government.

The difference between these organizational forms of law is not primarily one of outcomes. Statutes C and M may penalize exactly the same forms of behavior, and these prohibitions may be found constitutional by a court when challenged under the First Amendment. Yet the law will in each instance have reached its judgment within a different institutional and discursive space;[33] it will have employed different concepts of the legal subject, different kinds of legal rules, different patterns of legal reasoning, and different allocations of power within legal institutions.

There are, I think, two reasons for these systematic differences. First, community, management, and democracy represent different normative commitments. If the law commits itself to arranging social life according to the dictates of a shared cultural identity, it will structure itself according to the requirements of community. If the law chooses to order social life instrumentally to achieve specific results or to protect a realm of collective self-determination, it will structure itself according to the principles of management or democracy. I shall use the term "authority" to capture this sense of a set of fundamental commitments that hold our allegiance. The institutional and discursive spaces of community, management, and democracy are different because decisions within each are settled by reference to distinct kinds of authority.

Second, authority inheres not merely in abstract purposes, but also in historically specific social arrangements. Our legal and national experience has led us to associate the values of community, management, and democracy with particular social structures that for us carry their own internal logic and integrity. We are of course free to reinterpret these values, or to repudiate them altogether and to commit ourselves to other forms of social ordering. But we are not free arbitrarily to divorce these values from the particular forms of social ordering through which their meanings have been conveyed. We are not free to write on a clean slate. Thus processes of historical differentiation function to distinguish the institutional and discursive spaces of community, management, and democracy.

The Interdependence of Democracy, Community, and Management

Although democracy, community, and management are each distinctive in ways that flow from their fundamentally disparate purposes, they are nevertheless interrelated in important and systematic ways. It is clear, for example, that democracy presupposes management, for without management democratic government could never organize to accomplish the specific ends selected by the processes of self-determination.[34] Yet democracy is truncated within managerial domains, because management represses and objectifies the autonomous subject. Management is equally impossible within democratic domains, because management requires that goals be taken as given, whereas self-determination requires that social space be structured so as to enable all goals potentially to be called into question. It follows that the continued health of both democracy and management requires that the law fix and maintain an appropriate boundary between the two.

An analogous point can be made about the structural interconnection between democracy and community. The social order of democracy exists only because of our commitment to the value of self-determination.[35]

This commitment has the peculiar property of demanding that the application and enforcement of other community values be suspended within the boundaries of democracy. It is thus easy to mistake democracy for an autochthonous social formation. But if we inquire into the origins of this antecedent commitment to self-determination, it becomes immediately clear that the commitment is historically contingent, and that it arises because democracy happens to be embedded within a culture that desires to foster the end of self-government.

Thus it would be self-defeating for democratic authority to expand to the point of displacing the very culture that fosters the unique value necessary for the maintenance of a democratic social order. In this way the project of democracy "recognizes the impossibility of the complete realization of democracy."[36] Democracy must sustain a complementary but hostile relationship with community. Democracy negates community within the arena of democracy's application, yet democracy depends upon community both to provide external support for the continued existence of that arena and to establish within that arena the grounds of social cohesion necessary to facilitate the processes of collective self-determination.

The continued health of democracy requires, therefore, that the law fix and sustain an appropriate boundary between democracy and community. The location of that boundary will no doubt be unstable and contestable. It will in part depend upon the law's interpretation of the extent and reach of the ambient culture's desire for self-government. But it will also depend upon the law's sense of the legal support required for the continued viability of community itself.

These conclusions can be supplemented by analyzing the concepts of person presupposed by management, democracy, and community. Instrumental reason objectifies persons, but persons who are objects exist merely as things to be regulated. Hence they cannot themselves define and direct instrumental rationality. It follows that managerial domains, which are inhabited by objectified persons, must necessarily presuppose other forms of social order inhabited by persons who are agents capable of selecting among possible social ends.

Democracy, of course, imagines persons as just such autonomous agents who continually choose their purposes and ends. The difficulty, however, is that persons who do not already have an identity are incapable of meaningful choice. Choices have significance only within the context of an anterior horizon of commitments.[37] This suggests that democracy always presupposes community, which alone can fashion persons with the identity capable of giving content to the value of autonomy.[38]

The clear implications of this analysis are that the managerial domains of the administrative state must be carefully evaluated for their adverse effects on democracy and community, and that even democracy itself must be limited when it threatens to preempt the community upon which it depends.

Forms of Social Order and Constitutional Adjudication

It may be helpful to review briefly the argument I have so far advanced. Law seeks to support and establish forms of social order that will make possible the realization of certain values or purposes. I have sketched three such structures: democracy, which seeks to embody the purpose of self-determination; management, which seeks to attain the benefits of instrumental reason; and community, which seeks to sustain the identity implicit in common cultural norms.

Democracy, management, and community each exert a powerful and distinct influence on the institution of the law, and in particular on the nature of judicial reasoning. Courts generally feel an obligation to justify their decisions. This obligation is especially pressing in constitutional adjudication, where courts must assess the validity of democratically en-acted and otherwise legitimate laws. Courts can justify their decisions, however, only if they can reason from basic premises which they share with their audience. Purposive social structures like democracy, manage-ment, and community provide such premises. This is because we are generally convinced that fulfillment of their purposes entails distinct and internally consistent forms of logic that have been made cogent through experience. That is why these social structures establish an authority capable of conferring a recognizable grammatical shape upon a court's overarching pattern of discursive and doctrinal justification.

These consequences are plainly visible within First Amendment juris-prudence. Doctrines of freedom of expression are primarily determined by the social domains to which courts allocate communicative acts. Thus the point of Chapter 6 is to show that courts apply to speech within managerial domains the same instrumental logic that they apply to man-agerial domains generally. This logic is fundamentally incompatible with what are ordinarily regarded as the most basic principles of general First Amendment doctrine. I attempt to show in Chapters 4, 5, and 8 that many of these more familiar principles of First Amendment doctrine are in fact derivable from the distinctive logic of democratic authority, and that they may have little relevance where that authority is not itself deemed to be applicable.

The gulf that separates this methodological perspective from the dominant approach to First Amendment law can perhaps best be illustrated by contrasting it with Frederick Schauer's intelligent and influential book *Free Speech: A Philosophical Enquiry*.[39] As Schauer's subtitle suggests, he seeks to analyze First Amendment jurisprudence philosophically in order to assess why expression ought to be protected. His premise is that because the First Amendment safeguards "freedom of speech," there must be some philosophical "free speech principle" that uniquely protects expression.

The essays in this volume, on the other hand, begin from the very different premise that value is embodied in a social system taken as a whole, not in its constituent parts, and that therefore speech cannot be abstracted from its concrete social context. It follows that we will comprehend a good deal more about the shape of our actual First Amendment jurisprudence by understanding the connection of speech to the specific social orders of democracy, community, and management than by searching for any general "free speech principle."

This conclusion distinguishes the essays in this volume from much contemporary First Amendment scholarship, which aims to ascertain a fundamental and essential rationale for protecting freedom of expression. In my view this quest is self-defeating, for the necessary concomitant of imposing any such single rationale would be the effacement of important and indispensable forms of social differentiation. So, for example, Geoffrey Stone has recently proposed "distrust of government regulation" as the comprehensive "bedrock" of First Amendment jurisprudence.[40] But, as I demonstrate in Chapter 6, courts routinely trust and defer to government officials within managerial domains, and these domains would be unable to accomplish their purposes were this not the case. Similarly, Martin Redish has proposed that the "one true value" of the First Amendment is "individual self-realization."[41] Yet courts routinely permit actions to enforce social norms and redress dignitary harms within domains dedicated to community,[42] and, as I argue in Chapters 4 and 5, it is clear that such domains would suffer irreparably were courts to act otherwise.

These examples illustrate that both the conceptualization and protection accorded speech will vary drastically depending upon the social domain to which the speech is judicially assigned. In fact what are ordinarily called personal "rights" to freedom of expression might perhaps most fundamentally be understood as mechanisms by which law defines and establishes such domains. It is for this reason crucial to explore how courts decide to locate the boundaries between social domains. Sometimes, to be sure, courts do not self-consciously construct such boundaries at all; they simply follow *stare decisis*, which ensures that the border between social domains will remain relatively stable. *Stare decisis* makes it probable that given aspects of social life will be analyzed according to generally consistent forms of judicial logic, and it thus helps provide constitutional adjudication with the appearance of "normal science."

But *stare decisis* can be broken, and the boundary between social domains can always be contested. In such circumstances courts must justify not merely their decisions but the authority under which their decisions are reached. They must justify, that is, assigning regulated conduct to one social domain or another. At such moments the dialectical relationship of the law to its ambient culture stands starkly exposed. Sometimes courts will simply reflect the form of social order they perceive to be already operative in the relevant patch of social life. Sometimes, however, courts will intervene to seek to establish the form of social order they independently perceive to be necessary or appropriate.

In either case courts must convincingly articulate and justify the set of authoritative premises that will guide legal regulation of the matter at hand. These premises encapsulate the purposes that the law wishes to accomplish. As the law dedicates itself to particular purposes, so does it also define itself by revealing its values and vision. The public justification of these values thus must finally depend upon an articulation of the identity of the political community that the law purports to represent. Ultimately there can be no warrant for the decision to allocate a particular aspect of social life to a specific social domain other than that the decision is a wise and convincing interpretation of ambient cultural values.

This is a powerful conclusion, for it implies yet another sense in which community is fundamental. The conclusion in fact requires us to distinguish two distinct senses in which community is relevant for law. On the one hand, community is a particular social order thematized and established by the law with discrete and ascertainable boundaries. We have already seen why this particular social order is fundamental with respect to its complementary domains of democracy and management. On the other hand, however, community is also a comprehensive social milieu that makes possible the very existence of the rule of law as we now know it, which is to say as an enterprise that depends upon practices of justification.[43]

Community in this larger, more embracing sense is a prerequisite for the institution of law itself. In particular, as I argue in Chapter 1, community in this more inclusive sense underwrites the very possibility of constitutional adjudication. Judicial articulation of constitutional law must ultimately depend upon what I term "responsive interpretation," which is the effort to read the Constitution in the light of what John Dewey once called "The Great Community" of the nation.[44] Those who would deny the existence of such a community, like contemporary postmodernists, pose a fundamental and searching challenge to the continuing project of constitutional interpretation, as they do also to the very notion of the rule of law.[45]

Moments in constitutional law when courts must justify their allocation of conduct to particular social domains have for good reason caused intense discomfort among academic commentators. They leave courts exposed and vulnerable. Courts cannot merely thematize and incorporate ambient cultural norms, as where the law seeks to establish community in the narrower sense of a specific social domain. Instead courts must themselves display those norms; they must actively step forward and reason as representative members of the community. Stripped of the technical comforts of precedent, courts have no choice but to stake their choice of authority on the naked quality of their judgment in speaking for the common faith and fate of the nation.

These tend to be dramatic and uncertain moments, when legitimacy depends precariously upon character and leadership. Because such moments can erupt at any time, constitutional adjudication characteristically assumes a strange and intoxicating rhythm, simultaneously stable and flexible, simultaneously bound and willful, simultaneously doctrinal and political.

Conclusion

I have attempted in this introduction to summarize the intellectual program of the essays in this volume. My précis, however, enjoys the advantage of hindsight. Several of the essays that follow were written at a time when the general outline of this program was far from clear, and the reader should therefore not expect perfect consistency. Each essay attempts to unfold its topic on the basis of the insights available to it at the time, and on the whole these insights have proven to be complementary rather than contradictory. There are, of course, particular aspects of the essays that I would not now wholeheartedly endorse. For example, in Chapter 6, which is the oldest article in the collection, I establish a binary opposition between governance and management which today seems to me overly crude; I would now be much more inclined to stress the triangular relationship among management, democracy, and community. But since the major thrust of Chapter 6 is to make visible the central role of managerial authority in contemporary constitutional law, and since the concept of governance serves mainly as a foil to this end, I am content to let the essay stand.

With the possible exception of Chapter 5, the essays that follow were written to respond to particular exigent problems of constitutional or common law. The intellectual program I have summarized in this introduction emerged only as it was necessary or useful in illuminating these specific problems. I have decided to let the essays retain their original focus on particular issues, because I fundamentally believe that the best test of the structural analysis I am offering is its ability helpfully to engage salient legal questions. I have therefore chosen to leave the essays largely unedited, with only minor amendments primarily to avoid serious redundancy and to maintain a rudimentary consistency. I have also chosen to excise some of the denser and more technical legal material.

The general outline of the book is, I hope, self-explanatory. Part I explores the realm of community, which I identify in Chapters 1 and 2 as the foundation of both constitutional interpretation and human dignity. Chapter 3 introduces the concept of individualism, and it argues that despite the claims of modern pluralists to respect the value of diversity, pluralism in fact fits comfortably within the authority of community.

Part II shifts the focus to democracy and the domain of human autonomy. Chapter 4 discusses the First Amendment's pervasive attempts to free public discourse from the imposition of community norms. Chapter 5, which is in many respects the centerpiece of the book, offers a general theoretical formulation of democratic authority and of its relationship to community.

Part III turns to an investigation of the world of management. Chapter 6 demonstrates how the Court has used public forum doctrine to establish managerial domains for the regulation of speech, while Chapter 7 addresses important managerial issues raised by contemporary efforts to revitalize a Meiklejohnian account of First Amendment jurisprudence.

The concluding chapter I have called a "reprise" because it evaluates arguments for the regulation of racist speech, which requires a comprehensive discussion of the full spectrum of relationships among democracy, community, and management. The essay therefore revisits and summarizes many of the themes developed in earlier chapters.

I

Community and Human Dignity

1

Theories of Constitutional Interpretation

Modern democracy invites us to replace the notion of a regime founded upon laws, of a legitimate power, by the notion of a regime founded upon the legitimacy of a debate as to what is legitimate and what is illegitimate—a *debate which is necessarily without any guarantor and without any end.*
— Claude Lefort

In 1979 Ernest Chambers was a barber who had for nine years represented a predominantly black district of Omaha in the Nebraska unicameral legislature. He had been brought up in "a religious strait-jacket" in the fundamentalist Church of God and Christ, but as he had grown older he had come to renounce Christianity and all belief in God. Consequently he was uncomfortable when the chaplain hired by the legislature opened each session with prayer. In fact he felt compelled to leave the legislative chamber, so that he and the chaplain were "almost in a race to see whether [the chaplain could] get to the front before [Chambers could] get out the back door."[1]

The chaplain of the Nebraska legislature during that time was Robert E. Palmer, a Presbyterian clergyman who had ministered to the legislators since 1965. His prayers were short, almost perfunctory. He strove to make them nonsectarian, to reflect "just civil religion in America," which he understood to consist of "the Judeo-Christian tradition," the "kind of religious expressions that are common to the vast, overwhelming majority of most all Americans." He viewed the purpose of his prayers to be the provision of "an opportunity for Senators to be drawn closer to their understanding of God as they understand God, in order that the divine wisdom might be theirs as they conduct their business for the day." And so he would, for example, pray "in the name of Jesus—our Friend, our Saviour, our Example, our Guide," and he would "ask" that the senators come to realize that "they are part of the team working together to win the game for the benefit of the people of this state."[2]

Chambers attempted to convince his colleagues to end the practice of legislative prayer. When they refused, he took the characteristically American step of filing suit in federal court. His claim was elegantly simple: the payment of a state salary to the minister of a single Christian denomination for fourteen years for the purpose of offering official prayers to the state legislature was a violation of the establishment clause of the First Amendment to the United States Constitution. That clause provides: "Congress shall make no law respecting an establishment of religion."[3]

The trial court held that while the payment of the chaplain's salary violated the establishment clause, the observance of legislative prayer did not.[4] The appellate court went even further and declared that the whole "prayer practice" was unconstitutional.[5] The case was then accepted for decision by the United States Supreme Court, by which time the concrete concerns of Ernest Chambers and Robert Palmer had dwindled to little or no moment. Chambers' lawsuit had become merely a medium through which the Court could ponder the legal meaning for the entire nation of the establishment clause. The methods by which the Court ascertains this constitutional meaning are of the utmost legal and political importance. Ernest Chambers' lawsuit would prove to be the occasion for an unusually clear and dramatic display of these methods.

Judicial Review and Constitutional Interpretation

Sometimes, although rarely, the words of the Constitution appear to speak for themselves. In such circumstances the Constitution does not seem to require interpretation. Article I, Section 3, Clause 1 of the Constitution, for example, states that "the Senate of the United States shall be composed of two Senators from each State." If a third California senator should one day present herself for accreditation in Washington, D.C., no court in the country would think twice before disapproving of the application. From a phenomenological point of view, there would be no question of "interpreting" the constitutional language, for its meaning and application would appear clear and obvious.[6]

The most famous expression of the experience of this clarity is by Justice Owen Roberts, who in 1936 wrote that the "judicial branch of the government has only one duty,—to lay the article of the Constitution which is involved beside the statute which is challenged and to decide whether the latter squares with the former."[7] In legal circles, this approach is sometimes characterized as a "plain meaning" or "textualist" theory of interpretation. Yet, strictly speaking, the approach is not a theory at all; it is instead a description of what happens when constitutional meaning is not problematic.

But if for any reason that meaning has become questionable, it is no help at all to instruct a judge to follow the "plain meaning" of the constitutional text. A meaning that has ceased to be plain cannot be made so by sheer force of will.[8] In Chambers' lawsuit, for example, either the meaning of the establishment clause with respect to the issue of legislative prayer is "plain," or it is not. If the latter, the question of constitutional meaning cannot be resolved by staring harder at the ten words of the clause. What is required instead is a means of interpreting the text so as to mediate between the clause and its application.[9]

Because judges must be able to justify their decisions, they must also be able to justify the means of interpretation that they employ to reach those decisions, particularly if their choice affects the ultimate result or significance of a case. Judges must be able to explain why they have decided to interpret the Constitution through one set of inquiries rather than another. In legal (although not in philosophical or literary) parlance, judges require and must be able to articulate a "theory" of constitutional interpretation.

Any such theory of interpretation, however, must accommodate itself to the role of judicial review within American democracy. When a court sets aside a statute as unconstitutional, it in essence deems the statute invalid in the name of the Constitution. Courts have claimed the power to do this because, in the famous words of John Marshall in Marbury v. Madison, the decision that established the institution of judicial review, "it is emphatically the province and duty of the judicial department to say what the law is."[10] The implicit premise of this claim is that the Constitution is a form of "law," just like the law which courts ordinarily interpret and apply. Fidelity to law is a preeminent value in a nation that, as Marshall put it in *Marbury*, prides itself in being "a government of laws, and not of men."[11]

But as the force of Marshall's argument in *Marbury* also required him to acknowledge, the Constitution is something more than ordinary law; it is "the fundamental and paramount law of the nation." The Constitution is "fundamental" because it is the vehicle through which "the people . . . establish, for their future government, such principles as, in their opinion, shall most conduce to their own happiness." The Constitution is therefore "the basis on which the whole American fabric has been erected."[12] The question arises, therefore, why it should be the province and duty of the federal judiciary to discern in that "American fabric" the "principles" and "opinion" of "the people," when that judiciary is not elected by and hence structurally responsible to the people. Why shouldn't that task be allocated instead to the democratically elected branches of government, which are presumptively in closer contact with the popular mind?

This question, which is sometimes termed the "counter-majoritarian" difficulty,[13] has proved durable enough to sustain the work of generations of constitutional scholars. The question makes a powerful political point. Judicial determinations of unconstitutionality nullify the actions of democratically elected branches of government. Such determinations are for all practical purposes final; often the only formal recourse is the cumbersome and impractical process of constitutional amendment. Who are these nine Justices, one might well have asked the Court in 1857 after the *Dred Scott* decision,[14] to instruct the nation so definitively about the "American fabric"?

Constitutional Interpretation in Marsh v. Chambers

The United States Supreme Court voted 6 to 3 against Ernest Chambers. If one were simply to view the Constitution as ordinary law, this outcome would have been something of a surprise. The relevant precedents of the Court pointed unambiguously to the unconstitutionality of the practice of legislative prayer. As Justice William J. Brennan pointed out in his dissent, it is "obvious that, if the Court were to judge legislative prayer through the unsentimental eye of our settled doctrine, it would have to strike it down as a clear violation of the Establishment Clause."[15]

In ordinary adjudication, courts follow the principle of *stare decisis*, which is to say that they follow the doctrinal rules laid down in controlling precedents.[16] In American law, the principle constitutes a fundamental aspect of "the rule of law,"[17] for it requires courts to decide cases on the basis of public and predictable rules, applied in an evenhanded manner, upon which persons can rely in the conduct of their lives.[18] In constitutional adjudication, "adherence to precedent can contribute to the important notion that the law is impersonal in character, that the Court believes itself to be following a 'law which binds [it] as well as the litigants.' "[19] The principle of *stare decisis* helps to ensure that our constitutional order retains the kind of stability and continuity that are prerequisite for institutional legitimacy.

If the Court in Ernest Chambers' case had followed the principle of *stare decisis*, it would have deemed controlling, as did the Court of Appeals below,[20] the three-part doctrinal test laid down in Lemon v. Kurtzman:

> Every analysis in this area must begin with consideration of the cumulative criteria developed by the Court over many years. Three such tests may be gleaned from our cases. First, the statute must have a secular legislative purpose; second, its principal or primary effect must be one that neither advances nor inhibits religion; finally, the statute must not foster "an excessive government entanglement with religion."[21]

The primary purpose of religious prayer cannot reasonably be deemed to be secular; nor can its principal effect be understood as anything other than enhancing religion. As for the potential for "excessive government entanglement with religion," it is apparent that official sponsorship of prayer necessarily entangles the state in decisions about which forms of prayer are appropriate or inappropriate. The word was passed to Reverend Palmer, for example, that Jewish senators in the Nebraska legislature were offended by his many references to Christ.[22] Eighty years before, when a state senator conveyed a similar message to the legislative chaplain of the state senate of California, a local clergyman thundered that the senator's words "were those of an irreverent and godless man" and that his offense was a "crowning infamy."[23] The point of the "entanglements" prong of the *Lemon* rule is to ensure that the state not be embroiled in religious quarrels of this kind.

"In sum," as Justice Brennan remarked, "I have no doubt that, if any group of law students were asked to apply the principles of *Lemon* to the question of legislative prayer, they would nearly unanimously find the practice to be unconstitutional."[24] A fascinating aspect of the *Chambers* decision, however, is that the majority neither disagreed with this assessment nor attempted to alter the *Lemon* doctrine. In fact it ignored *Lemon* altogether, making no effort whatever to justify its decision by reference to past precedents.

Instead, the Court, in an opinion written by Chief Justice Warren Burger and joined by five other Justices, focused its analysis on the fact that the "opening of sessions of legislative and other deliberate bodies with prayer is deeply embedded in the history and tradition of this country." The Court noted that most states have traditionally opened their legislative sessions with prayer, and that Congress has continuously employed chaplains to offer legislative prayer since the eighteenth century. Indeed, on 22 September 1789, three days before Congress approved the language of the First Amendment (and the establishment clause) and sent it to the states for ratification, Congress enacted a statute providing for the payment of congressional chaplains.[25]

Although the Court conceded that "standing alone, historical patterns cannot justify contemporary violations of constitutional guarantees," it concluded that the evidence in Chambers' case was different, for it definitely established "not only . . . what the draftsmen intended the Establishment Clause to mean, but also . . . how they thought that Clause applied to the practice authorized by the First Congress—their actions reveal their intent." "Clearly," the Court concluded, "the men who wrote the First Amendment Religion Clauses did not view paid legislative chaplains and opening prayers as a violation of that Amendment."[26]

The premise of the majority's opinion is thus that the meaning of the Constitution is better ascertained through strong evidence of the intent of the Framers than through fidelity to past precedents and doctrine. The reason is apparently that the intent of the Framers best embodies those principles which "the people" desired to instantiate in their Constitution. In the eyes of the majority, therefore, it is more important that the Constitution be interpreted in a manner which accurately expresses these principles than that it be interpreted in a manner which remains faithful to the principle of *stare decisis*.[27]

The principle of *stare decisis*, moreover, is inconsistent with a quite different method of constitutional interpretation. William Brennan, in a dissent joined by one other Justice, also gave only cursory attention to the rules of *Lemon*. In fact he appeared to agree with the majority that "the path of formal doctrine . . . can only imperfectly capture the nature and importance of the issues at stake in this case."[28] But rather than focusing on the intentions of the Framers of the First Amendment, Brennan offered instead an "account" of "the underlying function of the Establishment Clause" and of the relationship between that function and the practice of legislative prayer.

According to Brennan, the establishment clause embodies the twin principles of "separation between church and state" and "neutrality" as between diverse religions. These two principles, in turn, serve four purposes. They guarantee "the individual right to conscience" by ensuring that persons are not coerced to support (through taxes or otherwise) religious practices with which they disagree; they "keep the state from interfering in the essential autonomy of religious life"; "they prevent the trivialization and degradation of religion by too close an attachment to the organs of government"; and they "help assure that essentially religious issues, precisely because of their importance and sensitivity, not become the occasion for battle in the political arena."[29]

Brennan convincingly demonstrated that Nebraska's authorization of legislative prayer was inconsistent with each of these four purposes. Indeed, as Brennan noted, the majority said "almost nothing contrary to" this functional analysis, relying instead almost entirely on evidence of the historical intent of the Framers. The majority ultimately differed from the dissent, therefore, neither on the application of doctrine nor on the function of the establishment clause, but rather on the relevance of evidence of original intent for constitutional interpretation.

Brennan explicitly rejected such evidence as definitive of constitutional meaning, arguing that "the Constitution is not a static document whose meaning on every detail is fixed for all time by the life experience of the Framers." He contended that the Constitution must be understood instead as "a document meant to last for the ages," the bearer of an "inherent adaptability" that could not be cabined by any "static and lifeless" meaning. His proposed analysis of the establishment clause's "underlying function" was meant to illustrate how courts could discern the *contemporary* significance of "the majestic generalities of the Bill of Rights."[30] His dissent pictured the Constitution as a living, evolving entity whose full meaning could be ascertained neither by doctrinal precedent nor by evidence of original intent. The dissent, therefore, was predicated upon yet a third form of constitutional interpretation.

The outcome of Ernest Chambers' lawsuit thus appears as a triangular structure in which three distinct theories of interpretation compete for control of the Constitution. In one corner is a form of interpretation that strives to implement the Constitution through the articulation of explicit doctrinal rules. In a second corner is a form of interpretation that attempts to construe the Constitution to reflect the original intent of its Framers. In yet a third corner is a form of interpretation that reads the Constitution in a manner designed to express the deepest contemporary purposes of the people. Each of these three theories is immediately recognizable and familiar to those who practice constitutional adjudication.

Constitutional Interpretation and Constitutional Authority

The purpose of constitutional adjudication is to assess the constitutional validity of state actions, like the hiring of legislative chaplains. But courts can achieve this purpose only to the extent that they have the authority to evaluate, in the name of the Constitution, the validity of otherwise perfectly legal state actions. Every act of constitutional interpretation invokes and depends upon this authority, and for this reason "constitutional interpretation is essentially about the sources of authority in American political life."[31] What in fact distinguishes the three theories of interpretation displayed in *Chambers*—theories that I shall respectively call doctrinal, historical, and responsive interpretation—is that each appeals to a different conception of constitutional authority.

The Authority of Law

There is, first, the authority of the Constitution as law. The Constitution controls state actions because the Constitution is the highest law, above all merely quotidian state activity. The concept of the "constitution as hard law, law written in virtually capital letters (LAW), law as meaning reliable law," has been termed "by far the most important idea of the Constitution."[32] Because "courts are the mere instruments of the law,"[33] they are peculiarly fitted to interpret a Constitution whose authority lies in its character as law. It is therefore no accident that in *Marbury* Marshall appealed precisely to this image of constitutional authority in establishing the institution of judicial review.

If the Constitution predominates because it is law, its interpretation must be constrained by the values of the rule of law, which means that courts must construe it through a process of reasoning that is replicable, that remains fairly stable, and that is consistently applied.[34] In American adjudication the principle of *stare decisis* has been an essential component of the rule of law.[35] The principle is of particular importance on those occasions when constitutional adjudication involves vague textual referents (like "equal protection of the laws," or "due process of law"), with regard to which there is "only limited evidence of exactly how the Framers intended the [text] to apply."[36] On these occasions the principle of *stare decisis* holds courts to a consistent and stable interpretation of Constitution.

Without such consistency and stability, it would be difficult to understand the Constitution as having any existence as law. Suppose, for example, that the Supreme Court were to decide one day in decision A that the practice of legislative prayer was constitutional, perhaps because in its view the Framers had so intended. Imagine that a month later the Court were to decide in decision B, without any reference to A, that the practice was unconstitutional, perhaps because the Court's view of the Framers' intent had changed. And assume that one month later the Court were to determine in decision C, without any reference to A or B, that the practice was partially constitutional, perhaps because its reading of the historical evidence had once again altered. In such circumstances state legislators would simply not know what to do; they would have no rule of law by which to decide whether or not they could constitutionally hire legislative chaplains.[37]

It is of course implausible to suppose that the Court would so swiftly and radically change its assessment of the historical evidence. But the question is whether this implausibility derives from the unequivocal state of the historical record or rather from the Court's implicit obligation to remain faithful to its own prior determinations. Since historical evidence is often equivocal, particularly with respect to matters of contemporary constitutional moment, it is the latter obligation, I would suggest, that plays an important role in enabling courts to create stable and predictable rules upon which persons can rely in the arrangement of their lives and institutions.[38] This obligation receives formal acknowledgment in the principle of *stare decisis*.

This means that the principle of *stare decisis* often underlies the capacity of constitutional adjudication to generate a system of constitutional *law*. Thus the *Chambers* decision creates a rule of constitutional law only because of the implicit commitment of the Court to act in the future in ways that are consistent with the *Chambers* holding. Put another way, the legal implications of *Chambers* depend upon the implicit and necessary expectation that the Court will in the future treat *Chambers* in a way that it declined in *Chambers* to treat *Lemon*.[39]

Of course the principle of *stare decisis* is an immensely flexible instrument, allowing courts to treat precedents on the one hand as the source of specific and binding formal rules[40] and on the other as an amorphous mass of material to be rendered consistent through the virtue of "integrity."[41] What every application of the principle requires, however, is that a court focus its analysis on the doctrine that has emerged from relevant prior cases. The principle of *stare decisis* therefore creates a chain of cases, in which each decision is an interpretation of immediately prior decisions.

Construing the Constitution in a manner that is faithful to its authority as law thus leads to what I shall call "doctrinal" interpretation. The implication of doctrinal interpretation is that the actual text of the Constitution is remitted to one end of a growing line of precedents. Even if the very first judicial decision to interpret the establishment clause had concentrated its attention on the specific words of the clause or the intentions of its Framers, the practice of doctrinal interpretation would require the second decision to focus chiefly on the meaning of the first decision, the third decision chiefly on the meaning of the second, and so forth. In this process the text of the Constitution recedes until, as one prominent commentator has put it, it comes to seem "rather like . . . a remote ancestor who came over on the Mayflower."[42]

The vast majority of constitutional decisions rely primarily upon doctrinal interpretation. Novices are often quite struck by the relative absence of the Constitution from constitutional opinions, which seem oriented instead toward specific doctrinal "tests," like the *Lemon* test, derived from prior judicial decisions. But this should be no surprise if the most powerful justification for the Constitution's authority is that it is law, and if the most defensible justification for judicial review is that it is the peculiar province and duty of the courts to expound the law.

The Authority of Consent

If doctrinal interpretation rests on the equation of constitutional authority with law, what I shall call "historical" interpretation rests instead on the equation of constitutional authority with consent. The story is simple and familiar. The Framers of the Constitution proposed a compact to limit the power of government; the people signified their agreement to that compact by their ratification of the Constitution, and that agreement is what gives the Constitution its authority. The interpretation of the Constitution should therefore be designed to give effect to the terms of that original act of agreement.

The story behind historical interpretation has enormous resonance in a liberal society like our own. It conceives of the Constitution as binding in the same way that a promise is binding, as a single voluntary act of willful self-regulation. In interpreting such a Constitution, courts can portray themselves as merely the passive enforcers of the democratic will that "ordained and established" the Constitution. Thus, as former Attorney General Edwin Meese III could observe, "A Jurisprudence of Original Intention . . . reflects a deeply rooted commitment to the idea of democracy. The Constitution represents the consent of the governed to the structures and powers of the government. The Constitution is the fundamental will of the people; that is why it is the fundamental law."[43]

Different variants of historical interpretation emphasize different forms of evidence as probative of that original exercise of "fundamental will." For some commentators the constitutional "text" is a privileged form of evidence because "the text *is* the intention of the authors or of the framers,"[44] whereas for others the "relevant inquiry must focus on the *public* understanding of the language when the Constitution was developed."[45] By far the most common form of historical interpretation, and the one used by Chief Justice Burger in *Chambers*, regards the intentions of the Framers as the best evidence of the agreement represented by the Constitution.[46]

This form of historical interpretation has become quite controversial in recent years, in part because some members of the resurgent Right have attempted to use historical interpretation as a means of constricting the discretion of supposedly liberal judges. The notion is that judges will have less room to maneuver if they are bound to the specific factual intentions of the Framers. But this notion is a vulgar misinterpretation of the principles of historical interpretation, as is elegantly illustrated by an example suggested by Paul Freund. Article I, Section 8, Clause 14 of the Constitution gives to Congress the power "to make Rules for the Government and Regulation of the land and naval forces." It can be said with complete certainty that no one in the eighteenth century had the intent to endow Congress with the power to make rules for the regulation of an air force. But no reasonable person would conclude from this undisputed fact that Congress does not now have this power.[47] This is because the intent behind the clause would naturally be understood as giving Congress the power to regulate the "military" or the "armed forces," or some other such general concept.

The point of Freund's example is that the intent of the Framers cannot be understood as the kind of simple historical fact that resists interpretation. It must instead be conceived as a purpose which can be characterized in terms that are more or less general.[48] Once this move is taken, however, historical interpretation assumes a flexibility inimical to the political purposes of the Right.

Historical interpretation is a rather uncommon phenomenon in modern constitutional adjudication. In part this may be due to the logical and evidentiary difficulties involved in the effort to unearth historical intentions. It is hard enough to ascertain the intention of a living individual. It is harder still to determine the intention of a group of living individuals, like a legislature or a Congress. The difficulty is compounded when the group of individuals is two centuries remote in time and the evidence of their thoughts and purposes is scattered, fragmentary, ambiguous, and conflicting. And the task is made almost impossible when the relevant intention pertains to questions which in all probability never occurred to that group of individuals and which are meaningful only in light of circumstances that would to them be inconceivable.

It is the rare case indeed that, like *Chambers*, seems to present strong evidence of original intention on the precise question to be adjudicated. Even in such a case, as Brennan points out in his dissent, the logic of democratic consent requires that the intentions of those who ratified the Constitution be controlling, rather than the intentions of those who merely proposed constitutional language for popular adoption.[49] And, as Brennan cheerfully notes, " 'We know practically nothing about what went on in the state legislatures' during the process of ratifying the Bill of Rights."[50]

It is important to understand, however, that these obstacles to historical interpretation, while formidable, are not necessarily fatal. First, in any given case the available historical evidence of intent may be more or less compelling. Second, the nature of the evidence that will count as probative of intent may itself be entirely a matter of "generally accepted conventions,"[51] and hence shaped in a manner designed to ease the course of historical inquiry. For example, historical interpretation now focuses on the intent of the Constitution's Framers, rather than of its ratifiers, because the former are by common convention taken to be conclusive of the latter. Similarly, *The Federalist Papers* are by common convention now presumed to constitute authoritative (and convenient) evidence of the intent of the Framers, although any historian could easily demonstrate the empirical inadequacy of the presumption. This tension between the kind of evidence of intent necessary to legitimate political authority and the kind of evidence of intent necessary to persuade professional historical judgment illustrates the truth of Nietzsche's remark that "history, so far as it serves life, serves an unhistorical power."[52] Third, historical interpretation need not focus on the intentions of the Framers or ratifiers at all, but may attempt instead to ascertain consent through inquiries aimed at altogether different kinds of evidence.

Ultimately, therefore, the infrequency of historical interpretation in contemporary constitutional interpretation may stem less from evidentiary difficulties than from the intrinsic limitations of any theory of interpretation resting on the authority of consent. If that authority is understood to arise at the moment of the Constitution's ratification, then in fact no living person has "consented" to the First Amendment, or indeed to most of the Constitution. Why, it may be asked, should the consent of our predecessors have authority over us?[53] When faced with this difficulty, consent theorists often resort to notions of "implied" or "tacit" consent, notions that rapidly drain the concept of consent of its ability to legitimate authority. These notions have a stopgap, jerrybuilt quality that renders them ultimately unsatisfactory.[54] Hanna Pitkin has demonstrated that principled consent theorists like Locke or Joseph Tussman, when seriously pressed with the absence of actual consent, transform the issue into a question of hypothetical consent. "True authority" thus "emerges as being one to which [persons] *ought to consent*, quite apart from whether they have done so."[55]

A similar transformation is visible in the arena of constitutional interpretation. It is said that even if the "legitimacy" of the Constitution cannot rest upon a prior act of consent, it may nevertheless be founded on the fact that persons now ought to view it as "a *good* Constitution and therefore one worthy of continuing support."[56] This is essentially the form of constitutional authority appealed to by Justice Brennan in his dissent in *Chambers*. Because interpretation founded on this form of authority must ultimately be accountable to contemporary concepts of value, I shall call it "responsive" interpretation.

The Authority of Ethos

The classic statement of responsive interpretation is by Oliver Wendell Holmes:

> When we are dealing with words that are also a constituent act, like the Constitution of the United States, we must realize that they have called into life a being the development of which could not have been foreseen completely by the most gifted of its begetters. It was enough for them to realize or to hope that they had created an organism; it has taken a century and has cost their successors much sweat and blood to prove that they created a nation. The case before us must be considered in the light of our whole experience and not merely of what was said a hundred years ago.[57]

For Holmes the authority of the Constitution is not exhausted in a single creative act of consent, but continues to inhere in the national "being" that the Constitution has "called into life." Hence the nature of that authority can be captured neither by rules laid down in judicial precedents nor by notions of original intention. The authority must rather be conceived as flowing from the "whole experience" of nationhood. That experience legitimately claims our allegiance because we are necessarily included within it, and hence responsible both for what it has been and what it might become. What is authoritative is thus neither more nor less than our common commitment to the flourishing of the mutual enterprise of nationhood.

The radical and paradoxical implication of this perspective is that the Constitution explicitly loses its character as a specific document or a discrete text. It becomes instead, as Karl Llewellyn bluntly put it, a "going Constitution," a "working Constitution" which has a content that "is in good part utterly extra-Documentary" and which represents the "*fundamental* framework" of "the governmental machine."[58] In this way the Constitution is transformed into what Kant might call the "regulative" idea of the enterprise of constitutional adjudication, the "imaginary focus from which the concepts" of that enterprise "seem to proceed, even though there is nothing knowable at that focus."[59]

The Constitution as a regulative idea defines the *telos* and shape of constitutional interpretation: it demands, in Hanna Pitkin's formulation, a continual effort to articulate the authority of our "fundamental nature as a people" and hence concomitantly to summon us "to our powers as co-founders and to our responsibilities," in the full knowledge that "how we are able to constitute ourselves is profoundly tied to how we are already constituted by our own distinctive history."[60] In this sense responsive interpretation requires judges to view the Constitution as a form of what Philippe Nonet and Philip Selznick have called "responsive law," law that submits to "the sovereignty of purpose" by functioning as "a facilitator of response to social needs and aspirations."[61]

There is a tension, however, between using law to implement a succession of merely present purposes, and using law to sustain the "general ends" constitutive of our "fundamental framework" of governance. The authority of constitutional law inheres only in the latter, for it alone claims fidelity to the "whole experience" that has comprised "our distinctive history." To maintain its legitimacy, therefore, responsive interpretation must be oriented toward the kind of general ends that have been closely linked over the long run to a historical instantiation of national identity. But such ends can provide the basis for adjudication only if they can also "be made objective enough and authoritative enough to control adaptive rule making."[62] In this regard Justice Brennan's dissent in *Chambers* is paradigmatic. His effort to inquire into "the underlying function of the Establishment Clause" is specific enough to engender legal consequences but general enough to express a deep vision of the secular nature of the American state.

Although the theory of responsive interpretation sounds exotic, responsive interpretation is in fact rather common in judicial opinions (certainly much more so than historical interpretation). In the area of the First Amendment's guarantee of freedom of speech, for example, the outcome of cases depends upon whether judges perceive the purpose of that freedom to be that of assuring an "unfettered interchange of ideas for the bringing about of political and social changes desired by the people,"[63] or instead that of fostering "individual liberty and dignity."[64] In the area of the constitutional right to privacy, the outcome of cases depends upon whether judges conceive the purpose of the due process clause to be that of safeguarding those "liberties that are 'deeply rooted in this Nation's history and tradition,' "[65] or instead that of protecting intimate decisions of a kind that "define one's identity."[66]

Responsive interpretation is in fact a vast umbrella sheltering a myriad of different approaches to the Constitution. It need not have the specifically liberal cast that is visible in Brennan's dissent in *Chambers*. It can be used by those who stress the constitutional priority of democratic decision-making and hence who emphasize judicial caution and prudence, as well as by those who stress the constitutional primacy of individual rights. It has commonly been used by judges and scholars of both the Right and the Left.

Responsive interpretation does, however, have an important vulnerability. It contains within it no particularly persuasive response to the counter-majoritarian difficulty. If doctrinal interpretation portrays courts as merely the instruments of the law, if historical interpretation portrays courts as merely the instruments of an original democratic will, responsive interpretation portrays courts instead as arbiters of the fundamental character and objectives of the nation. And why, it may be asked, should courts be entrusted to act in that capacity, particularly when in doing so they set aside alternative visions of the national character propounded by democratically elected branches of government?

One possible response to this question, which is increasingly visible in the literature, is to stress Hans-Georg Gadamer's theory that all interpretation necessarily involves a conversation between a reader and a text, and so effects a merger between a text and a reader's own purposes and perspectives. Even if this theory is accepted, however, it does not repair the vulnerability of responsive interpretation. This is because the theory's thrust is entirely to describe the conditions that make reading possible, and hence it can offer no guidance to the judge who, having determined the original intent of the Framers to the best of his ability (and therefore in a manner necessarily influenced by his own perspective), must decide whether to be bound by that determination (like Chief Justice Burger in *Chambers*), or instead to set it aside in favor of a more self-consciously responsive approach (like Justice Brennan in *Chambers*). The implications of hermeneutic insights for theories of constitutional interpretation are thus quite modest, a fact that is recognized by its more sophisticated proponents.

The acknowledgment of these limitations is, for example, the point of David Hoy's distinction between the "application" of a text, which is "a prior cognitive operation where we first find the text to be saying something to us," and the "appropriation" of a text, which is "a willful, self-conscious act": "Application is not an option and is not subjective. But appropriation (e.g., making the text seem more rather than less relevant) is an optional strategy, such that it can be used or avoided."[67] Responsive interpretation is a matter of appropriation, and as such cannot be defended by the hermeneutic turn.

The Interrelationship among Forms of Constitutional Authority

We are thus in a position to connect each of the three theories of constitutional interpretation displayed in *Chambers* to a different conception of constitutional authority. Doctrinal interpretation, which follows the principle of *stare decisis*, invokes the authority of the Constitution as law. Historical interpretation, which implements an original act of will, is validated by the authority of the Constitution as consent. Responsive interpretation, which engages in an ongoing process of national self-definition, appeals to the authority of the Constitution as, for lack of a better word, ethos.

I will not make the strong claim that these are the only possible conceptions of constitutional authority (and hence the only possible theories of constitutional interpretation), but I will make the more modest descriptive claim that these three conceptions dominate the actual practice of constitutional adjudication. All the many methods of constitutional interpretation that have proliferated in the legal literature of the past decade, ranging from those that stress the values of democratic participation to those that stress the values of autonomous individualism,[68] ultimately rest upon one or another of these three conceptions of constitutional authority.

Each of these forms of authority is by itself incomplete and incapable of sustaining the enterprise of constitutional adjudication. The authority of the Constitution as law, for example, requires the authority of either consent or ethos in order to initiate a chain of precedents. The authority of consent and that of ethos, on the other hand, each require doctrinal elaboration in order to find embodiment as law. The authority of consent anchors constitutional interpretation in the democratic principles that are necessary and desirable in a country like the United States, while the authority of ethos offers an indispensable flexibility in the interpretation of a document designed to last for the lifetime of the nation.

Yet if these three forms of authority are on one level systematically interdependent, they are at a different level potentially divergent and incompatible.[69] As the *Chambers* decision illustrates, a court in a constitutional case may be called upon to decide which form of authority should govern its efforts, and its decision may determine the outcome of the case. Because this decision is most often understood to depend upon an antecedent characterization of the Constitution (as, for example, "law," "compact," or "ethos"), arguments about theories of interpretation commonly modulate into arguments about the inherent "nature" of the Constitution. To the extent that the three theories of constitutional interpretation are perceived as incompatible, it is due to the fact that they are seen as flowing from incompatible notions of the Constitution itself.

But this vision of constitutional authority is fundamentally flawed, for it hypostatizes the Constitution as external to the processes of its own interpretation. It imagines that the nature of the Constitution can somehow be determined in a manner which is independent of the practice of constitutional interpretation, and that the practice is therefore logically controlled by this antecedent determination of constitutional authority.[70] A better account of the practice of constitutional interpretation, however, would situate constitutional authority instead in the *relationship* obtaining between participants in that practice and the Constitution. Paradoxically, then, constitutional interpretation is not merely about the Constitution but about the more radical and profound question of how we stand in connection to the Constitution.

The Nature of the Authority of Law

If we ask, for example, what it means to defer to the authority of the Constitution as law, the answer is that this authority embodies the values of stability, predictability, and reliance which are necessary to the legitimacy of any modern legal system. Not only are these values themselves important, but they are also the means by which the law orders behavior so as to achieve justice and other desired objectives. The authority of the Constitution as law flows precisely from the acknowledgment of these values.

Once this point is made clear, however, it is also evident that these values, no matter how important, may or may not be compelling in particular circumstances. The values of the rule of law are most pressing when there is agreement that the law is generally just and otherwise fulfilling its proper purposes. In such circumstances doctrinal interpretation and the principle of *stare decisis* hold the law steady on its course. But if there is disagreement about the justice of the law or about its purposes or about its effectiveness in achieving those purposes, then the balance can begin to tip away from the values of stability and predictability.[71] At a certain point, when dissatisfaction with the status quo reaches a sufficient magnitude, we can expect to see the doctrinal chain snapped.[72]

This means, however, that the authority of the Constitution as law does not stand outside the processes of constitutional interpretation, like an axiom in a geometrical proof, but rather is implicated within that very process. In any specific case we may question whether that authority is compelling enough to mandate a particular result. Thus it is not the antecedent "nature" of the Constitution that requires doctrinal interpretation, but rather the decision to recognize and be bound by the values embodied in the authority of the Constitution as law. By acknowledging these values we create a certain relationship to the Constitution, one in which the authority of the rule of law becomes visible and pressing.

In the American legal system this authority appears both flexible and inevitable. It is not disabled even if in particular cases we deny its mandate and break with the principle of *stare decisis*. When the chain of doctrine is broken and precedent is either explicitly or effectively overruled, a new decision must be announced, and for that decision itself to have any effect, it must be crafted in the form of a rule of law that will be respected according to the principle of *stare decisis*. In this way doctrinal interpretation is presupposed even in the moments of its repudiation. Thus although the practice of constitutional adjudication at times may and sometimes must depart from doctrinal interpretation, it is a form of interpretation to which the practice will also inevitably return.

The Symmetrical Nature of the Authority of Consent and the Authority of Ethos

If doctrinal interpretation views the Constitution only dimly at one end of a long corridor of precedents, historical and responsive interpretation each confront the Constitution, so to speak, face to face. The directness of this inquiry liberates courts from the chains of doctrine and empowers them to alter and amend precedents. It also empowers them to uncover and articulate substantive constitutional values. For historical interpretation, this power rests on a court's claim to speak with the authority of an original act of consent. For responsive interpretation, this power rests on a court's claim to speak with the authority of our deepest national identity and commitments. Although these claims appear on their surface to be very different, as different as Burger's majority opinion in *Chambers* from Brennan's dissent, in fact they share an underlying structural similarity.

The authority of consent rests on the capacity of the individual to assume obligations voluntarily. Absent special circumstances to the contrary, a person's contracts are viewed as binding and authoritative. This fact has important consequences for constitutional interpretation. Imagine the dismay you would feel, for example, if you had worked for and achieved the ratification of a constitutional amendment, say the Equal Rights Amendment, only to have it interpreted by a court in a manner flatly contrary to your intent and to the intent of the amendment's supporters and ratifiers. In such circumstances you would want a judge to subordinate her personal perspectives and to implement faithfully the act of consent by virtue of which the amendment had become authoritative. You would no doubt experience a judge's departure from this duty as a betrayal.

The appeal of historical interpretation trades on this experience of betrayal. It is important to understand, however, that this experience does not depend upon anything so simple as the physical casting of a vote. Constitutional amendments are ratified by state legislatures or special state conventions. Your experience of betrayal would not depend upon whether you personally were a member of one of these special ratifying bodies, but rather upon your identification with those who had physically signified their consent. What would count is your sense that the members of the state legislatures or conventions who had actually assented to the Equal Rights Amendment spoke "for" you.

This same identification can extend in time as well as in space. Thus when confronted with constitutional provisions that are a century or more old, historical interpretation can be understood implicitly to assert an identification, a community of interest, with the framers or ratifiers of those provisions. *Their* consent, so the implicit assertion would go, is *our* consent; they spoke "for" us. It follows that the authority of historical interpretation will in significant measure depend upon the persuasiveness of that assertion. That is why in *Chambers* Chief Justice Burger offers an extended discussion of "the unambiguous and unbroken history of more than two hundred years," which he claims establishes that "the practice of opening legislative sessions with prayer has become part of the fabric of our society."[73] The power of Burger's opinion rests in the end upon a claimed continuity of identification with those who had proposed and ratified the First Amendment.

This claim, however, is neither more nor less than a characterization of the national ethos. It is a claim about our national identity and history. Thus while the debate between majority and dissent in *Chambers* can at one level be seen as a struggle between historical and responsive interpretation, it can at a deeper level be understood as a disagreement about whether we can identify with our ancestors or whether we have over the centuries become so different from them, so much more secular or diverse, that we have lost any persuasive identification with the consent of those who ratified the First Amendment.[74]

This deep symmetry between historical and responsive interpretation stems from the fact that both ultimately flow from the authority of a will that affirms its own identity.[75] Responsive interpretation makes this authority explicit because it openly affirms responsibility for the nature of our national ethos. While historical interpretation seemingly presents itself as a self-denying submission to the identity of past ratifiers, closer analysis reveals that that identity is authoritative only insofar as we can be persuaded to adopt it as our own.[76] In either case, the authority of the Constitution ceases to stand apart from the processes of its interpretation. That authority flows not from the antecedent nature of the Constitution but rather from the particular relationship we have forged with the Constitution.

In this regard, however, responsive interpretation is unique, for it alone explicitly thematizes this relational nature of constitutional authority. Both historical and doctrinal interpretation purport to submit to a Constitution whose authority is independent and fixed, either in the preexisting consent of the ratifiers or in the preexisting rules of controlling precedents. Although this submission is illusory, it is an illusion capable of disarming dissent. Responsive interpretation, however, disavows this illusion and frankly locates constitutional authority in the relationship between the Constitution and its interpreters. As a consequence, responsive interpretation generates an intense and singular kind of political dynamics.

A good example is Brown v. Board of Education.[77] The decision did not turn on what the ratifiers of the Fourteenth Amendment thought,[78] or on what the Court had previously held in Plessy v. Ferguson.[79] Instead, the ideal of racial equality had become so pressing to the Court that there was no alternative but to interpret the Equal Protection Clause in light of its imperatives. But because this interpretation rested upon an open avowal of a national ideal, *Brown* represented a courageous gamble. The Court's embrace of the value of racial equality could have been a misreading of the national ethos; indeed the Court's gamble was intensely controversial and came close to failing precisely because that ethos was in fact so divided.[80]

By refusing to interpret the Constitution as if it were a source of external compulsion, either of past precedent or of past consent, responsive interpretation always places a court in such an exposed position, purporting to speak for the fundamental ethos of the contemporary community but justified in the end only by the wisdom of its own insight. Under conditions of cultural division, that position can be the platform for a special form of leadership (as in *Brown*), or it can be the cause of the most unhappy form of vulnerability (as in Roe v. Wade).

Roe, which at the time of its decision stood without significant historical or precedential support,[81] illustrates the structural vulnerability of responsive interpretation to the charge that it articulates values that are merely local and partisan rather than general and truly constitutive of the nation. The charge is unlikely to surface when there is cultural consensus, because the enunciation of contemporary values will under such circumstances be unobtrusive and perhaps even unnoticed. But in the absence of consensus the frank ambition of responsive interpretation to "speak for" the character of the nation, while expressive of the outlook of some, will necessarily constitute a hegemonic imposition upon others. Thus the enterprise of responsive interpretation can become the locus of an overt struggle for the definition of national identity. In the legal academy, responsive interpretation has been profoundly controversial because of the unease generated by perceived judicial participation in such a struggle.

Paradoxically, however, the root cause of this unease is precisely responsive interpretation's explicit thematization of the relational nature of constitutional authority, a form of authority that it in fact shares with both historical and doctrinal interpretation.

The Inevitability of Responsive Interpretation

Responsive interpretation is in some respects similar to what has been called "noninterpretivism,"[82] which can roughly be defined as that form of constitutional interpretation which seeks "the principal stuff of constitutional judgment in one's rendition of society's fundamental values rather than in the document's broader themes."[83] Noninterpretivism, and by extension responsive interpretation, is frequently attacked as breaking faith with a judge's obligation to interpret the Constitution rather than to enact her own desires.

Understood in a psychological sense, the attack is clearly justified. If a judge believes that the Constitution means X but she decides Y because she prefers Y, the judge's decision is presumptively illegitimate. But this framing of the issue is ultimately trivial, for it proceeds on an assumption of bad faith, and it prejudges the critical question, which is the nature of that Constitution to which the judge should maintain fidelity. If responsive interpretation is defined as rendering judgment upon the basis of extraconstitutional factors, then it will of course be vulnerable, but only in an uninteresting and merely stipulative sense. Properly understood, however, responsive interpretation avoids this vulnerability by including the additional claim that our "fundamental nature as a people" is part of the legitimate authority of the Constitution.

One objection to responsive interpretation, therefore, is that it mistakes the "root premise" of American constitutionalism, which is that "the Supreme Court, like the other branches of government, is constrained by the *written* constitution."[84] The point is that responsive interpretation, which explicitly dissolves the Constitution as a specific written text, rests on an unacceptable notion of the Constitution. The force of this objection, which is considerable, derives from the circumstance in which the words of the Constitution appear to speak plainly to us. Recall the case of the third California senator, which a court could settle merely by reading the text of the document. In such a case it seems as if the document itself were authoritative, as if meaning flowed naturally from that handwritten, hand-signed parchment kept under glass in the National Archives.[85] It would appear to follow that any theory of interpretation which abandons that document is illegitimate.

This reasoning, however, proves far too much. It is true that when the document's meaning is unproblematic we feel constrained to regard its language as authoritative without further inquiry. But when for whatever reason the document's meaning does seem problematic, we are necessarily forced outside the text in search of some authority to guide our interpretation of the text. Thus every theory of constitutional interpretation is at some level inconsistent with the notion of a narrow fidelity to a written document. Doctrinal interpretation, for example, which is the sine qua non of constitutional adjudication, applies not the words of the document but legal rules that judges have subsequently created. Most constitutional cases are decided on the basis of doctrinal "tests" that have very little to do with the text of the parchment which resides in the National Archives. Even historical interpretation looks for authority not to the text of the written document but rather to the consent of those who agreed to it. The charge that responsive interpretation abandons the written document, therefore, is an accusation that would disqualify virtually *all* forms of constitutional interpretation.

A second objection to responsive interpretation, however, is that it abandons the document in a particularly unacceptable way. Historical interpretation focuses on an original act of consent because that consent "points toward" the document and illuminates its specific meaning. Doctrinal interpretation, it might be said, focuses on rules of precedent because such rules also "point toward" the document and are attempts to elucidate its meaning. Responsive interpretation, on the other hand, seems to turn away from the document altogether in an effort to uncover present values.

This objection captures what I take to be a major animus of the contemporary debate, and for that reason it needs to be carefully parsed. It is true that because historical interpretation looks to the consent of the ratifiers, the historical document actually ratified is central to the interpretive enterprise. But doctrinal interpretation can be said to "point toward" that document only in the most attenuated metaphorical sense, a sense in which it is equally true to say that responsive interpretation "points toward" the document.

Responsive interpretation rests on the claim that the Constitution is not "static and lifeless," to use Brennan's words in *Chambers*. Instead, as Holmes put it, the Constitution is understood as having "called into life a being" that, like any "organism," must grow and develop on the basis of its "experience."[86] Thus the ambition and challenge of responsive interpretation is to determine which aspects of our contemporary ethos may be regarded as legitimate "growth from the seeds which the fathers planted," and hence as bearing "the essential content and the spirit of the Constitution."[87] Only these aspects of the national ethos are genetically related to the document and thus may properly form the basis for responsive interpretation. In this sense responsive interpretation does indeed "point (backward) toward" the document, in at least as strong a metaphorical sense as does doctrinal interpretation.

Admittedly the organic metaphor that underlies this account of responsive interpretation is highly problematic. It is important to understand, however, that responsive interpretation could equally well rest upon other and perhaps more convincing metaphors. It could invoke, for example, the image of an evolving "tradition" that is constitutive of cultural meaning.[88] Or it could adopt the sociological language of communitarianism, as in this passage from Philip Selznick:

> A social contract is a *constitutive* contract. Its function is to create a political community by founding the legitimacy of government on the consent of the governed. Once the community is formed it has a logic and a dynamic of its own. Even the fundamental obligations of government and citizenry—obligations of loyalty, self-restraint, and care—flow from the nature of the community and of its historical premises, not from the terms of an agreement.[89]

Each of these metaphors can be used to describe a national ethos that changes over time and yet also manages to retain a distinctive identity. Each portrays a national ethos in which we are implicated and to which we are therefore responsible. Each is thus capable of sustaining the enterprise of responsive interpretation.

In these heady days of postmodernism, of course, it is easy enough to deny the truth of all these metaphors and to repudiate the very existence of any overarching national ethos. The political consequences of such a denial, however, are grim. They were in fact first systematically articulated by Thomas Hobbes, and today the premises of his work remain visible in the writings of those influenced by economics and public choice theory. A clear example can be found in the views of Robert Bork, who argues that there is no such thing as a distinctive national ethos but only a vast collection of individual preferences.[90] It follows from this perspective that any attempt to interpret the Constitution on the basis of the authority of a national ethos will necessarily degenerate into an unwarranted imposition of private judicial preferences.[91]

Two preliminary points should be made about this perspective. First, it is inconsistent with historical interpretation, with which it is sometimes associated. Historical interpretation rests on the implicit assertion that the national ethos supports an identification with the ratifiers of the Constitution. But if there are only discrete individual preferences, and if the nation does not have any national ethos, there is no reason whatever why the consent of those long dead should hold any particular authority for the present generation. Second, as the example of Hobbes illustrates, this perspective has difficulty offering a plausible account of political authority as anything other than a collective need for forceful and clear rules of conduct to save individuals from the destructive consequences of their own egoism. But this form of authority, stressing as it does the values of continuity and predictability, is compatible only with the authority of the Constitution as law, which is to say with doctrinal interpretation. The actual implication of this perspective, therefore, is that the principle of *stare decisis* should hold until interrupted by contemporaneous processes of constitutional amendment.

The consequences of denying the existence of a national ethos are thus dramatic, far-reaching, and singularly unattractive. It transforms the overriding concern of constitutional adjudication into the maintenance of rules (any rules), for only such rules stand between us and the chaos of individual desires. Because the primary objective of these rules will be the preservation of order, those subject to constitutional rules will necessarily be reduced "to mere objects of the administered life."[92] The Constitution is concomitantly converted into a form of "repressive law" that "gives short shrift to the interests of the governed."[93]

This transformation is relevant to an assessment of the position of scholars like Bork. Although the existence or absence of a national ethos appears at first blush to be an empirical question that is independent of the perspective of a court, in fact matters are not so simple. As the example of Brown v. Board of Education illustrates, a court can, through the eloquent articulation of public ideals, actually help to solidify a national ethos. The national ethos to which responsive interpretation appeals, in other words, may in significant ways be affected by the very practice of responsive interpretation. The question facing a court, therefore, is whether it should interpret the Constitution in ways that may express or establish a national ethos, or whether it should do so in ways that may confirm its absence. I think this question answers itself, which is why constitutional interpretation has never at any time proceeded on Hobbesian premises.

There is, however, yet a fourth objection to responsive interpretation, one which exerts considerably more influence than the Hobbesian perspective. It does not deny that the nation has an ethos which forms an important component of its public life, but it contends that it is inappropriate for judges to appeal to that ethos as a form of constitutional authority, because the conservation and articulation of that ethos should be placed in the hands of democratically elected officials rather than judges. The objection, in other words, rests on an institutional analysis of how courts ought to function in a democracy. It is of course on precisely such institutional considerations that the counter-majoritarian difficulty is ultimately founded. The stubborn persistence of the difficulty suggests the presence of powerful truths that cannot be brushed aside.

They are, however, only partial truths. If the Constitution is not to degenerate into merely repressive law, authoritative only because of the need for clear and predictable rules, courts interpreting the Constitution must be allowed to speak from the authority of a national ethos, in the form of either historical or responsive interpretation. Taken to its logical conclusion, therefore, the counter-majoritarian difficulty leads to exactly the same unacceptable vision of constitutional law as that which flows from overtly Hobbesian premises.[94] But this consequence is unacceptable to proponents of the counter-majoritarian difficulty, for the institutional considerations by which they seek to circumscribe judicial power are themselves based on a particular account of the national ethos, one that characteristically stresses the importance of majority will in the form of government created by the Constitution.[95] Proponents of the counter-majoritarian difficulty are thus torn between their account of appropriate institutional principles and the fact that these principles, if fully implemented, would preclude judges from appealing to the very national ethos from which the principles flow.

Institutional objections to responsive interpretation are consequently riven by internal tensions. For this very reason, however, institutional objections have rarely if ever implied a simple repudiation of responsive interpretation. Instead, they have characteristically generated counsels of caution, urgent recommendations that responsive interpretation be used only sparingly and in ways consonant with the underlying conception of the national ethos upon which the institutional objections are themselves based. They have led, in other words, to forms of responsive interpretation based upon a particular understanding of the national ethos as founded upon majoritarian principles.[96]

Conclusion: Constitutional Interpretation and Constitutional Culture

The fact that identical judges use different theories of constitutional interpretation in different cases is often used as evidence of the unprincipled nature of constitutional law. And, indeed, if the choice of an interpretive theory depended on the nature of the Constitution, and if that nature were antecedently and externally given, it would be difficult to condone the ways in which judges actually use interpretive theories. But if, as I have argued, constitutional interpretation depends instead upon a relational concept of constitutional authority, judges can legitimately select a specific interpretive theory in light of the circumstances of a particular case.

The interpretive theory judges choose will express their understanding of the pertinent and controlling form of constitutional authority, which is to say that it will both evince and enact their vision of the relevant constitutional culture. Judges can use historical interpretation with respect to an issue in a case if they believe that the national ethos supports an identification with a past act of consent relevant to that issue. They can use responsive interpretation if they discern with respect to that issue the presence of a national ethos that in a pertinent way historically embodies the essential content and spirit of the Constitution, and that precludes identification with any past act of consent. Or they can select doctrinal interpretation if they determine that the values of the rule of law outweigh the inadequacy of controlling precedents.

No matter which theory of constitutional interpretation judges adopt, they cannot escape from the responsibility of cultural articulation and judgment. The pattern of their judgments reveals a good deal about the nature of fundamental authority in our democratic state. It suggests, for example, that visions of a national ethos and community, and hence of a "humanly meaningful authority,"[97] are at the core of our practice of constitutional adjudication. This is encouraging news to set against the view of those who, like Theodor Adorno and Max Horkheimer, perceive the tidal current of this century as flowing toward "undeviating organization,"[98] with its concomitant conditions of bureaucracy, alienation, deracination, and instrumental rationality. But it is also cause for concern if, as appears increasingly likely to be the case for many of us, the vision of national ethos authoritatively enacted by the Supreme Court is contrary to our own. Our consolation in such circumstances is the strength that Claude Lefort identifies with modern democracy: the ever-present possibility that our protests will create a reconstituted political perspective that will in turn alter the character of future judicial appointments.

But that possibility, of course, simply pulls Ernest Chambers round full circle, back to his original efforts to convince his fellow legislators of the deep impertinence of legislative prayer.

2

The Social Foundations of Privacy: Community and Self in the Common Law Tort

Privacy is commonly understood as a value asserted by individuals against the demands of a curious and intrusive society.[1] Thus it is remarked that "privacy rests upon an individualist concept of society,"[2] and that one of "the main enemies of privacy in our own time" is "Community."[3] Consistent with this understanding, the function of the common law tort of invasion of privacy is usually said to be protecting the "subjective" interests of individuals against "injury to the inner person."[4] The stated purpose of the tort is to provide redress for "injury to [a] plaintiff's emotions and his mental suffering."[5]

The origins of the tort of invasion of privacy lie in a famous article called "The Right to Privacy," published in 1890 by Samuel Warren and Louis Brandeis.[6] Arguing powerfully for legal recognition of "the right to privacy, as a part of the more general right to the immunity of the person,—the right to one's personality,"[7] the article sparked the development of the modern tort,[8] which has now evolved into four distinct branches: unreasonable intrusion upon the seclusion of another, unreasonable publicity given to another's private life, appropriation of another's name or likeness, and publicity that unreasonably places another in a false light before the public.[9] In this essay I shall analyze the first two of these branches,[10] attempting to demonstrate that the tort does not simply uphold the interests of individuals against the demands of community, but instead safeguards rules of civility that in some significant measure constitute both individuals and community. The tort rests not upon a perceived opposition between persons and social life but rather upon their interdependence. Paradoxically, that very interdependence makes possible a certain kind of human dignity and autonomy that can exist only within the embrace of community norms.

Interpreted in this way, the common law tort of invasion of privacy offers a rich and complex apprehension of the texture of social life in America. That apprehension is sensitive not merely to the prerogatives of social norms in defining persons and communities but also to the limitations of those prerogatives when faced with competing demands from, for example, the requirements of public governance and accountability.

The Tort of Intrusion: Privacy, Civility, and the Self

The conceptual structure that underlies the branch of the tort which regulates unreasonable intrusion can be illuminated by consideration of an elementary case, Hamberger v. Eastman.[11] *Eastman* was decided by the New Hampshire Supreme Court in 1964, and constituted the state's first official recognition of the tort of invasion of privacy. I choose the case because it is so entirely unexceptional and representative in its reasoning and conclusions. The plaintiffs were a husband and wife who alleged that the defendant, their landlord and neighbor, had installed an eavesdropping device in their bedroom. The New Hampshire Supreme Court, adopting William Prosser's novel proposal that the tort of invasion of privacy be divided into four distinct branches,[12] characterized the plaintiffs' complaint as "the tort of intrusion upon the plaintiffs' solitude or seclusion."[13]

The plaintiffs alleged that as a result of the discovery of the eavesdropping device they were "greatly distressed, humiliated, and embarrassed," that they sustained "intense and severe mental suffering and distress, and ha[d] been rendered extremely nervous and upset." The New Hampshire Supreme Court had little difficulty in finding that, "by way of understatement," the type of intrusion suffered by the plaintiffs "would be offensive to any person of ordinary sensibilities." It did not matter, said the court, that the plaintiffs could not establish that anyone ever "listened or overheard any sounds or voices originating from the plaintiffs' bedroom,"[14] since the gravamen of the plaintiffs' cause of action rested solely on the intrusive installation of the offensive device.

At first glance *Eastman* tells a rather simple story. "Marital bedrooms," as the United States Supreme Court has had occasion to observe in the first of its modern constitutional right to privacy cases, are "sacred precincts,"[15] in which we expect privacy and into which it is plainly highly offensive to intrude.[16] An invasion of privacy is "an injury to personality. It impairs the mental peace and comfort of the individual and may produce suffering more acute than that produced by a mere bodily injury."[17] The plaintiffs in *Eastman* experienced just such mental suffering, and the New Hampshire Supreme Court in *Eastman* decided that the common law ought to provide redress for that injury.[18]

In all probability this story accurately reflects how the vast majority of judges and lawyers understand the tort of invasion of privacy. It is a story, however, that places an intense and narrow focus on the actual mental suffering of specific individuals. The limitations of this focus become apparent once it is understood that the eavesdropping device in *Eastman* was defined as an invasion of privacy not merely because the plaintiffs were in fact discomforted but rather because the installation of the device was "offensive to any person of ordinary sensibilities."[19] In the later language of the second *Restatement of Torts*, the placement of the eavesdropping device was actionable because it "would be highly offensive to a reasonable person."[20]

The "reasonable person" is of course a figure who continually reappears in American common law, most especially in the law of torts. The important point about the reasonable person is that he is no one in particular; "he is not to be identified with any real person."[21] He is rather, as a standard text would have it, "an abstraction," a representative of "the normal standard of community behavior," who embodies "the general level of moral judgment of the community, what it feels ought ordinarily to be done."[22] Thus in *Eastman* the installation of the eavesdropping device is transformed into an actionable invasion of privacy because the general level of moral judgment in the community finds it highly offensive for landlords and neighbors to spy on marital bedrooms. The *Eastman* court states that "it is only where [an] intrusion has gone beyond the limits of decency that liability accrues."[23] The tort of invasion of privacy, we may thus conclude, is at least as concerned with policing these "limits of decency" as with redressing the mental distress of particular plaintiffs.

The *Restatement* characterizes these limits as those whose transgression would be "highly offensive." At first blush this notion of offense appears to describe the actual mental distress alleged to have been suffered by the *Eastman* plaintiffs. *Webster's Third New International Dictionary*, for example, defines "offensive" as that which gives "painful or unpleasant sensations" or causes "displeasure or resentment." But the displeasure or painful sensations at issue in the *Eastman* case cannot be those of the plaintiffs, for their particular mental condition is not determinative of whether the installation of the eavesdropping device is an actionable invasion of privacy. So it must be the "reasonable person" who suffers. But that leaves us with something of an enigma, for the reasonable person is only a generic construct without real emotions.

Thus the pain or displeasure at issue in defining liability cannot be understood as actual sensations or emotions. Because the reasonable person is not simply an empirical or statistical "average" of what most people in the community believe, the mental distress at issue in defining liability also cannot be understood as a mere empirical or statistical prediction about what the majority of persons in a community would be likely to experience. Instead, because the reasonable person is a genuine instantiation of community norms, the concept of offensiveness at issue in *Eastman* must be understood as predicated upon a quality that inheres in such norms.

The dictionary suggests the nature of that quality when it states that the adjective "offensive" "describes what is disagreeable or nauseating or painful because of outrage to taste and sensibilities or affronting insultingness." The pain or displeasure associated with the offensive can be understood as flowing from this "outrage" or "affront." Outrage and affront, however, are ways of describing how it is appropriate to feel when certain social norms have been transgressed. Hence when the law asks whether the reasonable person would find certain invasions of privacy "highly offensive," it is seeking not to predict actual emotions but rather to characterize those social norms whose violation would appropriately cause affront or outrage.

Thus a more precise characterization of the conceptual structure underlying *Eastman* is that a plaintiff is entitled to relief if it can be demonstrated that a defendant has transgressed the kind of social norms whose violation would properly be viewed with outrage or affront, and that the function of this relief is to redress "injury to personality." This legal structure typifies the tort of intrusion. It rests on the premise that the integrity of individual personality is dependent upon the observance of certain kinds of social norms.

This premise, of course, also underlies much of sociological thought. For purposes of analyzing the privacy tort, the most systematic and helpful explication of the premise may be found in the work of Erving Goffman. He most explicitly states the premise in his early article "The Nature of Deference and Demeanor," where he offers an image of social interactions as founded on rules of "deference and demeanor." Rules of deference define conduct by which a person conveys appreciation "*to a* recipient or *of* this recipient, or of something of which this recipient is taken as a symbol, extension, or agent." Rules of demeanor define conduct by which a person expresses "to those in his immediate presence that he is a person of certain desirable or undesirable qualities."[24]

Taken together, rules of deference and demeanor constitute "rules of conduct which bind the actor and the recipient together" and "are the bindings of society." By following these rules, not only do individuals confirm the social order in which they live, but they also establish and affirm "ritual" and "sacred" aspects of their own and others' identities. Thus Goffman states that each individual "must rely on others to complete the picture of him of which he himself is allowed to paint only certain parts":

> Each individual is responsible for the demeanor image of himself and the deference image of others, so that for a complete man to be expressed, individuals must hold hands in a chain of ceremony, each giving deferentially with proper demeanor to the one on the right what will be received deferentially from the one on the left. While it may be true that the individual has a unique self all his own, evidence of this possession is thoroughly a product of joint ceremonial labor, the part expressed through the individual's demeanor being no more significant than the part conveyed by others through their deferential behavior toward him.[25]

According to Goffman, then, we must understand individual personality as *constituted* in significant aspects by the observance of rules of deference and demeanor; or, to return to the more prosaic language of *Eastman*, by the rules of decency recognized by the reasonable man. Violation of these rules can thus damage a person by discrediting his identity and injuring his personality. Breaking "the chain of ceremony" can deny an individual the capacity to become "a complete man" and hence "disconfirm" his very "self."[26]

It is for this reason that the law regards the privacy tort as simultaneously upholding social norms and redressing "injury to personality." We must be clear, however, that in any particular case individuals may or may not have internalized pertinent rules of deference and demeanor, and hence may or may not suffer actual injury to personality. The device of the reasonable person focuses the law not on actual injury to the personality of specific individuals but rather on the protection of that personality which would be constituted by full observance of the relevant rules of deference and demeanor, those whose violation would appropriately cause outrage or affront. I shall call such rules "civility rules," and I shall call the personality that would be upheld by these civility rules "social personality."

The concept of social personality points simultaneously in two distinct directions. On the one hand, the actual personalities of well-socialized individuals should substantially conform to social personality, for such individuals have internalized the civility rules by which social personality is defined. It is for this reason that the tort of intrusion, even though formally defined in terms of the expectations of the "reasonable person," can in practice be expected to offer protection to the emotional well-being of real plaintiffs. On the other hand, social personality also subsists in a set of civility rules that, when taken together, give normative shape and substance to the society that shares them. In fact, these rules can be said to define the very community that the "reasonable person" inhabits. They constitute the "special claims which members [of a community] have on each other, as distinct from others,"[27] and hence which create for a community "its distinctive shape, its unique identity."[28] Thus even if particular plaintiffs are not well socialized and hence have not suffered actual injury because of a defendant's violation of civility rules, the law nevertheless endows such plaintiffs with the capacity to bring suit, thereby upholding the normative identity of the community inherent in the concept of social personality.

This interpretation of the tort explains what would otherwise be a puzzling aspect of its legal structure. Most torts require, as distinct elements of a prima facie case, allegation and proof that the violation of a relevant social norm has actually caused some harm or damage. For example, if you drive your car carelessly and have an accident, a lawsuit against you for negligence can succeed only if it establishes that your negligent behavior has actually caused some demonstrable injury.[29] The basic idea is "no harm, no foul." But the tort of invasion of privacy is qualitatively different because the injury at issue is logically entailed by, rather than merely contingently caused by, the improper conduct. An intrusion on privacy is *intrinsically* harmful because it is defined as that which injures social personality.

The legal profile of the invasion of privacy tort reflects this logical structure. In contrast to the usual cause of action for negligence, the privacy tort enables a plaintiff to make out his case without alleging or proving any actual or contingent injury, such as emotional suffering or embarrassment. The privacy tort shares this profile with other torts that redress "dignitary harms."[30] In the area of defamation, for example, where the law also seeks to uphold civility rules,[31] a plaintiff could at common law successfully prosecute a suit, and even receive substantial sums in "general damages," despite a defendant's credible proof that the plaintiff had suffered no actual or contingent injury whatever.[32] In their 1890 article, Warren and Brandeis conceived of the "remedies for an invasion of the right of privacy" as analogous to "those administered in the law of defamation."[33] In 1939 the first *Restatement of Torts* stated flatly that damages in a privacy action "can be awarded in the same way in which general damages are given for defamation."[34] In its second edition the *Restatement* was somewhat more circumspect,[35] stating:

> One who has established a cause of action for invasion of his privacy is entitled to recover damages for
>   (a) the harm to his interest in privacy resulting from the invasion;
>   (b) his mental distress proved to have been suffered if it is of a kind that normally results from such an invasion; and
>   (c) special damage of which the invasion is a legal cause.[36]

The *Restatement* thus enables a plaintiff to maintain a suit, and even to receive damages, because of harm to an "interest in privacy," notwithstanding the absence of allegations or proof of actual injury, such as mental distress. This in effect renders the invasion of privacy tort theoretically independent of any merely empirical or contingent consequences of the violation of the underlying civility rule.[37] The most plausible interpretation of this legal structure is that the *Restatement* has empowered plaintiffs to use the tort to uphold the interests of social personality, which are *necessarily* impaired by a defendant's breach of a civility rule.

The strength of this conclusion, however, should be qualified somewhat because of the paucity of reported decisions on point. I have been able to locate only a very few decisions where plaintiffs have been unable or unwilling to present any evidence of actual injury. But in those few cases courts have followed the implications of the *Restatement*'s analysis and awarded damages,[38] even if only nominal.[39]

The minuscule number of such decisions is itself instructive, however, for it indicates that as a practical matter virtually every plaintiff will allege and be able to produce some credible evidence of contingent and actual injury in the form of emotional suffering. The very credibility of this evidence suggests how dependent our personalities in fact are upon the observance of civility rules, and hence confirms the close congruence between social personality and the actual individual personalities of those who use the legal system. The strength of this congruence is illustrated by the confidence with which we instinctively feel the plausibility of the emotional suffering alleged by plaintiffs in the *Eastman* case, even though we have absolutely no empirical knowledge of who those plaintiffs really are. This confidence can be grounded only on the almost irresistible assumption that the personalities of those plaintiffs have been forged by the same rules of civility as have shaped our own personalities.

The privacy tort thus represents a complex pattern in which legal interventions supportive of general rules of civility occur at the behest of specific aggrieved individuals. This pattern can be viewed as an attempt to disperse enforcement authority. In contrast to the criminal law, in which all power to prosecute infractions of important legal norms is concentrated in the hands of accountable public officials, the privacy tort devolves the authority of enforcement into the hands of private litigants. Concomitant with this decentralization—or perhaps because of it—the privacy tort is also concerned with the specific interests of those plaintiffs who take the trouble to bring violators of civility rules before adjudicative tribunals. This concern is particularly visible in how the tort is structured to redress the claims of those who have suffered actionable injuries.

We may roughly distinguish between two kinds of plaintiff interests. The first arises because of contingent psychological injuries that plaintiffs may suffer as a result of the violation of civility rules. Mental anguish and humiliation are common and routine examples of such injuries. But there are more exotic forms of such damage as well. In *Eastman*, for example, the husband alleged that the discovery of the eavesdropping device in his bedroom had rendered him impotent; his wife alleged that she had been made frigid. Although these injuries are idiosyncratic, they nevertheless deserve redress, and the tort is structured to provide that redress.[40]

The second kind of interest arises from the dignitary harm which plaintiffs suffer as a result of having been treated disrespectfully. Violations of civility rules are intrinsically demeaning, even if not experienced as such by a particular plaintiff.[41] This is because dignitary harm depends not on the psychological condition of an individual plaintiff but rather on the forms of respect that a plaintiff is entitled to receive from others.[42] We need to ask how the law can provide redress for the dignitary harm that results when these forms of respect are, in important ways, violated.

The answer can perhaps be found in those not infrequent cases where juries use the pretext of "psychic and emotional harm" to return "large verdicts, although little objective evidence is available"[43] to support them.[44] The *Restatement* shrewdly characterizes such damages as "vindicating" a plaintiff:

> For certain types of dignitary torts, the law serves the purpose of vindicating the injured party. Thus, in suits for defamation [or] invasion of privacy ... the major purpose of the suit may be to obtain a public declaration that the plaintiff is right and was improperly treated. This is more than a simple determination of legal rights for which nominal damages may be sufficient, and will normally require compensatory or punitive damages.[45]

The *Restatement*'s conclusion that large damage awards which are seemingly unrelated to any contingent harm represent a form of vindication is an informed and convincing interpretation.[46] To say that the plaintiff in an invasion of privacy suit requires vindication, however, is to imply that he is somehow in need of exoneration. But this implication is puzzling, for the plaintiff has been the victim, not the perpetrator, of a transgression. The shame of the victim, however, is made explicable by the fact that he has been denied respect, and consequently his status as a person to whom respect is due has been called into question.

The victim of the breach of a civility rule, in other words, suffers a special kind of injury: he is "threatened" with being "discredited" because he has been excluded from the "chain of ceremony" that establishes the respect normally accorded to full-fledged members of the community.[47] Since the boundaries of a community are marked by the "special claims which members have on each other, as distinct from others,"[48] the defendant's disregard of the plaintiff's claim to be treated with respect potentially places the plaintiff outside the bounds of the shared community. The plaintiff can accordingly be vindicated only by being reaffirmed as a member of the community. It is plausible to interpret the seemingly excessive damages that sometimes characterize invasion of privacy actions as such an affirmation, which occurs through the simultaneous enrichment of the plaintiff and the punishment of the defendant.[49] The privacy tort, in other words, functions not merely to uphold the chain of ceremony, but also, in appropriate cases, to reforge it when it has been fractured.

Privacy and Civility: Some Theoretical Implications

We have come a long way, then, from the first simple story we were able to tell about the *Eastman* case. The underlying structure of the privacy tort is as much oriented toward safeguarding rules of civility and the chain of ceremony they establish as it is toward protecting the emotional well-being of individuals. This understanding of the tort has several important theoretical implications, both for the concept of privacy and for the functioning of the law.

The Normative Nature of Privacy: The Reconciliation of Community and Autonomy

Consider first the concept of privacy that underlies the tort. It is obviously quite different from the "neutral concept of privacy"[50] which some commentators have proposed, and which attempts to define privacy in purely descriptive and value-free terms. Ruth Gavison, for example, has defined privacy as a gradient that varies in three dimensions: secrecy, anonymity, and solitude. She believes that an individual's loss of privacy can be objectively measured "as others obtain information [about him], pay attention to him, or gain access to him."[51] The presence or absence of privacy is thus a fact capable of ascertainment without regard to normative social conventions.

A "neutral" concept of privacy has certain obvious advantages and uses. It is useful, for example, in the cross-cultural analysis of privacy, because it creates an object of analysis that is independent of the various perceptions of the cultures at issue. It is also useful for efforts to create a functional account of privacy. The hypothesis that "privacy" is necessary to cause certain consequences will be cleaner and more easily verifiable if the "privacy" at issue is conceived as a measurable fact. Thus Robert Merton rests his claim that privacy is "an important functional requirement for the effective operation of social structure" on a neutral definition of privacy as "insulation from observability." Privacy is necessary, argues Merton, because without it "the pressure to live up to the details of all (and often conflicting) social norms would become literally unbearable; in a complex society, schizophrenic behavior would become the rule rather than the formidable exception it already is."[52]

Whatever the virtue of such neutral definitions of privacy, they are most certainly not at the foundation of the common law, which rests instead upon a concept of privacy that is inherently normative. The privacy protected by the common law tort cannot be reduced to objective facts like spatial distance or information or observability; it can only be understood by reference to norms of behavior. A defendant who stands very close to a plaintiff in a crowded elevator will not be perceived as having committed a highly offensive intrusion; but the case will be very different if the defendant stands the same distance away from the plaintiff in an open field. In the common law, as in everyday life, issues of privacy refer to the characterization of human action, not to the neutral and objective measurement of the world.

Thus the sphere of privacy protected by the tort can be perceived only through the exercise of what Simmel calls "moral tact."[53] Gavison argues that privacy defined in terms of social norms "is simply a conclusion, not a tool to analyze whether a certain invasion should be considered wrong in the first place."[54] But in the end this objection simply highlights that the common law attempts not to search out and articulate first ethical principles, as would a certain kind of moral philosopher, but instead to discover and refresh the social norms by which we live, the very norms that to Gavison provide only the starting point for respectable critique.

Civility rules of course protect dignitary interests other than those of privacy. But because the common law has not attempted to define privacy in the neutral manner advocated by Gavison, it has on the whole been almost indifferent to any systematic effort to distinguish between those civility rules which protect privacy and those which safeguard other dignitary interests. The single act of a defendant is often the basis for a lawsuit alleging various kinds of dignitary harms, ranging from invasion of privacy to defamation and to the intentional infliction of emotional distress.[55]

The common law attempts to distinguish privacy from other forms of social respect primarily through the specification of the formal elements of the privacy tort. The formal elements of the branch of privacy law known as "intrusion," the precise privacy law tort at issue in *Eastman*, require a plaintiff to allege that a defendant has intentionally intruded upon the plaintiff's solitude or seclusion in a manner that would be highly offensive to a reasonable person.[56] The formal elements of the tort of intentional infliction of emotional distress, on the other hand, require a plaintiff to allege that the defendant has, by means of extreme and outrageous conduct, intentionally caused the plaintiff severe emotional distress.[57]

Obviously these elements overlap substantially, and it is not surprising that plaintiffs will frequently allege both intrusion and intentional infliction of emotional distress.[58] But the elements of the two torts are logically distinct, for the intrusion tort focuses narrowly on policing what Simmel

calls that "ideal sphere [which] lies around every human being" and
which "cannot be penetrated, unless the personality value of the individual is thereby destroyed,"[59] whereas the tort of intentional infliction of
emotional distress focuses on preventing the intentional violation of civility rules for the purpose of causing harm to the personality. Thus the
latter tort prohibits evil intentions, while the former guards against the
penetration of private space. But this formal distinction is less helpful
than it might appear, for the penetration of private space is often not
"highly offensive" unless perpetrated with improper intent,[60] and so the
boundary between the two torts is obscured.

That the common law lives comfortably with such ambiguity is evidence that it is primarily interested in maintaining the forms of respect
deemed essential for social life, and relatively indifferent to whether particular forms of respect should be denominated as privacy. Certain kinds
of respect are in ordinary discourse understood to be concerned with
privacy, and the common law roughly incorporates this understanding
into the formal elements of the privacy tort. But the common law makes
no great effort to analyze that understanding systematically so as to isolate
the private as a distinct object of protection.

The intrusion branch of the privacy tort has intuitively obvious connections to ordinary understandings of privacy. Certainly in common
usage a basic meaning of privacy is that of a private space, like a bathroom
or a home, from which others may be excluded.[61] The forms of respect
that underlie such spaces are well displayed by Erving Goffman in his
essay "The Territories of the Self." Goffman defines a territory as a "field
of things" or a "preserve" to which an individual can claim "entitlement to possess, control, use, or dispose of." Territories are defined
not by neutral, objective factors, like feet or inches, but instead are contextual. Their boundaries have a "socially determined variability" and
depend upon such factors as "local population density, purpose of the
approacher, . . . character of the social occasion and so forth."[62]

That territories are defined by normative and social factors as opposed
to neutral or objective criteria is well illustrated by the decision of Huskey
v. National Broadcasting Co. In that case Arnold Huskey, a prisoner at
the United States Penitentiary at Marion, Illinois, sued NBC because its
cameras had filmed him while in the prison's "exercise cage," a room
roughly twenty-five feet by thirty feet with a concrete floor and surrounding fence. Huskey was wearing only gym shorts, leaving several distinctive
tattoos exposed. Huskey claimed that NBC had intruded on his seclusion,

because he had expected that "the only ones able to see him would be persons 'to whom he might be exposed as a necessary result of his incarceration': the guard assigned to watch him, other prison personnel and other inmates."[63] NBC argued that it could not "be held liable for intrusion upon Huskey's seclusion because he was not secluded"; the exercise cage was " 'open to view and used by other prisoners.' "[64]

The court refused to accept the "neutral" fact of Huskey's visibility as determinative of the territory from which he could rightfully exclude others:

> Huskey's visibility to some people does not strip him of the right to remain secluded from others. Persons are exposed to family members and invited guests in their own homes, but that does not mean they have opened the door to television cameras. Prisons are largely closed systems, within which prisoners may become understandably inured to the gaze of staff and other prisoners, while at the same time feeling justifiably secluded from the outside world (at least in certain areas not normally visited by outsiders).[65]

The court concluded that the success of Huskey's claim would have to await further development of the factual record regarding the actual customs and usages of the exercise cage. These customs and usages, not the "objective" facts of visibility, secrecy, anonymity, and solitude, defined the territory in which Huskey could legally claim the right to undisturbed "seclusion."

Goffman's central and profound point is that territories, defined in this normative way, are a vehicle for the exchange of meaning; they serve as a kind of language, a "ritual idiom,"[66] through which persons communicate with one another. We indicate respect for a person by acknowledging his territory; conversely, we invite intimacy by waiving our claims to a territory and allowing others to draw close. An embrace, for example, can signify human compassion or desire, but if it is unwelcome it can instead be experienced as a demeaning indignity.[67] The identical physical action can have these two very different meanings only because its significance is constituted by the norms of respect which define personal space. It is characteristic of "territories of the self" to be used in this "dual way, with comings-into-touch avoided as a means of maintaining respect and engaged in as a means of establishing regard."[68]

Goffman's analysis suggests that by lending authoritative sanction to the territories of the self, the tort of intrusion performs at least three distinct functions. First, it safeguards the respect due individuals by virtue of their territorial claims.[69] Second, it maintains the language or "ritual idiom" constituted by territories, thus conserving the particular meanings carried by that language. Third, the tort preserves the ability of individuals to speak through the idiom of territories, and this ability, as Goffman notes,

> is somehow central to the subjective sense that the individual has concerning his selfhood, his ego, the part of himself with which he identifies his positive feelings. And here the issue is not whether a preserve is exclusively maintained, or shared, or given up entirely, but rather the role the individual is allowed in determining what happens to his claim.[70]

An individual's ability to press or to waive territorial claims, his ability to choose respect or intimacy, is thus deeply empowering for his sense of himself as an independent or autonomous person. As Jeffrey Reiman has noted, "Privacy is an essential part of the complex social practice by means of which the social group recognizes—and communicates to the individual—that his existence is his own. And this is a precondition of personhood."[71]

There is now a fierce debate in law and political philosophy between, speaking roughly, liberals and communitarians.[72] The former stress those aspects of the self which are independent and autonomous, the latter emphasize those aspects which are embedded in social norms and values. In the intrusion tort, however, this debate is miraculously transcended, for the tort presides over precisely those social norms which enable an autonomous self to emerge.

Some norms, like those prohibiting murder, cannot be waived by the consent of individuals. But the norms policed by the intrusion tort are different. They mark the boundaries that distinguish respect from intimacy, and their very ability to serve this function depends upon their capacity for being enforced or waived in appropriate circumstances. In the power to make such personal choices inheres the very essence of the independent self. This mysterious fusion of civility and autonomy lies at the heart of the intrusion tort.

The Legal Enforcement of Civility Rules: Hegemony and Community

My analysis so far has assumed that the common law incorporates civility rules from society in some relatively unproblematic way. The assumption reflects the common law's understanding of its own project. The elements of intrusion require it to enforce rules of civility as perceived by the "reasonable person," who is meant to embody "the general level of moral judgment of the community." The discernment and application of these civility rules is in general entrusted to a jury, which is a randomly selected group of persons designed to be representative of the community.[73] The prevailing image is that of a legal system transparently reflecting community norms.

This image, however, requires three important qualifications. First, social life is thick with territorial norms that contribute substantially to "the concrete density and vitality of interaction."[74] For obvious reasons, however, the common law can maintain only a small subset of these norms. The law itself claims to enforce only the most important of them, only those whose breach would be "highly offensive." This selection criterion serves the interest of legal institutions, which otherwise would be inundated with trivial lawsuits. It also, and somewhat less obviously, preserves the flexibility and vitality of social life, which undoubtedly would be hardened and otherwise altered for the worse if every indiscretion could be transformed into legal action.

Second, the legal system must translate civility rules into workable legal doctrine. The complex, tacit, and contextual territorial principles described by Goffman must be stiffened into the relatively clear, explicit, and precise elements of a formal cause of action. This transmutation is captured by Paul Bohannan's notion of "*double* institutionalization," which means that the law must domesticate general social norms so that they are compatible with the needs and functioning of the legal system.[75] Civility rules must thus assume the character of legal doctrine; they must be formulated according to the logic of the rule of law, which means that they must be articulated in such a way that "people will be able to be guided" by them.[76] They must be capable of generating rules of precedent to constrain future judicial decisions. These transformations imply that legal doctrine is often, as Bohannan puts it, "out of phase with society."[77] If the objective of the law is to shape and alter social norms, this tension between law and custom is desirable. But if the law's purpose is to maintain social norms, as is manifestly the case for the common law tort of intrusion, this dissonance works against the very rationale of the law.

Third, and most important, it is something of a fiction to speak of a single, homogeneous community within a nation as large and diverse as the United States. There is every reason to expect that civility rules regarding privacy will differ "among communities, between generations, and among ethnic, religious, or other social groups, as well as among individuals."[78] It is said, for example, that Warren and Brandeis wrote their famous article because Warren, a genuine Boston Brahmin, was outraged that common newspapers had had the effrontery to report on his private entertainments.[79] As such the class content of the privacy norms advanced by the article is plain.[80]

That content is also explicit in the writings of E. L. Godkin, which Warren and Brandeis cite with approval. Godkin characterized privacy as "one of the luxuries of civilization, which is not only unsought for but unknown in primitive or barbarous societies." He illustrated the social consequences of the point by reciting the

> story of the traveller in the hotel in the Western mining town, who pinned a shirt across his open window to screen himself from the loafers on the piazza while performing his toilet; after a few minutes he saw it drawn aside roughly by a hand from without, and on asking what it meant, a voice answered, "We want to know what there is so darned private going on in there?" The loafers resented his attempts at seclusion in their own rude way.[81]

Godkin's story is plainly meant to demonstrate the class basis of privacy norms. In a world in which privacy norms are heterogeneous, however, the common law must choose which norms to enforce. It must pick sides in the confrontation between the traveler and the loafers. And this choice cannot be avoided by an appeal to the judgment of the "reasonable person," for it must first be determined to which community the reasonable person belongs.

In defamation law, the question of which community the law will serve is explicitly thematized as a doctrinal issue. Some courts have said that the law will uphold the values of "a considerable and respectable class in the community";[82] others have adopted the perspective of " 'right-thinking persons.' "[83] But this question is not explicitly addressed in the doctrine of the more recent tort of invasion of privacy, which speaks only in the majestic and abstract accents of the "reasonable person." Thus the civility rules recognized by the common law tort of intrusion are presented as "universalist norms, applicable to the society as a whole rather than to a few functional or segmental sectors, highly generalized in terms of principles and standards."[84]

Whether this claim to universalist status is justified, however, cannot be determined from the mere fact of a judicial decision. It could be that the civility rules enforced by a judicial decision are genuinely expressive of generally accepted norms in a society. I doubt, for example, if anyone would seriously question *Eastman*'s assertion that eavesdropping on marital bedrooms constitutes a serious violation of generally accepted civility rules. But the converse could also be true, and it is possible that the civility rules enforced by a particular court may be understood as hegemonically imposed by one dominant cultural group onto others.

This suggests that care must be taken in evaluating the universalist pretensions of the tort of intrusion. Under conditions of cultural heterogeneity, the common law can become a powerful instrument for effacing cultural and normative differences.[85] The significance of this effacement, however, lies not only in its hegemonic consequences but also in the commitment that it reveals to the task of constructing a common community through the process of authoritatively articulating rules of civility. The common law tort purports to *speak for* a community. Yet this very ambition to forge a community simultaneously requires the common law to displace deviant communities. Under such conditions, community and hegemony necessarily entail each other.

The Tort of Public Disclosure

The core of the invasion of privacy tort is commonly understood to lie in the branch of the tort that attempts to regulate the publicizing of private life.[86] The elements of that branch are described by the *Restatement* in the following manner:

> One who gives publicity to a matter concerning the private life of another is subject to liability to the other for invasion of privacy, if the matter publicized is of a kind that
> (a) would be highly offensive to a reasonable person, and
> (b) is not of legitimate concern to the public.[87]

This branch of the tort (which for convenience I shall call simply "public disclosure") differs from intrusion in three fundamental ways. First, intrusion concerns the physical actions of a defendant, whereas public disclosure involves the dissemination of information. The tort in *Eastman* was complete when the defendant placed the eavesdropping device in the plaintiffs' marital bedroom. Liability did not depend upon whether the defendant actually listened to the device or acquired any information from it, or whether he revealed any such information to others. An essential element of the tort of public disclosure, on the other hand, is a defendant's public disclosure of private information.

Second, whereas both intrusion and public disclosure turn on what a "reasonable person" would find "highly offensive," the tort of public disclosure penalizes only certain kinds of highly offensive revelations of private life—namely, those in which a defendant has given "publicity" to the offensive information. To give "publicity" to information is to make it public. This concept of publicity has no analogue in the tort of intrusion.

Third, the tort of public disclosure requires a plaintiff to establish that the offensive information "is not of legitimate concern to the public." The concept of "legitimate concern" also has no analogue in the tort of intrusion.

In the following sections of this essay I shall address the first and third of these important differences.

The Offensive Disclosure of Private Facts: Civility and the Protection of Information Preserves

The public disclosure tort regulates forms of communication rather than behavior. To be actionable, a communication must be about "a matter concerning the private life of another" and the matter must be "of a kind that would be highly offensive to a reasonable person." At first glance these two criteria appear to concern only the content of the information contained in a communication. Either the information is about private life or it is not; either the information is highly offensive or it is not. In fact, however, these two criteria do not concern merely the information that may be contained in a communication. They serve instead as standards for the evaluation of communicative acts, and are used to assess not merely communicative content but also such varied aspects of these acts as their timing, justification, addressees, form, and general context.

This distinction between the regulation of information and the regulation of communicative acts is illustrated by the facts of a venerable case, Brents v. Morgan, which was the first decision to recognize the invasion of privacy tort in the state of Kentucky. In 1926 in the town of Lebanon, Kentucky, W. R. Morgan, a veterinarian, owed $49.67 to George Brents, a garage mechanic. Brents made several unsuccessful efforts to collect the debt, and in frustration finally put up a sign, five feet by eight feet, in the window of his garage facing one of the principal streets of the town. The sign stated:

Notice.
Dr. W. R. Morgan owes an account here of $49.67. And if promises would pay an account this account would have been settled long ago. This account will be advertised as long as it remains unpaid.

Dr. Morgan sued Brents for damages, alleging that the sign had "caused him great mental pain, humiliation, and mortification," that it exposed him "to public contempt, ridicule, aversion, and disgrace," and that it had caused "an evil opinion of him in the minds of tradesmen and the public generally."[88] Morgan's complaint was styled in the language of a typical libel or defamation suit. But in Kentucky, as elsewhere, truth was a complete defense to an action for defamation, and Dr. Morgan did in fact owe Brents $49.67.

The Kentucky Supreme Court, however, held that although truth may be a defense against an action for defamation, it does not constitute a defense against the "new branch of the law [which] has been developed in the last few years [and] which is denominated the right of privacy." The right of privacy concerned "the right of a person to be free from unwarranted publicity, or the right to live without unwarranted interference by the public about matters with which the public is not necessarily concerned."[89] The court concluded that Brents's posting of the sign violated Morgan's right of privacy. The facts of the case have been cited ever since as a paradigmatic illustration of invasion of privacy.[90]

The *Restatement* would have us ask two questions about the content of Brents's notice. First, we are instructed to inquire whether the information on the sign concerns "the private life" of Dr. Morgan. This inquiry, however, is somewhat puzzling, for it is not certain in what sense Dr. Morgan's debt, and his refusal to pay it, are private facts. Certainly these facts were known to Brents and were not viewed as secret by either party. And surely Brents would have been within his rights to discuss them with his wife or his banker or his accountant. We would even feel nothing improper about his relating them to a perfect stranger who was attempting to determine the worth of Brents's garage in the expectation of purchasing the business.

This suggests that we cannot determine whether the information on the sign concerns private facts simply by examining the content of the information; we must instead have some notion of the circumstances surrounding the revelation of that information. The same information can be viewed as private with respect to some kinds of communications but not with respect to others. To say that the information on Brents's sign concerns "private life," therefore, is really to say that he should not have revealed it in the manner in which he did.

This conclusion is dramatically illustrated by the line of cases holding that a defendant who reveals the past crimes of a rehabilitated felon can be liable for invasion of privacy. The California Supreme Court, for example, held in Briscoe v. Reader's Digest Association[91] that a plaintiff who is leading an exemplary and respectable life can bring an action for public disclosure on the basis of a story in a national magazine revealing that he was convicted of hijacking a truck eleven years earlier.[92] The Court distinguished between publishing "the facts of past crimes" and publishing the identity "of the *actor* in reports of long past crimes."[93] Liability could be predicated on the latter communication but not on the former.

It is obvious, however, that the identity of the plaintiff was, at the time of his conviction, as public a fact as the events of his crime. The characterization of the information as private, therefore, cannot possibly turn solely upon either its content or the extent to which it has previously been disseminated. It must instead depend upon an assessment of the total context of the communicative act by which that information is revealed. The court's conclusion makes sense only if it is read as resting on the perception that it is somehow deeply inappropriate for the defendant to have revealed the plaintiff's identity in that way, or at that time, or to that audience.

The California Supreme Court had in fact explicitly articulated this sense of inappropriateness in Melvin v. Reid, the precedent *Briscoe* relied upon. *Melvin* upheld a plaintiff's claim of invasion of privacy against a defendant who had made a movie about the plaintiff's past life that accurately identified her as a notorious prostitute and an accused felon. The court branded the movie as one made in "willful and wanton disregard of that charity which should actuate us in our social intercourse and which should keep us from unnecessarily holding another up to the scorn and contempt of upright members of society."[94]

If the conclusion that a communicative act reveals the "private life" of a plaintiff ultimately turns on whether, under the circumstances, the communication wantonly disregards social norms of appropriateness, so also, and in a more obvious way, does the second question propounded by the *Restatement*. In assessing whether Brents's sign is an actionable invasion of privacy, the *Restatement* would have us ask whether the information contained in the sign "is of a kind that would be highly offensive to a reasonable person."

The *Restatement*'s formulation of the question invites us to focus on the content of the sign and to assess it according to community norms. We might say, for example, that community norms view the commission of a crime as inherently stigmatic, and hence that the communication of such information would be highly offensive. But the facts of *Brents* do not fit easily within this understanding of the question. Dr. Morgan's debt and his delinquency on that debt are not inherently offensive in the same way as the commission of a crime. Information about the debt, for example, would not be highly offensive as between Morgan and his banker, or as between Brents and Morgan, or as between Morgan and his wife or children. Indeed, twenty-four years after *Brents* the Kentucky Supreme Court held in Voneye v. Turner that it was neither offensive nor an invasion of privacy to communicate to a debtor's employer the fact of a debt and of the debtor's refusal to pay it.[95] As one court put it, "An employer 'is not in a category with the general public which cannot have any legitimate interest in a purely private matter between a creditor and a debtor,' "[96] in large part because

> when one accepts credit, he impliedly consents for the creditor to take reasonable steps "to pursue his debtor and persuade payment . . ." It is only when the creditor's actions constitute oppressive treatment of a debtor, including the unreasonable giving of undue publicity to private debts, that such actions have been held to be an actionable invasion of a debtor's right of privacy.[97]

The offensiveness of the sign in *Brents*, therefore, is a matter not merely of the content of the information that it contains, but also of the "oppressive" manner in which it disseminates that information. This distinction is illustrated by the case of Vassiliades v. Garfinckel's, Brooks Bros., in which a woman sued her surgeon for public disclosure because he had shown "before" and "after" pictures of her cosmetic surgery on a television program. The trial court had directed a verdict for the defendant, in part on the theory that "the photographs were not highly offensive because there was nothing 'uncomplimentary or unsavory' about them." The appellate court reversed, stating that the trial court had misconceived the issue. The question was not whether the content of the photographs was offensive, but rather "whether the publicity of Mrs. Vassiliades' surgery was highly offensive to a reasonable person."[98]

This formulation of the offensiveness requirement, however, essentially asks whether the communicative act at issue, considered in its full context, is "highly offensive."[99] But this inquiry is virtually identical to the inquiry underlying the "private facts" requirement. Both focus broadly on the appropriateness of the communicative act in question, rather than narrowly on the specific content of that communication. The distinct contribution of the "offensiveness" requirement is primarily that it makes explicit the notion that the law will not regulate every inappropriate revelation, but only those which are "highly offensive." Thus the public disclosure tort, like the intrusion tort, penalizes only serious transgressions.

As with intrusion, the elements of the public disclosure branch of the tort roughly approximate an everyday understanding of privacy. When we speak in ordinary language about violations of privacy, we often have in mind inappropriate revelations of intimate facts that ought not be disclosed.[100] The twin requirements of "private facts" and "offensiveness" are a rough attempt to specify when such revelations are inappropriate. But, as with intrusion, the public disclosure tort does not depend upon a neutral or objective measure of when disclosures should be subject to legal liability. Instead the tort draws upon the social norms governing the flow of information in modern society. And these norms, like those that define private space, have a "socially determined variability" and so are sensitive to such factors as the "character of the social occasion,"[101] the purpose, timing, and status of the person making the disclosure, the status and purposes of the addressee of the disclosure, and so on. Information about a debtor, which may be perfectly appropriate to disclose to his employer or banker or wife, would be inappropriate to disclose to his neighbors. Information that may be widely known in some circles may be inappropriate to reveal in others.

We can understand information, then, as confined within "boundaries"[102] that are normatively determined. These boundaries function analogously to those which define the spatial territories analyzed by Goffman. And indeed Goffman specifically notes that one kind of territory is an "information preserve," which contains the "set of facts about himself to which an individual expects to control access," and which is "traditionally treated under the heading of 'privacy.'"[103] Goffman's point is that just as individuals expect to control certain spatial territories, so they

expect to control certain informational territories. The almost physical
apprehension of this informational space is evident, for example, in Warren and Brandeis' famous complaint that "the press is overstepping in
every direction the obvious bounds of propriety and of decency."[104] Because the boundaries of an individual's informational space are "relative
to the customs of the time and place, and . . . determined by the norm of
the ordinary man,"[105] the public disclosure branch of the tort can be said
to maintain those civility rules which establish information preserves in
the same way that the intrusion branch upholds the civility rules which
define spatial territories.

Information preserves, like spatial territories, provide a normative
framework for the development of individual personality. Just as we feel
violated when our bedrooms are invaded, so we experience the inappropriate disclosure of private information "as *pollutions* or *defilements*."[106]
Although the social norms that define information territories concern
communications between defendants and third parties, we nevertheless
depend upon those norms and experience their breach to be "just as
violent and morally inadmissible as listening behind closed doors."[107]
Thus courts enforcing the public disclosure tort see themselves as protecting persons from "indecent and vulgar" communications that would
"outrage or cause mental suffering, shame or humiliation to a person of
ordinary sensibilities,"[108] or that would have the effect of "degrading a
person by laying his life open to public view,"[109] or that would threaten
plaintiffs with a "literal loss of self-identity."[110]

The civility rules which delineate information preserves must therefore
be understood as forms of respect that are integral to both individual and
social personality. They make up an important part of the obligations that
members of a community owe to one another. This perspective helps to
clarify a perplexing feature of the public discourse tort. The tort has
always seemed somewhat strange because a plaintiff can recover damages
for the public disclosure of "private" facts only by definitively and widely
re-broadcasting those same "private" facts through an official adjudicative process. Although few may have heard of Mrs. Vassiliades' plastic
surgery as a result of her doctor's announcements over the television—in
fact, Mrs. Vassiliades could identify only two persons who had seen the
broadcast—her surgical alteration is now forever imprinted in the law
books, and the very process of her trial no doubt made the fact of her
surgery known to many of her acquaintances who otherwise would not
have been aware of it. If the public disclosure tort is understood simply as
a mechanism for protecting the secrecy of private facts, it would seem to

be entirely self-defeating.[111] But if the tort is instead understood as a means of obtaining vindication for the infringement of information preserves, the disclosure of information in the course of a judicial action may be of only secondary importance so long as the plaintiff is ultimately reintegrated into that chain of ceremony which defines and embraces members of the community.

This suggests that the public disclosure tort fulfills the first two of the three functions we previously identified for the intrusion tort—safeguarding the respect due individuals by virtue of their territorial claims, and protecting the "ritual idiom" through which such respect finds social expression.[112] The idiom at issue in the context of public disclosure, however, appears somewhat different than the idiom at issue in intrusion. Intrusion regulates dyadic relationships, which involve the appropriateness of direct interactions between plaintiffs and defendants, whereas public disclosure regulates triadic relationships, which involve the appropriateness of defendants' disclosures of private information about plaintiffs to third-party addressees.

This difference has significant consequences. The intrusion tort regulates situations in which a plaintiff's direct control over whether to assert or to waive pertinent civility rules is constitutive of the most intimate aspects of her social existence. In public disclosure, on the other hand, the pertinent civility rules specifically control only the relationship between a defendant and his audience. It is therefore awkward to speak of these rules as norms that intrinsically establish the intimate life of a plaintiff. Thus the idiom at issue in public disclosure is chiefly expressive of respect, and does not characteristically function in the dual way of the civility norms protected by intrusion, which mark the boundary between respect and intimacy. It follows from this that the public disclosure tort cannot systematically be linked to the third function that we attributed to the intrusion tort, that of preserving the ability of individuals to use the language of territories to develop a sense of their own autonomy. Viewed in this light, limitations on the tort of public disclosure carry somewhat less profound social implications than do limitations on the tort of intrusion.

The Concept of "Legitimate Public Concern": The Tension between Civility and Public Accountability

The tort of public disclosure requires that a plaintiff demonstrate that a defendant's communication "is not of legitimate concern to the public."

This requirement, which is sometimes called the "privilege to report news"[113] or the "privilege to publicize newsworthy matters,"[114] is acknowledged by all common law courts that have recognized the public disclosure tort. The requirement is the single most important distinction between the intrusion and public disclosure branches of the invasion of privacy tort.[115] If the former seeks to regulate all highly offensive violations of spatial territories, the latter permits information territories to be freely broken if the information at issue is "newsworthy."

The reason for this difference is not obscure: it lies in the distinction between a territory conceived as a physical space and a territory conceived as an array of information. Preservation of the former requires no more than the regulation of discrete forms of physical conduct; preservation of the latter, however, implies no less than control over the diffusion of information throughout an entire society. The common law long ago came to recognize the importance of that diffusion for maintaining social order and solidarity. In his 1826 *Treatise* on defamation law, for example, Thomas Starkie noted the "difficulties" involved in the regulation of information about persons, because the

> subject matter is more subtle and refined, and does not admit of the broad and plain limits and distinctions which may be established in respect of forcible injuries; for instance, in the case of battery of the person, the law can, without hesitation, pronounce, that any, the least degree of violence shall be deemed illegal, and entitle the complainant to his remedy; but, communications concerning reputation cannot be so prohibited; every day's convenience requires, that men, and their affairs, should be discussed, though frequently at the hazard of individual reputation; and it conduces mainly to the ends of morality and good order, to the safety and security of society, that considerable latitude should be afforded to such communications. The dread of public censure and disgrace is not only the most effectual, and therefore the most important, but in numberless instances the only security which society possesses for the preservation of decency and the performance of the private duties of life.[116]

From the perspective of individuals, respect for information preserves is a matter of common decency. From a more general perspective, however, decency would itself be undermined if individuals could hide immoral acts within the secrecy of information preserves. Moreover, as Starkie observes, legal protection of information territories would have other social costs, including those associated with transactions based upon imperfect information.[117]

Long before the Constitution was relevant to the regulation of the invasion of privacy tort,[118] the common law was sensitive to just such policy concerns regarding the diffusion of information. Warren and Brandeis, for example, flatly asserted that "the right to privacy does not prohibit any publication of matter which is of public or general interest."[119] The first decision to recognize a right of privacy, Pavesich v. New England Life Insurance Co., stated with equal firmness that "the truth may be spoken, written, or printed about all matters of a public nature, as well as matters of a private nature in which the public has a legitimate interest."[120] From the beginning, therefore, the task of the common law has been to balance the importance of maintaining individual information preserves against the public's general interest in information.

In conceptualizing the claims of the public, courts have tended to follow two distinct forms of inquiry. The first is directed toward the social status of the plaintiff, the second toward the social significance of the information at issue. Both inquiries ultimately lead to the same question: the nature of the public and its right to demand information.

The first inquiry is best illustrated by the example of public officials or candidates for public office. The obvious political importance of the dissemination of full information about such individuals has led courts to view them as having only extremely attenuated claims to information preserves.[121] Although the flap in early 1988 over the disclosure of Gary Hart's extramarital affair indicates that this view is still somewhat controversial,[122] it is profoundly unlikely that courts will intervene to decide what information may or may not be disclosed about a public official or candidate.[123] The underlying metaphor is that of the expropriation of private property, for "public men are, as it were, public property."[124] The claims of public officials to a "private" information preserve are simply overridden by the more general demands of the public for political accountability.

Courts have reached a similar conclusion with regard to "voluntary public figures." In the words of the *Restatement*:

> One who voluntarily places himself in the public eye, by engaging in public activities, or by assuming a prominent role in institutions or activities having general economic, cultural, social or similar public interest, or by submitting himself or his work for public judgment, cannot complain when he is given publicity that he has sought, even though it may be unfavorable to him . . . The legitimate interest of the public in [such an] individual may extend beyond those matters which are them-

selves made public, and to some reasonable extent may include information as to matters that would otherwise be private.[125]

Although the reasoning of the *Restatement* is almost entirely in terms of
the voluntary public figure's waiver of any right to an information preserve, this logic is ultimately incomplete. For in almost every case a public
figure will bring an action for the disclosure of information which he has
not voluntarily made public, and it would be patent fiction to assert that
in such circumstances he has "waived" his claim to the protection of this
information. In such cases, therefore, the law's refusal to protect the
public figure's information preserve must be justified in terms of a substantive analysis of the public's "legitimate interest" in the information at
issue.

The second line of inquiry that courts have used to interpret the "legitimate public concern" requirement contains just such a substantive
analysis. This inquiry focuses not on the social status of the plaintiff but
rather on the nature of the information at issue. As the *Restatement* asserts,
"Included within the scope of legitimate public concern are matters of the
kind customarily regarded as 'news.' "[126] The question posed by this line
of analysis is why the public's interest in "news" should override individual claims to the integrity of their information preserves.

This question is illuminated by the work of Alvin Gouldner, who has
offered a theoretical account of the sociological status of the "public":

> A "public" emerges when there is an attenuation between culture, on the
> one side, and patterns of social interaction, on the other. Traditional
> "groups" are characterized by the association and mutual support of
> both elements; by the fact that their members have patterned social
> interactions with one another which, in turn, fosters among them com-
> mon understandings and shared interests, which, again in turn, facilitates
> their mutual interaction, and so on. A "public" "refers to a number of
> people exposed to the same social stimuli," and having something in
> common even without being in persisting interaction with one another
> . . . "Publics" are persons who need not be "co-present," in the "sight
> and hearing of one another."[127]

The implication of Gouldner's analysis is that in large and diverse modern societies, in which common personal and patterned social interactions
are quite limited, news provides precisely those "same social stimuli" that
gather together the population into a "public."[128] "News," writes
Gouldner, "is a public (and a public-generating) social phenome-

non." Thus the "emergence of the mass media and of the 'public' are mutually constructive developments."[129] To restrict the news is therefore simultaneously to restrict the public.

The public, however, has certain overriding claims to resist such restriction. One such claim, raised in the context of public officials, is political. Because American law views the public, in its role as the electorate, as ultimately responsible for political decisions, the public is presumptively entitled to all information that is necessary for informed governance. This theory is well canvassed in the First Amendment literature,[130] and it is responsible for the frequent reiteration by the Supreme Court that "expression on public issues 'has always rested on the highest rung of the hierarchy of First Amendment values.' "[131]

But although the application of the theory of political governance to the public disclosure tort is uncontroversial, it is far too narrow to explain the broad scope of "legitimate public concern" that courts have felt compelled to protect. An excellent illustration is the classic case of Sidis v. F-R Publishing Corp., which involved a famous child prodigy named William James Sidis who in 1910 at the age of eleven had lectured distinguished mathematicians on the subject of four-dimensional bodies. His graduation from Harvard College at the age of sixteen attracted "considerable public attention." But Sidis unfortunately never lived up to his promise. Soon after his graduation he slipped into a public obscurity from which he was rudely retrieved in 1937 by a biographical sketch in the "Where Are They Now?" section of *The New Yorker*. The sketch was "merciless in its dissection of intimate details of its subject's personal life, and this in company with elaborate accounts of Sidis' passion for privacy and the pitiable lengths to which he has gone in order to avoid public scrutiny." The Second Circuit characterized the article as "a ruthless exposure of a once public character, who has since sought and has now been deprived of the seclusion of private life." The court nevertheless concluded that Sidis could not recover for invasion of privacy, because the "public interest in obtaining information" was "dominant over the individual's desire for privacy."[132]

The court's decision to favor the interests of the public over Sidis' claim to an information preserve cannot be explained by a narrowly political theory of the public. The information contained in the article was not relevant to the governance of the nation. Nor, except in a purely tautological sense, can the court's decision be explained on the grounds that Sidis' pathetic condition was "news," for by 1937 he had faded completely from public view. On what grounds, then, could the court conclude that the public was entitled to the information contained in the article?

The court reasoned that Sidis "was once a public figure" who had "excited both admiration and curiosity"; the article was "a matter of public concern" because it contained "the answer to the question of whether or not [Sidis] had fulfilled his early promise."[133] In effect, then, the court equated the notion of legitimate public concern with efforts to answer reasonable questions about public matters. Thus the court's analysis ultimately rested on the assumption that the public has a right to inquire into the significance of public persons and events.

This assumption has deep historical and sociological roots. Gouldner notes, for example, that "to make matters 'public' means to open them even to those who are not known personally, to those who do not ordinarily come into one's sight and hearing. On the paradigmatic level, to make things public is to take them (or to allow them to go) beyond the *family*, where all is in the sight and hearing of others." Because relations outside the family lack "affection, emotional dependency, tact, and . . . direct power over one another, there will be far fewer constraints in what may be questioned in public." Thus public actions "are open to a critique by strangers who have fewer inhibitions about demanding justification and reasonable grounds," and for this reason such action must "routinely have to give an accounting of itself, either by providing information about its conduct or justification for it." "The public," in short, "is a sphere in which one is accountable," and being accountable "means that one can be *constrained* to reveal *what* one has done and *why* one has done it."[134]

Gouldner's claim, of course, is not that public discussion is invariably characterized by a rational inquiry into accountability. Anyone familiar with the "unfair, intemperate, scurrilous and irresponsible"[135] character of much of our public discourse, or with the susceptibility of that discourse to manipulation by what Walter Lippmann called "publicity men,"[136] would know otherwise. Indeed, the discovery of the many irrational elements of our public discourse in the 1920s led to a serious "crisis" of democratic theory.[137] Gouldner's point is rather that the very attempt to assess the meaning of public phenomena implies "a cleared and safe space" in which the value of competing assessments may be "questioned, *negated* and *contradicted*." The public search for accountability, in other words, creates a structure of communication that is inherently "*critical*."[138]

Gouldner's observations suggest that the public, as a collection of strangers united by access to common stimuli, is a social formation that has its own distinctive dynamic. An important aspect of this dynamic is the constant need to evaluate the significance of those stimuli whose public dissemination establishes the public's own continued existence. This need generates a critical logic in which no given evaluation can be rendered invulnerable to contradiction. The power of this logic is plainly visible in the reasoning of the *Sidis* opinion. The case in effect creates "a cleared and safe space" in which rival interpretations of the meaning of public persons and events may compete. The *Sidis* court refuses to circumscribe that space by withholding the information necessary for any given interpretation.

Thus *Sidis* ultimately rests on what might be termed a normative theory of public accountability, on the notion that the public *should* be entitled to inquire freely into the significance of public persons and events, and that this entitlement is so powerful that it overrides individual claims to the maintenance of information preserves. The theory is highly influential in modern case law, and it has led courts to interpret the "legitimate public concern" requirement as protecting the disclosure of all information having "a rational and at least arguably close relationship" to public persons or events "to be explained."[139]

The theory of public accountability offers a justification for the *Restatement*'s rules regarding "voluntary public figures," for such persons are by definition already public, and hence subject to the free competition of rival interpretive assessments. Thus even if voluntary public figures cannot plausibly be understood to have "waived" their right to foreclose inquiry into nonpublic aspects of their lives, the public nevertheless has the right to scrutinize those aspects if they are relevant to its evaluation of the significance of public action.[140]

The theory also accounts for the *Restatement*'s treatment of what it calls "involuntary public figures." These are individuals who, without their consent or approval, have become involved in public events like crimes, disasters, or accidents. The *Restatement* concludes that such persons

> are regarded as properly subject to the public interest, and publishers are permitted to satisfy the curiosity of the public ... As in the case of the voluntary public figure, the authorized publicity is not limited to the event that itself arouses the public interest, and to some reasonable extent includes publicity given to facts about the individual that would otherwise be purely private.[141]

Because concepts of consent and waiver are obviously inapplicable, the *Restatement* cannot explain exactly why the information preserves of involuntary public figures should be subject to "authorized publicity." The theory of public accountability, however, would justify the dissemination of information necessary to assess the significance of the public events in which such persons have become embroiled. Publicity would be actionable only when it bears "no discernible relationship" to the public events that require explanation.[142]

The theory of public accountability, with its requirement that the legal system permit public events and persons to be critically assessed, flatly contradicts the fundamental purpose of the public disclosure tort, which is to subject public communications to civility rules. This tension can be seen by comparing *Sidis* with *Briscoe*. In *Sidis* a public figure was deemed accountable to the demands of public inquiry despite the passage of time and the successful quest for anonymity; in *Briscoe* the passage of time and the successful achievement of anonymity were deemed to signify that a public figure had "reverted to that 'lawful and unexciting life' led by others," so that "he no longer need 'satisfy the curiosity of the public.' "[143] In *Sidis* public accountability runs roughshod over civility; in *Briscoe* civility forecloses the potential evaluation of a public person and event, and hence impedes the critical process of public accountability.

The reconciliation of this tension is an essential problematic of the public disclosure tort. *Sidis* itself allows for the possibility that the public accountability of public figures may be theoretically limited by the requirements of civility, but it predicts that these limits will be so attenuated as to be practically nonexistent:

> We express no comment on whether or not the newsworthiness of the matter printed will always constitute a complete defense. Revelations may be so intimate and so unwarranted in view of the victim's position as to outrage the community's notions of decency. But when focused upon public characters, truthful comments upon dress, speech, habits, and the ordinary aspects of personality will usually not transgress this line. Regrettably or not, the misfortunes and frailties of neighbors and "public figures" are subjects of considerable interest and discussion to the rest of the population. And when such are the mores of the community, it would be unwise for a court to bar their expression in the newspapers, books, and magazines of the day.[144]

The development of the law has in general supported *Sidis'* prediction. Even the California Supreme Court has come to characterize *Briscoe*, its own precedent, as "an exception to the more general rule that 'once a man has become a public figure, or news, he remains a matter of legitimate recall to the public mind to the end of his days.' "[145] Thus the logic of public accountability has proved virtually overpowering with respect to the discussion of public persons or events. Any information with a "discernible relationship" to such public matters will likely be deemed "of legitimate concern to the public," and hence its dissemination to the public will not be actionable.[146]

That leaves open, however, the question of when information about nonpublic persons or events may also be protected as "of legitimate concern to the public." This question is nicely illustrated by the case of *Meetze v. Associated Press*, in which the South Carolina Supreme Court held that a story reporting the birth of a healthy baby boy to a married twelve-year-old mother was of legitimate public interest, despite the mother's request that there be no "publicity."[147] The birth was not a public event until the Associated Press made it so, and for this reason the court's holding cannot be explained by any theory of public accountability. The publication of the story cannot be justified on the grounds of the public's need to understand public events or persons. Instead, the court's protection of the story must depend upon a different theory, one which addresses the question of when events or persons may be made public in the first instance.

One such theory is that of political governance. Because we understand the public, in its role as the electorate, to be the ultimate source of political authority, it follows that information pertinent to informed governance should be made public. As Walter Lippmann observed at the dawn of the modern First Amendment era, "News is the chief source of the opinion by which government now proceeds."[148] But this theory, although uncontroversial, is too narrow to account for a case like *Meetze*, and the South Carolina Supreme Court made no attempt to use it. Instead, the court defended its interpretation of the "legitimate public concern" requirement on the grounds that it "is rather unusual for a twelve-year-old girl to give birth to a child. It is a biological occurrence which would naturally excite public interest."[149]

This notion of "naturally" exciting public interest is puzzling. The precise issue posed by *Meetze* is whether a mother's information preserve should be forced to yield to the curiosity of the public. That the public is in fact curious may well be true, but it merely restates the problem. As the court itself notes, "The phrase 'public or general interest' in this connection does not mean mere curiosity."[150] But this brings us back full circle, for we cannot distinguish between "natural" and "mere" curiosity without some criterion of when it is justifiable to drag nonpublic matters into the light of public scrutiny.

The second *Restatement*, in a widely cited and influential commentary,[151] offers just such a criterion. It suggests that the question of whether giving publicity to nonpublic matters is of legitimate public concern should be decided by reference to "the customs and conventions of the community":

> In the last analysis what is proper becomes a matter of the community mores. The line is to be drawn when the publicity ceases to be the giving of information to which the public is entitled, and becomes a morbid and sensational prying into private lives for its own sake, with which a reasonable member of the public, with decent standards, would say that he had no concern. The limitations, in other words, are those of common decency, having due regard to the freedom of the press and its reasonable leeway to choose what it will tell the public, but also due regard to the feelings of the individual and the harm that will be done to him by the exposure.[152]

At first blush, the *Restatement*'s interpretation appears to explain why, for example, the South Carolina Supreme Court, thirty years after *Meetze*, would in Hawkins v. Multimedia, Inc.[153] uphold a finding of liability against a newspaper for publicly disclosing the identity of a teenage father of an illegitimate child in a story about teenage pregnancies. It is plausible to suggest that "community mores" would be more offended by such a story than by an article identifying the married twelve-year-old mother of a baby son.[154]

Upon further reflection, however, the gloss placed upon the *Restatement* by a decision like *Hawkins* is inadequate, for it essentially equates the "customs and conventions of the community" that determine whether nonpublic matters are of legitimate public concern with the social norms that underlie the twin requirements of "offensiveness" and "private facts." It thus collapses the "legitimate public concern" test into the very criteria that define whether disclosures are actionable, thereby rendering the test superfluous. As a result the capacity of the news to make persons and events public would be completely subordinated to the civility rules enforced by the public disclosure tort.

Most courts, however, have refused to subordinate the news in this manner. In Kelley v. Post Publishing Co., for example, a newspaper was sued for publishing the photograph of a hideously deformed body of a child after a fatal automobile accident. While the display of such a photograph might well exceed the bounds of common decency, the court in *Kelley* ruled that it was not actionable for the newspaper to publish the photograph, on the grounds that any contrary conclusion would prevent the publication of pictures "of a train wreck or of an airplane crash if any of the bodies of the victims were recognizable."[155]

Kelley's reasoning rests on two widely shared and important premises. The first is that we want information about events like disasters to be made public; the second is that we want this information disseminated even if doing so would violate the civility rules that would otherwise be enforced by the tort.[156] It is clear that the *Restatement* shares these premises, for it explicitly states that "authorized publicity includes publications concerning homicide and other crimes, arrests, police raids, suicides, marriages and divorces, accidents, fires, catastrophes of nature . . . and many other similar matters of genuine, even if more or less deplorable, popular appeal."[157]

Thus the *Restatement*, and in fact almost all courts, interpret the "legitimate public concern" requirement as insulating from legal liability news that is uncivil and "deplorable."[158] But this implies that the "community mores" which determine whether the disclosure of nonpublic matters is of legitimate public concern cannot be the same as the civility rules which determine whether communications are "highly offensive" disclosures of "private" facts. The *Restatement* tells us that the community mores at issue in the "legitimate public concern" test are instead those which identify "matters . . . customarily regarded as 'news.'"[159] So it is the mores that define news which circumscribe the scope of the press's "reasonable leeway to choose what it will tell the public."[160]

But while this interpretation of the "legitimate public concern" requirement has the virtue of internal coherence, it simultaneously raises a distinct and pressing issue of public policy: Why should the press be confined by the customary definition of "news"? It is true that the mores which define newsgathering define the boundaries of public life as we now know it, but why should the law hinder attempts to enlarge that life, particularly if there is a public desire for the information constitutive of such enlargements?

The answer, of course, is that once persons or events are made public, the logic of public accountability will all but displace rules of civility. In the public sphere all persons and events are subject to an unblinking scrutiny that searches for meaning and significance; in the sphere of community such scrutiny is experienced as demeaning and as utterly destructive of the conventions that give meaning to human dignity.[161] The two spheres are deeply incommensurate and can coexist only in an uneasy tension. The common law therefore resists enlargement of the public sphere because it is inconsistent with the maintenance of social personality. What is ultimately at stake in this resistance is thus the protection of both individual dignity and community identity, as constituted by rules of civility, from the encroachments of the logic of public accountability.

In the modern tort the reach of this logic is as a practical matter determined by the application of the "legitimate public concern" test to nonpublic matters. The test thus bears an enormous social pressure, and it is not surprising to find that the common law is deeply confused and ambivalent about its application.[162] One jurisdiction abandons the field to the public sphere and refuses to enforce communal norms of civility,[163] while another gives full sway to " 'the customs and conventions of the community,' "[164] while yet a third holds that "in borderline cases the benefit of doubt should be cast in favor of protecting the publication."[165] Some courts confine the sphere of legitimate public concern to information that is, in Gouldner's phrase, "*de*contextualized,"[166] so that they "distinguish between fictionalization and dramatization on the one hand and dissemination of news and information on the other."[167] Other courts hold that "it is neither feasible nor desirable for a court to make a distinction between news for information and news for entertainment in determining the extent to which publication is privileged."[168]

In these various and conflicting interpretations of the "legitimate public concern" test one can trace the wavering line between the insistent demands of public accountability and the expressive claims of communal life. Common law courts, like the rest of us, are searching for ways to mediate between these two necessary and yet conflicting regimes. We can understand the public disclosure tort, then, as holding a flickering candle to what Max Weber in 1918 called the "fate of our times," which is of course the "rationalization and intellectualization and, above all, . . . the 'disenchantment of the world.' "[169]

Concluding Thoughts: The Fragility of Privacy

I hope I have made good on my initial claim that the common law tort of invasion of privacy reflects a complex and fascinating apprehension of the social texture of contemporary society. The tort safeguards the interests of individuals in the maintenance of rules of civility. These rules enable individuals to receive and to express respect, and to that extent are constitutive of human dignity. In the case of intrusion, these rules also enable individuals to receive and to express intimacy, and to that extent are constitutive of human autonomy. In the case of both intrusion and public disclosure, the civility rules maintained by the tort embody the obligations owed by members of a community to one another, and to that extent define the substance and boundaries of community life.

The tort's preservation of civility rules appears in its clearest and least qualified form in the branch of the tort that protects the seclusion of individuals from intrusion. But when civility rules attempt to control communication, as in the branch of the tort that regulates the public disclosure of private information, the common law must confront the tension between such rules and the demands of public accountability. The common law has been torn between maintaining the civility which we expect in public discourse, and giving ample "latitude"[170] to the processes of critical evaluation that are also intrinsic to that discourse.

This interpretation of the tort carries with it several significant implications for the understanding of privacy in contemporary society. First, it suggests that in everyday life we do not experience privacy as a "neutral" or "objective" fact but rather as an inherently normative set of social practices that constitute a way of life, our way of life. The privacy protected by the common law has no special function, like the protection of secrecy or the maintenance of role segregation, although it may, to a greater or lesser extent, accomplish each of these purposes. In the tort, "privacy" is simply a label that we use to identify one aspect of the many forms of respect by which we maintain a community. It is less important that the purity of the label be maintained than that the forms of community life of which it is a part be preserved.

Second, privacy understood as subsisting in the ritual idiom of civility rules can exist only where social life has the density and intensity to generate and sustain such rules. It is important to stress, however, that social life does not always have these characteristics. Certain kinds of "total institutions," for example, deliberately violate civility rules so as to degrade and mortify inmates.[171]

A less exotic and more significant example of the loss of civility rules can be found in the writings of James Rule, who has extensively studied large-scale surveillance organizations like consumer credit rating agencies. Rule found that attempts to limit the organizations' access to personal information in the name of privacy were invariably transformed into requirements that they ensure the accuracy and instrumentally appropriate use of such information. This transformation ultimately rested on the unimpeachable assumption that organizations could reach better, more precise decisions with greater information, and on the more questionable assumption that "both organizations and individuals shared an interest in [this] enhanced efficiency." What Rule found striking was the absence of any strong privacy claims that could limit the *absolute* amount of information obtainable by such organizations.[172]

This absence, however, is rendered explicable by Rule's own account of the nature of the "privacy" interest at stake, which in his view amounted to no more than " 'aesthetic' satisfactions in keeping private spheres private." In the instrumental world of large surveillance organizations, in other words, the realm of the private has dwindled to the domain of the "instinctive."[173] This strongly suggests that relationships between individuals and large organizations like credit rating agencies are not sufficiently textured or dense to sustain vital rules of civility, and that as a result privacy has lost its social and communal character. But if the value of privacy can be conceptualized only in personal or subjective terms, it should be no surprise that its value has not proved politically powerful.

Third, the specific areas of social life that are governed by rules of civility are vulnerable to displacement by exogenous institutions. The preemption of civility by the rational accountability characteristic of the public sphere is only one example of such exogenous pressure. Another would be the claims of the state to control and regulate communal life. Stanley Diamond has eloquently documented how the modern state has "cannibalized" the "spontaneous, traditional, personal, [and] commonly known" aspects of "custom."[174] This tension between the prerogatives of state power and the norms of communal life is plainly visible in Fourth Amendment jurisprudence, which attempts to subordinate the conduct of state law enforcement officials to the community's normatively sanctioned "expectations of privacy," while simultaneously balancing against these expectations "the government's need for effective methods to deal with breaches of public order."[175] In this balance it is not uncommon for the instrumental needs of the state to override community norms.

The ultimate lesson of the tort, then, is the extreme fragility of privacy norms in modern life. That fragility stems not merely from our ravenous appetite for the management of our social environment but also from the undeniable prerogatives of public accountability. The way of life that happens to constitute us, and to bestow our privacy with its meaning, appears to be merely arbitrary when placed against this great need to assess the meaning of public phenomena. And we are thus led to attempt to rationalize the value of privacy, to discover its functions and reasons, to dress it up in the philosophical language of autonomy, or to dress it down in the economic language of information costs. But this is to miss the plain fact that privacy is for us a living reality only because we enjoy a certain kind of communal existence. Our very dignity inheres in that existence,[176] which, if it is not acknowledged and preserved, will vanish, as will the privacy we cherish.

3

Cultural Heterogeneity and Law: Pornography, Blasphemy, and the First Amendment

Twenty-five years ago legal academics viewed the law of obscenity as the regulation of sex. Laws prohibiting obscenity were understood to stem from "traditional notions, rooted in this country's religious antecedents, of governmental responsibility for communal and individual 'decency' and 'morality.' "[1] They protected our common cultural "environment."[2] The constitutional issue posed by such laws, therefore, was whether the First Amendment permitted expression to be suppressed for the purpose of preserving "the purity of the community and . . . the salvation and welfare of the 'consumer.' "[3]

During the 1980s, however, this view of obscenity changed, in large measure because of the remarkable work of Catharine MacKinnon and Andrea Dworkin.[4] For MacKinnon and Dworkin the issue is neither decency nor community morality but rather the oppression of women. They use the term "pornography" to signify their concern with the sexually explicit subordination of women as distinguished from mere prurience.[5] Pornography is for them "an institution of gender inequality," which not only causes discrete acts of sexual violence against individual women, but which, more fundamentally, hurts "individuals, not *as* individuals in a one-at-a-time sense, but as members of the group 'women.' "[6] Women as a group are harmed because "pornography constructs the social reality of gender," and hence in a deep sense all women are "defined in pornographic terms" as sexually unequal.[7] The efforts of MacKinnon and Dworkin pose an important constitutional question: whether the First Amendment will permit expression to be suppressed for the purpose of preventing this assault on the "status"[8] of women as a group.[9]

This question implicates many of the same issues as those raised by government attempts to regulate speech vilifying particular minorities or ethnic cultures.[10] At the most general level, the question interrogates the obligations of a legal order when society does not consist of a single, unified community, but is instead heterogeneous and made up of diverse and competitive groups. In this essay I shall suggest three different ways of understanding these obligations. I shall then explore the historical and sociological underpinnings of these perspectives by examining the crime of blasphemy in England and America. Finally, I shall bring these perspectives to bear on the constitutional challenge posed by the contemporary feminist critique of pornography.

Law in a Heterogeneous Society

Consider the options available to a legal order in a society consisting of heterogeneous groups. The law can place the authority of legal sanctions behind the cultural perspectives of a dominant group; or it can foster a regime in which diverse groups can escape from such domination and maintain their distinctive values; or it can ignore group values and perspectives altogether and recognize only the claims of individuals. I shall call these three options, respectively, assimilationism, pluralism, and individualism.[11] Most legal orders, and certainly our own, contain elements of each of these three options, and are, for example, individualist with respect to one issue but assimilationist with respect to another.

Assimilationist law places the force of the state behind the cultural perspective of a particular, dominant group. If a society is relatively homogeneous, so that the values of this group are representative of the society as a whole, assimilationist law can be said to be expressive of common community norms. But if the society is heterogeneous, assimilationist law can instead be understood as an attempt, which may be more or less hegemonic in character, to extend the values of a dominant group to the larger society.[12] An example of an assimilationist law is the federal anti-bigamy statute, which was upheld in Reynolds v. United States on the grounds, inter alia, that "polygamy has always been odious among the northern and western nations of Europe."[13] Another example is the requirement that schoolchildren salute the flag, which was upheld in Minersville School District v. Gobitis on the grounds that a state can enforce "the traditions of a people" and hence "create that continuity of a treasured common life which constitutes a civilization."[14]

In both of these examples law was used to support the values of a dominant culture, notwithstanding the dissenting values of marginal or subordinate groups. From the perspective of these latter groups, assimilationist law can often appear based in "cultural chauvinism, social hypocrisy, and disdain for diversity."[15] Assimilationist values, however, have deep roots in American history.[16] With respect to newly arrived immigrants, for example, our "most prevalent ideology" has been the concept of "Anglo-conformity," which "demanded the complete renunciation of the immigrant's ancestral culture in favor of the behavior and values of the Anglo-Saxon core group."[17] Assimilationist values in this country are probably best exemplified by the "Americanization" movement that flourished during the early years of the twentieth century.[18]

Opposed to assimilationist values are those of pluralism, which embrace, rather than reject, group heterogeneity. The concept of pluralism is sometimes associated by legal scholars with a vision of politics as a "struggle among self-interested groups for scarce social resources" in which any concept of the common good is "incoherent, potentially totalitarian, or both."[19] But pluralism has a prior and deeper meaning, one in which the affirmative value of diversity is explicitly acknowledged and celebrated.[20] In 1909, for example, William James used the term in this sense in his Hibbert Lectures, entitled *A Pluralistic Universe*.[21] Fifteen years later James's literary executor, Horace Kallen, coined the term "cultural pluralism" to express the importance of "manyness, variety, differentiation," as opposed to what Kallen viewed as the dead uniformity of Americanization. For Kallen, "democracy involves, not the elimination of differences, but the perfection and conservation of differences. It aims, through Union, not at uniformity, but at variety . . . It involves a give and take between radically different types, and a mutual respect and mutual cooperation based on mutual understanding."[22]

The values of pluralism, like those of assimilationism, also have deep roots in American history. They reach back beyond Walt Whitman's chants in praise of the United States as "the modern composite nation," the "Nation of many nations,"[23] to the very structure of our federalism, which seeks to the extent possible to preserve the heterogeneity inherent in local and regional differentiation.[24]

If assimilationist law attempts to unify society around the cultural values of a single dominant group, pluralist law attempts to create ground rules by which diverse and potentially competitive groups can retain their distinct identities and yet continue to coexist.[25] These ground rules can range from the requirement of state neutrality respecting conflicting re-

ligions, to the enforcement of norms of mutual respect, as exemplified by
the group libel statute upheld in Beauharnais v. Illinois. That statute
imposed criminal penalties on any expression that exposed " 'citizens of
any race, color, creed or religion to contempt, derision, or obloquy.' " In
Beauharnais the Court stressed that the need to foster "the manifold
adjustments required for free, ordered life in a metropolitan, polyglot
community" justified the legal provision of "such group-protection on
behalf of the individual."[26]

Pluralist law rests on two premises: that diversity is to be safeguarded,
and that diversity inheres in the various perspectives of differing groups.
"In a multi-ethnic society," the historian John Higham has written, "the
assimilationist stresses a unifying ideology, whereas the pluralist guards
distinctive memory." The pluralist guards his distinctive memory because
for him "individuals can realize themselves, and become whole, only
through the group that nourishes their being."[27] Hence pluralism "stresses
the rights of the ethnic group over the rights of the individual."[28] As Justice
Black dryly noted in his dissent in *Beauharnais,* the Court had in effect held
that the value of providing group protection was more important than that
of safeguarding an "individual's choice" to speak.[29]

This focus on group rights has always been controversial in America
because it appears "to predetermine the individual's fate by his ethnic
group membership."[30] Americans have traditionally attached great importance to the image of the independent individual capable of transcending his or her particular social or ethnic background; "we strongly assert
the value of our self-reliance and autonomy."[31] Thus if pluralist law
protects the ability of groups to maintain their distinctive identities, law
based on the value of individualism focuses instead on the protection of
individuals vis-à-vis groups. If pluralism celebrates the diversity of cultures, individualism acclaims instead the diversity of persons.

The distinction between the two forms of law is illustrated by the case
of Wisconsin v. Yoder, where the Supreme Court held that the free
exercise clause of the First Amendment prohibited the state of Wisconsin
from requiring that Amish children attend public or private schools until
the age of sixteen.[32] In his opinion for the Court, Chief Justice Burger
noted that such a requirement would pose the "very real threat of undermining the Amish community and religious practice as they exist today," and would require the Amish to "either abandon belief and be
assimilated into society at large, or . . . to migrate to some other and more
tolerant region."[33] Burger thus construed the First Amendment as pro-

tecting the identity of the Amish community and as shielding that community from forced assimilation into the dominant culture.

Justice Douglas argued in dissent, however, that the Constitution safeguarded instead the rights of individual Amish children to choose whether or not to become part of the Amish community. Douglas viewed religion as "an individual experience," and hence interpreted the First Amendment as guaranteeing the rights of children "to break from the Amish tradition":

> It is the future of the student, not the future of the parents, that is imperiled by today's decision. If a parent keeps his child out of school beyond the grade school, then the child will be forever barred from entry into the new and amazing world of diversity that we have today. The child may decide that that is the preferred course, or he may rebel. It is the student's judgment, not his parents', that is essential if we are to give full meaning to what we have said about the Bill of Rights and of the right of students to be masters of their own destiny.[34]

For Burger the "amazing world of diversity" to be protected inheres in the continuing traditions of the Amish community; for Douglas that diversity is constituted instead by the decisions of individuals to embrace or reject those traditions. Burger's opinion rests on the values of pluralism, Douglas' on the values of individualism.[35]

The contrast between individualism and assimilationism can appear equally stark. The latter upholds the cultural values of the dominant group; the former protects the rights of individuals to dissent from those values. In *Gobitis* the Supreme Court supported the values of assimilationism by upholding the right of a majority to require dissenters to swear allegiance to the flag and to the cultural perspective for which it stood.[36] But three years later the Court dramatically reversed itself, and in West Virginia State Board of Education v. Barnette issued the classic defense of "intellectual individualism": "If there is any fixed star in our constitutional constellation, it is that no official, high or petty, can prescribe what shall be orthodox in politics, nationalism, religion, or other matters of opinion." *Barnette* rested squarely on the individual's "right to differ as to things that touch the heart of the existing order,"[37] a right that is deeply incompatible with assimilationist law.

We are thus in a position to draw rough distinctions between three different kinds of law: assimilationist, pluralist, and individualist. Each postulates a different kind of relationship between cultural heterogeneity and the legal order. Assimilationist law strives toward social uniformity by imposing the values of a dominant cultural group; pluralist law safeguards diversity by enabling competing groups to maintain their distinct perspectives; individualist law rejects group values altogether in favor of the autonomous choices of individuals.[38]

It is tempting to view these three kinds of law as sharply distinct and mutually exclusive. But they are not. There are in fact subtle and fascinating connections between them. In the next section I shall explore these connections using the example of the crime of blasphemy, which in both England and America has been one legal response to the presence of religious diversity. By examining the complex interrelationships among individualist, pluralist, and assimilationist law, I hope to offer a theoretical structure that will assist in the analysis of the feminist critique of pornography.

The Crime of Blasphemy

In England, blasphemy was a common law crime. It was one of the four branches of criminal libel, the other three being obscenity, sedition, and defamation.[39] All four branches of libel sought to ensure that speech did not violate established norms of respect and propriety. The particular province of blasphemy was to prevent disrespect toward God, which according to Blackstone could be manifested "by denying his being or providence; or by contumelious reproaches of our Saviour Christ."[40]

Blasphemy in English Law: From Assimilationism to Pluralism

Although blasphemy and obscenity originally shared a common concern with regulating the profane,[41] blasphemy was in its early years most closely allied to sedition, since attacks on God and religion were viewed as equivalent to attacks on the social order.[42] The classic statement in this regard was delivered by Sir Matthew Hale in *Taylor's Case*, in which the defendant was accused of "uttering . . . divers blasphemous expressions, horrible to hear, (viz) that Jesus Christ was a bastard, a whoremaster, religion was a cheat; and that he neither feared God, the devil, or man." Hale ruled

> that such kind of wicked blasphemous words were not only an offence to God and religion, but a crime against the laws, State and Government,

and therefore punishable . . . For to say, religion is a cheat, is to dissolve all those obligations whereby the civil societies are preserved, and that Christianity is parcel of the laws of England; and therefore to reproach the Christian religion is to speak in subversion of the law.[43]

Underlying *Taylor's Case* is "the plain principle that the public importance of the Christian religion is so great that no one is allowed to deny its truth."[44] Proceeding on this principle, the law of blasphemy was successfully used to prosecute individuals for publishing such works as Thomas Paine's *Age of Reason*,[45] Shelley's poem "Queen Mab,"[46] and the popular Discourses of an early deist, by a minister and Fellow of Sydney Sussex College at Cambridge, which urged that the miracles reported in the New Testament be interpreted allegorically rather than literally.[47] In 1841 the English Commissioners on Criminal Law could report that "the common law of England punishes as an offence any general denial of the truth of Christianity, without reference to the language or temper in which such denial is conveyed."[48]

Until quite recently, then, the crime of blasphemy was a paradigmatic example of assimilationist law. Christians were the dominant group in England, and blasphemy made Christian values "parcel of the laws" in England. Christian values rested on the asserted truth of certain theological and doctrinal propositions, and blasphemy prohibited those propositions from being controverted. As the Court of King's Bench was reported to have succinctly stated in Rex v. Woolston: "The Christian religion is established in this kingdom; and therefore [it] would not allow any books to be writ, which should tend to alter that establishment."[49] Not only did the law of blasphemy offer no protection to subordinate or minority religions,[50] but it seemed likely that even non-Anglican Christian denominations were "protected only to the extent that their fundamental beliefs [were] held in common with the established Church."[51]

About the middle of the nineteenth century, however, the crime of blasphemy began to change. One can detect the transformation in Lord Denman's charge to the jury in Regina v. Hetherington:

Upon the question whether it is blasphemous or not I [make] this general observation . . . namely, that the question is not altogether a matter of opinion, but that it must be, in a great degree, a question as to the tone, and style, and spirit, in which such inquiries are conducted. Because, a difference of opinion may subsist, not only between different sects of Christians, but also with regard to the great doctrines of Chris-

tianity itself; and . . . even discussions upon that subject may be by no
means a matter of criminal prosecution, but, if they be carried on in a
sober and temperate and decent style, even those discussions may be
tolerated, and may take place without criminality attaching to them; but
that, if the tone and spirit is that of offence, and insult, and ridicule,
which leaves the judgment really not free to act, and, therefore, cannot
be truly called an appeal to the judgment, but an appeal to the wild and
improper feelings of the human mind, more particularly in the younger
part of the community, in that case the jury will hardly feel it possible to
say that such opinions, so expressed, do not deserve the character [of
blasphemy] affixed to them in this indictment.[52]

For Lord Denman the crime of blasphemy did not inhere so much in
the substance of what was said as in the style in which it was said. It was
not blasphemous to deny "the great doctrines of Christianity" so long as
that denial was advanced "in a sober and temperate and decent style." But
if Christianity was attacked in a "tone and spirit . . . of offence, and insult,
and ridicule," then the attack was blasphemous. Attacks that were not
civil were irrational; they did not leave "the judgment really . . . free to
act," and were instead appeals "to the wild and improper feelings of the
human mind."
   In 1883 Lord Coleridge made explicit this altered view of blasphemy.
Whatever the "old cases" may have said, he explained, "the mere denial
of the truth of Christianity is not enough to constitute the offence of
blasphemy."[53] To be blasphemous, expression must instead be "calculated and intended to insult the feelings and the deepest religious convictions of the great majority of the persons amongst whom we live."[54]
The point of blasphemy law for Coleridge was thus to prevent "outrages
to the general feeling of propriety among the persons amongst whom we
live."[55] It followed for him that "if the decencies of controversy are
observed, even the fundamentals of religion may be attacked without the
writer being guilty of blasphemy."[56]
   Today the crime of blasphemy in England is essentially a restatement
of Coleridge's view of the law.[57] It is a view that has been attacked as
resting on a highly vulnerable distinction between style and substance.[58]
The concept of assimilationist law, however, is helpful in casting Coleridge's view in a more sympathetic light, for the concept invites us to
focus on the nature of the social group that Coleridge's view was designed
to protect. Coleridge had in effect altered the group whose values were to
be implemented by blasphemy law. That group was no longer Christians

holding allegiance to certain theological and doctrinal propositions; it was instead Christians holding allegiance to "the decencies of controversy." The members of this latter group, whom Coleridge explicitly understood to consist of "the great majority of the persons amongst whom we live," were not offended by the mere fact of religious difference,[59] but were outraged when Christianity was not treated with the respect they felt it deserved. They understood this respect to be coincident with the requirements of reason: blasphemy would permit attacks on Christianity if cast in the form of "an appeal to the judgment," but it would penalize such attacks if they constituted instead "an appeal to the wild and improper feelings of the human mind" that did not leave "the judgment really . . . free to act."

To the modern eye, it is clear that the concept of reason underlying the reformulation of blasphemy law is not universal, but rather the product of the mores of a particular culture. It is perhaps more generally true that in matters of deep human meaning, like religion (or sex), what counts as reason, as an appeal to the judgment rather than to "the wild and improper feelings of the human mind," is ultimately determined by the proprieties of discourse.[60] That is why the purported style/substance distinction proposed by Coleridge cannot withstand close logical scrutiny: in the end the distinction rests not on logic at all but instead on a specific cultural sense of "the decencies of controversy."

The particular group whose values these "decencies" were meant to reflect is in retrospect apparent enough. In 1930, during parliamentary debates on a proposed law to abolish the common law crime of blasphemy,[61] it was repeatedly observed that "what it really comes to is that, where opinions are strongly held by an educated man, those opinions will be expressed in a way which the law cannot touch, while those expressed by an uneducated man, simply because he is uneducated, will come under the penalties of the law."[62] After Coleridge, then, the crime of blasphemy reflected the values of educated and "respectable" Christians.[63] Because the crime imposed these values on society as a whole, it remained deeply assimilationist in character and aspiration.

There were no successful prosecutions for blasphemy in England between 1922 and 1977.[64] In the 1970s, however, interest arose in the potential use of blasphemy to check cultural manifestations that were viewed as objectionable.[65] Ultimately this interest came to focus on a magazine entitled *Gay News*, which in 1976 published a poem by Professor James Kirkup entitled "The Love That Dares to Speak Its Name."

The poem described in explicit detail acts of sodomy and fellatio with the body of Christ immediately after his death, and ascribed to Christ during his lifetime promiscuous homosexual practices with the apostles and with other men. The poem was accompanied by a drawing of the Crucifixion featuring the body of Christ in the embrace of a Roman centurion.[66] In 1977 Mrs. Mary Whitehouse, an English moral crusader, brought a private prosecution for blasphemy against Gay News Ltd., the publisher of *Gay News*, and against Denis Lemon, its editor.[67] Lemon was convicted and sentenced to nine months' imprisonment (suspended for eighteen months) and fined £500, and Gay News Ltd. was fined £1000.[68]

The case attracted widespread notice,[69] and eventually wound its way up to the House of Lords.[70] The actual grounds of the appeal turned on the rather technical question of whether the prosecution ought to have demonstrated a specific intent to blaspheme on the part of the defendants. But the real underlying issue was whether the crime of blasphemy in 1979 in England was an embarrassment that should be discouraged.[71] In 1979 the Law Lords, by a 3–2 vote, upheld the conviction.[72] The decisive and to American eyes most compelling opinion was by Lord Scarman. What makes his opinion particularly pertinent for this discussion, however, is its fascinating attempt to envision a law of blasphemy based on pluralist, rather than assimilationist, foundations.

Scarman was willing to assume that Lemon could establish that "he had no intention to shock Christian believers" and had published "the poem not to offend Christians but to comfort practising homosexuals by encouraging them to feel that there was room for them in the Christian religion." But Scarman deemed Lemon's intent to be irrelevant, because the whole point of blasphemy law was "to protect religious feeling from outrage and insult."[73] Hence "the character of the words published matter; but not the motive of the author or publisher." If in Kirkup's poem "the argument for acceptance and welcome of homosexuals within the loving fold of the Christian faith [had] been advanced 'in a sober and temperate . . . style,' . . . there could have been no criminal offence committed." But for Scarman "the jury (with every justification) [had] rejected this view of the poem and drawing."[74]

Scarman's rejection of the requirement of intent flowed from his understanding of "legal policy in the society of today"; in his view, that policy should strive to find a "way forward for a successful plural society."[75] Although Scarman, as a judge, could not expand the common law crime of blasphemy to protect the religious feelings of non-Christians, he wanted to use the *Lemon* case as a platform to urge that the common law be changed by legislation to protect the sensibilities of all religious groups. His repudiation of the requirement of intent was integral to that ambition. He made this powerfully clear at the very outset of his opinion:

> My Lords, I do not subscribe to the view that the common law offence of blasphemous libel serves no useful purpose in the modern law. On the contrary, I think that there is a case for legislation extending it to protect the religious beliefs and feelings of non-Christians . . . In an increasingly plural society such as that of modern Britain it is necessary not only to respect the differing religious beliefs, feelings and practices of all but also to protect them from scurrility, vilification, ridicule, and contempt . . . When [in the 19th century] Lord Macaulay protested in Parliament against the way the blasphemy laws were then administered, he added (Speeches, p. 116): "If I were a judge in India, I should have no scruple about punishing a Christian who should pollute a mosque." . . . When Macaulay became a legislator in India, he saw to it that the law protected the religious feelings of all. In those days India was a plural society: today the United Kingdom is also. I have permitted myself these general observations at the outset of my opinion because, my Lords, they determine my approach to this appeal. I will not lend my voice to a view of the law relating to blasphemous libel which would render it a dead letter, or diminish its efficacy to protect religious feeling from outrage and insult. My criticism of the common law offence of blasphemy is not that it exists but that it is not sufficiently comprehensive. It is shackled by the chains of history.[76]

Scarman offers a compelling vision of blasphemy law transformed by statute into an instrument of pluralism. If the common law crime of blasphemy protects only the hegemonic status of Christianity, Scarman wants the law altered to ensure that distinct and competing religious groups treat one another with sensitivity. He believes it imperative "in an increasingly plural society" to use the law to enforce respect for the "religious beliefs, feelings and practices of all."[77] Reformulated in this way, the law of blasphemy would be part of a pluralist legal framework designed to maintain the integrity of diverse religious groups.[78]

Scarman's opinion represents a major and thoroughgoing effort to reestablish blasphemy on a pluralist, rather than assimilationist, basis. What is most interesting about the opinion, however, are the intrinsic limitations of that effort. For Scarman's opinion necessarily rests on the crucial (and unobtrusive) assumption that all religious groups in a "plural society" can be measured by a common metric of "outrage and insult." As we have seen in our analysis of mid-nineteenth-century blasphemy law, however, the metric used by Scarman itself reflects particular cultural values, and there is no reason to assume that in modern England diverse religious groups would in fact share this same sense of the "decencies of controversy." Scarman's opinion therefore implicitly presupposes that religious groups *should* tolerate disagreement if conducted in a temperate and sober style. Despite the purity of Scarman's pluralist intentions, his effort paradoxically rests on a quintessentially assimilationist value.

This suggests that assimilationism and pluralism may not be mutually exclusive concepts. Efforts to establish pluralism will always shade, at one point or another, into assimilationism. The very respect for diversity on which pluralist law is based may well run contrary to the beliefs of some groups; pluralist attempts to create a legal framework based on the value of toleration will then end up imposing this value on groups who do not share it. Even if diverse groups do share some basic notions of respect and tolerance, the definitive meaning of these values will be given uniform and authoritative interpretation by legal institutions, and hence fail to reflect the various meanings that these values will have to different groups in a heterogeneous society.[79] Indeed, at the most basic level, the definition and recognition of who and what will count as a group within a pluralist legal framework will necessarily rest on assimilationist values. Should Scarman's view of blasphemy become the law of England, for example, English judges would face the uncomfortable, assimilationist task of determining which practices and beliefs would count as religions, and hence which feelings the crime of blasphemy ought to protect.

The most general statement of the point is that the meaning of diversity must itself reflect and express the norms of a dominant community, so that the legal ambition to respect diversity must itself enforce these norms. It follows that pluralist law must necessarily remain anchored to assimilationist law; the distinction depends, so to speak, on the length of the chain, on the degree and manner in which the particular value of diversity penetrates the law.

There is a somewhat sharper line of demarcation, however, between pluralism and individualism, as can be illustrated by contemplating what would happen in the United States to any statute that attempted to define the crime of blasphemy in the manner suggested by Lord Scarman. We can learn a great deal about the difference between pluralism and individualism by analyzing why the prospects for such a statute would be so very bleak.

Blasphemy in American Law: The Individualist First Amendment

One's first thought, of course, is that the religion clauses of the First Amendment would flatly bar the enforcement of any blasphemy statute, pluralist or not.[80] Harry Kalven, for example, has written that the religion clauses of the First Amendment provide the basis for "a first great principle of consensus," which is that *"in America, there is no heresy, no blasphemy."*[81] The difficulty with this narrow focus on constitutional language, however, is that it ignores the framework of assumptions and values that will necessarily inform the interpretation of that language. The importance of this framework can be illustrated by an examination of the fate of blasphemy laws in the states prior to the 1920s. Although blasphemy prosecutions during that period were challenged as unconstitutional because of state guarantees of religious freedom that were strikingly similar in form to the First Amendment,[82] courts uniformly interpreted these state constitutional guarantees as permitting the imposition of criminal penalties for blasphemy.[83]

The first and most influential case was People v. Ruggles, in which a defendant in New York was charged with blasphemy for having stated that *"Jesus Christ* was a bastard, and his mother must be a whore."[84] The New York Constitution of the time had not only "discarded religious establishments,"[85] but had also, in order "to guard against that spiritual oppression and intolerance wherewith the bigotry and ambition of weak and wicked priests and princes have scourged mankind," guaranteed that "the free exercise and enjoyment of religious profession and worship, without discrimination or preference, shall for ever hereafter be allowed within this State to all mankind."[86] Nevertheless, the New York Supreme Court, in an opinion by Chief Justice Kent, had no difficulty in upholding the conviction:

> The free, equal, and undisturbed enjoyment of religious opinion, whatever it may be, and free and decent discussions on any religious subject, is granted and secured; but to revile, with malicious and blasphemous contempt, the religion professed by almost the whole community, is an abuse of that right. Nor are we bound, by any expressions in the constitution, as some have strangely supposed, either not to punish at all, or to punish indiscriminately the like attacks upon the religion of *Mahomet* or of the grand *Lama;* and for this plain reason, that the case assumes that we are a christian people, and the morality of the country is deeply ingrafted upon christianity, and not upon the doctrines or worship of those impostors.[87]

Kent distinguished between the formal establishment of religion through the compulsory power of the state, and the voluntary adoption by the "people of this state, in common with the people of this country, [of] the general doctrines of christianity, as the rule of their faith and practice." To "scandalize" Christ was punishable not because it defied established religion, but because it was "a gross violation of decency and good order" that struck "at the root of moral obligation, and weaken[ed] the security of the social ties."[88]

Ruggles set a pattern that would continue for more than 110 years.[89] Prosecutions for blasphemy, in their full assimilationist form, were deemed permissible, notwithstanding constitutional rights of religious freedom. It was not until quite recently that legal professionals have become convinced that prosecutions for blasphemy would violate such constitutional rights. A 1968 conviction for blasphemy in Maryland, for example, was set aside two years later when a Maryland appellate court held that the state's 1723 blasphemy statute was "contrary to the terms of the First Amendment's prohibition of laws respecting an establishment of religion or prohibiting the free exercise thereof."[90] At the time of the Maryland decision, Delaware was in the process of prosecuting for blasphemy two teenagers who had called Jesus Christ a bastard. The teenagers had been jailed and were free on bail pending trial. In light of the Maryland decision, the Delaware attorney general's office decided to drop charges. In 1971 in Pennsylvania, two shopkeepers were charged with blasphemy for displaying a poster reading: "Jesus Christ—Wanted for sedition, criminal anarchy, vagrancy, and conspiracy to overthrow the established government. Dressed poorly; said to be a carpenter by trade; ill-nourished; associates with common working people, unemployed and bums. Alien; said to be a Jew." After the intervention of the American Civil Liberties Union, the county prosecutor asked that the local magistrate drop the charges.[91]

In each of these cases, a local attempt to enforce a blasphemy statute was checked by legal professionals who believed that the statute was contrary to the religious freedom guaranteed by the First Amendment. The literal terms of the First Amendment could not have dictated this belief, for these terms are not different from those in state constitutions that had consistently been construed to allow the punishment of blasphemy.[92] It is rather that the religion clauses of the First Amendment are now interpreted in light of very different assumptions and values from those informing earlier interpretations of equivalent language in state constitutions. It is important, therefore, to explore the values that we bring to contemporary constitutional adjudication. These values are well displayed in the important case of Cantwell v. Connecticut, one of the first and most influential decisions to apply the religion clauses of the First Amendment to the states.

In that case Jesse Cantwell, a Jehovah's Witness, entered a Catholic neighborhood and played for two Catholic men a phonograph record that contained an attack on all organized religious systems as "instruments of Satan and injurious to man," and that further singled "out the Roman Catholic Church for strictures couched in terms which naturally would offend not only persons of that persuasion, but all others who respect the honestly held religious faith of their fellows." Cantwell was charged and convicted of the common law crime of inciting breach of the peace.[93]

Chief Justice Kent would certainly have viewed Cantwell's vitriolic attack on organized religion as "an abuse of" the right of free exercise of religion. Indeed, in *Ruggles* he said that to construe the guarantee of "free exercise and enjoyment of religious profession and worship" in the New York Constitution "as breaking down the common law barriers against licentious, wanton, and impious attacks upon christianity itself, would be an enormous perversion of its meaning."[94] And Lord Scarman would certainly have deemed Cantwell's conduct to be intolerable "for a successful plural society," because Cantwell had demonstrated a complete lack of respect for the religious sensibilities of others by gratuitously insulting and offending members of the Catholic religion.

It was open, therefore, to the United States Supreme Court to interpret the First Amendment in light of either the assimilationist values of Kent or the pluralist values that Scarman attempted to use thirty-nine years later to reconstruct the common law crime of blasphemy. But the Court took neither of these paths. Instead it set aside Cantwell's conviction and offered this important gloss on what it called "the interest of the United States that the free exercise of religion be not prohibited and that freedom to communicate information and opinion be not abridged":

> In the realm of religious faith, and in that of political belief, sharp differences arise. In both fields the tenets of one man may seem the rankest error to his neighbor. To persuade others to his own point of view, the pleader, as we know, at times resorts to exaggeration, to vilification of men who have been, or are, prominent in church or state, and even to false statement. But the people of this nation have ordained in the light of history, that, in spite of the probability of excesses and

abuses, these liberties are, in the long view, essential to enlightened opinion and right conduct on the part of the citizens of a democracy. The essential characteristic of these liberties is, that under their shield many types of life, character, opinion and belief can develop unmolested and unobstructed. Nowhere is this shield more necessary than in our own country for a people composed of many races and of many creeds.[95]

According to *Cantwell*, then, the First Amendment should be interpreted in a manner consistent with social heterogeneity. Kent had brought to his construction of the New York Constitution the assumption that the values of Christianity provided "that moral discipline, and . . . those principles of virtue, which help to bind society together."[96] The Court in *Cantwell*, on the other hand, brought to its reading of the First Amendment the assumption that society consists of "many creeds" and is divided by "sharp differences," in which "the tenets of one man may seem the rankest error to his neighbor." The presupposition of social uniformity that underlies Kent's assimilationist vision seems to have vanished from *Cantwell*'s account, which is much closer in spirit to the "plural" society described by Scarman. But for Scarman social diversity implied the enactment of pluralist values, so that the law could be used to protect religious differences from "vilification, ridicule, and contempt." For *Cantwell*, on the other hand, the fact of diversity led in exactly the opposite direction, toward the constitutional requirement that the law tolerate "exaggeration," "vilification," and even "excesses and abuses."

It is not difficult to perceive the line that divides *Cantwell* from *Ruggles*; but what distinguishes *Cantwell* from Scarman's pluralist vision? The key lies in the fact that while *Cantwell* focuses its analysis on the religious speaker, Scarman concentrates on the offense suffered by the religious audience. There is a deeply significant asymmetry in these approaches: the speaker stands alone, whereas the outrage of the audience is generic. For Scarman the law responds not to the outrage of offended individuals but to the common outrage of the members of a religious group whose group identity has been attacked. *Cantwell* explicitly rejects this focus on the group, choosing instead to use the law as a "shield" so that "many types of life, character, opinion and belief can develop unmolested and unobstructed." In essence *Cantwell* requires that established religious groups, who have already developed their distinctive character and beliefs, must suffer offense so that new religious groups can be born.[97] Underlying *Cantwell*, then, lies the classic American commitment to "voluntarism,"[98] to the belief that "religion is . . . a matter of individual choice."[99]

The contrast between Scarman and *Cantwell* might thus be formulated in this manner: for Lord Scarman religious heterogeneity presupposes a social world in which diverse religious groups already exist as part of a stable and established social fabric, whereas for *Cantwell* religious diversity presupposes a social world in which the dynamic of individual choice causes new religious groups continually to evolve. Both Scarman and *Cantwell* recognize the existence of groups, but Scarman assumes that the function of law is to protect the integrity of established and stable groups, whereas *Cantwell* assumes that the function of law is to protect the capacity of individuals to form new and different groups. The individual is the locus of value for *Cantwell*; the group is the locus of value for Scarman. The distinction between the two, in short, is that between individualism and pluralism. Unlike the gradient that holds together pluralism and assimilationism, the distinction between *Cantwell* and Scarman is quite sharp, for it turns on the more or less dichotomous determination of whether the law should be used to enforce the norms of groups as against individuals, or to protect instead the prerogatives of individuals as against groups.[100]

In interpreting the Constitution in light of the values and assumptions of individualism, *Cantwell* speaks for what unquestionably has become the great tradition of First Amendment thought. Of course there have been dissenting voices in that tradition, but it is fair to characterize cases like *Beauharnais* and *Yoder* as ripples on the surface of a deeper and more powerful current of individualist decisions. It is worth pausing for a moment to inquire into the sociological causes of these decisions. Why in the 1930s did we begin to interpret the First Amendment to our national Constitution (as distinct from our state constitutions) in light of the principles of individualism? Was it that the natural heterogeneity of American society was more easily visible from a national, rather than a local, viewpoint? Or was it instead that the federal enforcement of individualism was integral to the process of forging a distinctively national culture, a culture designed to transcend local and regional identifications? In the answers to these questions lie the roots of our own constitutional perspectives, perspectives that, for example, account for our instinctive rejection of Lord Scarman's proposals for the use of blasphemy law.

If individualism is sharply demarcated from pluralism, it bears a considerably more complex relationship to assimilationism. Paradoxically, individualism and assimilationism are discontinuous and yet interdependent. As Charles Taylor has observed, the concept of "the autonomous, self-determining individual," which lies at the heart of individualism, presupposes a particular "social matrix" and depends for its continuing vitality on "a certain type of culture":

> The crucial point here is this: since the free individual can only maintain his identity within a society/culture of a certain kind, he has to be concerned about the shape of this society/culture as a whole. He cannot . . . be concerned purely with his individual choices and the associations formed from such choices to the neglect of the matrix in which such choices can be open or closed, rich or meager. It is important to him that certain activities and institutions flourish in society. It is even important to him what the moral tone of the whole society is—shocking as it may be to libertarians to raise this issue—because freedom and individual diversity can only flourish in a society where there is a general recognition of their worth. They are threatened by the spread of bigotry, but also by other conceptions of life—for example, those which look on originality, innovation, and diversity as luxuries which society can ill afford given the need for efficiency, productivity, or growth.[101]

Taylor's analysis suggests that at certain points the desires of autonomous individuals may very well clash with the kind of general culture necessary to support autonomous individualism, and at those points individualist law will in effect be transformed into assimilationist law.

This transformation is visible in *Cantwell*, which notes two different assimilationist justifications for the imposition of limitations on individual freedom of speech. The first justification refers to "statements likely to provoke violence and disturbance of good order." *Cantwell* states that "when clear and present danger of riot, disorder, interference with traffic upon the public streets, or other immediate threat to public safety, peace, or order, appears, the power of the State to prevent or punish is obvious."[102] Thus individual expression can be prevented and punished when it functions to cause harms or conduct that can be regulated to protect the assimilationist values of public safety and order. By its evocation of the "clear and present danger" test, *Cantwell* indicates that speech can be penalized only when there is a very strict causal connection between speech and subsequent action or harm. The strictness of the causal nexus is in part designed to maximize the amount of speech constitutionally exempt from the regulation of assimilationist values.

The second limitation on individual expression proposed by *Cantwell* refers to "profane, indecent, or abusive remarks directed to the person of the hearer." *Cantwell* states that "resort to epithets or personal abuse is not in any proper sense communication of information or opinion safeguarded by the Constitution, and its punishment as a criminal act would raise no question under that instrument."[103] This limitation on speech is qualitatively different from the clear and present danger test, for it is grounded on the concept that speech can be regulated because it is itself intrinsically undesirable, regardless of its causal connection to subsequent harms or conduct. *Cantwell* expresses this limitation on speech by reference to a distinction similar to that used in mid-nineteenth-century English blasphemy law. English law distinguished between "sober and temperate" expression, which was addressed to the "judgment," and expression infected by a tone of "offence, and insult, and ridicule," which was addressed to "the wild and improper feelings of the human mind." *Cantwell* offers an analogous distinction between speech that communicates "information or opinion" and speech that is "profane, indecent, or abusive."

Just as the style/substance distinction in English blasphemy law did not describe inherent properties of speech but rather reflected cultural values relating to the "decencies of controversy," so the distinction offered by *Cantwell* should be understood not as describing inherent properties of language, but rather as expressing the cultural values underlying individualism.[104] For *Cantwell* the general culture necessary to sustain autonomous individualism rests on norms of interpersonal respect, and these norms in turn function as assimilationist values that limit the autonomous speech of particular individuals. "Profane, indecent, or abusive" speech violates these norms.

Cantwell's understanding of these assimilationist norms, however, has been strikingly influenced by the individualism underlying the opinion. The norms recognized by *Cantwell* differ fundamentally from the assimilationist norms implicit in the English cases. Individuals in the English cases have the right to take offense at communications that insult their particular status as, say, practicing Christians.[105] But the norms of respect upheld in *Cantwell* are quite different, for integral to that decision is the notion that the Constitution prohibits Connecticut from punishing Jesse Cantwell's speech simply because it is outrageous to the Catholicism of his audience. Instead the law can constitutionally intervene to censor only those statements that consist of "abusive remarks directed to the person of the hearer."[106] The specific social status of an audience is immaterial to these kinds of statements, because every person has the right not to be personally abused.

Thus even when it explicitly recognizes assimilationist values that can

directly regulate speech, *Cantwell* does so in a manner that follows the
logic of individualism to its natural conclusion. *Cantwell* enforces a constitutional symmetry between speaker and audience: it allows the law to
redress audience outrage only when that outrage stems from characteristics potentially shared by all individuals, rather than when it stems from
characteristics that are constitutive of particular social or religious
groups.[107] The assimilationist values underlying *Cantwell* are thus real
and palpable, but they are also extremely thin, for there is only so much
that we all, as Americans, potentially share in common. The abstract and
rather bloodless nature of these values is the price we pay for having a
First Amendment grounded in individualism rather than pluralism.

Pornography and Pluralism

It is precisely the abstract nature of these values that is challenged by
MacKinnon's and Dworkin's critique of pornography. The censorship of
obscenity, as can now plainly be seen, is a paradigmatic expression of
assimilationist law, in which the dominant culture in a community is set
free to limit individual expression so as to enforce "community standards" and hence define the "tone" and "quality" of its community life.[108]
But the pressure of First Amendment individualism has forced obscenity
law to rest on the kind of thin values which are compatible with that
individualism. Obscenity law thus speaks in the abstract language of "prurience,"[109] a vice that is potentially universal and equally dangerous to all
individuals. It does not focus at all on the particular outrage inflicted by
pornography on women.

   Feminists like Dworkin and MacKinnon demand that the law be transformed to take cognizance of that outrage. The problem, however, is that
this outrage stems from the characteristics of a specific group (women); it
is not the outrage of a generic audience composed of undifferentiated
individuals. Dworkin and MacKinnon want the law to recognize that
pornography demeans women, not just persons, and in this ambition they
are like the two Catholic men in *Cantwell* who would seek redress for the
specific insult to their Catholicism. The feminist demand for the regulation of pornography is so controversial, in other words, because implicit
within it lies the entire difference between pluralism and individualism.

   There are several advantages to conceptualizing the pornography controversy in terms of the tension between pluralism and individualism. It
focuses analysis on the essential grievance motivating the feminist cri-

tique; it does so in a way that exposes the exact tension with basic First Amendment principles; and it offers the intellectual tools to refine and sharpen the precise points in controversy, and so illuminates what is most fundamentally at stake. The first of these advantages can best be illustrated comparatively, through a brief discussion of three other constitutional understandings of the controversy that are prominent in the current literature.

Three Common Justifications for Regulating Pornography

A common justification offered for the suppression of pornography is that it causes discrete acts of sexual violence against individual women. This justification is not theoretically problematic, but its nature and strength depend entirely on the empirical evidence offered in its support. Given its most generous interpretation, the systematic evidence presently available does not demonstrate that pornography automatically leads to sexual violence, but rather that it causes "attitudinal" changes in men which make them more likely to countenance sexual violence against women.[110] For this evidence to justify the censorship of pornography, it must be argued that the relationship between such attitudinal changes and subsequent behavior constitutes a sufficiently close causal nexus as to justify the regulation of pornography.

This is precisely the kind of argument that was traditionally offered to support the regulation of blasphemy. It was contended that blasphemy induced attitudinal changes toward religion that would lead persons to countenance antisocial acts: "Public contumely and ridicule of a prevalent religion . . . threaten the public peace and order by diminishing the power of moral precepts."[111] It is also the kind of argument used by the Supreme Court in the notorious case of Debs v. United States. There the Court upheld the conviction of Eugene Debs for delivering an antiwar speech to the state convention of the Socialist Party of Ohio, on the grounds that the "natural tendency and reasonably probable effect" of the speech would be to induce attitudinal changes in the audience that would increase their willingness to obstruct the recruitment of American forces for World War I.[112]

As these examples illustrate, the government would acquire enormous and intolerable powers of censorship if it were given the authority to penalize any speech that would tend to induce in an audience disagreeable attitudinal changes with respect to future conduct. To avoid the potential for such censorship the Supreme Court has held that penalizing speech because it causes contingent future harmful acts by inducing attitudinal changes is constitutional only if the speech "is directed to inciting or producing imminent lawless action and is likely to incite or produce such action."[113] Pornography obviously does not meet this test.[114] Given the present state of the evidence, then, the contention that pornography should be generally regulated because of its causal connection to future acts of sexual violence is profoundly at odds with the basic First Amendment principle that seeks to circumscribe broad government discretion to curtail speech.[115]

The second justification sometimes offered for the suppression of pornography is the argument that pornography is not speech but rather "an act of male supremacy."[116] It is contended that "pornography is not expression depicting the subordination of women, but is the *practice of subordination* itself."[117] The power and reach of this argument can be appreciated by calling to mind J. L. Austin's concept of "performative utterances." There are certain occasions when a person's speech makes us think "that he is *doing* something rather than merely *saying* something." Announcing "I do" at a wedding ceremony, for example, is to perform the act of getting married. Performative utterances seem like actions because by common "convention" the acts that they perform are understood to subsist in speech.[118] It may be argued that, in a similar way, certain kinds of social relationships are by convention understood to be constituted in large measure (although not entirely) by speech. Relationships of respect, for example, inherently involve communication, so that to speak disrespectfully is to perform an act of disrespect. From the feminist perspective, pornography is just such a disrespectful act.

This argument can be extended by noting that relationships of inferiority and superiority are also in large measure (although not entirely) constituted by speech. The status of social superiors is established and confirmed by the tokens of respect that are their due; conversely, the status of social inferiors inheres in part in the disrespect with which they can be treated. Pornography can thus be seen as the practice of subordination because it is the pervasively disrespectful treatment of women. Even if women as a group defy the stigmatizing imputations of pornography, society's countenance of its widespread distribution indicates that this defiance is powerless before the conventional judgment of inferiority that is everywhere pornographically displayed.[119]

There is nothing illogical about this argument; it rests on rather profound insights into the manner in which social relations are constituted by speech as well as by physical actions. In its pure form, however, the argument is incompatible with any viable notion of freedom of expression, for social relations are pervasively made up of speech.[120] Consider the following three examples, which deal only with relationships of respect: I can, as a literary critic, speak disrespectfully and authoritatively about a new novel; or I can, as an outraged moralist, speak disrespectfully and with great effect about the actions of an acquaintance; or I can, as a political partisan, speak disrespectfully and influentially about the character of the president. In each of these examples I have acted disrespectfully, and with potentially devastating consequences to the social standing of the object of my speech. We can argue about whether or not the law should intervene to punish me in any particular case, but surely it goes too far to claim that freedom of speech is not pertinent to any of these examples because they each involve an act rather than communication.

The argument that pornography can be regulated because it is the practice of subordination, rather than speech, thus proves too much to be useful for First Amendment purposes. Social relations to a great extent inhere in communications that have the quality of performative utterances,[121] and it would be entirely inconsistent with any modern understanding of the Constitution to remove such communications in wholesale fashion from the purview of the First Amendment.

A third justification that has been offered to support the regulation of pornography is that "pornography is more accurately treated as a physical rather than a mental experience" because it contains "neither propositional, emotive, nor artistic content."[122] Pornography lacks "intellectual appeal,"[123] and is "non-rational, almost physical . . . material which is purely designed to excite sexual fantasies, largely as an aid to masturbation."[124] Pornography "thus contains none of the properties that are defined by the technical sense of the word 'speech,' and is thus outside the scope of the Free Speech Principle."[125]

This argument appears inconsistent with the contention that pornography should be regulated because it is the practice of sexual subordination. It is hard to understand how pornography can communicate attitudes of disrespect toward women if it is entirely devoid of propositional, emotive, and artistic content. If one must choose between these two characterizations of pornography, I think that it is more accurate to conclude that pornography does convey specific attitudes toward women, and that it does so in the same manner as any intentional act of communication. The notion that even a "hard-core" pornographic film could be completely empty of content strikes me as fanciful, since at a minimum the film will be understood as attempting to communicate the author's perception of what his audience will find sexually arousing. The concept of sexual arousal is of course a complex, substantive matter, filled with implications for the social understanding of gender.

To be fair to the proponents of the argument that pornography lacks all ideational content, however, it should be noted that the argument was originally developed to justify the regulation of obscenity rather than pornography. Although the argument purports to analyze the intrinsic properties of speech, it is in fact grounded on the same assimilationist values as those that underlie the prohibition of obscenity. The argument's analysis of speech may be fallacious, but its grasp of these values is considerably more formidable.

Like English blasphemy law in the nineteenth century, the argument turns on the fusion of reason and civility; it rests on a distinction analogous to the opposition between speech addressed to the "judgment" and speech addressed to "the wild and improper feelings of the human mind." "Obscenity," so the argument goes in its most explicit form, "pertains, not to the realm of ideas, reason, intellectual content and truth-seeking, but to the realm of passion, desires, cravings and titillation."[126] The implication of the distinction is that obscenity can be regulated because the culture of autonomous individualism depends on reason and is undermined by passion. Reformulated in this way, the argument is a serious attempt to articulate the assimilationist values that necessarily form the foundation of First Amendment individualism.[127] But as such the argument ignores the particular concerns raised by Dworkin's and MacKinnon's critique of pornography.

Pornography and the First Amendment

These three justifications for the regulation of pornography are a fair sampling of some of the stronger arguments available in the current literature. Yet they all seem deeply unsatisfactory, either because they conflict with basic First Amendment principles or because they miss the essential point of the feminist critique. It is as if commentators are searching for some adequate way to conceptualize the bold new claims presented by the attack on pornography.[128] In fact, however, the structure of these claims should be familiar, for they are closely analogous to the question of group libel addressed in *Beauharnais*.[129]

In *Beauharnais* the Court held that state law could punish speech calculated to expose ethnic or religious groups to "contempt, derision, or
obloquy," on the grounds that "a man's job and his educational opportunities and the dignity accorded him may depend as much on the reputation of the racial and religious group to which he willy-nilly belongs,
as on his own merits."[130] The structure of the Court's reasoning applies
equally well to membership in a gender as to membership in a religious
or ethnic group. If pornography subjects the group "women" to contempt and derision by "eroticiz[ing] dominance and submission or portray[ing] women in a degrading manner as objects to be sexually exploited
and manipulated,"[131] the dignity accorded to each woman will suffer,
regardless of her personal merits.

Of course as a matter of technical precedent *Beauharnais* comes to us as
damaged goods. Its reasoning was crippled by New York Times Co. v.
Sullivan,[132] and its holding was unmistakably undone by Philadelphia
Newspapers, Inc. v. Hepps.[133] More important, *Beauharnais* depends on
the argument that group libel is simply a variant form of individual defamation, and this argument requires that the defendant in a group libel
case be given the opportunity to establish the truth of his publication.[134]
What is at issue in the feminist critique of pornography, however, is not
the falsity of the assertion that women are objects to be sexually exploited,
but rather the insult and contempt that is communicated when that assertion is made in a particular way. Pornographically expressed, the assertion is a form of "personal abuse," only it is abuse targeted at a group
rather than at an individual addressee.

Because the feminist campaign against pornography aims to suppress a
specific message of abuse, some have rejected the purposes of the campaign as "viewpoint discrimination"[135] or "thought control."[136] On one
level this objection is easily met. Anti-pornography legislation can effectively be drafted in formally gender-neutral terms that prohibit sexual
insult to either men or women. Such a reformulation would be more
consistent with the pluralist goal of maintaining respect between competing groups, in this case between the groups of men and women.

On a deeper level, however, this reformulation of anti-pornography
legislation remains vulnerable to the charge of viewpoint discrimination,
for the legislation would still penalize messages of gender insult. It would
still contain "an 'approved' view of women, of how they may react to
sexual encounters, of how the sexes may relate to each other."[137] But
when used in this way, the charge of viewpoint discrimination would
apply with equal force to *Cantwell's* exclusion from First Amendment

protection of "profane, indecent, or abusive remarks directed to the person of the hearer."[138] *Cantwell* also establishes an "approved" view of how persons should relate to each other and how they should react to personal, religious, or even political disagreements.

The decisive issue, then, is not the presence vel non of viewpoint discrimination, but rather the justification for such discrimination. Reflecting its individualist presuppositions, First Amendment law has long asserted that the social costs of viewpoint discrimination are tolerable if they involve only those face-to-face messages that would be deemed universally abusive; it has characterized these messages as "of such slight social value as a step to truth that any benefit that may be derived from them is clearly outweighed by the social interest in order and morality."[139] But First Amendment law contains no such confident assertion if the discrimination occurs against those messages that are abusive only to particular groups. As judicial reaction to the feminist anti-pornography campaign illustrates,[140] such discrimination is much more likely to be understood as intolerable viewpoint discrimination, perhaps because of an instinctive perception that intergroup struggle is a central aspect of our political culture.

The virtue of the distinction between pluralism and individualism is that it forces us to make these different assessments explicit and to subject them to appropriate examination. There are in fact two generic grounds for apprehension concerning the relationship between pluralism and our system of freedom of expression. The first relates to the tenuous nature of group identity in American culture, the second to the distinct kinds of assimilationist values that underlie pluralism and individualism.

Zechariah Chafee noted the first reason for unease long ago when he observed that the ultimate objection to group libel was its potential for strangling public discussion: "Once you start group libel laws, every influential body of men will urge that it has an equal claim to be protected by such legislation. And the wider the protection, the narrower becomes the field for unimpeded discussion of public affairs."[141] Chafee's observation rests on assumptions similar to those that underlie *Cantwell*; he perceives group life in America as dynamic and unstable. Because groups are constantly evolving, the meaning of group identity is ambiguous, and hence there is no natural brake to claims for group protection.[142] That is perhaps why the English are more comfortable than we in using pluralist principles to regulate speech: categories of group identity have in England been made so much more definite by history and tradition.

American perceptions of group identity are exemplified by our ambiv-alent perception of race, which is for us the paradigmatic example of group identity made distinct through history and tradition. On the one hand we doubt whether a distinct group racial identity should really exist; we sincerely believe that race shouldn't matter and that the law should be color-blind. On the other hand, when we acknowledge the existence of that identity, we do so in a way that flattens racial uniqueness into an ethnic culture that is functionally no different from the cultures of other ethnic Americans, like that of the Irish, the Italians, the Scandinavians, and so forth. When we think in terms of pluralism, in other words, even the unique category of race dissolves into a cascade of groups, each force-fully pressing its case to be recognized as the bearer of a valuable ethnic identity. Chafee is right that the First Amendment would suffer harm if the law were used to regulate expression so as to enforce respect among all such potential groups.

But this conclusion does not settle the question of pornography. It leads instead to the question of whether there is a basis for distinguishing gender groups from all other kinds of groups, or, to put it another way, whether there is a principled manner in which the values of pluralism can be confined to pornography and not applied to expression generally. Catharine MacKinnon has written that "the situation of women is *not really like anything else.*"[143] From a constitutional point of view, much depends on the substantiation of this claim. We have been fairly success-ful in confining strict scrutiny under the equal protection clause to only a small number of potential groups. The question is whether we can be equally successful in the area of freedom of expression.

The second and ultimately more substantial ground for concern about the relationship between the First Amendment and pluralism turns on the kind of assimilationist values that support pluralist law. As the example of *Cantwell* illustrates, individualism tightly circumscribes the assimilationist values that can be used to characterize speech as intrinsically harmful and therefore unprotected. In the individualist realm of the First Amendment, assimilationist values are thin and universal, for they must potentially apply to all persons. Such values also tend to be weak, because in order to foster a general culture of autonomous individualism, it is necessary to minimize interference with the expression of autonomous individuals. At the margins the assimilationist values associated with the First Amend-ment authorize censorship of "fighting words," or "personal abuse," or "obscenity." But in the vast majority of cases these values strain to tolerate individual differences. Thus within the realm of the First Amendment we say that because "one man's vulgarity is another's lyric,"[144] "uninhibited, robust, and wide-open"[145] discussion of public issues can be attained only by suspending ordinary assimilationist norms of civility and interpersonal respect.[146] Pluralist law, on the other hand, presupposes assimilationist values that are richer and more aggressive. These values enable pluralist law not only to identify which groups deserve legal protection, but also to specify the norms of civility and respect that will obtain between these groups. In this sense pluralism contemplates a far wider and more influential role for assimilationist law than does individualism. The regulation of pornography proposed by MacKinnon and Dworkin invites the law not only to define and enforce conceptions of group identity within the area of gender, but also to impose norms of respect and civility between genders. Individualist law, in contrast, stresses the value of personal choice, of leaving individuals free to battle over the shape and meaning of gender identity, so that "many types of life, character, opinion, and belief can develop unmolested and unobstructed."[147]

If the pluralist perspective of MacKinnon and Dworkin is perceived to be in tension with the First Amendment, it is because we instinctively identify that Amendment with the individualist tradition that has evolved since the 1930s. It is hard for us to imagine a system of freedom of expression that does not ultimately embody the value of "assuring individual self-fulfillment."[148] Yet it is precisely this value that MacKinnon and Dworkin call into question. To assess the constitutional implications of their critique, therefore, we must engage in a substantive interpretation of the fundamental purposes of the First Amendment and inquire whether we value freedom of expression because it furthers individual or group life. As the English example illustrates, either approach is compatible with a system of freedom of expression. The question of which we choose turns on the kind of social world that we want to use the First Amendment to help construct.

To elect the pluralist option is not to abandon the First Amendment, but rather to forsake the individualist assumptions underlying contemporary First Amendment law. A full assessment of the claim that pornography can constitutionally be regulated should accordingly impel us toward a more thorough investigation of these assumptions. We need to reexamine our commitment to a First Amendment informed primarily by individualist principles.

II

Democracy and Human Freedom

4

The Constitutional Concept of Public Discourse: Outrageous Opinion, Democratic Deliberation, and Hustler Magazine v. Falwell

The recent "revival" of the view that politics should be understood as a "deliberative process"[1] raises significant questions for First Amendment jurisprudence. It invites reconsideration of the function and extent of constitutional protection for public speech. Frank Michelman, an astute participant in the revival, has for example convincingly argued that public deliberation cannot achieve its purposes if it is "considered or experienced as coercive, or invasive, or otherwise a violation of one's identity or freedom."[2]

Although the United States Supreme Court has increasingly fashioned First Amendment doctrine around the concept of what it calls "public discourse,"[3] it has developed the concept in ways that seem plainly incompatible with Michelman's point. Emblematic is the Court's 1988 opinion in Hustler Magazine v. Falwell, in which Chief Justice Rehnquist used the notion of "public discourse" to provide constitutional immunity for speech that was justifiably experienced as profoundly invasive and violative of identity.[4] The Court has often explicitly and forcefully reiterated this approach: "In public debate our own citizens must tolerate insulting, and even outrageous, speech in order to provide 'adequate "breathing space" to the freedoms protected by the First Amendment.' "[5]

The purpose of this essay is to assess the justification and structure of the concept of public discourse that underlies these strong conclusions. It uses the *Falwell* decision as a specific focus for analysis. The first section, "Hustler Magazine v. Falwell," appraises torts like defamation and the intentional infliction of emotional distress, which form the basis of the *Falwell* case, and illustrates how they regulate communication in order to enforce a particular kind of community life. The First Amendment doctrines invoked by *Falwell* prohibit this enforcement within the realm of public discourse. The second section, "The First Amendment and Public Discourse," explores the theory of public discourse that justifies this prohibition. That theory, in brief, turns on the demarcation of a distinct realm of speech within which legal application of the ordinary norms of community life is constitutionally suspended. This suspension ensures that in the culturally heterogeneous environment of the United States, public debate can proceed within an arena that is legally neutral with respect to the norms of particular communities. It also creates an arena within which new forms of community life can be exemplified and advocated. We can begin to discern in this function the sources of the First Amendment's deep commitment to the values of individualism. The suspension of community norms is conceptually and socially unstable, however, because speech that contravenes those norms is experienced as coercive and violative of personal identity, and hence as incompatible with constructive public debate.

The third part, "Public Discourse and the *Falwell* Opinion," demonstrates how the First Amendment doctrines employed by the *Falwell* opinion follow from its conception of public discourse. The constitutional separation of public discourse from community life illuminates why *Falwell* rejects "outrageousness" and illicit motivation as grounds for the regulation of public speech.[6] It also explains why *Falwell* turns on the curious and muddy distinction between fact and opinion,[7] for I argue that statements of fact are those which claim to be true regardless of the standards that define community life, whereas statements of opinion are those which claim to be true on the basis of the standards of a particular community.

The final section of the essay canvasses the various criteria used by the Court to distinguish public discourse from other speech. These criteria are generally conceded to be inadequate. I explore the reasons for this failure and then offer a reconceptualization of these criteria, attempting to uncover the values at issue in the classification of speech as public discourse.

Hustler Magazine v. Falwell

Hustler Magazine v. Falwell is a classic First Amendment case.[8] Its antagonists could have been selected by central casting to embody the fundamental constitutional tension between anarchic self-expression and strict civic virtue. The plaintiff was Jerry Falwell, a well-known religious fundamentalist and leader of the Moral Majority, a political organization that sought to inject traditional values into American public life. The defendants were *Hustler* magazine and its publisher, Larry Flynt, both notorious for their dedication to a vivid and perverse pornography. The subject of the dispute was a vicious and puerile satire that purported to describe an incestuous encounter between Falwell and his mother in an outhouse, and that was intended, as Flynt testified, to "assassinate" Falwell's integrity.[9]

Michael Sandel once observed that "liberals often take pride in defending what they oppose."[10] If that is true, there was much to be proud of in the *Falwell* opinion. Even those who maintained that the *Hustler* parody was constitutionally protected confessed to the "profound repugnance" that it inspired.[11] In the face of that repugnance, however, the Supreme Court, impressively massing behind an opinion by Chief Justice Rehnquist, held in ringing First Amendment tones that however "outrageous" the satire, however maliciously motivated or intensely painful its effects, a public figure like Falwell could not recover damages without demonstrating the existence of "a false statement of fact which was made with 'actual malice.' "[12] The *Falwell* opinion thus stands squarely in the tradition of Cohen v. California[13] as an important articulation of the First Amendment right to give offense.

The Background of the Case

The antagonism between Larry Flynt and Jerry Falwell could hardly be more natural. Flynt was to Falwell a "sleaze merchant,"[14] a purveyor of precisely the kind of moral corruption that Falwell sought to destroy. Falwell was to Flynt a phony, "a big windbag" who, like the fallen evangelists Jimmy Swaggart and Jim Bakker, needed to be "exposed."[15] For years Flynt had excoriated Falwell in the pages of *Hustler*, the raunchy flagship of Flynt's pornographic publications, as a "vicious hypocrite."[16] The breaking point came in November 1983, when *Hustler* featured on its inside front cover a parody of an advertisement for Campari liqueur. Campari ads had a well-known and recognizable format. They featured celebrities speaking about their "first time," meaning their first drink of Campari, but with a clear double entendre concerning their first sexual experience.

Hustler's version was entitled "Jerry Falwell talks about his first time." The spoof followed the usual Campari format; it featured a thoughtful photograph of Falwell, beneath which was set forth the following "interview":

FALWELL: My first time was in an outhouse outside Lynchburg, Virginia.

INTERVIEWER: Wasn't it a little cramped?

FALWELL: Not after I kicked the goat out.

INTERVIEWER: I see. You must tell me all about it.

FALWELL: I never *really* expected to make it with Mom, but then after she showed all the other guys in town such a good time, I figured, "What the hell!"

INTERVIEWER: But your mom? Isn't that a bit odd?

FALWELL: I don't think so. Looks don't mean that much to me in a woman.

INTERVIEWER: Go on.

FALWELL: Well, we were drunk off our God-fearing asses on Campari, ginger ale and soda—that's called a Fire and Brimstone—at the time. And Mom looked better than a Baptist whore with a $100 donation.

INTERVIEWER: Campari in the crapper with Mom . . . how interesting. Well, how was it?

FALWELL: The Campari was great, but Mom passed out before I could come.

INTERVIEWER: Did you ever try it again?

FALWELL: Sure . . . lots of times. But not in the outhouse. Between Mom and the shit, the flies were too much to bear.

INTERVIEWER: We meant the Campari.

FALWELL: Oh, yeah. I always get sloshed before I go out to the pulpit. You don't think I could lay down all that bullshit sober, do you?[17]

At the bottom of the parody, in small letters, was the disclaimer "ad parody—not to be taken seriously."[18]

Falwell was not amused. In fact he was "incensed."[19] He first read the parody on an airplane; when his flight landed he called his lawyer and said, "Get him." Falwell wanted " 'to protect myself and the memory of my mother,' and to end 'the kind of sleaze merchantry that Larry Flynt typifies.' "[20] Almost immediately thereafter he filed suit in the United States District Court for the Western District of Virginia, alleging defamation, invasion of privacy, and intentional infliction of emotional distress.[21]

Falwell's legal strategy reflected the growing trend of plaintiffs to combine in a single complaint two or more of the three so-called "dignitary torts or torts which focus on the protection of 'personality.' "[22] The strategy proved fortunate for Falwell. Because Virginia had no common law cause of action for invasion of privacy,[23] Falwell was forced to base his privacy claim on a Virginia statute prohibiting the use of a person's name or likeness for purposes of trade or advertising without his consent.[24] At the close of evidence, however, the district court ruled as a matter of law that Flynt's use of "Falwell's name and likeness . . . was not for purposes of trade within the meaning of the statute."[25] Falwell's libel claim was also eliminated when the jury returned a special verdict that the *Hustler* parody could not "reasonably be understood as describing actual facts about plaintiff or actual events in which plaintiff participated."[26] Since 1974 it has been assumed that dictum in Gertz v. Robert Welch, Inc. establishes an absolute constitutional privilege in defamation actions for the publication of opinion, as opposed to false fact,[27] and the jury's verdict was taken to mean that the Campari parody was opinion.[28]

All that remained, therefore, was Falwell's claim for intentional infliction of emotional distress. Virginia law specifies that in order to succeed a plaintiff must establish four elements:

> One, the wrongdoer's conduct was intentional or reckless. This element is satisfied where the wrongdoer had the specific purpose of inflicting emotional distress or where he intended his specific conduct and knew or should have known that emotional distress would likely result. Two, the conduct was outrageous and intolerable in that it offends against the generally accepted standards of decency and morality. This requirement is aimed at limiting frivolous suits and avoiding litigation in situations where only bad manners and mere hurt feelings are involved. Three, there was a causal connection between the wrongdoer's conduct and the emotional distress. Four, the emotional distress was severe.[29]

Falwell's evidence that Flynt had intended to cause him distress rested on Flynt's deposition testimony that he had intended to "upset" Falwell, that he had wanted "to settle a score" because Falwell had labeled Flynt's personal life "abominable," and that he had desired to "assassinate" Falwell's integrity.[30] Falwell's evidence that the *Hustler* parody had caused severe emotional distress consisted primarily of his testimony that reading the satire had inflicted a "very deep wound of personal anguish and hurt and suffering, such as nothing in my adult life I ever recall before."[31] This evidence satisfied the jury, which, sharing Falwell's opinion that the parody was "outrageous and intolerable," awarded Falwell $100,000 in compensatory damages and held Flynt and *Hustler* magazine each responsible for $50,000 in punitive damages.[32]

Flynt and *Hustler* appealed, offering two constitutional arguments.[33] First, they contended that because the *Hustler* parody was opinion and constitutionally privileged in a defamation action, it should also be privileged in a cause of action for intentional infliction of emotional distress. Second, they contended that even if the parody were not absolutely privileged, Falwell's admitted status as a public figure meant that "the actual malice standard of *New York Times Co. v. Sullivan* . . . must be met before Falwell can recover for emotional distress."[34]

The Fourth Circuit, however, rejected both arguments and upheld the jury's verdict. It brushed aside the first contention on the ground that the defamation tort was essentially concerned with false statements of fact, whereas an "action for intentional infliction of emotional distress concerns itself with intentional or reckless conduct which is outrageous and proximately causes severe emotional distress, not with statements per se." At issue in the case, therefore, was whether the defendants' publication was outrageous, not whether the publication was fact or opinion. Defendants' argument was for this reason "irrelevant in the context of this tort."[35]

The Court of Appeals rejected the second argument on similar grounds. It noted that although the tort of defamation was intrinsically concerned with false statements, the "actual malice" standard of *New York Times* "alters none of the elements of the tort; it merely increases the level of fault the plaintiff must prove in order to recover." Applying the actual malice standard to the tort of intentional infliction of emotional distress, on the other hand, "would add a new element" to the tort and fundamentally shift its focus from the outrageous character of a publication to its truth or falsity. Interpreting the *New York Times* standard as focusing "on culpability," the Fourth Circuit held that Virginia's requirement that infliction of emotional distress be "intentional or reckless" evidenced an exactly parallel focus. "The first amendment will not shield intentional or reckless misconduct resulting in damage to reputation, and neither will it shield such misconduct which results in severe emotional distress."[36]

The Supreme Court Opinion

The Supreme Court reversed. Chief Justice Rehnquist wrote for the Court, and his opinion was joined by all Justices except Justice Kennedy, who did not participate in the case, and Justice White, who wrote a short, one-paragraph concurrence designed primarily to dissociate himself from Chief Justice Rehnquist's strong reaffirmation of the *New York Times* actual malice standard.[37] Chief Justice Rehnquist's opinion is rhetorically adept, touching all the "right" First Amendment sentiments and eloquently evoking the nation's tradition of cutting political satire. But the argumentative structure of the opinion is obscure, making it difficult to discern a crisp course of reasoning.

In essence, however, the logical foundation of the *Falwell* opinion lies in its repudiation of the Fourth Circuit's interpretation of *New York Times*. The *Falwell* opinion makes clear that *New York Times* was concerned not so much with setting levels of "culpability" as with fulfilling a constitutional mandate to design rules calculated to facilitate "the free flow of ideas and opinions on matters of public interest and concern" that is "at the heart of the First Amendment."[38] The damages assessed against Flynt and *Hustler*, the Court argued, must be evaluated against the requirements of that same constitutional mandate. For this reason it is not sufficient simply to observe, as did the Fourth Circuit, that the torts of defamation and intentional infliction of emotional distress have different functions and elements. The decisive issue is rather how these elements affect "the world of debate about public affairs" protected by the Constitution.[39]

The holding of *Falwell* ultimately rests on three distinct propositions concerning that world. First, the constitutional value of a communication to "public discourse" does not depend upon its motivation. The American tradition of political satire, for example, represents a form of speech "often calculated to injure the feelings of the subject of the portrayal," and yet "from the viewpoint of history it is clear that our political discourse would have been considerably poorer without" it. Thus the regulation of improper intentions, although important for the civil law of torts, is constitutionally inappropriate "in the area of public debate about public figures."[40]

Second, in the world of public debate safeguarded by the First Amendment, "false statements of fact are particularly valueless" because "they interfere with the truthseeking function of the marketplace of ideas." It is especially important, on the other hand, "to ensure that individual expressions of ideas remain free from governmentally imposed sanctions," particularly those opinions or ideas involved in the criticism of "public men and measures." That freedom " 'is essential to the common quest for truth and the vitality of society as a whole.' "[41] The caricature at issue in *Falwell* should therefore receive particular constitutional solicitude, not only because it expresses an idea, but also because it involves the criticism of a public figure.

Third, nonfactual communications in public discourse cannot constitutionally be penalized because of their "outrageousness":

> "Outrageousness" in the area of political and social discourse has an inherent subjectiveness about it which would allow a jury to impose liability on the basis of the jurors' tastes or views, or perhaps on the basis of their dislike of a particular expression. An "outrageousness" standard thus runs afoul of our longstanding refusal to allow damages to be awarded because the speech in question may have an adverse emotional impact on the audience.[42]

While frankly acknowledging that this "refusal" has had its exceptions—as for example with respect to " 'fighting' words"[43] or to " 'vulgar,' 'offensive,' and 'shocking' " speech broadcast over the electronic media[44]—the Court in *Falwell* simply shrugged off this apparent inconsistency. It casually observed that "the sort of expression involved in this case does not seem to us to be governed by any exception to the general First Amendment principles"[45] that " 'speech does not lose its protected character . . . simply because it may embarrass others' "[46] or because " 'society may find [it] offensive.' "[47]

Each of these three propositions about "the world of debate about public affairs" is well rooted in traditional constitutional doctrine, and a good measure of the undeniable power of the *Falwell* opinion lies in its ability to evoke authentically such central themes of First Amendment jurisprudence. Although the opinion does not even attempt to explore the logical status and interrelationship of these claims, the three propositions, when taken together, offer a strongly normative image of a realm of public discourse that is obviously incompatible with the jury verdict in *Falwell* and that therefore requires the reversal of the Fourth Circuit's decision.

In the last two paragraphs of its opinion, the Court in *Falwell* shifted gears and announced a narrow prophylactic rule:

> Public figures and public officials may not recover for the tort of intentional infliction of emotional distress by reason of publications such as the one here at issue without showing in addition that the publication contains a false statement of fact which was made with "actual malice," *i.e.*, with knowledge that the statement was false or with reckless disregard as to whether or not it was true.

The Court did not claim that this carefully guarded rule was itself expressive of the normative characteristics of public discourse. Instead it proposed the rule as an explicitly instrumental device designed to ensure that the operation of the legal system not unduly curtail legitimate public discussion. The Court justified the rule with the familiar theory that constitutionally valueless expression must sometimes be protected so that speakers will not engage in self-censorship and hence diminish "speech relating to public figures that does have constitutional value." The Court insisted that it had to apply the rule to the tort of intentional infliction of emotional distress in order "to give adequate 'breathing space' to the freedoms protected by the First Amendment."[48]

The *Falwell* opinion thus combines a specific and extraordinarily narrow holding with reasoning best described as delphic. By refusing to reconcile inconsistencies between *Falwell* and prior decisions on offensive or abusive speech, the opinion fails to address the tension between such speech and freedom of expression, a tension central to *Falwell* and to First Amendment jurisprudence generally. The opinion tells us almost nothing about whether the Constitution protects outrageous communications that are privately disseminated rather than displayed in the pages of a nationally distributed magazine,[49] or whether it protects outrageous communications that are designed to hurt or embarrass private figures,[50] or whether it protects communications that, although injuring the same emotional tranquillity as that safeguarded by the tort of intentional infliction of emotional distress, are also violative of similar torts like invasion of privacy.[51] If the only operative legal standard is the "general first amendment principle" that speech cannot be regulated because it causes offense or embarrassment, then these questions are all easily answered: each of these hypothetical situations is constitutionally indistinguishable from the one actually presented by the *Falwell* case.

But this conclusion rings false; it jumps far too easily beyond the particular circumstances of the *Falwell* decision. If the implications of *Falwell* are not to reach so far, however, the decision must rest on some implicit constitutional theory considerably more complex than any announced by the Chief Justice.[52]

The Significance of the Falwell Opinion: Civility and Intentional Infliction of Emotional Distress

The full significance of the *Falwell* opinion becomes clear only when assessed from a historical and functional perspective. The tort of intentional infliction of emotional distress is one of a family of actions, which include defamation and invasion of privacy, that are designed to protect the respect to which the law believes persons are entitled. In serving this function, however, these torts also enforce those "generally accepted standards of decency and morality"[53] that define for us the meaning of life in a "civilized community."[54] Although our own experience of human dignity subsists in the performance of these standards, the *Falwell* opinion prohibits their enforcement in public discourse, at least in the absence of false statements of fact.

This prohibition represents a radical departure from the traditional perspective of the common law. For centuries the kind of ridicule represented by the *Hustler* parody was regulated by the common law tort of defamation. Communications were deemed defamatory if they exposed an individual "to hatred, contempt, or ridicule."[55] The object of the tort was the protection of reputation, which is to say the standing of a person in the eyes of others. But an important reason why the law protected reputation was, as Justice Stewart observed in an eloquent and influential formulation, to safeguard "the essential dignity and worth of every human being."[56]

The relationship between dignity and reputation is complex, but the essential idea is that our sense of identity and "worth" depends to a significant degree upon what others think of us.[57] Because individual identity evolves from forms of social interaction, we incorporate into our personality, into our very sense of self-worth and dignity, the institutionalized values and norms to which we have been socialized.[58] This insight was most acutely formulated by George Herbert Mead, who observed that "what goes to make up the organized self is the organization of the attitudes which are common to the group. A person is a personality because he belongs to a community, because he takes over the institutions of that community into his own conduct."[59]

More recently, the sociologist Erving Goffman has demonstrated how the very stability of human personality depends upon the continual reaffirmation of community values and attitudes through the enactment of forms of civility, which Goffman calls rules of "deference and demeanor."[60] In his most famous work, for example, Goffman documented how certain "total institutions," like mental hospitals, prisons, or the military, deliberately violate ordinary rules of deference and demeanor in an attempt to unhinge and alter the identity of new initiates.[61] This strategy works because a person's "self" can be "disconfirm[ed]" if a person is not permitted to participate in the forms of mutual respect which he has been socialized to expect.[62] The dignity and integrity of individual personality thus depend to no small degree upon the maintenance of this respect.

Defamatory communications may be defined as those whose content is not civil, because their meaning violates the respect which we have come to expect from each other. They thus threaten not only the self of the defamed person (causing, among other things, symptoms of "personal humiliation, and mental anguish and suffering"[63]), but also the continued validity of the rules of civility which have been violated. These rules represent the "special claims which members [of a community] have on each other, as distinct from others,"[64] and hence they embody the very substance and boundaries of community life. The definition and enforcement of these boundaries create for each community "its distinctive shape, its unique identity."[65] The common law's regulation of defamation contains numerous features that attempt to preserve the integrity of these rules of civility, and thus to safeguard not only the dignity and personality of defamed persons but also the identity and values of the community.[66]

In this process of regulation, the concept of truth played a curious and ambiguous role. At traditional common law, a libel victim was given a choice of "two remedies, one by indictment and the other by action."[67] If the plaintiff elected to proceed by way of criminal prosecution, the truth or falsity of the libel was deemed immaterial,[68] and the defendant was "not allowed to allege the truth of it by way of justification."[69] The crime of defamation was thus entirely oriented toward maintaining the integrity of civility rules. If a plaintiff elected to bring an action for civil damages, however, a defendant could plead the "justification" of truth as an affirmative defense. A plaintiff could not recover compensation if a defendant could prove that his own uncivil communication was true.

The traditional common law rule had a special twist, however: a "defamatory statement [was] presumed to be false,"[70] and a defendant had to overcome this presumption to avoid liability. Hence in cases like the *Hustler* parody, where truth was either difficult or impossible to establish because the defamatory communication did not contain factual statements, the defendant would be held liable. Thus private plaintiffs, and even public officials, could recover damages for the publication of satire containing defamatory ridicule.[71]

This tradition of focusing the tort primarily on the regulation of uncivil communications was most famously summarized by Learned Hand in an opinion upholding a libel judgment based upon a photograph that asserted nothing whatever about a plaintiff, either true or false, but that nevertheless exposed him "to more than trivial ridicule." Hand stated that "it is a non sequitur to argue that whenever truth is not a defense, there can be no libel; that would invert the proper approach to the whole subject." The function of the tort was to provide redress for uncivil communications, which subject persons to " 'ridicule, scandal, reproach, scorn, and indignity.' " "The only reason why the law makes truth a defense," wrote Hand, "is not because a libel must be false, but because the utterance of truth is in all circumstances an interest paramount to reputation."[72]

About the turn of the century, the traditional common law approach to truth began to change. Courts began to speak of a plaintiff's burden of proving falsity instead of a defendant's burden of proving truth. To shift the burden of proof in this manner is essentially to narrow the focus of the tort from communications whose content is uncivil to communications whose content is uncivil by reason of false statements of fact. The tort's altered focus is reflected in the elements of the cause of action for defamation contained in the first *Restatement of Torts*, which stated that "to create liability for defamation there must be an unprivileged publication of false and defamatory matter."[73] The *Restatement* did not completely abandon the focus of the traditional common law, however, for it also expressly retained a provision providing that an actionable communication "may consist of a statement of opinion."[74] Although conceding that the legal characterization of opinion may depend on "propriety" rather than "truth or falsity," the *Restatement* nevertheless insisted that "a defamatory communication may be made by derogatory adjectives or epithets as well as by statements of fact."[75] It even illustrated the point with an example containing political criticism:

> A, while making a political speech, accurately relates certain specific conduct of his opponent in blocking reform measures advocated by A. In the course of his argument, A declares that any person who would so conduct himself is no better than a murderer. A has defamed his opponent . . .[76]

The first *Restatement* thus contained within it two distinct visions of the tort of defamation,[77] one retaining the traditional focus on the regulation of uncivil communications, the other reflecting the newer focus on the regulation of communications that were uncivil by reason of false statements of fact. This dual focus was also evident in the tentative drafts of the second *Restatement*. They retained both the requirement that defamatory statements be "false"[78] and provisions enabling actionable defamation to consist solely of expressions of opinion.[79] Indeed, as recently as May 23, 1974, the American Law Institute approved the insertion into the second *Restatement* of a new section entitled "Ridicule," which provided that "a defamatory communication may consist of words or other matter which ridicule another."[80] The comment to the section stated:

> One common form of defamation is ridicule, which in effect is the expression of an opinion that the plaintiff is ridiculous, and so exposes him to contempt or derision, or other derogatory feelings. Humorous writings, verses, cartoons or caricatures which carry a sting and cause adverse rather than sympathetic or neutral merriment, may be defamatory.[81]

One month later, on June 25, 1974, the Supreme Court in Gertz v. Robert Welch, Inc. issued its famous dictum on the constitutional protection of opinion:

> We begin with the common ground. Under the First Amendment there is no such thing as a false idea. However pernicious an opinion may seem, we depend for its correction not on the conscience of judges and juries but on the competition of other ideas. But there is no constitutional value in false statements of facts.[82]

The *Gertz* dictum definitively preempted the traditional common law understanding of truth, decisively shifting the focus of the tort to communications that are uncivil by reason of false statements of fact.[83] Common law regulation of other kinds of uncivil communications, as for example those that offend against decency by reason of true statements of fact or by reason of ridicule, was for this reason displaced to torts like invasion of privacy[84] or the intentional infliction of emotional distress.

This is of course exactly what happened to Jerry Falwell in his suit against Flynt. Because the *Gertz* dictum had immunized plainly defamatory ridicule like the *Hustler* parody, Falwell was forced to offer a theory of his case that predicated liability on the basis of the comparatively more recent tort of intentional infliction of emotional distress. Although the latter tort has quite different elements from those of defamation, it nevertheless has a closely analogous sociological structure.

Until well into the twentieth century, the "long-recognized common-law rule" did not permit claims "for mental suffering only."[85] By 1939, however, at about the same time that the tort of defamation was shifting its focus to false statements of fact, Dean Prosser could write that "it is time to recognize that the courts have created a new tort" regulating "the intentional, outrageous infliction of mental suffering in an extreme form."[86] The new tort was recognized by the drafters of the second *Restatement* in 1948[87] and is now widely accepted.[88] Although the four elements of the tort set forth in Virginia law are entirely typical,[89] "the tort, despite its apparent abundance of elements, in practice tends to reduce to a single element—the outrageousness of the defendant's conduct."[90]

This reduction occurs because of the strong tendency to assume that "the extreme and outrageous character of the defendant's conduct is in itself important evidence that the distress has existed,"[91] so that the element of "severe" emotional distress is generally satisfied by a plaintiff's simple recitation that he has been upset. The tendency is illustrated by the *Falwell* case itself, where the independent evidence of Falwell's mental anguish was minimal, to say the least.[92] The implicit assumption that outrageous conduct necessarily produces emotional distress also satisfies the requirement that there be "a causal connection between the wrongdoer's conduct and the emotional distress."[93] Consequently the element of causality is most often met, as in the *Falwell* case, by the simple testimony of a plaintiff. Finally, the element of intent or recklessness is usually satisfied by the notion that a defendant "should have known" that outrageous conduct would produce emotional distress. The question thus becomes whether the defendant's conduct was itself intentional.

The "collapse"[94] of the tort's four elements into the single question of the outrageousness of the defendant's behavior is sociologically significant. Outrageous behavior is precisely conduct which "offends against the generally accepted standards of decency and morality,"[95] and which is therefore, in the influential words of the second *Restatement*, "utterly intolerable in a civilized community. Generally, the case is one in which the recitation of the facts to an average member of the community would arouse his resentment against the actor, and lead him to exclaim, 'Outrageous!' "[96] Because well-socialized members of a "civilized community" have incorporated into their very identities the "generally accepted standards of decency and morality" policed by the tort, they experience behavior which violates these standards as profoundly demeaning, disrespectful, and painful. The expectation of a spontaneous and negative emotional reaction to such behavior is so powerful that the *Restatement* (and most courts) use it to define the behavior to be regulated. It is no wonder that juries have been willing to do the same.

The reciprocal dependence of personality and civility thus undermines the formal structure of the tort and leads to the "collapse" of its distinct elements. Even though the tort as a doctrinal matter follows the pattern of a negligence action, in which a defendant is held liable if and only if his unacceptable conduct actually causes demonstrable injury, the practical structure of the tort instead resembles actions for defamation or invasion of privacy, which have no independent requirement that a plaintiff allege or prove actual injury.[97] From a sociological point of view, the tort functions, as do these latter actions, to penalize those defendants who breach civility rules, regardless of the contingent consequences of that behavior.

For this reason the tort of intentional infliction of emotional distress, like common law actions for defamation and invasion of privacy, in practice serves at least two distinct purposes. It not only provides relief for those whose personalities have been threatened by uncivil behavior, but it also serves to safeguard those "generally accepted standards of decency and morality" that define for us the meaning of life in a "civilized community."

Many of these standards, of course, inhere in norms of communication, norms that define the terms of civil discussion. As the Court stressed in Bethel School District No. 403 v. Fraser, these norms are particularly important for the maintenance of "public discourse," because " 'the habits and manners of civility [are] indispensable to the practice of self-government in the community and the nation.' "[98] Frank Michelman makes essentially the same point when he argues that public discussion cannot be "jurisgenerative" unless it "is not considered or experienced as coercive, or invasive, or otherwise a violation of one's identity or freedom."[99] Yet the *Falwell* opinion prohibits the tort of intentional infliction of emotional distress from enforcing, in the absence of a knowingly false assertion of fact, exactly those norms which define civility and hence which would restrain speech likely to be experienced as coercive and violative of identity.

As this discussion illustrates, moreover, the opinion's precise justification for this prohibition is patently inadequate. The Court states that "in the area of political and social discourse" the distinction between outrageous and non-outrageous opinion is not "principled" and hence constitutionally inappropriate, because it "has an inherent subjectiveness about it" that would permit liability to be imposed merely on the basis of "tastes" or preferences.[100] Although this reasoning accurately captures a central theme of First Amendment jurisprudence,[101] the reasoning seems deeply misplaced in the context of a tort that appeals to *inter*subjective, rather than to private, standards of judgment. Outrageous behavior is that which violates *community* values, rather than merely personal or idiosyncratic preferences.[102] The Court's reference to "tastes" fails to recognize that taste constitutes an appeal to social and common standards of evaluation, and thus that "taste, in its essential nature, is not private, but a social phenomenon."[103] Immanuel Kant's classic modern formulation of this point contrasts taste, which *"demands"* the agreement of others, with the sense of the agreeable or pleasant, concerning which "every one is content that his judgment, which he bases upon private feeling, and by which he says of an object that it pleases him, should be limited merely to his own person."[104]

To claim that speech is outrageous is to assert much more than that it is personally unpleasant or disagreeable; it is to claim that the speech is undesirable because it is inconsistent with common canons of decency. Such a claim may be controversial, but it need be neither arbitrary nor subjective. This is recognized even within the narrow confines of First Amendment doctrine, which draws the line between constitutionally protected and unprotected speech on the basis of such structurally similar claims as that speech is "prurient" (when measured by """"contemporary community standards""""[105]) and hence obscene, or that speech is of a kind whose "very utterance inflict[s] injury" and hence constitutes "fighting words,"[106] or that speech is "vulgar, offensive, and shocking," and hence not fit for broadcast over the radio during daytime hours.[107]

It is evident, then, that what is driving the *Falwell* opinion is not that the distinction between outrageous and non-outrageous speech is subjective or arbitrary, but rather that it is constitutionally inappropriate as a standard for the legal regulation of public discourse. The question, of course, is exactly why the distinction is inappropriate, and on this question the *Falwell* opinion is not forthcoming.

The opinion is clear, however, about its concern to protect constitutionally a special kind of "world of debate about public affairs,"[108] and it is with this concern that the construction of an adequate explanatory theory must begin.

The First Amendment and Public Discourse

There has traditionally been a strong affinity between First Amendment jurisprudence and the concept of the public. The "Court has emphasized that the First Amendment 'embraces at the least the liberty to discuss publicly . . . all matters of public concern.' "[109] It has stated more than once that "expression on public issues 'has always rested on the highest rung of the hierarchy of First Amendment values,' "[110] and that speech on matters "of public concern" is "entitled to special protection."[111] The same is true for speech about "public persons," a class consisting of "those who hold governmental office" and those "who, by reason of the notoriety of their achievements or the vigor and success with which they seek the public's attention, are properly classed as public figures."[112]

The concept of the public has a number of different meanings for First Amendment doctrine. One important meaning is the designation of speech that will be deemed constitutionally independent of the managerial authority of state institutions. This is the meaning that the concept of the public holds in contemporary "public forum" doctrine. But in the context of a case like *Falwell* the concept expresses quite a different meaning. It refers instead to the protection of speech from the control of community norms like those enforced by the tort of intentional infliction of emotional distress. This section explores some of the justifications and consequences of that protection.

Public Discourse and Community

The concept of "public discourse" at issue in a decision like *Falwell* is in many respects unique and counterintuitive. These qualities can perhaps best be made visible by comparing the First Amendment concept of public discourse to a competing notion that developed in the early nineteenth century in the common law privilege of "fair comment." Roughly speaking, the privilege, with many local and chronological variations, functioned to immunize the publication of honestly held but defamatory opinions about matters of public concern that were fair and communicated without malice.[113]

The origins of the privilege have been traced back to an 1808 decision involving the harsh criticism of three travel books.[114] Although the criticism was otherwise defamatory, the judge charged the jury as follows: "Every man who publishes a book commits himself to the judgment of the public, and anyone may comment upon his performance . . . [W]hatever their merits, others have a right to pass their judgment upon them—to censure them if they be censurable, and to turn them into ridicule if they be ridiculous."[115] Any other conclusion, the judge stated, would permit the author of a book to "maintain a monopoly of sentiment and opinion respecting it."[116]

As the privilege achieved recognition and expanded to embrace purely political discussion, the elements of the privilege also came more sharply into focus. Although articulated differently by various judges at various times, these elements included the requirements that the privileged comment represent the honest belief of the speaker;[117] that the comment state opinion rather than fact;[118] and that the comment concern matters "of public interest" rather than, for example, the merely "private character" of public persons like authors or politicians.[119] Successful invocation of the privilege also required that the comment be without malice,[120] meaning that the comment be made for "a well-defined public purpose" rather than "for some ulterior and improper purpose,"[121] and that the comment not be framed in too intemperate a fashion.[122]

At first blush, the privilege of fair comment resembles the constitutional privilege that emerges from *Falwell*: both privileges attempt to define an arena of specifically "public" discourse, and both rely for their rationale on the distinction between opinion and fact. But this resemblance is merely superficial, for in fact the two privileges presuppose radically different concepts of public discourse.

The privilege of fair comment defines a "world of debate about public affairs" that is pervasively normative, in that it focuses upon whether a public communication has been made "upon a proper occasion, from a proper motive, in a proper manner and . . . based upon reasonable or probable cause."[123] The privilege of fair comment thus envisions public debate as infused with and controlled by precisely "the habits and manners of civility" praised by the Court in Bethel School District No. 403 v. Fraser.[124] Although courts applying the privilege used various doctrinal tests, like the distinction between fact and opinion, the nature of malice, or the scope of the legitimate interests of the public, in the end these tests were merely tools by which courts could analyze such normative questions as whether it is civil and appropriate in public discourse to attribute base motivations to public persons,[125] to scrutinize the private character or personal life of such persons,[126] or to express one's evaluations of such persons with "contemptuous allusions, and sarcastic phrases, well calculated to humiliate, and . . . devoid of all cast of fair comment."[127]

The privilege of fair comment, in other words, functioned to interpret and uphold norms of civility, in the same manner as did the underlying tort of defamation. Although the existence of the privilege indicated that public discourse had for the common law its own somewhat distinct rules of civility, which permitted a freer play of opinion than in private life, the common law nevertheless subordinated that discourse to community notions of propriety and decency. In line with this subordination, the common law allocated to the jury, as the representative of the community, the determination as to the applicability of the privilege of fair comment.[128] By this means the common law firmly embedded the sphere of public discourse within a community defined by rules of civility and respect.

Exactly the opposite is true, however, of the sphere of public discourse defined by First Amendment doctrine. Since the 1930s the Supreme Court has regularly expressed a specifically constitutional vision of a "world of debate about public affairs" that transcends the bounds and perspectives of any particular community. An early and classic articulation of this vision appears in Cantwell v. Connecticut, in which a Jehovah's Witness had been convicted of the common law crime of inciting breach of the peace because of speech that was concededly highly offensive to his Catholic audience. The Court held that the speech was constitutionally protected:

> In the realm of religious faith, and in that of political belief, sharp differences arise. In both fields the tenets of one man may seem the rankest error to his neighbor. To persuade others to his own point of view, the pleader, as we know, at times, resorts to exaggeration, to vilification of men who have been, or are, prominent in church or state, and even to false statement. But the people of this nation have ordained in the light of history, that, in spite of the probability of excesses and abuses, these liberties are, in the long view, essential to enlightened opinion and right conduct on the part of the citizens of a democracy.
>
> The essential characteristic of these liberties is, that under their shield many types of life, character, opinion and belief can develop unmolested and unobstructed. Nowhere is this shield more necessary than in our own country for a people composed of many races and of many creeds.[129]

The passage is extraordinarily rich and allusive, and it merits close attention. It sketches a sphere of constitutional immunity that extends to speech about public subjects, like "religious faith" or "political belief" or "prominent" persons, even though such speech violates the most elementary civility rules against "exaggeration" or "vilification" or "excesses and abuses." The justification for this immunity is that America contains "many" diverse communities which are often in sharp conflict. If the state were to enforce the civility rules of one community, say those of Catholics, as against those of another, say Jehovah's Witnesses, the state would in effect be using its power and authority to support some communities and repress others. But the First Amendment forbids the state from doing this, in order that "many types of life, character, opinion and belief can develop unmolested and unobstructed."

Cantwell thus refuses to enforce civility rules within a constitutionally defined sphere of public discourse because it perceives communities as labile and evolving. If the common law privilege of fair comment reflects and enforces the civility rules of a fixed and established community that contains within itself a distinct sphere of public discourse, First Amendment doctrine since *Cantwell* instead maintains a sphere of public discourse in which communities themselves develop through competition for the allegiance of individual adherents. The constitutional "shield" established by *Cantwell* ensures that this competition occurs on a level playing field, in which no particular community can obtain an unfair advantage and use the power of the state to prejudge the outcome of this competition by enforcing its own special norms or civility rules. This special neutrality is reflected in the fact that the Constitution shifts the primary locus of decision-making away from the jury, which represents community standards, to the judge, who represents instead an impartial and overarching public order, and who exercises "independent review" to determine matters of "constitutional fact."[130]

This analysis suggests that the familiar image of constitutional neutrality articulated by *Cantwell* actually rests on the assumption that community life is constituted by the voluntary choices of its members. It is because of this assumption that *Cantwell* views the function of the First Amendment to be that of safeguarding the potential for new and more satisfactory choices.[131] This vision of social life, however, differs fundamentally from that assumed by the common law torts of defamation and intentional infliction of emotional distress, which conceive the self as instead constituted by community norms. These torts penalize speech that violates civility rules because they understand such speech as damaging the very identity of community members; First Amendment doctrine, on the other hand, rests on the possibility of using such speech to create new identities.

Ultimately, then, the logic of *Cantwell* places the Constitution firmly on the side of those individuals who would attempt to use speech to alter the terms of community life. This is an important source of the strong "intellectual individualism" that characterizes First Amendment doctrine.[132] The most eloquent expression of that individualism is perhaps Cohen v. California, in which the Court rejected the authority of the state to punish "unseemly" speech so as to maintain "a suitable level of discourse within the body politic":

> The constitutional right of free expression is powerful medicine in a society as diverse and populous as ours. It is designed and intended to remove governmental restraints from the arena of public discussion, putting the decision as to what views shall be voiced largely into the hands of each of us, in the hope that use of such freedom will ultimately produce a more capable citizenry and more perfect polity and in the belief that no other approach would comport with the premise of individual dignity and choice upon which our political system rests.[133]

The concept of a neutral sphere of public discourse, which derives from this commitment to individualism, has powerful implications for the civility rules enforced by the common law tort of intentional infliction of emotional distress. The specific "outrageousness" standard at issue in *Falwell*, for example, can have meaning only within the commonly accepted norms of a particular community. But the constitutional concept of public discourse forbids the state from enforcing such a standard within the "world of debate about public affairs,"[134] because to do so would privilege a specific community and prejudice the ability of individuals to persuade others of the need to change it. Outrageous speech calls community identity into question, practically as well as cognitively, and thus it has unique power to focus attention, dislocate old assumptions, and shock its audience into the recognition of unfamiliar forms of life.

Of course, on this account, an "outrageousness" standard is unacceptable not because it "has an inherent subjectiveness about it"[135] but rather because it would enable a single community to use the authority of the state to confine speech within its own notions of propriety.[136] *Falwell* itself gestures toward this latter explanation by defending its holding on the ground of the "oft-repeated" premise that " 'it is a central tenet of the First Amendment that the government must remain neutral in the marketplace of ideas.' "[137] The difficulty with this gesture, however, is that, like most modern commentary, it conceives of neutrality only at the level of ideas, rather than at the more general level of the structures that establish communal life. We might correct this difficulty by saying that the concept of public discourse requires the state to remain neutral in the "marketplace of communities."

It is important to note that this neutrality does not and cannot extend to public life generally, where it is natural and commonplace for law to regulate behavior in ways that implement one or another specific image of communal identity. We outlaw drug abuse or racial discrimination because we believe that such conduct is inconsistent with who we want to be. But the central thrust of modern First Amendment doctrine is to prohibit speech from being regulated in this way. The consequence of this prohibition is to ensure that the various forms of identity enacted by public law remain subject to the perennial evaluation of speech, and so to that limited extent vulnerable and provisional.[138] Thus the ambition of constitutional law to create a distinct realm of public discourse independent of the norms of any particular community has forced First Amendment doctrine sharply to separate communication from behavior. The common law privilege of fair comment, however, by subjecting public discourse to community norms like any other form of conduct, effaces this distinction between speech and action.

Constitutional law and common law, then, embody fundamentally different concepts of public discourse.[139]

The Structure of Public Discourse

The very notion that discourse can proceed independently of the norms of ordinary community life should pose something of a puzzle. *Cohen* tells us that "the arena of public discussion" constituted by the First Amendment is designed to produce "a more perfect polity."[140] But how can this be true if those who participate in that arena speak to one another across the deep chasms that divide American communities from each other? We may well ask how such persons can find common ground to support a discussion that will be to their mutual advantage.

Curiously, at about the time the Supreme Court was fashioning its special concept of public discourse, American sociologists were developing a strikingly analogous notion of the public, which they viewed as a form of social organization transcending particular communities and existing only in the presence of diverse and conflicting forms of communal life. In his 1933 article "The Concept of the Public," for example, Carroll Clark noted that "before a group can become a public there must be a confrontation of divergent attitudes involving the tacit or expressed rules that set the pattern of behavior and fix judgment of consequences." "Publics come into existence" only when "social organization is widened and complicated by economic and cultural differentiation that entail incompatible schemes of group behavior." But what could hold a public together as a viable social formation across the rifts of such cultural differentiation? Clark's answer, by no means idiosyncratic, is quite striking from the perspective of First Amendment scholarship: " 'A public is, in fact, organized on the basis of a universe of discourse . . .' "[141]

A public, in other words, is constituted precisely by the ability of persons to speak to one another across the boundaries of divergent cultures. From this perspective, of course, the social function of First Amendment doctrine, as reformulated during the 1930s and 1940s, becomes plain enough: it is to establish a protected space within which this communication can occur. Sociologically viewed, however, the continued existence of this space depends upon at least five preconditions.

First, a society must include a plurality of cultures and traditions. A society characterized by the norms of only one community will lack the impetus to liberate its public discourse from the regulation of those norms. At least in America, the recognition of "rich cultural diversities"[142] has spurred the disengagement of public discourse from the values of any single community. Since *Cantwell* the acknowledgment of these competing traditions has been a continual theme of First Amendment jurisprudence.

Second, even a culturally heterogeneous society cannot sustain public discourse unless the society values and wishes to preserve that heterogeneity. Just as Jerry Falwell sought to impose his notion of the outrageous onto Larry Flynt's satire, so too will powerful communities seek to use the authority of the state to impose their own norms on speech generally. The common law torts of defamation and invasion of privacy represent just such efforts to use law to subject communication to putatively "universal" cultural standards.[143] In the absence of a commitment to diversity, therefore, the fact of heterogeneity may well be submerged within a legal tendency toward uniformity. First Amendment jurisprudence is committed to diversity because of its methodological individualism, which, I have argued, ultimately derives from its voluntaristic conception of community life.[144] This conception converts the individual into the privileged unit of social action.[145]

Third, those participating in public discourse can communicate with one another only if they have something in common to talk about. Persons thus cannot constitute a public unless "they are exposed to similar social stimuli."[146] A primary and continuing source of these stimuli within public discourse is the news. News, as Walter Lippmann noted long ago, "comes from a distance,"[147] from beyond the "self-contained community"[148] in which we happen to live. The news functions as a medium of common information that brings together persons of widely disparate traditions and cultures. Thus "news is a public (and a public-generating) social phenomenon."[149] "The emergence of the mass media and of the 'public' are mutually constructive developments."[150] For this reason the First Amendment protects not merely the expression of ideas but also "the free communication of information."[151]

Fourth, persons must have a reason to enter into the realm of public discourse to communicate with those beyond their own communities.[152] Clark offers as exemplary the public sphere of the marketplace. Individuals from widely disparate cultural backgrounds participate together in a market, in which decisions are made not upon "mores" or "tradition" but rather upon commonly available "fact and news."[153] It is important to recognize, however, that the continued existence of the public space established by the market depends upon a common motivation for profit. With respect to "the arena of public discussion" established by the First Amendment, the common motivation must be understood as that of democratic self-governance and a shared political destiny. Because our government responds to the desires of "the whole People, who are the publick,"[154] individuals from diverse traditions and communities must attempt to communicate with each other if they wish to participate in that dialogue which will ultimately direct the actions of the entire nation.

Fifth, communication requires not merely common information but also commonly accepted standards of meaning and evaluation. Persons who do not share a minimum set of such standards simply cannot understand one another; they cannot participate in a common "universe of discourse." The necessity for these standards suggests that the emergence of public discourse rests upon a delicate balance: if persons in public discourse share too much, if they are simply members of the same community, the diversity requisite for the emergence of public discourse will not be present. But if, on the other hand, such persons share too little, if they have absolutely no common standards for the evaluation and assessment of meaning, public discourse cannot be sustained.[155]

The conduct of public discourse, in other words, requires persons to share standards, but not the kind of standards that fuse them into a community. But what can persons in public discourse share in the "absence of interaction in terms of the conventional and traditional definitions"[156] of specific communities? Persons can share the ability to engage in "intellectual processes," sociologists said, and they thus defined a "public" as "any group . . . that achieves corporate unity through critical interaction."[157] "In the public," it was said, "interaction takes the form of discussion. Individuals act upon one another critically . . . Opinions clash and thus modify and moderate one another."[158] In the words of a more contemporary theorist, Alvin Gouldner, the very existence of public discourse implies "a cleared and safe space" in which the interpretation of shared stimuli, like news, can occur in a "critical" manner, "meaning that what has been said may be questioned, negated and contradicted."[159]

The identification of public discourse with forms of "critical interaction" rests upon a very abstract logic. If membership in a community is "a constituent of . . . identity,"[160] the effort to communicate through public discourse with those who do not share that identity must entail a constant effort to distance oneself from the assumptions and certitudes that define oneself and one's community.[161] By being "critical" and "intellectual," public discourse can strive to generalize its appeal so as to reach persons from disparate cultures and traditions.

The problem, however, is that this conception of public discourse is highly schematic, and its value as an empirical description may be questioned. Even the most casual survey of American public deliberation would lead to the conclusion that it is "intellectual" and "critical" only in fits and starts, and that there are unending attempts by various cultures and traditions to seize control of public discussion and to subject it to particular community values and standards.[162] But the conception does have considerable power as a description of how meaningful public discussion can occur in the face of fundamental and concededly valid cultural divergence. In such circumstances, it may be said, persons ought to strive to engage in a mutual process of critical interaction, because if they do not, no uncoerced common understanding can possibly be attained.[163]

First Amendment doctrine attempts to protect an arena for just such a process of critical interaction. Resting upon a deep respect for the "sharp differences" characteristic of American life, First Amendment doctrine is committed to the maintenance of "the right to differ as to things that touch the heart of the existing order."[164] It thus creates "a cleared and safe space" within which can occur precisely that "uninhibited, robust, and wide-open"[165] debate on public issues that one would expect to emerge when dominant cultural traditions are denied access to the force of law to silence the clash of divergent perspectives. Contemporary constitutional doctrine looks to this debate to constitute that "universe of discourse" within which public opinion, and hence democratic policy, may be formed.

To more fully understand that doctrine, however, the notion of "critical interaction" upon which it depends must be analyzed somewhat more precisely.

The Nature of Critical Interaction within Public Discourse

The general idea of critical interaction is simple enough. Public discussion must facilitate communication among persons from widely varying traditions and cultures. Within public discourse, therefore, "the tenets of one man may seem the rankest error to his neighbor";[166] "one man's vulgarity is another's lyric";[167] and "one man's amusement, teaches another's doctrine."[168] In such circumstances participants in public debate must be tolerant; they cannot silence speech because of preexisting assumptions about what is reasonable or appropriate, for any such assumptions would prejudge the outcome and conduct of the debate.

At root, therefore, the concept of critical interaction depends upon the continuous possibility of transcending what is taken for granted. If, as the torts of defamation and intentional infliction of emotional distress suggest, speech within a community is ordinarily bounded by normative standards whose validity is assumed and enforced, critical interaction may be defined as that in which such standards have ceased to provide boundaries because they have themselves become potentially questionable. The First Amendment embodies this conception of critical discourse by performing the wholly negative function of shielding speakers from the enforcement of community standards.

When the standards to be suspended are civility rules, however, constitutional intervention can be quite problematic, for the observance of civility rules sustains and defines the very personalities of those within a community. For this reason, words that are deeply uncivil "by their very utterance inflict injury,"[169] and, as Alexander Bickel once remarked, such communication "amounts to almost physical aggression."[170] We might say, therefore, that civility rules that distinguish appropriate from inappropriate ways of speaking also tend to define a point (although certainly not the only point) at which speech shades into conduct, at which a community subordinates speech to the regulatory schemes that it imposes upon action generally.[171] This is explicitly true with respect to the tort of intentional infliction of emotional distress, which enforces a standard that makes no distinction at all between speech and conduct; but it is also characteristically true of the other dignitary torts, which carry the strong sense of a defendant's having used "words as instruments of aggression and personal assault."[172] For this reason the prohibition of the enforcement of civility rules is experienced less like the opening to debate of heretofore unquestionable topics, and more like the licensing of heretofore unacceptable patterns of behavior.

This fact has important consequences for the constitutional concept of public discourse, because the ultimate purpose of that discourse is to enable the formation of a genuine and uncoerced public opinion in a culturally heterogeneous society. The most complete contemporary investigation of this purpose appears in the work of Jürgen Habermas, who views the public as a "sphere" that grounds the legitimacy of modern states by providing a space for the creation of "a common will, communicatively shaped and discursively clarified." The objective is the attainment of "a consensus arrived at communicatively in the public sphere."[173] But such a consensus will carry legitimacy only if the state imposes upon public discussion the regulative structure of an "ideal speech situation," in which speech is "immunized against repression" and "all force" is excluded, "except the force of the better argument."[174] Within an ideal speech situation, discourse is seen as functioning as pure communication, as "removed from contexts of experience and action" and as consisting entirely of "bracketed validity claims of assertions, recommendations, or warnings."[175]

The radical implication of this perspective is that within the public sphere the state must regard speech as independent from the general context in which social action is routinely assessed. This means that many of the criteria for the evaluation of speech which ultimately derive from that context must be "bracketed" out. As Alvin Gouldner notes, the "rationality of 'public' discourse . . . depends on the prior possibility of separating speakers from their normal powers and privileges in the larger society, especially in the class system, and on successfully defining these powers and privileges as irrelevant to the quality of their discourse."[176]

All speech, of course, is simultaneously communication and social action,[177] and in everyday life it is quite difficult and unusual to separate these two aspects of speech. In most circumstances we attend as carefully to the social status of a speaker, and to the social context of her words, as we do to the bare content of her communication.[178] We thus cannot understand Habermas' and Gouldner's characterization of discussion within the public sphere as descriptive. It must be understood rather as articulating a regulative ideal for the legal structure of public discourse. This ideal is reflected, for example, in the First Amendment right to engage in public discourse anonymously, so that speakers can divorce their speech from the social contextualization which knowledge of their identities would necessarily create in the minds of their audience.[179]

At first glance, therefore, the aspiration of public discourse toward a condition of "deliberation and reflection and a critical spirit"[180] appears to complement the structure of critical interaction, which also regulates speech as pure communication that is severed from its social context. But on closer inspection this compatibility dissolves, for our conception of rational reflection and deliberation itself depends upon the observance of civility rules. Speech inconsistent with these rules is easily seen as irrational or valueless,[181] as the condescending disgust aroused in some readers by *Hustler*'s Campari parody illustrates.[182] More important, speech inconsistent with civility rules is likely to be experienced as violent and coercive.[183] John Dewey made this point in the very passage in which he expressed his "democratic faith" in

> the possibility of conducting disputes, controversies, and conflicts as cooperative undertakings in which both parties learn by giving the other a chance to express itself, instead of having one party conquer by forceful suppression of the other—a suppression which is not the less one of violence when it takes place by psychological means of ridicule, abuse, intimidation, instead of by overt imprisonment or in concentration camps.[184]

The dependence of rational deliberation upon rules of civility suggests that we must understand rational reflection as itself a form of social action that depends for its fulfillment upon a specific normative structure.[185] Public discourse consequently entails two distinct and incompatible requirements. There is, first, the requirement of negativity, of freedom from the boundaries of community expectations and norms. This requirement initiates the very possibility of public discourse by distinguishing it as pure communication able to reach out beyond the confines of any single community. This is the requirement of *critical interaction*. But there must also be a second requirement, one of *rational deliberation*, which entails consideration and evaluation of the various positions made possible by the space of critical interaction. The constitutional purpose of public discourse requires that rational deliberation be civil and noncoercive, which is to say that it must be consistent with the very norms that are negated by critical interaction.

The two requirements of public discourse thus stand in contradiction. The aspiration to be free from the constraints of existing community norms (and to attain a consequent condition of pure communication) is in tension with the aspiration to the social project of reasoned and non-coercive deliberation. The first aspiration is sustained by the values of neutrality, diversity, and individualism; the second by the deliberative enterprise of democratic self-governance. Although the success of public discourse depends upon both requirements, the primary commitment of modern First Amendment jurisprudence has unquestionably been to the radical negativity that characterizes critical interaction, which defines the initial, distinguishing moment of public discourse.[186] As a consequence the constitutional structure that regulates the domain of public discourse denies enforcement to the very norms upon which the success of the political enterprise of public discourse depends.

This contradiction is deeply disturbing. As Sabina Lovibond has recently reminded us, "the norms implicit in a community's . . . social practices are 'upheld,' in quite a material sense, by the sanctions which the community can bring to bear upon deviant individuals."[187] The sanctions that the law can bring to bear to support civility rules are unique, not so much because of their monopoly of physical force, but because they alone purport to define social norms in accents that are universal. These norms can, of course, continue to be enforced by means of private and social pressure. But in the heterogeneity of contemporary culture, only the law can authoritatively speak for norms that define a *common* ideal of rational deliberation. Only the law can rise above the particularity of specific social groups and definitively articulate those irreducible, minimum constraints of decency whose violation would be "utterly intolerable in a civilized community."[188] To the extent that a constitutional commitment to critical interaction prevents the law from articulating and sustaining a common respect for the civility rules that make possible the ideal of rational deliberation, public discourse corrodes the basis of its own existence.

This might be called the "paradox of public discourse." In general we have become so accustomed to the paradox that we scarcely notice it. But it is impossible to avoid in a decision like *Falwell*, where the First Amendment, in the name of freedom of critical interaction, blunts rules of civility that define the essence of reason and dignity within community life. Surely, we tell ourselves, Larry Flynt's parody cannot be the stuff of rational deliberation; yet the constitutional protection afforded the parody undercuts our assurance. In the absence of legal support, our condemnation of the parody, and the values underlying that condemnation, become somehow relativized and drained of authority.[189] We are left with a conflict between Flynt's concept of discourse and our own, with no umpire to decide between us. In this sense a decision like *Falwell* endangers our hold on the very concept of rational deliberation.

The intrinsic unease engendered by *Falwell* is thus explained in no small degree by the complex dependence of public discourse upon the very community norms that it negates, and by our queasy apprehension that those norms cannot entirely be maintained without the impersonal authority of law. The Court could have upheld Falwell's judgment only at the price of denying the premises of critical interaction, by subjecting that interaction to "repression" and "force" grounded in community values. It could set aside his judgment only at the price of severing one more thread in the rope that binds community existence, and hence that may ultimately sustain the very possibility of rational deliberation.[190] The jagged and uneven course of the Court's precedents involving the regulation of offensive speech is merely the legal reflection of this deeply disturbing tension between rational deliberation and critical interaction, both necessary and vital elements of public discourse.

The First Amendment, Community, and Public Discourse

First Amendment jurisprudence, as has often been noted, contains many diverse themes.[191] To claim, as I have done, that one important theme is the separation of public discourse from the regulation of community norms, is to invite two objections. First, it may be argued that because the Constitution has been interpreted since the 1930s to require norms of toleration and individualism, norms that are themselves constitutive of a particular kind of community,[192] there can be no coherent distinction between public discourse and community life. Second, it may be argued (with perhaps some inconsistency) that because the concept of community is altogether too elusive to be of analytic value, it is impossible to specify the kinds of norms whose enforcement within public discourse is prohibited by the First Amendment.

Although the premise of the first objection seems to me quite accurate, its conclusion does not. It is true that we interpret the First Amendment to create a distinct domain of public discourse because we believe in such values as neutrality, individualism, and diversity. Our understanding and implementation of these values define the boundaries of that domain, and for that reason, as I discuss below in greater detail in the section entitled "Defining the Domain of Public Discourse," the location of these boundaries must ultimately depend, at least in part, upon such community values. But *within* the boundaries established for public discourse, the First Amendment aspires to suspend legal enforcement of these as well as all other community values. Thus within the domain of public discourse even the national flag, the very symbol of the values of individualism and diversity, may be burned and desecrated.[193] The *Falwell* decision itself displays this radical negativity by immunizing speech contrary to norms of rationality, respect, and toleration—the very norms that justify the creation of our constitutional form of public discourse.

The second objection also begins with a sound premise. Although the concept of community is "the most fundamental and far-reaching of sociology's unit-ideas,"[194] it is also exceedingly "difficult to define."[195] In this essay I define a community as a social formation that inculcates norms into the very identities of its members.[196] But this understanding is vulnerable to the criticism that the inculcation of shared norms is a matter of degree, that some persons can share some norms but not others, that even within a community the meaning and application of shared norms can give rise to debate and disagreement, and so forth. And of course this criticism is perfectly reasonable and accurate. Taken to its logical extreme, it would seem to dissolve the notion of community altogether, because we can have no principled way to decide abstractly at just what point enough norms are sufficiently specific, inculcated, and shared so as to constitute a community. But the criticism need not be pushed so far, for differences of degree often become differences of kind. The more damaging thrust of the criticism, therefore, is that in practice it can be extremely difficult to distinguish exactly when particular norms are part of a community life.

This point is well taken. Fortunately, though, it is not fatal to the dialectic between community and public discourse that animates First Amendment doctrine. In the kind of cases we are considering, the First Amendment functions primarily as a shield to block the imposition of those norms that a state has already determined to enforce legally. The decision to define these norms and to recognize them as important and as widely shared is thus made in the first instance by the state itself. The precise question for constitutional adjudication in such circumstances is whether the legal enforcement of the norms is incompatible with the requirements of public discourse.

This incompatibility can arise for a number of different reasons. In many cases the issue for decision is most likely to be whether the norms that a state seeks to enforce are inconsistent with the neutrality essential to public discourse. The analysis of such questions does not depend upon whether the norms at issue in a particular case are in fact sufficiently inculcated or sufficiently shared so as to constitute an actual community.

The analysis does depend, however, upon whether the norms are of a kind that, if they were actually socialized into the identities of persons, would establish a community with a "distinctive shape, [a] unique identity."[197] An important challenge for First Amendment jurisprudence, therefore, is to distinguish between two kinds of social standards: those that have the potential to constitute a specific form of community life, and those that do not. Enforcement of the former, in contrast to the latter, conflicts with the neutrality of public discourse. The distinction between the two, as I shall attempt to demonstrate in the following section, underlies some of the most important and otherwise puzzling aspects of the *Falwell* decision.

Public Discourse and the *Falwell* Opinion

The *Falwell* opinion uses three propositions to define "the world of debate about public affairs" protected by the First Amendment. The first of these propositions is that "an 'outrageousness' standard" cannot constitutionally be used to penalize speech because it "would allow a jury to impose liability on the basis of the jurors' tastes or views." The second is that "the First Amendment prohibits" using "bad motive" as a test for imposing "tort liability . . . in the area of public debate about public figures." The third is that in public discourse "[f]alse statements of fact are particularly valueless," while the "First Amendment recognizes no such thing as a 'false' idea."[198] Each of these propositions, I would argue, can best be understood in the context of a constitutional prohibition on the enforcement of those standards that carry the potential to define a particular community identity.

The "Outrageousness" Standard

The "outrageousness" standard rejected by *Falwell* is a paradigmatic attempt to use the law to maintain the "boundaries" of a particular concept of community "identity,"[199] for it is designed to penalize speech that has gone "beyond all possible bounds of decency" and that is "to be regarded as . . . utterly intolerable in a civilized community."[200] Legal enforcement of an outrageousness standard would thus confine public discourse within the "bounds" of the particular "civilized community" defined by the standard. It would deprive public discourse of a position of neutrality as among differing definitions of community identity.

The *Falwell* opinion justifies its rejection of an outrageousness standard on the grounds of "our longstanding refusal to allow damages to be awarded because the speech in question may have an adverse emotional impact on the audience."[201] The three dignitary torts are the primary means by which the law awards damages to protect the "personality" of individuals from emotional harm caused by speech. These torts penalize speech that violates civility rules on the theory that the observance of such rules is necessary for the emotional well-being of properly socialized individuals. But these same civility rules concomitantly establish the identity of a community as "civilized," in exactly the same manner as does the outrageousness standard at issue in *Falwell*. The "longstanding refusal" to which the Court refers thus functions as a continuing effort to exempt public discourse from the enforcement of those kinds of norms commonly used to create community identity.

Falwell illustrates the depth of the Court's commitment to preserving the neutrality of public discourse from the imposition of such norms. Although the Court assumed that the *Hustler* parody would "doubtless [be] gross and repugnant in the eyes of most,"[202] it nevertheless refused to permit the parody to be penalized. This result comports with the reasoning of *Cantwell*: if public discourse is constitutionally protected because it is the medium for the formation of future communities, its structural independence from all civility rules must be guaranteed, even if such rules in fact are accepted by every contemporary community. The "marketplace of communities" must thus be understood as extending in time as well as in space. The individualist methodology of First Amendment doctrine ultimately means that individuals must be free within public discourse from the enforcement of all civility rules, so as to be able to advocate and to exemplify the creation of new forms of communal life in their speech.

The Distinction between Speech and Its Motivation

Falwell's rejection of the reasoning of the Fourth Circuit rests squarely on the premise that in public discourse the worth of speech cannot be measured by the integrity of its motivation. The opinion reaches the strong conclusion that, while "bad motive may be deemed controlling for purposes of tort liability in other areas of the law, we think the First Amendment prohibits such a result in the area of public debate about public figures."[203]

The reasoning of the *Falwell* opinion seems at first glance consistent with traditional First Amendment doctrine. Since *New York Times*, the Court has repeatedly insisted upon this separation of speech from intent, holding that even false defamatory speech uttered " 'from personal spite, ill will or a desire to injure' "[204] does not lose its constitutional protection. This separation is remarkable, for in ordinary life our assessment of the meaning and value of speech often depends upon our understanding of the purposes or intentions of a speaker.[205]

The justification for this separation in the context of the *Falwell* decision should by now be plain enough. The intent element of the tort of intentional infliction of emotional distress effectuates a civility rule concerning how persons should relate to one another. To use speech for the primary purpose of emotionally injuring another is to act in an uncivil way and hence to bring one's conduct within the regulation of a dignitary tort. Because it enforces a civility rule, the intent element at issue in *Falwell* maintains a particular vision of community life, and so is inconsistent with the neutrality necessary for public discourse.

This reasoning does not imply, however, that intent can never constitutionally be used to regulate public discourse, and any such implication in *Falwell* is plainly false. The actual malice standard of *New York Times*, for example, which *Falwell* itself applies, permits false defamatory speech to be punished if there is "sufficient evidence to permit the conclusion that the defendant in fact entertained serious doubts as to the truth of his publication."[206] The standard thus ultimately turns on the "state of mind of the defendant."[207] It cannot be true, therefore, that the "First Amendment prohibits" bad motive from "controlling" the legal characterization of speech within public discourse.

The reason the use of an intent requirement is constitutionally impermissible in the tort of intentional infliction of emotional distress but constitutionally acceptable in the actual malice standard is that the latter does not use the criterion of intent to enforce a civility rule. In explicating the actual malice standard, the Court has consistently stressed that the criterion of intent is not to be confused with morally charged notions like "personal spite, ill will or a desire to injure."[208] Indeed, the fundamental mistake of the Fourth Circuit in *Falwell* was to conflate the actual malice standard with the ethical concept of "culpability."[209] The purpose of the actual malice standard is not to demarcate any such "boundary between morally acceptable and unacceptable modes of political discussion";[210] it is rather to forge "an instrument of policy, to attain the specific end of minimizing the chill on legitimate speech."[211] The element of intent in the actual malice standard accomplishes this objective by placing a defendant, to the maximum extent possible, in control of the legality of his own speech. In the actual malice standard, therefore, the element of intent functions not to impose the norms of an ideal community, but instead to achieve a desired policy outcome. Thus the permissibility of regulating public discourse on the basis of the criterion of intent depends upon the precise use of the criterion in relation to community norms.

The Distinction between Fact and Opinion

The *Falwell* decision draws a sharp distinction between the communication of facts within public discourse, which can be subject to legal supervision for truth or falsity, and the communication of opinions or ideas within public discourse, which is constitutionally immunized from such supervision. Although this distinction may be commonplace, it is also deeply obscure, and it has proved resistant to most analytic attempts at clarification. I argue in this section that the thrust of the distinction can most convincingly be explained by reference to a constitutionally enforced separation of community norms and public discourse.[212]

Some Contemporary Understandings of the Distinction between Fact and Opinion

For many years the distinction between fact and opinion formed the backbone of the fair comment privilege, yet neither courts nor commentators were able to give a principled or convincing explanation of its theoretical foundations. The words "fact" and "opinion," as one writer observed, are "treated as if they possessed some 'magic quality' of self-elucidation," so that they are used "primarily" as "vague familiar terms into which one can pour whatever meaning is desired in order to reach a particular conclusion."[213] The confusion intensified after the Court's announcement in *Gertz* that defamatory opinion was constitutionally privileged.[214] Although courts recognize that it is "often quite difficult to determine whether a publication constitutes a statement of fact or statement of opinion,"[215] the absence of any satisfactory theory has left courts saddled with circular and unhelpful doctrinal tests, like those that urge judges to "consider all the words used" or "all of the circumstances surrounding the statement, including the medium by which the statement is disseminated and the audience to which it is published."[216] Such tests fail to specify in any theoretically useful manner exactly what a court should look for in the "words" or "medium" employed.

Rhetorical Hyperbole.   Part of the difficulty courts face is that in defamation law the notion of opinion has been confused with the concept of "rhetorical hyperbole," which, strictly speaking, has nothing to do with the distinction between fact and opinion. Modern case law on the subject takes as its point of origin the Supreme Court's decision in Greenbelt Cooperative Publishing Association v. Bresler, in which a newspaper had reported on negotiations between a city and Charles Bresler, a real estate developer, and had characterized Bresler's negotiating tactics as "blackmail." Bresler sued for defamation and was awarded damages by the trial court, apparently on the theory that the articles had "imputed to him the crime of blackmail." The Court rejected this interpretation of the meaning of the newspaper's language:

> It is simply impossible to believe that a reader who reached the word "blackmail" in either article would not have understood exactly what was meant: it was Bresler's public and wholly legal negotiating proposals that were being criticized. No reader could have thought that either the speakers at the meetings or the newspaper articles reporting their words were charging Bresler with the commission of a criminal offense. On the contrary, even the most careless reader must have perceived that the word was no more than rhetorical hyperbole, a vigorous epithet used by those who considered Bresler's negotiating position extremely unreasonable.[217]

In *Bresler*, therefore, the Court forcefully seized control over the interpretation of the meaning of a communication and definitively determined that an accusation of "blackmail" referred not to the crime of blackmail but rather to extremely unreasonable behavior. The Court used the term "rhetorical hyperbole" to signify this gap between the "literal" meaning of a defendant's words and the Court's interpretation of their "real" meaning. But having legally determined the "real" meaning of a communication, a court must still decide whether that meaning constitutes an assertion of fact or of opinion. Thus the concept of rhetorical hyperbole, which merely signifies a legally determinable separation between literal and actual meaning, concerns an inquiry that logically precedes the question of whether any specific meaning is fact or opinion.

Unfortunately, however, the Court, in a decision issued on the same day as *Gertz*, appeared to link the notion of rhetorical hyperbole to the kind of "opinion" that *Gertz* deemed constitutionally privileged. In Old Dominion Branch No. 496, National Association of Letter Carriers v. Austin, the Court reviewed a libel judgment against a labor union that had identified three plaintiffs as "scabs," and that had cited Jack London's famous definition of a scab as "a traitor to his God, his country, his family and his class." Although the case technically turned on the application of federal labor law to local labor disputes, the Court went out of its way to cite *Gertz* and *Bresler* and to conclude that the union's publication "cannot be construed as representations of fact" because it was "merely rhetorical hyperbole."[218] Ever since *Austin* there has been an unfortunate tendency to equate constitutionally protected opinion with rhetorical hyperbole,[219] instead of inquiring into whether the actual meaning made visible by the concept of rhetorical hyperbole is fact or opinion.

This confusion of opinion with rhetorical hyperbole is reflected even in the structure of the *Falwell* case itself. The jury in the case had returned a judgment that the Campari parody could not " 'reasonably be understood as describing actual facts about [plaintiff] or actual events in which [plaintiff] participated.' "[220] Everyone involved with the case, including the Court, assumed from this judgment that the parody involved an assertion of opinion rather than fact. But this conclusion does not follow.[221] The concept of rhetorical hyperbole requires us to recognize that even if traditions of satiric exaggeration do not permit us to read the assertions of the *Hustler* parody literally to say that Falwell actually had intercourse with his mother in an outhouse, these assertions can nevertheless be understood to convey a different message. In his Reply Brief to the Court, Flynt explicitly stated what he had intended the parody to mean: "that Falwell's message is 'b.s.' ... that this formidable public figure's teachings are nonsense."[222] If a reasonable reader were to agree with Flynt that the parody conveys this meaning, the precise question would then be whether *this* message is opinion or fact.

The Distinction between Judgments and Preference Expressions. Any attempt to analyze the constitutional privilege for opinion must distinguish between two very different kinds of statements. Following the Kantian distinction that we have already discussed, statements that merely express or describe the private feelings of a speaker must be distinguished from statements that make judgments about aspects of the world independent of a speaker.[223] The first kind of statement, which I shall call a "preference expression," is essentially a report on the inner condition of a speaker, and the only possible claim to truth it might contain lies in the factual accuracy of that report. The sentence "I don't like Jerry Falwell" is an example of a preference expression. Although the sentence does claim to be true, this claim is at most limited to the validity of its factual characterization of the subject of the pronoun "I."[224] The second kind of statement, which I shall call a "judgment," does not simply make known the private feelings or attitudes of a speaker, but rather makes claims that are independent of the speaker and that do not appear to be merely factual in nature. The sentence "Jerry Falwell is a hypocrite" is an example of a judgment. The claim of the sentence to be true does not turn on the attributes of its speaker, and we intuitively understand the claim to involve evaluation rather than merely factual description.

At common law, preference expressions rarely formed the basis for defamation actions. "Terms of abuse and opprobrium" that "had no real meaning except to indicate that the individual who used them was under a strong emotional feeling of dislike toward those about whom he used them" were traditionally viewed as "not of themselves actionable as libelous."[225] For this reason the vast majority of defamation cases that privilege communications as opinion concern judgments. The Campari parody in *Falwell*, for example, conveys just such a negative judgment on Falwell's "teachings."

The distinction between preference expressions and judgments forces us to understand the opinion privilege invoked by the *Falwell* decision in a deeper way. The decision distinguishes "false statements of fact," which are "particularly valueless," from statements of opinion. The latter are privileged to protect "the truth-seeking function of the marketplace of ideas": because " 'the best test of truth is the power of the thought to get itself accepted in the competition of the market,' " the "First Amendment recognizes no such thing as a 'false' idea."[226]

This rationale justifies privileging judgments, which make nonfactual truth claims about the world that can be the subject of discussion and criticism. But it cannot justify privileging preference expressions, which make only factual truth claims that can in no way constitute a marketplace of ideas.[227] If preference expressions are to be constitutionally privileged, therefore, it must be on the basis of a very different theory than that proposed in *Falwell*. Because preference expressions represent a special and marginal case, I discuss in the remainder of this essay the constitutional privilege for judgments, and I use the terms "opinions" and "ideas" to refer exclusively to judgments.[228]

Subjectivity. It is clear that the justification for the constitutional privilege accorded to judgments cannot be, as is sometimes asserted in the literature, that opinions are idiosyncratic and subjective[229] and hence incapable of being "characterized as true or false."[230] If judgments could not be said to be either true or false, the marketplace of ideas could not serve a "truth-seeking function," and the Court's whole constitutional rationale for protecting opinion would collapse.

The distinction between judgments and preference expressions suggests, moreover, that in ordinary experience judgments do not at all seem to involve merely personal or subjective assertions. In everyday life we make momentous decisions on the basis of our evaluation of the truth or falsity of judgments, whether such judgments occur in a doctor's medical diagnosis or in the grades of a school transcript or in a memorandum of legal advice. In many areas of the law, like legal and medical malpractice, the state freely predicates civil sanctions on the basis of its evaluation of the truth or falsity of opinions.[231] It could not do so if judgments were intrinsically subjective and incapable of being characterized as true or false.

Verifiability. The theory that has most influenced courts concerning the distinction between fact and opinion is the notion that an opinion is an assertion that "does not lend itself to verification and cannot, therefore, be regarded as one of fact."[232] Opinions are thus those statements which cannot be "proved true or false."[233] Simply stated in this fashion, however, the theory is subject to two fatal objections. First, the definition of opinions as unverifiable statements renders meaningless the constitutional rationale for protecting opinion. "The competition of the market" could not in any sense determine the validity of intrinsically unprovable statements, and hence a marketplace in such statements could not serve a valuable "truth-seeking function."

Second, there are statements which, although unverifiable, would commonly be recognized as statements of fact. For example, if I were to claim that the temperature at a certain spot in Antarctica was −100 degrees at 2:00 P.M. on October 17, 1497, the claim might be unverifiable because of the absence of data or evidence, yet it would be apparent to all that I was making a factual assertion.[234]

There is, however, a more sophisticated formulation of the verifiability test that asks not whether statements are verifiable but whether they are "objectively" verifiable,[235] whether they are "subject to *empirical* proof."[236] This formulation of the test offers two significant advantages. First, it shifts the focus of analysis away from the issue of *whether* a particular statement can be proved, to the question of *how* it can be proved. The latter question requires us to understand the particular kind of claim contained in a statement. Second, it offers a rough typology of two potential modes of "verification": the truth of some statements can be "empirically" or "objectively" established, but the validity of others can be determined only by the unimpeded discussion characteristic of the "marketplace of ideas."

Of course this version of the test cannot work unless we can establish some intelligible meanings for words like "empirically" or "objectively." These words are not self-defining, and in proposing definitions we need to keep in mind the purpose of the enterprise. "False statements of fact" are constitutionally valueless, the Court in *Falwell* tells us, because "they interfere with the truth-seeking function of the marketplace of ideas, and they cause damage to an individual's reputation that cannot easily be repaired by counterspeech, however persuasive or effective."[237] The Court's point may perhaps be fairly generalized in the following manner: for constitutional purposes the truth of certain kinds of statements— opinions—can be determined only by the free play of speech and counterspeech characteristic of the marketplace of ideas. But the functioning of the marketplace depends upon the accuracy of other kinds of statements—factual assertions—whose truth must be determined independently of any mere process of discussion.

The difficulty with this interpretation of the Court's analysis is that it appears to conceive of factual truth as independent of social processes of discussion and communication. This conception conjures up images of a long-discredited logical empiricism, in which the "verification" of facts was said to rest on " 'brute data' . . . whose validity cannot be questioned by offering another interpretation or reading" and "whose credibility cannot be founded or undetermined by further reasoning."[238] It is no doubt to these images that judicial use of the words "empirically" and "objectively" is meant to refer. But the vulnerability of such crude empiricism is now more or less taken for granted, because even if there were such a thing as "brute data," the meaning of those data would necessarily depend upon processes of inference that themselves are susceptible to further interpretation or reasoning.[239] All knowledge, therefore, ultimately depends, to one degree or another, upon social processes of discussion.[240]

Toward a Reformulation of the Distinction between Fact and Opinion

It is possible, however, to make sense of the Court's analysis if it is reformulated to take account of "the accepted contrast between" statements "which are expected to be highly diverse, and which are not expected and which are not required, to converge on the one hand," and statements "where there is a well established expectation of convergence" on the other.[241] In the area of "scientific enquiry," for example, "there should ideally be convergence on an answer, where the best explanation of that convergence involves the idea that the answer represents how things are, whereas in the area of the ethical . . . there is no such coherent hope."[242]

We expect scientific hypotheses ultimately to converge on a single answer because such hypotheses, in the words of Gilbert Harman, are "tested against the world,"[243] and the world exists independently of our perceptions of it. This abstract appeal to a "world" affects only the kind of claims we understand scientific statements to make; it does not affect the substance of those claims by naïve reliance upon "brute data." Thus we recognize a claim as scientific if it purports to describe something independent of scientific investigators in such a way that, given enough time and effort, we would expect the claim to be confirmed or disconfirmed by a consensus of investigators. The origins of this way of thinking go back to the work of Charles Peirce, who defined scientific truth as the "opinion which is fated to be ultimately agreed to by all who investigate," and who defined reality as "the object represented in this opinion." For Peirce, reality was thus "independent, not necessarily of thought in general, but only of what you or I or any finite number of men may think about it."[244]

If the notion of a "world" allows us to anticipate that scientific thought will converge on a single description of nature, matters are very different with regard to ethical thought, which is ultimately "a matter of belonging to a certain culture,"[245] a matter of "the conventions of groups."[246] So long as there are divergent groups or cultures, we have no special grounds to expect a consensus to emerge about any particular ethical claim. If I were to argue, for example, that eating pork or marrying the widow of one's brother is morally wrong, I would ultimately have to appeal to norms already accepted within my culture or community. To the extent that you did not share those norms, I would have no particular reason to expect that you would agree with me. (You *may* be convinced, of course, but that is another matter.)[247] The lack of any "coherent hope" of convergence in ethical matters, then, is ultimately founded upon the diversity of groups and cultures.

We can thus distinguish between statements that make claims whose validity purports to be independent of the standards or perspectives of any finite group of persons, and statements that instead make claims founded upon the "complex of obligations binding us, as members of a community, to sustain the institutions which provide structure for our collective life."[248] Judgments are intrinsically statements of the latter sort. That is because "there must be underlying grounds of judgment which human beings, qua members of a judging community, share, and which serve to unite in communication even those who disagree *(and who may disagree radically)* . . . Judgment implies a community that supplies common grounds or criteria by which one attempts to decide." Hence "we require a definition of community in order to know how the judgment shall proceed."[249]

Thus the distinction between convergent and nonconvergent claims is related in an important way to the First Amendment distinction between public discourse and community. Because the truth or falsity of judgments is determinable only by reference to the standards of a particular community, any government effort to penalize false judgments in public discourse would in effect use the force of the state to impose the standards of a specific community. This would of course violate the constitutional principle that the arena of public discussion be neutral as to community standards. It might well be said, therefore, that from a constitutional point of view the evaluation of such statements must be left to the free play of speech and counterspeech through which communities compete within public discourse for the allegiance of individuals.

But because the truth or falsity of statements of fact is in theory determinable by reference to standards that, as Peirce notes, transcend all possible communities, government efforts to penalize false statements of fact are in theory consistent with a position of neutrality vis-à-vis the standards of any particular community. "The independence of the fact-finder, the witness, and the reporter," as Hannah Arendt has movingly demonstrated, places them "outside the community to which we belong and the company of our peers."[250] It is true that the punishment of false statements of fact appears, at first blush, to be inconsistent with the requirement of an ideal speech situation that all force be excluded "except the force of the better argument."[251] But statements of fact are not arguments, and the very ability to argue presupposes accurate facts. "Freedom of opinion," Arendt notes, "is a farce unless factual information is guaranteed and the facts themselves are not in dispute. In other words, factual truth informs political thought."[252] Thus the integrity of public discourse itself depends upon factual accuracy, a point to which *Falwell* itself appeals.[253]

If Peirce is correct, however, the validity of any factual characterization of the world ultimately depends upon the convergence of an infinite number of perspectives, because any given perspective can be biased and reflect only the particular standards of a specific community. Whenever the state attempts to determine definitively the truth or falsity of a specific factual statement, it truncates a potentially infinite process of investigation and therefore runs a significant risk of inaccuracy.[254] Thus although legal fact-finding may in theory be neutral, in practice we can expect it to be often inaccurate and inappropriately influenced by the sentiment and prejudice of a particular community. Any respectable First Amendment theory should allow for this phenomenon; it is no doubt part of the underlying explanation of why the Court in *Falwell* did not permit liability to be imposed for false statements of fact *simpliciter* but instead imposed the additional requirement of "actual malice," so as "to give adequate 'breathing space' to the freedoms protected by the First Amendment."[255]

We can thus advance a rough justification for the position adopted in

Falwell that false statements of fact have no constitutional value within public discourse, but that false opinions can be regulated only by the marketplace of ideas. The justification depends upon reformulating the constitutional distinction between fact and opinion in the following manner. Statements of fact make claims about an independent world, the validity of which are in theory determinable without reference to the standards of any given community, and about which we therefore have a right to expect ultimate convergence or consensus. Statements of opinion, on the other hand, make claims about an independent world, the validity of which depends upon the standards or conventions of a particular community, and about which we therefore cannot expect convergence under conditions of cultural heterogeneity.[256] If this reformulation is correct, it implies that *Falwell*'s distinction between fact and opinion stems from the same central First Amendment concern as that which guided *Falwell*'s other characterizations of public discourse: the preservation of the neutrality of public discourse from the domination of community mores.

This reformulation enables courts to distinguish fact from opinion constitutionally by determining the kinds of validity claims made by particular statements. If a literary critic writes, for example, that a certain novelist did not deserve the Nobel Prize, the statement makes sense only by reference to the specific canons of aesthetic judgment invoked by the critic. Because these canons define a particular group, the statement should be characterized as opinion. But if the critic writes that the novelist paid $50,000 to certain Swedish officials, she makes a claim that any person, regardless of her specific community, should in theory ultimately come to accept if confronted with the relevant evidence, and thus the statement should be regarded as one of fact.

Sometimes the very same statement can be regarded as either fact or opinion, depending upon the claim that it is interpreted as making. For example, if a restaurant reviewer states that the egg rolls at a Chinese restaurant were "frozen," the statement should be deemed one of fact if the reviewer is taken to mean that the egg rolls were below the freezing temperature of water, a reference that in principle should be confirmable by anyone at all. But if, as is more likely, the reviewer is taken to mean that anyone who has a proper understanding of the appropriate temperature for the correct presentation of egg rolls would consider them unacceptably cool, her statement depends for its validity upon the standards of proper Chinese cooking and should be understood as opinion.

The kind of validity claim made by a statement frequently depends upon the genre of expression within which it is embedded. The example of the restaurant reviewer demonstrates how in many circumstances the internal dynamics of a particular genre will virtually compel a specific interpretation of the validity claim of a statement.[257] This is why courts attempting to apply the fact/opinion distinction have so often focused their analysis on the "medium" and context of a communication.

This focus, however, is ultimately relevant only to the secondary issue of what a statement means; the more fundamental question of the state's constitutional power to regulate a statement rests on our willingness to use the law to enforce the cultural standards by reference to which an opinion is judged true or false. Outside the sphere of public discourse there are plainly circumstances in which good reasons exist for using law in this fashion. To pick a particularly obvious example, laypersons must often depend upon the opinions of experts, like lawyers or doctors, and hence as to laypersons these opinions are not really debatable. It makes sense, therefore, for the law to hold such experts legally accountable, within a certain range, for the truth or falsity of their opinions. When the law does this, it is in essence hegemonically establishing authoritative cultural standards upon which persons can rely.[258]

The establishment of such standards, however, is exactly what the neutrality of public discourse forbids. The constitutional regulation of opinion, therefore, will plainly be affected by the boundaries we set to the domain of public discourse.

Defining the Domain of Public Discourse

If the First Amendment extends special constitutional protection to public discourse by insulating it from the enforcement of community norms,[259] it is necessary to distinguish public discourse from other speech. In contemporary doctrine, however, this distinction is notoriously ill conceived and unreliable.[260] In fact it is commonly accepted that the Court's efforts in this direction have resulted in a dreadful mess.[261] It is important to assess the causes of this failure, however, before attempting to hazard any recharacterization of the specific domain of public discourse. In doing so one must begin with the observation that contemporary doctrine has attempted to mark the boundaries of the domain of public discourse in roughly two ways. The first focuses on the content of speech, the second on the manner of its dissemination.

The Domain of Public Discourse in Contemporary Doctrine

The Content of Speech: Matters of Public Concern

Contemporary doctrine delineates the domain of public discourse primarily through an assessment of the content of speech. The Court has a standard account of this approach: "We have recognized that the First Amendment reflects a 'profound national commitment' to the principle that 'debate on public issues should be uninhibited, robust, and wide-open' and have consistently commented on the central importance of protecting speech on public issues."[262] As a doctrinal matter, therefore, the Court has most comprehensively attempted to define public discourse by distinguishing speech about "matters of public concern" from speech about "matters of purely private concern."[263]

Although the "public concern" test rests on a clean and superficially attractive rationale, the Court has offered virtually no analysis to develop its logic.[264] Indeed, as matters now stand, the test of "public concern" "amounts to little more than a message to judges and attorneys that no standards are necessary because they will, or should, know a public concern when they see it."[265] To begin to comprehend the causes for this failure, one must note the ambiguity in the adjective "public" in the phrase "public concern." Sometimes the adjective signifies that the speech at issue is about matters that ought to be of interest to those who practice the art of democratic self-governance. I shall call this the "normative" conception of public concern. Sometimes, however, the adjective connotes that the speech at issue concerns matters that large numbers of people already know, and thus are "public" in a purely empirical sense. I shall call this the "descriptive" conception of public concern.

The doctrinal test that the *Falwell* opinion uses to distinguish public discourse from other speech hovers equivocally between these two conceptions of public concern. Under the rule proposed by *Falwell*, which tracks traditional First Amendment doctrine in the area of defamation, the *New York Times* actual malice standard applies if the plaintiff is a public figure or a public official.[266] The "public official" branch of this doctrine flows directly from the normative concept of public concern, which reflects the core purpose of *New York Times* to protect speech about matters pertinent to democratic self-governance. But the "public figure" branch is ambiguous, half justified by the notion that speech about public figures is normatively relevant to democratic self-governance,[267] and half by the notion that speech about public figures concerns matters of "notoriety" that have, in a purely descriptive sense, already caught "the public's attention."[268] In the end, therefore, the public official/public figure test must be justified by reference to either the normative or descriptive conception of public concern.[269] An understanding of the ills that underlie contemporary doctrine must begin with an analysis of each of these two distinct conceptions of public concern.

The Normative Conception of Public Concern. The Court is most comfortable with the normative conception of public concern, and in most instances its use of the phrase signifies that the content of the speech at issue refers to matters that are substantively relevant to the processes of democratic self-governance. But it is not difficult to see why this conception of public concern would lead directly to a doctrinal impasse. Democratic self-governance posits that the people, in their capacity as a public, control the agenda of government. They have the power to determine the content of public issues simply by the direction of their interests. This means that every issue that can potentially agitate the public is also potentially relevant to democratic self-governance, and hence potentially of public concern. The normative conception of public concern, insofar as it is used to exclude speech from public discourse, is thus incompatible with the very democratic self-governance it seeks to facilitate.

The Court fully recognizes this difficulty. It underlies the Court's firm and correct conviction that "governments must not be allowed to choose 'which issues are worth discussing or debating' ... To allow a government the choice of permissible subjects for public debate would be to allow that government control over the search for political truth."[270] It also lies at the root of the Court's initial rejection in *Gertz* of Justice Brennan's plurality opinion in Rosenbloom v. Metromedia, Inc., which proposed to apply the *New York Times* requirement of actual malice to all speech involving matters of "public or general interest."[271] The Court repudiated this proposal because of its doubts concerning "the wisdom of committing ... to the conscience of judges" the task of determining " 'what information is relevant to self-government.' "[272]

Certain speech, of course, is clearly and obviously recognizable as substantively relevant to democratic self-government. Most speech about public officials falls into this category. But it does not follow from this fact that speech less easily recognizable can with confidence be ruled out as irrelevant to matters of public concern. Robert Bork, for example, once proposed limiting constitutionally protected speech to that "concerned with governmental behavior, policy or personnel."[273] Bork's proposal was attractive because it seemed to follow so directly from the logic of democratic self-governance, and to offer a clean and precise definition of speech about matters of public concern.

On closer inspection, however, Bork's proposal proved inadequate, because it missed the fundamental point that the First Amendment safeguards public discourse not merely because it informs government decision-making, but also because it enables a culturally heterogeneous society to forge a common democratic will. The formation of this will depends upon the ability of public discourse to sustain deliberation about our identity as a people, as well as about what specifically we want our government to do. That is why most would unquestionably consider as public discourse the public discussion of such issues as the proper role of motherhood, the disaffection of the young, and the meaning of American citizenship, even if this discussion did not occur within the specific context of any proposed or actual government action.[274]

The public realm, as Hanna Pitkin has eloquently remarked, is where the "people determine what they will collectively do, settle how they will live together, and decide their future, to whatever extent that is within human power." To decide these things, however, is to engage in a process of "collective self-definition," of determining "who we shall be, for what we shall stand."[275] To classify speech as public discourse is, in effect, to deem it relevant to this collective process of self-definition and decision-making. There is obviously no theoretically neutral way in which this can be done. Speech can be deemed irrelevant for national self-definition only in the name of a particular, substantive vision of national identity. If this is done with the authority of the law, possible options for democratic development will be foreclosed.

The problem can be illustrated by Samuel Warren and Louis Brandeis' famous article "The Right to Privacy," published in 1890, which virtually created the common law tort of invasion of privacy.[276] The origins of the article were said to lie in the outrage which Warren, a genuine Boston Brahmin, felt at newspaper reports of his private entertainments.[277] Warren and Brandeis argued that such gossip was not of public concern and that it usurped "the space available for matters of real interest to the community."[278] Yet in retrospect it is clear that public fascination with the doings of the rich and the aristocratic at the turn of the century may have played an integral part in the general movement toward the creation of the welfare state, with its progressive tax and other instruments of wealth redistribution. Although reports of Samuel Warren's particular dinner parties may well have lacked significance, they formed part of this much larger process by which the people, as a public, came to alter their vision of the nation. As a result Warren and Brandeis' dismissal of such gossip as merely "idle" and as the bearer only of "triviality" has come to seem to us merely unattractive and self-serving class prejudice.[279]

The fundamental theoretical difficulty faced by writers like Warren and Brandeis, who would place limits on what *ought* to be pertinent to the formation of a common democratic will, is that any effort substantively to circumscribe public discourse is necessarily self-defeating, for it displaces the very democratic processes it seeks to facilitate.

The Descriptive Conception of Public Concern.   The descriptive conception of public concern promises a way out of this impasse. It appears to offer courts a means of maintaining the boundaries of public discourse in a manner that remains neutral with respect to the competing claims of speech to be relevant to issues of democratic governance. The descriptive conception defines "speech involving matters of public concern" as speech about issues that happen actually to be of interest to the "public," which is to say to "a significant number of persons."[280] The conception thus flows from a purely empirical notion of the public; it classifies as public discourse expression about the common stimuli that in fact establish the existence of a public.[281]

The influence of the descriptive conception is visible in the Court's doctrinal efforts to make constitutional protection depend upon the "public figure" status of plaintiffs.[282] These efforts have led some courts to classify speech as public discourse depending upon whether it is about a plaintiff who "statistical surveys" indicate enjoys "name recognition" among "a large percentage of the well-informed citizenry."[283]

The attempt to define public discourse in purely descriptive terms, however, is subject to the powerful objections of being both over- and underinclusive. The definition is overinclusive because it extends constitutional protection to speech about matters that seem trivial and irrelevant to democratic self-governance.[284] The definition would classify as public discourse speech about prominent celebrities, even if such celebrities have only negligible "involvement in or influence on public policy matters."[285] Examples such as Johnny Carson and Carol Burnett come immediately to mind.[286] The definition is underinclusive because it would exclude from public discourse speech about matters which, although unknown, obviously pertain to the processes of democratic self-governance. The exposé of heretofore secret government misconduct, or the discussion of an especially high but as yet unnoticed rate of teen-age suicide, concern issues that ought to be well known, even if they in fact are not; any acceptable definition of public discourse must include them.

Both objections to the descriptive conception of public concern rest on the assumption that the true touchstone of public discourse must lie in a substantive evaluation of whether the content of speech is relevant for self-governance. The argument that the descriptive conception is over-inclusive assumes that speech about matters that are manifestly irrelevant can be identified in a principled way. The argument that the definition is underinclusive assumes that speech about matters that are manifestly relevant can be identified. Therefore, to the extent that these objections carry weight, and they seem to me very strong, we are brought around full circle and returned to our initial lack of any principled method of determining what kinds of issues ought to be excluded from the domain of public discourse.

The descriptive conception of public concern nevertheless retains a certain appeal, because it focuses attention on the social preconditions for the maintenance of public discourse. One of these preconditions is the exposure of the participants in public deliberation to common stimuli. Speech about well-known matters concerns the very stuff that makes public discussion possible. Such speech thus reinforces and amplifies the bonds of public life. Although speech about Johnny Carson differs in important ways from speech about explicit government policy, the ability of the public to deliberate about government policy depends upon the fund of experience common to members of the public, and speech about commonly known matters increases the depth of that experience. Speech about prominent celebrities may therefore influence in subtle and indirect ways public deliberation of public policy: it may provide common points of reference for debate, or crystallize common concerns, or shape common metaphors of understanding. Learning of a prominent athlete or entertainer's struggles with drugs or alcohol may well lead the public to a different and perhaps more (or less) sympathetic understanding of the social problem of substance abuse. Discussion of the World Series may lead to an altered perception of the national character.

The claim of speech about well-known matters to constitutional protection as public discourse thus depends on the assumption that public speech is indivisible, that communication for one purpose, such as gossip, will influence communication for another, such as self-government. This assumption underlies that "overwhelming" dialectic which Harry Kalven once predicted would lead the definition of public discourse "from public official to government policy to public policy to matters in the public domain."[287]

But the extent of interdependence among forms of public speech is an empirical question, and without empirical data all that can be said is that public discourse will probably be impoverished, to some unspecifiable degree, whenever the enforcement of community civility standards diminishes speech about well-known matters. It does not follow from this that speech about well-known but seemingly trivial issues must be included within public discourse. But it does counsel great caution in the exclusion of such speech from public discourse.

The Manner in Which Speech Is Disseminated: Of the Media/ Nonmedia Distinction and Other Conundrums

If the strand of contemporary doctrine that attempts to define public discourse in terms of the content of speech is ultimately inadequate and self-contradictory, it at least has the advantage of explicit judicial thematization. The second strand of contemporary doctrine, which focuses on how speech is disseminated rather than on its content, is much more obscure, and must be gathered together out of the dark corners of the Supreme Court's opinions. But although the Court has not yet attempted to formulate this second strand of doctrine in the shape of formal rules, its influence on the Court's judgments is nevertheless distinctly visible.

The origin of the phrase "matters of public concern" in First Amendment doctrine, for example, lies in the important 1940 decision of Thornhill v. Alabama. In *Thornhill*, the Court considered the question of whether labor picketing was constitutionally protected expression. The Court began its analysis with this premise: "The freedom of speech and of the press guaranteed by the Constitution embraces at the least the liberty to discuss publicly and truthfully all matters of public concern without previous restraint or fear of subsequent punishment."[288] The Court thus defined public discourse not merely in terms of the content of the speech at issue but also in terms of the manner in which that speech was disseminated. The basic idea was that speech must be communicated "publicly" in order to qualify as public discourse.

This focus on the manner of dissemination is plainly discernible in the *Falwell* opinion, which refers to "the area of public debate about public figures."[289] Although the second use of the adjective "public" in this phrase refers to the content of speech, its first use concerns instead the manner in which speech is communicated. It points toward a "genre" in which speech is distributed in such a way as to be understood as "public" debate. *Falwell* refers again to this genre in the prophylactic rule that it formulates at its conclusion. *Falwell* explicitly confines the rule to recoveries for the tort of intentional infliction of emotional distress "by reason of publications such as the one here at issue."[290] The point, although never explicit, is apparently that Flynt communicated his attack on Falwell in a public way rather than in a private letter or in a personal late-night telephone call. The Court's formulation of the rule implies that if Flynt were to convey the very same words as those in the *Hustler* parody to Falwell in a private manner, they might not be included within the domain of public discourse, and might not receive the same degree of constitutional protection. The Court's citation of Justice Harlan's carefully phrased conclusion in Street v. New York strengthens this implication: " 'It is firmly settled that . . . the public expression of ideas may not be prohibited merely because the ideas are themselves offensive to some of their hearers.' "[291]

The boundaries of public discourse, therefore, are to some extent dependent upon the ways in which speech is disseminated. Although the judgment that speech is being communicated in a "public" manner ultimately depends upon the particular context of a specific communicative act, at least three generic factors have influenced the Court's approach to this question: the intent of the speaker, the size of the speaker's audience, and the identity of that audience. The Court's sensitivity to the intent of a speaker that her speech form part of public discourse[292] manifests itself in the Court's image of "the lonely pamphleteer who uses carbon paper or a mimeograph."[293] Even if that pamphleteer manages to distribute her message to only a very few people, the Court will nevertheless consider her efforts as part of "the flow of information to the public."[294] The reason cannot be that the pamphleteer's message has in fact been received by the large number of people who constitute the public. It must instead be that when a speaker disseminates messages "at large" in this way, it signifies that she *intends* her speech to be widely distributed and to form part of public debate.

The Court has sometimes been influenced in these matters by a rather special concept of intention, which turns not on the actual purposes or motivations of any specific person, but rather on the generic intent attributable to a particular form of communication. The very act of distributing pamphlets on the street carries with it, so to speak, its own presumptive intent. This notion of generic intent appears in Justice Powell's plurality opinion in *Dun & Bradstreet*, which concludes that a credit report is not within the domain of public discourse in part because the report is "solely in the individual interest of the speaker and its specific business audience" and is "solely motivated by the desire for profit."[295] Justice Powell's evaluation of motivation does not turn on the actual state of mind of the Dun & Bradstreet employees who wrote the credit report, an issue upon which no evidence appeared in the record. It is rather a generic attribution of intent to a particular genre of speech. Justice Powell's reasoning can thus be understood as pointing toward a general legal conclusion that commercial credit reports are written primarily for the purpose of profit, and that this purpose counts against their classification as public discourse.

The Court's use of this concept of generic intent is also evident in Miller v. California, in which the Court excluded obscene speech from the domain of public discourse, in part because obscene speech portrays "hard-core sexual conduct for its own sake, and for the ensuing commercial gain."[296] The Court's attribution of intention to the generic category of obscene speech could not possibly have constituted an empirical description of the particular motivations of individual writers or filmmakers. It must instead be interpreted as an ascriptive attribution of a specific social purpose to an entire genre of speech. The Court explicitly contrasted this purpose to the one it deemed appropriate to public discourse, which is an intent to bring about " 'political and social changes desired by the people.' "[297]

A second factor relevant to the determination of whether speech has been disseminated in a public manner relates to the size of its audience. The importance of this factor arises from the social foundations of public discourse. Widely distributed speech itself becomes a shared stimulus of the kind necessary for the creation of public discourse; thus the "emergence of the mass media and of the 'public' are mutually constructive developments."[298] If speech about well-known matters deepens public experience, widely distributed speech makes even heretofore secret matters well known, and thus extends the range of public experience. The same potential for impoverishing public discourse inheres in censorship of either kind of speech.

This fact, together with the concept of generic intent, can perhaps shed some light on the difficulties faced by the Court on the question of whether to distinguish constitutionally between media and nonmedia defendants.[299] Speech disseminated through the mass media is by definition widely distributed, and hence is singularly "public-generating."[300] The generic intent attributable to such speech, moreover, is at least presumptively that of desiring to contribute to public discourse.[301] Thus media speech, simply by virtue of the manner of its distribution, presents a strong prima facie claim to be classified as public discourse.[302] Of course this claim is defeasible; obscene speech, for example, can be distributed through the mass media. But the existence and strength of the claim makes the exclusion of media speech from public discourse difficult and controversial.

Media speech is thus unique because it carries within it this prima facie claim to constitute public discourse, a claim based entirely on the manner of its distribution rather than on its content. This singularity explains the Court's continual attraction to a distinction between media and nonmedia defendants.[303] But on close inspection the uniqueness of media speech lies only in the particular way in which it grounds its claim to be public discourse, a claim whose substance it shares with many other kinds of communication. Five members of the Court can therefore state, without internal contradiction, that "the rights of the institutional media are no greater and no less than those enjoyed by other individuals or organizations engaged in the same activities."[304]

A third factor that has influenced the Court in determining whether speech has been disseminated in a public manner is the identity of the audience to whom the speech is addressed. Speech that is widely distributed is assumed to be addressed to the public. The same assumption applies to speech that is actually communicated to only a few people, so long as it is distributed to strangers "at large." The question of audience arises, therefore, only in those cases where speech is specifically addressed to a few designated persons. In such a context, the Court has implied that the very same speech can be public discourse when communicated to one audience, but be constitutionally unprotected if communicated to another.[305] Even speech "communicate[d] privately"[306] to one person can be public discourse, if that person is, for example, a government official,[307] rather than someone merely in contractual privity with the speaker.[308]

The Failure of Contemporary Doctrine

The failure of contemporary doctrine, then, stems from two distinct causes. First, the criterion of "public concern" lacks internal coherence. Second, the importance ascribed by the Court to the circumstances surrounding the dissemination of speech exerts extraordinary pressure toward specific, contextual judgment. Even if the "public concern" test could be given coherent and definitive meaning, the classification of speech as public discourse would nevertheless depend upon a wide array of particular variables inherent in specific communicative contexts. Notwithstanding the importance of the normative and descriptive concepts of public concern, the complex contextualizing force of circumstances will sometimes exclude from public discourse even speech whose content plainly pertains to democratic self-governance and well-known persons.

Chaplinsky v. New Hampshire, in which the defendant publicly called a city marshal a "damned Fascist" and a "racketeer," provides an extreme example of this phenomenon. The specific context of the defendant's speech convinced the Court that the communication at issue was a species of " 'personal abuse' " rather than public discourse, and that it therefore enjoyed no constitutional protection.[309] *Chaplinsky* is remarkable precisely because the subject of the defendant's speech was the official conduct of a public officer, a fact that would ordinarily qualify speech prima facie as public discourse. *Chaplinsky* illustrates, therefore, the powerful force of circumstances in the classification of speech. The same point might be made hypothetically by imagining what would happen if Flynt had privately mailed the Campari parody to Falwell's mother or had telephoned Falwell in the middle of the night to read him the words of the parody. In such circumstances no court would classify the speech as public discourse, despite the unchanged content of Flynt's communication.

The many factors relevant to the classification of speech as public discourse thus resist expression in the form of clear, uniform, and helpful doctrinal rules. The Court's effort to fashion simple doctrinal tests is no doubt due to the imperative of articulating crisp and predictable constitutional guidelines so that speakers will not face a margin of legal uncertainty that might induce self-censorship. It is consequently all the more remarkable that the Court's doctrine should be so demonstrably overwhelmed by the pressure of contextualization. Because of this pressure the Court's attempt to explain what it actually means to inquire whether speech involves " 'matters of public concern' " has collapsed into the conclusion that the inquiry " 'must be determined by [the expression's] content, form, and context . . . as revealed by the whole record.' "[310]

An Alternative Conception of the Domain of Public Discourse

The underlying cause of this pressure toward contextualization becomes clear when we recall that the First Amendment establishes a distinct domain of public discourse in order to implement our common belief in such values as neutrality, diversity, and individualism. It follows that the domain of public discourse will extend only so far as these values override other competing commitments, such as those entailed in the dignity of the socially situated self,[311] in the importance of group identity,[312] or in the necessary exercise of community authority.[313] The boundaries of the domain of public discourse are located precisely where the tension between these competing sets of values is most intense, and where some accommodation must consequently be negotiated.

The boundaries of public discourse thus define the relative priorities of our national values. They mark the point at which our commitments shift from one set of goals to another. In locating these boundaries we use the Constitution to facilitate social conditions that reflect the hierarchy of our values, and in this way exercise "our capacity for human self-constituting."[314] Because our values come to us not in the abstract but rather through the critical apprehension of our cultural inheritance, this process of self-constituting is also a process of self-discovery. For this reason "how we are able to constitute ourselves is profoundly tied to how we are already constituted by our own distinctive history."[315]

Courts manifest their respect for this distinctive history when they attempt to fix the boundaries of the domain of public discourse by reference to the social norms that create for us the "genre" of public discourse. These norms form part of our cultural inheritance; they determine when we instinctively perceive speech as public. The common law tort of invasion of privacy, which looks to "the customs and conventions of the community" in order to determine whether speech is about matters "of legitimate public interest,"[316] demonstrates the power of these norms. Such customs and conventions, like all community norms, are highly contextual. They have a "socially determined variability"[317] which requires judgment to "take account of what the *situation* requires, not what an abstraction demands."[318] Their perception and application require the exercise of what Georg Simmel calls "moral tact."[319]

It is through the exercise of such "tact" that Justice Murphy in *Chaplinsky* "knew" that the defendant in the case was engaged in a private fracas rather than a public debate.[320] The norms interpreted by this tact represent a tacit reconciliation of the competing demands of public discourse and community life. The law can ignore them only at the price of resolving conflicts of value through abstractions cut off from the conventions that give meaning to everyday experience.

There are, however, two reasons why it is impossible to maintain a pure fidelity to these norms. First, any such fidelity would require the kind of extreme contextualization ordinarily associated with the common law dignitary torts, and such contextualization would conflict with the need for First Amendment rules to be clear and predictable in order to minimize self-censorship. Second, and more important, a pure methodology of moral tact conflicts with the constitutional function of public discourse, which is to establish "a cleared and safe space" in which a common democratic will may be forged. The application of social norms must thus continually be examined in order to determine whether they actually serve this function.

The logic of democratic self-governance, however, cannot itself provide an unqualified guide for doctrinal formulation. The normative concept of public concern lacks coherence precisely because all speech is potentially relevant to democratic self-governance, and hence according to democratic logic all speech ought to be classified as public discourse. But this conclusion is unacceptable, for our commitment to the values of public discourse does not automatically and always override other competing commitments. The conclusion is also internally inconsistent, because the paradox of public discourse requires that critical interaction must at some point be bounded. Critical interaction suspends the civility rules that make possible rational deliberation. Hence the very possibility of rational deliberation might be endangered if the boundaries of critical interaction were to sweep too extensively. An uncontrollable expansion of critical interaction threatens to undermine the very purpose for which we establish public discourse.

Sensitivity to this potential dynamic is evident in a decision like Bethel School District No. 403 v. Fraser, in which the Court permitted a school to censor "lewd speech" on the grounds that it was "a highly appropriate function of public school education to prohibit the use of vulgar and offensive terms in public discourse" so as to " 'inculcate the habits and manners of civility.' "[321] It is also apparent in FCC v. Pacifica Foundation, in which the Court permitted the FCC to enforce "contemporary community standards" to prohibit the broadcasting of " 'patently offensive' " speech at " 'times of the day when there is a reasonable risk that children may be in the audience.' "[322] In reaching this conclusion the Court reasoned that "broadcasting is uniquely accessible to children" and hence could frustrate "the government's interest in the 'well-being of its youth' " "and in supporting 'parents' claim to authority in their own household.' "[323] In both cases, therefore, the Court refused to expand the arena of critical interaction in such a way as to impair significantly the processes by which communities socialize the young and cause them to identify with community norms that the Court viewed as necessary for rational deliberation.[324]

Thus, just as the exercise of moral tact is by itself an insufficient guide to the demarcation of the boundaries of public discourse, so also is the logic of democratic self-governance. In fact, the placement of these boundaries appears to require accommodation to three very different kinds of concerns and judicial methodologies. The logic of democratic self-governance presses toward solutions that maximize the domain of public discourse. The paradox of public discourse requires a social and functional analysis of the dynamic interrelationship between critical interaction and rational deliberation. And the need to reconcile the values of public discourse with those of community life exerts pressure toward specific and contextual judgments.

The real problem with contemporary doctrine is not that it fails to attain some overarching reconciliation among these competing considerations, for it is doubtful that such a reconciliation can be theoretically achieved, but rather that it fails to articulate with sufficient clarity what is actually at stake in the definition of public discourse. We need to establish a domain of public discourse that is amply sufficient to the needs of democratic self-governance, but that is also reasonably sensitive to competing value commitments, to the preexisting social norms that define the genre of public speech, and to the social consequences implied by the paradox of public discourse. Doctrinal formulation should assist courts in the evaluation of these considerations, rather than masking them under opaque phrases and tests.

Implicit in this conclusion is the proposition that the boundaries of public discourse cannot be fixed in a neutral fashion. From the perspective of the logic of democratic self-governance, any restriction of the domain of public discourse must necessarily constitute a forcible truncation of possible lines of democratic development. Because this truncation must ultimately be determined by reference to community values, the boundaries of a discourse defined by its liberation from ideological conformity will themselves be defined by reference to ideological presuppositions.[325] *Fraser, Pacifica Foundation, Chaplinsky,* and *Miller* are all examples of such ideologically determined boundaries to the domain of public discourse.

This kind of ideological regulation of speech is deeply distasteful, and it is best that it remain so. Democratic self-governance could easily be eviscerated if such regulation became the rule rather than the exception. The ultimate fact of ideological regulation, however, cannot be blinked. In the end, therefore, there can be no final account of the boundaries of the domain of public discourse.[326] We can and do have firm convictions about the core of that domain, but its periphery will remain both ideological and vague, subject to an endless negotiation between democracy and community life.

Conclusion

Public discourse lies at the heart of democratic self-governance, and its protection constitutes an important theme of First Amendment jurisprudence. This essay has traced the implications of that theme for a single case, Hustler Magazine v. Falwell, and has examined the illumination that the theme can shed on some significant and troublesome aspects of First Amendment doctrine. These include the protection of offensive speech, the distinction between fact and opinion, and the use of motivation as a criterion for the regulation of speech. The primary dynamic that underlies each of these doctrinal areas is the separation of public discourse from the domination of civility rules that define the identity of communities. The First Amendment preserves the independence of public discourse so that a democratic will within a culturally heterogeneous state can emerge under conditions of neutrality, and so that individuals can use the medium of public discourse to persuade others to experiment in new forms of community life. The ultimate dependence of public discourse upon community life, however, suggests that this neutrality and freedom is always limited, for the very boundaries of public discourse must be located in a manner that is sensitive to ensuring the continued viability of the community norms that inculcate the ideal of rational deliberation.

We might say, therefore, that the public discourse which is the object of contemporary First Amendment doctrine is like the wind described by Herman Melville that "spins *against* the way it drives."[327] It is for this reason inherently unstable, and may in fact be a passing phenomenon. What is now called the "civic republican tradition" may actually give rise to "a universal community" founded upon a "common commitment to a moral understanding"[328] that will transform public discourse into the kind of communal deliberation traditionally protected by the common law privilege of fair comment. Against the pull of that communitarian solidarity it is indeed difficult to hold on to the radical negativity demanded by contemporary First Amendment doctrine. In the end only time, and our ultimate convictions, will tell.

5

Between Democracy and Community: The Legal Constitution of Social Form

In this essay I discuss the concept of "democratic community" from the specific perspective of the American legal system. This perspective, in Ronald Dworkin's elegant and accurate formulation, entails the continual effort to grasp the internal point of social institutions.[1] The enterprise is neither purely descriptive nor entirely normative. It instead involves a hermeneutic apprehension of social practices, which are understood as existing independently of the observer and yet as subsisting in purposive structures whose requirements are perennially subject to debate and determination. The American legal system, through the medium of doctrine, aspires to uncover the meaning of social practices and to translate them into governing principles of conduct.

In brief, I argue that for the past sixty years American constitutional law has regarded democratic community as a complex dialectic between two distinct and antagonistic but reciprocally interdependent forms of social organization, which I call "responsive democracy" and "community." I define these forms of social organization in terms of the hermeneutic project of the law. When the law attempts to organize social life based on the principle that persons are socially embedded and dependent, it instantiates the social form of community. When it attempts to organize social life based on the contrary principle that persons are autonomous and independent, it instantiates the social form of responsive democracy. My thesis is that the tension between responsive democracy and community has a characteristic shape. Although the principles of responsive democracy and community often conflict in the outcomes they require for specific cases, American constitutional law has nevertheless recognized that the maintenance of a healthy and viable democracy necessarily entails the maintenance of a healthy and viable community.[2] The concept of "democratic community," therefore, although unstable and contest-

able, has an essential and respected place in the history of our constitutional jurisprudence.

This chapter has a simple structure. The first part, "Community,"
considers legal perspectives on the form of social organization I call
community. The second part, "Democracy," addresses our constitutional
understandings of responsive democracy. The final section explores the
distinct and controversial domain of democratic community.

Community

Although the concept of "community" is "the most fundamental and
far-reaching of sociology's unit-ideas,"[3] it has proven exceedingly "difficult to define."[4] The temptation is to think of community as exemplified
by a particular culture, having a specific content, and actually situated in
time and space. This is certainly what Tönnies had in mind when he
charted the development from "Gemeinschaft" to "Gesellschaft."[5] In the
1960s modernization theory displayed similar assumptions using the more
sophisticated (but essentially analogous) dimensions of Talcott Parsons'
pattern variables.[6]

The enterprise of attempting to locate historical "community" empirically, however, has collapsed into a hopeless muddle. In his amusing
study of American historiography, for example, Thomas Bender docu-
ments how historians have found community to be always and continuously dissolving. Respectable monographs, when "placed in serial
order, . . . offer a picture of community breakdown repeating itself in the
1650s, 1690s, 1740s, 1780s, 1820s, 1850s, 1880s, and 1920s."[7]

Whenever we look, apparently, we can be certain to find community
slipping away. Bender suggests, therefore, that we abandon the concept of
community as occupying "a specific space" and instead think of it as "a
fundamental and enduring form of social interaction."[8] The methodological inquiry would thus shift away from the question of whether a particular culture represents community, and toward the question of how
communal forms of social interaction are instantiated and how they in-
tersect with other kinds of social organization. The shift, in essence,
would require us to abandon a concept of community that has determinate content, and to substitute instead a concept of community that entails a substantively empty but formally specific structure of social
ordering.

Following Bender's suggestion, and building on the work of Michael

Sandel, I define "community" as a form of social organization that provides for its members "not just what they *have* as fellow citizens but also what they *are*, not a relationship they choose (as in a voluntary association) but an attachment they discover, not merely an attribute but a constituent of identity."[9] Within community, therefore, social order is maintained through the inculcation among members of deep and parallel forms of personal identities. This formulation permits us to ground community in the empirical processes of primary socialization. George Herbert Mead, for example, has persuasively demonstrated how these processes establish common structures of identity in individual personalities:

> What goes to make up the organized self is the organization of the attitudes which are common to the group. A person is a personality because he belongs to a community, because he takes over the institutions of that community into his own conduct. He takes its language as the medium by which he gets his personality, and then through a process of taking the different roles that all the others furnish he comes to get the attitude of the members of the community. Such, in a certain sense, is the structure of a man's personality . . . The structure, then, on which the self is built is this response which is common to all, for one has to be a member of a community to be a self.[10]

The work of Erving Goffman illustrates that the creation and maintenance of these common structures of identity occur not only during early and primary socialization but also throughout the lifetime of community members through forms of everyday social interaction. By following rules of "deference and demeanor," community members both confirm the social order in which they live and constitute "ritual" and "sacred" aspects of their own selves. They thus continuously and inescapably "rely on others" to complete their own identities:

> Each individual is responsible for the demeanor image of himself and the deference image of others, so that for a complete man to be expressed, individuals must hold hands in a chain of ceremony, each giving deferentially with proper demeanor to the one on the right what will be received deferentially from the one on the left. While it may be true that the individual has a unique self all his own, evidence of this possession is thoroughly a product of joint ceremonial labor, the part expressed through the individual's demeanor being no more significant than the part conveyed by others through their deferential behavior toward him.[11]

In the forms of social interaction that Goffman classifies as "ceremonial," persons create shared identities by reference to common social
expectations or norms. Because a community subsists in the "special
claims which members [of a community] have on each other, as distinct
from others,"[12] these norms, when taken together, also define for a community "its distinctive shape, its unique identity."[13] That is why Richard
Rorty can define immoral action as "the sort of thing which, if done at all,
is done only by animals, or by people of other families, tribes, cultures, or
historical epochs. If done by one of us, or if done repeatedly by one of us,
that person ceases to be one of us. She becomes an outcast."[14]

We can define community, therefore, as a form of social organization
that strives to establish an essential reciprocity between individual and
social identity. Both are instantiated in social norms that are initially
transmitted through processes of primary socialization and are thereafter
continually reaffirmed through the transactions of everyday life. It is for
this reason that Sandel can speak of community as inhering in attachments that are discovered and not merely chosen. In the social particularity and historical contingency of that discovery lies the "mystic
foundation" of which Pascal so movingly speaks: "Custom is the whole of
equity, for the sole reason that it is accepted; that is the mystic foundation
of its authority. Anyone who tries to trace it back to its first principles will
destroy it."[15] The essential truth of Pascal's observation is reflected in the
shape of contemporary ethical theory, which, in its most sensitive applications, seeks not closed deductive systems but rather reflective equilibria
that are ultimately anchored in the contingent particularity of our given
perspectives.

I do not mean to imply, however, that persons in communities are
robots, automatons programmed to follow fixed social norms. If we conceptualize the operation of social norms from the perspective of individual actors, we might perhaps imagine a subtle and inescapable language
that can communicate various messages. For example, I can convey respect by maintaining a discreet distance and obeying applicable norms of
privacy. Or, in the identical situation, I can instead indicate contempt by
violating these norms and inappropriately intruding into a partner's personal space. Although the choice is mine, the choice is made meaningful
only because of the existence of commonly shared norms. The message
conveyed by my choice, in turn, reflects on the identity of its intended
audience. In Charles Taylor's words, "Our 'dignity' . . . is our sense of
ourselves as commanding (attitudinal) respect."[16] The point is powerfully

supported by sociological work demonstrating the extent to which reiterated infractions of social norms, conveying indignities large and small, can profoundly unhinge identity.[17]

I also do not mean to imply that communities are static and unchanging. Social norms are typically contestable, subject to interpretation and reinterpretation.[18] What is at stake in such contests is the shape of our dignity, our common identity, our community. Although it is implausible to contend that we can redefine ourselves altogether, it is clear that to some unspecifiable extent we can reimagine some of the norms of which we are composed. We can, by degrees, alter what we are and so affect the nature of our community. This reimagination can occur slowly, invisibly and by accretion. Or it can occur in jumps, as for example when distinct groups separate from and divide a community. In such circumstances a communal form of social organization can continue to exist only if there are authoritative cultural institutions, like state educational systems, which work to articulate the norms that reciprocally define individual and social identity and inculcate these norms in a manner that spans social divisions. That is why, if social divisions are sharp enough, groups will typically struggle to capture (or retain control of) authoritative cultural institutions.

The formal universality of the law, exemplified by its assertion of control over all cultural groups within the jurisdictional boundaries of the state, makes the law a particularly significant prize in these struggles. That the law functions to enunciate minimum acceptable standards to which all citizens of the state, regardless of cultural affiliation, must conform, is commonly recognized. It is less obvious that for centuries the common law in England and America has also functioned to define and enforce norms that are part of a communal form of social organization, norms that simultaneously establish both personal and community identity. Of course the common law has not enforced all such norms, just those deemed exceedingly important by those who control the law; I call these norms "civility rules." The extent to which the law has performed this task is of course subject to historical investigation, but it is I think clear that at least the doctrinal structure of the common law "dignitary" torts of defamation,[19] invasion of privacy, and intentional infliction of emotional distress can best be explained in terms of the legal definition and enforcement of civility rules.

Each of these torts penalizes uncivil communication on the assumption that the self of the addressee of such speech is intrinsically damaged, either through the loss of essential dignity and respect or through the infliction of emotional distress and injury. Communication is understood to cause such injury because common law doctrine conceptualizes the self as dependent on the observance of civility rules for the maintenance of its integrity. In this way the law conceives civility rules as the measure of a common identity. By enforcing these rules the law also determines which speech is "utterly intolerable in a civilized community"[20] and thereby defines the boundaries and meaning of community life. Under conditions of cultural heterogeneity, therefore, the common law can and has functioned as a powerful hegemonic force for the articulation of authoritative visions of community life.

Democracy

American constitutional law is rich in its characterizations of democracy. Democracy has clearly implied what Frank Michelman calls "self-rule," the belief that "the American people are politically free insomuch as they are governed by themselves collectively."[21] This commitment to self-rule is sometimes equated with majoritarianism.[22] Even so powerful a constitutional theorist as Frederick Schauer can argue that "any distinct restraint on majority power, such as a principle of freedom of speech, is by its nature anti-democratic, anti-majoritarian."[23] But the essence of constitutional law lies in its normative principles, and if majoritarianism is understood as such a principle rather than as a mere rule of procedure, its foundation most naturally rests on some form of utilitarian preference maximization. There is rather strong evidence that American constitutional law has decisively rejected that ideal.[24]

A far more persuasive account of the project of American constitutional law is one that begins with "the distinction between autonomy and heteronomy: Democratic forms of government are those in which the laws are made by the same people to whom they apply (and for that reason they are autonomous norms), while in autocratic forms of government the law-makers are different from those to whom the laws are addressed (and are therefore heteronomous norms)."[25] Simple majoritarianism fits awkwardly with the value of autonomy, because it contemplates the heteronomous imposition of majority will on the minority.[26] The solution to this difficulty, clearly envisioned by Rousseau, lies in postulating social processes anterior to majoritarian decision-making that somehow connect the democratic system as a whole to the autonomous will of the entire citizenry.

A wide range of modern theorists have understood democracy in exactly this way. Hans Kelsen, for example, defines democracy as an "ideal type" of government implementing the value of autonomy and resting on "the principle of self-determination." In explaining exactly how a collectivity can serve to realize the autonomy of its individual members, Kelsen initially reflects Rousseau's formulation in *The Social Contract*, but then quickly gives that formulation a distinctively modern spin:

> A subject is politically free insofar as his individual will is in harmony with the "collective" (or "general") will expressed in the social order. Such harmony of the "collective" and the individual will is guaranteed only if the social order is created by the individuals whose behavior it regulates. Social order means determination of the will of the individual. Political freedom, that is, freedom under social order, is self-determination of the individual by participating in the creation of the social order.[27]

Because it is unconvincing to imagine that the individual will can be "in harmony" with the general will in all matters of political moment, Kelsen ultimately locates the value of self-determination in the ability of persons to participate in the process by which the social order is created. The social order is thus conceived as anterior to particular acts of majoritarian decision-making. The creation of the social order is itself open to the participation of all because it preeminently occurs through processes of communication:

> The will of the community, in a democracy, is always created through a running discussion between majority and minority, through free consideration of arguments for and against a certain regulation of a subject matter. This discussion takes place not only in parliament, but also, and foremost, at political meetings, in newspapers, books, and other vehicles of public opinion. A democracy without public opinion is a contradiction in terms.[28]

For Kelsen, then, democracy serves the principle of self-determination because it subjects the political and social order to public opinion, which is itself the product of a communicative exchange open to all. The normative essence of democracy is thus located in the communicative processes necessary to instill a sense of self-determination, and in the subordination of political decision-making to these processes.

This logic is widely shared. It leads Benjamin Barber, for example, to conclude that "there can be no strong democratic legitimacy without ongoing talk."[29] It leads John Dewey to remark that "democracy begins in conversation."[30] It leads Durkheim to observe that "the more that deliberation and reflection and a critical spirit play a considerable part in the course of public affairs, the more democratic the nation."[31] It leads Claude Lefort to claim that "modern democracy invites us to replace the notion of a regime governed by laws, of a legitimate power, by the notion of a regime founded upon *the legitimacy of a debate as to what is legitimate and what is illegitimate*—a debate which is necessarily without any guarantor and without any end."[32]

In fact, the notion that democratic self-determination turns on the maintenance of a structure of communication open to all commands an extraordinarily wide consensus. Jürgen Habermas characterizes that structure as shaped by the effort to attain "a common will, communicatively shaped and discursively clarified in the political public sphere."[33] John Rawls views it as a process of "reconciliation through public reason."[34] Frank Michelman regards it as the practice of "jurisgenerative politics" through the "dialogic 'modulation' of participants' pre-political understandings."[35] For all three thinkers the goal of the structure is to facilitate the attainment of "agreement" that is "uncoerced, and reached by citizens in ways consistent with their being viewed as free and equal persons."[36]

Coercion is precluded from public debate because the very purpose of that debate is the practice of self-determination. The goal is "agreement" (or the attainment of "a common will") because in such circumstances the individual will is by hypothesis completely reconciled with the general will. It is important to understand, however, that this goal is purely aspirational, what Kant might call a "regulative idea."[37] In fact it is precisely because absolute agreement can never actually be reached that the debate that constitutes democracy is necessarily "without any end," and hence must be independently maintained as an ongoing structure of communication. Adopting the term used by the U.S. Supreme Court, I call this structure of communication "public discourse."[38]

Without public discourse, the simple kind of majoritarian rule Schauer equates with democracy loses its grounding in the principle of self-determination, and merely represents the heteronomous submission of a minority to the forceful command of a majority. This would be true even if majority and minority positions were determined accurately by sensitive voting procedures.[39] With a structure of public discourse in place, on the other hand, both majority and minority can each be understood to have had the opportunity to participate freely in a "system"[40] of communication on which the legitimacy of all political arrangements depends. Whether that opportunity will actually establish the value of autonomous self-determination for both majority and minority is a complex and contingent question, dependent on specific historical circumstances. But in the absence of that opportunity, realization of the value of autonomous self-determination will be precluded under conditions characteristic of the modern state.[41]

It should by this point be obvious that the concept of democracy that I am sketching, which I call "responsive democracy," has little to do with the usual paraphernalia of descriptive social science. It does not specifically address systems of representation, voting mechanisms, interest groups, and the like. Its essence lies instead in its hermeneutic apprehension of the meaning of our democratic institutions. I claim that American constitutional law has for the past sixty years employed the ideal of responsive democracy to shape the nation's political landscape.

This is most obvious in the Court's First Amendment jurisprudence, which most directly concerns the articulation of democratic aspirations. If Schauer were correct in his equation of democracy with majoritarianism, First Amendment restrictions on majoritarian lawmaking would indeed be anti-democratic. But from the very beginning of the First Amendment era[42] the Court has instead consistently viewed the First Amendment "as the guardian of our democracy,"[43] and it has characterized freedom of expression as "vital to the maintenance of democratic institutions."[44] It has thematized the democratic values protected by the First Amendment in terms that explicitly evoke the principle of self-determination:

> The maintenance of the opportunity for free political discussion to the end that government may be responsive to the will of the people and that changes may be obtained by lawful means, an opportunity essential to the security of the Republic, is a fundamental principle of our constitutional system.[45]

A brief overview of four significant implications of the concept of responsive democracy illustrates both its central importance to the structure of American constitutional law and its complex relation to the concept of community.

First, the function of responsive democracy is to reconcile, to the extent possible, the will of individuals with the general will. Responsive democracy is therefore ultimately grounded on a respect for individuals seen as "free and equal persons."[46] In the words of Jean Piaget:

The essence of democracy resides in its attitude towards law as a product of collective will, and not as something emanating from a transcendent will or from the authority established by divine right. It is therefore the essence of democracy to replace the unilateral respect of authority by the mutual respect of autonomous wills.[47]

The fundamental project of responsive democracy thus points sharply toward the individualism that pervades American constitutional law.[48] Hence the project necessarily presupposes a very different image of the person than does community. Responsive democracy begins with the premise of independent citizens who desire to fashion their social order in a manner that reflects their values and commitments. Community, on the other hand, begins with the opposite premise of citizens whose very identity requires the maintenance of particular forms of social order. Responsive democracy posits persons with autonomous selves; community posits persons with socially embedded selves. Responsive democracy strives to open up the field of social choice, community to restrict it.

These differences are most obvious in the contrasting regulation of public discourse within community and responsive democracy. Community conceives public discourse as the medium through which the values of a particular life are displayed and enacted. The common law thus freely regulates public speech that violates civility rules.[49] Responsive democracy, on the other hand, conceives public discourse as the communicative medium through which individuals select the forms of their communal life. It therefore resists the closure of that medium through the enforcement of civility rules that reflect preexisting social commitments. It requires that "in public debate our own citizens must tolerate insulting, and even outrageous, speech."[50] The point, as the Court stated in the landmark case of Cantwell v. Connecticut, is that the First Amendment mandates a social order in which "many types of life, character, opinion and belief can develop unmolested and unobstructed."[51] This conception of social life as labile and evolving flows directly from the individualist premises of responsive democracy, and it has led the Court to interpret the First Amendment sharply to restrict the enforcement in public discourse of community-reinforcing torts like defamation, invasion of privacy, and intentional infliction of emotional distress.[52]

Second, the individualist premises of responsive democracy necessarily imply some form of public/private distinction. This is because the state undermines the raison d'être of its own enterprise to the extent that it coercively forms the "autonomous wills" that responsive democracy seeks to reconcile into public opinion. The importance of this public/private distinction is most paradigmatically visible in the protection for individual conscience provided by the religion clauses of the First Amendment, which safeguard "the right of each individual voluntarily to determine what to believe (and what not to believe) free of any coercive pressures from the State."[53] "In the domain of conscience there is a moral power higher than the State."[54] The public/private distinction can also be seen in the branch of substantive due process doctrine that establishes the so-called constitutional "right to privacy," which protects the capacity "to define one's identity that is central to any concept of liberty."[55]

The public/private distinction must, of course, be understood as inherently unstable and problematic, for all government regulation influences, to one degree or another, the formation of individual identity.[56] For this reason the distinction must, from the perspective of responsive democracy, be regarded as a pragmatic instrument for identifying those aspects of the self considered indispensable for the exercise of political and moral autonomy and hence as beyond the coercive formation of the state.[57] In creating this sheltered haven, American constitutional law not only limits the reach of the democratic state, but it also curtails the ability of communities to use the force of law to require individuals to conform to community norms.

Third, responsive democracy is inherently incomplete. This is because the "autonomous wills" postulated by democratic theory do not and cannot appear *ex nihilo*. The only reason that a person possesses a personality capable of autonomous choice is that the person has internalized "the institutions of [the] community into his own conduct."[58] This process of socialization, which is prerequisite for personal identity, is not itself a matter of independent election. It is instead attributable to accidents of birth and acculturation. It most typically occurs through institutions like the family and the elementary school. In these settings a child's identity is created in the first instance through decidedly undemocratic means; it "comes to be by way of the internalization of sanctions that are de facto threatened and carried out."[59] Responsive democracy thus necessarily presupposes important (not to say foundational) aspects of the social world organized along nondemocratic lines.

The incompleteness of responsive democracy implies that its very stability depends on the maintenance of appropriate forms of community life.[60] Responsive democracy presupposes an overarching commitment to the value of self-determination.[61] Although responsive democracy must conceptualize that commitment as grounded in a collective act of autonomous consent, it is clear that such consent is chiefly mythical.[62] We must therefore understand the commitment as springing instead from principles instilled in persons as part of their socialization into community values.[63] This creates an obvious tension with the public/private distinction, a tension that is most manifest in the institution of coercive public education. The tension is pragmatically (if not entirely satisfactorily) reconciled in the conceptual distinction between the child who must learn and the adult who can choose.[64]

A good example of how American constitutional law recognizes the paradoxical dependence of responsive democracy on community forms of life may be found in the branch of substantive due process doctrine that insulates from majoritarian decision-making fundamental institutions "deeply rooted in this Nation's history and tradition."[65] Unlike the constitutional right to privacy, which subordinates community norms to individual rights, this strand of substantive due process doctrine enables deeply important community arrangements to circumscribe the competence of responsive democracy.[66] It is particularly forceful in its protection of the family, as the locus of primary socialization, from "statist" interference.[67]

Fourth, responsive democracy, like all forms of government, must ultimately be capable of accomplishing the tasks of governance. As Alexander Meiklejohn notes, "Self-government is nonsense unless the 'self' which governs is able and determined to make its will effective."[68] Democratic governments must therefore have the power to regulate behavior. But because public discourse is understood as the communicative medium through which the democratic "self" is itself constituted, public discourse must in important respects remain exempt from democratic regulation. We use the speech/action distinction to mark the boundaries of this exemption. All "words are deeds,"[69] so this distinction is purely pragmatic. The communicative processes necessary to sustain the principle of collective self-determination we designate as "speech" and thus insulate them from majoritarian interference.

This insulation, together with the public/private distinction and the dependence of responsive democracy upon the survival of essential community institutions, illustrates the extent to which constitutional limitations are a necessary implication of responsive democracy. Whether or not these limitations are enshrined in a written document or enforced by an independent judiciary, they must exist as operative restraints on majoritarian decision-making if responsive democracy is to remain faithful to its own normative premises. It is therefore vastly oversimplified to brand judicial review as anti-democratic because of the notorious "counter-majoritarian difficulty."[70] Although generations of constitutional lawyers have adopted this perspective, the American tradition of judicial review is better interpreted as itself evidence of a commitment to the principles of responsive democracy.

Democratic Community

On one level it is relatively easy to imagine an unproblematic account of the concept of "democratic community." If democracy is defined in terms of majoritarian decision-making procedures, we can envision a government in which such procedures are used to enact community values into law. We could call such a government a democratic community, and we could accurately ascribe this status to most contemporary democracies. Even our own government would qualify, for in America laws enacted through majoritarian procedures commonly function to place the force of the state behind the norms of the national community. A good example would be the many anti-discrimination laws that resulted from the civil rights movement, which serve graphically to express our communal commitment to egalitarian ideals.

But this account of "democratic community" is unsatisfactory if what we mean by democracy is not the external mechanics of a decision-making procedure but rather the normative project of responsive democracy. For this project appears in important respects to contradict the purposes of community. Thus if we put ourselves in the position of a lawmaker who must fashion law to create forms of social order, we will face a constant choice whether to design legal doctrine to sustain the common, socially embedded identities of citizens, or instead to design doctrine so as to protect the space for autonomous citizens independently to create their own social arrangements. To put the matter concretely, we must, if we are judges, decide whether constitutionally to permit or to prohibit the prosecution of flag burners.[71] To opt for the former is to enable law to be used to maintain popular identification with a particular conception of our community; to opt for the latter is instead to clear a public space in which hurtful and offensive (and therefore profoundly different) conceptions of our community can be displayed with impunity. Or, to offer another example, we must decide whether to allow persons to sue for compensation for emotional harms caused by unconscionably outrageous speech in public discourse.[72] If the function of law is to uphold norms that reciprocally define personal and communal identity, such suits ought to be permitted. They ought to be prohibited, however, if the function of law is instead to enable independent persons to advocate and exemplify new forms of life.

Such examples can be multiplied indefinitely; they are the stuff of everyday constitutional adjudication. They suggest a vision of responsive democracy and community as deeply antagonistic forms of social order. That vision, it is fair to say, is uniquely characteristic of the legal order of the United States, owing no doubt to the reciprocally reinforcing influences of our immense cultural diversity and the centrality of individualism to what Samuel Huntington has aptly termed our "American Creed."[73] The sharp polarity of that vision runs like a rift throughout our constitutional tradition, dividing in contemporary times "liberal" from "conservative" justices.[74]

But this polarity is misleading, for whereas it signifies the real tension between community and responsive democracy at the level of particular cases, it obscures the fact that at a more general systemic level, responsive democracy actually requires the maintenance of healthy and vigorous forms of community life. This is true for at least three reasons. First, as I have already discussed, responsive democracy is predicated on a commitment to the value of self-determination, which presupposes community institutions designed to inculcate this value. Hence the importance to democracy of establishing, as a matter of sheer "conscious social reproduction," a "nonneutral" educational system aimed at "cultivating the kind of character conducive to democratic sovereignty."[75]

Second, responsive democracy attempts to reconcile individuals with the general will by establishing processes of deliberation that will instantiate a sense of self-determination. The formal opportunity to speak and to hear constitutes a necessary but not sufficient condition for the creation of this sense of self-determination. Necessary also is the feeling of participation that at root must rest on an identification with the aspirations of a culture that attempts to reconcile differences through deliberative interaction. This identification is essential for the functioning, as well as for the reproduction, of responsive democracy, and it too must ultimately depend on the inculcation of particular forms of identity through community institutions.

Third, responsive democracy aspires to conditions of deliberation, to some form of "reconciliation through public reason." Such deliberation, in turn, presupposes civility and respect, for speech lacking these qualities is likely to be experienced as coercive and irrational, as an instrument "of aggression and personal assault."[76] The exercise of public reason is thus always inseparable from and made possible by historically particular community norms that give content to the values of respect and civility. In this sense also, responsive democracy requires the continued maintenance of healthy forms of community life.

The concept of democratic community, therefore, cuts a complex figure in our constitutional tradition. At the level of specific cases, responsive democracy and community appear oppositional, dictating conflicting perspectives and conclusions. But at the systemic level they appear reconcilable, perhaps even interdependent. This strange disjunction renders the concept of democratic community intrinsically unstable and contestable. In any particular circumstance it can always be argued either that legal enforcement of community norms is necessary for the survival of community, and hence for the ultimate health of responsive democracy, or that such enforcement is not necessary for the maintenance of community and therefore merely a betrayal of the principles of self-determination required by responsive democracy. The first form of argumentation was stressed during the McCarthy era, whereas the Warren Court subsequently recast vast stretches of American constitutional law according to the individualist premises of responsive democracy. More recently, courts have once again retrenched, enabling, for example, legal restrictions on speech where necessary to inculcate "the habits and manners of civility . . . indispensable to the practice of self government."[77]

The tension in American law between community and responsive democracy closely resembles the contemporary debate among American political philosophers between proponents of communitarianism and advocates of liberalism. The manner in which our law has accommodated this tension contains a useful lesson for the philosophical debate, for it starkly illuminates the extent to which the problem resists resolution *tout court* and requires instead situational and pragmatic adjustment. This can be illustrated by what I have elsewhere termed the "paradox of public discourse." The specific purpose of public discourse is the achievement of some form of "reconciliation through public reason," yet because the identity of democratic citizens will have been formed by reference to community norms, speech in violation of civility rules will characteristically be perceived as both irrational and coercive. Thus the First Amendment, in the name of responsive democracy, suspends legal enforcement of the very civility rules that make rational deliberation possible.

The upshot of this paradox is that the separation of public discourse from community depends in some measure on the spontaneous persistence of civility. In the absence of such persistence, even a Court imbued with the principles of responsive democracy may be required on purely pragmatic grounds to permit the enforcement of civility rules. Exemplary is the Court's decision in Chaplinsky v. New Hampshire, in which "fighting words"—words "which by their very utterance inflict injury"—were held to be unprotected by the First Amendment because they "are no essential part of any exposition of ideas, and are of such slight social value as a step to truth that any benefit that may be derived from them is clearly outweighed by the social interest in order and morality."[78]

The practical accommodation between responsive democracy and community characteristic of American constitutional law is also visible in its delineation of the distinct domain of public discourse. Responsive democracy requires that public discourse be broadly conceived as a process of "collective self-definition"[79] that will necessarily precede and inform government decision-making. Although the Court has sometimes attempted to define public discourse by distinguishing speech about "matters of public concern" from speech about "matters of purely private concern,"[80] it is evident that this definition is conceptually incoherent. This is because democratic self-governance posits that the people control the agenda of government. They have the power to determine the content of public issues simply by the direction of their interests. This means that every issue that can potentially agitate the public is also potentially relevant to democratic self-governance, and hence potentially of public concern. The distinction between "matters of public concern" and "matters of purely private concern," insofar as it is used to exclude speech from public discourse, is therefore incompatible with the very democratic self-governance it seeks to facilitate.

It does not follow, however, that all communication ought therefore to be classified as public discourse, for any such conclusion would preempt virtually all community control of speech and hence endanger the survival of the very community on which responsive democracy itself depends. For this reason the Court has been forced to define public discourse by evaluating the totality of circumstances surrounding particular speech acts, by reviewing a communication's "content, form, and context . . . as revealed by the whole record."[81] This inquiry, however, is neither more nor less than a determination of whether, in the circumstances presented, the values of self-determination embodied in public discourse ought to prevail over the values of the socially embedded self protected by community controls on speech. Thus the law will protect outrageous speech when disseminated in the pages of a nationally distributed magazine,[82] because the reading public ought with good reason to be regarded as autonomous self-governing citizens. But it will permit the regulation of such speech within the workplace, because the managerial control and social interdependence of the employment setting would render a similar attribution of autonomy patently out of place.[83] The distinction between responsive democracy and community is thus pragmatically and situationally justified.

This messy solution can be theoretically illuminated by George Herbert Mead's distinction between the "I" and the "me." Mead identified the socialized structure of the individual personality with what he called the "me." He was quite aware, however, that there could be no such thing as a completely "institutionalized individual." Persons always retain the inherent and irreducible capacity to modify or transcend socially given aspects of themselves. Mead identified this capacity as the "I":

> The "I" is the response of the organism to the attitudes of the others; the "me" is the organized set of attitudes of others which one himself assumes. The attitudes of the others constitute the organized "me," and then one reacts toward that as an "I."

The "I" is spontaneous, unpredictable, and formless; the "me" is structured and relatively static. Mead viewed each as a fundamental and indispensable aspect of the self. He associated the "me" with "social control," and the "I" with "self-expression." "Taken together," he wrote, "they constitute a personality as it appears in social experience. The self is essentially a social process going on with these two distinguishable phases."[84]

The sharp contrast between community and responsive democracy can be understood as flowing from the distinction between these two phases of the self. Law in the service of community upholds the values associated with the "me," which is to say the community norms and attitudes that form the structure of personality. Law in the service of responsive democracy safeguards the values associated with the "I," which is to say the potential for individual modification and transcendence of that structure.

But just as the "me" and the "I" are necessarily complementary and interdependent, so also are the social forms of community and responsive democracy. The tension between the two is irreducible and constant; the law merely provides the vehicle for its social embodiment. It throws the weight of the state behind one or another phase of the self, as circumstances require.

We are thus led to an image of democratic community as a complex dialectic between two equally necessary but opposing phases of the self and their corresponding social formations. The law is the instrument of this dialectic, tacking to and fro as directed between contradictory values. The result is a hodgepodge of conflicting legal judgments, certain to frustrate purists of either camp, but nevertheless explicable as an ongoing process of dynamic, contextual, and practical accommodation. In this regard, the ultimate revelation of the law is merely the shape and contours of our own deepest commitments.

III

Management and Instrumental Reason

6

Between Governance and Management: The History and Theory of the Public Forum

In 1972 the United States Supreme Court introduced for the first time the concept of the "public forum" into First Amendment jurisprudence. The concept enjoyed immediate success, and within twelve years had assumed the status of "a fundamental principle of First Amendment doctrine."[1] In the process the concept evolved into an elaborate, even byzantine scheme of constitutional rules designed to ascertain when members of the general public can use government property for communicative purposes.[2] In general outline, these rules focus tightly "on the character of the property at issue"[3] in order to determine whether it is a "public or nonpublic" forum.[4] If the property is a public forum, the government's ability to regulate the public's expressive use of the property is subject to strict constitutional limitations; if it is a nonpublic forum, the government is given great latitude in the property's regulation.

Although public forum doctrine has developed with extraordinary speed, it has done so in a manner heedless of its constitutional foundations. The Court has yet to articulate a defensible constitutional justification for its basic project of dividing government property into distinct categories, much less for the myriad of formal rules governing the regulation of speech within these categories. These rules have proliferated to such an extent as to render the doctrine virtually impermeable to common sense. The doctrine has in fact become a serious obstacle not only to sensitive First Amendment analysis but also to a realistic appreciation of the government's requirements in controlling its own property. It has received nearly universal condemnation from commentators[5] and is in such a state of disrepair as to require a fundamental reappraisal of its origins and purposes. This essay is intended as a modest step in that direction.

The first section traces the history of public forum doctrine with an eye toward uncovering the underlying values that have led the Court to back itself into its present uncomfortable position. The second section assesses the present condition of what Melville Nimmer called the "complex maze of categories and subcategories" which constitute modern public forum doctrine.[6] Almost none of the special rules characteristic of the doctrine can withstand analytic scrutiny.

The third section proposes a constitutional theory that is responsive to the values which the history of public forum doctrine reveals have animated the Court, and the theory in turn leads to a reformulation of the doctrine that is consistent with contemporary constitutional principles. To summarize this reformulation in a brief and somewhat delphic manner, public and nonpublic forums should be distinguished not because of the character of the government property at issue, but rather because of the nature of the government authority in question. There are two kinds of government authority, corresponding to two distinct regimes of First Amendment regulation. The first is what I call "managerial" authority, with which the state is characteristically invested when it acts to administer organizational domains dedicated to instrumental conduct. In such contexts the government may constitutionally regulate speech as necessary to achieve instrumental objectives. The second kind of authority can be termed "governance." It is characteristic of the authority which the state exercises over what Hannah Arendt has called the "public realm": the arena in which members of the general public meet to accommodate competing values and expectations, and hence in which all goals or objectives are open to discussion and modification.[7] The government's ability to restrict speech in the public realm is limited by what are generally conceived to be traditional principles of First Amendment adjudication. If the government exercises the authority of governance over a resource which a member of the general public wishes to use for communicative purposes, the resource is a public forum. The resource is a nonpublic forum if it is subject to the managerial authority of government. The fourth section of this essay will discuss in detail the constitutional criteria that distinguish management from governance, and hence public from nonpublic forums.

A number of constitutional consequences flow from this reformulation of public forum doctrine, one of the most important of which is that public forums do not, as the Court has sometimes remarked, occupy "a special position in terms of first amendment protection,"[8] but are instead resources governed by normal and generally applicable First Amendment standards. These standards do not ordinarily apply, however, in nonpublic forums, in which the state is instead permitted to regulate speech as necessary to achieve certain specified objectives. When a court reviews government action in a nonpublic forum, it must decide whether it should independently evaluate the state's instrumental justification for the regulation of speech, or whether it should defer on this question to the judgment of government officials. The question of deference, which accounts for some of the most controversial aspects of contemporary public forum doctrine, is discussed in the fifth section.

The History of Public Forum Doctrine

The phrase "public forum" is traditionally attributed to Harry Kalven's classic 1965 article, "The Concept of the Public Forum: Cox v. Louisiana."[9] In *Cox*,[10] the Court addressed the troublesome issue of street demonstrations in the vicinity of a courthouse. Kalven used the occasion to attempt a major reconsideration of "the problems of speech in public places." Kalven's basic point was:

> In an open democratic society the streets, the parks, and other public places are an important facility for public discussion and political process. They are in brief a public forum that the citizen can commandeer; the generosity and empathy with which such facilities are made available is an index of freedom.[11]

The concept of the "public forum" was not for Kalven primarily a tool for categorizing different kinds of government property; his central concern was rather with the protection of that "uninhibited, robust and wide-open" speech "on public issues" which New York Times Co. v. Sullivan[12] had recently placed at the center of First Amendment concerns.[13] Streets and parks were constitutionally important because they were peculiarly fitted to foster such speech. But Kalven's use of the phrase "public forum" to express this importance proved in the long run unfortunate, for it tended to focus attention on categories of public property rather than on the relationship between such categories and the underlying constitutional value of public discussion.

Kalven's Reconstruction of the Early Precedents: Of Streets and Private Homes

Kalven cannot be entirely exonerated from contributing to this misunderstanding, however, for his claim that the "concept of the public forum" is "implicit in the earlier cases" appeared to imply that Supreme Court precedents of the 1930s and 1940s had given special constitutional protection to a specific category of public property.[14] This implication, however, was quite mistaken. The precedents relied upon by Kalven did indeed restrict the government's ability to regulate speech within public forums, but they also imposed exactly the same kind of restrictions on the government's ability to regulate speech in circumstances that did not involve public forums.

An important holding relied upon by Kalven for his interpretation of "the earlier cases" was Schneider v. State, in which the Court had considered the constitutionality of municipal ordinances prohibiting the distribution of handbills in streets and other public places. The ordinances were defended on the grounds that they were necessary in order to prevent littering. The Court balanced this justification against the ordinances' impact on the exercise of First Amendment rights, and concluded that "the purpose to keep the streets clean and of good appearance is insufficient to justify an ordinance which prohibits a person rightfully on a public street from handing literature to one willing to receive it."[15]

Kalven was undoubtedly right in reading *Schneider* as having "an impressive bite" in protecting First Amendment concerns,[16] but it is somewhat more doubtful whether this bite came, as Kalven seemed to claim, from a specific concern for speech in public places. Only four years after *Schneider*, the Court in Martin v. City of Struthers struck down a municipal ordinance prohibiting the door-to-door distribution of handbills. As in *Schneider*, the Court weighed the First Amendment right to distribute and receive information against the state's interest in preventing a "minor nuisance,"[17] and, as in *Schneider*, the Court concluded that the First Amendment right must prevail. In *Martin*, however, there was no question of protecting speech in public places, there was only the question of protecting speech.

Martin and *Schneider*, taken together, suggest that a specific concern for speech in what Kalven later called a "public forum" was not a major component of the Court's analysis. This conclusion is reinforced by a review of the Court's First Amendment decisions in the 1930s and 1940s, when virtually every protection extended to speech occurring in public forums was also extended to speech that did not occur in such forums. If the Court held that street demonstrations could not be subject to the whim of official discretion,[18] it also held that the distribution of pamphlets in private homes could not be subject to such discretion.[19] If the

Court protected provocative speech in the streets,[20] it also protected such speech in private halls.[21]

In short, the precedents indicate that the Court's primary concern was to protect speech that today might be called public discourse, and that the geographical location of that discourse played a relatively minor role in that concern. There was, however, one major exception to this generalization, an exception that formed the basis of Kalven's historical reconstruction. That exception was Justice Roberts' famous dictum in his plurality opinion in Hague v. CIO:

> Wherever the title of streets and parks may rest, they have immemorially been held in trust for the use of the public and, time out of mind, have been used for purposes of assembly, communicating thoughts between citizens, and discussing public questions. Such use of the streets and public places has, from ancient times, been a part of the privileges, immunities, rights, and liberties of citizens. The privilege of a citizen of the United States to use the streets and parks for communication of views on national questions may be regulated in the interest of all; it is not absolute, but relative, and must be exercised in subordination to the general comfort and convenience, and in consonance with peace and good order; but it must not, in the guise of regulation, be abridged or denied.[22]

Because of its apparent emphasis on the special importance of speech in streets and other public places, the passage has been cited as the origin of the concept of the public forum.[23] But the passage is deceptive, for the holding of Justice Roberts' opinion is simply that official discretion to suppress speech in public places is constitutionally invalid, and Roberts was equally willing to reach this conclusion with respect to speech in private places.[24] Moreover, the passage appears to distinguish streets and other public places on the basis of "common law notions of adverse possession and public trust," notions that have no logical connection to First Amendment values.[25] The transition from "immemorial" usage to constitutional judgment seems so abrupt as to be simply a non sequitur.

The transition, however, makes a great deal more sense once it is understood that its purpose is to distinguish an early precedent, Davis v. Massachusetts, in which the Court had upheld a conviction for making a public address on the Boston Common without first having obtained a permit from the mayor.[26] The defendant in *Davis* had argued that the Common was "the property of the inhabitants of the city of Boston, and dedicated to the use of the people of that city and the public in many ways," including the making of public addresses. The Court rejected this claim, stating that "the common was absolutely under the control of the legislature," and that "for the legislature absolutely or conditionally to forbid public speaking in a highway or public park is no more an infringement of the rights of a member of the public than for the owner of a private house to forbid it in his house."[27]

If the reasoning of *Davis* were spelled out, it would take the form of a syllogism. The major premise of the argument is that when the government acts in a proprietary capacity, like "the owner of a private house," it can abridge or prohibit speech. The minor premise of the argument is that the government in fact acted in a proprietary capacity with respect to the Boston Common. The conclusion of the syllogism is that the ordinance requiring a citizen to obtain a permit prior to speaking on the Boston Common is constitutional.

The Court in *Davis* defended the minor premise of this syllogism on the basis of state property law. It defended the major premise on the basis of what today would be called the "rights/privilege distinction." The Court reasoned that because Boston "owned" the Common and could therefore "absolutely exclude all right to use," it necessarily also retained the power "to determine under what circumstances such use may be availed," including circumstances abridging speech, since "the greater power contains the lesser."[28]

The municipality in *Hague*, relying on *Davis*, had made a similar argument, contending that "the city's ownership of streets and parks is as absolute as one's ownership of his home, with consequent power altogether to exclude citizens from the use thereof."[29] Justice Roberts' assertion that streets and parks had "immemorially been held in trust for the use of the public" was meant to deny the minor premise of this argument, that the city was the proprietor of its streets. This explains Roberts' odd conjunction of common law property rights and constitutional principle. What is particularly interesting about Roberts' opinion, however, is that it did not seek to deny the major premise of the municipality's argument. It did not dispute that government could abridge speech were it to act in a proprietary capacity; it merely held that the government's power over streets and parks was not proprietary in nature.

Viewed in this light, the thrust of Justice Roberts' famous opinion in *Hague* is not that speech in streets and parks is especially important or unique, but rather that the government could not exercise proprietary control over such places. Even though the government "owned" the streets in a technical sense, it still could not freely manage them in the way that a property owner could manage his house. The streets were in some sense "external" to the government, and consequently in regulating them the government was subject to the ordinary constitutional restraints prohibiting the abridgment of speech.

This interpretation of *Hague* is confirmed by the Court's subsequent opinion in Jamison v. Texas, a decision relied upon by Kalven. In *Jamison*, the Court considered the constitutionality of a Dallas ordinance prohibiting the distribution of leaflets upon the streets and sidewalks. The city relied upon *Davis* in defending the ordinance, but its argument was summarily dismissed by the Court, which said that *Davis* had been repudiated by *Hague*. The law, said the Court, was that "one who is rightfully on a street which the state has left open to the public carries with him there as elsewhere the constitutional right to express his views in an orderly fashion. This right extends to the communication of ideas by handbills and literature as well as by the spoken word."[30]

Jamison makes explicit the basis of Justice Roberts' opinion in *Hague:* constitutional rights are not lost simply because one is on a street that happens to be "owned" by the state. But although First Amendment rights do not disappear simply because the state claims to have proprietary control over the places where they are exercised, such rights are on the other hand not particularly puissant *because* they are exercised in a public place. They are simply the same as First Amendment rights exercised "elsewhere."

There is, in this reasoning, no implicit concept of a public forum, at least insofar as the phrase is meant to signify a special geographical location or category of government property where speech merits unusual protection.

The Evolution of Modern Public Forum Doctrine

Whatever the accuracy of Kalven's reconstruction of the early precedents, his concept of a public forum was to prove profoundly influential in the development of First Amendment doctrine. In 1972 the Supreme Court, explicitly acknowledging its debt to Kalven, began to use the phrase "public forum" as a term of art.[31] For the next few years the Court experimented with various definitions of the phrase. By 1976, however, the Court was prepared to fix the framework of public forum doctrine as we now know it. That framework was heavily indebted to the Court's 1966 decision in Adderley v. Florida.

Adderley v. Florida: The Resurrection of the *Davis* Syllogism

In *Adderley* the Court was faced with a challenge to the convictions of thirty-two students who had been arrested for trespass on the grounds of a county jail. The students had been protesting the jail's segregative practices and had refused to disperse at the request of the sheriff, the custodian of the jail. The Court, speaking through Justice Black, summarily rejected the students' claim that their demonstration was protected by the First Amendment:

> Nothing in the Constitution of the United States prevents Florida from even-handed enforcement of its general trespass statute against those refusing to obey the sheriff's order to remove themselves from what amounted to the curtilage of the jailhouse. The State, no less than a private owner of property, has power to preserve the property under its control for the use to which it is lawfully dedicated. For this reason there is no merit to the petitioners' argument that they had a constitutional right to stay on the property, over the jail custodian's objections, because this "area chosen for the peaceful civil rights demonstration was not only 'reasonable' but also particularly appropriate . . ." Such an argument has as its major unarticulated premise the assumption that people who want to propagandize protests or views have a constitutional right to do so whenever and however and wherever they please. That concept of constitutional law was vigorously and forthrightly rejected in two of the cases petitioners rely on, *Cox v. Louisiana* [379 U.S.] at 554–555 and 563–564. We reject it again. The United States Constitution does not forbid a State to control the use of its own property for its own lawful nondiscriminatory purpose.[32]

At first glance the Court's argument appears inconsistent with the Court's earlier precedents concerning freedom of expression in the streets and other public places. After all, the streets, no less than the jailhouse curtilage, are "property under [the] control" of the state. If the state could act like "a private owner of property" with respect to the curtilage, then why not also with respect to the streets?

It might be thought that *Adderley* can be distinguished because the early precedents, in the words of *Jamison*, applied only to "one who is rightfully on a street which the state has left open to the public." In *Adderley*, Florida's trespass law prohibited the students from being "rightfully" on the jailhouse grounds. This distinction, however, cannot be sustained. Under an ordinance like that at issue in *Hague*, citizens who are "rightfully" on the streets cannot demonstrate unless they first receive approval from the Director of Public Safety. Under a statute like that at issue in *Adderley*, students can rightfully assemble and demonstrate on the jail-house grounds until ordered to disperse by the sheriff.[33] In both cases the legality of the demonstration depends upon the approval of a state official. In both cases this power of approval is discretionary and unconstrained by articulated guidelines.[34] In *Hague* the Court held that the First Amendment precluded the exercise of such power over speech, whereas in *Adderley* it did not.

In *Hague*, however, as in *Jamison*, the Court was concerned with determining the facial validity of ordinances that directly regulated recognized modes of communication, such as leafletting, parading, and assembling. In *Adderley*, on the other hand, the statute at issue was a general trespass statute that addressed conduct rather than a medium of communication.[35] Just as the prohibition against murder can be applied without constitutional difficulty to the terrorist who uses assassination as a mode of political expression, so a general proscription against trespass can be applied even to those who trespass in order to communicate.[36] Read in this light, *Adderley* is a very narrow decision, concerned not so much with the government's power to control speech as with its ability to enact and enforce general regulations of conduct.[37]

Subsequent cases, however, have not read *Adderley* in so narrow a fashion. The reason lies in *Adderley*'s discussion of Edwards v. South Carolina,[38] a case decided several years earlier in which the Court had vacated the convictions of black protesters who had demonstrated on the grounds of the South Carolina State House. The protesters had been charged with the common law crime of breach of the peace, which, like the trespass statute at issue in *Adderley*, appeared to be a neutral regulation of conduct rather than of speech. Justice Black distinguished *Edwards* on a number of grounds. One was that the common law crime at issue in *Edwards* was "so broad and all-embracing as to jeopardize speech, press, assembly and petition." But a second and ultimately more influential ground of distinction was that the demonstrators in *Edwards* "went to the South Carolina State Capitol grounds to protest," whereas the demonstrators in *Adderley* "went to the jail." This difference was constitutionally significant because "traditionally, state capitol grounds are open to the public. Jails, built for security purposes, are not."[39]

Justice Black's reliance on "traditional" usage was no doubt meant to echo Justice Roberts' reference to the "immemorial" use of the streets for "purposes of assembly, communicating thoughts between citizens, and discussing public questions." Black's language implied that even if a general trespass statute could not be applied to prevent demonstrations in the streets or on the grounds of a state capitol, they could be so applied on the grounds of the jailhouse *because* there was no history of communicative behavior associated with the jail. But this implication made sense only if Justice Black, like Justice Roberts in *Hague*, was writing within the confines of the *Davis* syllogism. From this perspective, Black's forceful analogy of the government to a "private owner of property" seemed to reassert the major premise of the syllogism, that the government could directly abridge speech when acting in a proprietary manner. And his reference to the absence of a tradition of public access to the jail seemed to refer to the minor premise and to imply that the jail was in fact under the government's proprietary control. And so *Adderley*'s conclusion, that Florida officials could use their discretion under the trespass statute to abridge speech within the jailhouse curtilage, seemed to flow naturally from an application of the *Davis* syllogism.[40]

Adderley's actual grounds of decision are ambiguous. But subsequent opinions of the Court which have developed the theory of the public forum, and which have on the whole been concerned with the regulation of speech rather than of conduct, have interpreted *Adderley* as resurrecting and relying upon the *Davis* syllogism. The irony of this interpretation is that at the time of *Adderley* the syllogism was fast becoming untenable because of the crumbling of the rights/privilege distinction.[41] But it was upon this foundation that the Court would later choose to erect the edifice of modern public forum doctrine.

The Moment of Ambivalence: *Grayned, Mosley*, and the Categorization of Public Property

For the decade after *Adderley*, the Court remained uncertain about the status of the *Davis* syllogism. In 1972, the Court appeared ready to reject it outright. In that year the Court decided Grayned v. City of Rockford, in which it upheld a municipal ordinance prohibiting "the making of any noise or diversion which disturbs or tends to disturb the peace or good order" of a school class while "on public or private grounds adjacent to any building in which a school or any class thereof is in session." Faced with a statute that regulated speech in a manner that did not differentiate among private property, streets, or school grounds, the Court, speaking through Justice Marshall, used the occasion to repudiate the major premise of the *Davis* syllogism. The Court stated flatly that "the right to use a public place for expressive activity may be restricted only for weighty reasons."[42] This was a blunt rejection of the notion that there were certain kinds of public property on which the government, like the owner of a private home, could abridge speech simply by virtue of its proprietary interest.

In place of the *Davis* syllogism, the Court proposed that speech on all public property be subject to "reasonable 'time, place and manner' regulations" which are "necessary to further significant governmental interests." In determining whether such regulations are reasonable, the "crucial question" is

> whether the manner of expression is basically incompatible with the normal activity of a particular place at a particular time. Our cases make clear that in assessing the reasonableness of a regulation, we must weigh heavily the fact that communication is involved; the regulation must be narrowly tailored to further the State's legitimate interest.[43]

Whereas the major premise of the *Davis* syllogism divides public property into two kinds, proprietary and nonproprietary, *Grayned* took the opposite tack, concluding that all public property be subject to a single, unified First Amendment test. Whereas the *Davis* syllogism classifies public property without reference to First Amendment principles, *Grayned* set forth a regime of constitutional regulation explicitly designed to serve the First Amendment value of maximizing social communication. In this focus on the constitutional value of public discussion, *Grayned* exemplified the spirit of Kalven's 1965 article, which it duly acknowledged.[44]

For this reason *Grayned* has remained a touchstone case for many commentators. It is important to stress, however, that the Court in *Grayned* did not use or adopt Kalven's phrase "public forum." *Grayned* was concerned to reject the perspective that divided public property into constitutionally distinct classifications, and the concept of the public forum implied the contrary conclusion, that some public property was subject to unique, especially restrictive First Amendment regulation. But in a decision issued on the same day as *Grayned* and also authored by Justice Marshall, the Court did adopt the phrase, once again explicitly acknowledging its debt to Kalven.

That decision was Police Department of Chicago v. Mosley.[45] At issue in *Mosley* was a Chicago ordinance prohibiting picketing or demonstrating "on a public way" within 150 feet of any primary or secondary school building while the school was in session. The ordinance exempted "peaceful picketing of any school involved in a labor dispute." Noting that the statute distinguished legal from illegal picketing based upon "the message on a picket sign," the Court held:

> Once a forum is opened up to assembly or speaking by some groups, government may not prohibit others from assembling or speaking on the basis of what they intend to say. Selective exclusions from a public forum may not be based on content alone, and may not be justified by reference to content alone.[46]

The reasoning of the Court was far from clear, but it seemed to turn on the distinction between a public forum and other government property.[47] The Chicago ordinance was unconstitutional, the Court ruled, because it attempted to exclude speech from a public forum "based on content alone," and that "is never permitted."[48] The negative inference was that such an exclusion would have been permissible had it occurred in a nonpublic forum, and that public and nonpublic forums were therefore controlled by different First Amendment rules. Thus *Grayned*'s effort to subject all public property to a single, unified regime of First Amendment regulation was undercut on the very day it was issued.

Mosley was not explicit about how government property assumed the status of a public forum, but it implied that this transformation occurred when the state "opened up" the property "to assembly or speaking by some groups."[49] The exact nature of this opening-up process was left ambiguous. It was not clear whether the "public ways" at issue in *Mosley* were public forums because the Chicago ordinance opened them up for use in peaceful labor picketing, or because Chicago permitted them to be used for other, nonpicketing forms of communication. In either case, the public forum status of the property was triggered not by traditional usage but rather by government decisions concerning the deployment of its property. The concept of the public forum advanced in *Mosley* was designed to force these decisions to be made in a nondiscriminatory way, so that the government could not "select which issues are worth discussing or debating in public facilities."[50] In this sense *Mosley*, like *Grayned*, did not accept the major premise of the *Davis* syllogism, for *Mosley* implied that if the government opened up its property to members of the public for communicative use, the government's power to abridge speech was subject to constitutional limitations, even if the property was under the government's proprietary control.

Despite this similarity, however, the two cases were in tension as to the question of whether government property could be divided into distinct categories that were governed by distinct regimes of First Amendment regulation. The tension reflects a similar strain in Kalven's article. Kalven wanted simultaneously to stress the general value of facilitating "robust" public discussion and to stress the particular value of speech in public places. *Grayned* is responsive to the first concern, *Mosley* to the second. Modern public forum doctrine developed from *Mosley*, not *Grayned*.[51]

The Period of Experimentation: *Lehman* and *Conrad*

After *Mosley*, the concept of the public forum moved to the forefront of the Court's attention. For the next three years the Court explored possible meanings for the concept, as well as various First Amendment rules that might be attached to it. Underlying this experimentation was the Court's effort to vindicate Kalven's perception that the public forum should enjoy an especially protected First Amendment status. But this perception distorted the Court's earlier precedents, and the Court's attempts to vindicate it during the early 1970s proved unsuccessful, leading the Court to propose harsh and unrealistic constitutional rules for the public forum.

In 1974, two years after *Mosley*, the Court decided Lehman v. City of Shaker Heights. *Lehman* adopted from *Mosley* the phrase "public forum," and for the first time the Justices gave the phrase serious and divisive doctrinal attention. In *Lehman*, a political candidate challenged the policy of a municipal rapid transit system which sold space on car cards to commercial advertisers, but which refused to permit the cards to be used for paid political advertisements. On its face the case seemed to be squarely controlled by *Mosley*, for the rapid transit system had opened up the cards to the public for communicative use and yet was making distinctions based upon "the message on [the] . . . sign." The Court nevertheless upheld the policy, although it was unable to unite behind a majority opinion.

Justice Blackmun, joined by three other Justices, wrote a plurality opinion rejecting the claim that the car cards were a "public forum" as to which the First Amendment created "a guarantee of nondiscriminatory access."[52] First Amendment restraints on government regulation of public property, Blackmun wrote, depend upon "the nature of the forum and the conflicting interests involved . . . Here we have no open spaces, no meeting hall, park, street corner, or other public thoroughfare." Instead the car cards were part of a "commercial venture," and the municipality controlled them "in a proprietary capacity." The municipality had "discretion" to make "managerial decision[s]," including decisions as to the messages permitted to be displayed on the cards. The Constitution required only that these decisions not be "arbitrary, capricious, or invidious."[53]

In essence, Blackmun's opinion reached back behind *Mosley* to *Davis*. It seemed to hold that the government's exercise of proprietary control empowers it to abridge speech.[54] Blackmun made no effort to justify this holding. His conclusion that the municipality's control over car cards was proprietary in nature rested entirely upon a perceived analogy between the rapid transit system and a private commercial enterprise, so that the system could select which advertising to display "in much the same way [as] a newspaper or periodical, or even a radio or television station."[55]

If Blackmun's opinion was inconsistent with *Mosley*, it was even more so with *Grayned*. Blackmun's opinion assumed that government property which was a public forum was subject to distinct First Amendment rules. *Grayned*, on the other hand, had attempted to subject all government property to a single, uniform scheme of First Amendment regulation. *Grayned* had also concluded that public claims to speak on government property be determined by an independent judicial examination of "whether the manner of expression [was] basically incompatible with the normal activity of a particular place at a particular time." But the import of Blackmun's opinion in *Lehman* was that in situations of proprietary control the First Amendment delegated authority to determine such claims to the discretion of government officials.

The fifth vote for the Court's holding came from Justice Douglas, who wrote an idiosyncratic opinion based upon the view that the car cards violated "the right of the commuters to be free from forced intrusions on their privacy."[56] The views of the remaining four Justices were expressed in a dissent by Justice Brennan,[57] which turned explicitly on a theory of the public forum. Citing Kalven's 1965 article, Brennan began his argument with the observation that "the determination of whether a particular type of public property or facility constitutes a 'public forum' requires the Court to strike a balance between the competing interests of the government, on the one hand, and the speaker and his audience, on the other."[58] Once government property is designated a "public forum," the Constitution requires that it "be made available . . . for the exercise of first amendment rights" and that government regulation of the forum not discriminate "based solely upon subject matter or content."[59] Citing *Hague* and *Edwards*, Brennan argued that the Court had designated "public streets and parks" and state capitol grounds as public forums.[60]

For Brennan there was simply no question but that the car cards at issue in *Lehman* were a public forum, since by making the cards available for commercial advertising the municipality had "effectively waived any argument that advertising in its transit cars is incompatible with the rapid transit system's primary function of providing transportation."[61] He therefore concluded that the system's policy of discriminating among messages based upon their content was constitutionally invalid.

Brennan's dissent was the first effort to set forth a systematic doctrine of the public forum.[62] It was a curious mixture of *Mosley* and *Grayned*. Like *Mosley*, it divided government property into public and nonpublic forums, and imposed strict First Amendment regulations on the former. But it rejected *Mosley*'s criterion for distinguishing the two kinds of government property, using instead a variant of *Grayned*'s "basic incompatibility" test as the means of dividing public from nonpublic forums. In Brennan's hands, however, the *Grayned* test was subtly and fundamentally transformed. Whereas *Grayned* had used the test as a means of subjecting all public property to a single, unified regime of First Amendment regulation, Brennan used the test to separate kinds of government property. Property classified as a public forum was subject to stringent First Amendment rules, regardless of whether such rules were in any particular instance compatible with the ordinary use of the property. In effect Brennan shifted the focus of analysis from the circumstances of particular speech to the general characteristics of the property at issue.

This shift in focus was integral to Brennan's larger project, which was to distinguish two generic kinds of government property: public and nonpublic forums. The whole point of this project lay in the fact that these two kinds of property were to be subject to distinct regimes of First Amendment regulation. When Brennan came to define the First Amendment rules applicable to a public forum, he cited *Mosley* for the proposition that in such places content discrimination was strictly forbidden.[63] Although the tenor of Brennan's dissent was that public forums were subject to unique and particularly stringent First Amendment scrutiny, in fact the prohibition on content discrimination did not distinguish such scrutiny from that applicable to private places like public utility billing envelopes or drive-in movie theaters.[64] There was a sharp tension in Brennan's dissent between a desire to endow the public forum with a "special position in terms of first amendment protection,"[65] and an inability to define that protection coherently except in terms of First Amendment principles generally applicable to public discourse. The Court continues to struggle with the same tension to this very day.

Nine months after *Lehman* the Court attempted again to define the nature of the public forum. In Southeastern Promotions, Ltd. v. Conrad,[66] Justice Blackmun, writing for five Justices, held that because municipal auditoriums were "public forums," their directors could not be given the "discretion" to accept or reject proposed theatrical performances without complying with the procedural safeguards that Freedman v. Maryland[67] had imposed on prior restraints.[68] It held that the auditoriums were public forums because, like the car cards in *Lehman*, they were "designed for and dedicated to expressive activities."[69] Despite its procedural focus, the underlying message of *Conrad* was that in a public forum content discrimination was constitutionally invalid. In his dissent Justice Rehnquist asked if this meant that municipal opera houses had to show rock musicals, or indeed had to open their doors to "any potential producer on a first come, first served basis."[70]

The question went unanswered, but its implications were powerful, harshly pointing toward the unsteady foundations of "the all or nothing approach to content regulation in the public forum."[71] That public forum doctrine should have arrived at such a rigid view in only three years is a testament to its extraordinarily rapid development. The doctrine had not only identified a special kind of government property, the public forum, but it had imposed on that property stringent First Amendment regulations that seemed unrelated to the property's actual uses. By 1975, the Court could describe the issue in *Lehman* as "whether the city had created a 'public forum' and *thereby* obligated itself to accept all advertising."[72]

The reach and power of this reasoning is formidable. If government facilities designed and employed for expressive activities are thereby disabled from making distinctions based upon content, then the ordinary and daily use of a great many government facilities is simply unconstitutional. Government facilities routinely draw distinctions based upon content. Consider, for example, such facilities as a high school classroom, a prison auditorium, a lecture room in a military compound, a meeting room in a government bureaucracy, or a high school newspaper. Public forum doctrine had developed so rapidly that the Court apparently had not had the opportunity to think through these implications. But by the following year a majority of the Court had come to the conclusion that the implications were unacceptable; in 1976, they abandoned the liberal promise of *Conrad* and *Mosley* and decided a case that definitively fixed the framework of modern public forum doctrine.

Establishing the Basic Doctrinal Framework: Greer v. Spock

The pivotal decision was Greer v. Spock, which concerned requests by candidates for national office from fringe political parties for permission to enter the public areas of the Fort Dix Military Reservation for the purpose of distributing campaign literature and holding a meeting to discuss national political issues with U.S. Army personnel and their dependents. These public areas were open to the public without restriction at all times of the day and night.[73] They were crossed by ten paved roads, including a major state highway.[74] Nevertheless, the commanding officer of the reservation denied the candidates' request, citing two Fort Dix regulations. The first, Fort Dix Reg. 210-26, prohibited "demonstrations, picketing, sit-ins, protest marches, political speeches and similar activities . . . on the Fort Dix Military Reservation." The second, Fort Dix Reg. 210-27, prohibited the distribution of political leaflets on the reservation "without prior written approval" of the base commander.[75] The commander refused to approve the distribution of leaflets because "political campaigning on Fort Dix cannot help but interfere with our training and other military missions."[76]

The Court, speaking through Justice Stewart, upheld the decision of the base commander. The Court's reasoning was simple, powerful, and immensely influential. It appropriated the terminology of the public forum which the Court had developed during the preceding four years, but infused it with a new focus that harked back to Justice Roberts' "familiar words" in *Hague*. The Court identified public forums as areas that "have traditionally served as a place for free public assembly and communication of thoughts by private citizens." In such places, the Court said, "there cannot be a blanket exclusion of first amendment activity."[77] Since it was "historically and constitutionally false" that "federal military installations" have traditionally been characterized by such First Amendment activity, it followed that Fort Dix was not a public forum.[78]

Underlying *Greer*'s approach was an emphatic repudiation of *Mosley*'s definition of a public forum. *Mosley* had held that government property becomes a public forum if it is "opened up to assembly or speaking." *Greer* specifically held, however, that "the fact that other civilian speakers and entertainers had sometimes been invited to appear at Fort Dix did not of itself serve to convert Fort Dix into a public forum."[79] *Greer* also rejected "the principle that whenever members of the public are permitted freely to visit a place owned or operated by the Government, then that place becomes a 'public forum' for purposes of the first amendment."[80]

In place of *Mosley*'s approach, *Greer* defined a public forum as government property which had "traditionally served" as a locus for First Amendment activities. Although this definition would within eight short years ascend to the canonical status of "a fundamental principle of First Amendment doctrine,"[81] the Court in *Greer* was silent as to its justification. Justice Roberts had focused on a tradition of public access because in the 1930s the government's claim to proprietary control could plausibly be grounded on common law property rights, and hence it made sense to express the limitations on that control in the language of adverse possession and public trust. But by 1976 this reasoning was untenable. In what would later become an unfortunate pattern, however, the Court in *Greer* made no effort to articulate any connection between its definition of a public forum and a theory of the First Amendment.

Greer's incorporation of Justice Roberts' approach in *Hague* fundamentally buried *Grayned*'s inquiry into whether a "manner of expression" is "basically incompatible with the normal activity of a particular place at a particular time." *Greer* shifted the focus of analysis away from the impact on a specific institution's ability to function if members of the public were granted a constitutional right of access for communicative purposes. In fact, *Greer* did not focus on particular institutions or property at all, but instead inquired into the general characteristics of generic kinds of government institutions and property. Thus *Greer* did not examine the particular attributes of Fort Dix, but rather inquired into the abstract properties of military installations. Its conclusion was therefore generic: a "military installation like Fort Dix" was not a public forum.[82]

In the Court's view the distinctive characteristics of Fort Dix were relevant only to the issue of whether the public areas of the fort were in fact part of a military installation. The Court formulated this issue as a question of whether the military had "abandoned any claim of special interest in regulating the distribution of unauthorized leaflets or the delivery of campaign speeches for political candidates within the confines of the military reservation."[83] For the Court the existence and enforcement of Regulations 210-26 and 210-27 were sufficient to negate any inference of abandonment.

Having concluded that the public areas of Fort Dix were not a public forum, the Court relied heavily on *Adderley* to describe the powers of the government in a nonpublic forum:

> The guarantees of the first amendment have never meant "that people who want to propagandize protests or views have a constitutional right to do so whenever and however and wherever they please." *Adderley v. Florida*, 385 U.S. 39, 48. "The State, no less than a private owner of property, has power to preserve the property under its control for the use to which it is lawfully dedicated." *Id.*, at 47.[84]

Greer was prepared to rely on *Adderley* for the proposition that the government could regulate speech within the public areas of the fort as though the government were "a private owner of property." This was reading *Adderley* broadly, as though the opinion rested upon a resurrection of the *Davis* syllogism, rather than upon a narrow interpretation of the government's power to regulate conduct. And *Greer* was prepared to ride the *Davis* syllogism for all it was worth. It held that in a nonpublic forum the government could flatly prohibit First Amendment activities, as illustrated by Regulation 210-26, which barred all "demonstrations, . . . political speeches, and similar activities." It held that in a nonpublic forum the government could subject speech to a system of prior restraint, as illustrated by Regulation 210-27, which banned the distribution of "any publication . . . without the prior written approval of the Adjutant General."[85] The Court also held that in a nonpublic forum the government could authorize discretionary suppression of speech, subject only to the limitation that in actually exercising its discretion the government did not act "irrationally, invidiously, or arbitrarily." "Invidious" discrimination was prohibited, but distinctions based upon content were not.[86]

Greer's resurrection of the major premise of the *Davis* syllogism was decisive for the future development of public forum doctrine, although the Court made no effort to explain or justify its use of the premise constitutionally. It simply assumed that in situations of proprietary control the government was empowered to abridge speech.

Although Justice Powell joined the Court's opinion, he also wrote a separate concurrence in which he argued that the issue before the Court should have been resolved by reference to *Grayned*'s "basic incompatibility" test. He recognized the tension between this test and the concept of the "public forum," noting that under the incompatibility test the First Amendment question could not be decided simply because "the area in which the right of expression is sought to be exercised [is] dedicated to some purpose other than use as a 'public forum.'" Powell concluded, however, that the regulations at issue met the *Grayned* test because there was a "functional and symbolic incompatibility" between the need for the military to remain a "specialized society separate from civilian society" and ordinary political electioneering.[87]

If Powell's opinion evinced unease with *Greer*'s use of public forum doctrine, Justice Brennan's dissent registered outright disgust. In fact Brennan virtually disowned the concept of the public forum, a concept which his own opinion in *Lehman* had been instrumental in advancing. "It bears special note," Brennan wrote, "that the notion of 'public forum' has never been the touchstone of public expression, for a contrary approach blinds the Court to any possible accommodation of first amendment values in this case."[88] Brennan reviewed precedents like *Edwards*, which he had once claimed established the existence of public forums,[89] and now concluded that the presence or absence of a public forum was irrelevant to their resolution:

> Those cases permitting public expression without characterizing the locale involved as a public forum, together with those cases recognizing the existence of a public forum, albeit qualifiedly, evidence the desirability of a flexible approach to determining when public expression should be protected. Realizing that the permissibility of a certain form of public expression at a given locale may differ depending on whether it is asked if the locale is a public forum or if the form of expression is compatible with the activities occurring at the locale, it becomes apparent that there is need for a flexible approach. Otherwise, with the rigid characterization of a given locale as not a public forum, there is the danger that certain forms of public speech at the locale may be suppressed, even though they are basically compatible with the activities otherwise occurring at the locale.[90]

Brennan had come to realize the profound tension between public forum doctrine and the Court's approach in *Grayned*. The distinction between public and nonpublic forums necessarily implied distinct regimes of First Amendment regulation. If the Court in *Conrad* had imposed unduly strict First Amendment rules on public forums, the Court in *Greer* had redressed the balance by virtually eliminating First Amendment restraints from the management of nonpublic forums. The result was that public and nonpublic forums were divided by a constitutional gulf of enormous and inexplicable proportions, a gulf that was inimical to the spirit and purpose of *Grayned*. The authority and irresistible attraction of *Hague*, an attraction that had even seduced Kalven, all but ensured that this gulf would run along the fault line of traditional usage, excluding most government facilities from the public forum category.

All this became evident to Brennan in *Greer*, and he responded by attempting to rehabilitate *Grayned*. He pointed to cases like Tinker v. Des Moines School District,[91] in which the Court had set aside school regulations barring speech without being in the least concerned with the question of whether the school was a "public forum." But by then it was too late; the public forum juggernaut had been launched.

The Birth and Death of the "Limited Public Forum"

The lasting legacy of *Greer* has been a public forum doctrine that sharply distinguishes public from nonpublic forums, and that cedes to the government virtual immunity from independent judicial scrutiny regarding the control of public access to the latter for communicative purposes. This immunity was founded upon *Greer*'s use of *Adderley* to reappropriate the major premise of the *Davis* syllogism, which gives to the government special prerogatives as a proprietor of its property. But since these prerogatives are indefensible to modern sensibilities, the Court has been torn between loyalty to the major premise of the *Davis* syllogism and repugnance at regulations of public access to nonpublic forums that are to contemporary eyes simply intolerable. The sad and fascinating story of the birth and death of the "limited public forum" is an account of how the Court has attempted ineffectually to limit these intolerable regulations and yet to leave intact to the greatest extent possible the immunity conferred by *Greer* upon government control of access to the nonpublic forum.

In order to appreciate the doctrinal tension which led to the creation of the limited public forum, it must be understood that underlying *Greer* were really two distinct inquiries: whether the government could deny access to its property to individuals desiring to use the property for the purpose of engaging in communicative activity, and whether the government could condition such access upon criteria that *discriminated* on the basis of persons or the content of speech.[92] *Greer* collapsed these two questions. It held that if the government property at issue was not a public forum, access could either be denied wholesale or else granted on a case-by-case basis, so long as such discriminatory access was not granted "irrationally, invidiously, or arbitrarily." Conversely, if the property was deemed a public forum, "there cannot be a blanket exclusion of first amendment activity."[93] Although *Greer* did not explicitly state that access to a public forum could not be granted in a discriminatory fashion, this was by 1976 already firmly accepted doctrine.[94] For *Greer*, then, the determination of the public forum status of government property simultaneously answered the questions of both access and equal access.

Greer's conceptualization of these questions flowed to a significant degree from the internal logic of the major premise of the *Davis* syllogism. It should be recalled that the premise invested government with the power to impose discriminatory criteria of access to the nonpublic forum *because* of its power to invoke the proprietary prerogative of closing off public access to the forum altogether. From this perspective the only possible constitutional distinction between nonpublic and public forums was that in the latter the government lacked this proprietary power to impose "a blanket exclusion of first amendment activity."[95] Thus from the major premise of the *Davis* syllogism it followed that in the nonpublic forum the government could both preclude access altogether and create conditions of discriminatory access, and that in the public forum it could not completely prohibit access. The rule against imposing discriminatory criteria of access to the public forum stemmed from the Court's decision in *Mosley* and *Conrad*.

The problem with collapsing questions of access and of equal access, however, is that it creates tools of analysis that for modern purposes are simply too crude to be of any use. This became apparent within six months of *Greer*. In December 1976 the Court decided City of Madison Joint School District No. 8 v. Wisconsin Employment Relations Commission,[96] in which the Wisconsin Employment Relations Commission had issued an order prohibiting a local school board from allowing employee teachers, other than those chosen by the union that was the exclusive collective bargaining representative of the district's teachers, to speak at the board's open meetings about matters subject to collective bargaining between the union and the board. Under *Greer*'s approach, the fundamental question in *Madison Joint School District* was whether the board's meetings should be categorized as a public forum. If so, then not only would the commission's order be unconstitutional, but in addition the board would be constitutionally prohibited from holding private meetings by completely excluding the public. If the board's meetings were classified as a nonpublic forum, on the other hand, then not only were private meetings permissible, but the board could also impose discriminatory criteria of access to its meetings and the commission's order would pass constitutional muster.

To modern eyes, however, it seems simply bizarre to bind together the question of the constitutionality of the commission's order and the question of the board's ability to hold private meetings. To the Court in *Madison Joint School District*, as to any contemporary constitutional observer, it made good sense to prohibit certain kinds of discriminatory access, even though access to the relevant forum might in some circumstances be altogether eliminated. Although this insight flatly contradicts the major premise of the *Davis* syllogism, the Court nevertheless, without so much as acknowledging the public forum doctrine just announced in *Greer*, held both that the board could "hold nonpublic sessions to transact business," and that the commission's order was unconstitutional because at public meetings the board "may not be required to discriminate between speakers on the basis of their employment, or the content of their speech."[97] In an opinion by Chief Justice Burger, the Court characterized the commission's order as "the antithesis of constitutional guarantees."[98]

Madison Joint School District carried radical implications for the doctrinal framework created by *Greer*, for it appeared to open up the nonpublic forum to kinds of constitutional scrutiny that were inconsistent with the major premise of the *Davis* syllogism. But the Court ignored these implications for five years, acting as if the dichotomous categories created by *Greer*'s appropriation of the premise were still unproblematic.[99] The tension between *Greer* and *Madison Joint School District* finally came to the surface in 1981, however, when the Court decided Widmar v. Vincent. In *Widmar*, the University of Missouri had made its facilities generally available for use by registered student groups, but had refused to do so for a registered student group seeking to use the facilities for religious worship and discussion. The Court used public forum doctrine to analyze the case. It held that by generally opening up its facilities to student groups, the University had created a "public forum," and that therefore it could not discriminatorily exclude student groups from the forum unless the exclusion was "necessary to serve a compelling state interest and . . . [was] narrowly drawn to achieve that end."[100]

In reaching this conclusion, the Court, in an opinion by Justice Powell, refused to be bound by the concept of the public forum set forth in *Greer*. Citing *Madison Joint School District*, the Court specifically held that the university could be prohibited from discriminating "even if it was not required to create the forum in the first place." The Court went even further and intimated in dicta that there could be distinctions among different kinds of public forums. It stated:

> A university differs in significant respects from public forums such as streets or parks or even municipal theatres. A university's mission is education, and decisions of this Court have never denied a university's authority to impose reasonable regulations compatible with that mission upon the use of its campus and facilities. We have not held, for example, that a campus must make all of its facilities equally available to students and nonstudents alike, or that a university must grant free access to all of its grounds or buildings.[101]

If *Madison Joint School District* had fractured the simple dichotomous categories created by *Greer*, the approach proposed by *Widmar* threatened to demolish them entirely. *Widmar* postulated a kind of public forum in which the government could exclude the public altogether, and it intimated that there was a spectrum of different kinds of government institutions as to which First Amendment questions of access and equal access would be individually determined depending upon an analysis of each institution's special "mission." In such a context *Greer*'s dichotomous categories of public and nonpublic forums would cease to have meaning, and independent judicial inquiry into institutional mission would threaten the claims of proprietary prerogative to be immune from judicial scrutiny. Justice Powell, who had been uncomfortable with *Greer*'s departure from *Grayned*, was apparently using his opinion in *Widmar* to undermine public forum doctrine from within, returning it to the case-by-case flexibility and independent judicial scrutiny characteristic of the *Grayned* approach.

But fourteen months later the Court forcefully checked any further movement in this direction by proposing the new concept of the "limited public forum." In Perry Education Association v. Perry Local Educators' Association, the Court, in an opinion by Justice White, decisively reaffirmed *Greer*'s categorical framework. *Perry* reviewed precedents, including *Widmar* and *Madison Joint School District*, and announced that for constitutional purposes there were now three distinct kinds of government property. There was, to begin with, the "traditional" or "quintessential" public forum, which consists of localities that had "by long tradition or by government fiat . . . been devoted to assembly and debate." Exemplary were the "streets and parks" identified by Hague v. CIO. In such public forums the government "may not prohibit all communicative activity," and it can "enforce a content-based exclusion" only if it can demonstrate that it is "necessary to serve a compelling state interest and that it is narrowly drawn to achieve that end."[102] The traditional public forum, in short, was the public forum described by *Greer*, in which the questions of access and equal access are tied together and each is constitutionally guaranteed.

At the other end of the spectrum was the nonpublic forum, which *Perry* also viewed in essentially the same light as *Greer*. Quoting from *Greer* and *Adderley*, *Perry* reaffirmed that in the nonpublic forum " 'the State, no less than a private owner of property, has power to preserve the property under its control for the use to which it is lawfully dedicated.' "[103] Hence for *Perry* "the right to make distinctions in access on the basis of subject matter and speaker identity" is "implicit in the concept of the nonpublic forum." Regulation of public access for communicative purposes to a nonpublic forum must only be "reasonable and not an effort to suppress expression merely because public officials oppose the speaker's view."[104]

Like *Greer*, therefore, *Perry* permitted the government to impose conditions on public access to the nonpublic forum that discriminated on the basis of content. But whereas *Greer* had drawn the line at "invidious" discrimination, *Perry* sought to prohibit "viewpoint discrimination."[105] Although the Court's opinion in *Perry* made no effort to clarify the distinction between "content" and "viewpoint" discrimination, Justice Brennan's dissent characterized "content neutrality" as pertaining to the government's ability to choose "the subjects that are appropriate for public discussion," whereas viewpoint neutrality relates to discrimination "among viewpoints on those subjects."[106]

Although *Perry*'s accounts of the nonpublic and traditional public forums were minor variations of the categories proposed by *Greer*, *Perry* still had to account for the circumstances encountered by the Court in cases like *Widmar* and *Madison Joint School District*. These circumstances did not fit easily into the dichotomous categories of *Greer*, and *Perry* attempted to encompass them within a category creating yet a third kind of government property, which it called a "limited public forum."[107] In a formulation echoing that of *Mosley*, *Perry* held that a limited public forum is created when the "State has opened" public property "for use by the public as a place for expressive activity."[108] But whereas the government cannot preclude public access to a traditional public forum,[109] *Perry* was explicit that the government is required neither to create nor to maintain public access to a limited public forum.[110] So long as the state does permit access, however, it "is bound by the same standards as apply in a traditional public forum. Reasonable time, place, and manner regulations are permissible, and a content-based prohibition must be narrowly drawn to effectuate a compelling state interest."[111]

On the surface, the concept of the limited public forum appeared to be an attempt to respond to the kinds of anomalous circumstances that could not be analyzed in the coarse terms offered by *Greer*'s dichotomous categories. It seemed to rest on the simple maneuver of disaggregating the questions of access and equal access. Beneath the surface, however, the concept ruptured the connections between public forum doctrine and the major premise of the *Davis* syllogism. The logic underlying the premise was that the government could impose discriminatory criteria of access to its property if (and because) it could completely shut off such access. In the limited public forum, however, the government can completely block public access, and yet it is constitutionally prohibited from imposing discriminatory criteria of access. But if the Constitution prohibits this discrimination, why does it not also prohibit the government from imposing discriminatory criteria of access to the nonpublic forum? If the prerogatives of proprietary control are not respected in the limited public forum, why should they be respected in the nonpublic forum?

Perry contains no answers to these questions. What is striking about the opinion, however, is its obvious determination to preserve undiminished the government's freedom to regulate public access to its proprietary property, even at the price of obvious and fundamental doctrinal incoherence. This determination is evident both in the First Amendment rules that *Perry* chooses to impose on the limited public forum, and in the manner in which *Perry* chooses to distinguish limited from nonpublic forums.

Consider, first, *Perry*'s puzzling assertion that the government's ability to regulate public access to the limited public forum is "bound by the same standards as apply in a traditional public forum." The assertion is manifestly contrary to the very precedents used by *Perry* to create the concept of the limited public forum. In *Madison Joint School District*, for example, the Court had specifically held that the school board could limit public discussion to certain subjects, and in *Widmar* the Court had permitted the university to limit its facilities to one class of speakers, namely students. In a traditional public forum, however, as *Perry* was the first to admit, "the State must demonstrate compelling reasons for restricting access to a single class of speakers, a single viewpoint, or a single subject."[112] Neither *Widmar* nor *Madison Joint School District* was willing to accept the imposition of such a harsh First Amendment standard. And it appears that *Perry* itself had difficulties with the standard, for in a strange footnote it asserted that "a public forum may be created for a limited purpose such as use by certain groups . . . or for the discussion of certain subjects."[113]

In the context of the doctrinal structure created by *Perry*, the footnote eviscerates the rule that in regulating public access to the limited public forum the government is bound by the same First Amendment standards as bind the government's ability to regulate access to the traditional public forum. For *Perry* imposes no First Amendment constraints whatever on the government's ability to build discriminatory criteria into the very definition or purpose of the limited public forum, and thus as a practical matter the government remains as free to limit public access to a limited public forum as to a nonpublic forum. This can be seen in the facts of the *Perry* case itself. The Metropolitan School District of Perry Township had made an interschool mail system available to the union that was the exclusive bargaining agent of the district's teachers (PEA), but not to a rival union (PLEA). The district had granted mail system access to outside groups like the Cub Scouts, the YMCA, and other civic and church organizations. The Court ultimately ruled that the system was a nonpublic forum and that PLEA's exclusion was "reasonable." But the Court went out of its way to conclude that even if it were assumed *arguendo* that the access granted to the system had "opened it up" into a limited public forum, "the constitutional right of access would in any event extend only to other entities of similar character":

> While the school mail facilities thus might be a forum generally open for use by the Girl Scouts, the local boys' club, and other organizations that engage in activities of interest and educational relevance to students, they would not as a consequence be open to an organization such as PLEA, which is concerned with the terms and conditions of teacher employment.[114]

In the end, therefore, it made no difference to the outcome of the case whether the mail facilities were categorized as a limited or a nonpublic forum. In either case the school system remained free to build discriminatory criteria of access into the very definition of its mail system. The doctrinal structure created by *Perry* ultimately renders illusory the harsh First Amendment constraints formally made applicable to the limited public forum. In *Widmar* and *Madison Joint School District*, on the other hand, less stringent First Amendment constraints were used so as actually to limit the government's freedom to control access to the nonpublic forum.

The chimerical quality of the limited public forum is also evident in the manner by which *Perry* chooses to distinguish, or rather not to distinguish, limited public forums from nonpublic forums. It had been black letter law since *Greer* that "a place owned or operated by the Government" does not become "a 'public forum' for purposes of the first amendment" simply because "members of the public are permitted freely to visit" it.[115] The origin of the rule lay in *Greer*'s forceful rejection of the view expressed in *Mosley* that once the government had "opened up" its property for expressive use by the public, it was thereafter disabled from regulating that use by imposing distinctions between persons and subjects. *Greer* had itself specifically held that the mere fact that "civilian speakers and entertainers had sometimes been invited to appear at Fort Dix did not of itself serve to convert Fort Dix into a public forum."[116] In subsequent cases the Court adamantly reiterated this rule,[117] and *Perry* went out of its way to reaffirm it, explicitly holding that the fact that the school district had provided "selective access" to its mail facilities to certain outside organizations like the YMCA and the Cub Scouts "does not transform government property into a public forum."[118]

The problem, of course, is that the rule lies squarely athwart *Perry*'s own definition of a limited public forum, which is keyed primarily to the opening up of government property to the public for expressive use. According to *Perry* both limited and nonpublic forums are characterized by a "selective" or discriminatory degree of access to proprietary government property. The question, then, is what criteria distinguish one from the other. *Perry* offers no such criteria; it gives no hint as to how the "opening up" that creates a limited public forum differs from the "opening up" that leaves a forum nonpublic.[119] The unavoidable inference is that *Perry* chose to let the distinction remain ambiguous so as to leave the government ample room to continue to characterize its property as a nonpublic forum.

The most plausible interpretation of *Perry*, then, is that the Court had come to recognize the inadequacy of *Greer*'s dichotomous categories, but that it was unprepared to modify them in any way that would seriously undermine the government's freedom to control public access to property that was not a traditional public forum. Under these circumstances the concept of the limited public forum was doomed from the start. The coup de grâce was delivered in 1985 when the Court in Cornelius v. NAACP Legal Defense & Education Fund held that the distinction between limited public and nonpublic forums turns on the government's intent in opening up the forum:

> The government does not create a public forum by inaction or by permitting limited discourse, but only by intentionally opening a nontraditional forum for public discourse. [*Perry Education Ass'n v. Perry Local Educator's Ass'n.*, 460 U.S. at 46]. Accordingly, the Court has looked to the policy and practice of the government to ascertain whether it intended to designate a place not traditionally open to assembly and debate as a public forum. [460 U.S. at 47]. The Court has also examined the nature of the property and its compatibility with expressive activity to discern the government's intent.[120]

Cornelius' focus on intent solved a good many problems. It explained why the government did not have to create the limited public forum in the first place, and why it could shut it down at will. It rendered intelligible the fact that the government could restrict a limited public forum to particular subjects or speakers. Most important, however, is that the focus on intent had the virtue of candor, for it tactfully withdrew the concept of the limited public forum as a meaningful category of constitutional analysis. If a limited public forum is neither more nor less than what the government intends it to be, then a First Amendment right of access to the forum is nothing more than the claim that the government should be required to do what it already intends to do in any event.

Cornelius shrinks the limited public forum to such insignificance that it is difficult to imagine how a plaintiff could ever successfully prosecute a lawsuit to gain access to such a forum.[121] If the reach of the forum is determined by the intent of the government, and if the exclusion of the plaintiff is the best evidence of that intent, then the plaintiff loses in every case. There is only one way out of this vicious circle, and it is not very satisfactory. It would require the Court to distinguish between the intent to include the class of speakers or subjects of which the plaintiff is the representative, and the intent to exclude the plaintiff. One problem with this distinction is that it is precious and in practice unworkable. Another problem is that it is inconsistent with the very precedents which had initially prompted *Perry* to propose the concept of the limited public forum. In *Madison Joint School District*, the commission's order explicitly intended to exclude a class of school employees from speaking about matters that were subject to collective bargaining, and yet the Court found in effect that such an intent was unconstitutional. In *Widmar*, the university explicitly intended to exclude the class of students seeking to use campus facilities for religious purposes, and yet the Court found that intent to be unconstitutional.

The central insight of both *Widmar* and *Madison Joint School District* was that even if government property were a nontraditional public forum, objective circumstances respecting the use of the property can have serious constitutional consequences for a First Amendment right of access, government intent notwithstanding. *Cornelius* flatly rejected this insight, and in the process essentially transformed the limited public forum into an empty category. As a result, the Court is now left with a public forum doctrine that ties together questions of access and equal access, and that offers no principles of review with respect to the large number of circumstances in which discriminatory access is constitutionally suspect although the access need never have originally been granted. In short, the Court has taken a long step backward toward the dichotomous framework of *Greer*.

The Present Condition of Public Forum Doctrine

Public forum doctrine has for this reason come to revolve with increasing intensity around the line separating the traditional public forum from the nonpublic forum. The placement and rationale of that line is therefore a matter of some importance, but the Court appears to have given it little or no consideration. *Cornelius* is typical when it defines traditional public forums as "those places which 'by long tradition or by government fiat have been devoted to assembly and debate.' "[122]

The definition, however, will simply not do. The reference to "government fiat" is ill considered. It echoes *Cornelius'* own definition of a limited public forum or a public forum by designation,[123] and implies that if government fiat can create a traditional public forum, then it can also terminate it. This would dissolve the traditional public forum into the same vicious circle as that which dissolved the limited public forum. At least since *Greer*, however, the Court has been continuously clear that the state, whatever its intent, cannot cut off access to the traditional public forum by "a blanket exclusion of first amendment activity."

The reference to "long tradition," by contrast, directly continues a line of analysis that stems back to *Greer*, and before that to *Hague*. The standard seems to be that if government property has "immemorially been held in trust for the use of the public and, time out of mind, . . . been used for purposes of assembly, communicating thoughts between citizens, and discussing public questions,"[124] then the property should be deemed a traditional public forum.

The question is why such a tradition should acquire constitutional immunity from alteration by the state. It would seem insufficient to answer this question simply by reference to the historical fact of the tradition, since it is the peculiar constitutional status of this fact which needs to be explained. For *Hague*, of course, the passage of time signified a change in ownership, so that a long tradition of public usage meant that the government could no longer claim to be the proprietor of the property in question. Thus the presence of tradition was meaningful because of the minor premise of the *Davis* syllogism. But in our own time, when the major premise of that syllogism carries such scant constitutional weight, this meaning is largely beside the point.[125] We do not now view the technicalities of property ownership as determinative.[126] The Court moved decisively away from these technicalities in *Greer* when it determined the nonpublic forum status of Fort Dix by focusing on the generic characteristics of military installations, rather than on technical issues of easement or adverse possession that were tied to the particular circumstances of the fort.[127]

The question therefore remains as to why a tradition of public usage should provide the point of distinction between public and nonpublic forums. Unless the Court can articulate why tradition matters,[128] contemporary doctrine will be left to focus dully on the brute passage of historical time. This is a recipe for crude and arbitrary results.[129] Airports, railroad terminals, and parks, for example, share many characteristics that are seemingly pertinent to the assessment of traditional public forum status,[130] but they differ in chronological age and thus have correspondingly different "traditions." If the Court were to differentiate among these forums on this basis alone, the result, as the Court recently perceived in a related context, would constitute "linedrawing of the most arbitrary sort."[131] Even if the Court's present emphasis on tradition is accepted, therefore, it remains unfounded and incomplete.

The line dividing public and nonpublic forums, however arbitrary, marks the boundary between deeply divergent regimes of constitutional regulation. With respect to the traditional public forum, which the Court has repeatedly stressed "occupies a special position in terms of first amendment protection,"[132] the Court has developed a scheme of constitutional rules that it says applies specifically "in such places":

> The government may enforce reasonable time, place, and manner regulations as long as the restrictions "are content-neutral, are narrowly tailored to serve a significant government interest, and leave open ample alternative channels of communication." Additional restrictions such as an absolute prohibition on a particular type of expression will be upheld only if narrowly drawn to accomplish a compelling governmental interest.[133]

Despite the Court's tendency to speak of traditional public forums as unique locations, the constitutional rules promulgated by the Court for their governance are identical to the First Amendment rules which it has generally imposed on government efforts to regulate speech. The Court has said that government action ranging from zoning ordinances to the prohibition of certain kinds of insertions in public utility billing envelopes can be justified as time, place, and manner regulations.[134] And the Court has also specifically held that any government restriction on "the speech of a private person" can be "sustained" if "the government can show that the regulation is a precisely drawn means of serving a compelling state interest."[135]

During the 1930s and 1940s the Court did not view public streets and parks as constitutionally unique, but rather concluded that speech in such areas was generally a form of public discourse, and hence that government regulation of such speech ought to be subject to the same kind of constitutional review as government regulation of public discourse generally. Decisions of the modern Court have been drawn willy-nilly toward a similar conclusion, and the modern Court's constant efforts to locate and apply special First Amendment rules to the public forum have, with one exception, met with continual frustration. The exception in fact aptly illustrates the misguided nature of the Court's efforts, for it is analytically indefensible.

The exception, continually reiterated since *Greer*, is the rule that there cannot be a blanket exclusion of First Amendment activities from a public forum.[136] In United States v. Grace, the Court said that "destruction of public forum status" is "presumptively impermissible." This rule attempts to establish "the special position in terms of first amendment protection" of the public forum by equating restrictions on access with restrictions on speech.[137] But this equation is false, for it fails to distinguish between the regulation of expression and the regulation of conduct, and hence cannot distinguish between an ordinance banning all political demonstrations and an ordinance authorizing the construction of a nonpublic forum office building on land that previously underlay a public street. It simply makes no sense to say that the latter is "presumptively impermissible," even if it results in a blanket exclusion of First Amendment activities in what was previously a public forum. Ordinary principles of First Amendment jurisprudence would have no special difficulty in evaluating the differential impact of these two ordinances on constitutional rights. But in its eagerness to establish some special and ultimately illusory First Amendment status for the public forum, the Court has brushed aside these principles, and as a consequence has backed itself into an untenable position.

If the First Amendment standards imposed on the public forum have tended to be unduly strict, those imposed on the nonpublic forum have, to the contrary, tended to be unduly lax. Putting to one side for the moment the prohibition on viewpoint discrimination, government restrictions on access to the nonpublic forum need only be "reasonable in light of the purpose served by the forum."[138] The Court has never precisely defined what it means by this "reasonableness" standard, but at a minimum it is clear that it is designed to provide the government the utmost flexibility in managing the nonpublic forum. As the Court said in *Cornelius*, the "Government, as an employer, must have wide discretion and control over the management of its personnel and internal affairs."[139]

Language like this prompted Justice Blackmun, in his dissent in *Cornelius*, to denigrate the "reasonableness" standard as "nothing more than a rational-basis requirement,"[140] which is the genuinely toothless restraint that the due process clause and the equal protection clause impose on all government action.[141] If Justice Blackmun is correct, then the reasonableness standard is simply a doctrinal restatement of the major premise of the *Davis* syllogism. If the standard creates no constitutional restrictions that are not already generally imposed on the state by the due process and equal protection clauses, then the standard offers no additional First Amendment protection for speech. If the major premise of the *Davis* syllogism is incorrect, however, then the fact that the government is regulating speech is constitutionally pertinent, and the "reasonable-ness" standard should not be reduced to a rational basis test.

The latter conclusion seems to me inescapable.[142] The Fourteenth Amendment imposes constitutional restrictions upon the "States" as such, not upon the states acting in some capacities and not others. And of course the federal government is in all of its capacities the creation of and therefore bound by the provisions of the Constitution, including the First Amendment. Almost twenty years ago a noted commentator could con-clude that "the point is now plain: the state is the state, bound by uniform constitutional constraints regardless of the capacity in which it purports to act."[143] Thus the fact that the government is acting as an employer or a proprietor will not exempt it from the distinct requirements of the equal protection clause,[144] the due process clause,[145] the commerce clause,[146] or the privileges and immunities clause of Article IV.[147] And, as the Court has plainly recognized in other contexts, there is no good reason why that fact should exempt the government from the requirements of the First Amendment.[148] The Court has in effect acknowledged the unavoidable logic of this position by imposing a First Amendment prohibition on viewpoint discrimination even upon the government acting in its propri-etary capacity.

While no one on the modern Court has explicitly defended the extreme perspective associated with the major premise of the *Davis* syllogism, there has been support for the milder position that "the role of govern-ment as sovereign is subject to more stringent limitations than is the role of government as employer, property owner, or educator."[149] This po-sition, understood generously, holds that although the government acting in a proprietary capacity is subject to the constraints of the First Amend-ment, these restraints should be substantively interpreted with the needs of a government proprietor in mind.[150] The consequence of such a po-sition would be a reasonableness standard which identified and enforced pertinent First Amendment concerns, but which tailored such concerns to the context of proprietary government action.

As a matter of simple internal consistency, this is the kind of reason-ableness standard which the Court must have meant to adopt in *Perry*. But as such the standard is a failure. It identifies neither the particular pro-prietary prerogatives that need to be protected nor the specific First Amendment concerns by which the exercise of these prerogatives are to be evaluated. For all practical purposes, public forum doctrine is presently a blank check for government control of public access to the nonpublic forum for communicative purposes.[151] To date, the Court has been willing to hold that the First Amendment prohibits restrictions on such access only if such restrictions can be justified by "no conceivable governmental interest."[152]

Toward a Reformulation of Public Forum Doctrine

When Melville Nimmer came to analyze public forum doctrine, he saw within it two competing lines of cases. The first, which is associated with the public forum theory that has triumphed in the Court's recent opinions, "assumes that whether or not publicly owned premises are to be regarded as 'public forums' and hence open to the public for communication purposes turns upon factors divorced from the proposed speech itself." The second line of cases, which springs from *Grayned*, "is not concerned with whether the public premises are dedicated to uses which would include the speech activities in issue. Instead, the question put is whether the speech activities would be incompatible with the use to which the premises are dedicated or primarily devoted."[153] What has truly bewildered most commentators about modern public forum doctrine is that the Court has continually repudiated the second line of cases, despite what commentators view as its obvious superiority.[154]

The attraction of *Grayned* is not difficult to appreciate. Its logic begins from the constitutionally congenial premise that the state should not suppress speech unless there is a good reason to do so. The reason for discouraging speech on government property is that it may interfere with the use of that property. If such interference occurs, the state may justifiably prohibit speech; conversely, the absence of interference indicates that the state may lack sufficient grounds to abridge speech. The doctrine proposed by *Grayned* thus invites courts to focus precisely on the relationship between speech and the reasons for its regulation, and it is designed to maximize the speech which the government is constitutionally required to tolerate, consistent with the appropriate and needful use of its property. This design flows naturally from the First Amendment's central objective of ensuring "uninhibited, robust, and wide-open" public debate.[155]

Contemporary public forum doctrine, on the other hand, begins from the constitutionally questionable premise that the government is in effect constitutionally unconstrained in its use of certain kinds of state property. It thus does not focus on speech and the justifications for its suppression, but rather on the kind of government property at issue. If the property does not bear a tradition of public usage for expressive activity, First Amendment rights can be effectively prohibited, even if the exercise of these rights would be compatible with the ordinary use of the property. The doctrine thus appears to invite the superfluous suppression of speech.

Why, then, has the Court stood by public forum doctrine with such formidable determination? The history of public forum doctrine provides a clue. In contrast to *Grayned*, public forum doctrine divides government property into distinct schemes of First Amendment regulation. From the moment of the doctrine's first contemporary appearance in *Greer*, the Court has consistently used it to demarcate a class of government property in which the First Amendment claims of the public are radically devalued and immune from independent judicial scrutiny. The Court has relentlessly pursued this goal despite such obstacles as the threat of obvious doctrinal incoherence and the absence of underlying constitutional justification.

This history strongly suggests that the motivation and conceptual core of contemporary public forum doctrine has been the preservation of this strange realm of First Amendment devaluation, so that, paradoxically, the doctrine now functions primarily to define and protect nonpublic forums. If the doctrine is to be supported by a defensible constitutional theory, therefore, it must be one capable of explaining and justifying this function. In this section I will sketch the outline of such a theory and then test its implications against the actual pattern of the Court's public forum decisions. The theory will in turn lead to a radical reformulation of the object and structure of public forum doctrine.

The Management of Speech within Government Institutions

The devaluation of First Amendment rights characteristic of the nonpublic forum cases is strikingly similar to that developed by the Court in a closely related line of cases dealing with the First Amendment claims of individuals who are members of a government institution.[156] In these cases the Court has concluded that First Amendment claims must be subordinated to the authority necessary to administer state organizations.

The constitutional rationale for this conclusion is straightforward. Government institutions, like most organizations, have a "hierarchy of formal authority" by which resources are coordinated and manipulated so as to achieve institutional ends.[157] This authority extends to persons as well as to things, and it extends to the speech of persons as well as to their actions.[158] The exercise of this authority is inconsistent with what most judges and scholars would recognize as First Amendment rights. This can be seen by analyzing a simple case, one that must occur on a daily basis throughout the country. In a government bureaucracy an official says to her subordinate, "Tomorrow is the big staff meeting on project X. I want you to draft a position paper taking position A, and I want you to have it on my desk first thing tomorrow morning for review. After I make the changes I think necessary, I want you to attend the staff meeting and present the paper."

This common situation is a First Amendment nightmare. The subordinate's presentation to the staff meeting is expression that is subject to the prior restraint of his superior, and such prior restraints are "the most serious and the least tolerable infringement on first amendment rights."[159] The superior is able to dictate whether her subordinate will take position A rather than position B, and hence to subject her subordinate's speech to viewpoint discrimination, despite the fundamental constitutional principle that "the first amendment forbids the government to regulate speech in ways that favor some viewpoints or ideas at the expense of others."[160] And the subordinate's speech is subject to the discretionary control of his superior, despite the "long line" of decisions striking down as "unconstitutional censorship" those statutes making the exercise of First Amendment rights "contingent" upon the "discretion" of a public official.[161]

It is clear, therefore, that if the most common forms of organizational authority are to withstand constitutional scrutiny, they must be analyzed in a very different fashion from what is appropriate when government regulates the speech of a member of the general public. The superior's control over the speech of her subordinate is somehow constitutionally different from the mayor's control over speech in the Boston Common. It is tempting to wish away this constitutional anomaly by arguing that the subordinate has "waived" his First Amendment rights by "consenting" to the terms and conditions of government employment. But this argument will not offer a satisfactory explanation of the way that speech is ordinarily managed within government institutions. First, it is well established that " 'courts indulge every reasonable presumption against waiver' of fundamental constitutional rights and . . . we 'do not presume acquiescence in the loss of fundamental rights.' "[162] A government employee may be taken to have consented to employment, but not, except in some patently fictional sense, to every violation of constitutional rights that a government employer may perpetuate. Second, waiver must be voluntary, but the constant threat of loss of employment and other sanctions within an organizational context makes deeply problematic any determination that constitutional rights have been voluntarily waived.

Third, and most important, the government's need to manage speech within its institutions is the same whether or not an institution's members have voluntarily agreed to participate within it. Government institutions, like most organizations, can be viewed as "formally established for the explicit purpose of achieving certain goals."[163] The goal of the school system is education; the goal of the judicial system is the just and efficient adjudication of cases and controversies; and so on. Managerial authority over speech is necessary for an institution to achieve these goals. A government institution's interest in internally regulating speech is therefore its interest in the attainment of the very purposes for which it has been established, and this interest remains the same whether or not its members consent to the exercise of government authority.

As a result, the Court has in fact determined the constitutional validity of a government institution's internal regulation of speech not by referring to concepts of waiver, but rather by asking whether the regulation is necessary in order to achieve the institution's legitimate objectives. Prisoners, for example, do not voluntarily agree to enter confinement, yet the Court has explicitly held that their First Amendment rights are subordinate to the attainment of "the legitimate penological objectives of the corrections system."[164] Elementary and high school students are compelled to attend school, yet the Court has held that student speech, "in class or out of it, which for any reason—whether it stems from time, place, or type of behavior—materially disrupts classwork or involves substantial disorder or invasion of the rights of others is, of course, not immunized by the constitutional guarantee of freedom of speech."[165] Military draftees are forced to enter the armed forces, and yet the Court has held that "speech likely to interfere with . . . vital prerequisites for military effectiveness . . . can be excluded from a military base."[166] Government employees, on the other hand, voluntarily agree to work for the government, and yet the Court has not used the doctrine of waiver to dismiss employee claims of First Amendment freedom but has instead analyzed these claims on their merits.[167] The Court has held that employee speech may be regulated so as to promote "the efficiency of the public services [the government] performs through its employees."[168]

The Court has also held that the fair and expeditious administration of the judicial system justifies subjecting the pretrial speech of litigants to prior restraints issued at the discretion of a trial judge, and that such judicial authority extends equally to plaintiffs, who have voluntarily submitted to a court's jurisdiction, and to defendants, who have not.[169]

The constitutional question in each case is whether the authority to regulate speech is necessary for the achievement of legitimate institutional objectives. This question, however, has rather subtle implications for the concept of independent judicial review. Suppose, in the bureaucratic example I have sketched, that the subordinate complains in court that he has a First Amendment right to present at the staff meeting position B, which he personally believes in, instead of position A, which his superior has required him to present. In assessing his claim, the court will have to evaluate two distinct kinds of potential damage to the bureaucracy. The first concerns the possible negative impact of presenting position B instead of A. This damage depends upon the consequences of the particular speech at issue; it turns on whether position B or the manner of its presentation is incompatible with the attainment of institutional goals.

The second kind of potential damage, however, is quite different. It concerns the possible undermining of the superior's managerial authority should the court countermand her directive. It is evident that if the court were to engage in the practice of second-guessing her managerial authority regarding speech, that authority would *pro tanto* diminish. The potential for this kind of damage implies that before engaging in judicial review a court must determine whether such review would itself diminish the authority at issue to such an extent as to impair the ability of the bureaucracy to attain its legitimate ends. The decision to withhold independent judicial scrutiny, and hence to defer to the judgment of institutional authorities, does not turn at all upon the nature or circumstances of the particular speech at issue, but rather turns upon the relationship between the practice of judicial review and the nature of the managerial authority at issue.

The question of judicial deference can be illustrated by comparing two Supreme Court decisions. In Brown v. Glines, the Court upheld a military regulation prohibiting Air Force members from circulating petitions on military bases without prior approval of their commanders. The commanders were empowered to censor any petition they felt would create "a clear danger to the loyalty, discipline, or morale" of their troops. The

Court held that "speech likely to interfere with . . . vital prerequisites for military effectiveness . . . can be excluded from a military base."[170] But the Court did not choose to scrutinize whether the plaintiff's particular petition would interfere with the prerequisites for military effectiveness; instead it focused on the potential damage to military authority that would occur if courts were to engage in the practice of independently reviewing military commands. The Court asserted that the "military mission" requires the maintenance of a form of authority founded on "instinctive obedience," and the Court therefore held that "the rights of military men must yield somewhat 'to meet certain overriding demands of discipline and duty . . .' " These demands are incompatible with the practice of independent judicial review "because the right to command and the duty to obey ordinarily must go unquestioned."[171] Hence the Court concluded that the nature of military authority requires that courts as a general matter defer to the judgment of military officials on the question of whether particular petitions would adversely affect the loyalty, discipline, or morale of the troops. The Court was prepared to review that authority only in the exceptional circumstance when it could with plausibility be claimed that it had been exercised "irrationally, invidiously, or arbitrarily."[172]

In Tinker v. Des Moines Independent Community School District, on the other hand, the Court struck down a school regulation prohibiting the wearing of black arm bands to protest the Vietnam War. The Court determined that the legitimate end of the school system is not the creation of students who are "closed-circuit recipients of only that which the State chooses to communicate," but rather the inculcation of "the independence and vigor of Americans who grow up and live in this relatively permissive, often disputatious, society." The attainment of this end did not, in the circumstances presented by the case, justify the maintenance of a pervasive and unquestioned form of authority. The Court held that "in our systems, state-operated schools may not be enclaves of totalitarianism. School officials do not possess absolute authority over their students." School officials, unlike military commanders, cannot prohibit expression on the basis of an "undifferentiated fear or apprehension of disturbance," but can only act on the basis of "facts which might reasonably have led [them] to forecast substantial disruption of or material interference with school activities."[173]

The constitutional standard adopted by the Court required the school to present evidence sufficient to convince a judge that plaintiffs' speech was incompatible with the educational process. In effect, then, the Court in *Tinker* held that the constitutionality of the school's regulation would be determined by independent judicial review of whether the regulation was necessary for the attainment of the school's educational objectives. The harm which such judicial review might cause to the general authority structure of the school did not justify deference to school officials, for the nature of educational authority was perceived as quite different from that of military authority. Because in *Tinker* there was no evidence that the wearing of arm bands would potentially disrupt legitimate school activities, or that plaintiffs' speech had actually disrupted these activities, the Court found the school regulation unconstitutional.

By focusing on the relationship between plaintiffs' arm bands and the school environment, *Tinker* pursued a form of analysis essentially congruent with that of *Grayned*. It asked whether the potential consequences of plaintiffs' proposed speech were incompatible with the normal functioning of the school, and it maintained that this question should be answered through independent judicial inquiry. *Glines*, on the other hand, concentrated on the generic characteristics of military authority and held that these characteristics justified the Court in generally deferring to the judgment of military officials on the question of whether particular speech was incompatible with the attainment of military objectives. As a result *Glines* created a special realm, similar to that delineated in the Court's nonpublic forum decisions, in which First Amendment rights were radically devalued. In *Glines* this realm was founded not upon the major premise of the *Davis* syllogism or any other such indefensible constitutional notion, but rather upon the logic of judicial deference.

Public Forum Doctrine and the Management of Speech within Government Institutions

This analysis suggests that First Amendment doctrine distinguishes between speech within government organizations and general public discourse. Such a distinction was in fact recognized long ago by Immanuel Kant, who observed

> Many affairs which are conducted in the interest of the community require a certain mechanism through which some members of the community must passively conduct themselves with an artificial unanimity, so that the government may direct them to public ends, or at least

prevent them from destroying those ends. Here argument is certainly not allowed—one must obey. But so far as a part of the mechanism regards himself at the same time as a member of the whole community or of a society of world citizens ... he can certainly argue without hurting the affairs for which he is in part responsible as a passive member. Thus it would be ruinous for an officer in service to debate about the suitability or utility of a command given to him by his superior; he must obey. But the right to make remarks on errors in the military service and to lay them before the public for judgment cannot equitably be refused him as a scholar.[174]

Elaborating Kant's insight into an explicit constitutional theory, we might say that government is invested with a special form of authority, which I shall call "management," when administering the "mechanism" of its own institutions. Managerial authority is controlled by First Amendment rules different from those that control the exercise of the authority used by the state when it acts to govern the general public. For convenience, I shall call the latter kind of authority "governance."[175] In situations of governance the state is bound by what we have come to regard as ordinary principles of First Amendment jurisprudence. These principles are complex and variegated. The general public engages in multiple forms of speech, including public discourse and other kinds of communication. The primary purpose of a theory of managerial authority is to carve out of this general jurisprudence a distinct and demarcated realm in which state regulation of speech can conform to the instrumental logic characteristic of organizations. When it exercises the authority of management, the state can constitutionally control speech so as to facilitate the institutional attainment of organizational ends. This instrumental logic even extends so far as to justify courts' deferring to the judgment of institutional officials respecting the need to manage speech, if such deference is itself thought necessary for the achievement of institutional goals.

   This theory of managerial authority is quite useful in explaining modern public forum doctrine. Not only does it illuminate the actual pattern of the Court's public forum doctrine decisions, but it also provides for them a coherent constitutional justification.

The Theory of Managerial Authority and Public Forum Doctrine

Public forum doctrine distinguishes between public and nonpublic forums, and it holds that each is governed by a distinct regime of First

Amendment rules. Although the Court has struggled to define an especially protected First Amendment status for the public forum, its efforts
have proved unsuccessful, and the Court's decisions have moved inevitably toward the conclusion that the government's actions within the public
forum are simply subject to the same First Amendment restraints as are
government actions generally. We can thus characterize government authority over the public forum as a matter of governance.

The Court's views concerning the kind of authority exercised by the
government over nonpublic forums, however, have been a good deal
murkier. Although the Court has said that the authority of government
institutions to control access by members of the general public to internal
organizational resources must be "reasonable in light of the purpose
served by the forum"[176] and so has invested this authority with the same
instrumental logic as that which characterizes managerial authority, it has
in fact shown no inclination to take this logic seriously. Under the spell
of the major premise of the *Davis* syllogism, the Court has instead tended
to view the government's discretion in controlling public access to the
nonpublic forum as a matter of inherent power. The problem with the
Court's view, of course, is that no one has yet been able to articulate a
defensible constitutional justification for this power.

Decisions like *Glines*, however, indicate that the persistently comprehensive control of speech in nonpublic forums which the Court has used
public forum doctrine to protect can best be explained and justified in
terms of the logic of management and judicial deference. These decisions
suggest that the Court has in its nonpublic forum cases been concerned
all along not with the attribution of substantive power, but rather with the
protection of managerial authority from the potentially deleterious effects
of judicial review. Reconceptualizing the nonpublic forum cases in terms
of the underlying theory of *Glines* would have the advantage of explicitly
orienting the Court toward the very values which have in fact animated it
during the history of public forum doctrine, thus permitting the Court to
begin to analyze and express those values in a principled manner. Public
forum doctrine would be released from the disastrous influence of the
major premise of the *Davis* syllogism, and the Court's nonpublic forum
cases and its decisions dealing with the internal management of speech
would be brought together under a single and defensible doctrinal framework.

Reconceptualizing the nonpublic forum cases in terms of the logic of
Glines would also explain why the Court has repeatedly rejected what has

appeared to commentators to be the ineluctable logic of *Grayned*. *Grayned*'s "incompatibility" test takes into account only the specific harm incident to a plaintiff's proposed speech; it does not recognize the generic damage to managerial authority flowing from the very process of independent judicial review of institutional decision-making. By focusing on this damage, the Court can begin explicitly and systematically to explore the conditions under which judicial deference is and is not appropriate. The Court's present focus "on the character of the property at issue"[177] is a theoretical dead end, because there is no satisfactory theory connecting the classification of government property with the exercise of First Amendment rights. But there is great potential for a rich and principled jurisprudence if the Court were to focus instead on the relationship between judicial review and the functioning of institutional authority.

To conceive the issue in this way, for example, is to see at once that the very decisions which led *Perry* to formulate the concept of the limited public forum involve the exercise of managerial authority in contexts in which the Court believed that judicial deference was inappropriate. In this sense the limited public forum cases display a strong analogy to the structure of *Tinker*. The analogy is clear in Madison Joint School District No. 8 v. Wisconsin Employment Relations Commission.[178] The decision recognized that a school board is invested with a different kind of authority in running an open school board meeting from what is involved in governing the general public. Although ordinary First Amendment principles would plainly prohibit the state from imposing an agenda on public discussion,[179] *Madison Joint School District* understood that a board must retain the flexible power to fix agendas for open school board meetings.[180]

In assessing the constitutional limitations of the board's managerial authority over such meetings, however, the Court chose not to defer to the judgment of the Wisconsin Employment Relations Commission that teachers who were not authorized union representatives be prohibited from speaking about matters subject to collective bargaining. The commission was not engaged in the day-to-day supervision of the school board or of its meetings. Its role was rather to oversee certain board decisions respecting its relations with its employees, much as a court might oversee certain decisions of an administrative agency. For this reason the Court correctly believed that it could independently review the merits of the commission's decision without potentially endangering a necessary structure of managerial authority. Advancing its own conception of the social purposes and meaning of the American institution of open school board meetings, the Court concluded that the commission's decision was without merit, since there was no "justification" for excluding teachers from the "public discussion of public business" characteristic of such meetings.[181]

The structural analogy between *Tinker* and *Widmar* is similar, although less complete. The regulation at issue in *Widmar* involved prohibiting students from using university facilities for religious worship and religious discussion. *Widmar* plainly recognized that the university was invested with managerial authority to regulate speech as necessary for the attainment of institutional ends. The Court explicitly noted that a "university's mission is education, and decisions of this Court have never denied a university's authority to impose reasonable regulations compatible with that mission upon the use of its campus and facilities."[182] Thus *Widmar* did not require a university to "make all of its facilities equally available to students and nonstudents alike,"[183] although similar discrimination among persons in the general public would pose an "obvious first amendment problem."[184] As in *Tinker*, however, the Court concluded that the "mission" of education did not depend upon the exercise of pervasive, managerial authority: university students participate in an environment that "is peculiarly 'the marketplace of ideas.' "[185] For this reason the Court addressed the merits of the university's regulation without apparent concern for potential damage to a structure of authority necessary for the attainment of educational objectives.[186]

Unfortunately, *Widmar*'s analysis of the merits of the case is disappointing. The natural and appropriate inquiry for *Widmar* to have undertaken was whether the university's regulation was compatible with its educational "mission." But *Widmar* did not follow through on its own insight. Although it explicitly recognized that a "university differs in significant respects from public forums such as streets or parks,"[187] it nevertheless adopted and applied, without explanation or justification, the strict scrutiny test which the Court had developed in the context of streets and parks. The abrupt recourse to doctrinal formalism illustrates the intellectually crippling effects of contemporary public forum doctrine.

Taken together, *Widmar* and *Madison Joint School District* indicate that within public forum doctrine there are circumstances in which the Court will invest the government with managerial authority, and yet will not defer to the exercise of that authority.[188] In the absence of deference, however, a court must independently evaluate the relationship between the regulation of speech and the attainment of institutional goals. As *Tinker* illustrates, this means that a court must perform an analysis similar in structure and intent to the "incompatibility" test of *Grayned*. Both *Grayned* and *Tinker* held that the government must bear the burden of demonstrating that the consequences of particular speech claims are so undesirable as to justify their denial. This allocation of the burden of proof follows from the important First Amendment principle that the state ought to tolerate the maximum possible speech, consistent with its own orderly operation. At a minimum this principle implies that speech should not be suppressed unless there is a good reason for doing so, and this implication places the burden of persuasion squarely on the government.

The Object of Public Forum Doctrine

Because of its reliance on the *Davis* syllogism, the Court presently views public forum doctrine as concentrating "on the character of the property at issue."[189] But the extraordinary similarities between public forum doctrine and the Court's decisions dealing with the internal management of speech suggest that the thrust of public forum doctrine lies in a different direction. Both lines of decisions involve the government's invocation of managerial authority to control speech. When that authority is called into question by the First Amendment claims of a member of a government institution, we tend to conceptualize the issue as one of the internal management of speech; when it is called into question by the First Amendment claims of a member of the general public, the same issue is conceptualized as a matter of public forum doctrine. Thus the core of public forum doctrine is a concern with the nature of managerial authority rather than with the character of government property.

Public forum doctrine is invoked when members of the general public bring the scope of managerial authority into question. It is important to be clear, however, about what it means to bring managerial authority into question. If a newspaper editorializes that a city council should give municipal employees a salary increase, the editorial may well affect the council's managerial relationship with its employees. But the editorial would not call the council's managerial authority into question, and we would not even be tempted to view the editorial as raising issues of public forum doctrine. This is because the council's authority over the newspaper is so clearly a matter of governance rather than management. The limits of managerial authority are called into question only when those who are arguably subject to its control resist its direction, rendering problematic its nature and reach. In public forum cases this characteristically occurs when members of the general public seek to use a resource over which the government claims managerial control.

The object of public forum doctrine, then, is the constitutional clarification and regulation of government authority over particular resources. Public forum cases require courts to decide whether a resource is subject to a kind of authority "like" that characterized by the government's relationship to a newspaper editorial, which is to say like that involved in the governance of the general public, or whether it is subject to a kind of authority "like" that characterized by the government's control over the internal operation of its own institutions, which is to say to the authority of management. If the latter, the questions in a public forum case will concern the legitimate objectives of the managerial authority, the instrumental relationship between the attainment of those objectives and the regulation of speech, and the institutional impact of judicial review.

Reformulating Public Forum Doctrine

Public forum doctrine, then, is susceptible to a simple and helpful reformulation. From a constitutional point of view, there is a fundamental distinction between two kinds of authority: management and governance. Two distinct regimes of First Amendment regulation correspond to these forms of authority. When the state acts to govern the speech of the general public, it is subject to the restrictions of what we would ordinarily think of as the "usual" principles of First Amendment adjudication. Prior restraints are presumptively unconstitutional, as are viewpoint discrimination, official discretion, agenda setting, and so forth. These principles do not automatically apply, however, when the government manages speech within its own institutions. When acting with managerial authority, a government institution may to a significant degree control speech as necessary to attain its legitimate organizational goals, as these goals are understood by a court.

When a member of the general public seeks to use a resource for expressive purposes and the government claims to exercise managerial authority over the resource, the nature of the government's authority must be determined. If that authority is deemed to be a matter of governance, the resource will be viewed as a public forum, and the government will be constitutionally prohibited from controlling the use of the resource for speech except in ways permitted by ordinary First Amendment principles. The great decisions of the 1930s and 1940s, in which the Court extended the protections of the First Amendment to expression in streets and parks, should essentially be viewed as the Court's determination that despite the government's ownership of these resources, its authority over them was a matter of governance rather than management. So interpreted, these decisions did not establish a "special position"[190] for the public forum, but to the contrary assimilated it into the most general framework of First Amendment analysis.

If, on the other hand, it is determined that the government may properly exercise managerial authority over the resource at issue, the question for judicial decision is whether the government's regulation of speech is necessary for the achievement of its legitimate institutional ends. If a court determines that it should decide this question, it must engage in an investigation analogous to that proposed by *Grayned*, placing upon the government the burden of demonstrating the necessity for the regulation. But a court has another option, which is to defer on this question to the judgment of institutional authorities. The primary justification for such deference is that the resource is subject to a kind of managerial authority that requires insulation from routine judicial oversight for its effective functioning.

As reformulated in this manner, public forum doctrine does not so much determine the outcome of particular cases, as orient courts toward the kind of reasoning whereby outcomes should be reached. The reformulation of the doctrine has several important advantages. It flows from the values and concerns which the history of public forum doctrine suggests have been the mainspring of the doctrine's development, and yet it does so in a manner that sweeps away the Court's antiquated focus on the inherent "proprietary" power of the government and that avoids the vicious circularity of the Court's concentration on government intent. It abandons the Court's fruitless and frustrating quest to define the constitutionally "special position" of the public forum; and with respect to the nonpublic forum it avoids the mistake of crudely binding together questions of access and of equal access, instead subsuming both under a sensible and functionally oriented standard. The reformulation is firmly rooted in the practical problems of administering government institutions, and yet it is also grounded in contemporary constitutional jurisprudence. It maximizes the speech which government must tolerate, consistent with a sophisticated understanding of the necessities of organizational management and an appreciation of the social meaning of particular government institutions.

The reformulation will not of course magically dispel the difficult issues that underlie public forum adjudication, but it will orient courts toward inquiries which are defensible and productive. In the remaining sections I will discuss in detail two important inquiries: the distinction between governance and management, and the distinction between structures of managerial authority which require judicial deference and those which do not.

The Distinction between Management and Governance

At present, public forum doctrine distinguishes public from nonpublic forums on the basis of a "long tradition" of use for "assembly and debate." The difficulty with this approach is that the Court has been unable to explain why such a tradition should have special constitutional consequences. As reformulated, however, public and nonpublic forums should be distinguished according to whether government authority over a resource is "like" that characteristic of the internal management of a state institution, or instead "like" that characteristic of the governance of the general public. This reformulation raises the question, however, of how to determine whether government authority over a resource is a matter of governance or of management.

The Question of Institutional Boundaries

This question has an immediate and almost irresistible answer, which is that governmental authority is a matter of management if a resource lies "within" a government organization, but that it is a matter of governance if a resource is located "outside" the organization's boundaries. It is in fact quite difficult to think about the question of governmental authority without recourse to this spatial metaphor of organizational boundaries.

The problem is that the metaphor does not have any obvious analytic content. As a matter of private ordering, the boundaries of an organization are ordinarily understood to be fixed by consent. I am within an organization when I consent to recognize its authority over me.[191] But this understanding is not helpful in fixing the boundaries of government institutions for public forum doctrine, because the doctrine deals with governmental authority over resources rather than people, and because the state has the power to sweep resources and individuals into its organizations regardless of their consent.[192]

Another common way of thinking about organizational boundaries relates to the organization's power of action. As one study observes, "The organization is the total set of interstructured activities in which it is engaged at any one time and over which it has discretion to initiate, maintain, or end behaviors . . . The organization ends where its discretion ends and another's begins."[193] In the case of government organizations, however, this definition is also unhelpful, since state institutions possess the discretion of state power, and the extent to which this power may be exercised is precisely the constitutional issue to be determined.

Modern organization theory, moreover, has come to view organizations "as open systems," whose "boundaries must necessarily be sieves, not shells, admitting the desirable flows and excluding the inappropriate or deleterious elements."[194] As a consequence, boundaries "are very difficult to delineate in social systems, such as organizations."[195] Depending upon one's perspective, one can view "suppliers, customers, inmates, and other types of persons" as "members" within "the organization's domain."[196] The problem is further complicated by the fact that the dependence of organizations on their environment gives them incentives to reach out and extend their "control" over important external resources,[197] thus pushing their already open boundaries into a state of constant motion.

The indeterminate boundaries characteristic of government institutions is well illustrated by United States Postal Service v. Council of Greenburgh Civic Associations, in which a civic association challenged the constitutionality of a federal statute prohibiting the deposit of unstamped "mailable matter" in the mailboxes of private individuals.[198] The Court approached the case by concluding that the mailboxes were a nonpublic forum, and wrote:

> It is difficult to conceive of any reason why this Court should treat a letterbox differently for first amendment access purposes than it has in the past treated the military base in *Greer v. Spock*, . . . the jail or prison in *Adderley v. Florida*, . . . and *Jones v. North Carolina Prisoners' Union*, . . . or the advertising space made available in city rapid transit cars in *Lehman v. City of Shaker Heights* . . . In all these cases, this Court recognized that the first amendment does not guarantee access to property simply because it is owned or controlled by the government. In *Greer v.*

Spock, . . . the Court cited approvingly from its earlier opinion in *Adderley v. Florida*, . . . wherein it explained that " '[t]he State, no less than a private owner of property, has power to preserve the property under its control for the use to which it is lawfully dedicated.' "[199]

The passage relies on precedents in which the government was exercising managerial authority over property which it unambiguously owned. The major premise of the *Davis* syllogism, whatever its intrinsic merits, was thus applicable to the facts of these precedents.

What is striking about the passage, however, is *Greenburgh*'s effort to appropriate and rely on the premise. Since the mailboxes at issue in *Greenburgh* were purchased and owned by private individuais, this effort is plainly misguided. The government cannot seriously be said to have a proprietary relationship to privately owned mailboxes. But the real thrust of the *Greenburgh* opinion is not that the government is the proprietor of the mailboxes, but rather that the mailboxes should be viewed as part of the internal organization of the Postal Service. The opinion is quite explicit on this point, stating that the mailboxes are "an essential part of the Postal Service's nationwide system for the delivery and receipt of mail" and that they must be "under the direction and control of the Postal Service" if the Service is "to operate as efficiently as possible a system for the delivery of mail."[200] In effect, therefore, *Greenburgh* perceived the boundaries of the Postal Service as expanding outward to embrace the privately owned mailboxes of individuals, and hence concluded that the Service's regulation of access to these mailboxes should be regarded for constitutional purposes as a matter of managerial authority.

Although *Greenburgh*'s conclusion is clear enough, it is far from obvious how the conclusion may be rationally assessed. The usual markers of organization boundaries—consent and power—offer virtually no guidance in evaluating *Greenburgh*'s expansive perception of the institutional boundaries of the Postal Service.

Criteria for Distinguishing Management from Governance

The Court's decisions addressing the internal management of speech have uniformly concluded that within a government organization expression may be controlled so as to achieve institutional ends. This conclusion reflects the perception that in our culture the domain of an organization is one of "instrumental orientation,"[201] in which "organizational goals" are taken as "value premises."[202] The function of an organization is to

implement these premises, not to question them, and within its boundaries people and resources are arranged so as to attain this objective.
Outside of this organizational domain, however, lies a public realm in
which the attainment of institutional ends is taken to be a relevant, but
not controlling, consideration. In the public realm, assertions of value are
not accepted as "premises" but rather are recognized as claims subject to
evaluation and assessment. In "public life . . . we jointly, as a community,
exercise the human capacity 'to think what we are doing,' and take charge
of the history in which we are all constantly engaged by drift and inad-
vertence."[203] In a democracy like our own, the public realm coincides
with the arena in which common values are forged through public discussion and exchange.

From a constitutional perspective, then, the distinction between management and governance turns on the priority accorded to proposed
objectives. If government action is viewed as a matter of internal management, the attainment of institutional ends is taken as an unquestioned
priority.[204] But if it is instead viewed as a matter of governance, the
significant and force of all potential objectives are taken as a legitimate
subject of inquiry. The facts of *Greenburgh* nicely illustrate the difference.
To conceptualize the mailboxes as a nonpublic forum "within" the organization of the Postal Service implies that they are a resource at the
Service's disposal, and that they can and should be instrumentally manipulated so as most efficiently to achieve the Service's explicit and legitimate goals. To conceptualize the mailboxes as a public forum
"external" to the organization of the Service, on the other hand, implies
that the attainment of these goals cannot automatically commandeer the
use of the mailboxes, and that the Service's claims must be evaluated in
light of other competing social interests in the mailboxes' use.

In our democracy the accommodation of competing values occurs
through a process of public discussion, a process that is constituted and
guarded by principles of First Amendment jurisprudence. These principles characteristically balance or weigh institutional interests, like those
asserted by the Postal Service in *Greenburgh*, against the social value of
maintaining First Amendment rights and hence the very process of public
discussion. The *Schneider* case is an early and explicit example of such
balancing, where the government's interest in preventing litter was held
insufficient to justify an ordinance prohibiting the distribution of pamphlets. The implication of such balancing, however, is that in specific
circumstances particular institutional objectives can justifiably limit First

Amendment rights. If an institutional objective is of sufficient importance, and if the appropriation of a public resource is sufficiently necessary to the attainment of the objective, First Amendment principles may well permit rights of free expression respecting the resource to be subordinated in carefully limited kinds of ways.[205] But general First Amendment principles are designed to ensure that this subordination will always be provisional, the result of a hard-fought clarification of competing public values, and that it will never be, so to speak, a matter of course.

This analysis of the constitutional distinction between management and governance is helpful in giving analytic content to the metaphor of organizational boundaries. These boundaries partition off from a public realm a special domain of instrumental action. The limits of that domain are marked by the very instrumental social practices by which organizations are constituted. This can be seen in Sigmund Diamond's study of the early history of Virginia, "From Organization to Society: Virginia in the Seventeenth Century." In its early years the Jamestown colony of Virginia had been established not as a "colony" or "political unit," but rather as "the property of the Virginia Company of London," whose objective was to "return a profit to the stockholders of that company." The Company was "governed administratively through a chain of command originating in the Company's General Court." From the point of view of the General Court, the Virginia settlers "were not citizens of a colony; they were the occupants of a status in—to use an anachronistic term—the Company's table of organization."[206]

The regulation of social life in Jamestown was designed solely to achieve the Company's objective, and it consequently "stripped from people all attributes save the one that really counted in the relationship which the Company sought to impose on them—their status in the organization."[207] But as the social life of Jamestown grew more populous and complex, and as individuals began to recognize in each other statuses outside those instrumentally imposed by the Company,[208] institutional roles became less important to the settlers. The settlers "were no longer willing to accept the legitimacy of their organizational superiors," and "the burden of achieving order and discipline . . . became the responsibility not of an organization but of a society." The emergence of this society was marked by the development of an "authentic political system" in which the diverging values and objectives of the colonists were resolved.[209]

What is most interesting about Diamond's work is the suggestion that the transition from organization to society was constituted by a change in social practices. The settlers of Jamestown who lived within an organization had their roles and statuses functionally defined by the Virginia Company; the settlers who participated in a society enjoyed a wide variety of divergent roles and statuses that could not be said to be instrumentally arranged. The emergence of a political system depended upon the growth of a social system that was sufficiently complex as to engender in its members diverse roles, values, and expectations. This symbiotic relationship between diversity and a public realm illuminates why we view that realm as an arena in which conflicting values and expectations are recognized, legitimated, and accommodated.[210] The instrumental rationality of an organization, on the other hand, is hostile toward this diversity, and requires that the various roles and statuses of its members be subordinated toward the achievement of institutional objectives. Organizations thus strive to ensure that "their personnel should not be influenced by extra-organizational factors,"[211] and they attempt functionally to define for their members specifically organizational roles that predominate over the multiple roles and statuses characteristic of the general society.[212]

This analysis suggests that for constitutional purposes an organization's boundaries can be recognized by the predominance of functionally defined organizational roles. If a resource is embedded in social practices that are constituted by such organizational roles, the resource can be said to lie within an organization. It is a nonpublic forum and subject to the exercise of managerial authority. On the other hand, if a resource is used by individuals occupying widely different roles and statuses, with correspondingly divergent values and expectations, the resource lies in the public realm, and the state's authority over it is a matter of governance. The resource is a public forum.

Four Examples

This way of understanding the distinction between public and nonpublic forums may seem a bit abstract, but it in fact yields concrete and useful results, as can be seen by the analysis of four examples. Consider, first, what underlies the Court's perception of the public forum status of streets and parks. Streets and parks are part of the experience of all citizens. We ordinarily use streets and parks in a wide variety of roles and statuses, and hence we subject them to an enormous diversity of competing demands and uses. No one of these uses has automatic priority.[213] Officials who regulate streets, for example, are normally torn between facilitating effi-

cient vehicle traffic and accommodating the concededly legitimate demands of those who want to conduct parades, funerals, block parties, or
festivals.[214] It is this fact, and not a tradition of public usage for expressive
purposes, which underlies the Court's firm and correct conclusion that
streets should be seen as public forums.[215]

The multiplicity of competing roles and expectations characteristic of
streets and parks should be contrasted to the social practices surrounding
the advertising cards at issue in *Lehman*. There was never any reasonable
expectation that the cards were to be made available to the public on any
grounds other than those useful, financially or otherwise, to the rapid
transit system. The only role in which the advertising space could be
purchased was that of a consumer, and that role was in all pertinent
respects functionally defined by the transit system. The Court was thus
correct in concluding that the cards were not a public forum.

Greenburgh presents a theoretically more interesting decision, for in
that case the federal government had attempted by the enactment of a
criminal statute to change the social practices associated with mailboxes.
Anyone who has unthinkingly dropped a note in a friend's mailbox knows,
however, that in everyday life mailboxes are subject to uses other than
simply the deposit of stamped mailable matter, which is but another way
of saying that we use mailboxes all the time in roles other than those
specifically defined by the Postal Service. For this reason the Court's
decision in *Greenburgh* was incorrect: the mailboxes should have been
regarded as a public forum, and the constitutionality of the government's
effort to restrict access to them should have been evaluated as if it were
a restriction on the speech of the general public.[216]

The lesson of *Greenburgh* is that the government cannot by mere legislative fiat justify the exercise of managerial authority. Such authority can
only be sustained by the existence of antecedent social practices. Of course
the government can act in ways that alter social practices. Thus the
government might have sought to justify its claims in *Greenburgh* by
fundamentally altering the roles, expectations, and behavior enveloping
the use of mailboxes, as for example by placing them under lock and key
controlled by Postal Service personnel. But the regulations altering conduct in this way would themselves have to pass constitutional scrutiny
according to general First Amendment principles. It is important to recognize, however, that public forum doctrine will not itself have anything
to contribute to those principles; the doctrine merely establishes the
register within which constitutional review will take place.

The analysis of a fourth and final example will illustrate the complexities of distinguishing between management and governance. In *Greer*, members of a political party sought access to the "areas of Fort Dix open to the general public"[217] for the purpose of holding demonstrations and handing out leaflets. Civilians "without any prior authorization" were not only "regular visitors" to these "unrestricted areas," but they also "regularly pass[ed] through" them "either by foot or by auto, at all times of the day and night."[218] Although the record is not perfectly clear, if these areas were, from a civilian's point of view, like "any public street,"[219] and so subject to conflicting uses and roles, then the areas should have been regarded as a public forum, and the government's attempt to restrict speech within them should have been evaluated according to ordinary First Amendment principles. The military could no more convert them into a managerial domain by simple fiat than could the Postal Service transform private mailboxes into nonpublic forums by simple decree.

What complicates the situation in *Greer*, however, is that the plaintiffs in the case had sought access to the areas in order to meet "with service personnel."[220] The issue posed by *Greer* is thus not merely the nature of the military's authority over the open areas of Fort Dix, but also the nature of the military's control over its own service personnel. Whether or not this control should be viewed for First Amendment purposes as managerial in nature does not depend at all upon the distinction between public and nonpublic forums, or upon the social practices of members of the general public, but rather upon a substantive analysis of the prerogatives of military authority vis-à-vis military personnel.

The relationship between a government institution and its members is not a question that we have so far discussed in any detail, but in Pickering v. Board of Education the Court held that this relationship can at a certain point cease to be managerial in nature. In that case the Court ruled that in some circumstances the interest of a school board in controlling a teacher's written communication with a newspaper was "not significantly greater than its interest in limiting a similar contribution by any member of the general public," and hence that the constitutionality of the sanctions imposed on the teacher should be evaluated according to ordinary First Amendment principles.[221] *Pickering* suggests that the question of whether the restrictions on speech imposed in *Greer* should be viewed as a matter of management or of governance turns on whether the military's interest in controlling access to servicemen in the open areas of the fort is so attenuated as to be not "significantly greater than its interest" in controlling the speech of members of the general public in those areas.

Whether or not *Pickering*'s approach is ultimately adopted, the lesson of *Greer* is that not every First Amendment claim by members of the general public which calls managerial authority into question turns on questions of public forum doctrine. While it is true that the Court should have concluded that the military's authority over the open areas of the fort involved matters of governance rather than of management, the ultimate ability of the military to control the plaintiffs' access to those areas depended upon the quite different question of the military's authority over its own personnel. The final irony of *Greer* is that the decision which established the framework of contemporary public forum doctrine did not itself ultimately depend upon the distinction between public and nonpublic forums, but rather on the reach of government's managerial authority over the members of its own institutions.

The Meaning of "Public" in Public Forum Doctrine

Public forum doctrine is conventionally, although inaccurately, understood to be pertinent only when the public seeks to use government property for expressive purposes.[222] This focus on property has disoriented the Court's conceptualization of public forum doctrine, for it has led the Court to conceive of the public forum in terms of the opposition between the public and the private, rather than in terms of the opposition between the public and the specifically instrumental.

Property is traditionally associated with a sphere of personal and private freedom, in which the individual, "as against the Government," has the right to be "let alone" to enjoy "personal security, personal liberty and private property."[223] "One of the main rights attaching to property is the right to exclude others, . . . and one who owns or lawfully possesses or controls property will in all likelihood have a legitimate expectation of privacy by virtue of this right to exclude."[224] From its inception public forum doctrine has associated the "nonpublic" with this image of specifically "private" freedom. *Davis* analogized the government to "the owner of a private house,"[225] and *Adderley*, in language that has been continually repeated, compared the state to "a private owner of property."[226] It is simply self-contradictory, however, to claim for the government the prerogatives of a sphere of personal privacy, because the government cannot intelligibly claim that it should be "let alone" from its own processes.

It makes sense, on the other hand, to conclude that there are situations in which government can and must organize itself to act through institutions in an instrumental fashion. Such action proceeds toward the attainment of partial ends determined by the value premises of a particular institution, in contrast to the achievement of public ends determined by the community "as a whole."[227] In the context of public forum doctrine, then, the opposite of the public is not the private, but rather the specifically instrumental.[228]

Public forum doctrine rests on the distinction between a public realm, in which social values and ends are constituted, and organizational domains, in which these values are taken as premises and implemented. The distinction calls to mind the difference between what Jürgen Habermas has called a social framework of "symbolic interaction," and a social framework "of purposive-rational action." The latter is aimed at the realization of "defined goals under given conditions"; the former at the creation of "consensual norms, which define reciprocal expectations about behavior."[229]

The analogy cannot be pressed too far, however, for two reasons. First, government action in the public realm must at times also be instrumental, and so the ordinary principles of First Amendment jurisprudence which govern the public realm must facilitate such action and yet simultaneously cabin it so that it will not impede the more fundamental processes of symbolic interaction. Second, government action within organizational domains is at times designed for the specific purpose of facilitating symbolic interaction, as occurs, for example, in courtrooms and universities.

But Habermas' distinction is helpful because it reminds us that the public realm *must* retain the ability to foster symbolic interaction and cannot be dedicated entirely to purposive-rational action. And, conversely, it forces us to recognize that when organizational domains foster symbolic interaction, they do so for a purpose that frames and limits such interaction. Paradigmatic of such limitations are the restrictive rules of evidence and speech characteristic of a court. One can expect these limitations to be more severe when organizational purposes are narrow and specific, and to be more generous when organizational purposes are broad and diffuse.

The most analytically interesting example of an institution designed to foster symbolic interaction is the town meeting, whose very purpose is the creation of a forum for public discourse and decision-making. Even that constitutionally benign purpose, however, when implemented through the authority of a moderator, has the power to limit speech through the imposition of agendas and rules of order and decorum. Many of these limitations are plainly contrary to ordinary First Amendment principles.

This suggests that underlying public forum doctrine lies the notion of a public discourse that occurs without government purpose or design. The stubborn persistence of Justice Holmes's famous metaphor of a marketplace of ideas, despite its many deficiencies, may perhaps be attributed to the fact that it is a precise expression of this notion. The metaphor assumes that public opinion will be formed through a spontaneous process of exchange and communication. Without central planning or design, the market evaluates the partial purposes of the organizations that compete within it. The paradox, of course, is that the market is itself sustained by government rules of interaction. In the economic sphere these rules include the law of property and contracts; in the sphere of communication they include the principles of the First Amendment.

The concept of the "public" in public forum doctrine, then, is extraordinarily complex. In part it refers to government facilitation of symbolic interaction. This facilitation, however, must be of a particular kind. If it is oriented toward the achievement of particular purposes or goals, the government's intervention will be perceived as creating a nonpublic forum like a courtroom or a university. The facilitation must instead be passive enough to be appropriated and used by purely private purposes. This points toward a conclusion whose irony should not be missed: in the end the public realm created by public forum doctrine is nothing other than a governmentally protected space for the achievement of private ordering. The irony, of course, has a final twist, for in a democracy like our own, private ordering is the very stuff of public will.

Judicial Deference to Managerial Authority

If a court determines that a particular resource is a nonpublic forum and hence belongs to the instrumental domain of an institution, the governing principle of constitutional law is that public use of the resource for communicative purposes may be restricted if such use interferes with the effective functioning of the institution. In passing on the constitutionality of the institution's regulation of the resource, either a court can make its own independent assessment of the compatibility of public use with the attainment of legitimate institutional objectives, or it can defer on this question to the judgment of authorities within the institution. The Court's tendency to defer to institutional judgment in its recent nonpublic forum cases has been the single most controversial aspect of contemporary public forum doctrine, and it is at the heart of the Court's rejection of *Grayned*. In this section I will sketch a framework for analyzing the question of deference within the context of public forum doctrine.

The General Structure of Deference Analysis

Deference analysis can be conceptualized as divided into three stages. The first stage concerns what may be called the preconditions of deference. Deference occurs when courts retain control over the content of governing constitutional principles but decide that these principles are best implemented by institutional officials.[230] It is a necessary precondition of deference that a court believe that institutional authorities are aware of the constitutional principles that should guide their judgment and are in good faith attempting to enact those principles. Thus deference presupposes a relationship of trust between a court and institutional authorities. It is inappropriate if a court has reason to suspect that institutional authorities are unaware of or indifferent to the rule that speech should be regulated only when necessary to attain organizational ends, or if a court doubts that institutional authorities are applying the rule in good faith. Courts ordinarily perceive danger signals when they confront institutional decisions that on the merits seem, to use the language of *Lehman*, "arbitrary, capricious, or invidious,"[231] or, to adopt the phrase of *Cornelius*, "unreasonable."[232] In this limited sense, questions of deference and questions of substance are interrelated.

If the preconditions of deference are satisfied, a court can address the second stage of deference analysis, which entails an assessment of the arguments for deference. As a general rule, courts are required to make an "independent constitutional judgment"[233] in cases involving regulation of "supremely precious"[234] First Amendment freedoms. There must be a good reason, therefore, to suspend such judgment. It is sometimes argued that one such reason is the respect which courts should have for the "professional expertise" of government officials.[235] But this argument, if accepted, would prove too much, for the prerogatives claimed by expertise are potentially endless, and deference based solely upon such grounds would have no limit. The Court has quite properly been reluctant to engage in the wholesale sacrifice of First Amendment rights that automatic deference to expertise would undoubtedly produce.[236] Although the school officials in *Tinker* and the military commanders in *Glines* presumably shared equal endowments of professional expertise, the Court chose to defer in the second case but not in the first.

The contrast between *Tinker* and *Glines* suggests an alternative justification for deference. The distinction between the two cases can be interpreted as resting on differences in the kind of institutional authority at issue, differences which make deference arguably necessary for the attainment of institutional ends in the second case but not in the first. This distinction can be generalized into the following principle: courts should defer if the exercise of institutional authority at issue is of the kind that requires insulation from judicial review for its effective functioning. I shall call deference which meets this standard "warranted." The justification for warranted deference flows from the definition of the very constitutional right that is at issue. The right of access to a nonpublic forum is in essence the right of a member of the general public to use institutional resources for communicative purposes in a manner that is not incompatible with the attainment of institutional ends. It is anomalous to require that a court itself obstruct the attainment of these ends in order to vindicate such a right.

The difficulty, of course, is that an institution's regulation of its resources may affect constitutional values other than simply an individual's particular right to use these resources for communicative purposes. When this is the case, a court must determine whether the presence of such other constitutional values renders inappropriate the exercise of even warranted deference. This determination involves the third stage of deference analysis, which entails a balancing of the justification for warranted deference against the potential damage to constitutional principles other than those implicated in the management of the speech of particular individuals.

The characteristics of this third stage can be illustrated by considering decisions involving the internal management of speech. The internal management of speech always involves more than merely a particular right to speak by an institution's member; it in addition necessarily involves the definition of that member's larger organizational role. There is thus an intrinsic tension between the organization's functional definition of that role and the member's need to maintain fidelity to external roles and statuses. In particular, it is not uncommon for institutions to impose organizational roles that are so "pervasive" as to prevent their members from engaging in nonorganizational roles that have constitutional value to the larger society.[237] For example, the military may prohibit service personnel from observing required religious obligations,[238] or prisons may prohibit inmate correspondence with a court.[239] In such cases the issue is not merely the right to practice a particular religious rite or to send a specific letter to a judge, but rather the very ability to enact the constitutionally protected roles of being a religious person or a participant in the judicial process. The general damage to these roles must be weighed against the potential damage to institutional authority resulting from judicial review.[240]

This tension is well illustrated by Connick v. Myers, in which the Court concluded that great deference should be given to the authority of government officials to regulate the speech of their employees, holding that "government officials should enjoy wide latitude in managing their offices, without intrusive oversight by the judiciary in the name of the first amendment." The Court set a limit on this deference, however, strongly hinting that if an employee speaks "as a citizen," if his speech "substantially involve[s] matters of public concern," then deference would be inappropriate.[241] Whereas Pickering concerned the boundary between the management and governance of employee speech, Connick addressed the legitimate reach of purely managerial authority. Connick recognized that the organizational role of employee could be defined so pervasively as to destroy the constitutional role of citizen, and so it implied that when the latter role was potentially endangered, independent judicial determination of the relationship between institutional ends and the regulation of speech was justified, notwithstanding the potential damage to institutional authority.

This tension between organizational and constitutional roles, which is so central to the analysis of deference in the context of the organizational regulation of speech, does not exist in public forum doctrine. The doctrine involves members of the general public, who by definition are not subject to the imposition of organizational roles. At stake in public forum doctrine is simply the right to use a particular resource for communicative purposes, and since this right is itself defined by the same instrumental principles as inform the determination of warranted deference, the third stage of analysis in public forum doctrine tends as a general matter to be rather weak.

In fact the Court has given serious recognition to only one constitutional value that could potentially override warranted deference, and that is the value involved in prohibiting government institutions from making their resources available to the public in a manner that discriminates on the basis of viewpoint.[242] Although the Court has forcefully enunciated this value, the relationship between the prohibition of viewpoint discrimination and public forum doctrine is rather complex, and the constitutional values behind the prohibition can be expected to override warranted deference in only a limited number of circumstances.[243]

The Criteria of Warranted Deference

For this reason the Court in cases involving public forum doctrine has tended to concentrate on the question of whether deference is warranted. If it is assumed that with sufficient attention and evidence a court can determine as well as a government administrator whether any particular regulation of speech is necessary for the attainment of organizational ends, the case for warranted deference must rest on the adverse consequences of having a court, rather than an institutional official, make this determination. The analysis of warranted deference must thus turn on the identification and assessment of these consequences.

It is of course not possible to generate an exhaustive catalogue of these consequences. But their nature and variety can be illustrated by examining the relationship between courts and what the sociologist Erving Goffman has called "total institutions," for in such institutions both the need for organizational authority and the distance from judicial culture are at their respective maxima.[244] Analyzing this relationship will permit us to identify three distinct kinds of such consequences, whose relevance to other kinds of government institutions can then be evaluated.

Total institutions, like the military to which the Court deferred in *Greer*, are organizations that attempt to regulate "all aspects of life . . . in the same place and under the same single authority." Total institutions not only physically separate their members from the larger society, but they also attempt to the maximum extent possible to strip away from their members statuses associated with that society, and to impose instead a uniform institutional identity. To accomplish this task, total institutions characteristically have pervasive systems of authority which are rationalized in terms of the "avowed goals" of the institution and which are expressed in "a language of explanation that the staff, and sometimes the inmates, can bring to every crevice of action in the institution."[245]

Judicial review of administrative decisions in the context of total institutions poses the possibility of three distinct kinds of adverse consequences to managerial authority. The first concerns the contamination of the institution. Courts represent the values and expectations of the larger society, and if they override managerial authority in a total institution they import these values and expectations and threaten the institution's isolation. Of course the extent to which this isolation should be preserved is itself an independent and substantive question of constitutional law. In *Greer*, the Court was quite concerned that the military be "insulated from both the reality and the appearance" of being connected with civilian political life.[246] In the case of prisons, however, the recent demise of the "hands-off" doctrine indicates a desire to subject prisons at least to some significant extent to the constitutional values of the larger society.[247]

Judicial review of managerial authority in total institutions can cause a second kind of adverse consequence. Because total institutions are physically separated from society, authority in these institutions must control literally every aspect of their members' behavior. Hence such authority is not a matter of discrete and specific rules but rather of constituting an entire way of life, one which causes the members of these institutions "to self-direct themselves in a manageable way."[248] Judicial tampering with particular institutional rules will therefore affect not merely the behavior specifically governed by these rules but also the institutional culture or way of life which the authority structure as a whole is designed to create. Thus, judicial review of military orders may well undermine that "instinctive obedience" which is thought necessary for the achievement of the "military mission."[249] Similarly, it is claimed that judicial imposition of specific due process regulations on prisons has had the unanticipated consequence of transforming the general institutional culture by altering the manner in which inmates regard guards, and has thereby caused unexpected problems of inmate violence and security.[250]

Such unanticipated consequences to organizational culture are difficult enough to deal with when a court has assumed more or less comprehensive authority for the administering of an institution through the issuance of a structural injunction. They are much more troublesome, however, when, as is characteristically the case in decisions involving public forum doctrine, they arise from judicial review of discrete rules or regulations. In such circumstances a court does not accept responsibility for running an institution, and yet its decisions may set off a chain of effects that have adverse consequences for those who have accepted this responsibility.

The third kind of adverse consequences threatened by judicial review concerns the relationship between rules and unpredictable task environments. Because officials in total institutions manage every aspect of the lives of their members, they must often attempt to exercise their authority in the face of unique and unforeseeable circumstances. Strict rules, however, are unsuitable "where the action to be controlled is non-recurring" and where there are situations involving "personalised, individual application."[251] In such cases it is desirable that managers exercise discretion.[252] To the extent that judicial review entails the imposition of rules, it can thwart this discretion and hence alter and impair the kind of flexible authority structure necessary for attaining institutional ends.[253]

In the context of total institutions, therefore, the very process of judicial review poses three distinct kinds of potentially adverse consequences to organizational authority: contamination, destruction of organizational culture, and the loss of needed flexibility. These consequences are illustrative of the criteria that a court should consider in deciding whether deference is warranted. The pertinence and weight of these criteria will vary depending upon the specific kind of decision, authority, and institution that is at issue, and hence the decision whether to engage in warranted deference must be made on a case-by-case basis. This can be illustrated by contrasting the question of warranted deference in two decisions, *Lehman* and *Perry*, both of which involve decision-making by ordinary government bureaucracies.

In *Lehman*, the issue before the Court was whether a municipal rapid transit system could refuse to sell advertising space on car cards to those who wished to purchase the space for political advertisements. Although Justice Blackmun correctly concluded that the cards were a nonpublic forum, he incorrectly assumed that this conclusion required the Court to defer to all managerial decisions respecting the use of the cards. If Blackmun had instead analyzed the specific management decision at issue to determine whether deference was actually warranted, he would have seen that the Court should in fact have made its own independent determination of whether the acceptance of political advertising was incompatible with the system's effective functioning.[254]

The municipal transit system was, after all, a government bureaucracy immersed in the larger society, so there could be no contention that judicial review would illicitly "contaminate" management authority with general social values. Moreover, the decision to restrict the cards to commercial advertising was addressed to members of the general public who were potential customers for the purchase of advertising space; it did not affect or involve the relationship between the transit system and its own employees. The relationship between the system and its potential customers was a contractual one negotiated at arm's length, and hence the system could not have expected to influence its potential customers through the creation of a specifically organizational culture. Thus, the decision to refuse political advertising could not be said to have been part of a general system of authority designed to inculcate an organizational way of life, and judicial review of the merits of the decision would have been unlikely to have unanticipated effects on the structure of internal authority within the transit system. Nor could a very plausible argument be made that the decision inhabited an unpredictable environment, so that the transit system would have to retain a continual flexibility to alter the rule against political advertising. Indeed, the rule had been in place and unchanged for twenty-six years.[255] Deciding whether the acceptance of political advertising would have been incompatible with the ends of the transit system might have involved complex and difficult matters of business judgment, but as to these questions of judgment there was no particular reason to believe that a court could not have reached as accurate a decision as a transit official.

For all these reasons, deference in *Lehman* was not warranted.[256] The circumstances of *Perry*, on the other hand, created a demonstrably stronger case for judicial deference. *Perry* concerned a school board's management of an internal mail system whose "primary function" was "to transmit official messages among the teachers and between the teachers and the school administration."[257] The Court characterized the system as a nonpublic forum, and proceeded in effect to defer to the decision of the school board to exclude a minority union (PLEA) from access to its system. The Court assumed that PLEA should be treated as a member of the general public, and hence characterized the case as one involving public forum doctrine.

Whereas in *Lehman* the decision to refuse political advertising did not affect the relationship between the bureaucracy and its employees, in *Perry* the decision to exclude PLEA was directly connected to this relationship. PLEA's exclusion was part of the labor contract negotiated between the board and the union which had been certified as the teachers' exclusive bargaining representative (PEA), and the exclusion was no doubt one of PEA's demands.[258] The school board, like any large-scale employer, no doubt wished to use its authority as an employer to engender in its employees "not just a passive but an active attitude toward the furtherance of the organization's objectives . . . Active rather than merely passive participation and cooperation is almost essential if an organization is to attain even moderate efficiency."[259] The decision at issue in *Perry* is thus part of the larger question of the school system's organizational culture, and hence judicial review of that decision could risk causing unanticipated adverse effects on the general relationship between the board and its employees. The decision is also one that calls for the exercise of discretion rather than fixed rules. The potential ability of the board to alter its decision to exclude PLEA gives it leverage in negotiating with PEA, and in other circumstances the board might well decide to more generally open up the mail system.[260] Thus the imposition of a fixed judicial rule regarding the use of the mail system may well impair needed flexibility.

Although both *Lehman* and *Perry* involve decisions of large and rather ordinary government organizations, deference is warranted in the second case but not in the first. The contrast arises because of differences in the kinds of decisions subject to review in the two cases, and illustrates that the determination of warranted deference depends not upon the "type" of institution at issue but rather upon a reasoned application of the various criteria of warranted deference to the specific facts of an actual case. Because deference involves such a serious abdication of the judicial obligation independently to protect individual constitutional rights, courts should be cautious in finding warranted deference. Needless to say, courts should exercise independent review with respect to the decision of whether or not to defer.

Conclusion

"We had the experience but missed the meaning," T. S. Eliot writes in "The Dry Salvages."[261] The observation illuminates a great deal of the twisted and unhappy history of public forum doctrine. The Court has sharply experienced the necessity of protecting the administrative integrity of government institutions, and yet has been unable to capture the meaning of that experience. It has instead concentrated on questions of government property and the constitutional license of the proprietor, questions that are deservedly anomalous in modern First Amendment jurisprudence. Fortunately the Court's instincts have proved truer than its doctrine, for underlying its actual judgments there is discernible a more or less defensible pattern of decision.

In this essay I have traced that pattern, beginning with the line between governance and management. When the state acts to govern the speech of the general public, it often truncates the very process of discussion and exchange by which public ends and public actions are determined; for this reason, the First Amendment has tended to impose rather stringent restrictions on such governance. When the state acts internally to manage speech within its own institutions, on the other hand, public ends are taken as given and as socially embodied within the form and objectives of a government organization. First Amendment restrictions on the internal management of speech thus turn in the main on whether the management is necessary in order to attain organizational purposes.

The line between governance and management corresponds to the distinction between the public and nonpublic forum. If a resource is subject to managerial authority, it is a nonpublic forum, and its use for communicative purposes can be routinely subordinated to the discretion of state officials, frozen through prior restraints, and in many circumstances subjected to viewpoint discrimination. All of this is presumptively forbidden to the government when a resource is a public forum and can only be regulated according to the standards of governance. This is not because the public forum receives especially strict constitutional protection, but rather because restrictions on speech within the public forum are controlled by ordinary principles of First Amendment adjudication.

There is no magic talisman to distinguish public from nonpublic forums. As a society, however, we recognize managerial domains by the presence of an instrumental orientation embodied in the exclusion of roles and statuses inconsistent with the attainment of organizational ends. Contemporary public forum doctrine can be interpreted as groping toward a similar recognition when it makes the distinction between public and nonpublic forums turn on a tradition of public access for expressive purposes, since in most circumstances such a tradition will be deeply incompatible with the proscription of all but narrowly organizational roles and statuses. The tradition, however, is not constitutive of the distinction between public and nonpublic forums, but is rather probative of underlying social practices that are themselves determinative of the authority ceded to the government in the regulation of speech.

When reviewing government control of access to a nonpublic forum, a court must decide whether to determine independently if the control is necessary for the attainment of legitimate institutional ends, or whether to defer on this question to the judgment of institutional authorities. In most cases, the distinction between the two approaches turns on whether judicial deference is itself necessary in order for a state organization to function effectively. If the government decision at issue entails a kind of authority which requires flexibility and discretion to function effectively, or which is part of the creation of a specific organizational culture for the management of the affected institution, there are strong justifications for judicial deference.

The underlying pattern of contemporary public forum doctrine, in short, reflects an emerging sociology of institutional authority as well as a pervasive and important struggle between a public realm and an organizational domain of instrumental rationality. Seen in this light, public forum doctrine has much to teach us about the nature and limits of our democracy.

7

Meiklejohn's Mistake: Individual Autonomy and the Reform of Public Discourse

Some of our best and most influential constitutional scholars have recently revived the view that the essential objective of the First Amendment is to promote a rich and valuable public debate. Their claim is that First Amendment issues ought to be decided not by "reference to . . . personal autonomy, or the right of self-expression," but rather by reference to the Amendment's "positive purpose of creating an informed public capable of self-government."[1] Because this understanding of the First Amendment subordinates individual rights of expression to collective processes of public deliberation,[2] I shall call it the "collectivist" theory of the First Amendment.

Moved by the disreputable state of contemporary democratic dialogue in America, proponents of the collectivist theory of the First Amendment have used the theory to advance a powerful reform agenda, ranging from statutes designed to correct the corrosive effects of private wealth on elections, to legislation calculated to free the marketplace of ideas from the distorting effects of large media oligopolies. The Supreme Court has been largely hostile to this agenda, objecting to its tendency to achieve its purposes through the suppression of individual speech. Thus in Buckley v. Valeo the Court struck down limitations on independent campaign expenditures, stating that "the concept that government may restrict the speech of some elements of our society in order to enhance the relative voice of others is wholly foreign to the First Amendment."[3] And in Miami Herald Publishing Co. v. Tornillo the Court sought to protect a private and independent sphere of editorial autonomy by striking down a Florida statute providing candidates a right of reply when attacked by the press.[4]

Advocates of the collectivist theory of the First Amendment view these decisions as misguided, because they invoke private speech rights to circumscribe government efforts to enhance public debate. The touchstone of constitutional analysis should rather be, as Cass Sunstein has written, what "will best promote democratic deliberation."[5] Instead of fetishizing private rights, the Court should engage in a nuanced, contextualized, and pragmatic inquiry.

The most uncompromising contemporary version of the collectivist theory has been offered by Owen Fiss. According to Fiss, the Supreme Court has been enthralled by a "Free Speech Tradition" that is wrongly focused on "the protection of autonomy."[6] It has thus failed to "see that the key to fulfilling the ultimate purposes of the first amendment is not autonomy . . . but rather the actual effect" of speech:

> On the whole does it enrich public debate? Speech is protected when (and only when) it does, and precisely because it does, not because it is an exercise of autonomy. In fact autonomy adds nothing, and if need be, might have to be sacrificed, to make certain that public debate is sufficiently rich to permit true collective self-determination. What the phrase "the freedom of speech" in the first amendment refers to is a social state of affairs, not the action of an individual or institution.[7]

This is a characteristically clear and succinct statement of the central premise of the collectivist theory. The criterion for constitutional analysis ought to be whether public debate is "sufficiently rich" to enable "true collective self-determination," and this criterion is analytically independent of the value of autonomy.[8] Once this premise is granted, the collectivist theory of speech presents a cogent and powerful argument for revising traditional First Amendment jurisprudence.

The question I explore in this chapter is whether, and if so under what conditions, this premise can be rendered constitutionally coherent.

Alexander Meiklejohn and the Collectivist Theory

The most influential exposition of the collectivist theory of the First Amendment is by the American philosopher Alexander Meiklejohn; his work continues to inspire and guide the theory's contemporary advocates.[9] Because of its candid and unflinching exploration of the theory's assumptions and implications, Meiklejohn's work offers an especially clear revelation of the theory's essential constitutional structure.

Managing Public Discourse

Meiklejohn anchors the First Amendment firmly to the value of self-government:

> The primary purpose of the First Amendment is . . . that all the citizens shall, so far as possible, understand the issues which bear upon our common life. That is why no idea, no opinion, no doubt, no belief, no counterbelief, no relevant information, may be kept from them. Under the compact upon which the Constitution rests, it is agreed that men shall not be governed by others, that they shall govern themselves.[10]

Meiklejohn locates the essence of self-government, and therefore also "the final aim" of First Amendment freedom, in democracy's effort to ensure "the voting of wise decisions."[11] He sharply distinguishes this purpose from that of individual autonomy.

The First Amendment, Meiklejohn writes, "has no concern about the 'needs of many men to express their opinions' "; it provides instead for "the common needs of all the members of the body politic."[12] This orientation toward the needs of the collectivity, rather than the individual, underlies one of Meiklejohn's most quoted aphorisms: "What is essential is not that everyone shall speak, but that everything worth saying shall be said."[13] In Meiklejohn's view, the ultimate purpose of the First Amendment is to guard against "the mutilation" of "the thinking process of the community," not to protect the rights of persons to self-expression.[14]

Meiklejohn's account of the First Amendment requires a standard by which the quality of the community's thinking process can be assessed. How otherwise could it be known whether public discourse is actually meeting "the common needs of all the members of the body politic"? How else could it be determined if "everything worth saying" has been said, or if some particular regulation of speech "mutilates," rather than advances, democratic deliberation?

Meiklejohn does not flinch from the responsibility of providing such a standard. He proposes "the traditional American town meeting" as "a model" for the measurement of the quality of public debate. Meiklejohn argues that the town meeting "is not a Hyde Park"; it is not a scene of "unregulated talkativeness." It is rather "a group of free and equal men, cooperating in a common enterprise, and using for that enterprise responsible and regulated discussion." The objective of the enterprise is "to act upon matters of public interest," and speech is routinely and necessarily regulated so as to attain that objective:

> For example, it is usually agreed that no one shall speak unless "recognized by the chair." Also, debaters must confine their remarks to "the question before the house." If one man "has the floor," no one else may interrupt him except as provided by the rules. The meeting has assembled, not primarily to talk, but primarily by means of talking to get business done. And the talking must be regulated and abridged as the doing of the business under actual conditions may require. If a speaker wanders from the point at issue, if he is abusive or in other ways threatens to defeat the purpose of the meeting, he may be and should be declared "out of order." He must then stop speaking, at least in that way. And if he persists in breaking the rules, he may be "denied the floor" or, in the last resort, "thrown out" of the meeting. The town meeting, as it seeks for freedom of public discussion of public problems, would be wholly ineffectual unless speech were thus abridged.[15]

Meiklejohn explicitly describes the town meeting as having a structure of authority that I have characterized in Chapter 6 as "managerial." The meeting is regarded as an instrumental organization designed to achieve important and specific social ends, and its rules and regulations are deemed constitutionally justified insofar as they are necessary for the attainment of these ends. For Meiklejohn, the purpose of the meeting is "to act upon matters of public interest," and all facets of the meeting, including the speech of its participants, can be legally arranged so as to realize that objective. Meiklejohn is quite clear that "the talking must be regulated and abridged as the doing of the business under actual conditions may require." The quality of public debate, therefore, is to be measured by its capacity to facilitate public decision-making.

This criterion makes sense within the context of a town meeting. Participants in the meeting share "a common enterprise" and hence a common derivative understanding of the purpose and function of the regulatory standards by which the enterprise will be advanced. There is general agreement about such fundamental questions as the methods for setting the meeting's agenda, the procedures for governing debate within the meeting, the criteria for distinguishing relevant from irrelevant speech, and so forth. In this antecedent agreement lies the source of the moderator's constitutional authority to enforce rules of procedure by controlling speech within the "structured situation" of the meeting,[16] even to the extent of "denying the floor" to those who persistently refuse to accept the moderator's authority.

Meiklejohn does not theorize this agreement; he assumes it. Or, to be more precise, he assumes the institutional structure of the town meeting in which it lies embedded. In fact, the very form of a town meeting derives from shared assumptions of function and procedure; they give the meeting its shape and order, and they distinguish it from the "unregulated talkativeness" of "a Hyde Park." These assumptions thus stand in a position analytically distinct from, and prior to, any substantive decisions the town meeting might reach. The meeting is free to resolve as it wishes items properly presented for decision, but it is not free to abandon the shared assumptions of function and procedure that constitute it as a town meeting.

Meiklejohn views the town meeting as a model for public discourse because he conceptualizes democratic dialogue as serving the function of facilitating "the voting of wise decisions." He sees the exercise of democracy as analogous to an enormous town meeting. He thus imports into his conception of democracy a dichotomy between the substance of public decisions and the shared understandings of function and procedure that are analytically distinct from, and prior to, the content of specific public decisions. The consequence of this dichotomy is that for Meiklejohn the content of government decisions remains open for the determination of citizens, but the framework of democratic decision-making remains fixed and beyond the reach of citizen self-government. It is precisely on this point, on the range and meaning of self-government, that traditional First Amendment jurisprudence differs significantly from Meiklejohn.

Management and Democracy

Every interpretation of traditional First Amendment doctrine is, of course, contestable, but there is little dispute that one of the most important themes of that doctrine is the Amendment's function "as the guardian of our democracy."[17] The Amendment serves to limit majoritarian enactments, so "democracy" cannot in this context be equated with simple majoritarianism.[18] In fact, majoritarianism, from the perspective of traditional First Amendment doctrine, is merely a mechanism for decision-making that we adopt to reflect the deeper value of self-government, which in turn rests on the distinction between autonomy and heteronomy: "Democratic forms of government are those in which the laws are made by the same people to whom they apply (and for that reason they are autonomous norms), while in autocratic forms of government the law-makers are different from those to whom the laws are addressed (and are therefore heteronomous norms)."[19] What it means for laws to be "made" by the "same people to whom they apply" is not easy to understand. If, with Rousseau, we postulate a determinate fusion of individual and collective will, the difficulty dissolves.[20] But the postulate is unconvincing under modern conditions of heterogeneity.

Traditional First Amendment doctrine and a broad spectrum of modern political theories meet this difficulty by locating the normative essence of democracy in the opportunity to participate in the formation of the "will of the community" through "a running discussion between majority and minority."[21] On this account democracy attempts to reconcile individual autonomy with collective self-determination by subordinating governmental decision-making to communicative processes sufficient to instill in citizens a sense of participation, legitimacy, and identification. Although citizens may not agree with all legislative enactments, although there may be no determinate fusion of individual and collective will, citizens can nevertheless embrace the government as rightfully "their own" because of their engagement in these communicative processes. Following Supreme Court precedent, I shall use the term "public discourse" to refer to these communicative processes.[22]

Conceiving public discourse in this way has two important implications. First, censorship of public discourse must be understood as excluding those affected from access to the medium of collective self-determination. Censorship cuts off its victims from participation in the enterprise of autonomous self-government, and the fundamental democratic project of replacing the "unilateral respect of authority by the mutual respect of autonomous wills" is *pro tanto* circumscribed.[23]

Second, public discourse must be conceptualized as an arena within which citizens are free continuously to reconcile their differences and to (re)construct a distinctive and ever-changing national identity. Building on the work of Charles Taylor, we might define a "national identity" in this context as an orientation in "moral space," a framework within which we "can try to determine from case to case what is good, or valuable, or what ought to be done."[24] We commonly ground government regulation of behavior on specific visions of national identity. But if the state attempts to use such visions to censor public discourse, if the state excludes communicative contributions on the grounds of a specific sense of what is

good or valuable, the state stands in contradiction to the central project
of collective self-determination. It displaces that project for the sake of
heteronomously imposed norms. The internal logic of self-government
thus implies that with regard to the censorship of speech the state must
act as though the meaning of collective identity were perpetually indeterminate within the medium of public discourse, where the "debate as to
what is legitimate and what is illegitimate" must "necessarily" remain
"without any guarantor and without any end."[25]

Meiklejohn's model of the town meeting, however, precisely violates
this necessary indeterminacy of public discourse. While acknowledging
that "the voting of wise decisions" must be kept free from government
interference, it nevertheless authorizes the censorship of public discourse
on the basis of assumptions about function and procedure. Meiklejohn
cannot appeal to a neutral distinction between substance and procedure to
justify this contraction of the scope of democratic self-government, for
the procedural assumptions he wishes to enforce, no less than substantive
ones, are ultimately grounded in a distinctive and controversial conception of collective identity. His paradigm of the town meeting specifically
presupposes that the function of American democracy is to achieve an
orderly, efficient, and rational dispatch of common business, and it consequently implies that aspects of public discourse incompatible with that
function are constitutionally expendable. To the extent that public discourse is thus truncated, a particular concept of national identity is placed
beyond the reach of the communicative processes of self-determination.

The difficulty with Meiklejohn's analysis, therefore, is that it reflects an
insufficiently radical conception of the reach of self-determination, which
encompasses not merely the substance of collective decisions but also the
larger framework of function within which such collective decision-
making is necessarily conceived as taking place. It is precisely because he
is certain about the nature of that framework that Meiklejohn can, for
example, unproblematically appeal to the authority of a moderator. But
Kenneth Karst noted long ago that in fact the "state lacks 'moderators'
who can be trusted to know when 'everything worth saying' has been
said."[26] The state lacks such moderators because the very standards necessary to distinguish "relevant" from "irrelevant" speech (or "original"
from "repetitious" speech, or "orderly" from "disorderly" speech, or
even "rational" from "irrational" speech) are themselves matters of potential dispute.[27] We can settle disputes about the nature of these standards only by appealing to particular conceptions of the larger framework

of function that gives collective decision-making its telos. Conflicts about the nature of these standards ought therefore to be a matter for debate within public discourse. To use a particular version of these standards to censor public discourse would be, *pro tanto*, heteronomously to foreclose the open-ended search for collective self-definition.

The same point can be made with respect to the agenda-setting mechanisms of a town meeting. Public control over the presentation and characterization of issues within a town meeting seems unproblematic because of a shared agreement concerning efficient institutional function and procedure. But within democratic life generally, such agreement cannot be assumed without concomitantly diminishing the arena for self-determination. This is because "political conflict is not like an intercollegiate debate in which the opponents agree in advance on the definition of the issues. As a matter of fact, *the definition of the alternatives is the supreme instrument of power* . . . He who determines what politics is about runs the country, because the definition of the alternatives is the choice of conflicts, and the choice of conflicts allocates power."[28] The state ought not to be empowered to control the agenda of public discourse,[29] or the presentation and characterization of issues within public discourse, because such control would necessarily circumscribe the potential for collective self-determination.

These elementary examples can be given general theoretical formulation. Managerial structures necessarily presuppose objectives that are unproblematic and hence that can be used instrumentally to regulate domains of social life. The enterprise of public discourse, by contrast, rests on the value of collective autonomy, which requires that all possible objectives, all possible versions of national identity, be rendered problematic and open to inquiry. No particular objective can justify the coercive censorship of public discourse without simultaneously contradicting the very enterprise of self-determination. As a consequence public discourse always appears intolerably formless and incoherent to those who care about the instrumental accomplishment of particular purposes, whether they be the voting of wise decisions or the maintenance of rational debate. Public discourse seems to them to consist merely of "a Hyde Park" filled with "unregulated talkativeness."

Justice Harlan captured this aspect of public discourse in Cohen v. California. He observed that democratic dialogue "may often appear to be only verbal tumult, discord, and even offensive utterance." But Harlan understood that this disorder, this "verbal cacophony," is merely a "necessary side [effect]" of the fact that, "in a society as diverse and populous as ours," public discourse is organized not to accomplish anything in particular but instead to serve as a medium within which heterogeneous versions of collective identity can be free continuously to collide and reconcile.[30]

Self-determination, we might say, is something that *happens* within public discourse; there is no external Archimedean point from which it can be compelled or its outcome anticipated. We can decide, within public discourse, to form and set in motion specific organizations of order and instrumental rationality, like town meetings. But it would be a grave mistake to confuse these discrete institutions with the sea of tumult and discord that is public discourse itself.

The Contemporary Managerial Impulse

Meiklejohn's work displays a structure of analysis that is common to all versions of the collectivist theory of the First Amendment. The theory postulates a specific "objective" for public discourse, and it concludes that public debate should be regulated instrumentally to achieve this objective. The objective thus stands distinct from, and prior to, any process of self-determination that happens within public discourse. The collectivist theory, therefore, stands for the subordination of public discourse to a framework of managerial authority.

This structure of analysis is plainly visible in the work of Owen Fiss. Fiss writes that "the larger political purposes" of the First Amendment are to establish a "rich public debate." He accordingly views the "protection of autonomy" as "instrumental" for enhancing "the quality of public discourse." "Autonomy may be protected, but only when it enriches public debate."[31] If autonomy does not fulfill this function, then "we as a people will never truly be free" until the state is constitutionally empowered to "restrict the speech of some elements of our society in order to enhance the relative voice of others."[32]

Thus Fiss, like Meiklejohn, would use governmental power to censor speakers whose expression is deemed incompatible with the achievement of a rich and informative public dialogue. He is willing to deny these speakers access to the processes of democratic self-government because he desires to fashion a public dialogue capable of empowering "people to vote intelligently and freely, aware of all the options and in possession of all the relevant information."[33] Fiss wants this goal to be managerially imposed upon public discourse by the state. He believes that objections to such managerial authority flow from a misplaced concern with individual autonomy, from a misguided effort to erect "a zone of noninterference" around the speech of "each individual."[34]

What Fiss apparently does not recognize, however, is that the value of individual autonomy is inseparable from the very aspiration for self-government that propels his own proposed revision of First Amendment doctrine. Fiss plainly sees that First Amendment jurisprudence must provide for "the essential preconditions for an effective democracy," and that "democracy promises collective self-determination."[35] Yet his analysis extends the logic of self-determination only to the content of democratic decisions, and it withholds that logic from the procedural framework of democratic decision-making. Like Meiklejohn, Fiss conceptualizes this framework as exogenous to public discourse and hence as subject to majoritarian control. Fiss is therefore vulnerable to the same critique that we have already applied to Meiklejohn.

As Sheldon Wolin has written, "Collective identity is created by and perpetuated through public discourse."[36] But different conceptions of collective identity will imply different standards for measuring the quality of public debate. Fiss believes that public discourse is subject to a "distorting influence" when it is controlled by the ambient structure of the capitalist market.[37] But Fiss's belief makes sense only because he has a particular orientation in "moral space," a framework within which he can distinguish the "distorted" from the normal. It is precisely because he has such a framework that Fiss can urge that the state regulate speech by means of decisions that "are analogous to the judgments made by the great teachers of the universities of this nation every day of the week."[38] But to use the coercive power of the state to suppress public discourse on the basis of such a particular vision of national identity would be to decide in advance the very issue of collective identity that public discourse is meant to be the means of resolving.

What follows from this analysis is not that public discourse can never be regulated, but that it ought not to be managed in ways that contradict its democratic purpose. This purpose need not preclude "time, place and manner regulations" that function as "rules of the road" to coordinate and facilitate expression within public discourse. Nor need it rule out government action designed to supplement or augment communications within public discourse, as for example by establishing state-supported forums to enhance public debate.[39] But the democratic function of public discourse is inconsistent with government regulations that suppress speech within public discourse for the sake of imposing a specific version of national identity.

Traditional First Amendment jurisprudence uses the ideal of autonomy to insulate the processes of collective self-determination from such pre-emption. Although Fiss can see in this ideal only the vestige of an earlier era of "Jeffersonian democracy,"[40] in fact the protection of individual autonomy functions in First Amendment doctrine to ensure that government will respect public discourse as pervasively indeterminate.[41] It prevents the state from violating the central democratic aspiration to create a communicative structure dedicated to "the mutual respect of autonomous wills" by guaranteeing that democratic dialogue will remain continuously available to the potential contributions of its individual participants. Autonomy, properly understood, signifies that within the sphere of public discourse and with regard to the suppression of speech the state must always regard collective identity as necessarily open-ended.[42]

The ideal of autonomy essentially distinguishes First Amendment jurisprudence from other areas of constitutional law, which are most often associated with specific visions of collective identity. In the domain of equal protection, for example, with which Fiss is most famously associated, the federal government has for forty years aggressively sought to inculcate particular national values of equality. But legal imposition of these values acquires democratic legitimacy precisely because the First Amendment has already established an arena of public discourse within which they can be freely embraced or rejected. Far from being vestigial, then, the ideal of autonomy is instead foundational for the democratic project.

Justifications for the Collectivist Theory

Many who practice empirical political science would no doubt object to the identification of democracy with the value of autonomous self-government.[43] But within the world of constitutional law this identification stands virtually unchallenged, perhaps because of the absence of serious alternative normative accounts of democracy. Indeed, the principle that "the American people are politically free insomuch as they are governed by themselves collectively" is one "that no earnest, non-disruptive participant in American constitutional debate is quite free to reject."[44]

There are, of course, vast disparities between the dreary realities of American politics and the aspirational principle of self-determination. The extent to which our public discourse actually functions to instill participation, legitimacy, and identification is highly debatable.[45] Participants in the American constitutional tradition are thus forced to choose. They can either abandon the principle of self-determination and proffer a new and more convincing normative account of democracy, or they can propose reforms that will enable the principle of self-determination to be more effectively realized in American society.

Proponents of the collectivist theory have uniformly chosen the latter option. Their reform agenda is explicitly designed to further the value of self-governance. Exemplary is the work of Cass Sunstein, who argues that "the First Amendment is fundamentally aimed at protecting democratic self-government," which he understands to be a structure of "deliberation" designed to place "governing authority in the people themselves." But because Sunstein believes that the value of "private autonomy" is logically distinct from democratic self-government, he also urges that public discourse be managed so as to improve its "quality and diversity."[46] Like all modern proponents of the collectivist theory, therefore, Sunstein is rendered vulnerable to the charge of failing to appreciate the full radical force of the aspiration toward democratic self-governance.

Although a complete survey of the literature is beyond my scope here, it can generally be said that proponents of the collectivist theory, in a sincere and admirable effort to rejuvenate democratic self-governance, argue that public discourse should be regulated so as to achieve some specific ideal associated with a particular view of national identity, ranging from "equality"[47] to "diversity"[48] to "fairness."[49] But to the extent that the managerial logic of the collectivist theory requires that these regulatory criteria be themselves exempt from the logic of self-determination, the theory stands in essential tension with fundamental premises of democratic self-governance.

To avoid this contradiction, proponents of the collectivist theory emphasize the circumstances in which public discourse cannot convincingly be said to realize the values of self-governance, and therefore in which the managerial logic of the collectivist theory does not contradict basic democratic premises. They properly focus attention on three propositions: (1) public discourse serves the value of self-governance only when there is a plausible public/private distinction; (2) public discourse serves the value of self-governance only when public debate can plausibly be regarded as an exchange among free and autonomous persons; and (3) public discourse serves the value of self-governance only when public debate engenders the sense of participation, legitimacy, and identification necessary to reconcile individual with collective autonomy.

Each of these propositions spotlights a vulnerable link between public discourse and the value of self-determination. Where any of these links are broken, the focus of traditional First Amendment jurisprudence on autonomy is rendered problematic, and the collectivist theory emerges as a powerful alternative account of freedom of speech.

The Public/Private Distinction

Traditional First Amendment doctrine presupposes some form of a public/private distinction. It locates the essence of democracy in self-determination, which inheres in the responsiveness of government to its citizens. The thrust of the doctrine is thus to protect from "public" regulation the communicative processes of "private" citizens deemed necessary for self-governance.[50] The doctrine has rather little to say, however, about government speech itself, which is not theorized as central to self-determination.[51] When, therefore, a speaker crosses the divide from private citizen to public functionary, she passes beyond the scope of traditional First Amendment doctrine. In such circumstances the collectivist theory offers an attractive alternative account of First Amendment standards for regulating the speech of public functionaries.

This can plainly be seen in the one decision of the Supreme Court that unambiguously relies on the collectivist theory, Red Lion Broadcasting Co. v. FCC. At issue in *Red Lion* was the constitutionality of various FCC regulations of the broadcast media, including the fairness doctrine and subsidiary rules requiring that those personally attacked be given a right to reply. The Court held that because "broadcast frequencies constituted a scarce resource whose use could be regulated and rationalized only by the Government," and because those frequencies were "a public trust," a broadcast licensee could appropriately be regarded as "a proxy or fiduciary with obligations to present those views and voices which are representative of his community and which would otherwise, by necessity, be barred from the airwaves."[52]

Broadcast licensees, in other words, were not private parties whose views were to be shielded from government regulation out of respect for the indeterminacy of their contribution to the communicative process of self-determination. They were instead agents of a public objective. The Court appealed to a collectivist theory of speech to specify this objective, which it characterized as "the First Amendment goal of producing an informed public capable of conducting its own affairs." The Court had no difficulty finding that the fairness doctrine instrumentally served this goal.[53]

The Court's embrace of the collectivist theory was thus made possible by its characterization of broadcast licensees as public functionaries. This characterization could not plausibly have been driven by the logic of scarcity; even at the time of *Red Lion* there were, in most media markets, many more frequencies available than FCC regulation had actually allocated for use.[54] In any event, neither we nor the Court ordinarily regard the owners of scarce important communicative resources, like major metropolitan newspapers, for that reason alone to be public agents.[55] The Court's characterization must instead be understood as reflecting a political judgment about whether the broadcast media were sufficiently independent from the achievement of public purposes as to be regarded as private participants in the project of self-determination.[56] Unfortunately the Court never convincingly spelled out the rationale for its judgment, and our ability to assess the validity of such evaluations remains quite rudimentary.

This has not prevented some modern proponents of the collectivist theory from attempting to generalize from *Red Lion*. They argue that the collectivist theory is justified because the public/private distinction can have little persuasive applicability to the modern world. Thus Fiss writes not only that CBS can "be said to perform a public function" (and therefore to be "a composite of the public and private"), but also that the "same is true of the print media, as it is of all corporations, unions, universities, and political organizations." In fact, Fiss concludes, "the social world is largely constituted by entities that partake of both the public and private."[57]

Fiss's argument illustrates the danger of confusing descriptive and political accounts of the public/private distinction. His characterization is no doubt descriptively accurate, but the public/private distinction turns instead on questions of moral and political ascription. What is politically at issue in characterizing a speaker as public or private is precisely the scope of self-government. To repudiate the private status of speakers in the wholesale manner proposed by Fiss would necessarily entail an equally sweeping rejection of the realm of democratic self-determination. And this would be inconsistent with the very value of self-governance that Fiss acknowledges to be at the root of the collectivist theory.

The point, therefore, is that while particular applications of the collectivist theory may be sustained through local adjustments of the boundary between private citizens and public functionaries, the collectivist theory cannot be *generically* justified by this method without profoundly revising contemporary notions of democratic legitimacy.[58]

The Empirical Implausibility of Autonomy

Public discourse merits unique constitutional protection because it is the process through which the democratic "self," the agent of self-government, is itself constituted through the reconciliation of individual and collective autonomy. Constitutional solicitude for public discourse, therefore, presupposes that those participating in public discourse are free and autonomous. Public discourse could not serve the project of self-determination if the opinions and attitudes of speakers were deemed to be merely the effects of external causes. Under such conditions the collectivist theory would no longer be inconsistent with democratic values.

Advocates of the collectivist theory commonly attempt to justify their position by stressing that public discourse cannot now plausibly be interpreted as an arena of free communicative exchange. Thus Julian Eule, using a metaphor popular among proponents of the collectivist theory, argues that limitations on campaign finance expenditures are necessary because the voices of the wealthy "drown out the voices of others." The metaphor serves a double function. At one level it expresses the normative criterion—"ensuring that the public is exposed to a broad array of views"—that Eule believes ought to be managerially used to regulate public discourse. At a deeper level the metaphor serves the additional function of justifying the creation of this managerial authority. Eule specifically tells us that "the extent to which a well-financed corporate speaker can dominate the 'marketplace' has little to do with the persuasiveness of the speech."[59] Eule's point is that the perspectives of those engaged in public discourse are caused by such variables as the quantity of speech that money can buy,[60] and hence that such perspectives cannot be regarded as the freely adopted conclusions of rational agents. Managerial control is justified because the freedom necessary to link public discourse to self-determination has vanished.

This method of justifying collectivist theory is also explicit in the work of Owen Fiss, who writes that the market is "a structure of constraint" and that regulation is necessary "to counteract the skew of public debate attributable to the market."[61] The denial of autonomy is most developed, however, in the arguments of Cass Sunstein. Sunstein sets rigorous standards for the ascription of autonomy: "The notion of autonomy should refer . . . to decisions reached with a full and vivid awareness of available opportunities, with reference to all relevant information, and without illegitimate or excessive constraints on preference formation. When these conditions are not met, decisions should be described as unfree or nonautonomous."[62] Sunstein finds it "most difficult" to deem "individual freedom" relevant when attitudes "are a product of available information, existing consumption patterns, social pressures, and governmental rules." In fact, individual attitudes should "be regarded as nonautonomous insofar as they are reflexively adaptive to unjust background conditions." Government regulation to overcome such conditions "removes a kind of coercion." Sunstein proposes far-reaching reforms to subordinate public discourse to managerial control, and these reforms are ultimately justified by his equally far-reaching denial of the relevance of individual autonomy.[63]

The denial of freedom poses a fundamental and complex challenge to traditional First Amendment jurisprudence. We know that human beings, like all natural objects, are subject to laws of cause and effect. As social science grows more sophisticated, we can expect to better understand, predict, and control the manifold ways in which cultural environment affects and determines social behavior, including speech and attitude formation. This knowledge, however, is deeply incompatible with the very premise of democratic self-government. Citizenship presupposes the attribution of freedom; in fact the ascription of autonomy may be said to be the transcendental precondition for the possibility of democratic self-determination. This is because members of a polity, regarded only through the lens of social or natural science, cease to be citizens; they are visible only as effects of complex and multifarious causes.

I appreciate the paradoxical quality of this conclusion. We often speak of autonomy as a condition that needs to be attained through education, nurturance, the ameliorization of disabling circumstances, and so forth. This is the perspective from which Sunstein writes, and it implies that autonomy must be achieved rather than ascribed. But this perspective can be misleading when it comes to the design of structures of social authority. These structures will be different depending upon whether they are intended to foster interactions among citizens who are autonomous or among citizens who are not. This means that the autonomy *vel non* of the subject of legal regulation is presupposed in the very structure of law by which that subject is regulated. From the point of view of the designer of the structure, therefore, the presence or absence of autonomy functions as an axiomatic and foundational principle.[64] Managerial structures locate citizens within the constraints of instrumental reason, assuming thereby that citizens are objects of regulation, subject to the laws of cause and effect. Structures of self-governance, in contrast, situate citizens within webs of hermeneutic interactions, assuming thereby that citizens are autonomous and self-determining.

In most circumstances we find ways of finessing this tension between management and democracy. The explosive expansion of the regulatory state during the twentieth century, for example, has been fueled by acceptance and application of the insights of social science. Through sophisticated forms of social engineering we manipulate the conditions of our environment and the persons who inhabit it. We do not regard these government controls as fundamentally incompatible with the premises of democratic freedom because we conceive them to be freely adopted by the citizens of a democratic state. Analogous managerial controls over public discourse, however, cannot be conceptualized as democratically legitimate in the same way, for they *displace* the very processes of collective self-determination. To conceive public discourse as a realm of causation, and to use this conception to justify regulating public discourse in ways incompatible with its democratic purpose, is directly and uncompromisingly to challenge the last redoubt of self-governance.

Like the public/private distinction, therefore, the concept of autonomy must function within public discourse as a moral ascription that marks the boundaries of our commitment to democratic self-government. For this reason the denial of freedom within public discourse cannot *generically* justify the collectivist theory of speech without contradicting the central premise of our democratic enterprise. At most autonomy can be negated in discrete and local ways where First Amendment presumptions of autonomy have come to seem merely "fictions"[65] masking particularly intolerable conditions of private power and domination. The maintenance of democratic legitimacy, however, requires that sufficient domains of public discourse remain governed by presumptions of freedom so as to realize meaningfully our commitment to self-government.

The consequence of this conclusion is apparent in the work of J. Skelly

Wright, who yields to none in the vehemence of his denunciation of the "stifling influence of money" that perverts "the minds of the people" and thus has "a powerful impact" on the outcome of electoral campaigns. Yet Wright's proposed remedy is discrete and limited:

> An election campaign is finite in time and focuses on specific ballot decisions regarding specific alternatives. Expenditure limits and other curbs on campaign finance practices are analogous to rules of order at a town meeting, enforced so that the deliberative process is not distorted. The first amendment does not permit curbs on general discussion of political, economic, or social controversies. But, like the loud mouth and long talker at the town meeting, untrammeled spending during an election campaign does not serve the values of self-government.[66]

As Eule, Fiss, and Sunstein all plainly understand, wealth has equally powerful and stifling effects on the "general discussion of political, economic, or social controversies" as it does on election campaigns. But Wright recognizes that public discourse cannot be subject to generic managerial control without concomitantly sacrificing central First Amendment values. He therefore embraces a distinction that is, from an empirical point of view, merely arbitrary. But so long as the political function of the attribution of autonomy is kept clearly in mind, some such empirically arbitrary limitation will be necessary whenever autonomy is denied to justify employment of the collectivist theory of freedom of speech.

An important practical implication of this analysis is that the criteria we use to locate autonomy must be politically calibrated by their implications for the value of self-determination. Thus, for example, Sunstein's rigorous preconditions for autonomy are plainly unacceptable for use in the First Amendment context. They are far too stringent to apply practically to the rough-and-tumble world of actual politics. Applied literally, they would reserve self-government for philosopher-kings. Applied loosely, they would tie the qualification for self-government directly to political perspective, and hence constitute an open invitation to exclude the communicative contributions of those whose views are deemed "reflexively adaptive to unjust background conditions."[67] Similarly, Owen Fiss's attribution of coercion to the constraints of the capitalist social structure is too vague and indiscriminate to coexist peacefully with the value of collective self-determination.

To be frank, I am uncertain whether appropriate criteria of autonomy can ever be satisfactorily established, for the tension between democracy and the attempt to justify the collectivist theory by denying the autonomy of citizens is so very fundamental. One cannot but be struck by the sharp anomaly of regulating democratic elections on the premise that voters are not autonomous and free. It is hard to imagine what kind of an empirical showing could ever suffice to overcome the internal disequilibrium of such a position. And there will always be disturbing possibilities for manipulation and abuse in sanctioning the exclusion of categories of citizens from the polity because of their ascribed lack of freedom. Without denying in principle that such exclusions may be necessary or desirable, I would emphasize that a democratic state can tolerate them only in the most unusual and limited of circumstances.

The Conditions of Participation, Legitimacy, and Identification

Both the repudiation of the public/private distinction and the denial of autonomy are arguments exogenous to traditional First Amendment jurisprudence. They attempt to clear a space for the application of the collectivist theory by negating axiomatic foundations for the application of established First Amendment doctrine. There is yet a third argument for the collectivist theory, however, which adopts a stance that is internal to the received First Amendment tradition.

This argument begins from the premise that public discourse serves the value of self-government because it engenders the sense of participation, identification, and legitimacy necessary to reconcile individual with collective autonomy. Even if public discourse is formally free, it cannot fulfill this function if the actual practices of public debate cause citizens to experience alienation or disaffection. A democratic state must combat these effects if public discourse is to sustain the value of self-determination. This effort may even require the subordination of specific aspects of public discourse to managerial control.

The internal argument for the collectivist theory is visible in the work of J. Skelly Wright, who observes that election campaigns, even if formally free, cannot fulfill their democratic function if they are experienced by citizens as distant, unresponsive, and dominated by wealth. Wright astutely cautions "that it is hazardous to discourage civic spirit, hope, and participation; that disillusionment breeds alienation; that alienation breeds apathy; that apathy menaces the democratic idea."[68] He therefore defends campaign expenditure limitations as a means of fulfilling the very concerns that lie at the core of collective self-determination.

Because the internal argument for the collectivist theory remains firmly anchored in the values of participation and self-government, it does not imply that the collectivist theory ought generally to displace traditional interpretations of the First Amendment. It instead forces us to confront the possibility that the achievement of democratic values may, in discrete circumstances, require carefully bounded structures of managerial control.[69] The narrow objective of such structures must be the correction of conditions which cause disabling citizen disaffection.

So, for example, Wright believes that civic alienation from electoral campaigns has been caused by flagrant violations of "the ideal of equality," and he argues that campaign speech ought to be managed so as to instantiate that ideal. Wright understands, however, that even such a beneficent purpose does not alter the fact that citizens subject to managerial control become the heteronomous objects of regulation. His use of the internal argument thus leads Wright to cede priority of place to democratic values, thereby checking the slippage, so apparent in the recent work of Fiss and Sunstein, toward a disturbing loss of serious engagement with the ideal of collective self-government. Wright clearly sees that the organized structure of an election campaign, like the analogous structure of a town meeting, must remain a narrowly bounded island within a more general and uncensored sea of "discussion of political, economic, or social controversies."[70]

It seems to me better to use a spatial metaphor to express such a limited suspension of autonomous self-determination than to use the more common temporal image that, for example, may be found in the often retold parable of Ulysses and the Sirens.[71] Well-known dynamics of power suggest that in actual practice managerial displacements of self-governance are unlikely to be temporary. And certainly the total partition of public discourse from the value of self-determination, however limited in duration, would be unacceptable in a democratic state. In this sense the spatial metaphor properly focuses attention on the relationship between discrete areas of managerial control and the general health of ongoing and free processes of communication. The spatial metaphor emphasizes the necessarily ancillary and subordinate character of the managerial regulation of communicative processes.

According to the internal argument for the collectivist theory, managerial control of discrete domains of public discourse can be justified only by pressing necessity, which the internal argument comprehends in terms of circumstances rendering the formal conditions of freedom inimical to the achievement of actual democratic legitimacy. Only a democracy mesmerized by formal freedom could fail to be alarmed by such circumstances. But the internal argument also demands that we face unflinchingly the paradox entailed by establishing structures of managerial control that violate formal conditions of freedom in order to recuperate democratic values. Such structures necessarily lose what they hope to achieve. They may be acceptable for acts of local rehabilitation, but, if generally imposed, would frustrate the very raison d'être of the democratic enterprise.

We are thus thrown into a world of inconsistency and compromise, the unhappy home of both politics and constitutional adjudication. Our main hope is to keep clearly in view the values that ought to guide our judgment, including and especially the painful conflicts among them. Because its principled application will enforce this divided awareness, the internal argument for the collectivist theory of the First Amendment seems to me the theory's most attractive constitutional justification.

Conclusion

Contemporary advocates of the collectivist theory, by contrast, tend enthusiastically and uncritically to endorse the theory as a beneficent extension of the progressive, regulatory state. Resistance to the theory is attributed to Lochnerism,[72] to a nostalgic fixation on long-lost Jeffersonian independence.[73] The modern world, we are told, demands a sterner realism, an acknowledgment of pervasive and complex configurations of constraint and heteronomy that can be mastered only through active state intervention.

State intervention, however, implies managerial control, and we ought not to be quite so quick to embrace a world of "undeviating organization" (as members of the Frankfurt school would characterize it).[74] The nightmare vision of Michel Foucault demonstrates clearly enough the true nature of such a world. Structures of control acquire their own life, turn, and bite the progressive hand that establishes them. If we create organizations of heteronomy, we shall all, sooner or later, be condemned to inhabit them. We shall become the subjects of a power not our own.

I do not mean to imply that government regulation does not have its necessary uses. There is no "natural" social order, and government management is indispensable for achieving our desired purposes and ends. Indeed, a public discourse that did not ultimately establish managerial organizations designed to attain publicly decided objectives would be merely impotent. But more is at stake in the regulation of public discourse than the simple question of laissez faire. Quite beyond values of individual human liberty[75] and personal self-realization[76] lies the significance of the *collective* virtue of self-government. Traditional First Amendment doctrine, with its quaint focus on autonomy and the indeterminacy of national identity, is one of the last remaining areas of constitutional law to engage seriously the project of self-determination. If we discard that project as childish myth, so do we also discard our commitment to democracy, at least as our constitutional tradition has so far understood democracy.

Perhaps that understanding is now ripe for revision. If some are indeed prepared to abandon the Enlightenment framework that has so far governed our appreciation of democratic legitimacy, the debate should be joined directly, and not crabwise, through the unconscious evisceration of the very values in whose name we still purport to act. Certainly in the absence of a convincing alternative normative account of democracy, we ought not willingly and cheerfully abandon our last vestigial commitments to the project of collective independence and freedom, even for the most beguiling visions of progressive reform.

The collectivist theory of freedom of speech clearly has its uses, but the case has not yet been made for its displacement of traditional First Amendment jurisprudence. We should employ the theory when it is truly necessary to sustain the enterprise of self-governance, or when we need standards to govern the regulation of the speech of public functionaries. But these circumstances should be the exception rather than the rule, at least until we have developed a more attractive explanation of the significance of our democratic institutions than that offered by the goal of collective self-determination.

Reprise

The Racist Speech Problem

The curse of racism continues to haunt the nation. Everywhere we face its devastation, the bitter legacy of, in William Lloyd Garrison's prophetic words, our "covenant with death and . . . agreement with Hell."[1] This is the living consequence of the history that has produced us. We cannot overcome that history without changing ourselves and therefore also our legal order. Since Brown v. Board of Education,[2] vast stretches of our law have passed through the flame of this challenge.[3] The question is always what to preserve, what to alter.

Now it is the turn of the First Amendment. Largely inspired by Richard Delgado's "Words That Wound,"[4] an extraordinary spate of articles analyzing the constitutionality of restrictions on racist speech has appeared in the past few years.[5] The analysis is not merely academic. Motivated by an alarming increase in racist incidents,[6] universities throughout the nation have turned toward the task of restraining racist expression.[7] The justification for these restraints, and their relationship to First Amendment values, has become a matter of intense controversy.[8]

One approach has been to attempt to use legal regulation to eradicate all visible signs of that "racist sentiment" which, in the view of some, our history has caused to "[pervade] the life of virtually all white Americans."[9] Rules promulgated by the University of Connecticut, for example, plainly evinced this remarkable ambition. These rules prohibited "behavior that denigrates others because of their race [or] ethnicity."[10] They provided that the "use of derogatory names, inappropriately directed laughter, inconsiderate jokes, anonymous notes or phone calls, and conspicuous exclusion from conversations and/or classroom discussions are examples of harassing behaviors that are prohibited." The rules listed the "signs" of proscribed "Harassment, Discrimination and Intolerance," some of which were:

Stereotyping the experiences, background, and skills of individuals
Treating people differently solely because they are in some way different
from the majority
Responding to behaviors or situations negatively because of the back-
ground of the participants . . .
Imitating stereotypes in speech or mannerisms . . .
Attributing objections to any of the above actions to "hypersensitivity"
of the targeted individual or group.[11]

These rules were plainly not designed to regulate specific forms of
behavior or expression, but rather to encompass and to forbid all exterior
"signs" of an interior frame of mind. One can readily understand the
logic of this purpose. If our "common historical and cultural heritage"
has made us "all racists,"[12] then racism must be seen as an unredeemed
form of identity, whose every manifestation ought to be challenged and
sanctioned. Punitive legal regulations are thus faced with the task of
attempting to imagine and specify every possible indication of racism. But
because the racist personality can express itself in an infinite variety of
ways, the task is intrinsically elusive. The University of Connecticut rules
were clearly caught up in the frustrating spiral of this logic, a logic that,
when carried to its conclusion, can end only in the complete legal sub-
jugation of the individual.[13]

The incompatibility of this logic with even the most elementary standards of freedom of speech is obvious. Any communication can potentially express the racist self, and thus no communication can ever be safe
from legal sanction. It is therefore no surprise that the University of
Connecticut was forced to withdraw its regulations, although apparently
with reluctance and distress, because of a threatened lawsuit.[14] If the
ambition of legal regulation is to suppress manifestations of racist personality, the necessary consequence will be the wholesale abandonment of
all principles of freedom of expression.

To the extent that we care about First Amendment values, therefore,
we must make do with more modest aspirations.[15] The possibility of
effecting a reconciliation between principles of freedom of expression and
restraints on racist speech depends upon deflecting our focus away from
its spontaneous target, which is the racism of our cultural inheritance, and
toward the redress of particular and distinct harms caused by racist expression. The specification of these harms will lead to the definition of
discrete forms of speech, the legal regulation of which can then be assessed in light of relevant First Amendment values.

Such, in any event, will be the strategy of this essay. Its ambition is to be illustrative rather than comprehensive: the general issue of racist speech simply has too many facets to be encompassed here. Although the first part, "The Harms of Racist Speech," attempts to isolate and describe five specific kinds of harm, the second part, "The Values of the First Amendment," offers an account of only one of several possible relevant and important First Amendment values, that of democratic self-governance. In my view this value is primarily responsible for the constitutional safeguards that currently protect public discourse. The third and major part of this essay, "Racist Speech and Public Discourse," addresses the narrow issue of the constitutionality of regulating public discourse to ameliorate specific harms caused by racist speech. The fourth part, "The First Amendment and Harm to the Educational Environment," briefly examines the quite different constitutional issues posed by the regulation of racist speech within public institutions of higher learning.

One significant drawback of this analytic structure is that it renders the term "racist speech" into something of a cipher. As the University of Connecticut regulations illustrate, the term is inherently labile and ambiguous. It probably has as many definitions as there are commentators, and it would be pointless to pursue its endlessly variegated shades of meaning. I have decided, therefore, to focus on the constitutional implications of specific justifications for restraining racist expression, and to let the term "racist speech" absorb the content implied by these various justifications.

I should add that writing this essay has been difficult and painful. I am committed both to principles of freedom of expression and to the fight against racism. The topic under consideration has forced me to set one aspiration against the other, which I can do only with reluctance and a heavy heart.

The Harms of Racist Speech

Even a brief survey of the contemporary debate reveals it to be rich with textured and complex characterizations of the harms of racist expression. Here I will group these harms into five rough categories that represent the most prominent lines of thought and that are at the same time convenient for First Amendment analysis.[16]

The Intrinsic Harm of Racist Speech

A recurring theme in the contemporary literature is that racist expression ought to be regulated because it creates what has been termed "deontic" harm. The basic point is that there is an "elemental wrongness" to racist expression, regardless of the presence or absence of particular empirical consequences such as "grievous, severe psychological injury."[17] It is argued that toleration for racist expression is inconsistent with respect for "the principle of equality"[18] that is at the heart of the Fourteenth Amendment:[19]

> The thrust of this argument is that a society committed to ideals of social and political equality cannot remain passive: it must issue unequivocal expressions of solidarity with vulnerable minority groups and make positive statements affirming its commitment to those ideals. Laws prohibiting racist speech must be regarded as important components of such expressions and statements.[20]

If the basic harm of racist expression lies in its intrinsic and symbolic incompatibility with egalitarian ideals, then the distinct class of communications subject to legal regulation will be defined by reference to those ideals. For example, if the Fourteenth Amendment is thought to enshrine an anti-discrimination principle, then "any speech (in its widest sense) which supports racial prejudice or discrimination"[21] ought to be subject to regulation. But if the relevant ideals are thought to embody substantive racial equality, then the relevant class of communications should be defined as speech containing a "message . . . of racial inferiority."[22]

Harm to Identifiable Groups

A second theme in the current debate is that racist expression ought to be regulated because it harms those groups which are its target. There are two basic variations on this theme. One draws its inspiration from the tradition of group libel[23] and the decision of the Supreme Court in Beauharnais v. Illinois.[24] On this view, speech likely to cast contempt or ridicule on identifiable groups ought to be regulated to prevent injury to the status and prospects of the members of those groups. A second variation derives from the more contemporary understanding of racism as "the structural subordination of a group based on an idea of racial inferiority."[25] Racist expression is viewed as especially unacceptable because it locks in the oppression of already marginalized groups: "Racist speech is particularly harmful because it is a mechanism of subordination, reinforcing a historical vertical relationship."[26]

If the prevention of group harm is the basis for the regulation of communication, the definition of legally proscribed speech will depend upon one's understanding of the nature of the group harm at issue and the way in which communication is seen as causing that harm. Regulation that derives from a theory of group defamation, for example, would tend to safeguard all groups,[27] whereas regulation that derives from a theory of subordinate groups would sanction only speech "directed against a historically oppressed group."[28]

Harm to Individuals

A third prominent theme in the contemporary literature is that racist expression harms individuals. This theme essentially analogizes racist expression to forms of communication that are regulated by the dignitary torts of defamation, invasion of privacy, and intentional infliction of emotional distress. The law compensates persons for dignitary and emotional injuries caused by such communication, and it is argued that racist expression ought to be subject to regulation because it causes similar injuries. These injuries include "feelings of humiliation, isolation, and self-hatred" as well as "dignitary affront." The injuries are particularly powerful because "racial insults . . . conjure up the entire history of racial discrimination in this country."[29] In Patricia Williams' striking phrase, racist expression is a form of "spirit-murder."[30]

Regulating racist expression because of its negative impact on particular persons would suggest that the class of communications subject to legal sanction be narrowed to those that are addressed to specific individuals or that in some other way can be demonstrated to have adversely affected specific individuals. The nature of that class would vary, however, depending upon the particular kind of harm sought to be redressed. If the focus is on preventing "dignitary harm,"[31] the injury might be understood to inhere in the very utterance of certain kinds of racist communications;[32] if the focus is instead on emotional damage, independent proof of distress might be required to sustain recovery.[33] Regulation will also vary depending upon whether harm to individuals is understood to flow from the ideational content of racist expression or instead from its abusive nature.[34]

Harm to the Marketplace of Ideas

A fourth theme in the current debate is that racist expression harms the very marketplace of ideas that the First Amendment is designed to foster. A variety of different arguments have been brought forward to support

this position. It is argued that racist expression ought to be "proscribed
. . . as a form of assault, as conduct" inconsistent with the conditions of
respect and noncoercion prerequisite to rational deliberation.[35] It is argued that racist expression is inconsistent with the marketplace of ideas
because it "infects, skews, and disables the operation of the market . . .
Racism is irrational and often unconscious."[36] Finally, it is argued that
racism "systematically" silences "whole segments of the population,"[37]
either through the "visceral" shock and "preemptive effect on further
speech" of racist words, or through the distortion of "the marketplace of
ideas by muting or devaluing the speech of blacks and other non-
whites."[38]

The class of communications subject to legal sanction would depend
upon which of these various arguments is accepted. Depending upon
exactly how racist expression is understood to damage the marketplace of
ideas, the class might be confined to communication experienced as coercive and shocking, or it might be expanded to include communication
perceived as unconsciously and irrationally racist, or it might be expanded
still further to encompass speech explicitly devaluing and stigmatizing
victim groups.

Harm to Educational Environment

Each of the four categories of harm so far discussed can be caused by
racist expression within public discourse. There is, however, yet a fifth
kind of harm which is quite important to the contemporary controversy,
but which is relevant only to the specific educational environment of
institutions of higher learning. This is the harm that racist expression is
understood to cause to the educational mission of universities or colleges.
The prevention of this harm is central to the definition of a great number
of campus regulations.

Universities and colleges characteristically seek to regulate racist communications that "directly create a substantial and immediate interference with the educational processes of the University," without
articulating exactly how racist expression can cause that interference.[39]
Some campus regulations are more specific, focusing on the damage that
racist expression is understood to cause to particular individuals or groups.
For example, some regulations only proscribe racist expression that "will
interfere with the victim's ability to pursue effectively his or her education
or otherwise to participate fully in University programs and activities."[40]

Presumably this interference will occur for reasons similar to those that we have already canvassed.

In a number of instances, however, college or university regulations enunciate special educational goals that are understood to be inherently incompatible with racist expression. For example, Mount Holyoke College seeks to inculcate the value of diversity, which it views as plainly inconsistent with racist expression. Accordingly, Mount Holyoke's regulations provide:

> To enter Mount Holyoke College is to become a member of a community . . .
> Our community is committed to maintaining an environment in which diversity is not only tolerated, but is celebrated. Towards this end, each member of the Mount Holyoke community is expected to treat all individuals with a common standard of decency.[41]

Marquette University defines itself as "a Christian and Catholic institution . . . dedicated to the proposition that all human beings possess an inherent dignity in the eyes of their Creator and equality as children of God." Accordingly, Marquette's regulations seek to maintain "an environment in which the dignity and worth of each member of its community is respected" and in which "racial abuse or harassment . . . will not be tolerated."[42] Mary Washington College sets forth what appears to be a secular version of this same educational mission; its regulations provide that the "goal of the College is to help all students achieve academic success in an environment that nurtures, encourages growth, and develops sensitivity and appreciation for all people." Accordingly, "any activity or conduct that detracts from this goal—such as racial or sexual harassment—is inconsistent with the purposes of the college community."[43]

In such instances, racist expression interferes with education not merely because of general harms that it may inflict on groups or individuals or the marketplace of ideas,[44] but also, and more intrinsically, because racist expression exemplifies conduct that is contrary to the particular educational values that specific colleges or universities seek to instill.[45]

The Values of the First Amendment

As any constitutional lawyer knows, First Amendment doctrine is neither clear nor logical. It is a vast Sargasso Sea of drifting and entangled values, theories, rules, exceptions, predilections. It requires determined interpretive effort to derive a useful set of constitutional principles by which to evaluate regulations of expression. In recent years there has been an unfortunate tendency, by no means limited to the controversy surrounding racist speech, to avoid this difficult work by relying instead on formulaic invocations of First Amendment "interests" which can be captured in such conclusory labels as "individual self-fulfillment," "truth," "democracy," and so forth.[46] These formulas cast an illusion of stability and order over First Amendment jurisprudence, an illusion that can turn dangerous when it substitutes for serious engagement with the question of why we really care about protecting freedom of expression.

What is most disappointing about the expanding literature proposing restrictions on racist speech is the palpable absence of that engagement. The most original and significant articles in the genre concentrate on uncovering and displaying the manifold harms of racist communications; the harms of regulating expression are on the whole perfunctorily dismissed. This emphasis is readily understandable. It is a formidable task to attempt to carve out a new exception to the general protection of speech afforded by the armor of First Amendment doctrine. Even so staunch a defender of minority rights as Justice William Brennan might seem unsympathetic, given his observation in United States v. Eichman[47] that "virulent ethnic and religious epithets" ought to receive constitutional protection because of the " 'bedrock principle underlying the First Amendment . . . that the Government may not prohibit the expression of an idea simply because society finds the idea itself offensive or disagreeable.' "[48] In the face of such daunting obstacles, it is natural for proponents of restraints on racist speech to emphasize their affirmative case and to minimize countervailing considerations.

I agree, of course, that the question of regulating racist speech ought not be settled simply by reference to present doctrine. But it is equally important that the question ought not be settled without serious engagement with the values embodied in that doctrine. Regulations like those promulgated by the University of Connecticut and many other universities suggest that this lack of engagement is a real and practical problem.[49] Although earnest inquiry into the First Amendment values involved in the restraint of racist speech cannot by itself definitively solve the difficult constitutional issues we face, it can at least illuminate what is most deeply at stake for us in this controversy, and to that extent clarify the choices we must make.

Democracy, Public Discourse, and the First Amendment

This essay concentrates on the relevance for the regulation of racist speech of only one strand of First Amendment values. It is, however, an extraordinarily important strand, one which in my view accounts for a good deal of the shape of contemporary First Amendment doctrine. It concerns the relationship between freedom of expression and democratic self-governance. Its basic thrust is to provide certain kinds of protection to communication deemed necessary for the processes of democracy, communication that the Court has labeled "public discourse."[50]

I have in Chapter 5 analyzed in detail the structural prerequisites which public discourse must fulfill if it is to serve the essential democratic purpose of facilitating collective self-determination. Four of these prerequisites now require special emphasis, for they will be of importance when we examine the regulation of racist speech.

First, the function of public discourse is to reconcile, to the extent possible, the will of individuals with the general will. Public discourse is thus ultimately grounded in a respect for individuals seen as "free and equal persons."[51] In the words of Jean Piaget, "The essence of democracy resides in its attitude towards law as a product of the collective will, and not as something emanating from a transcendent will or from the authority established by divine right. It is therefore the essence of democracy to replace the unilateral respect of authority by the mutual respect of autonomous wills."[52] The individualism so characteristic of First Amendment doctrine thus flows directly from the central project of democracy.[53]

Second, some form of public/private distinction is necessarily implied by democracy understood as a project of self-determination. This is because the state undermines the raison d'être of its own enterprise to the extent that it itself coercively forms the "autonomous wills" that democracy seeks to reconcile into public opinion.[54] If the adjective "private" is understood to designate that which is beyond the coercive formation of the state, public discourse must be conceptualized as a process through which "private" perspectives are transformed into public power.

Third, democracy is on this account inherently incomplete. Democracy necessarily presupposes important (not to say foundational) aspects of the social world organized along nondemocratic lines. Public discourse must always exist in tension with other forms of communication ("nonpublic speech").

Fourth, because public discourse is understood as the communicative medium through which the democratic "self" is itself constituted, public discourse must in important respects remain exempt from democratic regulation. We use the speech/action distinction as one way of marking the boundaries of this exemption. These boundaries are purely pragmatic. We designate the communicative processes necessary to sustain the principle of collective self-determination as "speech" and thus insulate them from majoritarian interference.

Community, Civility Rules, and Public Discourse

Restraints on racist speech characteristically involve certain general First Amendment issues that I briefly review in this section in light of the functional concerns of public discourse. In so doing I confine myself to summarizing conclusions, the detailed arguments for which I have developed elsewhere in this book.

If democratic self-governance presupposes a social world in which "autonomous wills" are to be coordinated and reconciled, there is an important form of social organization, which I call "community," that rests on exactly the opposite presupposition. Building on the work of Michael Sandel,[55] I define a community as a social formation that inculcates norms into the very identities of its members. Far from being considered autonomous, persons within a community are understood to depend, for the very integrity and dignity of their personalities, upon the observance of these norms.

For hundreds of years an important function of the common law has been to safeguard the most important of these norms, which I call "civility rules." These rules apply to communication as well as to action, and their enforcement lies at the foundation of such communicative torts as defamation, invasion of privacy, and intentional infliction of emotional distress. Through these torts the common law not only protects the integrity of the personality of individual community members, but also serves authoritatively to articulate a community's norms and hence to define a community's identity.

There is an obvious tension between community and democracy. Public discourse within a democracy is legally conceived as the communicative medium through which individuals choose the forms of their communal life; public discourse within a community is legally conceived as a medium through which the values of a particular life are displayed and enacted. Democracy seeks to open the space of public discourse for collective self-constitution; community seeks to bound that space through the enforcement of civility rules. In the inevitable negotiation between democracy and community, the First Amendment has, since the 1940s, generally served the purposes of democracy by suspending the enforcement of civility rules in such landmark cases as Cantwell v. Connecticut, New York Times Co. v. Sullivan, Cohen v. California, and Hustler Magazine v. Falwell.[56]

There is, however, a complex and reciprocal relationship between democracy and community. Democracy necessarily presupposes some form of social institution, like community, through which the concrete identities of "autonomous" democratic citizens can be defined and instantiated. The paradigmatic examples of such institutions are the family and the elementary school. In these settings a child's identity is created in the first instance through undemocratic means; it "comes to be by way of the internalization of sanctions that are de facto threatened and carried out."[57]

This fact has important consequences for the practice of public discourse. The specific purpose of that discourse is the achievement of some form of "reconciliation through public reason."[58] Yet because the identity of democratic citizens will have been formed by reference to community norms, speech in violation of civility rules will characteristically be perceived as both irrational and coercive. This creates what I have elsewhere termed the "paradox of public discourse": the First Amendment, in the name of democracy, suspends legal enforcement of the very civility rules that make rational deliberation possible. The upshot of the paradox is that the separation of public discourse from community depends in some measure upon the spontaneous persistence of civility. In the absence of such persistence, the use of legal regulation to enforce community standards of civility may be required as an unfortunate but necessary option of last resort. A paradigmatic example of this use may be found in the "fighting words" doctrine of Chaplinsky v. New Hampshire.[59]

If community norms thus infiltrate and make possible the practice of democracy, so the ethical imperatives of democracy can be expected to reshape the terms of community life. A stable and successful democratic state will regulate the lives of its citizens in ways consistent with the underlying principle of "their being viewed as free and equal persons."[60] Such regulation will influence community institutions, moving them

closer to the realization of specifically democratic principles. The only
intrinsic limitation on the ability of the democratic state to regulate community institutions in this manner is the public/private distinction, which
requires that at some point the coercive formation of the identity of
individuals remain beyond the purview of the state.

The Domain of Public Discourse

This essay primarily concerns the regulation of racist expression within
public discourse. "Public discourse" may be defined as encompassing the
communicative processes necessary for the formation of public opinion,
whether or not that opinion is directed toward specific government personnel, decisions, or policies. Democratic self-governance requires that
public opinion be broadly conceived as a process of "collective self-
definition"[61] that will necessarily precede and inform any specific government action or inaction. Public discourse cannot encompass all
communication within a democracy, however, because both the public/
private distinction and the paradox of public discourse imply that the
processes of democratic self-governance depend upon the persistence of
other, nondemocratic forms of social organization, such as community.

Because the First Amendment extends extraordinary protection to public discourse, it is important to demarcate the boundary between such
discourse and other speech. I have discussed this issue in detail in Chapter
4 and will not repeat that analysis here. Suffice it to say that the boundary
is inherently uncertain and subject to perennial reevaluation. Factors that
the Supreme Court has used to delineate the boundary include the content of speech and the manner of its dissemination. Speech that can be
said to be about matters of "public concern" is ordinarily classified as
public discourse, as is speech that is widely distributed to the public at
large through the mass media. There are exceptions, however, like commercial speech, which flow from the influence of traditional conventions
that define for us a recognizable "genre" of public speech.

It is difficult to discuss profitably the abstract question of setting the
boundaries of public discourse. At the most general level, these boundaries mark the point at which our commitment to the dialogue of autonomous self-governing citizens shifts to other values, as for example to that
of the socially implicated self characteristic of community. Exactly where
we wish our commitments to alter entails highly specific and contextual
inquiries requiring case-by-case assessment.

I confine myself, therefore, to two preliminary observations. First, the constitutional protections extended to public discourse differ importantly from those extended to nonpublic speech. Thus even if the First Amendment were to immunize from legal regulation the circulation of certain racist ideas in newspapers, it would not follow that the expression of those same ideas could not be restrained by the government within the workplace, where an image of dialogue among autonomous self-governing citizens would be patently out of place.[62] The First Amendment values at stake in the regulation of nonpublic speech are complex and diverse, and I will not be able to review them here.[63]

Second, the category of racist expression cannot be excluded as such from the domain of public discourse. The racist content of a particular communication is only one of many factors relevant to the determination of whether the communication lies within or outside that domain. Thus the leaflet at issue in Beauharnais v. Illinois,[64] which was an effort "to petition the mayor and council of Chicago to pass laws for segregation,"[65] was plainly an effort to engage in public discourse, despite its overt and virulent racism. Similarly, the infamous Nazi march in Skokie was also an attempt to participate in public discourse, notwithstanding its repulsive political symbolism.[66] In both cases racists used well-recognized media for the communication of ideas in order to address and affect public opinion.[67]

Racist Speech and Public Discourse

We are now in a position to assess the justifications for the regulation of racist expression in light of the First Amendment values associated with public discourse. In some cases this assessment allows us to reach definite conclusions; in others it simply helps to clarify the issues raised by particular forms of regulation. In each case I use the term "racist speech" to encompass the class of communications that would have to be regulated in order to ameliorate the specific harm under consideration.

Public Discourse and the Intrinsic Harm of Racist Ideas

It is of course a commonplace of First Amendment jurisprudence that "the government must remain neutral in the marketplace of ideas."[68] The justification for this principle as applied to public discourse is straightforward. Democracy serves the value of self-determination by establishing a communicative structure within which the varying perspectives of individuals can be reconciled through reason. If the state were to forbid the expression of a particular idea, the government would become, with respect to individuals holding that idea, heteronomous and nondemocratic. This is incompatible with a form of government predicated upon citizens being treated "in ways consistent with their being viewed as free and equal persons."[69]

For this reason the value of self-determination requires that public discourse be open to the opinions of all. "Silence coerced by law—the argument of force in its worst form" is constitutionally forbidden.[70] In a democracy, as Piaget notes, "there are no more crimes of opinion, but only breaches of procedure. All opinions are tolerated so long as their protagonists urge their acceptance by legal methods."[71] The notion that racist ideas ought to be forbidden within public discourse because of their "elemental wrongness"[72] is thus fundamentally irreconcilable with the rationale for First Amendment freedoms.

The contemporary debate nevertheless contains three distinct arguments that racist ideas ought to be proscribed because of their "deontic" harm. The first is that the idea of racism is *"sui generis"* because it is "universally condemned."[73] The authors who make this claim, however, also stress "the structural reality of racism in America," a reality manifested not merely in an "epidemic of racist incidents" but also in the widespread racist beliefs of "upper-class whites" and important social "institutions."[74] In fact, it is probably fair to characterize these authors as proponents of regulating racist speech precisely because of their urgent sense of the *prevalence* of racist practices. Although the nightmare of these practices ought to occasion strong public response, their prevalence substantially undermines the conclusion that racism is "universally condemned" in any sense relevant for First Amendment analysis. Such practices can be understood only as manifestations of strongly held but otherwise unarticulated racist ideas.[75]

A second argument is that the failure to regulate racist ideas amounts to a symbolic endorsement of racist speech, which is intolerable in "a society committed to ideals of social and political equality."[76] In essence this argument repudiates the public/private distinction required by democratic self-governance.[77] But this repudiation strikes the root of the project of self-determination. If responsibility for ideas advanced by individuals in public discourse were to be attributed to government, the government could not then also be deemed *responsive* to those ideas in the way required by the principle of self-governance. Just as a library could not function if it were understood as endorsing the views of the authors whose books it collects and displays, so also in a democracy the government could not serve the value of collective autonomy if it were understood as endorsing the ideas expressed by private persons in public discourse.[78]

A third argument is that the free expression of racist ideas is inconsistent with our commitment to the egalitarian ideals of the Fourteenth Amendment. At root this argument rejects autonomy as the principal value of democracy and substitutes instead what Kenneth Karst has eloquently argued is "the substantive center of the fourteenth amendment: the principle of equal citizenship."[79] Although some political theorists have endorsed this position,[80] it runs against the overwhelming American commitment to the importance of "self-rule," to the fundamental belief that "the American people are politically free insomuch as they are governed by themselves collectively."[81]

Of course the principle of self-rule contains its own commitment to the value of equal citizenship, to the notion that, as a formal matter, citizens must be "viewed as free and equal persons."[82] But the meaning of this commitment is measured by the purpose of enabling the processes of self-determination. The appeal to the Fourteenth Amendment, on the other hand, is meant to signify commitment to a substantive value of equality that is not defined by reference to this purpose, so that the implementation of the value may adversely affect processes of self-determination.[83] The argument thus envisions the possibility of "balancing" Fourteenth Amendment values against First Amendment principles.

In balancing the value of equal citizenship against the principle of self-determination, however, we must ask who is empowered to interpret the meaning of the highly contestable value of equal citizenship. To the extent that the value of equal citizenship is used to justify limiting public discourse, the interpreter of the value cannot be the people, because the very function of the appeal to the Fourteenth Amendment is to truncate the communicative processes by which the people clarify their collective will.[84] In such circumstances the Ultimate Interpreter, whoever or whatever it may finally turn out to be, must impose its will without popular accountability. Our government currently contains no such interpreter, not even the Supreme Court, whose constitutional decisions are always shadowed by the potential of constitutional amendment or political reconstruction through subsequent appointments. The impossibility of locating such an interpreter suggests the difficulties that attend the argument from the Fourteenth Amendment.

Public Discourse and Harm to Identifiable Groups

The purpose of public discourse is to reconcile through reason the differences occasioned by a collection of "autonomous wills." Groups neither reason nor have an autonomous will; only persons do. This is the source of the profound individualism that characterizes First Amendment doctrine. The question is whether that individualism is compatible with the regulation of public discourse in order to prevent harm to groups.

It is rather common for the laws of other countries to restrain speech deemed harmful to groups, speech that, in the words of the Illinois statute at issue in *Beauharnais*, casts "contempt, derision, or obloquy" on a particular group.[85] Such laws embrace pluralism, because they subordinate individual expression to the protection of group status and dignity, typically on the theory that group membership is an essential ingredient of personal identity. Hence, as Gary Jacobsohn notes in his description of Israeli law, groups are seen "as units whose corporate identity carries with it . . . claim[s] upon the state for specific entitlement." Thus the law will in certain situations give "greater priority to fraternal and communal attachments over the subjective choices of individuals."[86]

In American law, by contrast, there is a tendency to view groups as mere "collections of individuals"[87] whose claims are no greater than those of their constituent members.[88] This tendency is virtually fixed by the individualist presuppositions of public discourse. Thus in Cantwell v. Connecticut the Court extended First Amendment protection to an anti-Catholic diatribe so violent that it "would offend not only persons of that persuasion, but all others who respect the honestly held religious faith of their fellows." The Court reasoned that this constitutional immunity was necessary so that "many types of life, character, opinion and belief can develop unmolested and unobstructed."[89] This reasoning presupposes that groups evolve through the informed choices of individuals.[90] The Court subordinated the sensibilities of members of established groups, such as Catholics, to the communicative structure necessary for these choices. It thus refused to allow unattractive and highly offensive representations of the Church to be excluded from public discourse.

Cantwell makes special sense because American religious groups have since the nineteenth century been organized on the principle of "voluntarism,"[91] on the notion that "religion is ... a matter of individual choice."[92] It might be argued, however, that race is quite another matter, one in which a certain kind of group identity is inescapably imposed upon a person by accident of birth. For this reason group identity might be seen as primary with respect to race, and the individualist foundations of public discourse—the assumption that racial groups are determined by processes of individual decision-making—repudiated as unrealistic. We might conclude, therefore, that the law ought to be pluralist in its regulation of racist speech, even if First Amendment doctrine might require individualist assumptions with respect to the constitution of other aspects of public discourse.

This argument is powerful and requires close attention. In analyzing it, we can draw on the distinction that has emerged in feminist writings between "sex," which refers to biological facts, and "gender," which refers to socially constructed roles.[93] To confuse the two, to predicate the social content of gender upon the biological fact of sex, is to fall into "the determinist or essentialist trap."[94] The political point of the distinction is to keep perpetually open for discussion and analysis the social meaning of being born female and included within the group "women."[95] Even if one is not free to opt out of the group, the possibility ought nevertheless to be preserved that the identity of the group be ultimately determined, in the language of Nancy Fraser, "through dialogue and collective struggle." Fraser writes that "in a society as complex as ours, it does not seem to me wise or even possible to extrapolate" the outcome of that dialogue "from the current, prepoliticized experiences and idiolects of women, especially since it is likely, in my view, that these will turn out to be the current prepoliticized experiences and idiolects only of *some* women."[96]

Fraser's point is that regardless of the biological basis of sex, the social meaning of gender is a political issue whose outcome, like that of all political issues, must be regarded as indeterminate. She thus applies the structure of democratic self-determination to the constitution of group identity. The individualist assumptions of that structure create a form of communication in which political indeterminacy is preserved; they guarantee that the dialogue envisioned by Fraser will remain open to the perspectives of *all* women. If the identity of the group "women" were understood to have a content determinate enough to employ the force of law to silence dissenting views, the law would hegemonically impose the perspective of only *some* women.

The same logic, I believe, holds true for racial groups. We must distinguish race as a biological category from race as a social category. Even though unfortunately "the attempt to establish a *biological* basis of race has not been swept into the dustbin of history,"[97] it would be deplorable to construct First Amendment principles on the basis of a biological view of race. What is most saliently at issue is rather "race as a social concept": "The effort must be made to understand race as *an unstable and 'decentered' complex of social meanings constantly being transformed by political struggle.*"[98] To the extent that the social meaning of race is thus profoundly controversial[99]—and it is controversial not merely for members of minority groups but also for the entire nation[100]—the individualist premises of public discourse will ensure that it remains open to democratic constitution.

This lack of closure may of course be threatening, for it casts the creation of group identity upon the uncertain currents of public discourse. The safe harbor of legal regulation may, by contrast, appear to promise members of minority groups more secure control over the meaning of their social experience. But that promise is illusory, for it is profoundly inconsistent with the analysis of racism prevalent in the contemporary literature. To the extent that racism is viewed as pervasive among whites, and to the extent that whites, as a dominant group, can be expected to hold the levers of legal power, there would seem to be little reason to trust the law to establish socially acceptable meanings for race. Such meanings cannot be determined by reference to easy or bright-line distinctions, as for example those between positive or negative ascriptions of group identity. The work of figures as diverse as William Julius Wilson, Shelby Steele, and Louis Farrakhan illustrates how highly critical characterizations of racial groups can nevertheless serve constructive social purposes.[101] To vest in an essentially white legal establishment the power to discriminate authoritatively among such characterizations and purposes would seem certain to be disempowering.[102]

The conclusion that group harm ought not to justify legal regulation is reflected in technical First Amendment doctrine in the fact that virtually all communications likely to provoke a claim of group harm will be privileged as assertions of evaluative opinion.[103] The following language, for example, gave rise to legal liability in *Beauharnais:* "If persuasion and the need to prevent the white race from becoming mongrelized by the negro will not unite us, then the aggressions . . . rapes, robberies, knives, guns and marijuana of the negro, SURELY WILL."[104] Justice Frankfurter interpreted this language as a false factual assertion: "No one will gainsay that it is libelous falsely to charge another with being a rapist, robber, carrier of knives and guns, and user of marijuana."[105] This interpretation, however, seems plainly incorrect. To accuse an individual of using marijuana is to assert that she has committed certain specific acts. To accuse African-Americans as a group of using marijuana, however, is not to make an analogous assertion. Some African-Americans will have used marijuana, and most will not have. The question is thus not the existence of certain specific acts, but rather whether those acts can appropriately be used to characterize the group. The fundamental issue is the nature of the group's identity, an issue that almost certainly ought to be characterized as one of evaluative opinion.

Because the social meaning of race is inherently controversial, most statements likely to give rise to actions for group harm will be negative assessments of the identity of racial groups, and hence statements of evaluative opinion. No serious commentator would advocate a trial to determine the truth or falsity of such statements; the point is rather that such statements should not be made at all because of the deep injury they cause. But in a context in which group identity is a matter for determination through political struggle and disagreement, the hypostatized injury of a group cannot, consistent with the processes that instantiate the principle of self-determination, be grounds to legally silence characterizations of group identity within public discourse.

Commentators who stress the theme of group harm vigorously emphasize the fact that racist speech does not injure random groups; it damages precisely those groups who have historically suffered egregious oppression and subordination.[106] But although the tragedy of this fact is obvious, its constitutional implications are not. Our history certainly warrants the assumption that racist speech will inflict terrible injuries on victim groups. But the question is whether these injuries are so unspeakable as to justify suspending the democratic constitution of group identities. One approach might be to avoid this tension by characterizing the injuries of racist speech in such a way that their legal redress would actually be required by the principles of public discourse. Thus it can be argued that the stigmatizing and disabling effects of racist speech effectively exclude its victims from participation in public discourse. This approach suggests an important line of analysis, but I wish to defer consideration of it until the section below entitled "Public Discourse and Harm to the Marketplace of Ideas," where it can be placed in a more comprehensive context.

Another method of avoiding the tension between group harm and democratic principles would be to claim that racist speech ought to be characterized as a "mechanism of subordination" within a larger system of suppression, rather than as a form of communication.[107] This claim requires us to determine the criteria by which speech can be designated as action and hence excluded from public discourse. The standard implicitly advanced by the claim is that if communication is intimately connected to larger social relationships that are deeply undesirable, the communication can for that reason be characterized as action.

The difficulty with this standard is that all communication grows out of and embodies social relationships; for this reason all communication is both speech and action. The function of public discourse is to create a protected space within which communication, even if embodying social relationships, can be protected as speech if formulated and disseminated in ways relevant for democratic self-governance. Such a space opens up the possibility of subjecting social relationships to rational reflection, dialogue, and (hence) *self*-control. It thus enables "self-rule" to be reconciled with rule "by laws."[108] If communication could be excluded from this space because it embodies social relations of which we disapprove, public discourse could no longer perform this function. There is no difference between excluding speech from public discourse because we condemn the social relationships it embodies and excluding speech from public discourse because we condemn the ideas by which those social relationships are embodied. In the end, therefore, the argument that racist speech is a form of action reduces to the claim, which we have already considered, that racist speech ought to be restrained because of its inconsistency with the egalitarian ideals of the Fourteenth Amendment.

Public Discourse and Harm to Individuals

There appear at first blush to be important differences between claims of group harm and claims of individual harm. To the extent that group identity is understood to be a matter of political struggle (and hence dialogic interaction), speech containing negative ascriptions of that identity cannot be censored without undermining the democratic nature of that struggle. But individual identity does not seem to rest on political struggle and dialogue in this way. Indeed, one's spontaneous image is of fully formed individuals entering the realm of public discourse to reach agreement on issues that concern their collective, rather than personal, lives. Speech damaging personal life can thus be restricted without undercutting the very purposes of public discourse.

This perspective, however, rests on a rather sharp distinction between individual and collective identity, a distinction that simply cannot be maintained. The very reason that racist speech harms individual persons is because it so violently ruptures the forms of social respect that are necessary for the maintenance of individual personality. These forms of respect, when taken together, constitute a collective, community identity. Hence the state can prevent the individual harm caused by racist speech only by enforcing pertinent standards of community identity. The interdependence of individual and collective identity is thus presupposed in the very concept of individual harm.

This interdependence lies behind well-established constitutional prohibitions on restricting public discourse because it is "offensive"[109] or "outrageous,"[110] or because it affronts "dignity" or is "insulting" or causes "public odium" or "public disrepute."[111] Such speech causes intense individual suffering because it violates community norms, yet the Court has required its toleration in order to prevent the state from using the authority of law to enforce particular conceptions of collective life.[112]

Questions of personal identity are in fact always at stake in discussions of collective self-definition. For this reason effective political dialogue requires that participants be constantly willing to be transformed. As Frank Michelman points out, public discourse is impossible so long as "the participants' pre-political self-understandings and social perspectives must axiomatically be regarded as completely impervious to the persuasion of the process itself."[113] As our collective aspirations change, so will our respective personal identities. Thus restrictions on public discourse designed to protect those identities from harm will necessarily also restrict self-determination as to our collective life. If group harm is an inevitable price of the political constitution of group identity, individual injury is an unavoidable cost of the political constitution of community identity.

It is important to emphasize the narrowness of this conclusion. In recent years an important theme of our national life has been the opposition to racism. We have enacted that opposition by legally regulating racist behavior like discrimination. Because action both creates and manifests identity, this regulation inhibits the formation and expression of racist identities. So also does regulation prohibiting certain kinds of racist communications in nonpublic speech, as for example in the workplace. In effect we have determined to use government force to reshape community institutions in order to combat racism. This is an appropriate and laudable use of democratic power. But it is legitimate precisely because we have adopted it in a manner consistent with the principle of self-determination; it reflects a national identity that we have freely chosen.

This legitimacy is made possible by public discourse, which serves the goal of self-determination because it is so structured that every call for national identity has the opportunity to make its case. There is a significant difference, therefore, between proscribing racial insults directed toward individuals in the workplace[114] and proscribing them in a political discussion or debate.[115] The harm to the individual victim may be the same, but for public discourse to enable *self*-government, racist speech within that discourse must be repudiated on the merits rather than be silenced by force of law.

Public Discourse and Harm to the Marketplace of Ideas

The most effective arguments for regulating racist speech are those that double back on the concept of public discourse itself and contend that such regulation is necessary for public discourse truly to instantiate the principle of self-determination. On the surface there appear to be two distinct lines of analysis. The first stresses the irrational and coercive qualities of racist speech, the second the untoward effects of racist speech in silencing victim groups. In the end these lines of argumentation cross and depend upon each other.

Racist Speech as Irrational and Coercive

Public discourse must be more than simply a register of private preferences in order to serve as a medium for the enactment of collective autonomy. If persons communicated in public discourse merely through polling organizations to make known their "votes" on public issues, democracy would degenerate into a heteronomous system of majoritarian rule. The purposes of collective self-determination require instead that public action be founded upon a public opinion formed through open and interactive processes of rational deliberation. The argument that racist speech is irrational and coercive, that it is nothing more than a kind of "linguistic abuse (verbal abuse on an unwilling target),"[116] thus cuts to the very root of public discourse.

The argument, however, points to a more general problem, for all communication that violates civility rules is perceived as both irrational and coercive.[117] Because civility rules embody the norms of respect and reason we are accustomed to receive from members of our community, communication inconsistent with those rules is experienced as an instrument "of aggression and personal assault."[118] The argument from coercion and irrationality thus poses a generic dilemma for First Amendment doctrine. If the state were permitted to enforce civility rules, it would in effect exclude from public discourse those whose speech advocated and exemplified unfamiliar and marginalized forms of life. But if the state were to suspend the enforcement of civility rules, it would endanger the possibility of rational deliberation by permitting the dissemination of abusive and coercive speech. This tension between the requirement that self-government respect all of its citizens "as free and equal persons," and the requirement that self-government proceed through processes of rational deliberation, creates the paradox of public discourse.

It might be thought that the specific case of racist speech dissolves this paradox, for such speech by hypothesis violates norms of both equality and civility and hence appears to be suppressible without harm to public discourse. But this conclusion is not accurate. The principle of equality at issue in the paradox of public discourse is formal; its extension to all persons is the fundamental precondition of the possibility of self-government. To the extent that the principle is circumscribed, so also is the reach of self-determination. The norm of equality violated by racist speech, on the other hand, is substantive; it reflects a particular understanding of how we ought to live. It is the kind of norm that ought to emerge from processes of public deliberation. Although the censorship of racist speech is consistent with this substantive norm of equality, it is inconsistent with the formal principle of equality, because such censorship would exclude from the medium of public discourse those who disagree with a particular substantive norm of equality. Such persons would thus be cut off from participation in the processes of collective self-determination.

First Amendment doctrine has tended to resolve the paradox of public discourse in favor of the principle of formal equality, largely because violations of that principle limit *pro tanto* the domain of self-government, whereas protecting uncivil speech does not automatically destroy the possibility of rational deliberation. The visceral shock of uncivil speech can sometimes actually serve constructive purposes, as when it causes individuals to question the community standards into which they have been socialized and hence enables them, perhaps for the first time, to acknowledge the claims of others from radically different cultural backgrounds.[119] There is in fact a long tradition of oppressed and marginalized groups using uncivil speech to force recognition of the intensity and urgency of their needs.[120]

Tolerating uncivil speech, moreover, does not necessarily undermine the process of rational deliberation, so long as the extent of such speech is confined and does not infect the process as a whole. The judgment that rational deliberation can continue in spite of the presence of uncivil speech is exactly the point of Harlan's opinion in Cohen v. California, in which the Court refused to permit the state to use the force of law "to maintain . . . a suitable level of discourse within the body politic":

> The constitutional right of free expression is powerful medicine in a society as diverse and populous as ours. It is designed and intended to remove governmental restraints from the arena of public discussion, putting the decision as to what views shall be voiced largely into the hands of each of us, in the hope that use of such freedom will ultimately produce a more capable citizenry and more perfect polity and in the belief that no other approach would comport with the premise of individual dignity and choice upon which our political system rests . . .
>
> To many, the immediate consequence of this freedom may often appear to be only verbal tumult, discord, and even offensive utterance. These are, however, within established limits, in truth necessary side effects of the broader enduring values which the process of open debate permits us to achieve. That the air may at times seem filled with verbal cacophony is, in this sense not a sign of weakness but of strength.[121]

It is of course a matter of judgment whether "open debate" within "the arena of public discussion" is indeed achieving "broader enduring values." How one makes that judgment will depend very much on one's circumstances. The call in recent literature to attend more carefully to "the victim's perspective" is well taken in this regard.[122] Members of dominant groups may be satisfied with the overall quality of public deliberation, but members of victim groups, at whom racist speech is systematically targeted, may feel quite otherwise.

It is at this point that the line of analysis stressing the irrational, coercive quality of racist speech crosses and depends upon the line of analysis stressing the silencing of victim groups. For, when pressed, the point is not that public discourse is pervasively disabled by racist speech, but rather that the concentrated effect of such speech on members of victim groups is to foreclose public discourse as an effective avenue of collective self-determination. In the contemporary debate this effect has been addressed under the rubric of "silencing."

Racist Speech as Silencing Minority Groups

The literature on silencing has burgeoned. So far as I can make out, the literature presents three distinct arguments to support the claim of silencing:[123] victim groups are silenced because their perspectives are systematically excluded from the dominant discourse;[124] victim groups are silenced because the pervasive stigma of racism systematically undermines and devalues their speech; and victim groups are silenced because the visceral "fear, rage, [and] shock" of racist speech systematically preempts response.[125] This section analyzes each of these arguments separately; the following section weaves them together into a more complex indictment of racist speech.

The first argument is that the language of public discourse, although seemingly neutral and objective, has a built-in bias that prevents the articulation of minority positions.[126] Thus racism in the dominant discourse is compressed into "the neutralized word 'discrimination,'" in which "the role of power, domination, and oppression as the source of the evil" is effaced, and "much of the political, historical, and moral content of 'equality' has been dropped."[127] Similarly, the understanding of whites that racism is an "intentional belief in white supremacy"—the perpetrators' perspective—has been folded into the very language of public debate, whereas the understanding of minorities that racism " 'refers *solely* to minority subordination' "—the victims' perspective—is banished from the language.[128]

Although the premise of this argument seems to me true, it does not by itself support the conclusion that racist speech ought to be regulated. All communication rests on foundations of unarticulated assumptions. The very function of dialogue is often to move toward enlightenment by uncovering and exposing these assumptions. Enlightenment can be gradual and progressive, or it can result from the shock of intense political struggle. That our language always encompasses both more and less than our intentions is thus an argument not for the suppression of racist speech, but rather for the encouragement of further public debate.

The point might be made, however, that public debate fails to achieve

such enlightenment because the pervasive racism of American society
devalues and stigmatizes minority contributions to this debate. The voice
of the victims goes unheard. There is thus a call for an "outsider jurisprudence" which will legitimate that voice and enable "legal insiders . . .
[to] imagine a life disabled in a significant way by hate propaganda."[129]

Once again, the premise of this argument appears sound, but its conclusion does not. Audiences always evaluate communication on the basis
of their understanding of its social context.[130] This is not a deformity of
public discourse, but one of its generic characteristics.[131] It poses the
question of how an audience's prepolitical understanding of social context
may be altered, a question that confronts all participants in public dialogue. The urgency of the question does not justify restricting public
discourse; it is rather a call for more articulate and persuasive speech, for
more intense and effective political engagement.

Taken together, the argument from the inherent bias of accepted discourse and the argument from the stigmatic devaluation of minority
speech fuse into a single indictment of public discourse as irrational. The
systematic derogation of the specific perspectives of victim groups is said
to be caused by the nation's particular history of racial oppression, rather
than by concerns that should properly affect a legitimately rational public
dialogue. Both arguments thus ultimately appeal to the concept of false
consciousness,[132] to the notion that there is an ideal vantage from which
the rationality of discourse can be "objectively" assessed.

It is one thing, however, to use the idea of false consciousness as a
weapon *within* public discourse to convince others of the need to break
with the prejudices of the past, and quite another to use the idea as a
justification to limit public discourse itself. The first is a familiar rhetorical strategy. It is consistent with the processes of public discourse because
its effectiveness ultimately depends upon its persuasive power. But the
second presupposes an intimacy with truth so vital as to foreclose opposing positions. The very point of using the idea of false consciousness to
limit public discourse is to justify legally disregarding certain perspectives, on the grounds that these perspectives could not possibly be respected as true expressions of autonomous individuality. Circumscribing
public discourse to ameliorate false consciousness thus does not protect
public discourse from harm, but rather contradicts its very purpose of
providing a medium for the reconciliation of autonomous wills.

The third argument for restraining racist speech turns not on the
characterization of public discourse as irrational, but rather on the char-

acterization of public discourse as coercive. Recent literature contains searing documentation of the profound personal injury of racist speech, and this injury may in particular circumstances be so shocking as to literally preempt responsive speech. Although the analogous harm of uncivil speech is randomly scattered throughout the population, the disabilities attendant upon racist speech are concentrated upon members of victim groups. Hence, where members of dominant groups perceive "isolated incidents,"[133] members of victim groups perceive instead a suffocating and inescapable "racism that is a persistent and constituent part of the social order, woven into the fabric of society and everyday life."[134]

Under such conditions it is to be expected that members of dominant and victim groups may well come to conflicting judgments about whether racist speech shocks significant segments of victim group population into silence. The recent literature proposing restraints on racist speech is eloquent on the need to "[listen] to the real victims" of such speech and to display "empathy or understanding for their injury."[135] And of course any fair and just determination about the regulation of public discourse would require exactly this kind of sensitivity. But there is also a tendency in recent literature to move from the proposition that a fair determination cannot be made unless "the victims of racist speech are heard,"[136] to the very different proposition that such a determination ought to use "the experience of victim-group members [as] a guide."[137] The latter proposition seems to me plainly false.

The issue on the table is whether irrationality and coercion have so tainted the medium of public discourse as to require shrinking the scope of self-government. That issue significantly affects every citizen, and its resolution therefore cannot be ceded to the control of any particular group. In fact I do not see how the issue can be adequately resolved at all unless some notion of civic membership is invoked that transcends mere group identification. If we cannot strive to deliberate together as citizens, distancing ourselves from (but not abandoning) our specific cultural backgrounds, the issue can be resolved only through the exercise of naked group power, a solution not at all advantageous to the marginalized and oppressed.[138]

Paradoxically, therefore, the question of whether public discourse is irretrievably damaged by racist speech must itself ultimately be addressed through the medium of public discourse. Because those participating in public discourse will not themselves have been silenced (almost by definition), a heavy, frustrating burden is de facto placed on those who would truncate public discourse in order to save it. They must represent themselves as "speaking for" those who have been deprived of their voice. But the negative space of that silence reigns inscrutable, neither confirming nor denying this claim. And the more eloquent the appeal, the less compelling the claim, for the more accessible public discourse will then appear to exactly the perspectives racist speech is said to repress.

Even if this burden is lifted, however, and it is simply accepted that members of victim groups are intimidated into silence, it would still not follow that restraints on racist speech within public discourse are justified. One might believe, for example, that such silencing occurs chiefly through the structural conditions of racism, rather than specifically through the shock of racist speech. "The problem," as the controversial chair of the Black Studies Department of New York's City College once remarked in response to the racist comments of an academic colleague, lies not with specific communicative acts but rather with "racism" itself, "insidious in our society and built into our culture."[139] If the chair's diagnosis were true, restraints on racist speech would impair public discourse without at the same time repairing the silence of victim groups.

Alternatively, one might believe that racist speech silences victim groups primarily because of its "ideas," because of its messages of racial inferiority, rather than because of its incivility. The distinction is important for the following reason: although it is consistent with the internal logic of public discourse to excise in extreme circumstances certain kinds of uncivil speech that are experienced as coercive, it is fundamentally incompatible with public discourse to excise specific ideas because they are "analogously" deemed to be coercive. Public discourse is the medium within which our society assesses the democratic acceptability of ideas; to exclude certain ideas as prima facie "coercive" and hence destructive of public discourse is to contradict precisely this function. Therefore "harm" to public discourse cannot justify restraints on racist ideas on the grounds that such ideas are perceived to be threatening or coercive.[140]

There are also other possibilities. One might believe, for example, that because it is difficult to distinguish ideas from incivility, and because it is essential to collective self-determination to protect all ideas, the law will as a practical matter be able to restrain only a small category of blatantly racist epithets, which, although deeply offensive and lacking in ideational content, have relatively little to do with the more widespread phenomenon of silencing. Or one might believe that racist speech silences primarily when shocking racist epithets are used in the face-to-face confrontations characteristic of the "fighting words" doctrine of *Chaplinsky*,[141] so that the essential insight of the argument from silencing is already reflected within First Amendment doctrine.

My own conclusion, in light of these alternative considerations, is that the case has not yet been made for circumscribing public discourse to prevent the kind of preemptive silencing that occurs when members of victim groups experience "fear, rage, [and] shock." I say this with considerable diffidence. Even if the empirical claim of systematic preemptive silencing is accepted (and I am not sure that I do accept it), it is in my view most directly the result of the social and structural conditions of racism, rather than specifically of racist speech. Because the logic of the argument from preemptive silencing does not impeach the necessity of preserving the free expression of ideas, public discourse could at most be regulated in a largely symbolic manner so as to purge it of outrageous racist epithets and names. It seems to me highly implausible to claim that such symbolic regulation will eliminate the preemptive silencing that is said to justify restraints on public discourse.

Racist Speech as Symbolic Cultural Oppression

When distinguished and parsed in this analytic manner, therefore, the various arguments for restraining racist speech in order to preserve the integrity of public discourse do not in my judgment support their desired conclusion. But the arguments can be braided together to fund an accusation more powerful than its separate strands.

In ordinary life, members of victim groups do not experience a string of distinct disadvantages. Rather, if representations in the current literature are accepted as true, these groups confront in public discourse an undifferentiated complex of circumstances in which they are systematically demeaned, stigmatized, ignored; in which the very language of debate resists the articulation of their claims; in which they are harassed, abused, intimidated, and systematically and egregiously injured both individually and collectively. The question is not whether these liabilities, when taken individually and singly, justify restraining racist speech within public discourse, but rather whether, when taken together as a complex whole, they render public discourse unfit as an instrument of collective self-determination for members of victim groups, and whether this unacceptable situation would be cured by restraints on racist speech.

What makes this question so very formidable is that it turns on the nexus between public discourse and the value of collective self-determination. Although the formal preconditions of that nexus can be described, its actual substantive realization must remain contingent upon conditions of history, culture, and social structure. Thus when members of victim groups claim that public discourse no longer serves for them the value of self-government, it is no answer to reply that they have been embraced within its formal preconditions. If members of victim groups in fact perceive themselves to be systematically excluded from public dialogue, that dialogue can scarcely achieve for them those "broader enduring values" that are its democratic justification. The very legitimacy of democratic self-governance is thus called into question.

The dependence of the value of public discourse upon matters of social perception poses complex and delicate questions, but the difficulty of these questions is profoundly magnified in the context of the controversy over racist speech. First, the truth of the claim that members of victim groups are cut off from meaningful participation within public discourse cannot be directly experienced and hence evaluated by members of dominant groups. Its resolution must therefore depend, to one degree or another, upon acceptance of the representations of members of victim groups. As a practical political matter, therefore, what is called into question is not merely the truth of these representations but also the trust and respect with which they are received by members of dominant groups.[142] Second, the focus on trust and respect is reinforced by the remedial claim that racist speech ought to be censored so as to open up public discourse to victim groups. Essentially this claim requires that self-determination be denied to some so that it may be made available to others. Thus society's willingness to circumscribe public discourse is transformed into a touchstone of the esteem with which it regards victim groups.

In fact, it is this transformation that most precisely supports the argument. The argument turns on the interpretive meaning that members of victim groups ascribe to their place in American life; the contention is that this meaning is one of exclusion. Such an interpretation cannot be reduced to any specific empirical claims or conditions. Instead the need of those who feel alienated is most exactly met by a gesture of social esteem. By conveying in the strongest possible terms messages of respect and welcome, the censorship of racist speech might go a long way toward allowing members of victim groups to reinterpret their experience as one of inclusion within the dialogue of public discourse. The objection we noted earlier, that the regulation of racist speech within public discourse could at most restrict the publication of highly offensive racist epithets and names, and that such regulation could serve only symbolic purposes, is thus no longer pertinent. For the argument now turns squarely on the politics of cultural symbolism.

The most salient characteristic of such politics is that the particular content of government regulation is less important than its perceived meaning. We have already noted how claims like those of individual injury or preemptive silencing define concrete classes of communications that are said empirically to cause a particular harm. But the claim of cultural exclusion is fundamentally different, for it implies no such specific referent. The claim, when pressed, is not that any specific class of communications actually causes members of victim groups to feel excluded, but rather that a particular regulatory gesture will be the occasion for members of victim groups to feel included.[143]

This suggests, however, that restraints on public discourse are only one of a wide variety of strategies that government can pursue to ameliorate the sense of cultural exclusion experienced by victim groups. Other alternatives might include anti-discrimination laws, affirmative action programs, redistribution of economic resources, restraints on racist forms of nonpublic speech, and so forth. All these modifications of community life could be interpreted as significant gestures of respect and inclusion. It is a matter of political choice and characterization to reject these alternatives as insufficient and to deem the limitation of public discourse as necessary to overcome the alienation of victim groups.

At root, therefore, the argument from cultural exclusion seeks to subordinate public discourse, whose very purpose is to serve as the framework for all possible forms of politics, to a particular political perspective. The argument begins with the sound premise that a cultural sense of participation is necessary for public discourse to serve the value of collective self-determination. But instead of conceiving of public discourse as a means of rousing the nation's political will to actions designed to facilitate that sense of participation, the argument instead turns on public discourse itself, and, as a matter of political perception and assertion, deems the limitation of that discourse to be prerequisite for the elimination of disabling alienation. The argument therefore does not ultimately rest on the importance of protecting public discourse from harm, but rather on the need to sacrifice public discourse in order to recuperate profound social dislocations.

Bluntly expressed, the argument requires us to balance the integrity of public discourse as a general structure of communication against the importance of enhancing the experience of political participation by members of victim groups. The argument thus reiterates the position that public discourse ought to be subordinated to the egalitarian ideals of the Fourteenth Amendment. It adopts a sophisticated version of that position, however, for it is able to contend that public discourse need be impaired in only slight and symbolic ways. Even so minimal a gesture as purging outrageous and shocking racist epithets could be sufficient to make members of victim groups feel welcome within the arena of public discourse, and thus to enable public discourse to serve for them the value of self-determination.[144] In this form the argument is analogous to that advanced in the controversy over prohibiting flag burning, in which it is also urged that public discourse ought to be minimally impaired for highly important symbolic reasons.[145] Just as it has been contended that any idea can be expressed without burning a flag,[146] so it can be asserted that any idea can be expressed without recourse to vile racist epithets.[147] In both cases, therefore, it can be argued that the *de minimis* effects on public discourse are outweighed by the significance of the interests at stake.[148]

I believe, however, that this invitation to balance ought to be declined. This is not because balancing can be ruled out in advance by some "absolutist" algorithm; the attraction of a purely formal democracy may itself in certain circumstances no longer command limitless conviction. It is rather because, in the American context, the temptation to balance rests on what might be termed the fallacy of immaculate isolation.[149] The effect on public discourse is acceptable only if it is *de minimis*, and it is arguably *de minimis* only when a specific claim is evaluated in isolation from other, similar claims. But no claim is in practice immaculately isolated. As the flag burning example suggests, there is no shortage of powerful groups contending that uncivil speech within public discourse ought to be "minimally" regulated for highly pressing symbolic reasons.[150]

This is evident even if the focus of analysis is narrowly limited to the structure of the claim at issue in the debate over racist speech. In a large, heterogeneous country populated by assertive and conflicting groups, the logic of circumscribing public discourse to reduce political estrangement is virtually unstoppable. The nation is filled with those who feel displaced and who would feel less so if given the chance to truncate public discourse symbolically. This is already plain in the regulations that have proliferated on college campuses, which commonly proscribe not merely speech that degrades persons on the basis of their race, but also, to pick a typical list, speech that demeans persons on the basis of their "color, national origin, religion, sex, sexual orientation, age, handicap, or veteran's status."[151] The claim of *de minimis* impact loses credibility as the list of claimants to special protection grows longer.

The point I want to press does not depend upon the intellectual difficulty of drawing lines to separate similar claims. It is rather that the remedial and political logic of equal participation applies with analogous force to a broad and growing spectrum of group claims. One might, of course, devise arguments, perhaps based on the specific history of the Fourteenth Amendment, to distinguish racial epithets from blasphemous imprecations, or from degrading and pornographic characterizations of women, or from vicious antigay slurs, or from gross ethnic insults. But the question is whether such arguments can withstand the compelling egalitarian logic that unites these various situations. My strong intuition is that they cannot, and hence that the claim of *de minimis* impact on public discourse is implausible.

In the specific context of the argument from cultural exclusion, moreover, a refusal to balance is far less harsh than it might superficially appear. The fundamental challenge is to enable members of victim groups to reinterpret their experience within the American political and cultural order as one of genuine participation. There are a host of ways to address this challenge short of truncating public discourse. The most obvious and potentially effective strategy would be to dismantle systematically and forcefully the structural conditions of racism. If we were so blessed as to be able to accomplish that feat—if we were truly able to eliminate such conditions as chronic unemployment, inadequate health care, segregated housing, or disproportionately low incomes—then we would no doubt also have succeeded in ameliorating the experience of cultural exclusion.

The First Amendment and Harm to the Educational Environment

If public discourse is bounded on one side by the necessary structures of community life, it is bounded on the other by the need of the state to create organizations to achieve explicit public objectives. These organizations, which are nonpublic forums, regulate speech in ways that are fundamentally incompatible with the requirements of public discourse.

Public discourse is the medium through which our democracy determines its purposes, and for this reason the legal structure of public discourse requires that all such purposes be kept open to question and reevaluation. Within nonpublic forums, on the other hand, government objectives are taken as established, and communication is regulated as necessary to achieve those objectives.

Although the Supreme Court has often held that "the First Amendment rights of speech and association extend to the campuses of state universities," and even that "the campus of a public university, at least for its students, possesses many of the characteristics of a public forum,"[152] in fact state institutions of higher learning are public organizations established for the express purpose of education. The Court has always held that "a university's mission is education," and it has never construed the First Amendment to deny a university's "authority to impose reasonable regulations compatible with that mission upon the use of its campus and facilities."[153] The Court has explicitly recognized "a university's right to exclude . . . First Amendment activities that . . . substantially interfere with the opportunity of other students to obtain an education."[154] Thus student speech incompatible with classroom processes may be censored; faculty publications inconsistent with academic standards may be evaluated and judged; and so forth.

The regulation of racist speech within public institutions of higher learning, therefore, does not turn on the value of democratic self-governance and its realization in public discourse. Instead, the constitutionality of such regulation depends upon the logic of instrumental rationality, and specifically upon three factors: (1) the nature of the educational mission of the university; (2) the instrumental connection of the regulation to the attainment of that mission; and (3) the deference that courts ought to display toward the instrumental judgment of institutional authorities. The current controversy regarding the constitutionality of regulating racist speech on university and college campuses may most helpfully be interpreted as a debate about the first of these factors, the constitutionally permissible educational objectives of public institutions of higher learning.[155]

Courts have advanced at least three different concepts of those objectives. The most traditional concept, which I refer to as "civic education," views public education as an instrument of community life, and holds that "respect for constituted authority and obedience thereto is an essential lesson to qualify one for the duties of citizenship, and that the schoolroom

is an appropriate place to teach that lesson."[156] Civic education conceptualizes instruction as a process of cultural reproduction in which community values are authoritatively handed down to the young. The validity
of those values is largely taken for granted, and there is a strong tendency
to use them as a basis for the regulation of speech in the manner of the
traditional common law.

The concept of civic education held sway in the years before the Warren Court and has recently been forcefully resurrected with regard to the
regulation of speech within high schools. Thus in Bethel School District
No. 403 v. Fraser[157] the Court upheld the punishment of a high school
student for having delivered an "offensive" and "indecent" student-
government speech. The Court reasoned that "the objectives of public
education" included "the 'inculcat[ion of] fundamental values necessary
to the maintenance of a democratic political system.'" Among these
values were "'the habits and manners of civility as . . . indispensable to
the practice of self-government'":[158]

> The undoubted freedom to advocate unpopular and controversial views
> in schools and classrooms must be balanced against the society's coun-
> tervailing interest in teaching students the boundaries of socially appro-
> priate behavior . . .
>   . . . [S]chools must teach by example the shared values of a civilized
> social order . . . The schools, as instruments of the state, may determine
> that the essential lessons of civil, mature conduct cannot be conveyed in
> a school that tolerates lewd, indecent, or offensive speech and conduct
> such as that indulged in by this confused boy.[159]

That the concept of civic education would lead to similar conclusions
if applied to institutions of higher learning is evidenced by Chief Justice
Burger's 1973 dissent in Papish v. University of Missouri Curators:

> In theory, at least, a university is not merely an arena for the discussion
> of ideas by students and faculty; it is also an institution where individuals
> learn to express themselves in acceptable, civil terms. We provide that
> environment to the end that students may learn the self-restraint nec-
> essary to the functioning of a civilized society and understand the need
> for those external restraints to which we must all submit if group exist-
> ence is to be tolerable.[160]

Because racist speech is both deeply uncivil and contrary to "the shared
values of [our] civilized social order,"[161] its restraint would be relatively
unproblematic if civic education were understood to be a constitutionally

acceptable purpose of public institutions of higher learning.[162] A number of public universities have fashioned their regulations on exactly this understanding. For example, the Policy Against Racism of the Board of Regents of Higher Education of the Commonwealth of Massachusetts argues that "institutions must vigorously strive to achieve diversity in race, ethnicity, and culture sufficiently reflective of our society. However, diversity alone will not suffice":

> There must be a unity and cohesion in the diversity which we seek to achieve, thereby creating an environment of pluralism. Racism in any form, expressed or implied, intentional or inadvertent, individual or institutional, constitutes an egregious offense to the tenets of human dignity and to the accords of civility guaranteed by law. Consequently, racism undermines the establishment of a social and academic environment of genuine racial pluralism.[163]

The policy clearly postulates the fundamental task of the university to be the inculcation of the value of "genuine racial pluralism," and it proscribes racist speech because of its incompatibility with that value.

A second concept of the mission of public education, which I refer to as "democratic education," begins with the very different premise that the "public school" is "in most respects the cradle of our democracy,"[164] and it therefore understands the purpose of public education to be the creation of autonomous citizens, capable of fully participating in the rough-and-tumble world of public discourse.[165] Democratic education strives to introduce that world into the generically more sheltered environment of the school.

The concept of democratic education was most fully expressed during the era of the Warren Court in Tinker v. Des Moines School District, in which the Court held that the purpose of public education is to prepare students for the "sort of hazardous freedom . . . that is the basis of our national strength and of the independence and vigor of Americans who grow up and live in this relatively permissive, often disputatious, society." The majority in *Tinker* explicitly rejected the premise of civic education that the purpose of public schooling is the transmission of canonical values. It concluded instead that "in our system, state-operated schools may not be enclaves of totalitarianism . . . [S]tudents may not be regarded as closed-circuit recipients of only that which the State chooses to communicate. They may not be confined to the expression of those sentiments that are officially approved."[166] According to *Tinker*, the object of public education is to lead students to think for themselves.

The chief characteristic of democratic education is its tendency to assimilate speech within public educational institutions to a model of public discourse. Recognizing that this ambition is "not without its costs in terms of the risk to the maintenance of civility and an ordered society," the Court nevertheless strongly advanced the concept of democratic education during the late 1960s and early 1970s, in part because it believed the concept essential to the maintenance of "our vigorous and free society."[167] If, as I have argued, racist speech is and ought to be immune from regulation within public discourse, we can expect courts guided by the concept of democratic education to be quite hostile to the regulation of racist speech within universities, preferring instead to see students realistically prepared for participation in the harsh but inevitable world of public discourse.

There is yet a third concept of public education, one most often specifically associated with institutions of higher learning. This concept, which I refer to as "critical education," views the university as an institution whose distinctive "primary function" is "to discover and disseminate knowledge by means of research and teaching."[168] Critical education locates the principal prerequisite for university life in "the need for unfettered freedom, the right to think the unthinkable, discuss the unmentionable, and challenge the unchallengeable":

> If a university is a place for knowledge, it is also a special kind of small society. Yet it is not primarily a fellowship, a club, a circle of friends, a replica of the civil society outside it. Without sacrificing its central purpose, it cannot make its primary and dominant value the fostering of friendship, solidarity, harmony, civility, or mutual respect. To be sure, these are important values; other institutions may properly assign them the highest, and not merely a subordinate priority; and a good university will seek and in some significant measure attain these ends. But it will never let these values, important as they are, override its central purpose. We value freedom of expression precisely because it provides a forum for the new, the provocative, the disturbing, and the unorthodox. Free speech is a barrier to the tyranny of authoritarian or even majority opinion as to the rightness or wrongness of particular doctrines or thoughts.[169]

The university as the purveyor of critical education serves important social purposes. These include not only the disciplined pursuit of truth, but also the exemplary enactment of a "model of expression that is meaningful as well as free, coherent yet diverse, critical and inspirational."[170]

The concept of critical education has strong affinities to the traditional "marketplace of ideas" theory of the First Amendment; both are driven by specifically cognitive rather than political concerns. It is thus not uncommon for courts who use the concept to speak of the "classroom" as "peculiarly the 'marketplace of ideas,' " deserving of protection because the "Nation's future depends upon leaders trained through wide exposure to that robust exchange of ideas which discovers truth 'out of a multitude of tongues, [rather] than through any kind of authoritative selection.' "[171]

The concept of critical education differs significantly from both civic and democratic education. In contrast to civic education, it rejects the notion of canonical values that are to be reproduced in the young. Public universities committed to critical education are not free to posit certain values (apart from the value of critical education itself) and to punish those who disagree. The logic of critical education would constitutionally require that a public university "not restrict speech . . . simply because it finds the views expressed by any group to be abhorrent."[172] This stands in stark contrast to the educational project of institutions like the University of Massachusetts, Mount Holyoke, Marquette, or Mary Washington, which are committed to the mission of civic education.

The concept of critical education would also sharply limit the ability of universities to censor uncivil speech. Speech can be uncivil for many reasons, including the assertion of ideas that are perceived to be offensive, revolting, demeaning, or stigmatizing. But critical education would require the toleration of all ideas, however uncivil.[173] This toleration would be consistent with the Court's 1973 holding that "the mere dissemination of ideas—no matter how offensive to good taste—on a state university campus may not be shut off in the name alone of 'conventions of decency.' "[174]

Critical education also differs in important respects from democratic education. The telos of critical education lies in the pursuit of truth rather than in the instantiation of the responsible autonomy of the citizen. The pursuit of truth requires not only an unfettered freedom of ideas but also honesty, fidelity to reason, and respect for method and procedures. Reason, as we have seen, carries its own special requirements of civility, which preclude coercion and abuse. Although enforcement of these requirements and values would be inconsistent with democratic education, it may well be required by critical education. Moreover, critical education requires freedom of ideas only with respect to that speech which forms part of the truth-seeking dialogue of the university. Thus, for example, nothing in the concept of critical education would prevent a university from penalizing malicious racist speech communicated *solely for the purpose* of harassing, humiliating, or degrading a victim.[175] The trick, of course, would be to distinguish such speech in a manner that does not chill communication intended to form part of a truth-seeking exchange.[176] This represents a formidable technical challenge, for it is all too easy to permit revulsion with the content of speech to infect regulation ostensibly justified by other reasons.[177]

Although there is not space to engage in a full-scale exploration of the purposes of higher education, some conclusions are clear enough. The Constitution would not permit a public university, in the name of civic education, to prohibit the teaching of communism because of its conflict with community values. Nor would the Constitution, in the name of democratic education, preclude a public university from enforcing regulations against highly offensive racial epithets within a classroom.

Examples like these incline me toward the concept of critical education, yet the extent to which state universities ought constitutionally to be *required* to pursue one or the other of these educational missions does not seem to me without difficulties.[178] The analysis is further complicated by the possibility that public universities may have various educational functions with constitutionally distinct characteristics. Thus it is conceivable that public universities may be permitted to pursue the mission of civic education within their dormitories, but be required to follow the requirements of democratic education with regard to their open spaces.[179] These are matters that require extended and careful consideration.

I conclude, therefore, by stressing two brief points. First, the constitutionality of restraints on racist speech within public universities does not depend upon the constitutionality of such regulation within public discourse. Second, the constitutionality of restraints on racist speech within public universities will depend to a very great extent upon the educational purposes that we constitutionally attribute to public institutions of higher learning, and upon the various modalities through which such institutions are understood to pursue those purposes. We ought to see debate turn toward the achievement of a fuller and more reflective comprehension of these questions.

Conclusion: The Question of Formal Democracy

This account of the constitutionality of university restrictions on racist speech suggests that a principal flaw of the contemporary debate has been its pervasive assumption that the relationship of racist speech to the First

Amendment can be assessed independently of social context. Communication, however, does not form a constitutionally undifferentiated terrain. The standards of First Amendment protection afforded to public discourse will not be the same as those applied to nonpublic speech, and these in turn will differ from those that govern the regulation of speech within government institutions like universities. The concrete circumstances of racist speech thus figure prominently in the constitutional equation.

Public discourse is the realm of communication we deem necessary to facilitate the process of self-determination. As that process is open-ended, reflecting the boundless possibility of social self-constitution, so we fashion public discourse to be as free from legal constraint as is feasible to sustain. But as self-determination requires the antecedent formation of a "self" through socialization into the particularity of a given community life, so public discourse must at some point be bounded by nonpublic speech, in which community values are embodied and enforced. And as the decisions of a self-determining democracy require actual implementation, so public discourse must at some other point be bounded by the instrumentally regulated speech of the nonpublic forum.

I have attempted to explain the unique protections that American First Amendment jurisprudence affords to public discourse through a self-consciously formal analysis; that is, I have attempted to uncover the formal prerequisites for the instantiation of the value of democracy as self-determination. Although this kind of formal analysis has the advantage of forcing us to clearly articulate the values in whose name we purport to act, it has the disadvantage of obscuring the messy complications of the world. Formal analysis is always subject to the critique that actual, substantive conditions have undermined its very point and meaning.

From a formal perspective, democracy fulfills the purposes of autonomous self-government because we accept an image of independent citizens deliberating together to form public opinion. We therefore structure constitutional policy according to the requirements of that image. But it is an image blatantly vulnerable to the most forceful empirical attack.[180] Citizens are not autonomous; they are manipulated by the media, coerced by private corporations, immured in the toils of racism. Citizens do not communicate together; they are passive, irrational, and voiceless. Deliberation is impossible because of the technical and economic structure of the mass media; public opinion is therefore imposed upon citizens rather than spontaneously arising from them. The very aspiration to self-determination reinforces preexisting inequalities by empowering those with the resources and competence to take advantage of democratic processes; it systematically handicaps socially marginalized groups who lack this easy and familiar access to the media of democratic deliberation. And so forth: the litany is by now depressingly familiar.

Of course these criticisms, and others like them, contain important elements of truth. They therefore force us to choose: either we decide to retain the ideal of democracy as deliberative self-determination and work to minimize the debilitating consequences of these criticisms, or we decide that these criticisms have so undermined the ideal of deliberative self-determination that it must be abandoned and a different value for democracy embraced. If we choose the second alternative, we have the responsibility of articulating and defending a new vision of democracy. But if we choose the first, we have the responsibility of working to foster the constitutional values upon which we rely. We have the obligation of doing so, however, in ways that do not themselves contravene the necessary preconditions of the ideal of deliberative self-determination.[181] The function of formal analysis is to make clear the content of that obligation.

The strict implication of this essay, then, is not that racist speech ought not be regulated in public discourse, but rather that those who advocate its regulation in ways incompatible with the value of deliberative self-governance carry the burden of moving us to a different and more attractive vision of democracy. Or, in the alternative, they carry the burden of justifying suspensions of our fundamental democratic commitments. Neither burden is light.

Notes

Introduction

1. Lon F. Fuller, *The Principles of Social Order* 57 (Kenneth I. Winston, ed., 1981).

2. Philip Selznick, *The Moral Commonwealth: Social Theory and the Promise of Community* 358–59 (1992).

3. Mary Ann Glendon, *Rights Talk: The Impoverishment of Political Discourse* 48 (1991).

4. Harry Kalven, Jr., "Privacy in Tort Law—Were Warren and Brandeis Wrong?," 31 *Law and Contemporary Problems* 326, 341 (1966).

5. For a study of the concept of dignity in the context of community, see Robert Post, "The Social Foundation of Defamation Law: Reputation and the Constitution," 74 *California Law Review* 691, 707–19 (1986).

6. Charles Taylor, *Sources of the Self: The Making of the Modern Identity* 27 (1989).

7. For a sophisticated argument that the empirical absence of common cultural values requires the abandonment of the tort of invasion of privacy, see Randall P. Bezanson, "The Right to Privacy Revisited: Privacy, News, and Social Change, 1890–1990," 80 *California Law Review* 1133 (1992).

8. Selznick, *Moral Commonwealth*, at 289.

9. Walter Lippmann, *Drift and Mastery* 147 (1961) (originally published in 1914).

10. Griswold v. Connecticut, 381 U.S. 479, 496–97 (1965) (Goldberg, J., concurring).

11. Id. at 493.

12. The boundary between community and management is similarly contested in other areas of constitutional law. Fourth Amendment jurisprudence is a good example of such an area. There is a fierce controversy about the circumstances in which the government can search for and seize evidence without a warrant. The warrant requirement in essence constitutionally acknowledges the community value of "an expectation of privacy that society is prepared to recognize as reasonable." Skinner v. Railway Labor Executives Association, 489 U.S. 602, 616 (1989). The objection to requiring warrants is that "insistence on a warrant requirement would impede the achievement of the Government's objective." Id. at 623. The doctrinal controversy is thus ultimately about which aspects of social life ought to regulated in a manner that acknowledges the norms of community, and which ought to be given over purely to the logic of instrumental reason. For

a sampling of relevant cases, see New York v. Burger, 482 U.S. 691 (1987); O'Connor v. Ortega, 480 U.S. 709 (1987); New Jersey v. T.L.O., 469 U.S. 325 (1985).

13. Karl Marx, *Critique of Hegel's "Philosophy of Right"* 31 (Annette Jolin and Joseph O'Malley, trans., 1970).

14. Owen Fiss, "Free Speech and Social Structure," 71 *Iowa Law Review* 1405, 1407 (1986).

15. John Hart Ely, *Democracy and Distrust: A Theory of Judicial Review* 7 (1980).

16. Jürgen Habermas, *Communication and the Evolution of Society* 186–87 (Thomas McCarthy, trans., 1979).

17. See, e.g., Paul Brest, "The Substance of Process," 42 *Ohio State Law Journal* 131 (1981); Lawrence G. Sager, "The Incorrigible Constitution," 65 *New York University Law Review* 893 (1990).

18. For a discussion of such a society, see Martin H. Redish, "The Value of Free Speech," 130 *University of Pennsylvania Law Review* 591, 606–7 (1982).

19. Jean Piaget, *The Moral Judgment of the Child* 366 (Marjorie Gabain, trans., 1948).

20. Brown v. Hartlage, 456 U.S. 45, 60 (1982).

21. Letter from Justice Louis Brandeis to Robert Walter Bruere (Feb. 25, 1922) in 5 *Letters of Louis D. Brandeis* 46 (Melvin I. Urofsky and David W. Levy, eds., 1978).

22. 198 U.S. 45 (1905).

23. George Sutherland, "Principle or Expedient?," 44 *New York State Bar Association Proceedings and Reports* 278 (1921).

24. Chicago, Burlington and Quincy Railroad Co. v. Chicago, 166 U.S. 226, 235 (1897).

25. Roberts v. United States Jaycees, 468 U.S. 609, 619 (1984).

26. Eisenstadt v. Baird, 405 U.S. 438, 453 (1972).

27. For a discussion of these competing strands in contemporary substantive due process doctrine, see Robert Post, "Tradition, the Self, and Substantive Due Process: A Comment on Michael Sandel," 77 *California Law Review* 553 (1989).

28. Regina v. Butler, [1992], 1 S.C.R. 452; Regina v. Keegstra, [1990], 3 S.C.R. 697.

29. Alexis de Tocqueville, *Democracy in America* 506 (George Lawrence, trans., J. P. Mayer, ed., 1988).

30. 2 Fowler V. Harper and Fleming James, *The Law of Torts* §16.2 (1956).

31. Philip Selznick, "The Idea of a Communitarian Morality," 75 *California Law Review* 445, 459–60 (1987).

32. For an argument on this point, see Robert Post, "Rereading Warren and Brandeis: Privacy, Property, and Appropriation," 41 *Case Western Reserve Law Review* 647 (1991).

33. A concise and clear description of the discursive difference between community and management may be found in Jürgen Habermas, "Technology and Science as 'Ideology,' " in *Toward a Rational Society: Student Protest, Science and Politics* 81–122 (Jeremy J. Shapiro, trans., 1970). A longer and more sophisticated description may be found in Jürgen Habermas, *Knowledge and Human Interests* (Jeremy J. Shapiro, trans., 1971).

34. As Charles E. Lindblom writes: "In any large political system, the most democratic ruler imaginable must exercise organizing and coordinating controls over ordinary subject/citizens in a relation of asymmetry." "Democracy and the Economy," in *Democracy and the Market System* 116 (1988).

35. Our commitment to this value is no doubt related to the historical emergence of a capitalist system that, in Ernest Gellner's words, evoked an image of the "modern entrepreneur" as an "untrammeled, eternal inquirer" who inhabited a world that was "open to interminable exploration, offered endless possibilities of new combinations of means with no firm prior expectations and limits." *Nations and Nationalism* 22–23 (1983).

36. Chantal Mouffe, "Democratic Citizenship and the Political Community," in *Dimensions of Radical Democracy: Pluralism, Citizenship, Community* 238 (Chantal Mouffe, ed., 1992).

37. See Charles Taylor, *The Ethics of Authenticity* 31–41 (1992).

38. See Meir Dan-Cohen, "Conceptions of Choice and Conceptions of Autonomy," 102 *Ethics* 221 (1992).

39. Frederick Schauer, *Free Speech: A Philosophical Enquiry* (1982). For an example of Schauer's immediate and enormous influence, see Eric Barendt, *Freedom of Speech* (1985).

40. Geoffrey R. Stone, "Democracy and Distrust," 64 *Colorado Law Review* 1171, 1178 (1993).

41. Redish, "Value of Free Speech," at 593.

42. See, e.g., Contreras v. Crown Zellerbach Corp., 88 Wash. 2d 735, 565 P.2d 1173 (1977); Alcorn v. Anbro Eng'g, 2 Cal. 3d 493, 468 P.2d 216, 86 Cal. Rptr. 88 (1970).

43. Ronald Dworkin, *Law's Empire* 93 (1986).

44. John Dewey, *The Public and Its Problems* 211 (1927).

45. See Robert Post, "Post-Modernism and the Law," *London Review of Books* 3 (February 21, 1991).

1. Theories of Constitutional Interpretation

1. Testimony of Ernest Chambers, Marsh v. Chambers, 463 U.S. 783 (1983), joint appendix at 20, 23–24, 27.

2. Testimony of Robert E. Palmer, id. at 40–41, 45, 51, 83, 89; exhibit 1, 1975 Prayer Book, April 4, 1975, id. at 96; exhibit 2, 1977–78 Prayer Book, February 7, 1977, id. at 98.

3. Although the clause speaks only of Congress, it has been held to be binding on the states by virtue of the Fourteenth Amendment.

4. 504 F. Supp. 585 (D. Neb. 1980).

5. 675 F.2d 228 (8th Cir. 1982).

6. I stress the phenomenological character of this point. It is of course quite plausible to contend that all reading is necessarily active, and hence "interpretive." But not all reading requires a reader to inquire self-consciously into the meaning of a text. From a phenomenological point of view, therefore, some reading does not require that the process of interpreting a text be thematized.

7. United States v. Butler, 297 U.S. 1, 62 (1936).

8. It is necessary at this point to distinguish between textualism as a putative "theory" of interpretation, designed to reveal the meaning of an uncertain text, and textualism as a rule of evidence or priority, which is designed either to exclude from consideration data from beyond the four corners of the document or else to assign to the language of the text priority over such data. Textualism as a rule of evidence or priority would follow from, and presumably be justified by, an anterior theory of interpretation.

9. On the relationship between interpretation and situations where "meaning is doubtful," see Marcelo Dascal and Jerzy Wroblewski, "Transparency and Doubt: Understanding and Interpretation in Pragmatics and in Law," 7 *Law and Philosophy* 203 (1988). It is clear, as Dascal and Wroblewski point out, that the distinction between meaning that is plain, that "fits the case under consideration directly and unproblematically, as a glove to a hand," and meaning that is questionable, does not turn on the "inherent quality of a legal text" but is rather "pragmatic" in nature, turning on all the contingent and practical factors involved "in a given communicative situation." Id. at 215, 221.

10. Marbury v. Madison, 5 U.S. (1 Cranch) 137, 176 (1803).

11. Id. at 163. The phrase was made famous in America by John Adams, who had appointed Marshall to the bench; in *Marbury* Marshall wickedly used it to pinion John Adams' archenemy, Thomas Jefferson. For the derivation of the phrase, see Frank Michelman, "Foreword: Traces of Self-Government," 100 *Harvard Law Review* 4, 4 n.2, 40–41 (1986). For a discussion of other strange circumstances surrounding *Marbury*, see John A. Garraty, "The Case of the Missing Commissions," in *Quarrels That Have Shaped the Constitution* (1964).

12. Marbury v. Madison, 5 U.S. at 163, 175.

13. Alexander Bickel, *The Least Dangerous Branch* 16–17 (1962).

14. Dred Scott v. Sandford, 60 U.S. (19 How.) 393 (1857).

15. Marsh v. Chambers, 463 U.S. at 796 (Brennan, J., dissenting).

16. See Richard A. Wasserstrom, *The Judicial Decision: Toward a Theory of Legal Justification* 39–83 (1961).

17. For a discussion of the nature of the rule of law, see Joseph Raz, "The Rule of Law and Its Virtue," in *The Authority of Law* 210–19 (1979).

18. For further discussion, see Melvin Aron Eisenberg, *The Nature of the Common Law* 47–49 (1988).

19. Henry Paul Monaghan, "Stare Decisis and Constitutional Adjudication," 88 *Columbia Law Review* 723, 752 (1988) (quoting Archibald Cox, *The Role of the Supreme Court in American Government* 50 [1976]). See Vasquez v. Hillery, 474 U.S. 254, 265–66 (1986); Roscoe Pound, "What of Stare Decisis?," 10 *Fordham Law Review* 1, 2 (1941).

20. 675 F.2d at 233.

21. 403 U.S. 602, 612–13 (1971). See Comm. for Public Education and Religious Liberty v. Nyquist, 413 U.S. 756, 773 (1973).

22. Marsh v. Chambers, joint appendix at 49.

23. California Senate Journal, 37th Sess., 171–73, 307–8, 805–6, 808, 818–21 (1907).

24. Marsh v. Chambers, 463 U.S. at 801.

25. Id. at 786–88.

26. Id. at 788, 790.

27. This was essentially the position advocated by the Solicitor General in his brief for the United States as *amicus curiae*. The Solicitor General argued that in *Chambers* "analysis of the legislative chaplaincy practice under the *Lemon* test seems pointless" because "historical analysis . . . should alone suffice to demonstrate that the Nebraska chaplaincy" was consistent with "the intended meaning and scope of the Establishment Clause." Id., Brief for the United States, at 21–22.

28. Id. at 801.

29. Id. at 802–5.

30. Id. at 816–17. As Brennan has subsequently explained: "I frankly concede that I approach my responsibility as a justice, as a 20th century American not confined to [the] framers' vision in 1787. The ultimate question must be, I think, what do the words of the Constitution and Bill of Rights mean to us in our time." Address by William Brennan at Hyde Park, New York, *The Recorder* 8, Nov. 8, 1989.

31. Paul W. Kahn, "Reason and Will in the Origins of American Constitutionalism," 98 *Yale Law Journal* 449, 504 (1989).

32. William W. Van Alstyne, "The Idea of the Constitution as Hard Law," 37 *Journal of Legal Education* 174, 179 (1987). For a useful symposium on the subject, see 6 *Constitutional Commentary* 19–113 (1989).

33. Osborne v. Bank of the United States, 22 U.S. (9 Wheat.) 326, 381 (1824).

34. See Eisenberg, "Nature of Common Law," at 158–59.

35. See J. M. Balkin, "Constitutional Interpretation and the Problem of History," 63 *New York University Law Review* 911, 928 (1988).

36. Minneapolis Star & Tribune Co. v. Minnesota Commissioner of Revenue, 460 U.S. 575, 583 n. 6 (1983).

37. Lest this analysis seem too hypothetical, it should be noted that from 1967

until 1973 the Supreme Court decided thirty-one obscenity cases without opinion because it was unable to agree on a rule of law to distinguish obscene from nonobscene speech. See Frederick F. Schauer, *The Law of Obscenity* 44 (1976).

38. For a similar argument in the context of statutory interpretation, see Edward H. Levy, *An Introduction to Legal Reasoning* 30–33 (1949).

39. In speaking of "legal implications," of course, I am excluding the immediate impact of the decision on the parties to the case. The effect of the *Chambers* decision on the Nebraska state legislature is, at least for the purposes of Chambers' specific lawsuit, independent of the principle of *stare decisis.* That principle only determines the effect of the decision on other, similarly situated legislatures.

40. Frederick F. Schauer, "Formalism," 97 *Yale Law Journal* 509 (1988).

41. See Ronald Dworkin, *Law's Empire* (1986).

42. Paul Brest, "The Misconceived Quest for the Original Understanding," 60 *Boston University Law Review* 204, 234 (1980).

43. Speech of Attorney General Edwin Meese III before the American Bar Association, July 9, 1985, Washington, D.C., in *The Great Debate: Interpreting Our Written Constitution* 9 (1986).

44. Charles Fried, "Sonnet LXV and the 'Black Ink' of the Framers' Intention," 100 *Harvard Law Review* 751, 759 (1987). See H. Jefferson Powell, "The Original Understanding of Original Intent," 98 *Harvard Law Review* 885, 895–98 (1985). This version of historical interpretation might, for example, justify textualism as a rule of evidentiary exclusion. See note 8 above.

45. See Monaghan, "Stare Decisis," at 725.

46. See Raoul Berger, *Federalism: The Founders' Design* 13–20 (1987).

47. The undeniable force of this conclusion also illustrates the ease with which constitutional interpretation escapes from the specific and plain words of the constitutional text.

48. For an elaboration of this argument, see Ronald Dworkin, *A Matter of Principle* 33–57 (1985).

49. This was also James Madison's position; see 6 *The Writings of James Madison* 272 (Gaillard Hunt, ed., 1900); Powell, "Original Understanding," at 937–38.

50. Marsh v. Chambers, 463 U.S. at 815, n.32 (quoting 2 Bernard Schwartz, *The Bill of Rights: A Documentary History* 1171 [1971]).

51. Gerald C. MacCallum, Jr., "Legislative Intent," 75 *Yale Law Journal* 754, 766–69 (1966).

52. Friedrich Nietzsche, *The Use and Abuse of History* 11 (Adrian Collins, trans., 1957). Hence the notorious "illicit love affair" between "Clio and the Court"; Alfred H. Kelly, "Clio and the Court: An Illicit Love Affair," 1965 *Supreme Court Review* 119.

53. For a discussion, see Brest, "Misconceived Quest," at 225–26.

54. For the definitive analysis of this point, see David Hume, *A Treatise of Human Nature* 534–53 (1978) (L. A. Selby-Bigge, ed., 2d ed.).

55. Hanna Pitkin, "Obligation and Consent," in *Philosophy, Politics, and Society* 62 (Peter Laslett, W. G. Runciman, and Quentin Skinner, eds., 4th ser., 1972).

56. Daniel A. Farber, "The Originalism Debate: A Guide for the Perplexed," 49 *Ohio State Law Journal* 1085, 1099–1100 (1989).

57. Missouri v. Holland, 252 U.S. 416, 433 (1920).

58. Karl Llewellyn, "The Constitution as an Institution," 34 *Columbia Law Review* 1, 14–15, 26 (1934).

59. J. N. Findlay, *Kant and the Transcendental Object: A Hermeneutic Study* 241 (1981).

60. Hanna Pitkin, "The Idea of a Constitution," 37 *Journal of Legal Education* 167, 169 (1987).

61. Philippe Nonet and Philip Selznick, *Law and Society in Transition: Toward Responsive Law* 14–15, 78 (1978).

62. Id. at 79, 77.

63. Dun & Bradstreet, Inc. v. Greenmoss Builders, Inc., 472 U.S. 749, 759 (1985) (opinion of Powell, J.).

64. Id. at 787 (Brennan, J., dissenting).

65. Bowers v. Hardwick, 478 U.S. 186, 191–92 (1986).

66. Id. at 205 (Blackmun, J., dissenting).

67. David Couzens Hoy, "A Hermeneutical Critique of the Originalism/Nonoriginalism Distinction," 15 *Northern Kentucky Law Review* 479, 493, 495 (1988).

68. For a good survey, see Walter F. Murphy, James E. Fleming, and William F. Harris, Jr., *American Constitutional Interpretation* (1986).

69. Of course they need not be incompatible. Each of the three conceptions of authority can be understood in ways that render it functionally indistinguishable from the others. Thus an original act of consent can be construed as mandating on the one hand the rule of law, or on the other a continual, open sensitivity to the national ethos. The national ethos can be interpreted to require fidelity to precedent or submission to the founders' consent; the principle of *stare decisis* can be implemented in such a way as to express either the national ethos or the imperatives of an original act of consent.

The point, however, is that these potential convergences are merely contingent, and hence not truly dispositive of the distinctions that divide the three conceptions of constitutional authority. For example, a judge who argues that constitutional authority resides in an original act of consent that also happens to mandate sensitivity to an evolving national ethos is committed to the position that such sensitivity would be improper if the content of that consent were different. Thus for such a judge the discernment of consent would retain a privileged position.

70. For a path-breaking critique of this approach, see Philip Bobbitt, *Constitutional Fate: Theory of the Constitution* (1982).

71. As I write this, for example, the survival of a woman's constitutional right to terminate a pregnancy within the first two trimesters depends to no small extent upon the value assigned by the Supreme Court to the principle of *stare decisis*; see Webster v. Reproductive Health Services, 492, U.S. 490, 578 (1989) (opinion of Rehnquist, C. J.); id. at 558–59 (Blackmun, J., dissenting); Akron v. Akron Center for Reproductive Health, 462 U.S. 416, 419 (1983).

72. For examples, see United States v. Scott, 437 U.S. 83, 86–87 (1978); Garcia v. San Antonio Metropolitan Transit Authority, 469 U.S. 528 (1985). It is particularly important that past precedent not be entirely decisive "in cases involving the Federal Constitution, where correction through legislative action is practically impossible," Burnet v. Coronado Oil & Gas Co., 285 U.S. 393, 405–8 (1932) (Brandeis, J., dissenting), and hence where, since the practice of constitutional amendment is so cumbersome and impractical, correction can in many circumstances only come as a practical matter when the Court itself turns away from *stare decisis*. For this reason the Supreme Court has a "considered practice not to apply *stare decisis* as rigidly in constitutional as in nonconstitutional cases." Glidden Co. v. Zdanok, 370 U.S. 530, 543 (1962) (opinion of Harlan, J.). See Patterson v. McLean Credit Union, 491 U.S. 164, 172–73 (1989).

73. Marsh v. Chambers, 463 U.S. at 792.

74. This suggests that we should expect to see historical interpretation predominate (at least in cases of first impression) in the years immediately following the ratification of a constitutional provision. During that time there will be an obvious and perceptible identification with the process of consent. But as the years pass and as connections to that process fade, the assumption of identification may become increasingly less plausible or persuasive. Changed circumstances or altered cultural conditions may make the consent of the ratifiers seem foreign or alien, quite unlike our own consent. It is at such moments that one would anticipate a transition from historical to responsive interpretation. Llewellyn offers a marvelous description of this process in "Constitution as Institution," at 12–15.

75. In the words of Don Herzog, "The consent of the governed is a special case. It hangs not on the choices made by individuals but on the responsiveness of the state to the people, taken as a collective body." *Happy Slaves: A Critique of Consent Theory* 215 (1989).

76. It is of course possible to argue that we should be bound by the ratifiers' will even if it does not reflect our own. But then it must be explained why this is the case, and that explanation cannot invoke the authority of consent. One possible explanation is that the government couldn't function if decisions made according to appropriate democratic procedures were to lose their authority simply because the passage of time had altered the relevant democratic constit-

uency. But this explanation, stressing as it does the necessity for the Constitution to remain in effect as law in order to sustain the values of continuity, reliance, and predictability, would logically lead to a form of doctrinal rather than historical interpretation.

77. 346 U.S. 483, 489–95 (1954).

78. For a discussion of the incompatibility of *Brown* with any form of historical interpretation, see Monaghan, "Stare Decisis," at 728.

79. 163 U.S. 537 (1896).

80. See, e.g., Cooper v. Aaron, 358 U.S. 1 (1958).

81. John Hart Ely, *Democracy and Distrust* 2–3 (1980). In recent years, with the advantage of hindsight, more convincing arguments have been made that *Roe* could seriously have been justified as a form of doctrinal interpretation.

82. See Thomas C. Grey, "Do We Have an Unwritten Constitution?," 27 *Stanford Law Review* 703 (1975); David Lyons, "A Preface to Constitutional Theory," 15 *Northern Kentucky Law Review* 459 (1988).

83. See Ely, *Democracy and Distrust*, at 88 n.

84. Henry Paul Monaghan, "Our Perfect Constitution," 56 *New York University Law Review* 353, 375–76 (1981) (emphasis added).

85. For the fascinating suggestion that we may have actually enshrined the wrong document, see Akhil Reed Amar, "Our Forgotten Constitution: A Bicentennial Comment," 97 *Yale Law Journal* 281 (1987).

86. For a brief discussion of the history of "organic" metaphors of the Constitution, see Michael Kammen, *A Machine That Would Go of Itself: The Constitution in American Culture* 19–20 (1986).

87. The words are those of Chief Justice Charles Evans Hughes, in Home Building & Loan Assoc. v. Blaisdell, 290 U.S. 398, 443–44 (1934).

88. See, e.g., Hans-Georg Gadamer, *Truth and Method* (1975); Alasdair MacIntyre, *After Virtue* (1981).

89. Philip Selznick, "The Idea of a Communitarian Morality," 75 *California Law Review* 445, 451 (1987).

90. On the distinction between preferences and values, see Mark Sagoff, "Values and Preferences," 96 *Ethics* 301 (1986).

91. "Every clash between a minority claiming freedom and a majority claiming power to regulate involves a choice between the gratifications of the two groups. When the Constitution has not spoken, the Court will be able to find no scale, other than its own value preferences, upon which to weigh the respective claims to pleasure." Robert H. Bork, "Neutral Principles and Some First Amendment Problems," 47 *Indiana Law Journal* 1, 9 (1971).

92. Theodor W. Adorno and Max Horkheimer, *Dialectic of Enlightenment* 38 (John Cumming, trans., 2d ed., 1986). As Adorno and Horkheimer observe, "so long as the identity of the user of reason is disregarded," reason acquires an "affinity" with "force." Id. at 87.

93. See Nonet and Selznick, "Law and Society," at 29.

94. One possible conclusion, of course, is that there be no constitutional law at all, but only simple majority rule. The point in text assumes that those propounding the counter-majoritarian difficulty are attempting to offer a characterization of an appropriate, rather than nonexistent, form of constitutional law.

95. For a clear example of this form of argumentation, see Ely, *Democracy and Distrust*. For a general discussion, see Farber, "Originalism Debate," at 1097–1100.

96. See, e.g., Richard H. Fallon, Jr., "A Constructivist Coherence Theory of Constitutional Interpretation," 100 *Harvard Law Review* 1189, 1217–23 (1987).

97. The phrase is from John Schaar, *Legitimacy in the Modern State* 38 (1981).

98. See Adorno and Horkheimer, *Dialectic of Enlightenment*, at 87.

2. The Social Foundations of Privacy

1. See Thomas I. Emerson, *The System of Freedom of Expression* 549 (1970). For an excellent discussion and critique of this understanding, see C. Keith Boone, "Privacy and Community," 9 *Sociological Theory and Practice* 1, 1–3, 14–21 (1983).

2. Richard F. Hixson, *Privacy in a Public Society: Human Rights in Conflict* at xv (1987); see also Alan F. Westin, *Privacy and Freedom* 27 (1967); Steven J. Andre, "Privacy as an Aspect of the First Amendment: The Place of Privacy in a Society Dedicated to Individual Liberty," 20 *University of West Los Angeles Law Review* 87, 89 (1988–89).

3. Barrington Moore, *Privacy: Studies in Social and Cultural History* 267 (1984). Or, conversely, it is said that "privacy means alienation" and hence impedes the attainment of "authentic community." Alan Freeman and Elizabeth Mensch, "The Public–Private Distinction in American Law and Life," 36 *Buffalo Law Review* 237, 238–39 (1987).

4. Thomas I. Emerson, "The Right of Privacy and Freedom of the Press," 14 *Harvard Civil Rights–Civil Liberties Law Review* 329, 333 (1979).

5. Froelich v. Adair, 213 Kan. 357, 360, 516 P.2d 993, 997 (1973); see also Hazlitt v. Fawcett Publications, Inc., 116 F. Supp. 538, 544 (D. Conn. 1953).

6. Samuel D. Warren and Louis D. Brandeis, "The Right to Privacy," 4 *Harvard Law Review* 193 (1890). The article "is perhaps the most famous and certainly the most influential law review article ever written." Melville B. Nimmer, "The Right of Publicity," 19 *Law and Contemporary Problems* 203, 203 (1954). For a discussion of the historical circumstances surrounding the Warren and Brandeis article, see Don Pember, *Privacy and the Press: The Law, the Mass Media, and the First Amendment* 20–57 (1972). See also Robert Post, "Rereading Warren and Brandeis: Privacy, Property, and Appropriation," 41 *Case Western Law Review* 647 (1991).

7. See Warren and Brandeis, "Right to Privacy," at 207.

8. The tort is today recognized in one form or another in almost every jurisdiction in the nation. For a state-by-state overview, see *Libel Defense Resource Center, 50-State Survey 1988: Current Developments in Media and Invasion of Privacy Law* 924–67 (1988). The tort is still not recognized by English courts. John G. Fleming, *The Law of Torts* 572 (7th ed. 1987); see also Walter F. Pratt, *Privacy in Britain* 16–17 (1979).

9. *Restatement (Second) of Torts* (1977): §§652B, D, C, and E.

10. I defer analysis of the "false light" branch because of its close affiliation with the tort of defamation; I similarly defer analysis of the appropriation branch because of its subtle and complex relationship with concepts of property rights in personal image. See Post, "Rereading Warren and Brandeis."

11. 106 N.H. 107, 206 A.2d 239 (1964).

12. See William Prosser, "Privacy," 48 *California Law Review* 383, 389 (1960); compare id. with *Restatement of Torts* §867 (1939).

13. 106 N.H. at 110, 206 A.2d at 241.

14. 106 N.H. at 109, 111, 112, 206 A.2d at 240, 242.

15. Griswold v. Connecticut, 381 U.S. 479, 485 (1965).

16. For an historical account of the origins of these expectations, see Witold Rybczynski, *Home: A Short History of an Idea* 15–49 (1986).

17. *Eastman*, 106 N.H. at 112, 206 A.2d at 242 (quoting 3 Roscoe Pound, *Jurisprudence* 58 [1959]); see also Emerson, "Right of Privacy," at 333; John W. Wade, "The Communicative Torts and the First Amendment," 48 *Mississippi Law Journal* 671, 707–8 (1977).

18. "The action sounds in tort and when authorized is primarily to recover for a hurt to the feelings of the individual." Wheeler v. P. Sorensen Mfg. Co., 415 S.W.2d 582, 584 (Ky. 1967); see also Goodrich v. Waterbury Republican-Am, Inc., 188 Conn. 107, 128 n.19, 448 A.2d 1317, 1329 n.19 (1982); Froelich v. Adair, 213 Kan. 357, 362, 516 P.2d 993, 998 (1973); Billings v. Atkinson, 489 S.W.2d 858, 861 (Tex. 1973); Crump v. Beckley Newspapers, Inc., 320 S.E.2d 70, 87 (W. Va. 1984).

19. *Eastman*, 106 N.H. at 111, 206 A.2d at 242.

20. *Restatement (Second) of Torts* §652B. The *Restatement* provides that "one who intentionally intrudes, physically or otherwise, upon the solitude or seclusion of another or his private affairs or concerns, is subject to liability to the other for invasion of his privacy, if the intrusion would be highly offensive to a reasonable person."

21. Id. §283 comment c.

22. 2 Fowler V. Harper and Fleming James, *The Law of Torts* §16.2 (1956).

23. 106 N.H. at 111, 206 A.2d at 242.

24. Erving Goffman, "The Nature of Deference and Demeanor," in *Interaction Ritual: Essays on Face-to-Face Behavior* 47, 56, 77 (1967).

25. Id. at 90, 91, 84–85.

26. Id. at 51.

27. Joseph R. Gusfield, *Community: A Critical Response* 29 (1975).

28. Kai T. Erikson, *Wayward Puritans: A Study in the Sociology of Deviance* 11 (1966).

29. See *Restatement (Second) of Torts* §328A (1977).

30. The phrase comes from Harry Kalven, "Privacy in Tort Law—Were Warren and Brandeis Wrong?," 31 *Law and Contemporary Problems* 326, 341 (1966). Torts that redress dignitary harms share this structure with the larger category of "traditional intentional torts." See Daniel Givelber, "The Right to Minimum Social Decency and the Limits of Evenhandedness: Infliction of Emotional Distress by Outrageous Conduct," 82 *Columbia Law Review* 42, 49–50 (1982). For a roughly analogous distinction between "damage" torts and "interference" torts, see F. H. Lawson, " 'Das subjektive Recht' in the English Law of Torts," in 1 *Many Laws: Selected Essays* 176–92 (1977).

31. Robert Post, "The Social Foundations of Defamation Law: Reputation and the Constitution," 74 *California Law Review* 691, 707–19 (1986).

32. See id. at 697–98. In 1974 in Gertz v. Robert Welch, Inc., 418 U.S. 323, 348–50 (1974), the United States Supreme Court held that the First Amendment sharply limits awards of such general damages, although in a recent decision the Court has somewhat loosened this constitutional restriction. See Dun and Bradstreet, Inc. v. Greenmoss Builders, Inc., 472 U.S. 749, 753–61 (1985).

33. Warren and Brandeis, "Right to Privacy," at 219.

34. *Restatement of Torts* §867 comment d (1939).

35. The circumspection was no doubt due to the Supreme Court's recent constitutional decision in *Gertz*, discussed at note 32; see also *Restatement (Second) of Torts* §652H comment c (1977). Because the tort of intrusion does not involve speech, it is not subject to the kind of First Amendment limitations imposed by *Gertz*.

36. *Restatement (Second) of Torts* §652H (1977).

37. Thus in the tort of intrusion the second *Restatement* provides that a plaintiff can recover damages for the violation of his "interest in privacy," which means "the deprivation of his seclusion." Id. §652H comment a.

38. See, e.g., Socialist Workers Party v. Attorney General, 642 F. Supp. 1357, 1417–23 (S.D.N.Y. 1986).

39. See, e.g., Manville v. Borg-Warner Corp., 418 F.2d 434, 437 (10th Cir. 1969); Cason v. Baskin, 159 Fla. 31, 41, 30 So.2d 635, 640 (1947); Samuel H. Hofstadter and George Horowitz, *The Right of Privacy* 265–68 (1964). But see Brents v. Morgan, 221 Ky. 765, 774–75, 299 S.W. 967, 971–72 (1927); Hazlitt v. Fawcett Publications, Inc., 116 F. Supp. 538, 544 (D. Conn. 1953). In negligence actions, by way of contrast, awards of nominal damages are not permitted, because a plaintiff can succeed only if he demonstrates actual injury. *Restatement (Second) of Torts* §907 comment a (1977).

40. There is, however, a limit to the idiosyncrasies that the law will recognize. The second *Restatement* notes, for example, that a plaintiff may "recover damages for emotional distress or personal humiliation that he proves to have been actually suffered by him, *if it is of a kind that normally results from such an invasion and it is normal and reasonable in its extent.*" *Restatement (Second) of Torts* §652H comment b (1977) (emphasis added). The law will not tolerate too great a divergence between social and individual personality.

41. The formulation of this point is a bit tricky, because often the question of whether a civility rule has been violated depends upon the subjective attitude of a plaintiff. For example, if the eavesdropping device in *Eastman* had been placed with the consent of the plaintiffs, we would understand the defendant not as having transgressed a civility rule but rather as having entered into some mutual, erotic relationship with the plaintiffs. The point in the text, however, is that if the placement of the device has broken a civility rule—if, for example, the plaintiffs in *Eastman* had been unaware of its installation—then the plaintiffs would have been demeaned regardless of their subjective apprehension.

42. Cf. Joel Feinberg, "The Nature and Value of Rights," 4 *Journal of Value Inquiry* 243, 252 (1970): "Respect for persons . . . may simply be respect for their rights, so that there cannot be the one without the other; and what is called 'human dignity' may simply be the recognizable capacity to assert claims. To respect a person, then, or to think of him as possessed of human dignity, simply *is* to think of him as a potential maker of claims."

43. Vassiliades v. Garfinckel's, Brooks Bros., 492 A.2d 580, 594 (D.C. 1985).

44. On the issue of "excessive" damage awards, see, for example, *Libel Def. Resource Bull., No. 11*, Summer–Fall 1984, at 12–18; "Socking It to the Press," *Editor and Publisher*, Apr. 7, 1984, at 31.

45. *Restatement (Second) of Torts* §901 comment c (1977).

46. In the area of defamation, for example, the punishment of a defendant through the exaction of high civil damages can be interpreted as the law's attempt to "vindicate" a plaintiff's honor. See Post, "Foundations of Defamation Law," at 703–6.

47. Goffman, "Nature of Deference and Demeanor," at 51.

48. Gusfield, *Community*, at 29.

49. On the relationship between punishment and vindication, see Post, "Foundations of Defamation Law," at 704–5.

50. Ruth Gavison, "Privacy and the Limits of Law," 89 *Yale Law Journal* 421, 425–40 (1980).

51. Id. at 428.

52. Robert K. Merton, *Social Theory and Social Structure* 429 (1968).

53. Georg Simmel, *The Sociology of Georg Simmel* 324 (Kurt H. Wolff, trans. and ed., 1950).

54. See Gavison, "Privacy and the Limits of Law," at 426 n.18.

55. An example of a case in which all three torts were alleged is Hustler

Magazine v. Falwell, 485 U.S. 46, 48–49 (1988). For a more typical case, see Sawabini v. Desenberg, 143 Mich. App. 373, 372 N.W.2d 559 (Ct. App. 1985). For a statistical study of pleading practices with respect to dignitary torts, see Terrance C. Mead, "Suing Media for Emotional Distress: A Multi-Method Analysis of Tort Law Evolution," 23 *Washburn Law Journal* 24, 36–44 (1983).

56. *Restatement (Second) of Torts* §652B (1977).

57. Id. §46.

58. See, e.g., Galella v. Onassis, 353 F. Supp. 196 (S.D.N.Y. 1972), aff'd in part and rev'd in part, 487 F.2d 986 (2d Cir. 1973); Fletcher v. Florida Publishing Co., 319 So. 2d 100 (Fla. Dist. Ct. App. 1975), rev'd, 340 So. 2d 914 (Fla. 1976), cert. denied, 431 U.S. 930 (1977); Pemberton v. Bethlehem Steel Corp., 66 Md. App. 133, 502 A.2d 1101 (Ct. Spec. App.), cert. denied, 306 Md. 289, 508 A.2d 488, cert. denied, 479 U.S. 984 (1986); Nader v. General Motors Corp., 25 N.Y.2d 560, 255 N.E.2d 765, 307 N.Y.S.2d 647 (1970); Mead, "Suing Media," at 49.

59. See Simmel, *Sociology*, at 321.

60. See, e.g., Housh v. Peth, 165 Ohio St. 35, 40–41, 133 N.E.2d 340, 343 (1956).

61. As Joel Feinberg notes: "The root idea in the generic concept of privacy is that of a privileged territory or domain in which an individual person has the exclusive authority of determining whether another may enter, and if so, when and for how long, and under what conditions. Within this area, the individual person is—pick your metaphor—boss, sovereign, owner." *Offense to Others* 24 (1985) (citation omitted).

62. Erving Goffman, "The Territories of the Self," in *Relations in Public: Microstudies of the Public Order* 28–29, 31, 40 (1971). Goffman makes clear that the conduct of the individual claiming the territory is also relevant to the social recognition of the territory. Id. at 41–44.

63. 632 F. Supp. 1282, 1285 (N.D. Ill. 1986) (quoting the Complaint at ¶9).

64. Id. at 1287 (quoting Respondent NBC's Memorandum at 8).

65. Id. at 1288.

66. Goffman, "Territories of the Self," at 60.

67. See Craker v. Chicago and N.W. Ry., 36 Wis. 657, 660 (1875).

68. See Goffman, "Territories of the Self," at 60–61. For commentators making a similar point, see Charles Fried, *An Anatomy of Values: Problems of Personal and Social Choice* 142 (1970); James Rachels, "Why Privacy is Important," 4 *Philosophy and Public Affairs* 323, 327–29 (1975).

69. Since such respect is constitutive of the self, it is not surprising to find the early cases describing privacy norms in the language of "natural law": "The right of privacy has its foundation in the instincts of nature. It is recognized intuitively, consciousness being the witness that can be called to establish its existence. Any person whose intellect is in a normal condition recognizes at once that as to each

individual member of society there are matters private and there are matters public so far as the individual is concerned. Each individual as instinctively resents any encroachment by the public upon his rights which are of a private nature as he does the withdrawal of those of his rights which are of a public nature. A right of privacy in matters purely private is therefore derived from natural law." Pavesich v. New England Life Ins. Co., 122 Ga. 190, 194, 50 S.E. 68, 69–70 (1905).

70. Goffman, "Territories of the Self," at 60.

71. Jeffrey H. Reiman, "Privacy, Intimacy, and Personhood," 6 *Philosophy and Public Affairs* 26, 39 (1976).

72. For an overview of this debate, see Amy Gutmann, "Communitarian Critics of Liberalism," 14 *Philosophy and Public Affairs* 308 (1985); Robert B. Thigpen and Lyle A. Downing, "Liberalism and the Communitarian Critique," 31 *American Journal of Political Science* 637 (1987); John R. Wallach, "Liberals, Communitarians, and the Tasks of Political Theory," 15 *Political Theory* 581 (1987); Note, "A Communitarian Defense of Group Libel Laws," 101 *Harvard Law Review* 682, 689–92 (1988).

73. On the distinction between judge and jury with respect to the discernment and application of community norms, see Robert Post, "Defaming Public Officials: On Doctrine and Legal History," 1897 *American Bar Foundation Research Journal* 539, 552–54.

74. Simmel, *Sociology*, at 323.

75. Bohannan states: "Customs are norms or rules . . . about the ways in which people must behave if social institutions are to perform their tasks and society is to endure. All institutions (including legal institutions) develop customs. Some customs, in some societies, are *re*institutionalized at another level: they are restated for the more precise purposes of legal institutions. When this happens, therefore, law may be regarded as a custom that has been restated in order to make it amenable to the activities of the legal institutions." Paul Bohannan, "The Differing Realms of the Law," 67 *American Anthropologist* 33, 35–36 (special issue, Dec. 1965).

76. Joseph Raz, "The Rule of Law and Its Virtue," in *The Authority of Law* 210, 213 (1979).

77. Bohannan, "Differing Realms," at 37. Bohannan notes:

> Indeed, the more highly developed the legal institutions, the greater the lack of phase, which not only results from the constant reorientation of the primary institutions, but also is magnified by the very dynamic of the legal institutions themselves.
>
> Thus, it is the very nature of law, and its capacity to "do something about" the primary social institutions, that creates the lack of phase . . . It is the fertile dilemma of law that it must always be out of step with society, but that people must always (because they work better with fewer contradictions, if for no other reason) attempt to reduce the lack of phase. Custom must either

grow to fit the law or it must actively reject it; law must either grow to fit the custom, or it must ignore or suppress it. It is in these very interstices that social growth and social decay take place. (Id., citation omitted)

78. Anderson v. Fisher Broadcasting Co., 300 Or. 452, 461, 712 P.2d 803, 809 (1986). " ' "Class, occupation, education, and status within various communities and organizations may significantly affect the way in which an individual thinks of himself as a 'private' individual and what he understands by 'the moral right to privacy." ' " Id. at 461 n.8, 712 P.2d at 809 n.8 (quoting Diane L. Zimmerman, "Requiem for a Heavyweight: A Farewell to Warren and Brandeis's Privacy Tort," 68 *Cornell Law Review* 291, 349 n.304 [1983], quoting Velecky, "The Concept of Privacy," in *Privacy* 25 [John B. Young, ed., 1983]).

79. Alpheus Thomas Mason, *Brandeis: A Free Man's Life* 70 (1956).

80. "The Warren-Brandeis proposal was essentially a rich man's plea to the press to stop its gossiping and snooping." Pember, *Privacy and the Press*, at 23. In the classic tones of the beleaguered aristocrat, Warren and Brandeis complain: "The press is overstepping in every direction the obvious bounds of propriety and of decency. Gossip is no longer the resource of the idle and of the vicious, but has become a trade, which is pursued with industry as well as effrontery. To satisfy a prurient taste the details of sexual relations are spread broadcast in the columns of the daily papers. To occupy the indolent, column upon column is filled with idle gossip, which can only be procured by intrusion upon the domestic circle." Warren and Brandeis, "Right to Privacy," at 196.

81. E. L. Godkin, "The Rights of the Citizen: To His Own Reputation," *Scribner's*, July 1890, at 58, 65, 66.

82. Peck v. Tribune Co., 214 U.S. 185, 190 (1909).

83. Kimmerle v. New York Evening Journal, Inc., 262 N.Y. 99, 102, 186 N.E. 217, 218 (1933) (quoting Sydney v. MacFadden Newspaper Publishing Corp., 242 N.Y. 208, 212, 151 N.E. 209, 210 [1926]); see Post, "Foundations of Defamation Law," at 714–15.

84. Talcott Parsons, *Sociological Theory and Modern Society* 510 (1967).

85. A good illustration of this potential is the case of Bitsie v. Walston, 85 N.M. 655, 658, 515 P.2d 659, 662 (Ct. App.), cert. denied, 85 N.M. 639, 515 P.2d 642 (1973), a decision interpreting the "appropriation" branch of the privacy tort, in which the court held that the "traditional" norms of the Navajo tribe could not be equated with the "ordinary sensibilities" of the reasonable person. See also Benally v. Hundred Arrows Press, Inc., 614 F. Supp. 969, 982 (D.N.M. 1985), rev'd on other grounds sub nom. Benally v. Amon Carter Museum of Western Art, 858 F.2d 618 (10th Cir. 1988).

86. See, e.g., Kalven, "Privacy in Tort Law," at 333.

87. *Restatement (Second) of Torts* §652D (1977). Once again, it is important to stress that the specific elements of this tort can vary from state to state, but it is fair to conclude that the *Restatement* version contains by far the most common array of elements.

88. 221 Ky. 765, 766, 299 S.W. 967, 968 (1927).

89. Id. at 770, 299 S.W. at 969, 970. The court quoted language to the effect that the foundation of the right of privacy "is in the conception of an inviolate personality and personal immunity. It is considered as a natural and an absolute or pure right springing from the instincts of nature. It is of that class of rights which every human being had in his natural state and which he did not surrender by becoming a member of organized society." Id. at 773, 299 S.W. at 971 (quoting 21 Ruling Case Law §3, at 1197–98 [1929]).

90. See, e.g., *Restatement (Second) of Torts* §652D comment a, illustration 2 (1977).

91. 4 Cal.3d 529, 483 P.2d 34, 93 Cal. Rptr. 866 (1971).

92. In 1975 the United States Supreme Court held in Cox Broadcasting Corp. v. Cohn, 420 U.S. 469 (1975) that the First Amendment prohibited a plaintiff from suing for damages for invasion of privacy on the basis of "the publication of truthful information contained in official court records open to public inspection." Id. at 495. Subsequent cases, however, as well as the 1977 edition of the *Restatement*, have continued to view liability as appropriate if the publication of such information occurs after a sufficient lapse of time. See, e.g., Conklin v. Sloss, 86 Cal. App. 3d 241, 247–48, 150 Cal. Rptr. 121, 125 (Ct. App. 1978); Roshto v. Hebert, 439 So. 2d 428, 431 (La. 1983); *Restatement (Second) of Torts* §652D comment k (1977); cf. Capra v. Thoroughbred Racing Ass'n, 787 F.2d 463 (9th Cir.), cert. denied, 479 U.S. 1017 (1986). The second *Restatement* provides that if publicity is given to a public event after a sufficient lapse of time, it must be determined "whether the publicity goes to unreasonable lengths in revealing facts about one who has resumed the private, lawful and unexciting life led by the great bulk of the community. This may be true, for example, when there is a disclosure of the present name and identity of a reformed criminal and his new life is utterly ruined by revelation of a past that he has put behind him . . . The question is to be determined upon the basis of community standards and mores." *Restatement (Second) of Torts* §652D comment k (1977).

The Supreme Court has itself signaled that the holding of *Cox* is to be narrowly parsed. In Florida Star v. B.J.F., 491 U.S. 524 (1989), the Court emphasized that *Cox* did not "exhaustively" resolve the "tension between the right which the First Amendment accords to a free press, on the one hand, and the protections which various statutes and common-law doctrines accord to personal privacy against the publication of truthful information, on the other." Id. at 530. The Court specifically refused to hold that "truthful publication is automatically constitutionally protected, or that there is no zone of personal privacy within which the State may protect the individual from intrusion by the press, or even that a State may never punish publication of the name of a victim of a sexual offense." Id. at 541. It held only that "where a newspaper publishes truthful information which it has lawfully obtained, punishment may lawfully be imposed, if at all, only when narrowly tailored to a state interest of the highest order. . . ." Id.

93. *Briscoe*, 4 Cal. 3d at 537, 483 P.2d at 39–40, 93 Cal. Rptr. at 871–72.

94. 112 Cal. App. 285, 292, 291, 297 P. 91, 93–94, 93 (Ct. App. 1931).

95. 240 S.W.2d 588 (Ky. 1951). The court stated that conveying such information would not impair " 'the standing of an individual and bring him into disrepute with right thinking people in the community.' " The court explained: "A debtor when he creates an obligation must know that his creditor expects to collect it, and the ordinary man realizes that most employers expect their employees to meet their obligations and that when they fall behind in so doing the employer may be asked to take the matter up with them. Indeed, most debtors would prefer to have their delinquencies referred to their employers in a courteous and inconspicuous manner rather than to have a suit filed against them and their wages garnished." Id. at 591, 593 (quoting in part Neaton v. Lewis Apparel Stores, 267 A.D. 728, 48 N.Y.S.2d 492, 494 [App. Div. 1944]). The holding of the Kentucky court is typical of decisions dealing with this issue. See Hofstadter and Horowitz, *Right of Privacy*, at 173–76.

96. Harrison v. Humble Oil and Refining Co., 264 F. Supp. 89, 92 (D.S.C. 1967) (quoting Patton v. Jacobs, 118 Ind. App. 358, 78 N.E.2d 789 [App. 1948]).

97. Id. (quoting Cunningham v. Securities Investment Co. of St. Louis, 278 F.2d 600, 604 [5th Cir. 1960]).

98. 492 A.2d 580, 588 (D.C. 1985).

99. Consider, in this light, the ambiguity of the *Restatement*'s own gloss on the offensiveness requirement: "The rule stated in this Section gives protection only against unreasonable publicity, of a kind highly offensive to the ordinary reasonable man. The protection afforded to the plaintiff's interest in his privacy must be relative to the customs of the time and place, to the occupation of the plaintiff and to the habits of his neighbors and fellow citizens." *Restatement (Second) of Torts* §652D comment c (1977).

100. Such revelations violate what Elizabeth Beardsley has termed "the right of selective disclosure"; Beardsley states that "selective disclosure constitutes the conceptual core of the norm of privacy." Elizabeth L. Beardsley, "Privacy: Autonomy and Selective Disclosure," in *Privacy* 56, 70 (J. Roland Pennock and John W. Chapman, eds., 1971) (*Nomos* 13).

101. Goffman, "Territories of the Self," at 31, 40.

102. David J. Seipp, "English Judicial Recognition of a Right to Privacy," 3 *Oxford Journal of Legal Studies* 325, 333 (1983).

103. Goffman, "Territories of the Self," at 38–39.

104. Warren and Brandeis, "Right to Privacy," at 196. For another example of this almost physical apprehension, see Brents v. Morgan, 221 Ky. 765, 774, 299 S.W. 967, 971 (1927).

105. Wheeler v. P. Sorensen Mfg. Co., 415 S.W.2d 582, 585 (Ky. 1967).

106. Ferdinand David Schoeman, "Privacy and Intimate Information," in

Philosophical Dimensions of Privacy: An Anthology 403, 406 (Ferdinand David Schoeman, ed., 1984).

107. Simmel, *Sociology*, at 323.

108. Daily Times Democrat v. Graham, 276 Ala. 380, 382, 162 So. 2d 474, 476 (1964).

109. Diaz v. Oakland Tribune, Inc., 139 Cal. App. 3d 118, 126, 188 Cal. Rptr. 762, 767 (Ct. App. 1983) (quoting Melville Nimmer, "The Right to Speak from *Times* to *Time:* First Amendment Theory Applied to Libel and Misapplied to Privacy," 56 *California Law Review* 935, 959 [1968]) (emphasis omitted).

110. Briscoe v. Reader's Digest Ass'n, 4 Cal. 3d 529, 534, 483 P.2d 34, 37, 93 Cal. Rptr. 866, 869 (1971).

111. See, e.g., Anderson v. Fisher Broadcasting Co., 300 Or. 452, 462, 712 P.2d 803, 809 (1986); Gavison, "Privacy and the Limits of Law," at 458.

112. This conclusion implies that it is a great mistake to view the tort, as some have proposed, as simply a device for protecting secrecy. See, e.g., Richard A. Posner, "The Right of Privacy," 12 *Georgia Law Review* 393, 393 (1978); George J. Stigler, "An Introduction to Privacy in Economics and Politics," 9 *Journal of Legal Studies* 623 (1980). Secrecy depends upon a purely descriptive concept of privacy, which is quite different from the normative concept that actually underlies the tort. The difference is most apparent in the fact that the tort deems the right of privacy to be a "personal" right that "can be maintained only by a living individual whose privacy is invaded." *Restatement (Second) of Torts* §652I (1977). Thus corporations, which have secrets to protect but which are not entitled to claims of social respect, have "no personal right of privacy" and cannot bring a "cause of action" to enforce any such right. Id. at comment c. For this reason, as Jack Hirshleifer has argued, privacy in the common law must be interpreted as signifying "something much broader than secrecy; it suggests . . . a particular kind of social structure together with its supporting social ethic." Jack Hirshleifer, "Privacy: Its Origin, Function, and Future," 9 *Journal of Legal Studies* 649, 649 (1980). By preserving the civility rules that define a community, the tort constitutes nothing less than "a *way of organizing society.*" Id. at 650 (emphasis in original).

113. Kalven, "Privacy in Tort Law," at 336.

114. Virgil v. Time, Inc., 527 F.2d 1122, 1128 (9th Cir. 1975), cert. denied, 425 U.S. 998 (1976).

115. See, e.g., Fletcher v. Florida Publishing Co., 319 So. 2d 100, 111 (Fla. Dist. Ct. App. 1975), rev'd on other grounds, 340 So. 2d 914 (Fla. 1976), cert. denied, 431 U.S. 930 (1977).

116. Thomas Starkie, *A Treatise on the Law of Slander, Libel, Scandalum Magnatum, and False Rumours* at xx–xxi (1826).

117. See Simmel, *Sociology*, at 323.

118. The First Amendment did not become applicable to state law until 1925

in the case of Gitlow v. New York, 268 U.S. 652 (1925). It was not until 1964 that the First Amendment was deemed to control state defamation law. See New York Times Co. v. Sullivan, 376 U.S. 254 (1964). The first decision of the United States Supreme Court to apply the First Amendment to state privacy law was Time, Inc. v. Hill, 385 U.S. 374 (1967).

119. Warren and Brandeis, "Right to Privacy," at 214.

120. 122 Ga. 190, 204, 50 S.E. 68, 74 (1905).

121. See, e.g., Kapellas v. Kofman, 1 Cal. 3d 20, 36–38, 459 P.2d 912, 922–24, 81 Cal. Rptr. 360, 370–71 (1969); Stryker v. Republic Pictures Corp., 108 Cal. App. 2d 191, 194, 238 P.2d 670, 672 (Ct. App. 1952).

122. See, e.g., Jack Nelson, "Soul-Searching Press Ethics," *Nieman Report*, Spring 1988, at 15.

123. Sanford Levinson, "Public Lives and the Limits of Privacy," 21 *Political Science and Politics* 263 (1988); cf. Monotor Patriot Co. v. Roy, 401 U.S. 265, 273–75 (1971).

124. Beauharnais v. Illinois, 343 U.S. 250, 263 n.18 (1952); see also Mayrant v. Richardson, 10 S.C.L. (1 Nott and McC.) 347, 350 (S.C. 1818).

125. *Restatement (Second) of Torts* §652D comment e (1977); see also Robert D. Sack, *Libel, Slander, and Related Problems* 410–11 (1980).

126. *Restatement (Second) of Torts* §652D comment g (1977); see, e.g., Campbell v. Seabury Press, 614 F.2d 395, 397 (5th Cir. 1980); Virgil v. Time, Inc., 527 F.2d 1122, 1128–29 (9th Cir. 1975), cert. denied, 425 U.S. 988 (1976); Logan v. District of Columbia, 447 F. Supp. 1328, 1333 (D.D.C. 1978); Neff v. Time, Inc., 406 F. Supp. 858, 861 (W.D. Pa. 1976); Kapellas v. Kofman, 1 Cal. 3d 20, 36, 459 P.2d 912, 922, 81 Cal. Rptr. 360, 370 (1969); Jacova v. Southern Radio and Television Co., 83 So. 2d 34, 40 (Fla. 1955); Cape Publications, Inc. v. Bridges, 423 So. 2d 426, 427 (Fla. Dist. Ct. App. 1982), petition denied, 431 So. 2d 988 (Fla. 1983), cert. denied, 464 U.S. 893 (1983); Bremmer v. Journal-Tribune Publishing Co., 247 Iowa 817, 827–28, 76 N.W.2d 762, 768 (1956); Fry v. Ionia Sentinel-Standard, 101 Mich. App. 725, 729–30, 300 N.W.2d 687, 690 (Ct. App. 1980); Bruce W. Sanford, *Libel and Privacy: The Prevention and Defense of Litigation* 447 (1987 Supp.).

127. Alvin W. Gouldner, *The Dialectic of Ideology and Technology* 95 (1976); see also John W. Bennett and Melvin M. Tumin, *Social Life: Structure and Function* 140 (1948).

128. Harvey Molotch and Marilyn Lester, "News as Purposive Behavior: On the Strategic Use of Routine Events, Accidents, and Scandals," 39 *American Social Review* 101 (1974).

129. Gouldner, *Dialectic*, at 106, 95–96. As Tocqueville put it: "There is a necessary connection between public associations and newspapers: newspapers make associations, and associations make newspapers." 2 Alexis de Tocqueville, *Democracy in America* 112 (Phillips Bradley, ed., 1945) (Henry Reeve, trans., 1st ed., 1840).

130. See, e.g., Lillian R. BeVier, "The First Amendment and Political Speech: An Inquiry into the Substance and Limits of Principle," 30 *Stanford Law Review* 299 (1978); Alexander Meiklejohn, "The First Amendment Is an Absolute," 1961 *Supreme Court Review* 245.

131. NAACP v. Claiborne Hardware Co., 458 U.S. 886, 913 (1982) (quoting Carey v. Brown, 447 U.S. 455, 467 [1980]).

132. 113 F.2d 806, 807–9 (2d Cir.), cert. denied 311 U.S. 711 (1940).

133. Id. at 809.

134. Gouldner, *Dialectic*, at 101–3; see also Freeman and Mensch, "Public–Private Distinction," at 243.

135. Desert Sun Publishing Co. v. Superior Court, 97 Cal. App. 3d 49, 51, 158 Cal. Rptr. 519, 521 (Ct. App. 1979).

136. Walter Lippmann, *Public Opinion* 345 (1922).

137. Edward A. Purcell, *The Crisis of Democratic Theory: Scientific Naturalism and the Problem of Value* 95–114 (1973).

138. Gouldner, *Dialectic*, at 98 (emphasis in original); see also id. at 96–97.

139. Virgil v. Sports Illustrated, 424 F. Supp. 1286, 1289 n.2 (S.D. Cal. 1976); see, e.g., Gilbert v. Medical Economics Co., 665 F.2d 305, 308–9 (10th Cir. 1981); Campbell v. Seabury Press, 614 F.2d 395, 397 (5th Cir. 1980); Dresbach v. Doubleday & Co., 518 F. Supp. 1285, 1290–91 (D.D.C. 1981); Vassiliades v. Garfinckel's, Brooks Bros., 492 A.2d 580, 590 (D.C. 1985); Romaine v. Kallinger, 109 N.J. 282, 302, 537 A.2d 284, 294 (1988).

140. See, e.g., Bilney v. Evening Star Newspaper Co., 43 Md. App. 560, 570–73, 406 A.2d 652, 659–60 (Ct. Spec. App. 1979).

141. *Restatement (Second) of Torts* §652D comment f (1977); see, e.g., Campbell v. Seabury Press, 614 F.2d 395, 397 (5th Cir. 1980); Virgil v. Time, Inc., 527 F.2d 1122, 1129 (9th Cir. 1975), cert. denied, 425 U.S. 998 (1976); Logan v. District of Columbia, 447 F. Supp. 1328, 1333 (D.D.C. 1978); Jacova v. Southern Radio and Television Co., 83 So. 2d 34, 37, 40 (Fla. 1955); Waters v. Fleetwood, 212 Ga. 161, 167, 91 S.E.2d 344, 348 (1956); Bremmer v. Journal-Tribune Publishing Co., 247 Iowa 817, 827–28, 76 N.W.2d 762, 768 (1956); Hofstadter and Horowitz, *Right of Privacy*, at 116.

142. Howard v. Des Moines Register and Tribune Co., 283 N.W.2d 289, 302 (Iowa 1979), cert. denied, 445 U.S. 904 (1980); see also Sack, *Libel*, at 411–12.

143. Briscoe v. Reader's Digest Ass'n, 4 Cal. 3d 529, 538, 483 P.2d 34, 40, 93 Cal. Rptr. 866, 872 (1971) (quoting *Restatement of Torts* §867 comment c [1939]).

144. Sidis v. F-R Publishing Corp., 113 F.2d 806, 809 (2d Cir.), cert. denied, 311 U.S. 711 (1940).

145. Forsher v. Bugliosi, 26 Cal. 3d 792, 811, 608 P.2d 716, 726, 163 Cal. Rptr. 628, 638 (1980) (quoting William Prosser, "Privacy," 48 *California Law Review* 383, 418 [1960]); see also Dresbach v. Doubleday & Co., 518 F. Supp. 1285, 1289 (D.D.C. 1981); Romaine v. Kallinger, 109 N.J. 282, 303–4, 537

A.2d 284, 294–95 (1988); McCormack v. Oklahoma Publishing Co., 6 Media Law Reporter (BNA) 1618, 1622 (Okla. 1980).

146. With regard to such matters, courts have registered their appreciation of the "force" in "the simple contention that whatever is in the news media is by definition newsworthy, that the press must in the nature of things be the final arbiter of newsworthiness." Kalven, "Privacy in Tort Law," at 336.

147. 230 S.C. 330, 334, 95 S.E.2d 606, 608 (1956).

148. Walter Lippmann, *Liberty and the News* 12 (1920).

149. 230 S.C. at 338, 95 S.E.2d at 610. The court expressed "regret" that it could not "give legal recognition to Mrs. Meetze's desire to avoid publicity but the courts do not sit as censors of the manners of the Press." Id. at 339, 95 S.E.2d at 610.

150. Id. at 337, 95 S.E.2d at 609 (quoting 41 *American Jurist* "Privacy" §14 [1942]).

151. See, e.g., Gilbert v. Medical Economics Co., 665 F.2d 305, 307–08 (10th Cir. 1981); Wasser v. San Diego Union, 191 Cal. App. 3d 1455, 1461–62, 236 Cal. Rptr. 772, 776 (Ct. App. 1987); Bilney v. Evening Star Newspaper Co., 43 Md. App. 560, 572–73, 406 A.2d 652, 659–60 (Ct. Spec. App. 1979); Montesano v. Donrey Media Group, 99 Nev. 644, 651, 668 P.2d 1081, 1086 (1983), cert. denied, 466 U.S. 959 (1984).

152. *Restatement (Second) of Torts* §652D comment h (1977).

153. 288 S.C. 569, 344 S.E.2d 145, cert. denied, 479 U.S. 1012 (1986).

154. Thus in *Meetze* the court had offered "another reason why the facts do not show a wrongful invasion of the right of privacy. It would be going pretty far to say that the article complained of was reasonably calculated to embarrass or humiliate the plaintiffs or cause mental distress. Although Mrs. Meetze was only eleven years old when she married, the marriage was not void." 230 S.C. at 338, 95 S.E.2d at 610. Although this reason appears to pertain to whether the story at issue is "highly offensive," a case like *Hawkins* suggests that a lack of such offensiveness is equally pertinent to the judgment that the public's curiosity in Mrs. Meetze's delivery is not unjustified.

155. 327 Mass. 275, 278, 98 N.E.2d 286, 287 (1951).

156. A good example of the expression of these premises may be found in the remarks of the Dutch journalist Joop Swart at an exhibition of the winners of the World Press Photo Competition: "Some of the pictures you see here might shock you deeply. And some of you might be inclined to denounce them as sensational, distasteful, intruding into the privacy of the individual. But let me remind you that the photographers who made those pictures chose reality over escapism . . . Let us be grateful to them, because they expanded our world." John Morris, "In Press Photos, the World at Its Worst," *International Herald Tribune*, May 12, 1989, at 9, col. 3.

157. *Restatement (Second) of Torts* §652D comment g (1977).

158. See, e.g., Cape Publications, Inc. v. Bridges, 423 So. 2d 426, 427–28 (Fla. Dist. Ct. App. 1982); Waters v. Fleetwood, 212 Ga. 161, 91 S.E.2d 344 (1956); Beresky v. Teschner, 64 Ill. App. 3d 848, 381 N.E.2d 979 (App. Ct. 1978); Bremmer v. Journal-Tribune Publishing Co., 247 Iowa 817, 827–28, 76 N.W.2d 762, 768 (1956); Costlow v. Cusimano, 34 A.D.2d 196, 311 N.Y.S.2d 92 (App. Div. 1970).

159. *Restatement (Second) of Torts* §652D comment g (1977).

160. Id. at comment h.

161. See Erving Goffman, *Asylums* 23–32 (1961).

162. Compare Diane L. Zimmerman, "Requiem for a Heavyweight: A Farewell to Warren and Brandeis's Privacy Tort," 68 *Cornell Law Review* 291, 350–51 (1983), with Linda N. Woito and Patrick McNulty, "The Privacy Disclosure Tort and the First Amendment: Should the Community Decide Newsworthiness?," 64 *Iowa Law Review* 185 (1979).

163. Hall v. Post, 323 N.C. 259, 269–70, 372 S.E.2d 711, 717 (1988); Anderson v. Fisher Broadcasting Co., 300 Or. 452, 469, 712 P.2d 803, 814 (1986).

164. Virgil v. Time, Inc., 527 F.2d 1122, 1129 (9th Cir. 1975); cert. denied, 425 U.S. 998 (1976) (quoting *Restatement (Second) of Torts* §652D comment f [Tent. Draft. No. 21, 1975]).

165. Cordell v. Detective Publications, Inc., 307 F. Supp. 1212, 1220 (E.D. Tenn. 1968), aff'd, 419 F.2d 989 (6th Cir. 1969).

166. Gouldner, *Dialectic*, at 95.

167. Garner v. Triangle Publications, Inc., 97 F. Supp. 546, 550 (S.D.N.Y. 1951); see Hazlitt v. Fawcett Publications, Inc., 116 F. Supp. 538, 545 (D. Conn. 1953); Diaz v. Oakland Tribune, Inc., 139 Cal. App. 3d 118, 134–35, 188 Cal. Rptr. 762, 773 (Ct. App. 1983); Aquino v. Bulletin Co., 190 Pa. Super. 528, 536–41, 154 A.2d 422, 427–30 (Super. Ct. 1959). On the distinction between newspapers getting "the facts" and getting "the story," see Michael Schudson, *Discovering the News: A Social History of American Newspapers* 88–120 (1978).

168. Jenkins v. Dell Publishing Co., 251 F.2d 447, 451 (3d Cir.) (footnote omitted), cert. denied, 357 U.S. 921 (1958); cf. Winters v. New York, 333 U.S. 507, 510 (1948).

169. Max Weber, "Science as a Vocation," in *From Max Weber: Essays in Sociology* 129, 155 (H. H. Gerth and C. Wright Mills, eds. and trans., 1958).

170. Afro-American Publishing Co. v. Jaffe, 366 F.2d 649, 654 (D.C. Cir. 1966).

171. See Goffman, *Asylums*, at 14–35.

172. James Rule, Douglas McAdam, Linda Stearns, and David Uglow, *The Politics of Privacy* 70–71 (1980).

173. Id. at 71, 22. In an earlier work, Rule characterized the value of privacy as the presocial good of "autonomy." James Rule, *Private Lives and Public Surveillance* 349–58 (1973). He expressed his hope that "values of individual auton-

omy and privacy can prevail in these contexts over those of collective rationality." Id. at 354.

174. Stanley Diamond, "The Rule of Law Versus the Order of Custom," 38 *Social Research* 42, 44–47 (1971).

175. New Jersey v. T.L.O., 469 U.S. 325, 337 (1985); see also United States v. Montoya de Hernandez, 473 U.S. 531, 537 (1985); Skinner v. Railway Labor Executives' Ass'n, 489 U.S. 602, 618–20 (1989).

176. Richard Rorty, "Postmodernist Bourgeois Liberalism," 80 *Journal of Philosophy* 583, 586–87 (1983).

3. Cultural Heterogeneity and Law

1. Louis Henkin, "Morals and the Constitution: The Sin of Obscenity," 63 *Columbia Law Review* 391, 391 (1963).

2. Alexander Bickel, *The Morality of Consent* 74 (1975); see Paris Adult Theatre I v. Slaton, 413 U.S. 49, 58–61 (1973).

3. Henkin, "Morals and the Constitution," at 395.

4. See Catherine MacKinnon, *Feminism Unmodified: Discourses on Life and Law* (1987); Andrea Dworkin, *Pornography: Men Possessing Women* (1981).

5. Andrea Dworkin, "Against the Male Flood: Censorship, Pornography, and Equality," 8 *Harvard Women's Law Journal* 1, 15–17 (1985).

6. MacKinnon, *Feminism Unmodified*, at 148, 156.

7. Id. at 166; see also id. at 161: "Pornography *constructs* women and sex, defines what 'woman' means and what sexuality is, in terms of each other." The emphasis on the social construction of gender helps to explain why MacKinnon and Dworkin include in their definition of pornography " 'the use of men, children or transsexuals in the place of women.' " Id. at 146 n.1. Because MacKinnon and Dworkin are chiefly concerned with the nature of the female social role, they are relatively indifferent as to the question of whether that role is filled by men or transsexuals. Of course to the extent that the female role comes characteristically to be filled by persons other than women, the claim that the role is in fact that of the female gender becomes problematic.

8. Id. at 178.

9. See, e.g., American Booksellers Ass'n v. Hudnut, 771 F.2d 323, 328–32 (7th Cir. 1985), summarily aff'd, 475 U.S. 1001 (1986); James R. Branit, "Reconciling Free Speech and Equality: What Justifies Censorship?," 9 *Harvard Journal of Law and Public Policy* 429 (1986); Paul Brest and Ann Vandenberg, "Politics, Feminism, and the Constitution: The Anti-Pornography Movement in Minneapolis," 39 *Stanford Law Review* 607, 659–60 (1987); David P. Bryden, "Between Two Constitutions: Feminism and Pornography," 2 *Constitutional Commentary* 147, 152–53 (1985); Erwin Chemerinsky and Paul J. McGeady, "Outlawing Pornography: What We Gain, What We Lose," 12 *Human Rights Quarterly* 24

(no. 3, Spring 1985); Thomas I. Emerson, "Pornography and the First Amendment: A Reply to Professor MacKinnon," 3 *Yale Law and Policy Review* 130 (1984); Caryn Jacobs, "Patterns of Violence: A Feminist Perspective on the Regulation of Pornography," 7 *Harvard Women's Law Journal* 5, 41–45 (1984); Barry W. Lynn, " 'Civil Rights' Ordinances and the Attorney General's Commission: New Developments in Pornography Regulation," 21 *Harvard Civil Rights–Civil Liberties Law Review* 27 (1986); Geoffrey R. Stone, "Anti-Pornography Legislation as Viewpoint-Discrimination," 9 *Harvard Journal of Law and Public Policy* 461 (1986); Cass R. Sunstein, "Pornography and the First Amendment," 1986 *Duke Law Journal* 589, 591–92.

For a summary of recent developments in England, which have followed a similar course, see A. W. B. Simpson, *Pornography and Politics: A Look Back to the Williams Committee* 72 (1983): "At a theoretical level however it is clear that whereas the Williams Committee saw pornography primarily as a public nuisance problem, the harm flowing from it consisting in the offence it caused, many feminists do not accept this. Pornography is seen as a political problem in that it is a mechanism for securing a certain distribution of power in society, one in which women lose out and is in itself an act of violence; the slogan 'pornography is violence against women' rejects the notion that the harm produced by pornography is to be sought in the consequences of pornography, but not in the material itself."

10. For two recent discussions of these issues, see Donald A. Downs, *Nazis in Skokie: Freedom, Community, and the First Amendment* (1985); Richard Delgado, "Words That Wound: A Tort Action for Racial Insults, Epithets, and Name-Calling," 17 *Harvard Civil Rights–Civil Liberties Law Review* 133 (1982).

11. These three options do not, of course, exhaust the field. For example, a legal order may found its laws upon neither group values nor individual claims, but upon instrumental reason.

12. For an example of the interplay between expressive and hegemonic functions of assimilationist law in the area of defamation, see Robert Post, "The Social Foundations of Defamation Law: Reputation and the Constitution," 74 *California Law Review* 691, 702–3 (1986).

13. 98 U.S. 145, 164 (1878); see H. L. A. Hart, *Law, Liberty, and Morality* 39–43 (1963).

14. 310 U.S. 586, 597 (1940). Three years later the requirement was struck down in West Virginia State Bd. of Educ. v. Barnette, 319 U.S. 624 (1943).

15. M. R. Karenga, "The Problematic Aspects of Pluralism: Ideological and Political Dimensions," in *Pluralism, Racism, and Public Policy: The Search for Equality* 226 (Edwin G. Clausen and Jack Bermingham, eds., 1981); see Joseph R. Gusfield, "On Legislating Morals: The Symbolic Process of Designating Deviance," 56 *California Law Review* 54, 59 (1968). Assimilationist law can be particularly cruel when applied to immutable traits like race. In the South before

World War II, for example, defamation law enforced the values of the dominant white culture, making it defamatory to say that a Caucasian was black but not permitting blacks to sue for defamation upon being labeled white. This result followed from the fact that defamation law understood itself to be reflecting "the intrinsic difference between whites and blacks," a difference inhering in the fact that, "from a social standpoint, the negro race is in mind and morals inferior to the Caucasian." Wolfe v. Georgia Ry. & Elec. Co., 2 Ga. App. 499, 505–6, 58 S.E. 899, 901–2 (1907). In such extreme circumstances, where the dominant culture imposes an immutable hierarchy of caste, it is almost a misnomer to call the law assimilationist, since subordinate groups are given no option to join the dominant culture. They are instead required to submit to that culture's impositions.

16. See, e.g., Lawrence Friedman, *Total Justice* 111–20 (1987).

17. Milton M. Gordon, *Assimilation in American Life: The Role of Race, Religion, and National Origins* 89, 85 (1964); see William M. Newman, *American Pluralism: A Study of Minority Groups and Social Theory* 53–62 (1973).

18. See Gordon, *Assimilation*, at 98–101. For a brief overview of the "Americanization" movement, see Philip Gleason, "American Identity and Americanization," in William Petersen, Michael Novak, and Philip Gleason, *Concepts of Ethnicity* 79–96 (1982).

19. Cass R. Sunstein, "Interest Groups in American Public Law," 38 *Stanford Law Review* 29, 32 (1985); see, e.g., William N. Eskridge and Philip P. Frickey, *Cases and Materials on Legislation* 46–65 (1988); Daniel A. Farber and Philip P. Frickey, "The Jurisprudence of Public Choice," 65 *Texas Law Review* 873, 875 (1987).

20. See Richard Bernstein, "The Varieties of Pluralism," 5 *Current Issues in Education* 1, 14–16 (1985). For the history of the term "pluralism," see Rupert Breitling, "The Concept of Pluralism," in *Three Faces of Pluralism: Political, Ethnic, and Religious* 1–19 (Stanislaw Erlich and Graham Wootton, eds., 1980). For examples of the variant usages of the term, see Charles E. Larmore, *Patterns of Moral Complexity* 23 (1987); David Nicholls, *Three Varieties of Pluralism* (1974); *Religious Pluralism* (Leroy S. Rouner, ed., 1984); Crawford Young, *The Politics of Cultural Pluralism* (1976); Marie R. Haug, "Social and Cultural Pluralism as a Concept in Social System Analysis," 73 *American Journal of Sociology* 294 (1967).

21. William James, *Essays in Radical Empiricism and A Pluralistic Universe* (1971). James noted that "the pluralistic world is thus more like a federal republic than like an empire or a kingdom." Id. at 274. Harold Laski would later cite this observation as a part of his attempt to define a "pluralist," as distinct from a "monist," theory of state sovereignty. Harold J. Laski, *Studies in the Problem of Sovereignty* 10, 23–25 (1917).

22. Horace M. Kallen, *Culture and Democracy* 43, 61 (1924). For further exposition of Kallen's thought, see Horace M. Kallen, *Cultural Pluralism and the*

American Idea (1956); Sidney Ratner, "Horace M. Kallen and Cultural Pluralism," in *The Legacy of Horace M. Kallen* (Milton R. Konvitz, ed., 1987). Kallen's work has proved deeply influential for American educators. See, e.g., Donna M. Gollnick and Philip C. Chinn, *Multicultural Education in a Pluralistic Society* 22–30 (1986); Alfredo Castaneda, "Persisting Ideological Issues of Assimilation in America: Implications for Assessment Practices in Psychology and Education," in *Cultural Pluralism* 60–62 (Edgar G. Epps, ed., 1974); Nathan Glazer, "Cultural Pluralism: The Social Aspect," in *Pluralism in a Democratic Society* 3–21 (Melvin M. Tumin and Walter Plotch, eds., 1977); Andrew T. Kopan, "Melting Pot: Myth or Reality?," in *Cultural Pluralism* 49–54 (Edgar G. Epps, ed., 1974).

Sociologists and educators have introduced numerous variations into the concept of cultural pluralism. Michael Novak, for example, lists five different possible meanings for the concept. See his "Cultural Pluralism for Individuals: A Social Vision," in *Pluralism in a Democratic Society*, at 34–36; see also Newman, *American Pluralism*, at 63–82. Cultural pluralism is most often contrasted with the notion of "amalgamation," id. at 63, or, as it is commonly called, the idea of the "melting pot." See Gordon, *Assimilation*, at 115–31. The concept of amalgamation is that diverse cultural groups fuse and combine to form a new and distinctive cultural entity. From the point of view of the legal order, however, a given law would either reflect the perspective of this new entity, in which case the law would be assimilationist, or view the new entity as simply one of a number of competing cultural groups, in which case the law would be pluralist.

23. Walt Whitman, *Leaves of Grass and Selected Prose* 37, 518 (1950). Whitman also noted, however, that "the fear of conflicting and irreconcilable interiors, and the lack of a common skeleton, knitting all close, continually haunts me." Id. at 466. His fear, one might say, is realized in the conception of value-free pluralism advanced by contemporary political scientists and legal academics.

24. Harold Laski, for example, viewed American federalism as exemplifying pluralist values by effecting a "wide distribution of . . . sovereign powers" so as to protect a "variety of . . . group life." See Laski, *Problem of Sovereignty*, at 275; see Andrzej Rapaczynski, "From Sovereignty to Process: The Jurisprudence of Federalism after Garcia," 1985 *Supreme Court Review* 341, 404–5. Kallen was aware of the analogy between his views and the principles of federalism, noting that "in effect the United States are in the process of becoming a federal state not merely as a union of geographical and administrative unities, but also as a cooperation of cultural diversities, as a federation or commonwealth of national culture." Kallen, *Cultural Pluralism*, at 116.

25. Pluralism has been defined as aspiring toward "a plurality of cultures with their members seeking to live together in amity and mutual understanding and mutual cooperation, but maintaining separate cultures." Robert J. Havighurst, *Anthropology and Cultural Pluralism: Three Case Studies, Australia, New Zealand, and USA* 3 (1974).

26. 343 U.S. 250, 251 (quoting Ill. Rev. Stat. ch. 38, para. 471 [1949] [repealed 1961]), 259, 262 (1952).

27. John Higham, "Integration vs. Pluralism: Another American Dilemma," *Center Magazine*, July/Aug. 1974, at 68; see also Ronald R. Garet, "Communality and Existence: The Rights of Groups," 56 *Southern California Law Review* 1001, 1065–75 (1983).

28. James A. Banks, "Cultural Pluralism: Implications for Curriculum Reform," in *Pluralism in a Democratic Society* (Tumin and Plotch, eds.), at 228.

29. 343 U.S. at 270 (Black, J., dissenting).

30. Gordon, *Assimilation*, at 150; see also Isaac B. Berkson, *Theories of Americanization: A Critical Study, with Special Reference to the Jewish Group* 81–93 (1920).

31. Robert N. Bellah, Richard Madsen, William M. Sullivan, Ann Swidler, and Steven M. Tipton, *Habits of the Heart: Individualism and Commitment in American Life* 151 (1985); see also David Riesman, *The Lonely Crowd* 240–60 (1961).

32. 406 U.S. 205, 207 (1972). The Amish refused to permit their children to attend school after they had completed eighth grade.

33. Id. at 218.

34. Id. at 243–45 (Douglas, J., dissenting).

35. Of course there are many situations where the values of individualism and pluralism do not conflict. This was the case, for example, in the years immediately following Brown v. Board of Education, 347 U.S. 483 (1954), when the goal of desegregated education was consistent with both individualist and pluralist values. In later years, however, the question of affirmative action has separated those who view the anti-discrimination principle as grounded in the protection of individuals from those who view it as founded in the protection of groups. Compare, e.g., Wygant v. Jackson Bd. of Educ., 476 U.S. 267, 281 n.8 (1986) (Opinion of Powell, J.) with id. at 309–10 (Marshall, J., dissenting).

36. Minersville School Dist. v. Gobitis, 310 U.S. 586 (1940).

37. 319 U.S. 624, 641–42 (1943).

38. Although these three alternatives are by no means exhaustive, they do reflect a certain internal logic with respect to law that flows from the cultural values of its surrounding society. Pluralist law rests on the twin premises that diversity is valuable and that the value of diversity inheres in group, rather than individual, perspectives. Eliminate the first premise and law will become assimilationist; eliminate the second and law will become individualist.

39. See Gary Spencer, "Criminal Libel—A Skeleton in the Cupboard (1)," 1977 *Criminal Law Review* 383. English law sometimes recognizes a technical distinction between the crime of blasphemy, which is oral, and the crime of blasphemous libel, which is written. Nothing turns on this distinction, however, and I shall ignore it here.

40. 4 William Blackstone, *Commentaries on the Laws of England* 59 (1769). Benjamin Norton Defoe defined blasphemy as "vile or opprobrious Language,

tending to the Dishonour of God." Benjamin N. Defoe, *A Compleat English Dictionary* n.p. (1735). Samuel Johnson defined it as "an offering of some indignity unto God himself." Samuel Johnson, *A Dictionary of the English Language* n.p. (1756).

41. Leonard W. Levy, *Treason Against God: A History of the Offense of Blasphemy* 306–7 (1981). For English observers, "the line between blasphemy and obscenity was at times thin." Note, "Blasphemy," 70 *Columbia Law Review* 694, 701 (1970); see also Frederick F. Schauer, *The Law of Obscenity* 1–18 (1976); Comment, "Blasphemy and Obscenity," 5 *British Journal of Law and Society* 89 (1978).

42. See The Law Commission, *Working Paper No. 79: Offences Against Religion and Public Worship* 5–6 (1981), hereinafter *Working Paper No. 79*; Levy, *Treason Against God*, at 303–6; Gerald Dacre Nokes, *A History of the Crime of Blasphemy* 67 (1928).

43. 86 Eng. Rep. 189, 1 Vent. 293 (K.B. 1676). For discussions of *Taylor's Case*, see Hypatia B. Bonner, *Penalties upon Opinion* 28–32 (1934); Levy, *Treason Against God*, at 312–14; Nokes, *History*, at 46–61; Courtney Kenny, "The Evolution of the Law of Blasphemy," 1 *Cambridge Law Journal* 127, 129–31 (1922); I. D. Leigh, "Not to Judge But to Save: The Development of the Law of Blasphemy," 8 *Cambrian Law Review* 56, 58–63 (1977).

44. 2 James F. Stephen, *A History of the Criminal Law of England* 475 (1883).

45. Id. at 471–73; Rex v. Williams, 26 Howell's St. Tr. 653 (K.B. 1797); Rex v. Carlile (Richard) 1 St. Tr. N.S. 1387 (1819); cf. Rex v. Carlile (Mary), 1 St. Tr. N.S. 1033 (1921).

46. Regina v. Moxon, 4 St. Tr. N.S. 693 (1841).

47. Rex v. Woolston, 94 Eng. Rep. 112, 1 Barn. K.B. 162 (1729); see Bonner, *Penalties upon Opinion*, at 34–35.

48. Commissioners on Criminal Law, *Sixth Report* 83 (1841); see also Nokes, *History*, at 70.

49. 94 Eng. Rep. at 113, 1 Barn. K.B. at 163. As recently as 1867 the House of Lords held unenforceable a contract to rent a hall for giving lectures on "The Bible shewn to be no more Inspired than any other Book," on the grounds that the contract was for the criminal purpose of propagating blasphemy. Cowan v. Milbourn, 2 L.R.-Ex. 230, 235 (1867), overruled, Bowman v. Secular Society, Ltd. [1917] App. Cas. 406.

50. Regina v. Gathercole, 116 Eng. Rep. 1140, 1157, 2 Lewin 237, 254 (1838).

51. See *Working Paper No. 79*, at 82. This parochialism remains true even of contemporary English blasphemy law.

52. 4 St. Tr. N.S. 563, 590–91 (1841).

53. Regina v. Ramsay and Foote, 15 Cox C.C. 231, 236 (1883).

54. Regina v. Bradlaugh, 15 Cox C.C. 217, 230 (1883).

55. Id. at 231.

56. *Ramsay and Foote*, 15 Cox C.C. at 238.

57. See *Working Paper No. 79*, at 14.

58. Peter Jones, for example, has perceptively observed that "Coleridge intended his ruling in 1883 to imply" the distinction "between matter and manner." Peter Jones, "Blasphemy, Offensiveness, and Law," 10 *British Journal of Political Science* 129, 141–42 (1980). Jones explains (142–143):

> The intention behind the distinction is plain. Granted that it is possible to distinguish manner from matter, a law restricting only forms of expression need not prevent the assertion of any substantive point of view. The usual conflict between freedom of opinion and prevention of offense is therefore largely avoided . . .
> The failing of the matter-manner distinction is that it supposes that statements are capable of more or less offensive formulations which are nevertheless identical in meaning. The manner of an assertion is treated as though it were so much verbal wrapping paper whose features had no bearing upon the content of the parcel. In certain cases this assumption may not be unjustified . . . More often, however, manner and matter are so integrally related that it is impossible to distinguish the offensive manner from the offensive matter of a statement.

59. Writing in 1883, James Fitzjames Stephen could observe: "The present generation is the first in which an avowed open denial of the fundamental doctrines of the Christian religion has been made by any considerable number of serious and respectable people. For many centuries the maintenance, or even the expression of opinions, suspected or supposed to involve a denial of the truth of religion in general, was regarded in the same kind of light as high treason in the temporal order of things . . . A man who did not believe in Christ or God put himself out of the pale of human society; and a man who on important subjects thought differently from the Church, was on the high road to disbelief in Christ and in God, for belief in each depended ultimately upon the belief in the testimony of the Church. In our own days the physical sanctions of the law are so much more frequently appealed to, and are so much more effective than its moral sanctions, that it is only by an effort that we can understand the horror with which our ancestors regarded a man who held opinions which, in their view, were inconsistent with a real hearty assent to the principles on which they believed all human society, whether spiritual or temporal, to repose." Stephen, *History*, at 438.

60. This would not be true of instrumental reason, the success or failure of which is determined, in a more or less universal fashion, by its ability to predict and control nature. For a succinct discussion of the distinction between instrumental reason and "communicative action," see Jürgen Habermas, *Toward a Rational Society* 91–94 (Jeremy J. Shapiro, trans., 1970). For a fuller discussion, see Jürgen Habermas, *Knowledge and Human Interests* (Jeremy J. Shapiro, trans., 1971).

61. The law was never passed. See *Working Paper No. 79*, at 29.

62. 234 *Parl. Deb., H.C.* (5th Ser.) 535 (1930) (remarks of Mr. Kingsley Griffith); see also id. at 499: "We have writers to-day who can commit the offence of blasphemy with impunity, if the offence of blasphemy is an attack on the Christian religion. There are men like Sir Arthur Keith, Mr. H. G. Wells, Mr. Bertrand Russell, Mr. Aldous Huxley and others who are able to attack the Christian religion without any danger whatever of their being prosecuted, while poor men, expressing the same point of view more bluntly and crudely, expose themselves to fine and imprisonment. That is a thoroughly unsatisfactory state of the law. After all, if one concedes the right to attack religion . . . one has to concede to the people who care to do this thing the right to choose their style of doing it. Different styles are needed for different circumstances and different audiences. I do not suppose the kind of style that would go down in a select circle in the West End would be effective amongst the democracy of the East End." Remarks of Mr. Thurtle; see also id. at 558, remarks of Mr. Lansbury.

63. Id. at 565, remarks of Mr. Scrymgeour. The crime continued to protect the sensibilities of Christians but not of Jews or Moslems or other religious minorities. Outrageous assaults on Judaism or Islam were not blasphemous.

64. See *Working Paper No. 79*, at 17.

65. Id. at 17–18; see Jones, "Blasphemy, Offensiveness, and Law," at 129.

66. Regina v. Lemon, 1979 App. Cas. 617, 632 (per Lord Diplock), 660 (per Lord Scarman).

67. For a biographical study of Mary Whitehouse, who had previously been involved in anti-obscenity campaigns, see Michael Tracey and David Morrison, *Whitehouse* (1979). Whitehouse stated: "When the [Kirkup] poem arrived on my desk, and I read it, I had one overwhelming feeling that this was the recrucifixion of Christ with 20th century weapons—with words, with obscenities, and if I sat there and did nothing I would be a traitor. It was just as simple as that." Ingrid Anderson and Pamela Rose, "Who the Hell Does She Think She Is?," 3 *Poly Law Review* 13, 15 (1980) (interview with Mary Whitehouse).

68. 1979 App. Cas. at 660. An account of the trial may be found in Nicolas Walter, *Blasphemy in Britain: The Practice and Punishment of Blasphemy, and the Trial of Gay News* (1977). The trial judge concluded his charge to the jury by telling the jurors to answer the following questions about the poem: "Did it shock you when you first read it? What was your immediate reaction? Would you be proud or ashamed to have written it? Would you read it aloud to a Christian audience, and if you did would you blush? What reaction would you expect from an audience of fellow Christians?" Id. at 16. After the verdict the trial judge is reported to have "expressed his hope that, as a result of the case, the 'pendulum of public opinion would swing back towards a more healthy climate.' " Corinna Adam, "Protecting Our Lord," *New Statesman*, July 15, 1977, at 74, col. 1.

69. See, e.g., Richard Buxton, "The Case of Blasphemous Libel," 1978 *Criminal Law Review* 673.

70. Along the way the Court of Appeal upheld the fines but quashed the sentence on the grounds that "we do not consider this an appropriate case for a prison sentence." 1979 Q.B. 10, 30.

71. For later assessments of this issue, see J. R. Spencer, "Blasphemy: The Law Commission's Working Paper," 1981 *Criminal Law Review* 810; "Blasting Blasphemy," 129 *Solicitor's Journal* 489 (1985).

72. 1979 App. Cas. at 617. The European Commission on Human Rights later found no inconsistency between the conviction and the European Convention on Human Rights and Fundamental Freedoms. See Gay News Ltd. v. United Kingdom, 5 Eur. Comm'n H.R. 123 (1982).

73. *Lemon*, 1979 App. Cas. at 660, 658. Scarman rejected the notion that blasphemy was criminal because of its tendency to cause a breach of the peace. It is "a jejune exercise," he said, "to speculate whether an outraged Christian would feel provoked by the words and illustration in this case to commit a breach of peace. I hope, and happen to believe, that most, true to their Christian principles, would not allow themselves to be so provoked." Id. at 662.

74. Id. at 665, 662 (citations omitted). The weakness of the style/substance distinction is starkly displayed in *Lemon*, for, as Jones rightly points out in "Blasphemy, Offensiveness, and Law" (143): "When the expression of a view occurs in a literary work—as in the Gay News case—the mode of expression is essential to the enterprise. To say that Kirkup should have produced an academic speculation on Christ's attitude toward homosexuality after the manner of Bishop Montefiore would be to say that he should not have written a poem."

75. 1979 App. Cas. at 664–65.

76. Id. at 658.

77. Id. Scarman might have had in mind the Prevention of Incitement to Hatred Act which had been enacted in 1970 for Northern Ireland, and which states:

> A person shall be guilty of an offence under the Act if, with intent to stir up hatred against, or arouse fear of, any section of the public in Northern Ireland—
> (a) he publishes or distributes written or other matter which is threatening, abusive or insulting; or
> (b) he uses in any public place or at any public meeting words which are threatening, abusive or insulting;
> being matter or words likely to stir up hatred against, or arouse fear of, any section of the public in Northern Ireland on grounds of religious belief, colour, race or ethnic or national origins. (N. Ir. Pub. Gen. Acts ch. 24 §1 [1970])

The background of the statute is discussed in Patricia M. Leopold, "Incitement to Hatred—The History of a Controversial Criminal Offence," 1977 *Public Law* 389, 399–402. For a brief international survey of blasphemy statutes, some of which have the form suggested by Scarman, see *Working Paper No. 79*, at 40–52.

78. As Scarman well knew, blasphemy law, reinterpreted in this fashion, would

be consistent with the pluralist values of the recently enacted provisions of The Race Relations Act of 1976, 2 Pub. Gen. Acts 1723, ch. 74, §70, which Scarman was himself instrumental in proposing, and which essentially imposed criminal penalties for incitements to racial hatred. See I. A. MacDonald, *Race Relations—The New Law* 137 (1977). Scarman in fact explicitly drew the analogy between his vision of blasphemy and the Race Relations Act. *Lemon*, 1979 App. Cas. at 665.

79. That is why the anthropologist Paul Bohannan defines colonial law as law that stems from a "unicentric power system" in societies with two or more cultures Paul Bohannan, "The Differing Realms of Law," 67 *American Anthropologist* (special issue) 33, 38–39 (1965). Bohannan's definition implies that pluralist law will always be hegemonic in character. But this implication may or may not be true, depending upon the extent to which a heterogeneous society experiences what John Rawls has called "overlapping consensus." The presence of such a consensus may permit assimilationist ground rules for pluralist interaction to in fact serve an expressive rather than hegemonic function. See John Rawls, "The Idea of an Overlapping Consensus," 7 *Oxford Journal of Legal Studies* 1 (1987).

80. For an informed and sensitive discussion of this question, see Note, "Blasphemy."

81. Harry Kalven, *A Worthy Tradition: Freedom of Speech in America* 7 (1988) (emphasis in original).

82. During the period prior to the 1920s, of course, the First Amendment had no application to the states. By convention the first case taken to indicate a contrary conclusion is Gitlow v. New York, 268 U.S. 652 (1925).

83. See Annotation, "Offense of Blasphemy," 14 A.L.R. 880, 883–85 (1921). In fact the first reported case to strike down a blasphemy statute was in 1970. See State v. West, 9 Md. App. 270, 263 A.2d 602 (1970). Theodore Schroeder, however, has reprinted an unpublished 1895 opinion issued by a lower court in Kentucky sustaining on state constitutional grounds a demurrer to an indictment for blasphemy. Theodore Schroeder, *Constitutional Free Speech Defined and Defended in an Unfinished Argument in a Case of Blasphemy* 60–64 (1919).

84. 8 Johns. 290, 291 (N.Y. 1811) (emphasis in original).

85. Id. at 296; N.Y. Const. art. 38 (1777).

86. N.Y. Const. art. 38 (1777).

87. 8 Johns. at 295.

88. Id. at 294, 296.

89. See, e.g., State v. Chandler, 2 Del. (2 Harr.) 553 (1837); State v. Mockus, 120 Me. 84, 113 A. 39 (1921); Updegraph v. Commonwealth, 11 Serg. & Rawle 394 (Pa. 1824). Apart from Ruggles, the most famous American blasphemy decision was Commonwealth v. Kneeland, 37 Mass. (20 Pick.) 206 (1838), in which Chief Justice Lemuel Shaw upheld a conviction for blasphemy against state con-

stitutional challenge. The Kneeland case is discussed in *Blasphemy in Massachu-setts: Freedom of Conscience and the Abner Kneeland Case* (Leonard W. Levy, ed., 1973); Henry Steele Commager, "The Blasphemy of Abner Kneeland," 8 *New England Quarterly* 29 (March 1935). The same blasphemy statute that was at issue in Kneeland was also used in 1928 to prosecute Horace Kallen for blasphemy. "Boston Judge Recalls Warrant for Arrest on Statements in Sacco Arrest," *New York Times*, Aug. 29, 1928, at 8, col. 1. According to that article, Kallen, in addressing a memorial meeting for Sacco and Vanzetti, "said that 'if Sacco and Vanzetti were anarchists, so was Jesus Christ, Socrates,' and several others." Two years previously, the same Massachusetts blasphemy statute had been the basis for a notorious prosecution of Anthony Bimba. See Zechariah Chafee, "The Bimba Case," in *The Inquiring Mind* 108 (1974); William Wolkovich, *Bay State "Blue" Laws and Bimba* (1973); Note, "Blasphemy," at 708–9.

90. State v. West, 9 Md. App. 270, 276, 263 A.2d 602, 605 (1970).

91. The Delaware and Pennsylvania cases are discussed in Levy, *Treason Against God*, at 337–38.

92. Indeed in 1897 the United States Supreme Court had in dicta interpreted the First Amendment in the same manner as state courts had interpreted equiv-alent state constitutional provisions, stating flatly that the Amendment did not extend constitutional protection to "the publication of . . . blasphemous or inde-cent articles, or other publications injurious to public morals or private reputa-tion." Robertson v. Baldwin, 165 U.S. 275, 281 (1897).

The Court's interpretation was at the time consistent with the opinion of authoritative commentators. Thomas Cooley, for example, had written in 1868 that "the constitutional liberty of speech and of the press . . . implies a right to freely utter and publish whatever the citizen may please, and to be protected against any responsibility for the publication, except so far as such publications, from their blasphemy, obscenity, or scandalous character, may be a public of-fence." Thomas Cooley, *A Treatise on the Constitutional Limitations Which Rest upon the Legislative Power of the States of the American Union* 422 (1868). And Joseph Story, in interpreting the religion clauses of the First Amendment, had flatly stated that "it is impossible for those who believe in truth of Christianity, as a divine revelation, to doubt, that it is the especial duty of government to foster and encourage it among all the citizens and subjects. This is a point wholly distinct from that of the right of private judgment in matters of religion, and of the freedom of public worship according to the dictates of one's conscience." 2 Joseph Story, *Commentaries on the Constitution of the United States* 661 (3d ed. 1858). Story stressed that "in a republic, there would seem to be a peculiar propriety in viewing the Christian religion as the great basis, on which it must rest for its support and permanence." Id. at 662. He concluded that "the real object of the [first] amendment was, not to countenance, much less to advance Mahometanism, or Judaism, or infidelity, by prostrating Christianity; but to exclude all rivalry among Christian sects, and to prevent any national ecclesiastical establishment." Id. at 664.

93. 310 U.S. 296, 309, 300 (1940).

94. 8 Johns. 290, 296 (N.Y. 1811).

95. 310 U.S. at 307, 310.

96. *Ruggles*, 8 Johns. at 294.

97. In 1940, the year in which the *Cantwell* opinion was issued, the sect of Jehovah's Witnesses was only sixty-eight years old, having been founded in 1872 by Charles Taze Russell in Allegheny, Pennsylvania. Edwin S. Gaustad, *Historical Atlas of Religion in America* 115–16 (1962). In the 1930s, Jehovah's Witnesses began to proselytize actively for new membership, and the sect experienced "sudden progress after 1940, all but eclipsing the development of the first sixty years." Id. at 118.

98. Perry Miller, *The Life of the Mind in America* 40–43 (1965).

99. Bellah et al., *Habits of the Heart*, at 225.

100. For a discussion of the tension between pluralism and individualism, see Nathan Glazer, "The Constitution and American Diversity," *Public Interest*, Winter 1987, at 10–21; Gordon, "Models of Pluralism: The New American Dilemma," *Annals*, March 1981, at 179–88.

101. 2 Charles Taylor, "Atomism," in *Philosophy and The Human Sciences: Philosophical Papers* 205–9 (1985).

102. Cantwell v. Connecticut, 310 U.S. 296, 308–9 (1940).

103. Id. at 309–10.

104. From a strictly logical point of view, "profane, indecent, or abusive remarks" communicate opinion and information, just as do other kinds of statements.

105. This is also true of Scarman's pluralist reformulation of blasphemy law, which would enable individuals in all religious groups to use the law to protect them from insults to their religious beliefs.

106. 310 U.S. at 309.

107. The Supreme Court has demonstrated an equally determined universalism in its treatment of defamation law; it has conceptualized state libel laws as redressing injuries impairing "the essential dignity and worth of every human being," Gertz v. Robert Welch, Inc., 418 U.S. 323, 341 (1974) (quoting Rosenblatt v. Baer, 393 U.S. 75, 92 [1966] [Stewart, J., concurring]), rather than injuries that would harm merely the honor of particular social groups or roles. See Post, "Foundations of Defamation Law," at 699–719, 722–26.

108. Paris Adult Theatre I v. Slaton, 413 U.S. 49, 58 (1973); Miller v. California, 413 U.S. 15, 33 (1973). As such, of course, obscenity law has always been a thumb in the eye of the First Amendment individualist tradition.

109. *Miller*, 413 U.S. at 30.

110. See MacKinnon, *Feminism Unmodified*, at 187–89; Branit, "Reconciling

Free Speech and Equality," at 456–57; Jacobs, "Patterns of Violence," at 10–11; Daniel Linz, Stephen Penrod, and Edward Donnerstein, "The Attorney General's Commission on Pornography: The Gaps Between 'Findings' and Facts," 1987 *American Bar Foundation Research Journal* 713, 719–23.

111. 1 Christopher G. Tiedeman, *A Treatise on State and Federal Control of Persons and Property* 201 (1900); see State v. Mockus, 120 Me. 84, 94, 113 A. 39, 43 (1921); Updegraph v. Commonwealth, 11 Serg. and Rawle 394, 408–9 (Pa. 1822).

112. 249 U.S. 211, 216 (1919).

113. Brandenburg v. Ohio, 395 U.S. 444, 447 (1969) (per curiam).

114. See Emerson, "Pornography," at 135.

115. See Stone, "Anti-Pornography Legislation," at 475–76. This conclusion also applies to the argument that because "the nature and extent of the link between act and harm are difficult to establish" and because the harm is "potentially severe," "suggestive evidence" of a causal connection between pornography and sexual violence should be sufficient to justify legal censorship. See Sunstein, "Pornography," at 601. This argument was used by the majority of the Court in Gitlow v. New York, 268 U.S. 652 (1925), to uphold a statute suppressing anarchist speech. The Court noted that the exact causal connection between such speech and the potentially severe harm of revolution was difficult to fix. Id. at 669. It is of course possible to argue that the stringent constitutional standards that now apply to most speech should be modified and diluted for pornographic speech. The question, however, is why pornography is, in some constitutionally relevant sense, "different" from other forms of speech. The pluralist/individualist distinction seeks to offer an analytic framework within which this question can be meaningfully addressed.

116. MacKinnon, *Feminism Unmodified*, at 154; see id. at 175–76, 193–94.

117. Brest and Vandenberg, "Politics, Feminism, and the Constitution," at 659.

118. J. L. Austin, *Philosophical Papers* 233–52 (3d ed. 1979), especially 235.

119. It is in this sense, I think, that MacKinnon's recurring theme of feminine powerlessness should be understood. "Having power means, among other things, that when someone says, 'This is how it is,' it is taken as being that way." MacKinnon, *Feminism Unmodified*, at 164. Hence pornography "*constructs* women and sex," despite the dissent of women; "dissent from it becomes inaudible." Id. at 161, 166.

120. The very concept of social order, for example, can be understood as constituted by speech. This is nicely illustrated by the remarks of Francis Holt, an English writer who presented the following argument in support of an early form of the style/substance distinction in blasphemy:

> [T]he law does not prohibit reasonable controversy even upon fundamental subjects, so long as it is conducted with a tone of moderation, which

shews that argument is the only purpose; the writer abstaining from language and terms which are abusive and passionate, and, therein, indecorous
towards the establishment, and offensive to the consciences of individuals.
What is argumentative may be very properly left to be replied to by
argument; what is passionate, and therein a disturbance of the proper ocon-
omy of the state, cannot be so safely passed over to a defence by similar
weapons.—Such a sufferance would be the endurance of brawls. When the
law is moved against such writers, it is not persecution: it is a defence of the
public tranquillity and decency. (Francis Holt, *The Law of Libel* 70–71
[1816])

For Holt "public tranquillity" literally subsists in the public observance of rules
of "decency"; breaches in decorum are thus equivalent to brawls. "Passionate"
speech is the same as action because Holt understands the social order to inhere
in decorum, and decorum to depend upon the verbal exercise of civility and
dispassionate reason. Even today the Corpus Juris Secundum defines the term
"breach of peace" to include "all violations of the public peace or order, or
decorum." 11 C.J.S. "Breach of the Peace" §1 (1938 and Supp. 1987).

While we may now differ from Holt in our understanding of the particular
ways in which the social order is constituted by speech, we nevertheless continue
to view speech acts as integral to that order. In Chaplinsky v. New Hampshire,
315 U.S. 568 (1942), for example, the Court justified its conclusion that "fighting" words were unprotected by the First Amendment on the grounds that such
words "by their very utterance inflict injury." Id. at 572. Thirty years later, in
Cohen v. California, 403 U.S. 15 (1971), where a defendant was convicted of
disturbing the peace for writing "Fuck the Draft" on the back of his jacket,
Justice Blackmun could describe "Cohen's absurd and immature antic" as "mainly
conduct and little speech." Id. at 27 (Blackmun, J., dissenting). Whether or not
one agrees with Blackmun's characterization, his point clearly rests upon an
intelligible cultural perception.

121. Austin himself was well aware that the "contrast" between performatives
and other forms of communication was not at all sharp, and that indeed "stating
something is performing an act just as much as is giving an order or giving a
warning." Austin, *Philosophical Papers*, at 246, 251. Ultimately, then, Austin came
to the conclusion that "action is . . . usually, at least in part, a matter of convention." Id. at 237.

122. Frederick F. Schauer, *Free Speech: A Philosophical Enquiry* 182–83 (1982).

123. Id. at 183.

124. E. M. Barendt, *Freedom of Speech* 263 (1985).

125. Schauer, *Free Speech*, at 183.

126. John M. Finnis, " 'Reason and Passion': The Constitutional Dialectic of
Free Speech and Obscenity," 116 *University of Pennsylvania Law Review* 222, 227
(1967); see Paris Adult Theatre I v. Slaton, 413 U.S. 49, 67 (1973).

127. For an explicit argument to this effect, see William A. Stanmeyer, "Keep-

ing the Constitutional Republic: Civic Virtue vs. Pornographic Attack," 14 *Hastings Constitutional Law Quarterly* 561, 585–90 (1987). Politicians have long appreciated the power of this argument. See, e.g., Richard Nixon, "Statement About the Report of the Commission on Obscenity and Pornography, Oct. 24, 1970," in *Public Papers of the Presidents of the United States: Richard Nixon* 940–41 (1971).

128. The search is sometimes quite explicit. See, e.g., Sunstein, "Pornography," at 602–8.

129. Beauharnais v. Illinois, 343 U.S. 250 (1951); see William E. Brigman, "Pornography as Group Libel: The Indianapolis Sex Discrimination Ordinance," 18 *Indiana Law Review* 479 (1985).

130. 343 U.S. at 251, 263.

131. Jacobs, "Patterns of Violence," at 24.

132. 376 U.S. 254 (1964). The premise of Frankfurter's opinion in *Beauharnais* was that group libel was a form of defamation and hence completely outside the purview of the First Amendment. 343 U.S. at 258. *Sullivan* exploded this premise, holding that the regulation of "libel can claim no talismanic immunity from constitutional limitations. It must be measured by standards that satisfy the First Amendment." 376 U.S. at 269.

133. 475 U.S. 767 (1986). The burden of proof was placed on the defendant in *Beauharnais* to establish, by way of affirmative defense, not only that "all the facts in the utterance" were true, 343 U.S. 254 n.1, "but also that the publication [was] made 'with good motives and for justifiable ends.' " Id. at 265 (quoting Ill. Const. art. II, §4). *Hepps*, on the other hand, holds that the First Amendment requires that a "plaintiff bear the burden of showing falsity" when a defamation involves a matter of public concern. 475 U.S. 776.

134. 343 U.S. at 254–56, 258. Ten years earlier David Riesman had stressed this same analogy between group libel and individual defamation. David Riesman, "Democracy and Defamation: Control of Group Libel," 42 *Columbia Law Review* 727, 777–78 (1942). The analogy has been criticized in Hadley Arkes, "Civility and Restriction of Speech: Rediscovering the Defamation of Groups," 1974 *Supreme Court Review* 281, 299–302.

135. See Stone, "Anti-Pornography Legislation," at 467.

136. American Booksellers Ass'n v. Hudnut, 771 F.2d 323, 328 (7th Cir. 1985), aff'd mem. 475 U.S. 1001 (1986).

137. Id.

138. Cantwell v. Connecticut, 310 U.S. 296, 309 (1940). Of course if one construes the rule of *Cantwell* to turn on the manner of speech, rather than its content, the same point could be made about the regulation of pornography.

139. Chaplinsky v. New Hampshire, 315 U.S. 568, 572 (1942).

140. See American Booksellers, 771 F.2d 323.

141. Zechariah Chafee, *Government and Mass Communications* 125 (1965).

142. In this regard, I cannot resist noting that as I write this essay the Oriental Rug Retailers of America, a professional association of rug merchants, are demanding an apology from ex–White House Chief-of-Staff Donald Regan for a remark demeaning "rug-merchant type of stuff" before the congressional committee investigating the Iran–*contra* arms scandal. The president of the association asserted: "Your statement was thoughtless and implies distrust of all rug merchants, and especially our membership." *San Francisco Chronicle*, Aug. 7, 1987, at 9, col. 4.

143. MacKinnon, *Feminism Unmodified*, at 166 (emphasis in original).

144. Cohen v. California, 403 U.S. 15, 25 (1971).

145. New York Times Co. v. Sullivan, 376 U.S. 254, 270 (1964).

146. See Post, "Foundations of Defamation Law," at 731–39; Robert Post, "Defaming Public Officials: On Doctrine and Legal History" (Review Essay), 1987 *American Bar Foundation Research Journal* 539, 553–57.

147. Cantwell v. Connecticut, 310 U.S. 296, 310 (1940).

148. Thomas I. Emerson, *The System of Freedom of Expression* 6 (1970).

4. The Constitutional Concept of Public Discourse

1. Cass Sunstein, "Beyond the Republican Revival," 97 *Yale Law Journal* 1539, 1541 (1988).

2. Frank Michelman, "Law's Republic," 97 *Yale Law Journal* 1493, 1527 (1988).

3. See, e.g., Hustler Magazine v. Falwell, 485 U.S. 46, 55 (1988); Bethel School Dist. No. 403 v. Fraser, 478 U.S. 675, 682–83 (1986); Cornelius v. NAACP Legal Defense & Educ. Fund, 473 U.S. 788, 802 (1985).

4. See *Falwell*, 485 U.S. at 52–55.

5. Boos v. Barry, 485 U.S. 312, 322 (1988) (quoting *Falwell*, 485 U.S. at 56); see also Texas v. Johnson, 491 U.S. 397, 411–12 (1989).

6. See *Falwell*, 485 U.S. at 53–55.

7. See id. at 51–57.

8. The *Falwell* decision has been called "momentous," "a case of profound First Amendment significance." Rodney Smolla, "Emotional Distress and the First Amendment: An Analysis of *Hustler v. Falwell*," 20 *Arizona State Law Journal* 423, 442 (1988). For the background of the case, see Rodney Smolla, *Jerry Falwell v. Larry Flynt: The First Amendment on Trial* (1988).

9. Deposition Testimony of Larry Flynt, reprinted in Joint Appendix at 91, 141, *Falwell* (No. 86–1278).

10. Michael Sandel, "Morality and the Liberal Ideal," *New Republic*, May 7, 1984, at 15.

11. Falwell v. Flynt, 805 F.2d 484 (4th Cir. 1986) (Wilkinson, J., dissenting from denial of rehearing en banc).

12. *Falwell*, 485 U.S. at 56.

13. 403 U.S. 15 (1971).

14. Stuart Taylor, "Court, 8–0, Extends Right to Criticize Those in Public Eye," *New York Times*, Feb. 25, 1988, at A22, col. 2.

15. David G. Savage, "Justices Void Award Falwell Won from Flynt," *Los Angeles Times*, Feb. 25, 1988, pt. 1 at 23, col. 1.

16. See Plaintiff's Trial Exhibit 11 (excerpting Feb. 1980 issue of *Hustler* magazine), reprinted in Joint Appendix, at 209. In February 1980, *Hustler* had named Falwell its "Asshole of the Month." See generally Plaintiff's Trial Exhibits 11–15 (excerpting Feb. 1980, Nov. 1981, Dec. 1981, Feb. 1982, and Mar. 1983 issues of *Hustler* magazine), characterizing Falwell as a fanatic, a charlatan, and an egomaniac, and envisioning censorship and destruction of classic works of art under a Moral Majority regime, reprinted in Joint Appendix, at 208–24.

17. *Hustler*, Nov. 1983, reprinted in On Petition for a Writ of Certiorari to the United States Court of Appeals for the Fourth Circuit at E1, *Falwell* (No. 86–1278).

18. Id. *Hustler*'s table of contents listed the satire as "Fiction; Ad and Personality Parody." 485 U.S. at 48.

19. Stuart Taylor, "Sharp Words in High Court on *Hustler* Parody of Falwell," *New York Times*, Dec. 3, 1987, at A30, col. 1.

20. Id. (quoting Jerry Falwell).

21. See 485 U.S. at 48–49. Jurisdiction was established on the basis of diversity. The suit named as defendants Larry Flynt, Hustler Magazine, Inc., and Flynt Distributing Co., Inc. See Complaint, reprinted in Joint Appendix, at 4–5. According to Hustler Magazine v. Moral Majority, 796 F.2d 1148, 1149–56 (9th Cir. 1986), on November 15, 1983, Falwell sent out two mailings to solicit contributions "to help . . . defend his mother's memory in court." The first mailing, which was sent to approximately 500,000 "rank-and-file members" of the Moral Majority, described the *Hustler* parody; the second, which was sent to about 26,900 "major donors," included a copy of the parody with eight words blackened out. On November 18, Falwell solicited contributions from about 750,000 supporters of the *Old Time Gospel Hour*. In his mailing he included a copy of the parody and a letter "focused on the need to keep Falwell's religious television stations open in order to combat people like Larry Flynt." These solicitations produced in excess of $700,000 in contributions. On December 4 and December 11, Falwell also displayed the parody during a sermon broadcast nationwide on the *Old Time Gospel Hour*. Flynt retaliated by reprinting the parody in the March 1984 issue of *Hustler* and by suing Falwell for copyright infringement because of Falwell's use of the parody to solicit contributions. The Ninth Circuit, however, held the mailings and the television displays permissible under the fair use doctrine.

22. George H. Mead, "Suing Media for Emotional Distress: A Multi-Method Analysis of Tort Law Evolution," 23 *Washburn Law Journal* 24, 29, 43 (1983).

23. See Brown v. ABC, 704 F.2d 1296, 1302–3 (4th Cir. 1983) (applying Virginia law).

24. See Complaint, reprinted in Joint Appendix, at 16. Falwell's complaint relied on Va. Code Ann. §8.01–40 (1984), which provides, in part: "Any person whose name, portrait, or picture is used without having first obtained the written consent of such person . . . for advertising purposes or for the purposes of trade . . . may maintain a suit in equity . . . and may also sue and recover damages for any injuries sustained by reason of such use."

25. Falwell v. Flynt, 797 F.2d 1270, 1273 (4th Cir. 1986). The Fourth Circuit, upholding the ruling, relied primarily on interpretations of §51 of the New York Civil Rights Law, to which it found the Virginia statute "substantially similar." See id. at 1278; N.Y. Civ. Rights Law §51 (McKinney Supp. 1989).

26. Petition for Writ of Certiorari, at C1.

27. 418 U.S. 323, 339–40 (1974). For a brief survey of the impact of the *Gertz* dictum, see Philip Gleason, "The Fact/Opinion Distinction in Libel," 10 *Hastings Communications and Entertainment Law Journal* 763, 775–92 (1988).

28. See *Falwell*, 797 F.2d at 1275–76.

29. Womack v. Eldridge, 215 Va. 338, 342, 210 S.E.2d 145, 148 (1974), cited in *Falwell*, 797 F.2d at 1275 n.4.

30. Deposition Testimony of Larry Flynt, reprinted in Joint Appendix, at 136, 113, and 141. Flynt was obviously irrational and deeply disturbed during his deposition. He began the deposition by identifying himself as "Christopher Columbus Cornwallis I.P.Q. Harvey H. Apache Pugh." Id. at 91. He repeatedly directed uncontrolled and foul-mouthed remarks to the attorneys in the room, calling his own lawyer an "idiot" and a "liar" and telling him to "shut up." Id. at 99, 144, 119. He called Falwell's lawyer an "asshole." Id. at 93–95. Flynt claimed that his life was "in danger," that he had a photograph of Falwell having coitus with a sheep, that he had affidavits of persons who had seen Falwell committing incest with his mother, and that the Campari parody was "not intended to parody or exaggerate anything, but to convey the truth." Id. at 146, 124, 105, 140.

Flynt later moved to have the deposition suppressed on the grounds that he could not comprehend the obligation of his oath or give a correct account of events, in support of which he submitted the affidavits of two psychiatrists to the effect that during the deposition Flynt was in a psychotic, manic state. See Declarations in Support of Defendant's Motion to Exclude Deposition Testimony of Larry Flynt, reprinted in Joint Appendix, at 180–85. The trial court initially granted Flynt's motion, but later, on the first day of trial, reversed itself and admitted an edited version of the deposition into evidence. See *Falwell*, 797 F.2d at 1273.

31. Testimony of Jerry Falwell, reprinted in Joint Appendix, at 38. Falwell

testified: "I have never been to a psychiatrist or psychologist in my life for personal help. I am not sure but what I feel that as a Christian and a minister—I am not sure it would not be wrong for me to do it . . . I did not cut my schedule back; I did not stop anything I was doing, but I can tell you it has created the most difficult year of performance, physically, mentally, emotionally, in all of my life. Those who work near me can tell you that my ability to concentrate and focus on the job at hand has been greatly, greatly damaged." Id. at 42. An administrative subordinate of Falwell, Dr. Ron Godwin, testified at trial that Falwell had an extraordinarily busy schedule and that as a result of the *Hustler* parody Falwell neither cut back his schedule in any way nor lost his dynamism in speaking. See Testimony of Ronald Godwin, reprinted in Joint Appendix, at 52–53. Godwin stated that, shortly after reading the parody, Falwell seemed "more troubled, more serious, more concerned than I had ever seen him on any other issue, crisis or otherwise," and that thereafter it was "more difficult for me as an administrator to get Dr. Falwell's attention and to get him to be able to focus on the details of the organization we administer." Id. at 53, 54.

32. See Petition for Writ of Certiorari, at C3–C4.

33. See Falwell v. Flynt, 797 F.2d 1270, 1273–74 (4th Cir. 1986). Flynt and *Hustler* also argued that the trial court had misunderstood some points of state law and that it had issued a number of incorrect and prejudicial evidentiary rulings. See id. at 1277–78.

34. Id. at 1273–74 (citing New York Times Co. v. Sullivan, 376 U.S. 254 [1964]). The actual malice standard of *New York Times* requires a plaintiff to demonstrate that a defendant has published the communication at issue with "knowledge that it is false or with reckless disregard of whether it is false or not." *New York Times*, 376 U.S. at 280, quoted in 797 F.2d at 1274 n.2.

35. 797 F.2d at 1276.

36. Id. at 1275. The Fourth Circuit's opinion was instantly controversial, receiving widespread and largely negative notice. See, e.g., Jonathan L. Entin, "Privacy, Emotional Distress, and the Limits of Libel Law Reform," 38 *Mercer Law Review* 835, 853–58 (1987); Note, "*Falwell v. Flynt:* First Amendment Protection of Satirical Speech," 39 *Baylor Law Review* 313, 322–32 (1987); Note, "Emotional Distress When Libel Has Failed: The Faulty Logic of *Falwell v. Flynt*," 16 *Colonial Lawyer* 115 (1987); Note, "*Falwell v. Flynt:* Intentional Infliction of Emotional Distress as a Threat to Free Speech," 81 *Northwestern University Law Review* 993, 1004–8 (1987); Note, "*Falwell v. Flynt:* An Emerging Threat to Freedom of Speech," 1987 *Utah Law Review* 703, 719–26. But see Note, "Constitutional Law—Satire, Defamation, and the Believability Rule as Bar to Recovery—*Falwell v. Flynt*," 22 *Wake Forest Law Review* 915, 922–29 (1987). By a 6–5 vote, the Fourth Circuit denied a petition to rehear the case en banc, see 805 F.2d 484 (4th Cir. 1986), despite a brilliant and stinging dissent by Judge Wilkinson.

37. Justice White had powerfully expressed his dissatisfaction with the *New York Times* actual malice standard in his concurring opinion in Dun and Bradstreet, Inc. v. Greenmoss Builders, Inc., 472 U.S. 749, 765–74 (1985) (White, J., concurring in the judgment).

38. *Falwell*, 485 U.S. at 50.

39. Id. at 53.

40. Id. at 54–55.

41. Id. at 52, 51 (quoting Bose Corp. v. Consumers Union of United States, Inc., 466 U.S. 485, 503–4 [1984]).

42. Id. at 55.

43. See Chaplinsky v. New Hampshire, 315 U.S. 568, 572 (1942): for constitutional purposes, " 'fighting' words" are defined as those "which by their very utterance inflict injury or tend to incite an immediate breach of the peace."

44. See FCC v. Pacifica Found., 438 U.S. 726, 747 (1978).

45. *Falwell*, 485 U.S. at 56.

46. Id. at 55 (quoting NAACP v. Claiborne Hardware Co., 458 U.S. 886, 910 [1982]).

47. Id. at 55–56 (quoting *Pacifica*, 438 U.S. at 745).

48. Id. at 56, 52, 56. It should be noted, however, that the Court's proposed rule is a technical matter unacceptably casual in its formulation, for it fails to specify any relationship between the required false fact and the actionable infliction of emotional distress. It does not make clear whether the false fact must itself cause the consequent emotional distress, or whether the false fact must merely be "contained" in a publication that otherwise inflicts such distress. If the latter, the rule does not make clear whether the false fact must be of a certain kind, or whether any false fact, no matter how innocent, will render an entire publication constitutionally unprotected. It would seem, however, that the rule cannot perform its assigned function of protecting an area of "breathing space" unless strictly interpreted, that is, unless it were to require that the false fact stated with actual malice also be intended to and in fact cause intense emotional distress by reason of its outrageous character.

49. Imagine, for example, that instead of printing the parody in a publication "such as the one here at issue," Flynt had reached Falwell on the telephone and said (with utter malice) the very same words that he had printed in *Hustler*. Would Flynt receive the same constitutional protection?

50. Imagine, for example, that instead of publishing the parody about a public official or a public figure, Flynt had picked a private person's name at random from the telephone directory and had published in *Hustler* the identical Campari parody about him. Would Flynt receive the same constitutional protection?

51. The holding of *Falwell* explicitly applies only to actions "for the tort of intentional infliction of emotional distress." 485 U.S. at 56. But the purpose of the tort of invasion of privacy, like that of the tort of intentional infliction of

emotional distress, is often said to be the provision of redress for "injury to [a] plaintiff's emotions and his mental suffering." Froelich v. Adair, 213 Kan. 357, 360, 516 P.2d 993, 996 (1973); see Time, Inc. v. Hill, 385 U.S. 374, 384 n.9 (1967). The Court has in fact been deeply troubled by the tension between First Amendment rights and the protection of privacy. See, e.g., Florida Star v. B.J.F., 491 U.S. 524, 530–34 (1989). Indeed, only four months after *Falwell*, the Court resolved this tension in a manner arguably inconsistent with some of the more broadly stated principles contained in *Falwell*. See Frisby v. Schultz, 487 U.S. 474 (1988).

52. As Rodney Smolla has written, "The intellectual challenge posed by Falwell's suit is not how to construct a convincing rationale for rejecting his claim, but rather how to articulate limits on that rationale." Smolla, "Emotional Distress," at 427; see Paul A. LeBel, "Emotional Distress, the First Amendment, and 'This Kind of Speech': A Heretical Perspective on *Hustler Magazine v. Falwell*," 60 *University of Colorado Law Review* 315 (1989).

53. Womack v. Eldridge, 215 Va. 338, 342, 210 S.E.2d 145, 148 (1974).

54. *Restatement (Second) of Torts* §46 comment d (1977). For a detailed discussion of this function in the context of the tort of defamation, see Robert Post, "The Social Foundations of Defamation Law: Reputation and the Constitution," 74 *California Law Review* 691, 710–19, 732–39 (1986). For a detailed discussion of this function in the context of the tort of invasion of privacy, see Chapter 2 of this volume.

55. Parmiter v. Coupland, 151 Eng. Rep. 340, 342 (Exch. of Pleas 1840).

56. Rosenblatt v. Baer, 383 U.S. 75, 92 (1966) (Stewart, J., concurring).

57. The argument in the following three paragraphs is developed in considerably greater length in Post, "Foundations of Defamation Law," at 707–19.

58. See, e.g., A. Irving Hallowell, *Culture and Experience* (1955); Tamotsu Shibutani, *Society and Personality* 239–47 (1961); John L. Caughey, "Personal Identity and Social Organization," 8 *Ethos* 173 (1980).

59. George H. Mead, *Mind, Self, and Society* 162 (Charles W. Morris, ed., 1937).

60. See Erving Goffman, *Interaction Ritual* 47–91 (1967).

61. Erving Goffman, *Asylums: Essays on the Social Situation of Mental Patients and Other Inmates* (1961).

62. Goffman, *Interaction Ritual*, at 51.

63. Gertz v. Robert Welch, Inc., 418 U.S. 323, 350 (1974).

64. Joseph R. Gusfield, *Community: A Critical Response* 29 (1975).

65. Kai Erikson, *Wayward Puritans: A Study in the Sociology of Deviance* 10–13 (1966).

66. See Post, "Foundations of Defamation Law," at 711–15, 735–39.

67. 3 William Blackstone, *Commentaries* *125.

68. See De Libellis Famosis, 77 Eng. Rep. 250, 251 (K.B. 1605).

69. See 3 Blackstone, *Commentaries*, at *126. See 2 James Kent, *Commentaries on American Law* 18–24 (2d ed. 1832). In the eyes of the early common law, " 'the greater the truth, the greater the libel.' " David Riesman, "Democracy and Defamation: Control of Group Libel," 42 *Columbia Law Review* 727, 735 (1942) (quoting Lord Mansfield). On the subsequent history of the defense of truth in indictments for criminal defamation, see Laurence H. Eldredge, *The Law of Defamation* §64, at 324–27 (1978); Marc A. Franklin, "The Origins and Constitutionality of Limitations on Truth as a Defense in Tort Law," 16 *Stanford Law Review* 789, 790–805 (1964); and Roy Robert Ray, "Truth: A Defense to Libel," 16 *Minnesota Law Review* 43, 43–49 (1931).

70. Eldredge, *Law of Defamation* §63, at 323.

71. See, e.g., Doherty v. Kansas City Star Co., 144 Kan. 206, 59 P.2d 30 (1936); Brown v. Harrington, 208 Mass. 600, 95 N.E. 655 (1911); Ellis v. Kimball, 33 Mass. (16 Pick.) 132 (1834); Donald Serrell Thomas, *A Long Time Burning: The History of Literary Censorship in England* 56–61 (1969). Two caveats to the point in text are necessary. First, liability depended on the application of the common law privilege of "fair comment." Second, the common law ordinarily refused to predicate liability upon mere "name-calling" or vile "epithets." See Rodney Smolla, *Law of Defamation* §4.03 (3d ed. 1989).

72. Burton v. Crowell Publishing Co., 82 F.2d 154, 156, 154 (quoting Complaint, *Burton* [No. 258]), 156 (2d Cir. 1936).

73. *Restatement of Torts* §558 (1938).

74. Id. §566. The accompanying comment, comment a, noted that if a communication "expresses a sufficiently derogatory opinion as to the conduct in question, it is defamatory and, unless it is privileged as fair comment, is actionable."

75. Id. §566 comment a.

76. Id. §566 comment a illustration. The *Restatement* also noted, however, that *A*'s criticism might be privileged as "fair comment."

77. The inconsistency has been well explored by George Christie. See George C. Christie, "Defamatory Opinions and the *Restatement (Second) of Torts*," 75 *Michigan Law Review* 1621, 1625–28 (1977).

78. See *Restatement (Second) of Torts* §558 (Tent. Draft No. 20, 1974). The drafters strengthened the requirement on April 5, 1975. See *Restatement (Second) of Torts* §558(a) (Tent. Draft No. 21, 1975). The final version of §558 provides: "To create liability for defamation there must be: (a) a false and defamatory statement concerning another . . ."

79. See *Restatement (Second) of Torts* §566 (Tent. Draft No. 20, 1974). The Tentative Draft did, however, insert the following comment: "Even though an expression of a derogatory opinion is defamatory, the Constitution may restrict the maintaining of an action for defamation if it deals with a matter of public or general interest." Id. §566 comment a.

80. Id. §567A (Tent. Draft No. 20, 1974); see also 51 *ALI Proceedings* 302–39 (1974) (reporting the discussion on the eventual abandonment of §567A); Christie, "Defamatory Opinions," at 1628–30 (describing the proposal and initial endorsement of §567A). Dean Prosser, as Reporter, first introduced this section in 1965; he stated that "ridicule appears nowhere in the Restatement, and since it is a common form of defamation it seemed obvious that it should be somewhere." 42 *ALI Proceedings* 404 (1965).

81. *Restatement (Second) of Torts* §567A comment a (Tent. Draft No. 20, 1974).

82. 418 U.S. 323, 339–40 (footnote omitted) (1974).

83. See Randall P. Bezanson, "The Libel Tort Today," 45 *Washington and Lee Law Review* 535, 540–41 (1988).

84. See *Restatement (Second) of Torts* §652D (1977). The early privacy cases perceived a definite connection between the theory of truth in criminal libel ("the greater the truth, the greater the libel") and the rationale of the privacy tort. See, e.g., Roberson v. Rochester Folding Box Co., 171 N.Y. 538, 555–56, 64 N.E. 442, 447 (1902); see also Eldredge, *Law of Defamation*, §66 at 330–31 and n.41; Calvert Magruder, "Mental and Emotional Disturbance in the Law of Torts," 49 *Harvard Law Review* 1033, 1061 (1936). ("[The] 'right of privacy,' is a flank attack upon the doctrine that truth is an absolute defense in libel and slander.")

85. Southern Express Co. v. Byers, 240 U.S. 612, 615 (1916).

86. William Prosser, "Intentional Infliction of Mental Suffering: A New Tort," 37 *Michigan Law Review* 874 (1939). See generally Magruder, "Mental and Emotional Disturbance" (describing the emergence of a broad tort principle affording relief for emotional distress in the more outrageous cases).

87. See Willard H. Pedrick, "Intentional Infliction: Should Section 46 Be Revised?," 13 *Pepperdine Law Review* 1, 2–5 (1985).

88. For a state-by-state survey of the tort of intentional infliction of emotional distress, see *Libel Defense Resource Center, 50-State Survey 1988: Current Developments in Media Libel and Invasion of Privacy Law* 926–67 (Henry R. Kaufman, ed., 1988).

89. See note 29 above. Section 46 of the second *Restatement* now provides: "One who by extreme and outrageous conduct intentionally or recklessly causes severe emotional distress to another is subject to liability for such emotional distress . . ."

90. Daniel Givelber, "The Right to Minimum Social Decency and the Limits of Evenhandedness: Intentional Infliction of Emotional Distress by Outrageous Conduct," 82 *Columbia Law Review* 42, 42–49 (1982); see Note, "Threat to Free Speech," at 1004–8.

91. *Restatement (Second) of Torts* §46 comment j (1977).

92. The intrinsic and reciprocal relationship between the outrageousness of the *Hustler* parody and the existence of Falwell's distress is perceptively noted by

Rodney Smolla, who asks, "How could such an ad *not* inflict distress . . . ?" Smolla, *Jerry Falwell v. Larry Flynt*, at 158.

93. Womack v. Eldridge, 215 Va. 338, 342, 210 S.E.2d 145, 148 (1974).

94. See Givelber, "Minimum Social Decency," at 49. For a rare example of a court consciously resisting this "collapse," see Kazatsky v. King David Memorial Park, Inc., 515 Pa. 183, 197–98, 527 A.2d 988, 995 (1987).

95. *Womack*, 215 Va. at 342, 210 S.E.2d at 148.

96. *Restatement (Second) of Torts* § 46 comment d (1977). For a sampling of the immense influence of this comment, see Teamsters Local 959 v. Wells, 749 P.2d 349, 357 n.13 (Alaska 1988); Watts v. Golden Age Nursing Home, 127 Ariz. 255, 258, 619 P.2d 1032, 1035 (1980); Haldeman v. Total Petroleum, Inc., 376 N.W.2d 98, 104–5 (Iowa 1985); Roberts v. Auto-Owners Ins. Co., 422 Mich. 594, 602–5, 374 N.W.2d 905, 908–10 (1985); Dominguez v. Stone, 97 N.M. 211, 214, 638 P.2d 423, 426 (1981); Breeden v. League Servs. Corp., 575 P.2d 1374, 1376 (Okla. 1978); and Contreras v. Crown Zellerbach Corp., 88 Wash. 2d 735, 739–40, 565 P.2d 1173, 1176 (1977).

97. At common law, of course, the publication of a defamatory statement carried with it an irrebuttable presumption of injury. See Post, "Foundations of Defamation Law," at 697–99. In Gertz v. Robert Welch, Inc., 418 U.S. 323 (1974), the Supreme Court held this irrebuttable presumption of injury unconstitutional and required instead some showing of "actual injury," which could include proof of "personal humiliation, and mental anguish and suffering." Id. at 349–50. Eleven years later the Court held that the common law presumption was constitutional where the plaintiff is a private figure and the communication at issue does not involve "matter[s] of public concern." Dun and Bradstreet, Inc. v. Greenmoss Builders, Inc., 472 U.S. 749, 761 (1985) (plurality opinion).

98. 478 U.S. 675, 681–82 (1986) (quoting Charles Austin Beard and Mary Beard, *New Basic History of the United States* 228 [1968]). The Court noted that "the 'fundamental values necessary to the maintenance of a democratic political system' disfavor the use of terms of debate highly offensive or highly threatening to others." Id. at 683 (quoting Ambach v. Norwick, 441 U.S. 68, 77 [1979]).

99. Michelman, "Law's Republic," at 1527.

100. See 485 U.S. at 55. The Court reiterated this reasoning one month later in Boos v. Barry, 485 U.S. 312 (1988), when it rejected a statute that regulated speech offensive to the "dignity" of foreign diplomats, stating that such a " 'dignity' standard, like the 'outrageousness' standard that we rejected in *Hustler*," would be "inherently subjective." Id. at 322.

101. See, e.g., Cohen v. California, 403 U.S. 15, 21, 25 (1971).

102. For a lucid discussion of this distinction, see Mark Sagoff, "Values and Preferences," 96 *Ethics* 301 (1986).

103. Hans-Georg Gadamer, *Truth and Method* 34 (Garrett Barden and John Cumming, trans., 2d ed., 1975).

104. Immanuel Kant, *Critique of Judgment* 46 (J. H. Bernard, trans., 1968). Kant continues: "Thus he is quite contented that if he says, 'Canary wine is pleasant,' another man may correct his expression and remind him that he ought to say, 'It is pleasant *to me.*'" Id. at 57 (emphasis in original).

105. Miller v. California, 413 U.S. 15, 24 (1973) (quoting Kois v. Wisconsin, 408 U.S. 229, 230 [1972] [quoting Roth v. United States, 354 U.S. 476, 489 (1957)]).

106. Chaplinsky v. New Hampshire, 315 U.S. 568, 572 (1942).

107. FCC v. Pacifica Found., 438 U.S. 726, 747 (1978).

108. *Falwell*, 485 U.S. at 53.

109. Consolidated Edison Co. v. Public Serv. Comm'n, 447 U.S. 530, 534 (1980) (quoting Thornhill v. Alabama, 310 U.S. 88, 101 [1940]).

110. NAACP v. Claiborne Hardware Co., 458 U.S. 886, 913 (1982) (quoting Carey v. Brown, 447 U.S. 455, 467 [1980]).

111. Connick v. Myers, 461 U.S. 138, 145 (1983); see Philadelphia Newspaper, Inc. v. Hepps, 475 U.S. 767, 775 (1986); Thornhill v. Alabama, 310 U.S. 88, 101–2 (1940).

112. Gertz v. Robert Welch, Inc., 418 U.S. 323, 342 (1974).

113. See, e.g., *Restatement of Torts* §§606–7 (1938); 1 William Blake Odgers, *The Law of Libel and Slander* 34–68 (1887); Ralph E. Boyer, "Fair Comment," 15 *Ohio State Law Journal* 280 (1954); Charles Cooper Townsend, "The English Law Governing the Right of Criticism and Fair Comment," 30 *American Law Register* 517 (1891).

114. Carr v. Hood, 170 Eng. Rep. 983 n.*, 1 Camp. 355 n.* (K.B. 1808); see John E. Hallen, "Fair Comment," 8 *Texas Law Review* 41, 43–44 (1929).

115. *Carr*, 170 Eng. Rep. at 985 n.*, 1 Camp. at 358 n.*; see also Van Vechten Veeder, "Freedom of Public Discussion," 23 *Harvard Law Review* 413, 414 (1910) (on literary criticism as the first discourse to receive the privilege of fair comment).

116. *Carr*, 170 Eng. Rep. at 985 n.*, 1 Camp. at 357 n.*.

117. See Veeder, "Freedom of Public Discussion," at 425–26.

118. See Dix W. Noel, "Defamation of Public Officers and Candidates," 49 *Columbia Law Review* 875, 878–80 (1949); Titus, "Statement of Fact Versus Statement of Opinion—A Spurious Dispute in Fair Comment," 15 *Vanderbilt Law Review* 1203, 1203–5 (1962). A minority of American jurisdictions held that the privilege should extend also to false statements of fact, provided that the other conditions of the privilege were also met. See Noel, "Defamation," at 891; Robert Post, "Defaming Public Officials: On Doctrine and Legal History," 1987 *American Bar Foundation Research Journal* (Review Essay) 539, 552–53.

119. See Note, "Fair Comment," 62 *Harvard Law Review* 1207, 1207–11 (1949).

120. See Charles H. Carman, "*Hutchison v. Proxmire* and the Neglected Fair Comment Defense: An Alternative to 'Actual Malice,'" 30 *De Paul Law Review*

1, 11 (1980); Thayer, "Fair Comment as a Defense," 1950 *Wisconsin Law Review* 288, 306–7.

121. Veeder, "Freedom of Public Discussion," at 425.

122. See Note, "Fair Comment," at 1216.

123. Bausewine v. Norristown Herald, 351 Pa. 634, 645, 41 A.2d 736, 742, cert. denied, 326 U.S. 724 (1945); see Preveden v. Croation Fraternal Union of America, 98 F. Supp. 784, 786 (W.D. Pa. 1951).

124. 478 U.S. 675, 681 (1986).

125. See Boyer, "Fair Comment," at 290–92; Hallen, "Fair Comment," at 74–81; Noel, "Defamation," at 881–87; Note, "Fair Comment," at 1209–10.

126. See Boyer, "Fair Comment," at 290–92; Hallen, "Fair Comment," at 81–86; David Reisman, "Democracy and Defamation: Fair Game and Fair Comment II," 42 *Columbia Law Review* 1282, 1289–90 (1942); Note, "Fair Comment," at 1210–11.

127. Williams v. Hicks Printing Co., 159 Wis. 90, 102, 150 N.W. 183, 188 (1914); see also Balzac v. Porto Rico, 258 U.S. 298, 314 (1922).

128. See Philip Lewis, *Gatley on Libel and Slander* ¶¶748–50 (8th ed. 1981); *Restatement of Torts* §§618–19 (1938). The court, however, retained the authority to determine whether the "defamatory criticism" involved "a matter of public concern." Id. §618 (1).

129. 310 U.S. 296, 310 (1940). The holding of *Cantwell* also rested in part upon the free exercise clause of the First Amendment.

130. See Harte-Hanks Communications, Inc. v. Connaughton, 491 U.S. 657, 685–86 (1989); Bose Corp. v. Consumers Union of United States, Inc., 466 U.S. 485, 498–511 (1984).

131. The importance of this potential to American sensibilities can hardly be overestimated. It underlies, for example, John Dewey's assertion, which seems almost blandly trite, that "democracy is a way of life controlled by a working faith in the possibilities of human nature." John Dewey, "Creative Democracy—The Task Before Us," in *Classic American Philosophers* 389, 391 (Max Harold Fisch, ed., 1951).

132. West Va. State Bd. of Educ. v. Barnette, 319 U.S. 624, 641 (1943).

133. 403 U.S. 15, 23–24 (1971) (citing Whitney v. California, 274 U.S. 357, 375–77 [1927] [Brandeis, J., concurring]). The individualism of First Amendment doctrine is linked to the innermost logic of democracy. To the extent that personality and social structure are interdependent, and to the extent that democracy is a social structure in which persons must continually *choose* their values and commitments, democracy must at root presuppose citizens autonomous enough to create, rather than be created by, their communities. Hence Whitman's famous celebration of American government as founded upon "the theory of development and perfection by voluntary standards, and self-reliance," and as premised upon the "idea of perfect individualism." Walt Whitman, "Democratic

Vistas," in *Leaves of Grass, and Selected Prose* 460, 471 (John Kouwenhoven, ed., 1950). The concept of democracy thus itself contains quite radical implications that point toward a very different image of the self than that which justifies the regulation of defamation or intentional infliction of emotional distress. The tentative development of these implications, in a context quite distinct from that of First Amendment doctrine, appears in Justice Blackmun's dissent in Bowers v. Hardwick, 478 U.S. 186, 199 (1986) (Blackmun, J., dissenting). See Jed Rubinfeld, "The Right of Privacy," 102 *Harvard Law Review* 737, 783–99 (1989).

134. *Falwell*, 485 U.S. at 53.

135. Id. at 55.

136. The same point could be made about the Court's refusal to implement a "dignity" standard in Boos v. Barry, 485 U.S. 313, 322 (1988). Although not inherently subjective, a "dignity" standard is intrinsically connected to the particular norms of a specific community. As Richard Rorty has observed, " 'Intrinsic human dignity' is the comparative dignity of a group with which a person identifies herself. Nations or churches or movements are, on this view, shining historical examples not because they reflect rays emanating from a higher source, but because of contrast effects—comparisons with other, worse communities. Persons have dignity not as an interior luminescence, but because they share in such contrast-effects." Richard Rorty, "Postmodernist Bourgeois Liberalism," 80 *Journal of Philosophy* 583, 586–87 (1983). State regulation of speech on the basis of a "dignity" standard, therefore, would impose the "example" of a particular community.

137. 485 U.S. at 56 (quoting FCC v. Pacifica Found., 438 U.S. 726, 745–46 [1978]).

138. As Harold Lasswell wrote in 1941, at a time when public debates were closing down all over the world, a society "is acting as a public when it makes debatable demands for collective action," but it is acting as a crowd "whenever a topic is beyond debate." Harold D. Lasswell, *Democracy Through Public Opinion* 20 (1941). Gabriel de Tarde first introduced the distinction between the public and the crowd in *L'Opinion et la Foule* (1910).

139. To avoid terminological confusion, the remainder of this essay refers to "public discourse" only as the kind of public dialogue defined by constitutional doctrine.

140. Cohen v. California, 403 U.S. 15, 24 (1971).

141. Carroll D. Clark, "The Concept of the Public," 13 *Southwestern Social Science Quarterly* 311, 314, 315, 313 (1933) (quoting Robert E. Park and Ernest W. Burgess, *Introduction to the Science of Sociology* 254 [1924]); see C. A. Dawson and Warren E. Gettys, *An Introduction to Sociology* 621–22 (3d ed. 1948). For an example of the influence of defining the "public" in terms of a "universe of discourse," see Kenneth Ewart Boulding, *The Image* 132–47 (1956).

142. West Va. State Bd. of Educ. v. Barnette, 319 U.S. 624, 642 (1943).

143. See Post, "Foundations of Defamation Law," at 714–15.

144. On individualism as one of "the values of the American Creed," see Samuel P. Huntington, *American Politics: The Promise of Disharmony* 14 (1981).

145. This individualism differs, for example, from the more corporatist values that inform the regulation of speech in England.

146. John W. Bennett and Melvin M. Tumin, *Social Life: Structure and Function* 140 (1948).

147. Walter Lippmann, *Liberty and the News* 38 (1920).

148. Walter Lippmann, *Public Opinion* 263–75 (1922).

149. Alvin W. Gouldner, *The Dialectic of Ideology and Technology: The Origins, Grammar, and Future of Ideology* 106 (1976).

150. Id. at 95.

151. Schneider v. California, 308 U.S. 147, 163 (1939).

152. See John Dewey, *The Public and Its Problems* 27–28 (1927).

153. See Clark, "Concept of the Public," at 316.

154. *Cato's Letters, No. 32*, (as reprinted in the *New-York Weekly Journal*, Feb. 25 and Mar. 4, 1734), reprinted in *Freedom of the Press from Zenger to Jefferson* 15 (Leonard W. Levy, ed., 1966).

155. Robert Park, for example, noted that "whenever in any political society the diversity of interests and points of view from which the news is interpreted becomes so great that discussion is no longer possible, then there is no longer any public opinion . . . In that case nothing but force, in some form or other, is capable of maintaining sufficient order to permit, if not the normal, at least the necessary, social processes to go on. Under such circumstances it is vain to speak of freedom of speech or of the role of public opinion." Robert Park, "News and the Power of the Press," 47 *American Journal of Sociology* 1, 6 (1941); see A. Lawrence Lowell, *Public Opinion and Popular Government* 34–36 (1913). See generally W. Phillip Davison, "The Public Opinion Process," 22 *Public Opinion Quarterly* 91, 102 (1958) (arguing that the definition of a public does not "include those who . . . feel no community of interest with it").

156. E. B. Reuter and C. W. Hart, *Introduction to Sociology* 502 (1933).

157. Id. at 501–2.

158. Robert E. Park and Ernest W. Burgess, *Introduction to the Science of Sociology* 869 (1921). Park and Burgess argue that because "public opinion is determined by conflict and discussion, . . . both sides of an issue get considered," and "contentions are rejected because they will not stand up to criticism." Id. at 794–95. Thus, "the public . . . is always more or less rational. It is this fact of conflict, in the form of discussion, that introduces into the control exercised by public opinion the elements of rationality and fact." Id. at 795; see also Dawson and Gettys, *Introduction to Sociology*, at 621–22: "Divergent opinions, through inter-communication in a public, tend to inhibit and modify each other until the

matter is thought out more or less dispassionately and a common definition is reached. This shared opinion is termed *public opinion.*"

159. Gouldner, *Dialectic,* at 98 (emphasis omitted).

160. Michael J. Sandel, *Liberalism and the Limits of Justice* 150 (1982).

161. See generally Clark, "Concept of the Public," at 314–15 (discussing the distinction between public discourse in "primary societies" with a shared identity and secondary societies with economic and cultural diversity).

162. For an informative catalogue, see Times Film Corp. v. Chicago, 365 U.S. 43, 69–73 (1961) (Warren, C. J., dissenting).

163. Michelman makes this same point by noting that public deliberation requires that "participation in the process [result] in some shift or adjustment in relevant understandings on the parts of some (or all) participants." Michelman, "Law's Republic," at 1526; see also Seyla Benhabib, *Critique, Norm, and Utopia: A Study of the Foundations of Critical Theory* 312–13 (1986).

164. West Va. State Bd. of Educ. v. Barnette, 319 U.S. 624, 642 (1943).

165. New York Times Co. v. Sullivan, 376 U.S. 254, 270 (1964); see also Watts v. United States, 394 U.S. 705, 708 (1969) (per curiam).

166. Cantwell v. Connecticut, 310 U.S. 296, 310 (1940); see Hannegan v. Esquire, Inc., 327 U.S. 146, 158 (1946).

167. Cohen v. California, 403 U.S. 15, 25 (1971).

168. Winters v. New York, 333 U.S. 507, 510 (1948); see Miller v. California 413 U.S. 15, 40–41 (1973) (Douglas, J., dissenting).

169. Chaplinsky v. New Hampshire, 315 U.S. 568, 572 (1942).

170. Alexander Bickel, *The Morality of Consent* 72 (1975); see Thomas Emerson, *The System of Freedom of Expression* 496 (1970).

171. I am building here on J. L. Austin's insight that the difference between speech and action is "usually, at least in part, a matter of convention." J. L. Austin, *Philosophical Papers* 237 (3d ed. 1979); see id. at 245–47, 251.

172. Time, Inc. v. Hill, 385 U.S. 374, 412 (1967) (Fortas, J., dissenting).

173. 2 Jürgen Habermas, *The Theory of Communicative Action* 81–82 (Thomas McCarthy, trans., 1987).

174. 1 id. at 25–26 (Thomas McCarthy, trans., 1984). See generally Benhabib, *Critique, Norm, and Utopia,* at 282–83.

175. Jürgen Habermas, *Legitimation Crisis* 107 (Thomas McCarthy, trans., 1975).

176. Gouldner, *Dialectic,* at 98.

177. "Words," as Wittgenstein reminds us, "are deeds." Ludwig Wittgenstein, *Culture and Value* 46e (Peter Winch, trans., 1980).

178. See Reisman, "Democracy and Defamation," at 1306–7.

179. See Talley v. California, 362 U.S. 60 (1960). *Talley* concerned a Los Angeles ordinance requiring those who distributed handbills to identify both themselves and the handbills' authors. The holding is sometimes read as narrowly

resting on the need to avoid "the deterrent effect on free speech" that a general requirement of identification would create. See id. at 67 (Harlan, J., concurring). But the ordinance at issue in *Talley* was struck down on its face, and as Justice Clark pointed out in dissent: "The record is barren of any claim, much less proof, that [Talley] will suffer any injury whatever by identifying the handbill with his name . . . [T]here is neither allegation nor proof that Talley or any group sponsoring him would suffer 'economic reprisal, loss of employment, threat of physical coercion [or] other manifestations of public hostility.' " Id. at 69 (Clark, J., dissenting) (quoting NAACP v. Alabama, 357 U.S. 449, 462 [1958]). The breadth of *Talley*'s holding is therefore better justified by the principle discussed in the text—the same principle that causes prestigious scientific journals to circulate proposed articles anonymously for peer review. The hope is that by withholding the identity of the manuscript's author, journals will obtain an impartial evaluation of the contents of the article rather than a reflection of the status of its author.

180. Emile Durkheim, *Professional Ethics and Civic Morals* 89 (Cornelia Brookfield, trans., 1957). For Durkheim, the more democratic the government, the "greater [the] number of things . . . submitted to collective debate," a debate which must be "dominated by reflection" and lead to a "shedding [of] custom and tradition." Id. at 87–88.

181. This tendency is evident in the otherwise inexplicable arguments of Frederick Schauer and others that obscenity "is more accurately treated as a physical rather than a mental experience" because it contains "neither propositional, emotive, nor artistic content." Frederick Schauer, *Free Speech: A Philosophical Enquiry* 182–83 (1982); see E. M. Barendt, *Freedom of Speech* 248 (1985); Cass Sunstein, "Pornography and the First Amendment," 1986 *Duke Law Journal* 589, 603. For examples in the judicial literature, see Texas v. Johnson, 491 U.S. 411, 430–32 (1989) (Rehnquist, C. J., dissenting); and Cohen v. California, 403 U.S. 15, 27 (1971) (Blackmun, J., dissenting).

182. For an illustrative reaction, see Bruce Fein, "*Hustler Magazine v. Falwell*: A Mislitigated and Misreasoned Case" (Book Review), 30 *William and Mary Law Review* 905, 910 (1989) (arguing that the parody lacks "any plausible nexus to cerebral activity").

183. This experience has already led at least one commentator to criticize strongly the conclusions of the *Falwell* opinion:

> This analogy between intentional infliction of emotional distress and the tort of battery impeaches the constitutional logic of *Hustler* at its deepest level. Most of us would be reluctant to ever categorize any punch or kick as "speech" within the meaning of the First Amendment . . . [E]ven though . . . the punch may be a reaction or a "response" to a political speech with which one heatedly disagrees . . .
>
> But if a punch . . . does not amount to speech in the constitutional sense, why must "written speech" be treated as speech within the meaning

of the Constitution if the "written speech" is nothing more than a surrogate for the punch? (R. George Wright, "*Hustler Magazine v. Falwell* and the Role of the First Amendment," 19 *Cumberland Law Review* 19, 23 [1988])

Speech that is experienced as "nothing more than a surrogate for [a] punch" by virtue of its violation of civility rules cannot be, in Michelman's terms, truly "jurisgenerative." Michelman, "Law's Republic," at 1502.

184. Dewey, "Creative Democracy," at 393. Dewey's belief in the necessity of civility reflects an unresolved tension in his thought. Dewey habitually contrasted "the democratic method of forming opinions in political matters," by which he meant "persuasion through public discussion," with what he called "the methods in common use in forming beliefs in other subjects," by which he meant dependence "upon a person or group possessed of 'authority.' " John Dewey, *Freedom and Culture* 128–29 (1939). Dewey believed that "the usual procedure" of settling "issues, intellectual and moral, by appeal to the 'authority' of parent, teacher, or textbook" was deeply "inconsistent with the democratic method." Id. at 129. Yet he never questioned how, in the absence of some form of social "authority," participants in democratic processes could define, inculcate, and sustain the rules of civility that distinguish legitimate persuasion from coercive "ridicule" and "abuse."

185. See Benhabib, *Critique, Norm, and Utopia*, at 316.

186. Thus First Amendment doctrine has never embraced the ideal of a civil "town meeting" that Alexander Meiklejohn took to exemplify public deliberation. Alexander Meiklejohn, *Political Freedom: The Constitutional Powers of the People* 24–26 (1948). See Post, "Defaming Public Officials," at 555–56.

187. Sabina Lovibond, *Realism and Imagination in Ethics* 61 (1983).

188. *Restatement (Second) of Torts* §46 comment d (1977).

189. See Fein, "*Hustler Magazine v. Falwell*," at 910: "The refusal of the Supreme Court to demarcate a First Amendment line between the Falwell parody and political cartoons suggests a decay in society's moral convictions."

190. This same point is made by those "communitarians," who, like Michael Sandel, argue that "intolerance flourishes most where forms of life are dislocated, roots unsettled, traditions undone. In our day, the totalitarian impulse has sprung less from the convictions of confidently situated selves than from the confusions of atomized, dislocated, frustrated selves, at sea in a world where common meanings have lost their force." Sandel, "Morality," at 17.

191. See, e.g., Steven Shiffrin, "The First Amendment and Economic Regulation: Away from a General Theory of the First Amendment," 78 *Northwestern University Law Review* 1212 (1983).

192. See Lee Bollinger, *The Tolerant Society* (1986); Charles Taylor, *Philosophy and the Human Sciences* 205–9 (1985).

193. See Texas v. Johnson, 491 U.S. 431 (1989).

194. Robert A. Nisbet, *The Sociological Tradition* 47 (1966).

195. Thomas Bender, *Community and Social Change in America* 5 (1978).

196. See Sandel, *Liberalism*, at 150; cf. Josiah Royce, "The Nature of Community," in *Classic American Philosophers* 201, 208–10 (Max Harold Fisch, ed.) (arguing that a community consists of members whose identities have incorporated shared events of cooperation).

197. See Erikson, *Wayward Puritans*, at 11.

198. 485 U.S. at 55, 53, 52. (citing Gertz v. Robert Welch, Inc., 418 U.S. 323, 339 [1974]).

199. See id. at 50.

200. *Restatement (Second) of Torts* §46 comment d (1977).

201. 485 U.S. at 55.

202. Id. at 50.

203. Id. at 53.

204. Beckley Newspapers Corp. v. Hanks, 389 U.S. 81, 82 (1967) (per curiam) (quoting from trial court's jury instructions); see also Harte-Hanks Communications, Inc. v. Connaughton, 491 U.S. 657, 666–67 (1989); Greenbelt Coop. Publishing Ass'n v. Bresler, 398 U.S., 10 (1970); Garrison v. Louisiana, 379 U.S. 64, 73 (1964).

205. See, e.g., Kenneth Burke, *A Grammar of Motives* (1945). Aristotle noted long ago that the ability of speech to persuade depends to a significant degree upon our perception of "the personal character of the speaker," 2 *The Complete Works of Aristotle* 2155 (Jonathan Barnes, ed., 1984), which in turn depends in large measure upon our conviction that he entertains "the right feelings towards his hearers." Id. at 2194. "Persuasion is achieved," said Aristotle, "by the speaker's personal character when the speech is so spoken as to make us think him credible. We believe good men more fully and more readily than others; this is true generally whatever the question is, and absolutely true where exact certainty is impossible and opinions are divided." Id. at 2155. A speaker's presentation of character "may almost be called the most effective means of persuasion he possesses." Id.

Motive has such obvious importance for the evaluation of speech that in most areas of the law we would not dream of severing speech from the context of its purposes or intentions. See, e.g., United States v. American Livestock Comm'n Co., 279 U.S. 435, 437–38 (1929) (Holmes, J.). ("Motive may be very material when it is sought to justify what until justified is a wrong.") Think, for example, of areas like fraud or perjury, where the legal assessment of speech depends directly upon its intent.

206. St. Amant v. Thompson, 390 U.S. 727, 731 (1968).

207. Herbert v. Lando, 441 U.S. 153, 160 (1979).

208. Beckley Newspapers Corp. v. Hanks, 389 U.S. 81, 82 (1967) (per curiam).

209. Falwell v. Flynt, 797 F.2d 1270, 1275 (4th Cir. 1986).

210. See Post, "Defaming Public Officials," at 553.

211. Id.; see LeBel, "A Heretical Perspective," at 331–32. The *Falwell* opinion makes this point explicitly when it states that the use of the *New York Times* standard "reflects our considered judgment that such a standard is necessary to give adequate 'breathing space' to the freedoms protected by the First Amendment." *Falwell,* 485 U.S. at 56.

212. Six months after this article was published, the Supreme Court decided Milkovich v. Lorain Journal Co., 497 U.S. 1 (1990), in which the Court both unambiguously reaffirmed its precedents establishing a fact/opinion distinction and simultaneously refused "to create a wholesale defamation exemption for anything that might be labeled 'opinion.'" Id. at 18. The Court stated that the *Gertz* dictum should be interpreted as "merely a reiteration of Justice Holmes' classic 'marketplace of ideas' concept," and it indicated its concern that fashioning a further explicit privilege for opinion might engender a tendency to "ignore the fact that expressions of 'opinion' may often imply an assertion of objective fact." Id. It is fair to characterize Milkovich as a somewhat unclear decision that holds, in the words of Justice Brennan's dissent, "that a protection for statements of pure opinion is dictated by *existing* First Amendment doctrine." Id. at 24 (Brennan, J., dissenting). Understood in this way, Milkovich would not affect the analysis of this section. At most it would suggest that courts inclined to protect statements as nonfactual "ideas" ought to be cautious in their conclusions.

213. See Titus, "Statement of Fact," at 1205–6.

214. For a sampling of modern commentary, see Alfred Hill, "Defamation and Privacy Under the First Amendment," 76 *Columbia Law Review* 1205, 1227–44 (1976); W. Page Keeton, "Defamation and Freedom of the Press," 54 *Texas Law Review* 1221 (1976); Comment, "Statements of Fact, Statements of Opinion, and the First Amendment," 74 *California Law Review* 1001 (1986); Note, "The Fact–Opinion Determination in Defamation," 88 *Columbia Law Review* 809 (1988); Note, "The Fact–Opinion Distinction in First Amendment Libel Law: The Need for a Bright-Line Rule," 72 *Georgetown Law Journal* 1817 (1984); and Comment, "The Fact/Opinion Distinction: An Analysis of the Subjectivity of Language and Law," 70 *Marquette Law Review* 673 (1987).

215. Information Control Corp. v. Genesis One Computer Corp., 611 F.2d 781, 783 (9th Cir. 1980).

216. Id. at 784.

217. 398 U.S. 6, 8, 14 (footnote omitted) (1970).

218. 418 U.S. 264, 268 (emphasis omitted), 284–86 (1974).

219. See, e.g., Palm Beach Newspapers v. Early, 334 So. 2d 50, 53 (Fla. Dist. Ct. App. 1976), cert. denied, 354 So. 2d 351 (1977), cert. denied, 439 U.S. 910 (1978); Lawrence A. Epter, "The Clash of Outrage and the First Amendment: The Protection of Non-Mainstream Opinion," 27 *Duquesne Law Review* 437, 438

n.6 (1989); Note, "*Hustler Magazine, Inc. v. Falwell*: Laugh or Cry, Public Figures Must Learn to Live with Satirical Criticism," 16 *Pepperdine Law Review* 97, 112–13 (1988); Note, "Fact and Opinion After *Gertz v. Robert Welch, Inc.*: The Evolution of a Privilege," 34 *Rutgers Law Review* 81 (1981); cf. Harriette K. Dorsen, "Satiric Appropriation and the Law of Libel, Trademark, and Copyright: Remedies Without Wrongs," 65 *Boston University Law Review* 923, 929–37 (1985) (discussing rhetorical hyperbole analysis in libel cases as analogous to the general fact/opinion determination).

220. *Falwell*, 485 U.S. at 49 (quoting Appendix to Petition for Certiorari at C1).

221. The point can be illustrated by the following example. Suppose Flynt had written of Falwell that he "drinks like a fish." A jury could very well conclude that the statement does not describe an "actual" fact about Falwell, meaning that Falwell could not really be said to drink as a *fish* would drink. This conclusion would not imply, however, that the figurative meaning of Flynt's statement—that Falwell is an alcoholic—is not a statement of fact.

222. Reply Brief of Petitioner at 20, *Falwell* (No. 86–1278).

223. I am grateful to Bernard Williams for his efforts to help me clarify this distinction.

224. Some preference expressions, like crude racial insults, may merely evince or express, rather than describe, private feelings. Strictly speaking, such preference expressions have no propositional content at all, and thus cannot be said to be either true or false. The existence of this category of preference expressions, however, in no way affects the argument of this section.

225. Curtis Publishing Co. v. Birdsong, 360 F.2d 344, 348 (5th Cir. 1966); see *Restatement (Second) of Torts* § 566 comment e (1977). Some courts, however, have labeled as opinion assertions that merely reflect a person's "subjective assessment of [a] situation." Fleming v. Benzaquin, 390 Mass. 175, 185, 454 N.E.2d 95, 102 (1983); see also Johnson v. Delta Democrat Publishing Co., 531 So. 2d 811 (Miss. 1988).

226. *Falwell*, 485 U.S. at 52, 51 (quoting Abrams v. United States, 250 U.S. 616, 630 [Holmes, J., dissenting]).

227. For a collection of cases dealing with preference expressions consisting of crude and offensive racial insults, see Dean M. Richardson, "Racism: A Tort of Outrage," 61 *Oregon Law Review* 267 (1982). At least one court has upheld such an action brought by a public official. See Dominguez v. Stone, 97 N.M. 211, 638 P.2d 423 (1981).

228. In so doing, I ignore yet a third kind of statement that courts sometimes classify under the rubric of opinion. John Searle calls them "fictional statements," and notes that they are "made possible by the existence of a set of conventions which suspend the normal operation of the rules relating illocutionary acts and the world." John R. Searle, *Expression and Meaning* 67 (1979). Fictional state-

ments do not refer (in the ordinary sense) to the world at all, and are therefore not "about" anyone or anything. As a legal matter, the claim that statements are fictional and hence not actionable in defamation should depend upon whether the statements are "of and concerning" the plaintiff. Some courts, however, have incorrectly conceptualized the problem of fictional statements as an issue of opinion. See, e.g., Pring v. Penthouse Int'l, 695 F.2d 438 (10th Cir. 1982), cert. denied, 462 U.S. 1132 (1983).

229. See Lewis v. Time, Inc., 710 F.2d 549, 554–56 (9th Cir. 1983).

230. Marc A. Franklin and Daniel J. Bussel, "The Plaintiff's Burden in Defamation: Awareness and Falsity," 25 *William and Mary Law Review* 825, 868–80 (1984); see Smolla, "Emotional Distress," at 450. For an example of a decision alluding to this approach, see Mr. Chow v. Ste. Jour Azur S.A., 759 F.2d 219, 227–29 (2d Cir. 1985).

231. See, e.g., William Lloyd Prosser, Dan B. Dobbs, Robert E. Keeton, and David G. Owen, *Prosser and Keeton on the Law of Torts* §32, at 185–89 (5th ed. 1984).

232. Immuno, A.G. v. Moor-Jankowski, 145 A.D.2d 114, 143, 537 N.Y.S.2d 129, 147 (1989).

233. *Mr. Chow*, 759 F.2d at 229; see, e.g., Janklow v. Newsweek, 788 F.2d 1300, 1302–3 (8th Cir.) cert. denied, 479 U.S. 883 (1986); Keller v. Miami Herald Publishing Co., 778 F.2d 711, 718 (11th Cir. 1985); Ollman v. Evans, 750 F.2d 970, 981 (D.C. Cir. 1984), cert. denied, 471 U.S. 1127 (1985).

234. The existence of such unprovable factual statements was explicitly acknowledged in the Court's discussion in Philadelphia Newspapers, Inc. v. Hepps, 475 U.S. 767 (1986), in which the Court pondered whether plaintiffs or defendants should bear the burden of proving the falsity of defamatory statements of fact when the speech at issue involved matters of public concern. All members of the Court agreed that the case posed the question of who should bear the risk that certain statements of fact might be "*unknowably* true or false." Id. at 776 (emphasis added); see also id. at 785 (Stevens, J., dissenting). Although the Court held that plaintiffs would in such circumstances be constitutionally required to prove falsity, it fully conceded that its holding would "insulate from liability some speech that is false, but unprovably so," and hence defeat suits that were, "in some abstract sense, . . . meritorious." See 475 U.S. at 776. This reasoning would make no sense whatever if speech were constitutionally privileged as opinion merely because it was unprovable.

235. See *Mr. Chow*, 759 F.2d at 229; *Ollman*, 750 F.2d at 981; Hollander v. Clayton, 16 Media Law Reporter (BNA) 1447, 1448 (N.Y. App. Div. 1989).

236. *Keller*, 778 F.2d at 718 (emphasis added).

237. 485 U.S. at 52.

238. Charles Taylor, *Philosophy and the Human Sciences* 19 (1985).

239. "Observations are always 'theory laden.' " Gilbert Harman, *The Nature of Morality* 4 (1977).

240. This dependence was the basis of Wigmore's dissatisfaction with the fact/opinion distinction in evidence law. See 7 John Henry Wigmore, *Evidence* §1919, at 14–16 (James H. Chadbourn, rev. ed., 1978); see also Beech Aircraft Corp. v. Rainey, 109 S. Ct. 439, 449 (1988); Ralph Slovenko, "The Opinion Rule and Wittgenstein's Tractatus," 14 *University of Miami Law Review* 1 (1959). This same dependence also underlay some of Frederick Schauer's justly famous critique of the division between fact and opinion in defamation law. See Frederick Schauer, "Language, Truth, and the First Amendment: An Essay in Memory of Harry Canter," 64 *Virginia Law Review* 263 (1978).

241. Stuart Hampshire, "Morality and Conversion," in *Utilitarianism and Beyond* 145, 146 (Amartya Sen and Bernard Williams, eds., 1982).

242. Bernard Williams, "The Scientific and the Ethical," in *Objectivity and Cultural Divergence* 209, 212 (S. C. Brown, ed., 1984).

243. Harman, *Nature of Morality*, at 6.

244. Charles S. Peirce, *Philosophical Writings* 38, 39 (1955).

245. Williams, "The Scientific and the Ethical," at 220.

246. Harman, *Nature of Morality*, at 113.

247. As Williams stresses, the distinction between convergent and nonconvergent assertions does not predict whether convergence "will actually occur"; instead, "the point of the contrast is that even if [convergence on ethical matters] happens, it will not be correct to think that it has come about because convergence has been guided by how things actually are, whereas convergence in the sciences might be explained in that way if it does happen. This means, among other things, that we understand differently in the two cases the existence of convergence or, alternatively, its failure to come about." Williams, "The Scientific and the Ethical," at 212.

248. Lovibond, *Realism and Imagination*, at 65.

249. Ronald Beiner, *Political Judgment* 142–43 (1983).

250. Hannah Arendt, *Between Past and Future* 259–60 (1968).

251. See 1 Habermas, *Theory of Communicative Action*, at 25.

252. See Arendt, *Between Past and Future*, at 238.

253. See *Falwell*, 485 U.S. at 52; Dun and Bradstreet, Inc. v. Greenmoss Builders, Inc., 472 U.S. 749, 769 (1985) (White J., concurring).

254. Thus, for example, we would certainly rather trust the verdict of indefinite generations of historians than the verdict of any given jury on such questions as whether General William Westmoreland gave orders to his intelligence officers to underestimate enemy troop strength during the Vietnam War, or whether Ariel Sharon actually discussed with the Gemayel family the need to take revenge against Palestinians. See Sharon v. Time, Inc., 599 F. Supp. 538 (S.D.N.Y. 1984); Westmoreland v. CBS, 596 F. Supp. 1170 (S.D.N.Y. 1984).

255. *Falwell*, 485 U.S. at 156. See Time, Inc. v. Hill, 385 U.S. 374, 406 (1967) (Harlan, J., concurring in part and dissenting in part). ("Any nation which counts the *Scopes* trial as part of its heritage cannot so readily expose ideas to sanctions

on a jury finding of falsity.") The actual malice standard thus offers a double margin of protection to defendants. The standard not only provides a safeguard against the potential distortion and error of the state as a fact finder, but also reduces the potential chilling effect on defendants' speech by ceding to them the maximum possible control over the legality of their own speech.

256. Of course, this distinction can make sense only within a society that has come to see itself anthropologically, as a distinct culture that could possibly be otherwise. For example, a culture that viewed ethics as having a "foothold or anchorage in Being, apart from the existence of actually living minds," would also view ethical claims as convergent and, in that respect, no different from factual statements. See William James, "The Moral Philosopher and the Moral Life," in *The Will to Believe and Other Essays in Popular Philosophy and Human Immortality* 184, 197 (1956). The legal interpretation of the fact/opinion distinction will thus ultimately reflect our understanding of our culture's separation from nature. Cf. Robert Post, "A Theory of Genre: Romance, Realism, and Moral Reality," 33 *American Quarterly* 367 (1981) (tracing the decline of ontologically grounded ethics in America).

257. For a particularly clear example of this process, see Myers v. Boston Magazine Co., 380 Mass. 336, 403 N.E.2d 376 (1980).

258. See Alfred C. Aman, "*SEC v. Lowe:* Professional Regulation and the First Amendment," 1985 *Supreme Court Review* 93, 93–95. Commercial speech may be another instance in which First Amendment doctrine permits the truth or falsity of opinions to be regulated. The doctrine certainly points heavily in that direction, for it allows commercial speech, which is not public discourse, to be regulated if it is "misleading" or "more likely to deceive the public than to inform it." Central Hudson Gas and Elec. Corp. v. Public Serv. Comm'n, 447 U.S. 557, 563–64 (1980). The doctrine makes no distinction between opinion and fact.

259. I do not mean to imply, of course, that the First Amendment protects only public discourse. See Marc A. Franklin, "Constitutional Libel Law: The Role of Content," 34 *UCLA Law Review* 1657, 1671–73 (1987).

260. See R. George Wright, "Speech on Matters of Public Interest and Concern," 37 *De Paul Law Review* 27 (1987). For a more general discussion of the difficulties of the public/private distinction, see Duncan Kennedy, "The Stages of the Decline of the Public/Private Distinction," 130 *University of Pennsylvania Law Review* 1349 (1982).

261. See e.g., Franklin, "Constitutional Libel Law," at 1657.

262. Boos v. Barry, 485 U.S. 317, 318 (1988) (citations omitted) (quoting New York Times Co. v. Sullivan, 376 U.S. 254, 270 [1964]).

263. Dun and Bradstreet, Inc. v. Greenmoss Builders, Inc. 472 U.S. 749, 758–59 (1985) (plurality opinion); see Philadelphia Newspapers, Inc. v. Hepps, 475 U.S. 767, 775 (1986). For about a decade this distinction remained obscure. The Court had reasoned in *New York Times* that the First Amendment embodies

"a profound national commitment" to robust public debate, in order to assure the
" 'unfettered interchange of ideas for the bringing about of political and social
changes desired by the people.' " 376 U.S. at 270, 269 (quoting Roth v. United
States, 354 U.S. 476, 484 [1957]). The Court had thus proposed that speech
necessary for democratic self-governance be immunized from the community
civility standards enforced by the common law tort of defamation, unless a speaker
had published false statements of fact with "actual malice." See id. at 283. *New
York Times* extended this immunity to criticism of the "official conduct" of public
official plaintiffs, because such criticism was manifestly at the core of democratic
self-governance. See id. at 282. In keeping with this rationale, the Court soon
expanded the application of the actual malice rule to "anything which might
touch on an official's fitness for office," Garrison v. Louisiana, 379 U.S. 64, 77
(1964), as well as to the fitness of candidates for elective public office, see Mon-
itor Patriot Co. v. Roy, 401 U.S. 265, 271–72 (1971). The apogee of this line of
analysis was Justice Brennan's plurality opinion in Rosenbloom v. Metromedia,
Inc., 403 U.S. 29 (1971), which proposed to apply the *New York Times* requirement of actual malice to all speech involving matters of "public or general interest." Id. at 43.

The clarity of this reasoning was obscured in 1974, however, when the Court
in Gertz v. Robert Welch, Inc., 418 U.S. 323 (1974), struck a compromise
position which required that the actual malice standard be applied only if a
defamation plaintiff were a "public person," meaning a public official or a public
figure, but which also extended some constitutional protection to all speech,
whether or not it could be characterized as public discourse. See id. at 342, 347.
Gertz held that in the absence of actual malice, states could not enforce common
law rules regarding presumptive and punitive damages for defamatory speech,
and also that the Constitution required that plaintiffs prove a defendant at "fault"
before receiving damages. See id. at 347, 349–50. Although these constitutional
restrictions intruded less deeply into the operation of community civility rules
than did the restrictions required by the *New York Times* actual malice standard,
they were nevertheless quite important. See Post, "Foundations of Defamation
Law," at 713–14, 738–39. The rationale for these restrictions was unclear, however, because to the extent that they applied to speech unrelated to matters of
democratic self-governance, they could not be justified by the reasoning that
underlay *New York Times*. To date the Court has been unable or unwilling to offer
any alternative rationale.

In recent years, therefore, the Court has begun to reformulate the *Gertz* compromise in such a way as to make the distinction between public discourse and
other speech determinative for the reach of constitutional restrictions on the
enforcement of community civility rules. In *Dun & Bradstreet*, for example, the
Court reinterpreted *Gertz* to eliminate any constitutional restraints on common
law rules of presumptive and punitive damages so long as defamatory speech

involves only private plaintiffs and is about "matters of purely private concern." *Dun & Bradstreet*, 472 U.S. at 759–60 (plurality opinion). Although the Court did not expressly discuss whether it would also remove the constitutional requirement of "fault" in such circumstances, it nevertheless left the clear implication that "the constitutional requirement of fault in a private plaintiff defamation case applies only if the subject matter of the defamatory falsehood pertains to a matter of 'public concern.' " Cox v. Hatch, 761 P.2d 556, 559 (Utah 1988).

In the 1986 decision of Philadelphia Newspapers, Inc. v. Hepps, 475 U.S. 767 (1986) the Court held that where speech "is of public concern" a plaintiff must bear the burden of providing falsity, even if the plaintiff is a private figure. See id. at 775–76. The Court did not indicate who would bear this burden if a plaintiff were a private figure and a defendant's speech were "of exclusively private concern," although the Court did delphically remark that in such circumstances "constitutional requirements do not necessarily force any change in at least some of the features of the common-law landscape." Id. One commentator has concluded that "the logic of *Dun & Bradstreet*" would lead to the conclusion that in such circumstances the First Amendment would require no change in "the unvarnished rules of the common law." Smolla, "Emotional Distress," at 471.

264. See Stephen Allred, "From *Connick* to Confusion: The Struggle to Define Speech on Matters of Public Concern," 64 *Indiana Law Journal* 43, 75, 81 (1988); Toni M. Massaro, "Significant Silences: Freedom of Speech in the Public Sector Workplace," 61 *Southern California Law Review* 1, 25–27 (1987).

265. Arlen W. Langvardt, "Public Concern Revisited: A New Role for an Old Doctrine in the Constitutional Law of Defamation," 21 *Valparaiso University Law Review* 241, 259 (1987).

266. See *Falwell*, 485 U.S. at 56.

267. See, e.g., Time, Inc. v. Firestone, 424 U.S. 448, 454 (1976); Curtis Publishing Co., v. Butts, 388 U.S. 130, 146–55 (1967) (plurality opinion); id. at 163–65 (Warren, C. J., concurring).

268. *Gertz*, 418 U.S. at 342. Note, for example, the ambiguity of the Court's characterization of Jerry Falwell as a "public figure." See *Falwell*, 485 U.S. at 57 and n.5. The Court cited *Who's Who in America* to the effect that Falwell "is the host of a nationally syndicated television show and was the founder and president of a political organization formerly known as the Moral Majority. He is also the founder of Liberty University in Lynchburg, Virginia, and is the author of several books and publications." Id. at 57, n.5.

269. The difference between the constitutional protection afforded to speech about public persons and that afforded to speech of public concern about private persons indicates that the domain of public discourse is not an undifferentiated terrain. It instead contains different categories of speech which may receive different forms of constitutional protection. The distinction between speech about public persons and speech of public concern about private persons is thus

not a distinction between public discourse and other forms of communication, but rather a difference internal to the domain of public discourse itself. In fact the Court's justification for providing greater constitutional protection to speech about "public figures" than to speech about private figures involving matters of public concern turns almost entirely on considerations of individual equity, considerations that have little to do with defining and protecting speech necessary for democratic self-governance. See *Gertz*, 418 U.S. at 344–46; David J. Branson and Sharon A. Sprague, "The Public Figure–Private Person Dichotomy: A Flight from First Amendment Reality," 90 *Dickinson Law Review* 627, 634–37 (1986).

270. Consolidated Edison Co. v. Public Comm'n, 447 U.S. 530, 538 (1980) (citations omitted) (quoting Police Dep't v. Mosley, 408 U.S. 92, 96 [1972]); see Thomas v. Collins, 323 U.S. 516, 545 (1945) (Jackson, J., concurring).

271. 403 U.S. 29, 43 (1971).

272. *Gertz*, 418 U.S. at 346 (quoting *Rosenbloom*, 403 U.S. at 79 [Marshall, J., dissenting]).

273. Robert H. Bork, "Neutral Principles and Some First Amendment Problems," 47 *Indiana Law Journal* 1, 27 (1971).

274. Recall, in this context, that Cantwell v. Connecticut, 310 U.S. 296 (1940), itself viewed debates about "the realm of religious faith" as quintessential public discourse. See id. at 310.

275. Hanna Pitkin, "Justice: On Relating Private and Public," 9 *Political Theory* 327, 343, 346 (1981).

276. Samuel D. Warren and Louis D. Brandeis, "The Right to Privacy," 4 *Harvard Law Review* 193 (1890).

277. See Alpheus Thomas Mason, *Brandeis: A Free Man's Life* 70 (1946); Don Pember, *Privacy and the Press: The Law, the Mass Media, and the First Amendment* 20–25 (1972).

278. See Warren and Brandeis, "Right to Privacy," at 196.

279. Id. Don Pember, for example, writes that "the Warren-Brandeis proposal was essentially a rich man's plea to the press to stop its gossiping and snooping." Pember, *Privacy and the Press*, at 23.

280. Bernard C. Hennessy, *Public Opinion* 8–9 (3d ed. 1975).

281. Modern political scientists have in general abandoned the normative definition of the public characteristic of the sociology of the 1930s, and have instead preferred to investigate the concept of the public as a purely empirical phenomenon. For examples of this tendency, see W. Lance Bennett, *Public Opinion in American Politics* 12–63 (1980), which adopts a "situational perspective" that regards the public as "the collection of individuals who actually form and express opinions on a specific issue at a particular time," id. at 13; and V. O. Key, *Public Opinion and American Democracy* 8–17 (1961), which defines public opinion broadly to encompass all opinions held by individuals that "governments find it prudent to heed," id. at 16.

282. See Franklin, "Constitutional Libel Law," at 1665.

283. Waldbaum v. Fairchild Publications, Inc., 627 F.2d 1287, 1295 and n.20 (D.C. Cir.) cert. denied, 449 U.S. 898 (1980); see Harris v. Tomczak, 94 F.R.D. 687 (E.D. Cal. 1982).

284. The Court's development of the doctrine of the limited purpose public figure can be read as a response to this overinclusiveness. The doctrine holds that the mere fact that an individual is involved in a prominent "public controversy" is not enough to make her into a public figure; the controversy must be of a certain "sort," of a kind that is related to " 'the resolution of public questions,' " Time, Inc. v. Firestone, 424 U.S. 448, 455 (1976) (quoting Gertz v. Robert Welch, Inc., 418 U.S. 323, 351 [1974]).

285. Frederick Schauer, "Public Figures," 25 *William and Mary Law Review* 905, 917 (1984).

286. See Branson and Sprague, "Dichotomy," at 636–37; Franklin, "Constitutional Libel Law," at 1665.

287. Harry Kalven, "The *New York Times* Case: A Note on the Central Meaning of the First Amendment," 1964 *Supreme Court Review* 191, 221.

288. 310 U.S. 88, 101–2 (1940).

289. 485 U.S. at 53.

290. Id. at 56.

291. Id. (quoting Street v. New York, 394 U.S. 576, 592 [1969]).

292. See In re *Primus*, 436 U.S. 412, 426–31 (1978).

293. Branzburg v. Hayes, 408 U.S. 665, 704 (1972).

294. Id. at 705.

295. 472 U.S. 749, 762 (1985) (plurality opinion).

296. 413 U.S. 15, 34–35 (1973).

297. Id. (quoting Roth v. United States, 354 U.S. 476, 484 (1966)). The common law tort of invasion of privacy contains a similar tension between the intent associated with commercial enterprise and the intent associated with public discourse. See Tellado v. Time-Life Books, Inc., 643 F. Supp. 904 (D.N.J. 1986).

298. See Gouldner, *Dialectic*, at 95.

299. For two recent accounts of these difficulties, see Rodney Smolla, *"Dun & Bradstreet, Hepps,* and *Liberty Lobby:* A New Analytic Primer on the Future Course of Defamation," 75 *Georgetown Law Journal* 1519, 1561–64 (1987); Katherine W. Pownell, "Defamation and the Nonmedia Speaker," 41 *Federal Communications Law Journal* 195, 210–15 (1989).

300. Gouldner, *Dialectic*, at 106.

301. For a clear example of how this presumption operates in the common law, see Arrington v. New York Times Co., 55 N.Y.2d 433, 434 N.E.2d 1319, 449 N.Y.S.2d 941 (1982), cert. denied, 459 U.S. 1146 (1983).

302. For examples of judicial recognition of the strength of this claim, see Denny v. Mertz, 106 Wis. 2d 636, 318 N.W.2d 141, cert. denied, 459 U.S. 883

(1983); and Harley-Davidson Motorsports, Inc. v. Markley, 279 Or. 361, 366, 568 P.2d 1359, 1362–63 (1977).

303. See, e.g., Philadelphia Newspapers, Inc. v. Hepps, 475 U.S. 767, 779 n.4 (1986); Smolla, "New Analytic Primer," at 1564.

304. Dun & Bradstreet, Inc. v. Greenmoss Builders, Inc., 472 U.S. 749, 784 (1985) (Brennan, J., dissenting); see also id. at 773 (White, J., concurring in the judgment).

305. See Connick v. Myers, 461 U.S. 138, 148 n.8 (1983).

306. Id. at 146.

307. See id.; Givhan v. Western Line Consol. School Dist., 439 U.S. 410, 415–16 (1979).

308. Cf. *Dun & Bradstreet*, 472 U.S. at 762 (plurality opinion).

309. 315 U.S. 568, 572 (1942) (quoting Cantwell v. Connecticut, 310 U.S. 296, 309–10 [1940]).

310. *Dun & Bradstreet*, 472 U.S. at 761 (plurality opinion) (quoting Connick v. Myers, 461 U.S. 138, 147–48 [1983]).

311. See Florida Star v. B.J.F., 491 U.S. 527, 533 (1989); id. at 550–52 (White, J., dissenting); Frisby v. Schultz, 487 U.S. 474, 484–85 (1988); *Dun & Bradstreet*, 472 U.S. at 757–61 (plurality opinion).

312. See Beauharnais v. Illinois, 343 U.S. 250, 263 (1952).

313. See, e.g., Miller v. California, 413 U.S. 15 (1973) (authorizing the trier of fact in obscenity cases to apply "contemporary community standards").

314. Hanna Pitkin, "The Idea of a Constitution," 37 *Journal of Legal Education* 167, 168 (1987).

315. Id. at 169.

316. *Restatement (Second) of Torts* §652D comment h (1977); see Virgil v. Time, Inc., 527 F.2d 1122, 1129 (9th Cir. 1975), cert. denied, 425 U.S. 998 (1976).

317. Erving Goffman, *Relations in Public* 40 (1971).

318. Phillip Selznick, "The Idea of a Communitarian Morality," 75 *California Law Review* 445, 460 (1987).

319. See Georg Simmel, *The Sociology of Georg Simmel* 324 (Kurt H. Wolff, trans., 1950).

320. Similarly, it is through the exercise of such tact that the Court has elaborated the " 'common sense' distinction" between commercial speech and public discourse. See Zauderer v. Office of Disciplinary Counsel, 471 U.S. 626, 637 (1985) (citing Ohralik v. Ohio State Bar Ass'n, 436 U.S. 447, 455–56 [1978]).

321. 478 U.S. 675, 683, 681 (1986) (quoting Charles Austin Beard and Mary Beard, *New Basic History of the United States* 228 [1968]).

322. 438 U.S. 726, 731–32 (1978) (quoting In re *Pacifica Found. Station*, 56 F.C.C.2d 94, 98 [1975]).

323. Id. at 749 (quoting Ginsberg v. New York, 390 U.S. 629, 640, 639, [1968]); see Sable Communications, Inc. v. FCC, 492 U.S. 115, 126–28 (1989).

324. For a discussion of such processes, see Spence E. Cahill, "Children and Civility: Ceremonial Deviance and the Acquisition of Ritual Competence," 50 *Sociological Psychology Quarterly* 312 (1987).

325. It is therefore no accident that the Court has been led to identify "classes of speech" that "are no essential part of any exposition of ideas," the toleration of which "is clearly outweighed by the social interest in order and morality." Chaplinsky v. New Hampshire, 315 U.S. 568, 571–72 (1942).

326. In the words of the French political scientist Claude Lefort, "public space" in a democracy "is always indeterminate." Claude Lefort, *Democracy and Political Theory* 41 (David Macey, trans., 1988).

327. Herman Melville, "The Conflict of Convictions," in *Battle Pieces and Aspects of the War* 14, 17 (1960) (facsimile of 1866 ed.).

328. William M. Sullivan, *Reconstructing Public Philosophy* 159, 170, 161 (1982). John Dewey, for example, viewed the public as but a prelude to the emergence of "The Great Community." See Dewey, *The Public*, at 211.

5. Between Democracy and Community

1. Ronald Dworkin, *Law's Empire* 49–65 (1986).

2. I do not discuss legal treatment of the converse question, whether the maintenance of a healthy and viable community necessarily entails the maintenance of democracy. In our constitutional tradition, democracy has always functioned as an essential first premise.

3. Robert A. Nisbet, *The Sociological Tradition* 47 (1966).

4. Thomas Bender, *Community and Social Change in America* 5 (1978).

5. See Ferdinand Tönnies, *Community and Society* (Charles P. Loomis, trans., 1963).

6. See Bender, *Community*, at 21–23. See Talcott Parsons, *The Social System* 58–77 (1951).

7. Bender, *Community*, at 45–53.

8. Id. at 43.

9. Michael J. Sandel, *Liberalism and the Limits of Justice* 150 (1982).

10. George Herbert Mead, *Mind, Self, and Society* 162 (Charles W. Morris, ed., 1962). See also Sandel, *Liberalism*, at 152–64.

11. Erving Goffman, *Interaction Ritual: Essays on Face-To-Face Behavior* 47, 84–85 (1967).

12. Joseph Gusfield, *Community: A Critical Response* 29 (1975).

13. Kai Erikson, *Wayward Puritans: A Study in the Sociology of Deviance* 11 (1966).

14. Richard Rorty, *Contingency, Irony, and Solidarity* 59 (1989).

15. *Pascal's Pensées* 72 (Martin Turnell, trans., 1962).

16. Charles Taylor, *Sources of the Self: The Making of Modern Identity* 15 (1989).

17. Erving Goffman, *Asylums: Essays on the Social Situation of Mental Patients and Other Inmates* (1961).

18. See, for example, Ronald Dworkin's parable of the interpretation of the norms of courtesy. Dworkin, *Law's Empire*, at 46–49.

19. See Robert Post, "The Social Foundations of Defamation Law: Reputation and the Constitution," 74 *California Law Review* 691 (1986).

20. *Restatement (Second) of Torts* §46 comment d (1977).

21. Frank Michelman, "Law's Republic," 97 *Yale Law Journal* 1500–1501 (1988). Michelman notes that "no earnest, non-disruptive participant in American constitutional debate is quite free to reject [this] belief." Id. at 1500.

22. Robert Alan Dahl, *A Preface to Democratic Theory* 67 (1956).

23. Frederick Schauer, *Free Speech: A Philosophical Enquiry* 40 (1982). Schauer writes: "The more we accept the premise of the argument from democracy, the less can we impinge on the right of self-government by restricting the power of the majority. If the argument from democracy would allow to be said things that the 'people' do not want to hear, it is not so much an argument based on popular will as it is an argument against it." Id. at 41.

24. See, e.g., Cass Sunstein, "Naked Preferences and the Constitution," 84 *Columbia Law Review* 1689 (1984).

25. Norberto Bobbio, *Democracy and Dictatorship* 137 (Peter Kennealy, trans., 1989).

26. For an earnest if unsuccessful effort to meet this problem, see Carol C. Gould, *Rethinking Democracy: Freedom and Social Cooperation in Politics, Economy, and Society* 236–38 (1988).

27. Hans Kelsen, *General Theory of Law and State* 284–86 (Anders Wedberg, trans., 1961). What makes Kelsen's perspective distinctively modern, of course, is its shift from substance to process. Rousseau had presupposed a substantive correspondence between the content of the general will and the content of the will of individuals. In contrast, Kelsen postulates only an identification of individual wills with the process by which the general will is formed.

28. Id. at 287–88.

29. Benjamin R. Barber, *Strong Democracy: Participatory Politics for a New Age* 136 (1984). See Hanna Fenichel Pitkin and Sara M. Shumer, "On Participation," *Democracy* 43–54 (Fall 1982).

30. *Dialogue on John Dewey* 58 (Corliss Lamont, ed., 1959).

31. Emile Durkheim, *Professional Ethics and Civic Morals* 89 (Cornelia Brookfield, trans., 1958).

32. Claude Lefort, *Democracy and Political Theory* 39 (David Macey, trans., 1988).

33. Jürgen Habermas, *The Theory of Communicative Action* 81 (Thomas McCarthy, trans., 1987).

34. John Rawls, "Justice as Fairness: Political Not Metaphysical," 14 *Philosophy and Public Affairs* 230 (1985).

35. Michelman, "Law's Republic," at 1527.

36. See Rawls, "Justice as Fairness," at 229–30; Michelman, "Law's Republic," at 1526–27; Jürgen Habermas, *The Theory of Communicative Action* 25–26 (Thomas McCarthy, trans., 1984).

37. See J. N. Findlay, *Kant and the Transcendental Object: A Hermeneutic Study* 241 (1981).

38. Hustler Magazine v. Falwell, 485 U.S. 46, 55 (1988).

39. See Barber, *Strong Democracy*, at 136–37.

40. Owen Fiss, "Foreword: The Forms of Justice," 93 *Harvard Law Review* 38 (1979).

41. I do not mean to foreclose the possibility that under special conditions of charismatic leadership or identification with traditional authority, the value of self-determination can be achieved in the absence of a communicative structure of public discourse. I mean only to imply that such conditions will not ordinarily obtain in the modern rational and bureaucratic state.

42. For practical purposes, the effective use of First Amendment doctrine to protect free speech dates back only to the case of Stromberg v. California, 283 U.S. 359 (1931).

43. Brown v. Hartlage, 456 U.S. 45, 60 (1982). See Buckley v. Valeo, 424 U.S. 1, 93 n.127 (1976); Richmond Newspapers, Inc. v. Virginia, 448 U.S. 555, 587–88 (1980) (Brennan, J., concurring); Saxbe v. Washington Post Co., 417 U.S. 843, 862–63 (1974) (Powell, J., dissenting).

44. Schneider v. State, 308 U.S. 147, 161 (1939). See Virginia Pharmacy Bd. v. Virginia Consumer Council, 425 U.S. 748, 765 n.19 (1976); Thomas v. Collins, 323 U.S. 516, 530 (1945).

45. Stromberg v. California, 283 U.S. 359, 369 (1931). The principle of self-determination manifestly underlies the crucial repudiation of seditious libel in New York Times Co. v. Sullivan, 376 U.S. 254 (1964). The decision turned on Madison's differentiation of American and English forms of government: in England "the Crown was sovereign and the people were subjects," whereas in America the "people, not the government, possess absolute sovereignty." Id. at 274. Thus in America "the censorial power is in the people over the Government, and not in the Government over the people." Id. at 275.

46. Rawls, "Justice as Fairness," at 230. For a general account of the value of "autonomy" as "a constitutive normative ingredient of American democratic constitutionalism," see D. A. J. Richards, "Autonomy in Law," in *The Inner Citadel: Essays on Individual Autonomy* 246–58 (John Christman, ed., 1989).

47. Jean Piaget, *The Moral Judgment of the Child* 366 (Marjorie Gabain, trans., 1948).

48. For salient examples of the influence of individualism in constitutional law, see, e.g., City of Richmond v. J.A. Croson Co., 488 U.S. 469 (1989); Zablocki v. Redhail, 434 U.S. 374 (1978); Weber v. Aetna Casualty and Surety Co., 406 U.S. 164 (1972); Reynolds v. Sims, 377 U.S. 533 (1964).

49. See, e.g., Robert Post, "Defaming Public Officials: On Doctrine and Legal History," 1987 *American Bar Foundation Research Journal* 539, 552–54; Dominguez v. Stone, 97 N.M. 211, 638 P.2d 423 (1981).

50. Boos v. Barry, 485 U.S. 312, 322 (1988).

51. 310 U.S. 296, 310 (1940).

52. See, e.g., New York Times Co. v. Sullivan, 376 U.S. 254 (1964); Philadelphia Newspapers, Inc. v. Hepps, 475 U.S. 767 (1986); The Florida Star v. B.J.F., 491 U.S. 524 (1989); Cox Broadcasting Corp. v. Cohn, 420 U.S. 469 (1975); Hustler Magazine v. Falwell, 485 U.S. 46 (1988). For a classic statement of the First Amendment position, see Cohen v. California, 403 U.S. 15 (1971).

53. Grand Rapids School Dist. v. Ball, 473 U.S. 373, 385 (1985). See Lyng v. Automobile Workers, 485 U.S. 360, 369 (1988); Wallace v. Jaffree, 472 U.S. 38, 50–53 (1985); Abood v. Detroit Bd. of Educ., 431 U.S. 209, 235 (1977); Cantwell v. Connecticut, 310 U.S. 296, 303 (1940).

54. Girouard v. United States, 328 U.S. 61, 68 (1946). For a general discussion, see D. A. J. Richards, *Toleration and the Constitution* 67–164 (1986).

55. Roberts v. United States Jaycees, 468 U.S. 609, 619 (1984). An early and influential decision recognizing the right is Meyer v. Nebraska, 262 U.S. 390 (1923), in which the Court struck down a Nebraska statute that prohibited the teaching of foreign languages to young students. Justice McReynolds wrote: "In order to submerge the individual and develop ideal citizens, Sparta assembled the males at seven into barracks and intrusted their subsequent education and training to official guardians. Although such measures have been deliberately approved by men of great genius, their ideas touching the relation between individual and state were wholly different from those upon which our institutions rest; and it hardly will be affirmed that any legislature could impose such restrictions upon the people of a state without doing violence to both letter and spirit of the Constitution." Id. at 402.

56. See, e.g., Cass Sunstein, "Legal Interference with Private Preferences," 53 *University of Chicago Law Review* 1138–39 (1986).

57. Quite apart from the ultimate merits of Roe v. Wade, this line of analysis has rather significant implications for John Ely's influential criticism of the right to privacy in Roe as wholly lacking in "connection with any value the Constitution marks as special." John Hart Ely, "The Wages of Crying Wolf: A Comment on Roe v. Wade," 82 *Yale Law Journal* 949 (1973).

58. Mead, *Mind, Self, and Society*, at 162.

59. Habermas, *Theory of Communicative Action*, at 38.

60. For a theoretical statement of this position, see Charles Taylor, *Philosophy and the Human Sciences: Philosophical Papers* 205–9 (1985).

61. Joseph Raz, "Liberalism, Skepticism, and Democracy," 74 *Iowa Law Review* 779–84 (1989).

62. David Hume, *A Treatise of Human Nature* 534–53 (2d ed., L. A. Selby-Bigge, ed., 1978). Even if the ratification of the Constitution could be convincingly analogized to an explicit act of collective consent, it still would not follow that we, who are two centuries removed from the ratifiers, have also consented.

63. To the extent that America is a culturally heterogeneous nation, a common commitment to the value of responsive democracy must derive from something like the "idea of an overlapping consensus" that has been developed by John Rawls. John Rawls, "The Idea of an Overlapping Consensus," 7 *Oxford Journal of Legal Studies* 1 (1987). See Dahl, *Preface to Democratic Theory*, at 76–81. On the role of education in achieving that consensus, see Amy Gutmann, *Democratic Education* (1987).

64. For a stimulating analysis of the more general tension entailed by the dependence of the autonomous democratic citizen upon ongoing forms of disciplinary socialization, see Peter Fitzpatrick, " 'The Desperate Vacuum': Imperialism and Law in the Experience of Enlightenment," in *Post-Modern Law: Enlightenment, Revolution and the Death of Man* 90–106 (Anthony Carty, ed., 1990).

65. Moore v. East Cleveland, 431 U.S. 494, 503 (1977) (plurality opinion). See Bowers v. Hardwick, 478 U.S. 186, 192 (1986).

66. For a discussion of the differences between these two strands of substantive due process doctrine, see Robert Post, "Tradition, the Self, and Substantive Due Process: A Comment on Michael Sandel," 77 *California Law Review* 553 (1989).

67. Parham v. J.R., 442 U.S. 584, 603 (1979). Thus Pierce v. Society of Sisters, 268 U.S. 510, 535 (1925): "The fundamental theory of liberty upon which all governments in this Union repose excludes any general power of the state to standardize its children by forcing them to accept instruction from public teachers only. The child is not the mere creature of the state; those who nurture him and direct his destiny have the right, coupled with the high duty, to recognize and prepare him for additional obligations." See also, e.g., Hodgson v. Minnesota, 497 U.S. 417, 445–47 (1990) (opinion of Stevens, J.); Moore v. East Cleveland, 431 U.S. 494 (1977); Planned Parenthood of Central Missouri v. Danforth, 428 U.S. 52 (1976); Stanley v. Illinois, 405 U.S. 645 (1972); Griswold v. Connecticut, 381 U.S. 479 (1965); Poe v. Ullman, 367 U.S. 497, 551–52 (1961) (Harlan, J., dissenting).

68. Alexander Meiklejohn, *Political Freedom: The Constitutional Powers of the People* 14 (1948).

69. Ludwig Wittgenstein, *Culture and Value* 46e (Peter Winch, trans., 1980).

70. Alexander Bickel, *The Least Dangerous Branch: The Supreme Court at the Bar of Politics* 16–17 (1962).

71. See, e.g., United States v. Eichman, 496 U.S. 310 (1990); Texas v. Johnson, 491 U.S. 397 (1989).

72. See, e.g., Hustler Magazine v. Falwell, 485 U.S. 46 (1988).

73. Samuel P. Huntington, *American Politics: The Promise of Disharmony* 14 (1981).

74. See Robert Post, "Justice William J. Brennan and the Warren Court," 8 *Constitutional Commentary* 11–19 (1991).

75. Gutmann, *Democratic Education*, at 41–47.

76. Time, Inc. v. Hill, 385 U.S. 374, 412 (1967) (Fortas, J., dissenting). Alexander Bickel once remarked that deeply uncivil communication "amounts to almost physical aggression." Alexander Bickel, *The Morality of Consent* 72 (1975).

77. Bethel School Dist. No. 403 v. Fraser, 478 U.S. 675, 681 (1986) (quoting Charles Beard and Mary Beard, *New Basic History of the United States* 228 [1968]). See FCC v. Pacifica Found. 438 U.S. 726 (1978).

78. 315 U.S. 568, 572 (1942).

79. Hanna Pitkin, "Justice: On Relating Private and Public," 9 *Political Theory* 346 (1981).

80. Dun & Bradstreet, Inc. v. Greenmoss Builders, Inc., 472 U.S. 749, 761 (1985) (plurality opinion) (quoting Connick v. Myers, 461 U.S. 138, 147–48 [1983]).

81. Dun & Bradstreet, Inc. v. Greenmoss Builders, Inc., 472 U.S. 749, 761 (1985) (plurality opinion) (quoting Connick v. Myers, 461 U.S. 138, 147–48 [1983]).

82. Hustler Magazine v. Falwell, 485 U.S. 46 (1988).

83. See, e.g., Rogers v. EEOC, 454 F.2d 234, 237–38 (5th Cir. 1971); EEOC v. Murphy Motor Freight, 488 F. Supp. 381, 385 (D. Minn. 1980); Alcorn v. Anbro Engineering, Inc., 2 Cal. 3d 493, 468 P.2d 216, 86 Cal. Rptr. 88 (1970); Contreras v. Crown Zellerbach Corp., 88 Wash. 2d 735, 565 P.2d 1173 (1977); cf. Meritor Savings Bank v. Vinson, 477 U.S. 57, 65–66 (1986).

84. George Herbert Mead, *On Social Psychology* 230–40 (Anselm Strauss, ed., 1964).

6. Between Governance and Management

1. Minnesota State Bd. for Community Colleges v. Knight, 465 U.S. 271, 280 (1984). The increasing prominence of public forum doctrine is documented in Daniel A. Farber and John E. Nowak, "The Misleading Nature of Public Forum Analysis: Content and Context in First Amendment Adjudication," 70 *Virginia Law Review* 1219, 1221–22 (1984).

2. On the complex nature of contemporary public forum doctrine, see, e.g., Melville B. Nimmer, *Nimmer on Freedom of Speech: A Treatise on the Theory of the First Amendment* §4.09[D], at 4-70–4-73 (2d ed. 1984); Gary C. Leedes, "Pi-

geonholes in the Public Forum," 20 *University of Richmond Law Review* 499, 500–501 and n.13 (1986).

3. Perry Educ. Ass'n v. Perry Local Educators' Ass'n, 460 U.S. 37, 44 (1983).

4. Cornelius v. NAACP Legal Defense and Educ. Fund, 473 U.S. 788, 800 (1985).

5. Geoffrey R. Stone, "Content-Neutral Restrictions," 54 *University of Chicago Law Review* 46, 92–93 and n.182 (1987). In a world of disputatious academic criticism, the unrelenting and unanimous condemnation of contemporary public forum doctrine is truly remarkable. The critics' reasons for rejecting the doctrine are nearly always the same. Public forum doctrine is said to depend upon a "myopic focus on formalistic labels" that "serves only to distract attention from the real stakes" at issue in disputes over public use of government resources for communicative purposes. Id. at 93. The doctrine is said to exemplify the kinds of formalism that "produces incoherent results untouched by the interplay of considerations that should inform . . . decision-making under the first amendment." Keith Werhan, "The Supreme Court's Public Forum Doctrine and the Return of Formalism," 7 *Cardozo Law Review* 335, 341 (1986). The doctrine is condemned as "simply . . . an inadequate jurisprudence of labels," C. Thomas Dienes, "The Trashing of the Public Forum: Problems in First Amendment Analysis," 55 *George Washington Law Review* 109, 110 (1986), and indicted because it distracts "attention away from the first amendment values at stake in a given case." Farber and Nowak, "Misleading Nature," at 1224. It is attacked because it is without underlying "coherent principles," Note, "Public Forum Analysis After *Perry Educ. Ass'n v. Perry Local Educators' Ass'n*—A Conceptual Approach to Claims of First Amendment Access to Publicly Owned Property," 54 *Fordham Law Review* 545, 548 (1986), and imposes a "categorization" that fails "to reflect accurately the conflicting interests affected by restrictions on expression." Note, "A Unitary Approach to Claims of First Amendment Access to Publicly Owned Property," 35 *Stanford Law Review* 121, 121–22 (1982). For a sampling of the negative commentary attracted over the years by the doctrine, see also Ronald A. Cass, "First Amendment Access to Government Facilities," 65 *Virginia Law Review* 1287, 1308–9, 1317–37 (1979); David Goldberger, "Judicial Scrutiny in Public Forum Cases: Misplaced Trust in the Judgment of Public Officials," 32 *Buffalo Law Review* 175, 183 (1983); Kenneth Karst, "Public Enterprise and the Public Forum: A Comment on *Southeastern Promotions, Ltd. v. Conrad*," 37 *Ohio State Law Journal* 247 (1976); Deborah A. Schmedemann, "Of Meetings and Mailboxes: The First Amendment and Exclusive Representation in Public Sector Labor Relations," 72 *Virginia Law Review* 91, 112–15 (1986).

6. See Nimmer, *Freedom of Speech*, §4.09[D], at 4-71.

7. See Hannah Arendt, *The Human Condition* 22–78 (1959); Ronald Beiner, *Political Judgment* 152 (1983).

8. United States v. Grace, 461 U.S. 171, 180 (1983).

9. 1965 *Supreme Court Review* 1; see, e.g., Nimmer, *Freedom of Speech*, §4.09[D], at 4-69 n.163; Kenneth Karst, "Equality as a Central Principle in the First Amendment," 43 *University of Chicago Law Review* 20, 35 (1975). The U.S. Supreme Court had occasionally used the phrase "public forum" prior to 1965, although not in the context of a recognizable First Amendment theory. See, e.g., International Ass'n of Machinists v. Street, 367 U.S. 740, 796 (1961) (Black, J., dissenting); id. at 806 (Frankfurter, J., dissenting). The Supreme Court of California, however, had used the phrase in a surprisingly contemporary sense as early as 1946. See Danskin v. San Diego Unified School Dist., 28 Cal. 2d 536, 545–48, 171 P.2d 885, 890–91 (1946).

10. 379 U.S. 536, 559 (1965).

11. Kalven, "Public Forum," at 3.

12. 376 U.S. 254 (1964). See Harry Kalven, "The *New York Times* Case: A Note on 'the Central Meaning of the First Amendment,'" 1964 *Supreme Court Review* 191.

13. Kalven, "Public Forum," at 3.

14. Id.

15. 308 U.S. 147, 162 (1939).

16. Kalven, "Public Forum," at 18.

17. 319 U.S. 141, 143 (1943).

18. See, e.g., Hague v. CIO, 307 U.S. 496 (1939); Kunz v. New York, 340 U.S. 290 (1951).

19. See, e.g., Schneider v. State, 308 U.S. 147, 163–65 (1939). During this period many of the Court's cases invalidating official discretion to regulate speech simply did not distinguish between speech that occurred in public places like streets, and speech that occurred in private places like homes. See, e.g., Largent v. Texas, 318 U.S. 418 (1943); Lovell v. City of Griffin, 303 U.S. 444 (1938).

20. See, e.g., Cantwell v. Connecticut, 310 U.S. 296, 309–10 (1940).

21. See, e.g., Terminiello v. Chicago, 337 U.S. 1 (1949).

22. 307 U.S. at 515–16.

23. United States Postal Serv. v. Council of Greenburgh Civic Ass'ns, 453 U.S. 114, 131 n.7 (1981); see Nimmer, *Freedom of Speech*, 2, §4.09[D], at 4-68. The passage has been frequently cited in recent public forum decisions. See, e.g., City Council of Los Angeles v. Taxpayers for Vincent, 466 U.S. 789, 813–14 (1984); Perry Educ. Ass'n v. Perry Local Educators' Ass'n 460 U.S. 37, 45 (1983); Carey v. Brown, 447 U.S. 455, 460 (1980); Greer v. Spock, 424 U.S. 828, 835–36 (1976).

24. See Schneider v. State, 308 U.S. 147, 163–65 (1939).

25. Geoffrey R. Stone, "Fora Americana: Speech in Public Places," 1974 *Supreme Court Review* 233, 238.

26. 167 U.S. 43 (1897). At issue in *Davis* was a municipal ordinance providing

that "no person shall, in or upon any of the public grounds, make any public address . . . except in accordance with a permit from the mayor." Id. at 44.

27. Id. at 46–47.

28. Id. at 48.

29. 307 U.S. 496, 514 (1939). The statute at issue in *Hague* was similar to that in *Davis*. It prohibited "public parades or public assembly in or upon the public streets, highways, public parks or public buildings of Jersey City" without a permit from "the Director of Public Safety." Id. at 502 n.1.

30. 318 U.S. 413, 416 (1943).

31. Police Dept. of Chicago v. Mosley, 408 U.S. 92, 96, 99 and n.6 (1972).

32. 385 U.S. 39, 47–48 (1966) (footnote omitted). The passage has exerted great influence on the development of modern public forum doctrine. See, e.g., Cornelius v. NAACP Legal Defense and Educ. Fund, 473 U.S. 788, 799–801 (1985); City Council of Los Angeles v. Taxpayers for Vincent, 466 U.S. 789, 814 n.31 (1984); Perry Educ. Ass'n v. Perry Local Educators' Ass'n, 460 U.S. 37, 46 (1983); United States v. Grace, 461 U.S. 171, 177–78 (1983); Heffron v. Int'l Soc'y for Krishna Consciousness, 452 U.S. 640, 647 n.10 (1981); United States Postal Serv. v. Council of Greenburgh Civic Ass'n, 453 U.S. 114, 129–30 (1981); Greer v. Spock, 424 U.S. 828, 836 (1976).

33. The statute at issue stated: "Every trespass upon the property of another, committed with a malicious and mischievous intent, the punishment of which is not specially provided for, shall be punished by imprisonment not exceeding three months, or by fine not exceeding one hundred dollars." 385 U.S. at 40 n.1. Since the curtilage of the jailhouse was not marked with NO TRESPASSING signs, and since the public was not generally excluded from the grounds, id. at 52 (Douglas, J., dissenting), the students' demonstration only became an illegal "trespass" upon the disapproval of the sheriff.

34. Neither the statute in *Adderley* nor the ordinance in *Hague* contained guidelines for determining when demonstrations should be permitted. If it is argued that the discretion of the sheriff in *Adderley* was implicitly constrained by his concern for the orderly operation of the jail, it could with equal plausibility be argued that the director's discretion in *Hague* was implicitly constrained by a similar concern to preserve the orderly flow of traffic in the streets.

35. In his 1965 article on the public forum, Kalven had attacked Justice Goldberg's opinion in Cox v. Louisiana, 379 U.S. 536, 555 (1965), for distinguishing between "pure speech" and speech mixed with "conduct such as patrolling, marching, and picketing." Kalven, "Public Forum," at 22. Kalven's point was that all speech necessarily involves physical action, whether it is noise, litter, or gestures, and that the mere presence of such action cannot therefore be by itself the ground for diminishing the First Amendment protection that the speech would otherwise merit. Id. at 23. Kalven's point is sound, but even if it is accepted it does not follow, as the Court recognized in 1968, that there is no constitutional

difference between a statute addressed directly to expression or to a recognized medium of expression, and a statute addressed to conduct that indirectly impacts on particular acts of expression. See United States v. O'Brien, 391 U.S. 367, reh'g denied, 393 U.S. 900 (1968). In recent years the Court seems to have lost its grip on this important distinction. See, e.g., Clark v. Community for Creative Non-violence, 468 U.S. 288, 298 (1984).

36. Distinct constitutional problems may arise, however, if a neutral statute addressed to conduct is enacted or enforced for reasons that are prohibited by the First Amendment. See, e.g., Tinker v. Des Moines Indep. Community School Dist., 393 U.S. 503, 526 (1969) (Harlan, J., dissenting); Lawrence Tribe, *American Constitutional Law* 598 (1978); Stone, "Content-Neutral Restrictions," at 55–56; Geoffrey Stone, "Content Regulation and the First Amendment," 25 *William and Mary Law Review* 189, 227 (1983). Although it is arguable that in *Adderley* the sheriff transformed the demonstration into an illegal trespass primarily in order to silence the protesting students, Justice Black did not address the important issues arising from this interpretation of the facts. He noted simply that there was "not a shred of evidence in this record" that the sheriff had evicted the demonstrators because he "objected to what was being sung or said by the demonstrators or because he disagreed with the objectives of their protest." 385 U.S. at 47.

37. If *Adderley* is narrowly interpreted in this manner, its true descendants in the area of public forum doctrine are decisions like United States v. Albertini, 472 U.S. 675 (1985), which deal with the applicability of general and neutral statutes addressed to conduct. Most public forum cases, however, concern regulations directly applicable to speech or to recognized media of communication. See, e.g., Cornelius v. NAACP Legal Defense and Educ. Fund, 473 U.S. 788 (1985); City Council of Los Angeles v. Taxpayers for Vincent, 466 U.S. 789 (1984); United States v. Grace, 461 U.S. 171 (1983); Perry Educ. Ass'n v. Perry Local Educators' Ass'n, 460 U.S. 37 (1983); Heffron v. Int'l Soc'y for Krishna Consciousness, 452 U.S. 640, 647 n.10 (1981); United States Postal Serv. v. Council of Greenburgh Civic Ass'ns, 453 U.S. 114 (1981); Widmar v. Vincent, 454 U.S. 263 (1981); Jones v. North Carolina Prisoners' Labor Union, 433 U.S. 119 (1977); Greer v. Spock, 424 U.S. 828 (1976). Many of these cases cite and rely upon *Adderley*.

38. 372 U.S. 229 (1963).

39. 385 U.S. at 41–42.

40. Justice Black did stress that the sheriff's enforcement of the trespass statute was "even-handed," and that the students' eviction from the jail was not because "the sheriff objected to what was being sung or said." 385 U.S. at 47. This focus implied that Black was perhaps prepared in appropriate circumstances to modify the *Davis* syllogism by forbidding viewpoint discrimination even in situations where the government was exercising proprietary control.

41. See, e.g., Sherbert v. Verner, 374 U.S. 398 (1963); Hans A. Linde, "Con-

stitutional Rights in the Public Sector: Justice Douglas on Liberty in the Welfare State," 40 *Washington Law Review* 10 (1965); Robert M. O'Neil, "Unconstitutional Conditions: Welfare Benefits with Strings Attached," 54 *California Law Review* 443 (1966); William W. Van Alstyne, "The Demise of the Right–Privilege Distinction in Constitutional Law," 81 *Harvard Law Review* 1439 (1968).

42. 408 U.S. 104, 107–8, 115 (1972).

43. Id. at 115, 116–17. The Court reinterpreted *Adderley* to stand for the proposition that "demonstrators could be barred from jailhouse grounds not ordinarily open to the public, at least where the demonstration obstructed the jail driveway and interfered with the functioning of the jail." Id. at 121 n.49. In fact *Adderley* had contained no showing that the student demonstration had actually "interfered" with the functioning of the jail.

44. Id. at 116 n.34.

45. 408 U.S. 92 (1972). For the references to Kalven see id. at 95 n.3, 99 n.6.

46. Id. at 93, 95, 96. The Court used the phrase "public forum" a second time. Id. at 99.

47. See Perry Educ. Ass'n v. Perry Local Educators' Ass'n, 460 U.S. 37, 49 n.9 (1983).

48. 408 U.S. at 99.

49. *Mosley*, 408 U.S. at 96.

50. Id.

51. Hence the irony of Geoffrey Stone's enthusiastic appraisal that in *Grayned* "the right to a public forum came of age." Stone, "Fora Americana," at 251; see Stone, "Content-Neutral Restrictions," at 89 n.171.

52. 418 U.S. 298, 301 (1974). Justice Blackmun's opinion was joined by Chief Justice Burger and Justices White and Rehnquist.

53. Id. at 302–4.

54. Blackmun slightly modified the *Davis* syllogism by imposing on proprietary control the weak constraint that it not be "arbitrary, capricious, or invidious." Id. at 303.

55. Id.

56. Id. at 307 (Douglas, J., concurring).

57. Joining Justice Brennan were Justices Stewart, Marshall, and Powell.

58. 418 U.S. at 312 (Brennan, J., dissenting). Hence, "the Court must assess the importance of the primary use to which the public property or facility is committed and the extent to which that use will be disrupted if access for free expression is permitted." Id.

59. Id. at 313–15 (Brennan, J., dissenting). Brennan continued: "To insure that subject matter or content is not the sole basis for discrimination among forum users, all selective exclusions from a public forum must be closely scrutinized and countenanced only in cases where the government makes a clear showing that its action was taken pursuant to neutral 'time, place and manner'

regulations, narrowly tailored to protect the government's substantial interest in preserving the viability and utility of the forum itself." Id. at 316–17.

60. Id. at 312–13.

61. Id. at 314.

62. Many of the ideas in Brennan's dissent had first been expressed the previous year, in somewhat more inchoate form, in his dissent in Columbia Broadcasting Sys. v. Democratic Nat'l Comm., 412 U.S. 94, 192–201 (1972) (Brennan, J., dissenting).

63. 418 U.S. at 315–16 (Brennan, J., dissenting).

64. See, e.g., Consolidated Edison Co. v. Public Serv. Comm., 447 U.S. 530, 537–40 (1980); Erznoznik v. City of Jacksonville, 422 U.S. 205, 209–12 (1975). In fact, in *Adderley* the Court had strongly hinted that viewpoint discrimination would be forbidden even in a nonpublic forum.

65. United States v. Grace, 461 U.S. 171, 180 (1983).

66. 420 U.S. 546 (1975).

67. 380 U.S. 51 (1965).

68. 420 U.S. at 553–59. In *Conrad*, the directors of the Chattanooga Memorial Auditorium had refused an application to present the musical *Hair* on the grounds that it "would not be 'in the best interest of the community.' " Id. at 548. The Court held that the Constitution required that discretionary decisions to lease municipal auditoriums be subject to the following procedural requirements: "First, the burden of instituting judicial proceedings, and of proving that the material is unprotected, must rest on the censor. Second, any restraint prior to judicial review can be imposed only for a specified brief period and only for the purpose of preserving the status quo. Third, a prompt final judicial determination must be assured." Id. at 560.

69. Id. at 555. Blackmun distinguished *Lehman* on the uncertain grounds that in *Conrad* there was no "captive audience" analogous to the commuters on the rapid transit system. Id. at 556.

70. Id. at 572–73 (Rehnquist, J., dissenting).

71. Karst, "Public Enterprise," at 252.

72. Erznoznik v. City of Jacksonville, 422 U.S. 205, 209 n.5 (1975) (emphasis added).

73. 424 U.S. 828, 830, 851 (1976) (Brennan, J., dissenting). The main entrances to the reservation were not normally guarded, and at least one entrance contained the sign VISITORS WELCOME. Id. at 830.

74. Id. at 851 (Brennan, J., dissenting).

75. Id. at 831. Approval could be withheld only if it appeared "that the dissemination of [the] publication presents a clear danger to the loyalty, discipline, or morale of troops at [the] installation . . ." Army Reg. 210-10, Par. 5-5(c) (1970), cited in 424 U.S. at 431 n.2.

76. 424 U.S. at 833 n.3. The commanding officer also cited the danger of

giving "the appearance that you or your campaign is supported by me in my official capacity." Id.

77. Id. at 835–38. In 1965, in Cox v. Louisiana, 379 U.S. 536, 555, the Court had reserved judgment on this question. Three years later, in Amalgamated Food Employees Union Local 590 v. Logan Valley Plaza, Inc., 391 U.S. 308 (1968), the Court addressed the question in dicta: "Streets, sidewalks, parks and other similar public places are so historically associated with the exercise of First Amendment rights that access to them for the purpose of exercising such rights cannot constitutionally be denied broadly and absolutely." Id. at 315; see Lloyd Corp. v. Tanner, 407 U.S. 551, 559 (1972). The Court's statement in *Greer* was essentially a recapitulation of this dicta.

78. 424 U.S. at 838.

79. Id. at 838 n.10. The Court explained: "The decision of the military authorities that a civilian lecture on drug abuse, a religious service by a visiting preacher at the base chapel, or a rock musical concert would be supportive of the military mission of Fort Dix surely did not leave the authorities powerless thereafter to prevent any civilian from entering Fort Dix to speak on any subject whatever." Id.

80. Id. at 836.

81. Minnesota State Bd. for Community Colleges v. Knight, 465 U.S. 271, 280 (1984).

82. 424 U.S. at 838.

83. Id. at 837.

84. Id. at 836.

85. Id. at 831, 865–66.

86. Id. at 840, 838 n.10, 868 n.16 (Brennan, J., dissenting).

87. Id. at 843, 844 (Powell, J., concurring).

88. Id. at 859 (Brennan, J., dissenting). Brennan's dissent was joined by Justice Marshall.

89. Lehman v. City of Shaker Heights, 418 U.S. 298, 313 (1974) (Brennan, J., dissenting).

90. 424 U.S. at 859–60 (Brennan, J., dissenting).

91. 393 U.S. 503 (1969).

92. For an illuminating discussion of the distinction between issues of access and issues of discrimination, see Note, "The Public Forum: Minimum Access, Equal Access, and the First Amendment," 28 *Stanford Law Review* 117 (1975).

93. 424 U.S. at 840, 838 and n.10, 835.

94. See Erznoznik v. City of Jacksonville, 422 U.S. 205, 209–10 n.5 (1975).

95. 424 U.S. at 835.

96. 429 U.S. 167 (1976).

97. Id. at 176, 175 n.8. The Court also held that the board could confine its meetings "to specified subject matter." Id. at 175 n.8. It was not clear how this

could be reconciled with the Court's pronouncement that the board could not be required to discriminate between speakers on the basis of "the content of their speech." Id. at 176.

98. Id. at 175–76.

99. See, e.g., United States Postal Serv. v. Council of Greenburgh Civic Ass'ns, 453 U.S. 114, 130–33 and n.7 (1981).

100. 454 U.S. 263, 270 (1981). When measured by this stringent standard, the university's exclusion of the religious students was clearly unconstitutional.

101. Id. at 268 and n.5.

102. 460 U.S. 37, 45 (1983).

103. Id. at 46 (quoting United States Postal Serv. v. Council of Greenburgh Civic Ass'ns, 453 U.S. 114, 129–30 [1981]).

104. Id. at 49, 46.

105. 460 U.S. at 49–50 n.9. In 1981 the Court had reached a somewhat different conclusion, stating in United States Postal Serv. v. Council of Greenburgh Civic Ass'ns, 453 U.S. at 131 n.7, that government control of access to a nonpublic forum "must be content-neutral."

106. 460 U.S. at 59, 61 (Brennan, J., dissenting). The cogency of this distinction can be questioned. For example, it is not clear whether it is content or viewpoint discrimination if a citizen who wants to argue that a proper auditorium can only be financed through the imposition of a new and disagreeable property tax is ruled out of order by a school board which concludes that citizens can discuss the subject of building a new auditorium, but not the subject of property taxes. Justice Brennan's formulation, however, remains the best that is available. Cf. Paul B. Stephan, "The First Amendment and Content Discrimination," 68 *Virginia Law Review* 203, 218 (1982).

107. 460 U.S. at 47–48. The Court has also called this kind of public forum a "public forum by designation." Cornelius v. NAACP Legal Defense and Educ. Fund, 473 U.S. 788, 803 (1985); cf., Board of Airport Comm'rs v. Jews for Jesus, 482 U.S. 569, 572 (1987).

108. 460 U.S. at 45.

109. After *Greer* the Court continued to emphasize this point. See, e.g., United States Postal Serv. v. Council of Greenburgh Civic Ass'ns, 453 U.S. 114, 133 (1981) ("Congress . . . may not by its own ipse dixit destroy the 'public forum' status of streets and parks which have historically been public forums . . ."). One month after *Perry* the point would again be strongly emphasized. See United States v. Grace, 461 U.S. 171, 180 (1983) (quoting *Greenburgh*, 453 U.S. at 133).

110. "A State is not required to indefinitely retain the open character of the facility." 460 U.S. at 46.

111. Id.

112. Id. at 55.

113. Id. at 46 n.7 (citations omitted). This same internal contradiction is evident in the Court's other attempts to explicate the theory of the limited public forum. In Cornelius v. NAACP Legal Defense and Educ. Fund, 473 U.S. 788 (1985), for example, the Court says both that in a limited public forum "speakers cannot be excluded without a compelling governmental interest," id. at 800, and that a limited public forum "may be created by government designation of a place or channel of communication for use by the public at large for assembly and speech, for use by certain speakers, or for the discussion of certain subjects." Id. at 802.

114. 460 U.S. at 47, 48–50.

115. Greer v. Spock, 424 U.S. 828, 836 (1976).

116. Id. at 838 n.10. Even before *Greer*, the Court had held in Lehman v. City of Shaker Heights, 418 U.S. 298, 304 (1974), that the car cards of a municipal rapid transit system were not a public forum even though they had been opened up to commercial advertisements.

117. See, e.g., United States v. Grace, 461 U.S. 171, 177–78 (1983); United States Postal Serv. v. Council of Greenburgh Civic Ass'ns, 453 U.S. 114, 130 n.6 (1981); Jones v. North Carolina Prisoners Union, 433 U.S. 119, 134 (1977).

118. 460 U.S. at 47.

119. In fact, *Perry* evidenced some uncertainty as to whether the school's mail system was a nonpublic or a limited public forum. On this question it is said only that the school district had not "by policy or practice . . . opened its mail system for indiscriminate use by the general public." 460 U.S. at 47. The problem, of course, is that "indiscriminate use by the general public" is quite beside the point, since *Perry* conceded that a limited public forum could, like a nonpublic forum, be created on the basis of "selective access." Id.

120. 473 U.S. 788, 802 (1985). The opinion for the Court in *Cornelius* was written by Justice O'Connor and was joined by Chief Justice Burger and by Justices White and Rehnquist. Justices Brennan, Blackmun, and Stevens dissented. Justices Marshall and Powell did not participate in the case.

121. From this perspective, the limited public forum has simply become "a nontraditional forum" which the government has chosen to open "for public discourse." *Cornelius*, 473 U.S. at 802. The terms and conditions of that choice are for all practical purposes insulated from constitutional review.

122. Id. (quoting *Perry*, 460 U.S. at 45).

123. Id. at 803; see id. at 825–26 (Blackmun, J., dissenting).

124. *Perry*, 460 U.S. at 45.

125. Indeed, *Cornelius* does not even attempt to offer a property-oriented interpretation of public forum doctrine. Instead *Cornelius* states that "the Court has adopted a forum analysis as a means of determining when the Government's interest in limiting the use of its property to its intended purpose outweighs the interest of those wishing to use the property for other purposes." *Cornelius*, 473

U.S. at 800; see Board of Airport Comm'rs v. Jews for Jesus, 482 U.S. 569, 572 (1987). The problem, however, is that *Cornelius*' image of balancing renders incomprehensible its definition of a traditional public forum. If the Court were truly balancing, the existence of a tradition of public use could at most be probative of the interests to be weighed; the tradition could not possibly be always determinative of the outcome of that balancing, as it is under the Court's present definition of a traditional public forum.

126. This is well illustrated by United States Postal Serv. v. Council of Greenburgh Civic Ass'ns, 453 U.S. 114 (1981), in which the Court decided that a private citizen's mailbox was a nonpublic forum, even though it was not "owned" by the government.

127. For a recent example of the influence of *Greer*'s generic focus, see City Council of Los Angeles v. Taxpayers for Vincent, 466 U.S. 789, 814 (1984).

128. See generally Martin Krygier, "Law as Tradition," 5 *Law and Philosophy* 237, 251–54 (1986).

129. The Court has recognized this fact in other areas. For example, when the Court was attempting to determine if federal regulation impaired the ability of the states " 'to structure integral operations in areas of traditional governmental functions,' " it held that "what is 'traditional' " could not be determined by " 'looking only to the past,' since that would impose a static historical view." United Transp. Union v. Long Island R.R., 455 U.S. 678, 684, 686 (1982) (quoting Nat'l League of Cities v. Usery, 426 U.S. 833, 852 [1976]). The Court recognized, in other words, that for legal purposes a tradition must have meaning and that it cannot be reduced simply to the passage of time.

130. For a discussion of these examples, see Note, "Public Forum Analysis," at 556–58 (1986). The Court recently dodged the question of whether an airport was a public forum in Board of Airport Comm'rs v. Jews for Jesus, 482 U.S. 569 (1987). [After the publication of this essay, the Court finally answered this question in the negative. See International Society for Krishna Consciousness, Inc. v. Lee, 112 S. Ct. 2701 (1992)].

131. Garcia v. San Antonio Metro. Transit Auth., 469 U.S. 528, 544 (1985).

132. United States v. Grace, 461 U.S. 171, 180 (1983); see City Council of Los Angeles v. Taxpayers for Vincent, 466 U.S. 789, 813 (1984).

133. United States v. Grace, 461 U.S. at 177 (citations omitted).

134. City of Renton v. Playtime Theaters, Inc., 475 U.S. 41, 46 (1986); Pacific Gas and Electric Co. v. Public Utilities Comm. 475 U.S. 1, 20 (1986); Schad v. Borough of Mount Ephraim, 452 U.S. 61, 74–76 (1981). The Court selfconsciously generalized time, place, and manner analysis from the early public forum decisions. Buckley v. Valeo, 424 U.S. 1, 17–18 (1976).

135. Consolidated Edison Co. v. Public Serv. Comm'r, 447 U.S. 530, 540 (1980).

136. See, e.g., Board of Airport Comm'rs v. Jews for Jesus, 482 U.S. 569, 573 (1987); Cornelius v. NAACP Legal Defense and Educ. Fund, 473 U.S. 788, 800 (1985); Perry Educ. Ass'n v. Perry Local Educators' Ass'n, 460 U.S. 37, 45 (1983); Greer v. Spock, 424 U.S. 828, 835 (1976).

137. United States v. Grace, 461 U.S. 171, 180 (1983).

138. *Cornelius*, 473 U.S. at 806; see Perry Educ. Ass'n v. Perry Local Educators' Ass'n, 460 U.S. at 49.

139. 473 U.S. at 806.

140. Id. at 821 (Blackmun, J., dissenting).

141. See Dandridge v. Williams, 397 U.S. 471, 485–86 (1970); Williamson v. Lee Optical Co., 348 U.S. 483, 488 (1955).

142. The case against the major premise of the *Davis* syllogism is succinctly set forth in Seth F. Kreimer, "Allocational Sanctions: The Problem of Negative Rights in a Positive State," 132 *University of Pennsylvania Law Review* 1293, 1315–24 (1984).

143. William W. Van Alstyne, "The Constitutional Rights of Public Employees: A Comment on the Inappropriate Uses of an Old Analogy," 16 *UCLA Law Review* 751, 754 (1969) (footnote omitted).

144. See, e.g., Mississippi Univ. for Women v. Hogan, 458 U.S. 718 (1982); Sugarman v. Dougall, 413 U.S. 634 (1973); Turner v. City of Memphis, 369 U.S. 350 (1962).

145. Cleveland Bd. of Educ. v. Loudermill, 470 U.S. 532 (1985); Perry v. Sindermann, 408 U.S. 593 (1972).

146. South-Central Timber Dev., Inc. v. Wunnicke, 467 U.S. 82 (1984).

147. United Bldg. and Constr. Trades Council v. Camden, 465 U.S. 208 (1984).

148. See Branti v. Finkel, 445 U.S. 507 (1980); Perry v. Sindermann, 408 U.S. at 597–98; Pickering v. Board of Educ., 391 U.S. 563, 568 (1968).

149. Board of Educ. v. Pico, 457 U.S. 853, 920 (1982) (Rehnquist, J., dissenting); see Rankin v. McPherson, 483 U.S. 378, 395 (1987) (Scalia, J., dissenting); Buckley v. Valeo, 424 U.S. 1, 290–91 (1976) (Rehnquist, J., concurring in part, dissenting in part); William H. Rehnquist, "The First Amendment: Freedom, Philosophy, and the Law," 12 *Gonzales Law Review* 1, 10–12 (1976).

150. See Van Alstyne, "Constitutional Rights," at 769–71; Michael Wells and Walter Hellerstein, "The Governmental–Proprietary Distinction in Constitutional Law," 66 *Virginia Law Review* 1073, 1116 (1980).

151. "The reasonableness standard of judicial review used in [nonpublic forum] cases is essentially no review at all." Dienes, "Trashing of the Public Forum," at 117.

152. Board of Airport Comm'rs v. Jews for Jesus, 482 U.S. 569, 575 (1987). [Since the publication of this essay, the Court has somewhat softened this position, although primarily under the rubric of preventing viewpoint discrimination.

See Lamb's Chapel v. Center Moriches Union Free School Dist., 113 S. Ct. 2141 (1993)].

153. Nimmer, *Freedom of Speech*, §4.09[D], at 4-70, 4-72.

154. By far the great majority of commentators have advocated that some variant of the *Grayned* approach be adopted. See Nimmer, *Freedom of Speech*, §4.09[D], at 4-73–4-74; Tribe, *American Constitutional Law*, at 690–92; Cass, "First Amendment Access," at 1317–18; Karst, "Public Enterprise," at 261–62; Stone, "Content-Neutral Restrictions," at 93–94; Werhan, "Public Forum Doctrine," at 378–84, 423–24; Note, "The Public Forum," at 138; Note, "A Unitary Approach," at 143–51.

155. New York Times Co. v. Sullivan, 376 U.S. 254, 270 (1964).

156. The cases are discussed in Robert Post, "The Management of Speech: Discretion and Rights," 1984 *Supreme Court Review* 169, 196–201.

157. James G. March and Herbert A. Simon, *Organizations* 194 (1958). In an organization, "authority—that is, institutionalized control—is expected to extend downward through the various echelons of organization, enabling leadership to determine the consequences which ultimately flow from their decisions. While current theories of organization rarely assume this strict and rigid pattern to be fully maintained in practice, hierarchical structure is clearly seen as a standard against which deviations may be judged; the burden of proof seems to lie with exceptions to this rule." Robert B. Denhardt, *In the Shadow of Organization* 19–20 (1981); cf. Oliver E. Williamson, *The Economic Institutions of Capitalism* 206–39 (1985).

158. To bring a few illustrations to mind, consider, for example, how a school system controls the speech of students and teachers in a classroom, or how a judge manages the speech of lawyers, witnesses, parties and spectators in a courtroom, or how a military officer manipulates the speech of a new recruit ("Yes, what?" "Yes, *sir!*"). For an illustration of the "constant struggle to suppress . . . dissent" within government bureaucracies, see John Kenneth Galbraith, *The Anatomy of Power* 60 (1983).

159. Nebraska Press Ass'n v. Stuart, 427 U.S. 539, 559 (1976); see Organization for a Better Austin v. Keefe, 402 U.S. 415, 418–20 (1971); New York Times Co. v. United States, 403 U.S. 713 (1971) (per curiam).

160. City Council of Los Angeles v. Taxpayers for Vincent, 466 U.S. 789, 804 (1984).

161. Staub v. City of Baxley, 355 U.S. 313, 322 (1958); see City Council of Los Angeles v. Taxpayers for Vincent, 466 U.S. at 797–98 and n.15.

162. Johnson v. Zerbst, 304 U.S. 458, 464 (1938) (citing Aetna Ins. Co. v. Hannedy, 301 U.S. 389, 393 [1937] and Ohio Bell Tel. Co. v. Public Utilities Comm'n, 301 U.S. 292, 307 [1937]).

163. Peter M. Blau and W. Richard Scott, *Formal Organizations* 5 (1962). As Richard Elmore points out, viewing organizations as hierarchically arranged for

the achievement of explicit goals is only one of several models of organizational behavior. Richard Elmore, "Organizational Models of Social Program Implementation," 26 *Public Policy* 185 (1978). It is chiefly a "normative" model rather than a descriptive one, telling us "how organizations *ought* to function, not necessarily how they actually do." Id. at 198. It is a model that is necessary for First Amendment analysis, however, because the explicit and socially recognized goals attributed to a government organization provide the only constitutional justification for its suppression of speech. See generally Meir Dan-Cohen, *Rights, Persons, and Organizations* (1986).

164. Pell v. Procunier, 417 U.S. 817, 822 (1974).

165. Tinker v. Des Moines Indep. Community School Dist., 393 U.S. 503, 513 (1969). In Healy v. James, 408 U.S. 169 (1972), the Court held that a state university need not tolerate "associational activities . . . where they infringe reasonable campus rules, interrupt classes, or substantially interfere with the opportunity of other students to obtain an education." Id. at 189.

166. Brown v. Glines, 444 U.S. 348, 354 (1980).

167. See, e.g., Connick v. Myers, 461 U.S. 138, 142–44 (1983); Branti v. Finkel, 445 U.S. 507 (1980); Givhan v. Western Line Consol. School Dist., 439 U.S. 410 (1979); Mt. Healthy City School Dist. Bd. of Educ. v. Doyle, 429 U.S. 274 (1977); Perry v. Sindermann, 408 U.S. 593, 597–98 (1972); Pickering v. Board of Educ. 391 U.S. 563 (1968). The one recent exception, Snepp v. United States, 444 U.S. 507 (1980) (per curiam), is subject to criticism for precisely this reason.

168. Connick v. Myers, 461 U.S. at 142.

169. Seattle Times Co. v. Rhinehart, 467 U.S. 20 (1984). The judge's control over speech within a courtroom is of course extensive, and it extends indifferently to parties, witnesses, and spectators. The trial judge, as the Court recently emphasized, "has the responsibility to maintain decorum in keeping with the nature of the proceeding; 'the judge is not a mere moderator, but is the governor of the trial for the purpose of assuring its proper conduct.' " United States v. Young, 470 U.S. 1, 10 (1985) (quoting Quercia v. United States, 289 U.S. 466, 469 [1933]).

170. 444 U.S. 348, 353, 354 (1980).

171. Id. at 354, 357, 354 (quoting Parker v. Levy, 417 U.S. 733, 744 [1974]), 357.

172. Id at 357 n.15.

173. 393 U.S. 503, 508–14 (1969).

174. Immanuel Kant, "What is Enlightenment?" in *Foundations of the Metaphysics of Morals and What Is Enlightenment?* 85, 87 (L. Beck, trans., 1959).

175. On the distinction between management and governance, see Phillip Selznick, *Law, Society, and Industrial Justice* 75–120 (1969).

176. Cornelius v. NAACP Legal Defense and Educ. Fund, 473 U.S. 788, 806

(1985); see Perry Educ. Ass'n v. Perry Local Educators' Ass'n, 460 U.S. 37, 49 (1983).

177. *Perry*, 460 U.S. at 44.

178. 429 U.S. 167 (1976).

179. Consolidated Edison Co. v. Public Serv. Comm'n, 447 U.S. 530, 537–38 (1980).

180. 429 U.S. at 175 n.8.

181. Id. at 175. Indeed the Court went further and noted that "restraining teachers' expressions to the board on matters involving the operation of the schools would seriously impair the board's ability to govern the district." Id. at 177.

182. 454 U.S. 263, 267–68 n.5 (1981).

183. Id.; see Perry Educ. Ass'n v. Perry Local Educators' Ass'n, 460 U.S. 37, 46 n.7 (1983). ("A public forum may be created for a limited purpose such as use by certain groups, e.g., *Widmar v. Vincent* [student groups].")

184. Posadas de Puerto Rico Assocs. v. Tourism Co. of Puerto Rico, 478 U.S. 328, 360 (1986) (Stevens, J., dissenting).

185. 454 U.S. at 267–68 n.5 (quoting Healy v. James, 408 U.S. 169, 180 [1972]).

186. The Court had also refused to defer to the judgment of educational authorities in Healy v. James, 408 U.S. 169 (1972), which concerned the refusal of a state university to recognize Students for a Democratic Society as a campus organization. One can imagine a different outcome, however, if the First Amendment claims at issue in a case touch an educational institution in its more managerial aspects, as, for example, if students claim the right to choose the topics for discussion in the classroom. In such a situation the Court may well defer to the managerial discretion of the classroom teacher to control the speech of her students. It was no doubt important to the Court's decision in *Tinker* that the prohibition at issue had been promulgated not by a classroom teacher but rather by a systemwide meeting of the "principals of the Des Moines schools." Tinker v. Des Moines Indep. Community School Dist., 393 U.S. 503, 504 (1969).

187. 454 U.S. at 267–68 n.5.

188. Consider in this light the cases in which the Court has determined that the public has a First Amendment right of access to various judicial proceedings. See, e.g., Press-Enterprise Co. v. Superior Court, 478 U.S. 1 (1986); Press-Enterprise Co. v. Superior Court, 464 U.S. 501 (1984); Globe Newspaper Co., v. Superior Court, 457 U.S. 596 (1982); Richmond Newspapers, Inc. v. Virginia, 448 U.S. 555 (1980). These cases create strict rules for when a trial judge can exclude members of the public from various proceedings, and enforce these rules by independent appellate review. The implicit premise is that appellate review of such decisions will not impair a trial judge's managerial authority over her court-

room. In contrast, the Court has rejected as unduly impairing of managerial authority a constitutional requirement for independent appellate review of a trial judge's decisions respecting the issuance of pretrial restraining orders. See Seattle Times Co. v. Rhinehart, 467 U.S. 20 (1984).

189. Perry Educ. Ass'n v. Perry Local Educators' Ass'n, 460 U.S. 37, 44 (1983).

190. United States v. Grace, 461 U.S. 171, 180 (1983).

191. See Herbert A. Simon, *Administrative Behavior* 110–11 (1957).

192. See, e.g., Richard O. Carlson, "Environmental Constraints and Organizational Consequences: The Public School and Its Clients," in *Behavioral Science and Educational Administration: The Sixty-third Yearbook of the National Society for the Study of Education*, pt. II, 264–68 (Daniel E. Griffiths, ed., 1964).

193. Jeffrey Pfeffer and Gerald R. Salancik, *The External Control of Organizations: A Resource Dependence Perspective* 32 (1978).

194. W. Richard Scott, *Organizations: Rational, Natural, and Open Systems* 180 (1981); see John H. Freeman, "The Unit of Analysis in Organizational Research," in *Environments and Organizations* 336–38 (Marshall W. Meyer and Associates, eds., 1978).

195. Fremont E. Kast and James E. Rosenzweig, "General Systems Theory: Applications for Organization and Management," 15 *Academic Management Journal* 447, 450 (1972).

196. Howard Aldrich, "Organizational Boundaries and Inter-organizational Conflict," 24 *Human Relations* 279, 286 (1971); see Charles I. Barnard, *Organization and Management* (1948).

197. Pfeffer and Salancik, *External Control*, at 113; see James D. Thompson, *Organizations in Action* 39–44 (1967); cf. Oliver Williamson, *Markets and Hierarchies: Analysis and Antitrust Implications* (1975).

198. 453 U.S. 114 (1981). Mailboxes were defined as letterboxes "established, approved, or accepted by the Postal Service for the receipt or delivery of mail matter on any mail route." 18 U.S.C. §1725 (1982).

199. 453 U.S. at 129–30 (citations omitted).

200. Id. at 128–29, 126, 133.

201. See Denhardt, *In the Shadow*, at 38. Talcott Parsons, for example, has written that "the defining characteristic of an organization which distinguishes it from other types of social systems" is its *"primacy of orientation to the attainment of a specific goal."* Talcott Parsons, "Suggestions for a Sociological Approach to the Theory of Organizations—I," 1 *Administrative Science Quarterly* 63, 64 (1956). Or, as Charles Perrow has more simply written, "Organizations are established to do something; they perform work directed toward some end." Charles Perrow, *Organizational Analysis: A Sociological View* 133 (1970).

202. Herbert A. Simon, Donald W. Smithburg, and Victor A. Thompson, *Public Administration* 82 (1950).

203. Hanna Pitkin, "Justice: On Relating Private and Public," 9 *Political Theory* 327, 344 (1981).

204. Of course a court can and must ultimately determine for itself the nature of a government organization's legitimate institutional ends, or at least the nature of those ends constitutionally capable of justifying the regulation of speech.

205. *Greenburgh* is a muddy case because the Court plainly intimated in its footnotes that the statute at issue would survive challenge even if analyzed under such general First Amendment principles. United States Postal Serv. v. Council of Greenburgh Civic Ass'ns, 453 U.S. 114, 130 n.6, 131 n.7 (1981). Indeed, Justice Brennan concurred separately on precisely these grounds. Id. at 134 (Brennan, J., concurring). In the end, therefore, it made no difference to the Court's actual decision whether mailboxes were or were not conceptualized as a public forum. See Nimmer, *Freedom of Speech*, §4.09[D] at 4-74–4-75.

An example of the Court finding that the attainment of institutional ends should take priority over other uses of a resource, even though the resource is subject to the authority of governance rather than management, can be found in Regan v. Time, Inc., 468 U.S. 641 (1984), in which the Court upheld restrictions on the photographic reproduction of United States currency. The restrictions were designed "to avoid creating conditions which would 'facilitate counterfeiting.'" Id. at 644. Another more venerable example is Cox v. Louisiana, 379 U.S. 559 (1965), in which the Court upheld against facial attack a Louisiana statute prohibiting picketing or parading "in or near a building housing a court of the State of Louisiana" with the "intent of influencing any judge, juror, witness, or court officer, in the discharge of his duty." Id. at 560. The Court reasoned that because the statute was "precise" and "narrowly drawn," and that because "it is of the utmost importance that the administration of justice be absolutely fair and orderly," a "State may adopt safeguards necessary and appropriate to assure that the administration of justice at all stages is free from outside control and influence." Id. at 562.

206. Sigmund Diamond, "From Organization to Society: Virginia in the Seventeenth Century," 63 *American Journal of Sociology* 457, 459–72 (1958).

207. Id. at 468.

208. Diamond notes: "At one time in Virginia, the single relationship that existed between persons rested upon the positions they occupied in the Company's table of organization. As a result of the efforts made by the Company to get persons to accept that relationship, however, each person in Virginia had become the occupant of several statuses, for now there were rich and poor in Virginia, landowners and renters, masters and servants, old residents and newcomers, married and single, men and women; and the simultaneous possession of these statuses involved the holder in a network of relationships, some congruent and some incompatible, with his organizational relationship." Id. at 471.

209. Id. at 473, 474, 472.

210. Paradoxically, as Hannah Arendt writes, the "public realm, as the common world, gathers us together," and yet the "reality of the public realm relies on the simultaneous presence of innumerable perspectives and aspects in which the common world presents itself and for which no common measurement or denominator can ever be devised." Arendt, *Human Condition*, at 48, 52.

211. See Perrow, *Organizational Analysis*, at 51. Of course this effort can be only partially successful, since "the ideal organization does not exist. One major reason is that the people who perform organizational tasks must be sustained by factors outside the organization. The organization is not the total world of the individual; it is not a society. People must fulfill other social roles; besides, society has shaped them in ways which affect their ability to perform organizational tasks. A man has a marital status, ethnic identification, religious affiliations, a distinctive personality, friends, to name only a few. Today it is customary to call management's attention to the fact that they are dealing with whole persons, rather than with automatons, and that therefore they should be sensitive to human relations. It is less often acknowledged, however, that a great deal of organizational effort is exerted to *control* the effects of extra-organizational influences upon personnel. Daily, people come contaminated into the organization." Id. at 52.

212. See, e.g., Simon, Smithburg, and Thompson, *Public Administration*, at 79–82.

213. The very exceptions to this rule illustrate the basic point. Some federal parks, for example, are dedicated to the primary goal of wilderness preservation. If these parks are not in fact subject to competing demands and uses, they are not public forums, despite the Court's generalizations about "streets and parks." Perry Educ. Ass'n v. Perry Local Educators' Ass'n, 460 U.S. 37, 45 (1983). For this reason speech within such parks may be managed in ways necessary for the attainment of the goal of wilderness preservation, as for instance by prohibiting political demonstrations.

214. See, e.g., C. Edwin Baker, "Unreasoned Reasonableness: Mandatory Parade Permits and Time, Place, and Manner Regulations," 78 *Northwestern University Law Review* 937, 954–56 (1983). To the extent that public behavior with respect to any particular street is oriented toward a single, paramount goal, however, the street is not a public forum. California freeways, for example, are designed and used for the explicit objective of facilitating rapid vehicle traffic. The freeways are therefore not a public forum, and claims to use the freeways for expressive purposes—for demonstrations or for leafleting on their shoulders— should be evaluated in terms of their impact on the freeways' objective.

215. Of course a tradition of public use for expressive purposes can be highly probative of the conclusion that streets and parks are legitimately subject to a variety of competing uses.

216. It does not follow, of course, that the Court's judgment upholding the constitutionality of 18 U.S.C. §1725 is incorrect, since the statute could plausibly

be upheld even under ordinary principles of First Amendment jurisprudence.

217. 424 U.S. 828, 834 (1976).

218. Id. at 851 (Brennan, J., dissenting).

219. Flower v. United States, 407 U.S. 197, 198 (1972); see *Greer*, 424 U.S. at 850–51 (Brennan, J., dissenting).

220. 424 U.S. at 832.

221. 391 U.S. 563, 573 (1968). The Court held that "in a case such as the present one, in which the fact of employment is only tangentially and insubstantially involved in the subject matter of the public communication made by a teacher, we conclude that it is necessary to regard the teacher as the member of the general public he seeks to be." Id. at 574. For this reason, and because of the nature of the employee's speech, the Court adopted the test created in New York Times v. Sullivan, 376 U.S. 254 (1964), for application to regulations of public discourse, and held that the teacher could not be punished "absent proof of false statements knowingly or recklessly made by him." 391 U.S. at 574.

222. See, e.g., Board of Airport Comm'rs v. Jews for Jesus, 482 U.S. 569, 572, (1987); Cornelius v. NAACP Legal Defense and Educ. Fund, 473 U.S. 788, 814–15 (1985) (Blackmun, J., dissenting); Minnesota State Bd. for Community Colleges v. Knight, 465 U.S. 271, 280 (1984); City Council of Los Angeles v. Taxpayers for Vincent, 466 U.S. 789, 813–14 (1984); Perry Educ. Ass'n v. Perry Local Educators' Ass'n, 460 U.S. 37, 44 (1983); Cass, "First Amendment Access," at 1287–88; Werhan, "Public Forum Doctrine," at 338; Note, "Public Forum Analysis," at 545.

Despite the received wisdom, cases like *Greenburgh* illustrate that public forum doctrine can be applied to resources which the government does not in fact own. *Cornelius* has attempted to capture this insight by observing that public forum theory is pertinent whenever a "speaker" seeks "access to public property or to private property dedicated to public use." 473 U.S. at 801.

223. Olmstead v. United States, 277 U.S. 438, 478, 474–75 (1928) (Brandeis, J., dissenting).

224. Rakas v. Illinois, 439 U.S. 128, 143–44 n.12 (1978).

225. 167 U.S. 43, 47 (1897).

226. 385 U.S. 39, 47 (1966); see, e.g., Cornelius v. NAACP Legal Defense and Educ. Fund, 473 U.S. 788, 800 (1985); United States v. Grace, 461 U.S. 171, 178 (1983); Perry Educ. Ass'n v. Perry Local Educators' Ass'n, 460 U.S. 37, 46 (1983); United States Postal Serv. v. Greenburgh Civic Ass'ns, 453 U.S. 114, 129–30 (1981); Greer v. Spock, 424 U.S. 828, 836 (1976). In Lehman v. City of Shaker Heights, Justice Blackmun evoked the metaphor of a private "commercial venture," like any other "newspaper or periodical, or even . . . radio or television station." 418 U.S. 298, 303 (1974). On the influence of the metaphor of private property on public forum doctrine, see Stone, "Content-Neutral Restrictions," at 87.

227. Forrest McDonald, *Novus Ordo Seclorum: The Intellectual Origins of the Constitution* 71 (1985).

228. There is, however, a variant usage of the phrase "public forum" in which it does make sense to contrast the public forum with a sphere of personal privacy. In that usage the phrase designates private property which has become so imbued with public functions as to become subject to the constitutional limitations placed upon state action. See Hudgens v. NLRB, 424 U.S. 507, 538–43 (1976) (Marshall, J., dissenting); Columbia Broadcasting Sys. v. Democratic Nat'l Comm., 412 U.S. 94, 134 (1973) (Stewart, J., concurring); Lloyd Corp. v. Tanner, 407 U.S. 551, 573 (1972) (Marshall, J., dissenting).

229. Jürgen Habermas, *Toward a Rational Society* 92–93 (1971).

230. Deference should thus be distinguished from what I have elsewhere called "delegation," which occurs when courts delegate to institutional officials the power to determine the constitutional principles by which their decisions will be judged. See Post, "Management of Speech," at 215. Delegation would be consistent with the major premise of the *Davis* syllogism, as would a substantive conclusion that there were no pertinent constitutional principles to constrain the decisions of institutional officials.

231. Lehman v. City of Shaker Heights, 418 U.S. at 298, 303 (1974).

232. Cornelius v. NAACP Legal Defense and Educ. Fund, 473 U.S. 788, 806 (1985).

233. Bose Corp. v. Consumers Union of U.S., Inc., 466 U.S. 485, 508 n.27 (1984); see also Landmark Communications, Inc. v. Virginia, 435 U.S. 829, 842–45 (1978); New York Times Co. v. United States, 403 U.S. 713 (1971).

234. NAACP v. Button, 371 U.S. 415, 433 (1963).

235. See, e.g., Turner v. Safley, 482 U.S. 78, 84–86 (1987); Jones v. North Carolina Prisoners' Labor Union, 433 U.S. 119, 128 (1977); Procunier v. Martinez, 416 U.S. 396, 404–5 (1974).

236. See Central Hudson Gas and Elec. Corp. v. Public Serv. Comm'n, 447 U.S. 557 (1980); New York Times Co. v. United States, 403 U.S. 713 (1971); Freedman v. Maryland, 380 U.S. 51 (1965); Post, "Management of Speech," at 185–86. I do not want to overstate the case, however, for it seems to me that at a certain point considerations of expertise do become important. See note 256 below.

237. The "pervasiveness" of an organizational role is a term of art within organizational theory: "The range of pervasiveness is determined by the number of activities in or outside the organization for which the organization sets norms. Pervasiveness is small when such norms cover only activities directly controlled by the organizational elites; it is larger when it extends to other activities carried out in social groups composed of organizational participants; for example, army officers maintain 'formalities' in their club. Finally, an organization of its participants in social units which include nonparticipants and which are, at least in part,

governed by nonorganizational 'external' elites. Schools define 'desirable' leisure-time activities of students; some churches specify the candidates they wish their members to support in the political arena." Amitai Etzioni, *A Comparative Analysis of Complex Organizations* 163 (1961).

238. See, e.g., Goldman v. Weinberger, 475 U.S. 503 (1986).

239. See, e.g., Ex parte Hull, 312 U.S. 546, 549 (1941).

240. Although courts are willing to protect these extrinsic constitutional values to the extent of refusing to defer to the judgment of institutional authorities, they are on the whole not willing to protect them to the extent of modifying the underlying constitutional principle that speech in such institutions may be regulated if necessary to attain institutional ends. Courts are extremely reluctant to protect speech or behavior that by hypothesis impairs the ability of an organization to function. In this regard Goldman v. Weinberger, 475 U.S. 503 (1986), is illustrative. At issue in the case was the refusal of the military to permit an orthodox Jewish officer to wear a religiously required yarmulke. The Court's opinion upheld the action of the military, holding that it must "give great deference to the professional judgment of military authorities concerning the relative importance of a particular military interest." Id. at 507. Four Justices dissented, writing three separate opinions. Not one of these opinions took the position that the religious rights of the officer should be protected if they in fact endangered the ability of the military to perform its function. Instead, each opinion rejected the claim that the Court should defer to the judgment of military officials, and went on to determine independently that the officer's yarmulke would work no "substantial harm to military discipline and esprit de corps." Id. at 532 (O'Connor, J., dissenting); see id. at 517–20 (Brennan, J., dissenting); id. at 526 (Blackmun, J., dissenting).

241. 461 U.S. 138 146, 147, 152 (1983). At first glance *Connick* appears to require courts to balance the First Amendment rights of employees against the achievement of institutional goals. *Connick* states that if an employee's speech touches upon a matter of public concern, the employee's interests as a citizen must be balanced against the government's interests "in promoting the efficiency of the public services it performs through its employees." 461 U.S. at 142; see id. at 149–50. On closer analysis, however, the image of balancing dissolves into a purely instrumental calculation. Even if an employee's speech involves a matter of public concern, *Connick* holds that "full consideration" must be given to "the government's interest in the effective and efficient fulfillment of its responsibilities to the public," id. at 150, and that it must be recognized that "the Government, as an employer, must have wide discretion and control over the management of its personnel and internal affairs." Id. at 151. *Connick* states: "When close working relationships are essential to fulfilling public responsibilities, a wide degree of deference to the employer's judgment is appropriate. Furthermore, we do not see the necessity for an employer to allow events to

unfold to the extent that the disruption of the office and the destruction of working relationships is manifest before taking action. *We caution that a stronger showing may be necessary if the employee's speech more substantially involved matters of public concern."* Id. at 151–52 (emphasis added). The question is the nature of the "stronger showing" which must be made in order to justify regulating employee speech that "more substantially involve[s] matters of public concern." In light of the overall structure of the opinion, I think the most plausible interpretation of *Connick* is that in such circumstances the government cannot depend upon judicial deference to managerial anticipation of harm to institutional culture, but must instead bring sufficient evidence before a court to convince it that the government's restriction of speech is in fact necessary for the attainment of institutional goals. In that case, of course, the court will in effect be reaching an independent, nondeferential decision as to whether the regulation of employee speech is truly required by the need to achieve institutional objectives.

This interpretation of Connick is supported by the Court's decision in Rankin v. McPherson, 483 U.S. 378 (1987). In *Rankin* a low-level government clerk had been fired for a private remark which the Court interpreted as being about a matter of public concern. Although the Court in *Rankin* reasserted as a general matter the *Pickering* balancing test, id. at 384, 388, the Court's holding that the firing was unconstitutional in fact turned on its conclusion that "there is no evidence that [the remark] interfered with the efficient functioning of the office." Id. at 389. The Court's decision, in other words, depended not upon a balance of two competing values but upon a purely instrumental calculation performed without deference for the judgment of institutional authorities.

242. It is sometimes said that the public's use of a particular institutional resource is so essential for the maintenance of public discussion that courts should not defer to administrative judgment in its regulation. See, e.g., Adderley v. Florida, 385 U.S. 39, 49–56 (1966) (Douglas, J., dissenting). But the Court has never accepted such an argument, preferring instead to assume that public discussion will continue regardless of the use of any particular government resource. Of course this assumption, like any other, must stand or fall on the strength of its empirical foundations. A different case would be presented if the government owned all the meeting halls in town, instead of the government's hall being only one among many. On the related empirical question of whether the use of certain kinds of government resources is necessary to maintain the availability of inexpensive means of communication, and so to maintain an undistorted marketplace of ideas, compare the views of Justices Stevens and Brennan in City Council of Los Angeles v. Taxpayers for Vincent, 466 U.S. 789, 812 and n.30, 819–20 (1984).

243. For a full discussion of this point, see the unabridged version of this essay at 34 *UCLA Law Review* 1713, 1824–32 (1987).

244. Erving Goffman, *Asylums: Essays on the Social Situation of Mental Patients and Other Inmates* 4–5 (1961).

245. Id. at 6, 119–21, 83.

246. Greer v. Spock, 424 U.S. at 828, 839 (1976).

247. On the demise of the "hands-off" doctrine, see Emily Calhoun, "The Supreme Court and the Constitutional Rights of Prisoners: A Reappraisal," 4 *Hastings Constitutional Law Quarterly* 219 (1977); James B. Jacobs, "The Prisoners' Rights Movement and Its Impacts, 1960–1980," 2 *Crime and Justice: Annual Review of Research* 429 (1980). For an example of the Court's ambivalence regarding the importance of isolating prisons from the general society's First Amendment values, see Procunier v. Martinez, 416 U.S. 396 (1974).

248. Goffman, *Asylums*, at 87.

249. Brown v. Glines, 444 U.S. 348, 354, 357 (1980).

250. James B. Jacobs, *Stateville: The Penitentiary in Mass Society* 136 (1977); James N. Marquart and Ben M. Crouch, "Judicial Reform and Prisoner Control: The Impact of *Ruiz v. Estelle* on a Texas Penitentiary," 19 *Law and Society Review* 557 (1985).

251. Jeffrey Jowell, "The Legal Control of Administrative Discretion," 1973 *Public Law* 178, 202.

252. See Thompson, *Organizations*, at 117–21. Discretion, of course, is not a blank check. We commonly speak of discretionary decisions as to which the consideration of specific factors is either prohibited or required. See Post, "Management of Speech," at 219.

253. See Nathan Glazer, "Should Judges Administer Social Services?," 50 *Public Interest* 64, 75–77 (1978). Judicial intervention in the administration of one prison, for example, had the effect of depriving guards of discretion and fostering a "bureaucratic-legal order." Marquart and Crouch, "Judicial Reform," at 581–84. Guards felt they could "no longer maintain control and order within the penitentiary," and there was a sharply increasing "rate of serious disciplinary infractions." Id. at 580. See Jacobs, "Prisoners' Rights Movement," at 458–63.

254. Justice Blackmun hypothesized a number of possible justifications for the refusal to accept political advertising: "Revenue earned from long-term commercial advertising could be jeopardized by a requirement that short-term candidacy or issue-oriented advertisements be displayed on car cards. Users would be subjected to the blare of political propaganda. There could be lurking doubts about favoritism, and sticky administrative problems might arise in parceling out limited space to eager politicians." Lehman v. City of Shaker Heights, 418 U.S. 298, 304 (1974). He did not, however, independently scrutinize any of these reasons.

255. Id. at 300–301.

256. A rather different case would be presented if the transit system had never allowed any advertising cards on their cars. One can imagine a political candidate bringing a lawsuit in such circumstances, arguing that the transit system should

be required to install advertising cards for political announcements and that such cards were compatible with the attainment of the system's goals as evidenced by the practices of other jurisdictions. If the transit system replied that it had never provided such cards and had neither the administrative nor economic ability to do so now, my instinct is that a court would defer to the system's judgment without making an independent determination as to the merits of the case.

Such deference, of course, would have to be justified by reference to different principles than those examined in the text. Two such principles come to mind. The first turns on notions of relative competence. As courts are asked to leapfrog over existing practices, rather than marginally to alter those practices, problems of information and unanticipated consequences grow geometrically more difficult. The distinction might be conceptualized as that between a court making policy and a court overseeing the implementation of an existing policy: the former obviously demands far greater expertise. The distinction suggests a second way in which judicial deference in these circumstances might be understood. To make policy is to fundamentally define the nature and goals of an organization. Although this task is implicit in much public forum doctrine, courts might well believe that the task also has its limits.

Both these principles of deference are matters of degree, and both seem relevant primarily when a plaintiff asks a court to transcend the common-sense boundaries of its proper function. That is why these principles emerge from hypothetical illustrations rather than from actual cases. That these principles of deference express a generally shared sense of appropriate limitations on judicial decision-making is evidenced by the fact that public forum suits asking for courts to create official resources for private expressive use are quite rare.

Such suits are closely related, however, to a more common kind of litigation, which concerns the "opening up" of government institutions to public view. See, e.g., Houchins v. KQED, 438 U.S. 1 (1978). This kind of litigation does not so much involve claims by members of the general public to commandeer government resources for their own First Amendment purposes, as claims that the interior of a government institution should be made accountable and visible to the general public. They thus involve complicated questions not only of the reach of the government's managerial authority over its own resources and personnel, but also of the affirmative structural requirements of the First Amendment for the facilitation of public discourse. This is not the place for a full investigation of these questions, but only for the limited observation that the Court's decisions in this area appear to have been deeply influenced by considerations of deference much like those just discussed. Hence it is no surprise that the institution which the Court has been most aggressive about opening up to the public is the judicial system. Not only does the Court possess expertise in the area of judicial management, but it also can speak confidently about the nature and goals of courts. Thus the ordinary barriers to using constitutional law to set organizational policy are greatly diminished with respect to the judicial system.

257. Perry Educ. Ass'n v. Perry Local Educators' Ass'n, 460 U.S. 37, 39 (1983).

258. 460 U.S. at 40, 70 n.12 (Brennan, J., dissenting).

259. Simon, Smithburg, and Thompson, *Public Administration*, at 81.

260. Indeed, until 1978, shortly before the *Perry* lawsuit was initiated, the school board permitted both the minority and majority unions to use the mail system. 460 U.S. at 39; Perry Local Educators' Ass'n v. Hohlt, 652 F.2d 1286, 1287 (7th Cir. 1981), rev'd sub. nom. Perry Educ. Ass'n v. Perry Local Educators' Ass'n, 460 U.S. 37 (1983).

261. T. S. Eliot, *The Complete Poems and Plays* 133 (1962).

7. Meiklejohn's Mistake

1. Stephen Holmes, "Liberal Constraints on Private Power? Reflections on the Origins and Rationale of Access Regulation," in *Democracy and the Mass Media: A Collection of Essays* 21, 32–33, 47 (Judith Lichtenberg, ed., 1990).

2. See Daniel D. Polsby, "*Buckley v. Valeo:* The Special Nature of Political Speech," 1976 *Supreme Court Review* 1, 5–14.

3. Buckley v. Valeo, 424 U.S. 1, 48–49 (1976). See First Nat'l Bank of Boston v. Bellotti, 435 U.S. 765, 790–92 (1978); Citizens Against Rent Control v. Berkeley, 454 U.S. 290, 295 (1981). But see Austin v. Michigan Chamber of Commerce, 494 U.S. 652 (1990).

4. 418 U.S. 241 (1974). See L. A. Powe, Jr., "Tornillo," 1987 *Supreme Court Review* 345, 380–85. But see Red Lion Broadcasting Co. v. FCC, 395 U.S. 367 (1969).

5. Cass R. Sunstein, "Preferences and Politics," 20 *Philosophy and Public Affairs* 3, 28 (1991).

6. Owen M. Fiss, "Free Speech and Social Structure," 71 *Iowa Law Review* 1405, 1408–11 (1986).

7. Id. at 1411. For a survey of literature making similar arguments in the context of campaign financing, see Lillian R. BeVier, "Money and Politics: A Perspective on the First Amendment and Campaign Finance Reform," 73 *California Law Review* 1045, 1068–74 (1985).

8. Fiss writes: "We should learn to recognize the state not only as an enemy, but also as a friend of speech; like any social actor, it has the potential to act in both capacities, and, using the enrichment of public debate as the touchstone, we must begin to discriminate between them . . . [T]he approach I am advocating is not concerned with the speaker's autonomy, real or effective, but with the quality of public debate. It is listener oriented." Id. at 1416–17.

9. For an argument that Meiklejohn's great predecessor Zechariah Chafee

also expounded a version of the collectivist theory, see Mark A. Graber, *Transforming Free Speech: The Ambiguous Legacy of Civil Libertarianism* 144–47 (1991).

10. Alexander Meiklejohn, *Political Freedom: The Constitutional Powers of the People* 75 (1960).

11. Id. at 26. Compare with Stephen Holmes: "Competition among would-be policymakers ... is justified by the education of speakers and listeners in the practice of democratic government and by the expectation that public learning will occur so that collective decisions will be *better* (more intelligent, better informed) than decisions made without benefit of debate." Holmes, "Liberal Constraints," at 32.

12. Meiklejohn, *Political Freedom*, at 55. Meiklejohn thus attacks Zechariah Chafee, Jr., for having been "misled by his inclusion of an individual interest within the scope of the First Amendment," and he faults Oliver Wendell Holmes for his "excessive individualism." Id. at 57, 61.

13. Id. at 26.

14. Id. at 27.

15. Id. at 24–26.

16. White v. City of Norwalk, 900 F.2d 1421, 1425 (9th Cir. 1990). White reaches the correct but seemingly paradoxical conclusion that a town meeting is not a "public forum" for First Amendment purposes.

17. Brown v. Hartlage, 456 U.S. 45, 60 (1982). See also Schneider v. New Jersey, 308 U.S. 147, 161 (1939); Stromberg v. California, 283 U.S. 359 (1931).

18. See Steven H. Schiffrin, *The First Amendment, Democracy, and Romance* 56–58 (1990).

19. Norberto Bobbio, *Democracy and Dictatorship: The Nature and Limits of State Power* 137 (Peter Kennealy, trans., 1989).

20. Jean-Jacques Rousseau, *The Social Contract* (Maurice Cranston, trans., 1968).

21. Hans Kelsen, *General Theory of Law and State* 284–88 (Anders Wedberg, trans., 1949). See, e.g., Benjamin R. Barber, *Strong Democracy: Participatory Politics for a New Age* 136 (1984); James T. Farrell et al., *Dialogue on John Dewey* 58 (Corliss Lamont, ed., 1959); Jürgen Habermas, *Communication and the Evolution of Society* 186 (Thomas McCarthy, trans., 1979); Frank Michelman, "Law's Republic," 97 *Yale Law Journal* 1493, 1526–27 (1988).

22. See Hustler Magazine v. Falwell, 485 U.S. 46, 54 (1988).

23. Jean Piaget, *The Moral Judgment of the Child* 366 (Marjorie Gabain, trans., 1948).

24. Charles Taylor, *Sources of the Self: The Making of the Modern Identity* 27–28 (1989).

25. Claude Lefort, *Democracy and Political Theory* 39 (David Macey, trans., 1988).

26. Kenneth Karst, "Equality and the First Amendment," 43 *University of*

Chicago Law Review 20, 40 (1975). Karst writes that "even the repetition of speech conveys the distinctive message that an opinion is widely shared," which is of "great importance in an 'other-directed' society where opinion polls are self-fulfilling prophecies." Id. Compare Meiklejohn, *Political Freedom*, at 26 (citations omitted): "If, for example, at a town meeting, twenty like-minded citizens have become a 'party,' and if one of them has read to the meeting an argument which they have all approved, it would be ludicrously out of order for each of the others to insist on reading it again. No competent moderator would tolerate that wasting of the time available for free discussion."

27. See, e.g., Kenneth Karst, "Boundaries and Reasons: Freedom of Expression and the Subordination of Groups," 1990 *University of Illinois Law Review* 95.

28. Elmer E. Schattshneider, *The Semisovereign People: A Realist's View of Democracy in America* 66 (2d. ed. 1975).

29. See, e.g., Consolidated Edison Co. v. Public Serv. Comm'n., 447 U.S. 530, 538 (1980). ("To allow a government the choice of permissible subjects for public debate would be to allow that government control over the search for political truth.")

30. 403 U.S. 15, 24–25 (1971).

31. Owen M. Fiss, "Why the State?," 100 *Harvard Law Review* 781, 785–86 (1987).

32. Fiss, "Free Speech," at 1425.

33. Id. at 1410.

34. Fiss, "Why the State?," at 785.

35. Fiss, "Free Speech," at 1407. Thus Fiss writes: "The duty of the state is to preserve the integrity of public debate . . . to safeguard the conditions for true and free collective self-determination." Id. at 1416. See also Owen Fiss, "State Activism and State Censorship," 100 *Yale Law Journal* 2087, 2087–88 (1991). ("The principle of freedom that the First Amendment embodies is derived from the democratic nature of our society and reflects the belief that robust public debate is an essential precondition for collective self-determination.")

36. Sheldon S. Wolin, *The Presence of the Past: Essays on the State and the Constitution* 9 (1989).

37. Fiss, "Why the State?," at 790. See id. at 788. ("To be a consumer, even a sovereign one, is not to be a citizen.")

38. Fiss, "State Activism," at 2101. Needless to say, it is deeply inconsistent with democratic legitimacy to conceive of citizens as the pupils of their government. A great educator defines her educational mission in terms of what she believes to be best for her students. But democracy conceives of its citizens not as pupils to be guided by a beneficent state but as free and independent persons capable of deciding their own destiny.

39. It is true that such government action may influence national identity, and it is also true that at some point such action may become so pervasive or ines-

capable as to amount to governmental imposition of a state-authorized version of national identity. At that point, and for that reason, traditional First Amendment jurisprudence would be relevant to the assessment of such government action.

40. Fiss, "Why the State?," at 786.

41. First Amendment doctrine also preserves the indeterminacy of public discourse by insisting upon the immunity of public discourse from the imposition of community norms. Such norms typically embody fully realized conceptions of national identity.

42. The preceding two sentences in the text frame an important question regarding the status of corporate speech during elections—the subject of a fascinating and unsteady line of Supreme Court decisions. See Austin v. Michigan Chamber of Commerce, 494 U.S. 652 (1990); Federal Election Comm'n v. Massachusetts Citizens for Life, Inc., 479 U.S. 238 (1986); First Nat'l Bank v. Bellotti, 435 U.S. 765 (1978). Meir Dan-Cohen has demonstrated rather convincingly that most corporations cannot claim original autonomy rights to expression. Meir Dan-Cohen, "Freedoms of Collective Speech: A Theory of Protected Communications by Organizations, Communities, and the State," 79 *California Law Review* 1229 (1991). But even in the absence of any concern for the autonomous participation of corporations within democratic life, constitutional scrutiny must also be applied to justifications for state regulation of corporate electoral speech.

In Austin v. Michigan State Chamber of Commerce, 494 U.S. 652 (1990), the Court upheld a Michigan prohibition on independent expenditures from corporate treasury funds in support of, or in opposition to, any candidate for state office. In an opaque and difficult opinion, Justice Marshall stated that the statute was meant to redress "the corrosive and distorting effects of immense aggregations of wealth that are accumulated with the help of the corporate form and that have little or no correlation to the public's support for the corporation's political ideas." Id. at 660. On Marshall's account the Michigan statute seems to be an effort to enforce a particular image of collective identity, from which vantage the influence of corporate wealth can be excised as "corrosive and distorting."

But this raises the question of whether such an effort does not contradict the First Amendment principle that the state must always regard collective identity as necessarily open-ended within the sphere of public discourse. The question is a vexing one. On the one hand, the force of this principle does not seem to depend upon the denial of the autonomy of particular speakers, as may perhaps be glimpsed in the constitutional fate that ought to await any statute that attempted to prohibit independent corporate expenditures in support of Democrats but allow such expenditures for Republicans. See R.A.V. v. City of St. Paul, 112 S. Ct. 2538, 2543 n.4 (1992). But, on the other hand, government actions affect collective identity all the time in ways that are properly viewed as constitutionally unproblematic, as for example by subsidies to private speakers. These actions seem to be constitutionally permissible precisely because they do not suppress the autonomy of speakers.

43. See, e.g., Joseph A. Schumpeter, *Capitalism, Socialism, and Democracy* (3d ed. 1950).

44. Michelman, "Law's Republic," at 1500.

45. Less debatable, perhaps, is the claim that, under conditions characteristic of the modern bureaucratic state, democratic self-governance would be impossible in the absence of a public discourse that is, in relevant respects, free and unfettered.

46. Cass Sunstein, "Free Speech Now," 59 *University of Chicago Law Review* 255, 263, 313–14, 277, 303–4, 277 (1992).

47. J. Skelly Wright, "Money and the Pollution of Politics: Is the First Amendment an Obstacle to Political Equality?," 82 *Columbia Law Review* 609, 625–26 (1982).

48. Julian N. Eule, "Promoting Speaker Diversity: Austin and Metro Broadcasting," 1990 *Supreme Court Review* 105, 111–16. See Judith Lichtenberg, "Foundations and Limits of Freedom of the Press," in *Democracy and the Mass Media: A Collection of Essays* (Judith Lichtenberg, ed., 1990).

49. Daniel H. Lowenstein, "Campaign Spending and Ballot Propositions: Recent Experience, Public Choice Theory, and the First Amendment," 29 *UCLA Law Review* 505, 515 (1982).

50. I enclose in quotation marks the adjectives "public" and "private" to avoid semantic confusion with the obviously very different meaning of the term "public" in the phrase "public discourse." The distinction between public discourse and nonpublic speech tracks the boundary between the speech of persons in their role as citizens and the speech of persons in other aspects of their lives. The public/private distinction at issue in text, however, refers to the boundary between government and its citizens. These common but different usages of the terms "public" and "private" allow us to assert, without fear of anomaly, that "private" citizens can engage in "public" discourse. Needless to say, our vocabulary in this area deserves a good scrubbing.

51. See generally Mark G. Yudof, *When Government Speaks: Politics, Law, and Government Expression in America* (1983).

52. 395 U.S. 367, 376, 383, 389 (1969). See id. at 394. ("It does not violate the First Amendment to treat licensees given the privilege of using scarce radio frequencies as proxies for the entire community, obligated to give suitable time and attention to matters of great public concern.")

53. Id. at 392, 390. See id. at 394. ("To condition the granting or renewal of licenses on a willingness to present representative community views on controversial issues is consistent with the ends and purposes of those constitutional provisions forbidding the abridgment of freedom of speech and freedom of the press.") For a contrary view, see Lucas A. Powe, Jr., *American Broadcasting and the*

First Amendment (1987). Powe concludes that "the regulation of broadcasting has been characterized by the very abuses—favoritism, censorship, political influence, that the First Amendment was designed to prevent in the print media." L. A. Powe, Jr., "Scholarship and Markets," 56 *George Washington Law Review* 172, 185 (1987).

54. See 395 U.S. at 398 n.25. On the theoretical and empirical inadequacy of the scarcity rationale, see Daniel D. Polsby, "Candidate Access to the Air: The Uncertain Future of Broadcaster Discretion," 1981 *Supreme Court Review* 223, 256–62.

55. Miami Herald Publishing Co. v. Tornillo, 418 U.S. 241 (1974). But see Jerome A. Barron, "Law and the Free Society Lectures: Access—The Only Choice for the Media?," 48 *Texas Law Review* 766, 775 (1970).

56. Justice Brennan understood this quite clearly when, four years after *Red Lion*, he concluded that the actions of broadcast licensees constituted "governmental action." Columbia Broadcasting Sys., Inc. v. Democratic Nat'l Comm., 412 U.S. 94, 180 (1973) (Brennan, J., dissenting). He reached this conclusion "because the Government 'has so far insinuated itself into a position' of participation" in the policies of licensees "as to make the Government itself responsible for [their] effects." Id. at 181 n.12. The majority of the Court, however, refused to follow Brennan's lead, thus relegating Red Lion's holding to a confused fixation on physical scarcity.

57. Fiss, "Free Speech," at 1414. For arguments with a similar tendency, see Cass R. Sunstein, "Legal Interference with Private Preferences," 53 *University of Chicago Law Review* 1129 (1986); Sunstein, "Free Speech Now," at 277, 288; Eule, "Promoting Speaker Diversity," at 113–14.

58. Hence the theoretical force behind Lee Bollinger's acute insight that, having embarked upon the collectivist regulation of the broadcast media, the state was bound "to maintain a partial regulatory structure for its own sake." Lee C. Bollinger, Jr., "Freedom of the Press and Public Access: Toward a Theory of Partial Regulation of the Mass Media," 75 *Michigan Law Review* 1, 36 (1976).

59. Eule, "Promoting Speaker Diversity," at 115, 112, 113.

60. See id. at 129–30. Both Wright, "Money," and Lowenstein, "Campaign Spending," contain well-developed arguments along these lines.

61. Fiss, "Why the State?," at 787–88.

62. Sunstein, "Preferences," at 11.

63. Id. at 11, 21, 12, 27–32.

64. John Stuart Mill understood this clearly when in *On Liberty* he refused to support limitations on "beer and spirit houses," despite what appeared to him to be disturbing evidence of their uncontrolled abuse among members of the working class. He wrote that such limitations would be "suited only to a state of society in which the laboring classes are avowedly treated as children or savages, and placed under an education of restraint, to fit them for future admission to the

privileges of freedom. This is not a principle on which the laboring classes are professedly governed in any free country." John S. Mill, *On Liberty* 100 (Elizabeth Rapaport, ed., 1978).

65. Eule, "Promoting Speaker Diversity," at 129–30.

66. Wright, "Money," at 636, 625, 622, 639.

67. Thus Sunstein concludes that First Amendment protection ought not be extended to pornography or hate speech because they "have serious and corrosive effects on beliefs and desires." Sunstein, "Preferences," at 31–32.

68. Wright, "Money," at 638.

69. In this sense the internal argument displays a structure of analysis similar to what I have identified in Chapter 4 as the "paradox of public discourse."

70. Wright, "Money," at 609, 639.

71. See, e.g., John Elster, *Ulysses and the Sirens: Studies in Rationality and Irrationality* (1979); Sunstein, "Legal Interference." For a critique of the political use of the metaphor, see Jonathan Schonsheck, "Deconstructing Community Self-Paternalism," 10 *Law and Philosophy* 29 (1991).

72. See David Yassky, "Eras of the First Amendment," 91 *Columbia Law Review* 1699 (1991); Cass R. Sunstein, "Lochner's Legacy," 87 *Columbia Law Review* 873, 883–84 (1987).

73. Fiss, "Free Speech," at 1412.

74. Max Horkheimer and Theodor W. Adorno, *Dialectic of Enlightenment* 87 (John Cumming, trans., 1972).

75. C. Edwin Baker, *Human Liberty and Freedom of Speech* (1989).

76. Martin H. Redish, "The Value of Free Speech," 130 *University of Pennsylvania Law Review* 591 (1982).

Reprise

1. Dwight Lowell Dumond, *Antislavery: The Crusade for Freedom in America* 273 (1961) (quoting William Lloyd Garrison).

2. 347 U.S. 483 (1954).

3. For a representative discussion, see Owen Fiss, "Foreword: The Forms of Justice," 93 *Harvard Law Review* 1 (1979).

4. Richard Delgado, "Words That Wound: A Tort Action for Racial Insults, Epithets, and Name-Calling," 17 *Harvard Civil Rights–Civil Liberties Law Review* 133 (1982); see Marjorie Heins, "Banning Words: A Comment on 'Words That Wound,'" 18 *Harvard Civil Rights–Civil Liberties Law Review* 585 (1983); Richard Delgado, "Professor Delgado Replies," 18 *Harvard Civil Rights–Civil Liberties Law Review* 593 (1983).

5. Richard Delgado, "Campus Antiracism Rules: Constitutional Narratives in Collision," 85 *Northwestern University Law Review* 343 (1990); Mary Ellen Gale, "On Curbing Racial Speech," *Responsive Community*, Winter 1990–91, at

47; Marvin Glass, "Anti-Racism and Unlimited Freedom of Speech: An Untenable Dualism," 8 *Canadian Journal of Philosophy* 559 (1978); Joseph Grano, "Free Speech v. the University of Michigan," *Academic Questions*, Spring 1990, at 7; Kent Greenawalt, "Insults and Epithets: Are They Protected Speech?," 42 *Rutgers Law Review* 287 (1991); Thomas C. Grey, "Civil Rights vs. Civil Liberties: The Case of Discriminatory Verbal Harassment," *Sociological Philosophy and Policy*, Spring 1991, at 81; Graham Hughes, "Prohibiting Incitement to Racial Discrimination," 16 *University of Toronto Law Journal* 361 (1966); Thomas David Jones, "Article 4 of the International Convention on the Elimination of All Forms of Racial Discrimination and the First Amendment," 23 *Howard Law Journal* 429 (1980); David Kretzmer, "Freedom of Speech and Racism," 8 *Cardozo Law Review* 445 (1987); "Language as Violence v. Freedom of Expression: Canadian and American Perspectives on Group Defamation," 37 *Buffalo Law Review* 337 (1989); Kenneth Lasson, "Racial Defamation as Free Speech: Abusing the First Amendment," 17 *Columbia Human Rights Law Review* 11 (1985); Kenneth Lasson, "Group Libel Versus Free Speech: When Big Brother Should Butt In," 23 *Duquesne Law Review* 77 (1984); Charles R. Lawrence, "If He Hollers Let Him Go: Regulating Racist Speech on Campus," 1990 *Duke Law Journal* 431; Jean C. Love, "Discriminatory Speech and the Tort of Intentional Infliction of Emotional Distress," 47 *Washington and Lee Law Review* 123 (1990); Mari Matsuda, "Public Response to Racist Speech: Considering the Victim's Story," 87 *Michigan Law Review* 2320 (1989); Martha Minow, "On Neutrality, Equality, and Tolerance: New Norms for a Decade of Distinction," *Change*, Jan.–Feb. 1990, at 17; David F. Partlett, "From Red Lion Square to Skokie to the Fatal Shore: Racial Defamation and Freedom of Speech," 22 *Vanderbilt Journal Transnational Law* 431 (1989); Dean M. Richardson, "Racism: A Tort of Outrage," 61 *Oregon Law Review* 267 (1982); Rodney A. Smolla, "Rethinking First Amendment Assumptions About Racist and Sexist Speech," 47 *Washington and Lee Law Review* 171 (1990); Nadine Strossen, "Regulating Racist Speech on Campus: A Modest Proposal," 1990 *Duke Law Journal* 484; Ruth Wedgwood, "Freedom of Expression and Racial Speech," 8 *Tel Aviv University Studies in Law* 325 (1988); R. George Wright, "Racist Speech and the First Amendment," 9 *Mississippi College Law Review* 1 (1988); Note, "A Communitarian Defense of Group Libel Laws," 101 *Harvard Law Review* 682 (1988); Note, "The University of California Hate Speech Policy: A Good Heart in Ill-Fitting Garb," 12 *Journal of Communications and Entertainment Law* 593 (1990); Comment, "Freedom from Fear," 15 *Lincoln Law Review* 45 (1984) (authored by Kammy Au); Peter Edelman, "Punishing Perpetrators of Racist Speech," *Legal Times*, May 15, 1989, at 20.

6. See, e.g., Howard J. Ehrlich, *Campus Ethnoviolence and the Policy Options* 41–72 (1990); Nancy Gibbs, "Bigots in the Ivory Tower: An Alarming Rise in Hatred Roils U.S. Campuses," *Time*, May 7, 1990, at 104.

7. David Rieff writes that 137 American universities "have in the past two

years passed proscriptions on hate speech." David Rieff, "The Case Against Sensitivity," 114 *Esquire* 120, 124 (1990). "See Lessons from Bigotry 101," *Newsweek*, Sept. 25, 1989, at 48; William Julius Wilson, "Colleges' Anti-Harassment Policies Bring Controversy Over Free-Speech Issues," *Chronicle of Higher Education*, Oct. 4, 1989, at A1; Cheryl M. Fields, "Colleges Advised to Develop Strong Procedures to Deal With Incidents of Racial Harassment," *Chronicle of Higher Education*, July 20, 1988, at A11.

8. For a chronicle of the effect of this controversy on the American Civil Liberties Union (ACLU), see Hentoff, "The Colleges: Fear, Loathing, and Suppression," *Village Voice*, May 8, 1990, at 20; Hentoff, "What's Happening to the ACLU?," *Village Voice*, May 15, 1990, at 20; Hentoff, "Putting the First Amendment on Trial," *Village Voice*, May 22, 1990, at 24; Hentoff, "A Dissonant First Amendment Fugue," *Village Voice*, June 5, 1990, at 16; Hentoff, "An Endangered Species: A First Amendment Absolutist," *Village Voice*, June 12, 1990, at 24; Hentoff, "The Civil Liberties Shootout," *Village Voice*, June 19, 1990, at 26; "Policy Concerning Racist and Other Group-Based Harassment on College Campuses," *ACLU Newsletter*, Aug.–Sept. 1990, at 2.

9. Joel Kovel, *White Racism: A Psycho History*, 34 (1970); see Charles R. Lawrence, "The Id, the Ego, and Equal Protection: Reckoning with Unconscious Racism," 39 *Stanford Law Journal* 317, 321–26 (1987).

10. Department of Student Affairs, University of Connecticut, "Protect Campus Pluralism." The regulations provided that "every member of the University is obligated to refrain from actions that intimidate, humiliate, or demean persons or groups or that undermine their security or self-esteem." They defined "harassment" as "abusive behavior directed toward an individual or group because of race, ethnicity, ancestry, national origin, religion, gender, sexual preference, age, physical or mental disabilities," and they prohibited "harassment that has the effect of interfering with an individual's performance or creating an intimidating, hostile or offensive environment."

11. Id. The regulations instruct a student to inform the "Discrimination and Intolerance Response Network" if "you have experienced or witnessed any of the signs" and to "know that the University will not tolerate such behavior."

12. Lawrence, "The Id," at 322.

13. One is reminded of the escalating efforts of the Inquisition in sixteenth-century Spain to discover and punish all external signs of inward backsliding on the part of Moors and Jews who had outwardly converted to Catholicism in order to avoid expulsion. These efforts eventually led the Inquisition to conclude that eating couscous or disliking pork were themselves punishable as heresy. See Deborah Root, "Speaking Christian: Orthodoxy and Difference in Sixteenth-Century Spain," *Representations*, Summer 1988, at 118, 126, 129.

14. Nick Ravo, "Campus Slur Alters a Code Against Bias," *New York Times*, Dec. 11, 1989, at B1, B3.

15. Modest aspirations, however, will not be easy in the highly charged atmo-

sphere of many universities. See Robert Detlefsen, "White Like Me," *New Republic*, Apr. 10, 1989, at 18. The University of Connecticut is hardly unique in its use of punitive legal regulation to block all manifestations of racism. The Board of Regents of Higher Education of the Commonwealth of Massachusetts, for example, adopted on June 13, 1989, a "Policy Against Racism" that "prohibits all forms of racism." Board of Regents of Higher Education, Commonwealth of Massachusetts, "Policy Against Racism and Guidelines for Campus Policies Against Racism" 1 (June 13, 1989). This prohibition includes "all conditions and all actions or omissions including all acts of verbal harassment or abuse which deny or have the effect of denying to anyone his or her rights to equality, dignity, and security on the basis of his or her race, color, ethnicity, culture, or religion." The "Policy Against Racism" continues: "Racism in any form, expressed or implied, intentional or inadvertent, individual or institutional, constitutes an egregious offense to the tenets of human dignity and to the accords of civility guaranteed by law." Id. at 2.

16. These categories by no means exhaust the field. The European literature, for example, contains a well-developed jurisprudence of regulating racist speech based upon the harm of potential violence. See Roger Cotterrell, "Prosecuting Incitement to Racial Hatred," 1982 *Public Law* 378; Kretzmer, "Freedom of Speech," at 456; Patricia M. Leopold, "Incitement to Hatred—The History of a Controversial Criminal Offense," 1977 *Public Law* 389, 391–93. I do not discuss this category of harm because it is relatively unimportant in the American setting. I suspect that this is largely because of the accepted dominion of the *Brandenburg* version of the clear and present danger test. See Brandenburg v. Ohio, 395 U.S. 444, 447–49 (1969).

17. Wright, "Racist Speech," at 14–22, 10, 9.

18. Hughes, "Prohibiting Incitement," at 364.

19. See Lawrence, "If He Hollers," at 438–49.

20. Kretzmer, "Freedom of Speech," at 456.

21. Id. at 454.

22. See Matsuda, "Public Response," at 2357.

23. David Riesman, "Democracy and Defamation: Control of Group Libel," 42 *Columbia Law Review* 727 (1942).

24. 343 U.S. 250 (1952). For work in this vein, see Lasson, "Group Libel"; Lasson, "Racial Defamation"; Note, "Group Vilification Reconsidered," 89 *Yale Law Journal* 308 (1979).

25. Matsuda, "Public Response," at 2358.

26. Id.

27. See, e.g., Lasson, "Racial Defamation," at 48.

28. Matsuda, "Public Response," at 2357.

29. See Delgado, "Words That Wound," at 137, 143, 157.

30. Patricia Williams, "Spirit-Murdering the Messenger: The Discourse of

Fingerpointing as the Law's Response to Racism," 42 *University of Miami Law Review* 127, 151 (1987).

31. See Love, "Discriminatory Speech," at 158.

32. Richard Delgado, for example, proposes that courts create a tort for racial insult whenever a plaintiff can prove that "language was addressed to him or her by the defendant that was intended to demean through reference to race; that the plaintiff understood as intended to demean through reference to race; and that a reasonable person would recognize as a racial insult." Delgado, "Words That Wound," at 179.

33. See, for example, the proposed regulation of the University of Texas at Austin, which prohibits racial harassment and which defines racial harassment as "extreme or outrageous acts or communications that are intended to harass, intimidate or humiliate a student or students on account of race, color, or national origin and that reasonably cause them to suffer severe emotional distress." President's Ad Hoc Committee on Racial Harassment, The University of Texas at Austin, "Report of President's Ad Hoc Committee on Racial Harassment" 4–5 (Nov. 27, 1989). The drafters of the proposed regulation state that it is "much preferable for a racial harassment policy to focus on the real injury of severe emotional distress." Id. at 20.

34. Compare, for example, the former regulations of the University of Wisconsin, which reach "racist or discriminatory comments, epithets or other expressive behavior directed at an individual," Board of Regents of the University of Wisconsin System, Wis. Admin. Code UWS §17.06(2a) (Aug. 1989) (struck down as a violation of the First Amendment in UWM Post, Inc. v. Board of the Univ. of Wis. Sys., 774 F. Supp. 1163 [E.D. Wis. 1991]), with those of Stanford University, which reach only racist speech that is "addressed directly to the individual or individuals whom it insults or stigmatizes" and that consists of "insulting or 'fighting' words." Stanford University, "Fundamental Standard Interpretation: Free Expression and Discriminatory Harassment" 2 (draft, Mar. 15, 1990).

35. See Lasson, "Group Libel," at 123. "The speech clause protects the market-place of ideas, not the battleground." Id.

36. See Lawrence, "If He Hollers," at 468.

37. Id. at 447 n.66 (quoting MacKinnon, "Not a Moral Issue," 2 *Yale Law and Policy Review* 321, 340 [1984]).

38. Id. at 452, 470.

39. Office of Student Life Policy and Service, Rutgers University at New Brunswick. "University Student Life Policy Against Insult, Defamation, and Harassment" 1 (May 31, 1989) (revised); see also Doe v. University of Mich., 721 F. Supp. 852, 856 (E.D. Mich. 1989); Oberlin College, "Policy on Race Relations and Informal Procedures for Racial Grievances"; Office of the Dean for Student Affairs and the Special Assistants to the President, Massachusetts Institute of

Technology, "Information on Harassment" (Sept. 1989); State University of New York, College at Brockport, "Discriminatory Harassment" §285.02; University of Pennsylvania, "Harassment Policy" (Almanac Supp., Sept. 29, 1987) (as published originally in the Almanac of June 2, 1987).

40. University of California, "Universitywide Student Conduct: Harassment Policy" (Sept. 21, 1989). For an example of a regulation based upon group harm, see Clark University's "Code of General Conduct": "Harassment includes any verbal or physical conduct which has the intent or effect of unreasonably interfering with any individual's or group's work or study, or creating an intimidating, hostile, or offensive environment." Clark University, "Code of General Conduct and University Judicial Procedures" 1 (Fall Semester 1988). For other examples of similar kinds of regulations, see Emory University, "Policy Statement on Discriminatory Harassment"; Marquette University, "Racial Abuse and Harassment Policy" (May 5, 1989); Office of University News and Information of Kent State University, "Policy to Combat Harassment, For the Record," vol. 5, no. 5 (Feb. 6, 1989).

41. Mount Holyoke College, "The Honor Code: Academic and Community Responsibility" §III, "Community Responsibility, Introduction" (reprinted from the Student Handbook).

42. Marquette University, "Racial Abuse and Harassment Policy" 1 (May 5, 1989).

43. Mary Washington College, "Mary Washington College Student Handbook" 20 (1990–91).

44. "If the university stands for anything, it stands for freedom in the search for truth . . . [But] can truth have its day in court when the courtroom is made into a mud-wrestling pit where vicious epithets are flung?" James T. Laney, "Why Tolerate Campus Bigots?," *New York Times*, Apr. 6, 1990, at A35.

45. Thus James T. Laney, the president of Emory University, stated: "Educators are by definition professors of value. Through education we pass on to the next generation not merely information but the habits and manners of our civil society. The university differs from society at large in its insistence on not only free expression but also an environment conducive to mutual engagement." Id.

46. See, e.g., Delgado, "Words That Wound," at 175–79; Note, "A First Amendment Justification for Regulating Racist Speech on Campus," 40 *Case Western Reserve* 733 (1989–90).

47. 496 U.S. 310 (1990).

48. Id. at 319 (quoting Texas v. Johnson, 491 U.S. 397, 414 [1989]). See Brennan's remark in Texas v. Johnson to the same effect: "The First Amendment does not guarantee that . . . concepts virtually sacred to our Nation as a whole—such as the principle that discrimination on the basis of race is odious and destructive—will go unquestioned in the marketplace of ideas." *Johnson*, 491 U.S. at 418. Brennan supported this remark by citing Bradenburg v. Ohio, 395 U.S.

444 (1969), in which the Court extended First Amendment protection to a Ku Klux Klan rally featuring such revolting comments as: "Bury the n——s"; "A Dirty n——r"; and "Send the Jews back to Israel." Id. at 446 n.1.

49. Charles Lawrence, for example, writes that the University of Michigan regulations recently invalidated by a federal court, see note 39 above, were so patently unconstitutional that "it is difficult to believe that anyone at the University of Michigan Law School was consulted" in their drafting. See Lawrence, "If He Hollers," at 477 n.161. "It is almost as if the university purposefully wrote an unconstitutional regulation so that they could say to the black students, 'We tried to help but the courts just won't let us do it.' " Id. A great many contemporary university regulations are similar to those of the University of Michigan.

50. Hustler Magazine v. Falwell, 485 U.S. 46, 54 (1988).

51. John Rawls, "Justice as Fairness: Political Not Metaphysical," 14 *Philosophy and Public Affairs* 230.

52. Jean Piaget, *The Moral Judgment of the Child* 366 (Marjorie Gabain, trans., 1948).

53. See, for example, George Kateb, "Democratic Individuality and the Claims of Politics," 12 *Political Theory* 331, 332 (1984): "To speak, therefore, of individualism is to speak of the most characteristically democratic political and moral commitment. It would be a sign of defection from modern democracy to posit some other entity as the necessary or desirable center of life. There is therefore nothing special (much less, arbitrary) in assuming that the doctrine of the individual has the preeminent place in the theory of democracy."

54. See, e.g., Bowers v. Hardwich, 478 U.S. 186, 205–6 (1986) (Blackmun, J., dissenting).

55. See Michael J. Sandel, *Liberalism and the Limits of Justice* (1982).

56. Respectively, 310 U.S. 296 (1940), 376 U.S. 254 (1964), 403 U.S. 15 (1971), and 485 U.S. 46 (1988).

57. 2 Jürgen Habermas, *The Theory of Communicative Action* 38 (Thomas McCarthy, trans., 1987).

58. Rawls, "Justice as Fairness," at 223, 230.

59. 315 U.S. 568 (1942).

60. Rawls, "Justice as Fairness," at 230.

61. Hanna Fenichel Pitkin, "Justice: On Relating Private and Public," 9 *Political Theory* 327, 346 (1981).

62. See, e.g., Rogers v. EEOC, 454 F.2d 234, 237–38 (5th Cir. 1971), cert. denied, 406 U.S. 957 (1972); EEOC v. Murphy Motor Freight Lines, 488 F. Supp. 381, 385 (D. Minn. 1980); cf. Meritor Sav. Bank v. Vinson, 477 U.S. 57, 65–66 (1986). I do not mean to imply, however, that *all* speech within the workplace is excluded from public discourse. See, e.g., Connick v. Myers, 461 U.S. 138, 149 (1983); Givhan v. Western Line Consol. School Dist., 439 U.S. 410, 415–16. (1979).

63. It should be emphasized that I am using the adjective "public" in a discrete and stipulative sense to refer to that speech necessary for democratic self-governance. Thus I do not mean to imply that speech within the workplace is "nonpublic" in the sense that it is unimportant, or that it is "private" in the sense of being intrinsically insulated from governmental control or regulation. See Kenneth Karst, "Private Discrimination and Public Responsibility: Patterson in Context," 1989 *Supreme Court Review* 1, 10–11. My point is instead that if the regulation of nonpublic speech is in fact protected by the First Amendment, it will be on the basis of constitutional values other than democratic self-governance.

64. 343 U.S. 250 (1952). The leaflet is reproduced in Justice Black's dissenting opinion. Id. at 276 (Black, J., dissenting).

65. Id. at 267 (Black, J., dissenting).

66. See Collin v. Smith, 447 F. Supp. 676 (N.D. Ill.), aff'd, 578 F.2d 1197 (7th Cir.), cert. denied, 439 U.S. 916 (1978).

67. To exclude from public discourse the category of racist speech as such would be equivalent to establishing a per se exclusion of racist ideas from public discourse, a form of regulation whose constitutionality is assessed in the next section.

68. Hustler Magazine v. Falwell, 485 U.S. 46, 56 (1988) (quoting FCC v. Pacifica Found., 438 U.S. 726, 745–46 [1978]).

69. Rawls, "Justice as Fairness," at 230.

70. Whitney v. California, 274 U.S. 357, 375–76 (1927) (Brandeis, J., concurring).

71. Piaget, *Moral Judgment*, at 57; see id. at 63.

72. Wright, "Racist Speech," at 10.

73. Matsuda, "Public Response," at 2359; Kretzmer, "Freedom of Speech," at 458.

74. See Matsuda, "Public Response," at 2332–34. "Racist hate messages are rapidly increasing and are widely distributed in this country using a variety of low and high technologies." Id. at 2336. Kretzmer is also concerned with the potential spread of racist ideas. See Kretzmer, "Freedom of Speech," at 464–65.

75. I thus do not reach the theoretically more fundamental question of why it would make a constitutional difference that racist ideas are "universally condemned." See, for example, the Court's repudiation in United States v. Eichman, 496 U.S. 310, 318 (1990), of the Solicitor General's invitation to overrule Texas v. Johnson, 491 U.S. 397 (1989), on the grounds of "Congress' recent recognition of a purported 'national consensus' favoring a prohibition on flag-burning . . . Even assuming such a consensus exists, any suggestion that the Government's interest in suppressing speech becomes more weighty as popular opposition to that speech grows is foreign to the First Amendment." *Eichman*, 496 U.S. at 318.

76. Kretzmer, "Freedom of Speech," at 456; Matsuda, "Public Response," at

2338: "However irrational racist speech may be, it hits right at the emotional place where we feel the most pain. The aloneness comes not only from the hate message itself, but also from the government response of tolerance. When hundreds of police officers are called out to protect racist marchers, when the courts refuse redress for racial insult, . . . the victim becomes a stateless person. Target-group members can either identify with a community that promotes racist speech, or they can admit that the community does not include them."

77. Matsuda, "Public Response," at 2378.

78. Greenawalt, "Insults," at 304–5.

79. Kenneth Karst, "Citizenship, Race, and Marginality," 30 *William and Mary Law Review* 1, 1 (1988).

80. See, e.g., Norberto Bobbio, *Democracy and Dictatorship* 157–8 (Peter Kennealy, trans., 1989); Carol C. Gould, *Rethinking Democracy: Freedom and Cooperation in Politics, Economy, and Society* 90 (1988); J. Roland Pennock, *Democratic Political Theory* 3–161 (1979).

81. Frank Michelman, "Law's Republic," 97 *Yale Law Journal* 1493, 1500–1501 (1988).

82. Rawls, "Justice as Fairness," at 230.

83. See, for example, "Language as Violence," at 360 (remarks of Mari Matsuda): "I use the principle of equality as a starting point . . . [I]f I were to give primacy to any one right, and if I were to create a hierarchy, I would put equality first, because the right of speech is meaningless to people who do not have equality. I mean substantive as well as procedural equality."

84. That members of minority groups are now embraced within the circle of the people and afforded the formal equality required by First Amendment processes of self-determination is not, of course, due to any principle of the First Amendment, but rather to the principle of equal citizenship embodied in the Fourteenth Amendment; in this fundamental sense, therefore, no hierarchical relationship between the First and the Fourteenth Amendment can exist.

85. Beauharnais v. Illinois, 343 U.S. 250, 251 (1952) (citing Ill. Rev. Stat. ch. 38, 471 [1949]). Anti-blasphemy regulations are a common example of such laws. See *The Law Commission, Offences Against Religion and Public Worship* 39–53 (Working Paper No. 79, 1981). Many countries also have laws prohibiting group defamation. See, e.g., E. M. Barendt, *Freedom of Speech* 161–67 (1985); Lasson, "Group Libel," at 88–89; Matsuda, "Public Response," at 2341–48.

86. See Gary Jacobsohn, "Alternative Pluralism: Israeli and American Constitutionalism in Comparative Perspective," *Review of Politics*, Spring 1989, 159, 175, 170.

87. Id. at 175.

88. See, e.g., City of Richmond v. J.A. Croson Co., 488 U.S. 469 (1989).

89. 310 U.S. 296, 309, 310 (1940).

90. For an excellent study of the efforts of contemporary Americans to forge

new communities, like the Castro district in San Francisco, and hence to "reinvent themselves" by constructing "new lives, new families, even new societies," see Frances FitzGerald, *Cities on a Hill: A Journey Through Contemporary American Cultures* 23 (1986). FitzGerald views such efforts as "quintessentially American"; try to imagine, she suggests, "Parisians creating a gay colony or a town for grandparents." Id. If in Europe or Canada group identity precedes the attempt to ask "the essential questions of who we . . . are, and how we ought to live," id. at 20, 389–90, FitzGerald's work illustrates the extent to which group identity in America tends to follow on that attempt, and hence ultimately to rest on individualist premises.

91. See Perry Miller, *The Life of the Mind in America*, 40–43 (1965).

92. Robert Bellah, Richard Madsen, William M. Sullivan, Ann Swidler, and Steven M. Tipton, *Habits of the Heart: Individualism and Commitment in American Life* 225 (1985).

93. See, e.g., Deborah L. Rhode, *Justice and Gender* 5 (1989); Isabel Marcus, "Reflections on the Significance of the Sex/Gender System: Divorce Law Reform in New York," 42 *University of Miami Law Review* 55, 55–63 (1987).

94. See Marcus, "Sex/Gender System," at 61; see Angela P. Harris, "Race and Essentialism in Feminist Legal Theory," 42 *Stanford Law Review* 581 (1990).

95. See Harris, "Feminist Legal Theory," at 615–16.

96. Nancy Fraser, "Toward a Discourse Ethic of Solidarity," 5 *Praxis International* 425, 429 (1986).

97. Michael Omi and Howard Winant, *Racial Formation in the United States: From the 1960's to the 1980's* 59 (1986). For an example of the persistence of a biological model of race, see R. J. Herrnstein, "Still an American Dilemma," *Public Interest*, Winter 1990, at 3.

98. See Omi and Winant, *Racial Formation*, at 60, 68. Omi and Winant write of the "continuous temptation to think of race as an *essence*, as something fixed, concrete and objective." Id. at 68. See Anthony Appiah, "The Uncompleted Argument: Du Bois and the Illusion of Race," in Henry Louis Gates, *"Race," Writing and Difference* 36 (1986): "Talk of 'race' is particularly distressing for those of us who take culture seriously . . . What exists 'out there' in the world—communities of meaning, shading variously into each other in the rich structure of the social world—is the province not of biology but of hermeneutic understanding."

99. For a good example, see Judy Scales-Trent, "Black Women and the Constitution: Finding Our Place, Asserting Our Rights," 24 *Harvard Civil Rights–Civil Liberties Law Review* 9 (1989).

100. For a brief history of the interdependence of understandings of national identity and understandings of race, see Philip Gleason, "American Identity and Americanization," in William Peterson, Michael Novak, and Philip Gleason, *Concepts of Ethnicity* 57 (1982). A small but, I suspect, paradigmatic example of this

interdependence may be found in the following passage from a student letter to the *Daily Californian*:

> Advertising, television, schools and government are areas of society where racism is largely promoted. Its existence is not easily eradicated. Phrases like "blackmail," "black ball" and "black mood" are common ways "blackness" is communicated in negative terms . . . One of my professors frequently employs terms like "black lie" to mean the worst of all lies. It takes a conscious effort to disregard these statements and prevent such negative influence on one's psyche. But we must understand that daily use of this terminology reinforces the attack on African-American identity and value. (Robyn "Iset" F. Broughton, "Promote Afro-American Culture," *Daily Californian*, Sept. 12, 1989, at 4)

The writer's point is relevant to the perspectives of members of *both* minority and majority groups; in fact the point effectively demonstrates the essential reciprocity of these perspectives.

101. William Julius Wilson, "Social Research and the Underclass Debate," *Bulletin of the American Academy of Arts and Sciences*, Nov. 1989, at 30. Shelby Steele, *The Content of Our Character: A New Vision of Race in America* (1990). See "Black Power, Foul and Fragrant," *Economist*, Oct. 12, 1985, at 25, for a summary of Farrakhan's critical assessment of the condition of many African-Americans.

102. Note, in this regard, Nadine Strossen's evidence that regulations of racist speech have historically proved to be "particularly threatening to the speech of racial and political minorities." Strossen, "Regulating Racist Speech," at 556–59.

103. Or, in the language that the Court recently proposed in Milkovich v. Lorain Journal Co., 497 U.S. 1 (1990), claims of group harm will most likely be privileged as nonfactual assertions of "ideas." For a discussion of the close relationship between group defamation and nonfactual ideas, see David A. J. Richards, *Toleration and the Constitution* 190–93 (1986); see Greenawalt, "Insults," at 305–6.

104. Beauharnais v. Illinois, 343 U.S. 250, 250, 276 (1952) (ellipsis in original).

105. Id. at 257–58.

106. See, e.g., Matsuda, "Public Response," at 2358.

107. Id.

108. See Michelman, "Law's Republic," at 1501.

109. Cohen v. California, 403 U.S. 15, 16 (1971).

110. Hustler Magazine v. Falwell, 485 U.S. 46, 52 (1988).

111. Boos v. Barry, 485 U.S. 312, 316, 322 (1988). "In public debate our own citizens must tolerate insulting, and even outrageous speech in order to provide 'adequate breathing space to the freedoms protected by the First Amendment.' " Id. at 322 (quoting *Hustler Magazine*, 485 U.S. at 56); see Texas v. Johnson, 491 U.S. 397, 410–20 (1989).

112. The cases cited in the preceding three notes thus stand foursquare against

the application to public discourse of the tort of racial insult as proposed by Delgado, "Words That Wound," Love, "Discriminatory Speech," and Wright, "Racist Speech."

113. Michelman, "Law's Republic," at 1526; see Frank Cunningham, *Democratic Theory and Socialism* 188–91 (1987).

114. See, e.g., Contreras v. Crown Zellerbach Corp., 88 Wash. 2d 735, 565 P.2d 1173 (1977); Alcorn v. Anbro Eng'g 2 Cal. 3d 493, 468 P.2d 216, 86 Cal. Rptr. 88 (1970); Love, "Discriminatory Speech," at 128–33.

115. Cf. Dominguez v. Stone, 97 N.M. 211, 638 P.2d 423 (1981) (penalizing racist speech in public discourse).

116. Lasson, "Group Libel," at 122.

117. Thus "fighting words" are understood to be those that "by their very utterance inflict injury." Chaplinsky v. New Hampshire, 315 U.S. 568, 572 (1942). Outrageous words intentionally inflicting emotional distress are "nothing more than a surrogate" for a "punch or kick." R. George Wright, *"Hustler Magazine v. Falwell* and the Role of the First Amendment," 19 *Cumberland Law Review* 19, 23 (1988). "Ridicule" is experienced as a form of "intimidation." John Dewey, "Creative Democracy—The Task Before Us," in *Classic American Philosophers* 389, 393 (Max Harold Fisch, ed., 1951). Pornography is received not as "expression depicting the subordination of women, but [as] the *practice of subordination* itself." Paul Brest and Ann Vandenberg, "Politics, Feminism, and the Constitution: The Anti-Pornography Movement in Minneapolis," 39 *Stanford Law Review* 607, 659 (1987). And blasphemous communications are nothing more than a form of "brawls." Francis Ludlow Holt, *The Law of Libel* 70–71 (1816).

118. Time, Inc. v. Hill, 385 U.S. 374, 412 (1967) (Fortas, J., dissenting).

119. In the words of Terminiello v. Chicago: "A function of free speech under our system of government is to invite dispute. It may indeed best serve its high purpose when it induces a condition of unrest, creates dissatisfaction with conditions as they are, or even stirs people to anger. Speech is often provocative and challenging. It may strike at prejudices and preconceptions and have profound unsettling effects as it presses for acceptance of an idea. That is why freedom of speech, though not absolute . . . is nevertheless protected against censorship or punishment, unless shown likely to produce a clear and present danger of a serious substantive evil that rises far above public inconvenience, annoyance, or unrest . . . There is no room under our Constitution for a more restrictive view. For the alternative would lead to standardization of ideas either by legislatures, courts, or dominant political or community groups." 337 U.S. 1, 4–5 (1949) (citations omitted).

120. For an excellent discussion, see Kenneth Karst, "Boundaries and Reasons: Freedom of Expression and the Subordination of Groups," 1990 *University of Illinois Law Review* 95.

121. 403 U.S. 15, 23, 24–25.

122. See Matsuda, "Public Response," at 2340; see Lawrence, "If He Hollers," at 436.

123. I omit discussion of speech that silences through outright intimidation and threats. The regulation of such speech is not problematic under any theory.

124. For a good introduction to the concept of "discourse," see Paul A. Bové, "Discourse," in *Critical Terms for Literary Study* 50 (Frank Lentricchia and Thomas McLaughlin, eds., 1990).

125. Lawrence, "If He Hollers," at 452.

126. Id. at 474–75; see Kimberle Williams Crenshaw, "Race, Reform, and Retrenchment: Transformation and Legitimation in Antidiscrimination Law," 101 *Harvard Law Review* 1331, 1370–81 (1988).

127. Lucinda M. Finley, "Breaking Women's Silence in Law: The Dilemma of the Gendered Nature of Legal Reasoning," 64 *Notre Dame Law Review* 886, 889 (1989).

128. Note, "Racism and Race Relations in the University," 76 *Virginia Law Review* 295, 304 n.32 (1990) (quoting Roy L. Brooks, "Anti-Minority Mindset in the Law School Personnel Process: Toward an Understanding of Racial Mindsets," 5 *Journal of Law and Inequality* 1, 8–11 [1987]).

129. Matsuda, "Public Response," at 2323–26, 2375; Lawrence, "If He Hollers," at 458–61.

130. David Riesman, "Democracy and Defamation: Fair Game and Fair Comment II," 42 *Columbia Law Review* 1282, 1306–7 (1942).

131. See Paul Chevigny, *More Speech: Dialogue Rights and Modern Liberty* 53–72 (1988); Frank Michelman, "Conceptions of Democracy in American Constitutional Argument: The Case of Pornography Regulation," 56 *Tennessee Law Review* 291, 313 (1989).

132. For a general discussion of the concept of false consciousness, see Raymond Geuss, *The Idea of a Critical Theory: Habermas and the Frankfurt School* (1981).

133. Matsuda, "Public Response," at 2331.

134. Note, "Racism and Race Relations," at 295.

135. Lawrence, "If He Hollers," at 436.

136. Id. at 481.

137. Matsuda, "Public Response," at 2369. This tendency is explicitly thematized in Iris Marion Young's artless proposal that "a democratic public" should cede to "constituent groups that are oppressed or disadvantaged" a "veto power regarding specific policies that affect a group directly." Young, "Polity and Group Difference," 99 *Ethics* 250, 261–62 (1989).

138. The "grand tradition" of republican participation, the notion that "we can lift our public life above the fallen and compromised realm of factional politics," thus does not seem to me so easily abandoned as would appear from

recent literature stressing fidelity to the particular cultural "tradition" of minority groups. See Gerald P. Lopez, "The Idea of a Constitution in the Chicano Tradition," 37 *Journal of Legal Education* 162, 163–64 (1987). Even Young notes that a "heterogenous public . . . is a *public*, where participants discuss together the issues before them and are supposed to come to a decision that they determine as best or most just." Young, "Polity," at 267. Young therefore acknowledges that "it is possible for persons to maintain their group identity and to be influenced by their perceptions of social events derived from their group-specific experience, and at the same time to be public spirited, in the sense of being open to listening to the claims of others and not being concerned for their own gain alone. It is possible and necessary for people to take a critical distance from their own immediate desires and gut reactions in order to discuss public proposals. Doing so, however, cannot require that citizens abandon their particular affiliations, experiences, and social location." Id. at 257–58.

139. Joseph Berger, "Professors' Theories on Race Stir Turmoil at City College," *New York Times*, Apr. 20, 1990, at B1, col. 2.

140. Note that the argument in the text does not hold against the contention that certain ideas should be excluded from public discourse because they cause extensive harm to individuals or victim groups. Such harm is extrinsic to the function of public discourse. To evaluate the contention that public discourse ought to be limited because of harm to individuals or groups, therefore, we must assess the importance of democratic self-governance in light of our commitment to protecting stable personal and group identities.

The argument considered in the text that certain ideas ought to be excluded from public discourse because they are intrinsically coercive, on the other hand, turns upon harm to the function of public discourse itself. The argument is unsatisfactory because the concept of "coercion" must itself be defined by reference to a "moral baseline" determined by the practice in question. See A. Wertheimer, *Coercion* 217 (1987). Within the practice of public discourse, no idea can be deemed intrinsically coercive because the very function of public discourse presupposes a formal equality of persons and hence of ideas.

141. Chaplinsky v. New Hampshire, 315 U.S. 568 (1942).

142. See Lawrence, "If He Hollers," at 474–75. That this is a general characteristic of group claims can be seen by the development of an analogous dynamic among those who support the regulation of pornography. See, e.g., Catharine MacKinnon, "On Collaboration," in *Feminism Unmodified: Discourses on Life and Law* 198 (1987).

143. The success or failure of the gesture will depend entirely on the perception of members of victim groups. There is thus no guarantee that any particular regulatory scheme will in fact actually cause members of victim groups to reinterpret their position within public discourse. This inherent gap between regulatory design and the achievement of regulatory purpose, coupled

with the fact that only members of victim groups can experience and evaluate the claim of cultural exclusion, creates disturbing possibilities for strategic manipulation.

144. Of course so minimal a gesture might not be sufficient to achieve this purpose. The intrinsically speculative quality of the argument must be taken into account in its evaluation.

145. According to the Solicitor General, the state's interest in prohibiting flag burning turns on the importance of "safeguard[ing] the flag's identity 'as the unique and unalloyed symbol of the Nation.'" United States v. Eichman, 496 U.S. 310, 315 (1990) (quoting Brief for United States at 28, 29).

146. Texas v. Johnson, 491 U.S. 397, 430–32 (1989) (Rehnquist, C. J., dissenting).

147. I should be plain that I myself reject the premise of this argument and do not believe that the rhetorical meaning of speech can be disentangled from the manner of its presentation. Style and substance are always interdependent, for, in the words of Georg Lukács, "content determines form." Georg Lukács, *Realism in Our Time: Literature and the Class Struggle* 19 (John and Necke Mander, trans., 1962). I therefore do not think that the impact on public discourse of prohibiting certain kinds of words can ever properly be said to be *de minimis*. I nevertheless want to evaluate the case for balancing on the strong assumption of this kind of *de minimis* impact.

148. For a discussion of this argument in the context of flag burning, see *Eichman*, 496 U.S. at 322–23 (Stevens, J., dissenting).

149. In evaluating this balance, I do not mean to call into question the holding of *Chaplinsky*, which in my view attempts to distinguish private fracases from political debate. It is clear enough that racial epithets, when uttered in certain face-to-face situations, would constitute "fighting words" and hence not form part of public discourse. See Greenawalt, "Insults," at 306. The point of the argument in the text, however, is to evaluate restraints on racist epithets in what would otherwise clearly be deemed public discourse, as for example in political debates, newspapers, pamphlets, magazines, novels, movies, or records.

150. Anyone inclined to doubt this proposition should review again the current controversy over funding for the National Endowment for the Arts, or the prosecutions occasioned by the Mapplethorpe exhibition or the recordings of 2 Live Crew. See "Rap Band Members Found Not Guilty in Obscenity Trial," *New York Times*, Oct. 21, 1990, § 1, at 1, col. 1; "Cincinnati Jury Acquits Museum in *Mapplethorpe* Obscenity Case," *New York Times*, Oct. 6, 1990, § 1, at 1, col. 1; "Reverend Wildman's War on the Arts," *New York Times*, Sept. 2, 1990, § 6 (Magazine), at 22, col. 1.

151. Emory University, "Policy Statement on Discriminatory Harassment" (1988); see Doe v. University of Mich., 721 F. Supp. 852, 856 (E.D. Mich. 1989) (concerning sanctions for speech victimizing an individual "on the basis of race,

ethnicity, religion, sex, sexual orientation, creed, national origin, ancestry, age, marital status, handicap or Vietnam-era veteran status"). The regulations of Michigan State University include the prohibited category of "political persuasion." Michigan State University, "Your Ticket to an Adventure in Understanding" (1988). The regulations of West Chester University include the category of "lifestyle." West Chester University, "Ram's Eye View: Every Student's Guide to West Chester University" 61 (1990). The regulations of Hampshire College include that of "socio-economic class." Hampshire College, "College Policies: Updates and Revisions" (1988–89).

152. Widmar v. Vincent, 454 U.S. 263, 267 n.5 268–69 (1981).

153. Id. at 268 n.5.

154. Id. at 277 (citing Healy v. James, 408 U.S. 169, 189 [1972]).

155. This short discussion considers only issues pertaining to the *constitutionality* of the regulation of racist speech. It does not consider the *educational* issues raised by such regulation. These issues are, however, profound and revolve around the question of whether legal restraint is the heuristically most effective response to racist speech.

156. Pugsley v. Sellmeyer, 158 Ark. 247, 253, 250 S.W. 538, 539 (1923).

157. 478 U.S. 675 (1986).

158. Id. at 678, 681 (quoting Ambach v. Norwick, 441 U.S. 68, 77 [1979]), 681 (quoting Charles Austin Beard and Mary Beard, *New Basic History of the United States* 228 [1968]).

159. Id. at 681, 683. For a more recent example of the same kind of reasoning, see Hazelwood School Dist. v. Kuhlmeier, 484 U.S. 260, 271–72 (1988).

160. 410 U.S. 667, 672 (1973) (Burger, C. J., dissenting).

161. Bethel v. School Dist. No. 403 v. Frazer, 478 U.S. 675, 681 (1986).

162. For the development of this logic at the pre-university level, see, for example, Clarke v. Board of Educ., 215 Neb. 250, 338 N.W.2d 272 (1983).

163. Commonwealth of Massachusetts Board of Regents of Higher Education, "Policy Against Racism and Guidelines for Campus Policies Against Racism" 2 (June 13, 1989).

164. Alder v. Board of Educ., 342 U.S. 485, 508 (1952) (Douglas, J., dissenting). For a fully developed statement of this position, see Abington School Dist. v. Schempp, 374 U.S. 203, 241–42 (1963) (Brennan, J., concurring).

165. The tension between the concepts of democratic and civic education closely recapitulates the informative debate between Piaget and Durkheim over the question of how to teach moral values. Durkheim stressed the importance of discipline, authority, and constraint, whereas Piaget emphasized cooperation, agreement, and autonomy. See Piaget, *Moral Judgment*, at 341–71.

166. 393 U.S. 503, 508–9, 511 (1969).

167. Healy v. James, 408 U.S. 169, 194 (1972).

168. "Report of the Committee on Freedom of Expression at Yale," 4 *Human*

Rights 357, 357 (1975). This function is not one that we ordinarily attribute to high schools, much less to elementary schools.

169. Id. at 357–58; see Benno Schmidt, "Freedom of Thought: A Principle in Peril?," *Yale Alumni Magazine*, Oct. 1989, at 65, 65–66.

170. J. Peter Byrne, "Academic Freedom: A 'Special Concern of the First Amendment,'" 99 *Yale Law Journal* 251, 261 (1989). The presence of such a model "contributes profoundly to society at large. We employ the expositors of academic speech to train nearly everyone who exercises leadership within our society. Beyond whatever specialized learning our graduates assimilate, they ought to be persuaded that careful, honest expression demands an answer in kind. The experience of academic freedom helps secure broader, positive liberties of expression." Id.

171. Keyishian v. Board of Regents, 385 U.S. 589, 603 (1967) (quoting United States v. Associated Press, 52 F. Supp. 362, 372 [S.D.N.Y. 1943]); see Healy v. James, 408 U.S. 169, 180–81 (1972).

172. *Healy*, 408 U.S. at 187–88.

173. "If the university's overriding commitment to free expression is to be sustained, secondary social and ethical responsibilities must be left to the informal processes of suasion, example, and argument." "Report of the Committee," at 360.

174. Papish v. University of Mo. Curators, 410 U.S. 667, 670 (1973).

175. As a matter of policy, however, it is always dangerous to make the legality of speech depend primarily upon an assessment of a speaker's intent, for there is a powerful tendency to attribute bad motives to those with whom we fundamentally disagree.

176. The inability to make this distinction contributed to a court's recent decision to strike down as unconstitutional the regulations of the University of Michigan. See Doe v. University of Mich., 721 F. Supp. 852 (E.D. Michigan 1989); Grano, "Free Speech," at 7.

177. For an admirable attempt to meet this challenge, see Grey, "Civil Rights," and the regulations that Professor Grey drafted for Stanford University.

178. Cases like *Tinker* and *Healy* make clear, however, that the Supreme Court's First Amendment jurisprudence has rested on the assumption that there are constitutional limits to the freedom of public educational institutions to define their own educational mission.

179. Some universities have regulated racist speech in ways that turn on similar functional and geographic considerations. See *Doe*, 721 F. Supp. at 856; "Tufts Restores Free Speech After T-Shirt Confrontation," *San Francisco Chronicle*, Dec. 9, 1989, at B6, col. 1; Wilson, "Colleges Take 2 Basic Approaches in Adopting Anti-Harassment Plans," *Chronicle of Higher Education*, Oct. 4, 1989, at A38, col. 1; Melissa Russo, "Free Speech at Tufts: Zoned Out," *New York Times*, Sept. 27, 1989, at A29.

180. See, e.g., Edward A. Purcell, *The Crisis of Democratic Theory: Scientific Naturalism and the Problem of Value* (1973).

181. For a striking illustration of the untoward (and in retrospect horrifying) consequences of repudiating that obligation, see Herbert Marcuse, "Repressive Tolerance," in Robert Paul Wolff, Barrington Moore, and Herbert Marcuse, *A Critique of Pure Tolerance* 81 (1965).

Sources

Earlier versions of the chapters in this book were originally published as follows.

Chapter 1: "Theories of Constitutional Interpretation," 30 *Representations* 13 (1990). © 1990 by the Regents of the University of California. Used by permission.

Chapter 2: "The Social Foundations of Privacy: Community and Self in the Common Law Tort," 77 *California Law Review* 957 (1989). © 1989 by California Law Review, Inc. Used by permission.

Chapter 3: "Cultural Heterogeneity and Law: Pornography, Blasphemy, and the First Amendment," 76 *California Law Review* 297 (1988). © 1988 by California Law Review, Inc. Used by permission.

Chapter 4: "The Constitutional Concept of Public Discourse: Outrageous Opinion, Democratic Deliberation, and *Hustler Magazine v. Falwell*," 103 *Harvard Law Review* 601 (1990). © 1990 by the Harvard Law Review Association.

Chapter 5: "Between Democracy and Community: The Legal Constitution of Social Form," *Nomos* xxxv ("Democratic Community") 163 (1993).

Chapter 6: "Between Governance and Management: The History and Theory of the Public Forum," originally published in 34 *UCLA Law Review* 1713 (1987). Copyright 1987, The Regents of the University of California. All rights reserved.

Chapter 7: "Meiklejohn's Mistake: Individual Autonomy and the Reform of Public Discourse," 64 *University of Colorado Law Review* 1109 (1993). A version of this article was originally published under the title "Managing Deliberation: The Quandary of Democratic Dialogue," 103 *Ethics* 654 (1993).

Reprise: "Racist Speech, Democracy, and the First Amendment," 32 *William and Mary Law Review* 267 (1990).

451

Index

Accountability, 79–85

Actual malice, 124, 152–153, 391–392

Adderley v. Florida, 205–208, 217, 219, 223, 248–249, 255, 406–408

Adorno, Theodore, 49–50

Americanization, 91

Arendt, Hannah, 161, 200, 420

Assimilationist law: and blasphemy, 95–98, 100, 101–104, 366; and community, 90–91, 99–100, 357–358; defined, 90–91; and individualist law, 93–94, 100, 104, 112; and obscenity, 111–112; and pluralist law, 91–92, 115–116, 99–100, 103

Austin, J. L., 110

Authority, 13, 415; and community, 17–18; and consent, 32–35, 39, 41–44, 340–341; constitutional, 29–50, 273–274, 276–289; and constitutional interpretation, 15–16, 29–50; defined, 12–13; and democracy, 16, 19, 39–40, 49–50, 184–186, 271–278; and ethos, 35–38, 41–47; and governance, 19, 200; and judicial opinions, 15, 29–50; and management, 49–50, 240–267, 271–272, 423–424; and the rule of law, 30–32, 39–41, 273–274

Autonomy: ascription of, 282–286, 432–433; and civility rules, 63–64, 74; and community, 10–11, 63–64, 74, 189–190; and democracy, 7, 10–11, 14–15, 187–189, 272–278, 282–286; and determinism, 282–286; and the "I," 195–196; and management, 10–11, 14, 269–289; and privacy, 60–64; and public discourse, 184–196, 268–269, 272–278, 282–289, 329–331; and social norms, 10–11

Barber, Benjamin, 185

Beauharnais v. Illinois, 92, 105, 112–113, 294, 303, 306, 308–309

Bender, Thomas, 180

Bethel School District No. 403 v. Fraser, 133–134, 136, 176–177, 325

Bickel, Alexander, 144–145

Black, Justice Hugo, 92, 206–208, 407

Blackmun, Justice Harry, 211–215, 231–232, 409

Blasphemy: in American law, 101–108, 366–367; and assimilationist law, 94–104, 362, 366–367; in English law, 94–100, 362; and the First Amendment, 102–108; and individualist law, 103–108; and pluralist law, 97–105; and pornography, 108; and speech/action distinction, 368–369, 444

Bohannan, Paul, 65, 79, 347–348, 365

Bork, Robert, 46–47, 166

Brandeis, Justice Louis D., 8, 51, 57, 66, 73, 76, 166–167

Brennan, Justice William J., 9; and Marsh v. Chambers, 26–29, 34–35, 37–38, 41, 46; and public forum doctrine, 212–214, 218–219, 409; on racist speech, 298, 438–439

Brents v. Morgan, 68–71

Briscoe v. Reader's Digest Association, 70, 81–82

Brown v. Board of Education, 43, 47–48, 291

Brown v. Glines, 237–239, 241, 258–259

Buckley v. Valeo, 268
Burger, Chief Justice Warren, 27, 33, 38, 41–42, 92–93, 221, 325

Cantwell v. Connecticut, 103–108, 113–115, 137–138, 141, 188, 301, 306
Chafee, Zechariah, 114
Chambers, Ernest, 23–26, 29, 50
Chaplinsky v. New Hampshire, 173, 175, 177, 194, 301–302, 319, 447
City of Madison Joint School District No. 8 v. Wisconsin Employment Relations Commission, 220–226, 228, 242–244
Civic education, 324–329. See also Universities
Civility rules: and accountability, 84–85; and autonomy, 63–64, 74; and community identity, 55–59, 127–129, 132–134, 181–184, 300–301, 311; defined, 55–56, 183, 300; and democracy, 192–196, 301, 313–314; and the educational environment, 325–329; and fair comment privilege, 135–137; and the First Amendment, 127–153, 188, 191–192, 310–311; and individual identity, 54–59, 63–64, 74, 127–128, 132–134, 144–145, 181–182, 310–311; and instrumental reason, 333–334; legal enforcement of, 54–59, 64–67, 74, 86, 127–134, 144–145, 147–148, 183–184, 300; and the "Me," 195–196; and news media, 82–84; and pornography, 112–116, 120–134; and public discourse, 135–140, 147–148, 151–153, 177, 192–196, 300–302; and rational deliberation, 144–148, 301, 312–313; and reasonable person, 56; and rules of deference and demeanor, 54–55, 181–184; and social meaning, 63–64, 74; social prerequisites for, 4, 86–87; and speech/action distinction, 144–148, 192–193, 313–314, 385–386, 444. See also Community
Clark, Carroll, 140–142
Coercion, 113, 119, 133, 186–187, 285–286, 299–300; defined by reference to a baseline, 318, 446; racist speech as, 312–319, 446; uncivil speech as, 144–148, 192–193, 301, 313–314
Cohen v. California, 121, 139–140, 275–276, 301, 314
Coleridge, Lord, 96–98, 362
Collectivist theory of the First Amendment: defined, 268–269; justifications for, 278–288; and managerial authority, 270–278, 288–289; Alexander Meiklejohn and, 269–276
Commercial speech, 392
Community: and authority, 17–18, 41–44; and civility rules, 56, 81–85, 127–134, 180–184, 300–302; and collective identity, 3–4, 41–44, 56, 128–129, 132–134, 149–163, 180–184, 303–306; and consent, 41–44; constitutional interpretation, 41–50, 191–196; and construction of the person, 10–11, 127–129, 144–145, 180–184; and critical interaction, 146–148, 175; and decency/morality, 89–90, 91–107, 108–116, 127–134; defined, 2–4, 15, 17–18, 46, 180–184; and democracy, 7–8, 13–15, 175–176, 187–196, 268–269, 270–275, 276–289, 300–302, 305–306; and diversity, 4, 64–67, 99–100, 183, 348; and ethos, 35–38, 41–44; and fair comment privilege, 135–137; hegemony and, 4, 64–67, 183; and human dignity, 3–4, 23–50, 81–85, 122–134, 182–183, 291–292, 300–318, 319–323; and individual identity, 10–11, 53–54, 72–73, 81–85, 113–114, 122–134, 138, 144–145, 150–153, 181–182, 195–196, 291–293, 295, 299–300, 301–312, 441–442; and judicial decision–making, 17–18, 183–184; and legal system, 12, 65, 347; and management, 5–6, 13–15, 87, 268–269, 270–275, 276–289, 333–335; and the "Me," 195–196; neutrality in the marketplace of communities, 138–139, 151; and pluralism, 99–100; and press/media, 73–74, 82–85; privacy and, 51, 60–64, 71–85, 127–134; and public discourse, 120, 135–163, 174–177, 187–196, 268–269, 270–275,

276–289, 300–302, 430; and reason, 95–97, 112, 144–148, 363

Connick v. Myers, 260

Consent, authority of, 32–35, 38–39, 340; and authority of ethos, 39–44; and authority of law, 38–39; and historical interpretation, 29–30, 32–35

Constitutional interpretation: and assmilationism, 17–18, 101–103, 111–112; and authority, 15–16, 30–50; and authority of consent, 32–36, 41–44, 280–282; and authority of ethos, 17–18, 35–38, 41–49; and authority of law, 30–32, 38–41; and community, 6, 17–19, 45–48, 138, 174–177, 187–196; and counter–majoritarian difficulty, 25, 37–38, 48–49, 190–191, 342; and cultural heterogeneity, 43–44; and democracy, 9–10, 15–17, 26, 184–196, 271–289; and doctrinal interpretation, 29–32, 38–41, 45, 47, 49; and historical interpretation, 32–25, 38–45, 47, 49; and individualism, 103–108, 114–116, 138–139, 148–149, 187–188, 299; and justification, 25; and management, 6, 234–267, 268–289, 323–329, 423–424; and original intent, 27–29, 30–35; plain meaning, 24–25, 44–45, 336; and pluralism, 104–105, 113–116; and responsive interpretation, 29–30, 35–50; and social domains, 1–2, 15–18, 148–149, 174–177, 189–196, 272–276, 286–288, 329–330; and social values, 102–103, 107, 111–112, 115–116, 148–149, 174–177, 189–196, 269–289, 302, 366; and *stare decisis*, 17, 26–32, 38–41, 47; textualism, 24–25, 44–45, 336

Cornelius v. NAACP, 227–228, 231, 258, 412–413

Counter–majoritarian difficulty, 25–26, 37–38, 48–49, 190–191, 342

Cox v. Louisiana, 206, 407

Critical education, 327–329; *See also* Universities

Critical interaction, 79–80, 142–148, 175–177

Cultural heterogeneity: and hegemony, 64–67, 94–97, 183, 303–306; and legal authority, 4, 43–44; and public discourse, 136–138, 140–141, 143–144, 304, 402; and neutrality in the marketplace of communities, 138–139, 151

Davis v. Massachusetts, 203–204

Debs v. United States, 109–110

Defamation law, 57, 66, 94–104, 122–123, 124, 127–134, 150–163, 183–184, 345, 367, 379, 400; and actual malice, 152–153, 161; and fair comment privilege, 135–137; and falsity, 129–131, 159–162; and public discourse, 119–120, 122–134, 150–163; and rules of civility, 56–57, 128–134, 183

Deference, 237–239, 241–144, 246, 257–267, 417–418, 422–426

Delgado, Richard, 291

Democracy: and autonomy, 10–11, 272–276, 282–286, 299, 335; boundaries of, 8–9, 175–176, 189–190, 191–196, 244–252, 278–288, 302–303; and community, 8, 13–15, 23, 142, 174–177, 189–196, 301–302; constitutional law and, 1–2, 13, 15–18, 32–33, 184–191, 193–196, 270–288, 299–300; and constitutional limitations, 190–191; and construction of the person, 10–11, 187–188, 282; and counter–majoritarian difficulty, 6, 26, 37, 48–49, 184–185, 190–191; defined, 2, 6–7, 15, 184–191, 272–274, 299; and diversity, 142–144, 251–252, 303–304, 313–314, 444; and the First Amendment, 7, 187, 269–276, 297–302; and identification, 7–8, 192, 273, 280, 286–288, 319–323; and indeterminate national identity, 188, 195–196, 273–278, 305–306; and individualism, 9–10, 187–188, 192, 299, 306–308, 381–382, 439; and judicial review, 24–30, 190–191, 272–278; and legal system, 12; and legitimation, 273, 280, 282, 286–288, 319–323, 431; and managerial law, 7–8, 13–15, 239–267,

Democracy (*cont.*)
269–289; and participation, 192, 273,
280, 286–288, 319–323; and public
discourse, 7–8, 142, 145, 184–187,
191–196, 272–278, 299–303, 329–331;
and the public/private distinction,
188–189, 280–282, 299, 304–305,
401, 431, 440; and rational deliberation, 192–193, 312–323; and reconciliation of individual and collective
autonomy, 7–8, 184–187, 273, 280,
286–289, 299, 306; and self–
determination, 6–8, 184–187, 272–
276, 286–288, 299, 305–306, 319–323
Democratic community, 179, 191–196
Dewey, John, 18, 146, 185–186
Diamond, Sigmund, 251–252, 419
Diamond, Stanley, 87
Dignitary harms, 3; assimilationism and,
106–107; and civility rules, 55–57,
61–62, 127–140, 144–148, 181–184,
300, 311, 345; and intentional infliction of emotional distress, 122–123,
138–139, 144–148, 183–184; managerial domains and, 16–17, 87–88; and
privacy tort, 58–59, 122–134, 138–
139, 183–184; racist speech and, 295,
310–312
Dignity: community and, 10–11, 19, 51,
54–56, 58–59, 61–62, 88, 127–129,
138–139, 144–148, 151, 182–183,
311, 345, 379, 382; defined, 128–129;
privacy and, 51–52, 73–74, 87–88,
122–123, 127–134, 151, 345; racist
speech and, 295, 310–312; and social
norms, 10–11, 52–74, 138–139, 144–
148, 182–183, 311
Diversity, 4, 43–44, 90–94, 99–100,
104–107, 140–141, 143–144, 251–252,
279, 297, 303–304
Doctrinal interpretation, 29–32, 38–41,
45, 47, 49. *See also* Constitutional interpretation; Historical interpretation;
Responsive interpretation
Double institutionalization, 65, 347–348
Douglas, Justice William O., 93
Dun & Bradstreet, Inc. v. Greenmoss
Builders, Inc., 171, 393–394

Durkheim, Emile, 186, 385, 448
Dworkin, Andrea, 89, 108, 112, 116
Dworkin, Ronald, 179

Education, 189–190, 238–239, 296–297;
and civic education, 189–190, 324–
326, 328–329; and critical education,
327–329; and democratic education,
326–329
Edwards v. South Carolina, 207, 213
Eisenstadt v. Baird, 9
Eliot, T. S., 265
Ely, John Hart, 6–7
Equality: formal versus substantive, 305–
306, 313–314, 441; racist speech and,
294, 310, 313–314
Establishment clause, 10, 24–29
Ethos, authority of, 35–39, 41–44, 339;
and community, 42–44, 49
Eule, Julian, 282–283, 285

Factual statements: community and, 142,
160–163; convergence and, 159–163;
versus fictional statements, 389–390;
versus statements of opinion, 120,
153–163; verifiability and, 157–159,
390
Fair comment, 135–137, 380
Fairness doctrine, 279, 280–282
False consciousness, 316
False statements, 125, 129–131, 391–392
Falwell, Jerry, 121–123, 131–132, 141,
155–156, 373–374
Farrakhan, Louis, 308
FCC v. Pacifica Foundation, 176–177
Federalism, 91, 359
Federalist Papers, The, 34
Fighting words, 115, 173, 175, 193–194,
301–302, 318–319, 444, 447
First Amendment: and balancing, 250–
251; and collectivist theory, 268–289;
democracy and, 7, 142, 187, 269–276,
297–300; and harm, 291–292, 318;
and individualism, 101–108, 114–116,
120, 138–139, 141, 148–149, 187–
188, 300, 381–382; and public discourse, 134–178, 187–188, 272–278;
social domains and, 15–18, 187–196,

234–267, 272–278, 286–288, 329–330.
See also Fighting words; Freedom of
speech; Public discourse; Racist speech
Fiss, Owen, 269, 276–278, 281–283,
285, 427, 428
Flynt, Larry, 121–123, 131, 141, 148,
155–156, 373
Formalism, 331
Foucault, Michel, 288
Fourteenth Amendment, 43, 305–306,
310, 322–323, 441
Fourth Amendment, 87, 333–334
Frankfurter, Justice Felix, 308–309
Fraser, Nancy, 307
Freedom of speech: and abusive speech,
5, 107–108, 113, 144–148, 173, 192–
193, 303–331; assimilationism and,
106–107, 115–116, 366–367; and
campaign finance reform, 268, 282–
288, 430–431; and community, 101–
104, 134–163, 174–177, 366–367; and
democracy, 8–9, 142, 184–196, 269–
276, 297–302, 330–331; and the free
speech principle, 16, 111; and individualism, 101–108, 114–116, 138–139,
141, 148–149, 187–188, 299, 306–
308; and management, 15, 234–267,
268–289, 323–329; media and, 169–
173, 280–282, 268, 280–282; and pluralism, 101–108, 113–116, 306–310,
315–323; and public discourse, 134–
178, 184–196, 272–276, 297–323; and
social domains, 15–16, 180–196, 234–
267, 269–289, 329–330; speech/action
distinction, 110–111, 144–148, 190–
191, 193, 310, 313, 368–369, 385–
386, 444. *See also* Blasphemy;
Defamation law; Fighting words; First
Amendment; Offensiveness; Outrageousness; Pornography; Public discourse; Public forum doctrine; Racist
speech
Free exercise clause, 101–103
Free Speech: A Philosophical Enquiry
(Schauer), 16, 125
Free speech principle, 16, 111
Freund, Paul, 33
Fuller, Lon, 1

Gadamer, Hans–Georg, 37–38
Garrison, William Lloyd, 291
Gavison, Ruth, 60
Gender, 115–116, 307
Gertz v. Robert Welch, Inc., 123, 131–
132, 154–155, 165, 393–394
Godkin, E. L., 66
Goffman, Erving, 54–55, 62–65, 72–73,
128–129, 181–182, 261
Goldberg, Justice Arthur, 6
Gouldner, Alvin, 77–80, 85, 143, 145–
146
Grayned v. City of Rockford, 208–213,
217–219, 233–234, 239, 242–244, 246,
257–258, 408, 415
Greenbelt Cooperative Publishing Asso-
ciation v. Bresler, 154–155
Greer v. Spock, 215–224, 226–230, 234,
253–255, 261–262
Griswold v. Connecticut, 6, 52
Group harm, 89, 92, 99–100, 113, 294–
295, 306–310, 315–323, 341
Group identity, 105, 113–116, 306–309,
311, 322–323, 371, 445–446
Group libel, 92, 99–100, 112–116, 294–
295, 306, 370
Group rights, 92, 99–100, 112–116,
306–309, 311, 322–323, 371

Habermas, Jürgen, 6, 145–146, 186, 256
Hague v. CIO, 203–208, 215–216, 219,
229
Hale, Sir Matthew, 94–95
Hamberger v. Eastman, 52–59, 67
Hand, Learned, 129–130
Harlan, Justice John, 170, 275–276, 314
Harman, Gilbert, 159
Hart, Gary, 76
Hate speech regulation. *See* Racist speech
Hawkins v. Multimedia, Inc., 83
Hegemony, 43–44, 64–67, 99–100, 183–
184
Heteronomy, 269–278
Higham, John, 92
Historical interpretation, 36, 38–44, 47,
49, 340. *See also* Constitutional inter-
pretation; Doctrinal interpretation;
Responsive interpretation

Hobbes, Thomas, 46–48
Holmes, Justice Oliver Wendell, 35–36, 257
Horkheimer, Max, 49–50
Hoy, David, 38
Huntington, Samuel, 192
Huskey v. NBC, 62–63
Hustler Magazine v. Falwell, 119–137, 139, 146–153, 155–158, 161, 164, 170, 177, 301
Hustler Magazine v. Moral Majority, 372

Identification, 7–8, 192, 273, 280, 286–288, 319–323
Identity: autonomy and, 63–64, 282–286; community and, 46, 127–134, 138, 144–148, 150–151, 180–184, 273–274, 276–289, 310–312; democracy and, 184–190, 273–278, 282–286; and group harm, 294–295, 306–308; legal creation of, 10–11, 182–184; national, 43–44, 189–190, 192, 195–196, 273–278, 305–306, 339; and public discourse, 187–188, 272–278, 286–289, 306–308
Individualism: ascription and, 282–286; autonomy and, 9–10, 187–188, 272–278, 282–286; blasphemy and, 101–108; and civility, 81–88, 137–139, 189–190; collective self–determination and, 184–190, 299, 306–308; community and, 10, 135–140, 189–190, 300–302, 441–442; Constitution and, 101–108, 115–116, 138–139, 140–141, 184–190, 299, 306–308, 381–382; democracy and, 9, 184–196, 272–278, 306–308, 381–382, 439; diversity and, 140–141, 192; obscenity and, 108; pornography and, 108, 112–116; and privacy, 3, 51–88, 122–134; and public discourse, 139–140, 150–163, 184–196, 268–269, 272–278, 306–307, 381
Individualist law: assimilationist law and, 92–94, 102–104, 106–108, 111–112 defined, 92–94; pluralist law and, 92–94, 105–106, 108–110, 114–116, 360, 383
Information preserves, 73–74

Instrumental reason, 4–5, 12, 15, 239–240, 249–252, 362
Intentional infliction of emotional distress, 61–62, 123–125, 127–128, 131–134, 145, 150–151, 183–184
Intersubjectivity, 133–134, 139
Intrusion, tort of, 52–59, 85–86
Involuntary public figures, 80–81
Irrational speech, 95–97, 112, 144–148, 193–194, 274–275, 301, 312–315, 363

Jacobsohn, Gary, 306
James, William, 91
Jamison v. Texas, 205–207
Judicial decision–making: and ascription, 280–286; and authority, 15, 29–50; and deference, 237–239, 241–244, 246, 257–267; and justification, 15–18, 25; and rights, 16–17; and social domains, 15–18, 257–267, 272–278, 280–288, 329–331; and *stare decisis*, 17, 26–32, 38–41, 47
Judgment, 156–163

Kallen, Horace, 91
Kalven, Harry, 101, 201–202, 205, 209, 212
Kant, Immanuel, 36, 134, 186, 239–240
Karst, Kenneth, 274–275, 305, 428–429
Kelley v. Post Publishing Co., 84
Kelsen, Hans, 185, 399
Kennedy, Justice Anthony, 124–125
Kent, Chief Justice James, 101–104
Kirkup, James, 97–98

Lefort, Claude, 23, 50, 186
Legitimation, 23, 273, 280, 282, 286–288, 319–323
Lehman v. City of Shaker Heights, 211–215, 218, 253, 258, 263–265
Lemon v. Kurtzman, 27, 31, 32
Libel. *See* Defamation law
Limited public forum, 219–228, 412
Lippmann, Walter, 5, 79, 82, 142
Llewellyn, Karl, 36
Lochner v. New York, 8

Locke, John, 35
Lovibond, Sabina, 147

MacKinnon, Catharine, 89, 108, 112,
   115–116
Majoritarianism, 6–7, 48–49, 272–273,
   399
Malice, 152–153, 393, 406
Management: authority and, 234–247,
   261–265, 271–272; boundaries of, 87,
   239–241, 247–255, 265–267, 272–289,
   333–334; and community, 5–6, 13–15,
   87, 268–269, 270–275, 276–289, 333–
   335; constitutional law and, 1–2, 15–
   18, 234–267, 268–269, 271–289, 323–
   331; and construction of the person,
   10–11, 282–286; defined, 2, 4–6, 15,
   275; and democracy, 7–8, 13–15, 239–
   240, 249–257, 271–278, 286–289;
   governance and, 239–241, 244–255;
   judicial deference to, 237–239, 241–
   244, 257–265, 324, 417–418, 422–
   426; and legal system, 12; public
   discourse and, 268–269, 272–269,
   276–289; and universities, 323–330.
   See also Public forum doctrine
Marbury v. Madison, 25–26, 30
Marketplace of communities, 138–139,
   151
Marshall, Chief Justice John, 25, 30
Marshall, Justice Thurgood, 209
Marsh v. Chambers, 23–31, 33–35, 37–
   39, 41–42
Martin v. City of Struthers, 202
Marx, Karl, 6
Mead, George Herbert, 128, 181–182,
   195–196
Media, news: managerial law and, 5,
   280–282, 431–432; and privacy, 75–
   85, 354; and public discourse, 141–
   142, 171–172, 302; and the public
   sphere, 77–78, 82–85, 129, 141–142,
   171–172
Meese, Edwin, III, 32
Meetze v. Associated Press, 82–83, 354
Meiklejohn, Alexander, 19–20, 190, 269–
   276
Melville, Herman, 178

Melvin v. Reid, 70–71
Merton, Robert, 60
Miami Herald Publishing Co. v. Tor-
   nillo, 268
Michelman, Frank, 119, 133, 184, 186,
   311
Miller v. California, 171, 177
Minersville School District v. Gobitis,
   90, 93
Moral Commonwealth, The (Selznick), 3
Moral tact, 60–61, 175
Murphy, Justice Frank, 175

News, 77–78, 82–85, 141–142. See also
   Media, news
New York Times Co. v. Sullivan, 113–
   114, 124–125, 152, 164, 201, 301,
   392–393
Nietzche, Friedrich, 34
Nimmer, Melville, 200
Nonet, Philippe, 36
Noninterpretavism, 44
Nonpublic forum: and contemporary
   doctrine, 223, 228–229, 231–234; and
   deference, 237–239, 241–244, 246,
   257–265; and managerial authority,
   233–257

Obscenity, 89, 171, 363; assmilationist
   law and, 111–112; First Amendment
   and, 89–90, 111–112; and ideas, 385;
   versus pornography, 89–90, 108, 112
Offensiveness: blasphemy and, 94–95,
   362; civility rules and, 52–59, 68–74,
   325–329; community and, 52–74, 311;
   diversity and, 65–67; privacy and 52–
   74, 350; public discourse and, 310–
   311. See also Civility rules; Dignitary
   harms; Intentional infliction of emotional distress; Intrusion, tort of; Outrageousness; Privacy; Public
   disclosure; Racist speech
Old Dominion Branch No. 496, National Association of Letter Carriers v.
   Austin, 155
Opinion, statements of: community and,
   120, 160–163, 388; versus factual
   statements, 120, 153–163; and falsity,

Opinion, statements of (*cont.*)
  125, 156–157, 160–161; nonconver-
  gence and, 159–163, 391; preference
  expressions and, 156–157; and public
  discourse, 163, 388; rhetorical hyperbole, 154–155; subjectivism and, 57
Organizations, 234–235, 239–240, 247–
  252, 259–260, 415–416, 418, 420,
  422–423
Outrageousness, 96–100, 107, 119, 126–
  134, 150–151, 311, 444

Paine, Thomas, 95
Palmer, Robert E., 23–24
Papish v. University of Missouri Cura-
  tors, 325
Paradox of public discourse, 147–148,
  192–194, 301
Participation, 192, 273, 280, 286–288,
  319–323
Pascal, Blaise, 182
Pavesich v. New England Life Insurance
  Co., 76, 346–347
Peirce, Charles, 159–161
People v. Ruggles, 101–102, 104
Perry Education Association v. Perry
  Local Educators' Association, 222–
  227, 232, 242, 263–265
Person, legal construction of, 8, 10–12,
  14–15; and autonomy, 10–11, 282–
  286; and community, 10–11, 14–15,
  54–60, 127–134, 138, 180–184, 191–
  196, 300–301, 310–312; and democracy, 8–11, 14–15, 184–196, 282–286,
  300–301, 310–312, 381–382; and
  group identity, 98–100, 106–107,
  113–116, 306–308; and individualism,
  106–108, 113–116, 137–139, 187–188;
  and management, 10–11, 14–15, 239–
  240, 282–286; and pluralism, 98–100,
  106–109, 113–116, 306–309, 320–
  323; public discourse and, 137–139,
  184–196, 272–278, 306–312, 381–382;
  "reasonable," 53–54, 56, 66–67, 72;
  right of privacy and, 51–52, 53–59,
  61–72, 74–88, 127–134, 346
Philadelphia Newspapers v. Hepps, 113,
  394

Piaget, Jean, 7, 187–188, 299, 304,
  448
Pickering v. Board of Education, 254–
  255, 260
Pitkin, Hanna, 35–36, 166
Plessy v. Ferguson, 43
Pluralism, 90–92, 358, 359; assimilationism and, 91–92, 115–116, 303–306;
  and community, 19, 99–100, 115–116;
  cultural pluralism, 91, 358; First
  Amendment and, 107–108, 114–116;
  gender and, 108–116, 307; group
  identity and, 99–100, 114–115, 306–
  310, 445–446; individualism and, 92–
  93, 105–106, 108–110, 114–116, 307;
  pornography and, 108–116, 120–134;
  race and, 115, 306–310, 315–323; religion and, 99–100, 104
Pluralistic Universe, A (James), 91
Pluralist law: assimilationist law and,
  91–92, 97–100; defined, 92; and individualist law, 92, 104–105, 114–116,
  360
Police Department of Chicago v. Mosley, 208–213, 215–216, 220, 223, 226
Polygamy, 90–91
Pornography: Canadian regulation of, 9;
  First Amendment and, 112–116; and
  harm, 109–110, 368; and ideas, 111–
  112; versus obscenity, 89–90, 108,
  112; and pluralism, 108–116, 357; and
  speech/action distinction, 110–111,
  444
Postmodernism, 18, 46–48
Powell, Justice Lewis, 171, 217–218,
  221–223
Precedent. See *Stare decisis*
Preference expressions, 133–134, 156–
  159, 389
Press. See Media, news
Privacy: and accountability, 79–82, 84–
  85; and civility rules, 54–57, 72–74,
  86, 127–128, 346–347; and damages,
  56–59, 132–133, 345; descriptive accounts of, 60–61; and double institutionalization, 65; and First
  Amendment, 349; and hegemony, 64–
  67; and individualism, 3, 51; intrusion,

52–67; and managerial authority, 86–87; and moral tact, 61–64, 72; and newsworthiness, 75–85; normative account of, 60–64, 68–74, 86; and offensiveness, 52–54, 68–74, 350; public disclosure, 67–85; and public discourse, 187–188; and public sphere, 74–85; and secrecy, 351; and surveillance organizations, 86–87; and territories of the self, 61–64; and vindication, 58–59, 73–74. *See also* Intrusion, tort of; Public disclosure
Prosser, Dean William, 52, 131–132
Public concern, matters of: and public discourse, 164–169, 302, 394; and tort of public disclosure, 77–85. *See also* Privacy; Public disclosure; Public discourse
Public disclosure, 67–86; and accountability, 79–82, 84–85; and civility rules, 68–74, 86; and community, 74, 84–85; defined, 67; and information preserves, 72–73; and intrusion, 67–68, 74; and moral tact, 72–74; and newsworthiness, 75–85; and offensiveness, 72; and public figures, 76–77, 80–85; and public sphere, 74–85
Public discourse: autonomy and, 184–196, 272–280, 282–289; boundaries of, 163–177, 191–196, 272–289, 302–303, 312, 431; collective self-determination, 7, 184–187, 272–276, 299–302; community and, 120, 135–140, 148–163, 174–177, 191–196, 310–323, 384–385, 387, 430; critical interaction, 142–148; defined, 7, 140–144, 184–187, 273, 299, 302; democracy and, 7, 142, 145, 184–196, 272–278, 299–300, 312, 400; dignitary torts and, 135–153, 188, 300–302, 310–312; diversity, 140–141, 250–252, 303–304, 313–314, 444; identification and, 192, 273, 286–288, 319–323; individualism and, 138–140, 187–188, 299; legitimation and, 273, 280, 286–288, 319–323, 431; management and, 272–289; marketplace of communities, 138–139, 151; matters of public concern and, 164–174; paradox of, 147–148, 192–194, 301; participation and, 192, 273, 280, 286–288, 319–323; prerequisites for, 140–144, 286–288; public figures and, 164–170, 394–395, 396; rational deliberation, 146–148, 192–193, 312–323; structure of, 140–148; as universe of discourse, 142–144. *See also* Democracy; First Amendment; Freedom of speech; Public concern, matters of
Public figures, 76–85, 126–127, 164–170, 280–281, 394
Public forum doctrine: contemporary doctrine of, 199, 228–223, 404; and the *Davis* syllogism, 203–205, 208–211, 217, 220–224, 231–232, 239, 241, 244, 249, 255, 408; discretion and, 235–236, 262–263; distinguishing management from governance, 247–255; history of, 201–228; and instrumental reason, 256–257, 423; judicial deference and, 236–239, 257–265, 417–418, 422–426; limited public forums, 219–228, 412; managerial authority and, 19, 234–255, 261–265; and metaphors of property, 203–208, 210–214, 217, 223, 229, 246, 255–256, 421–422; nonpublic forums, 19, 231–234, 256–257; reformulation of, 233–247; total institutions and, 261–263; town meetings and, 256–257; tradition and, 203–205, 207–208, 216, 219, 228–230, 413; viewpoint discrimination and, 223, 231, 234–235, 260–261, 414–415
Public/private distinction, 188–189, 280–282, 299, 304–305, 401, 431, 440

Race, 115, 307–309, 442
Racist speech: Canadian regulation of, 9; coercive speech and, 296, 312–323; defined, 293; and democratic legitimacy, 319–323; dignitary harm and, 295, 310–312; English regulation of, 364–365; false consciousness and, 316; group harm and, 294–295, 306–311,

Racist speech (*cont.*)
446; and harms to educational environment, 296–297, 323–330; and
harms to individuals, 295, 310–312,
446; and harms to marketplace of
ideas, 295–296, 312–323; and harms
of violence, 436; intrinsic harm of,
293–294, 303–306; irrational speech
and, 312–315; and nonpublic discourse, 303, 311–312, 323–330; and
public discourse, 302–323; and public/
private distinction, 304–305; and racist personality, 291–292; and speech/
action distinction, 310, 313
Rational deliberation, 146–148, 192–
194, 296, 300–302, 312–323
Rawls, John, 186
Reason: and civility, 95–97, 112, 147–
148, 313–315, 363; and critical inter-
action, 142–148
Reasonable person, 52–53, 420; civility
rules and, 66–67
Redish, Martin, 16
Red Lion Broadcasting Co. v. FCC,
280–281
Regina v. Hetherington, 95–96
Regina v. Lemon, 97–100
Rehnquist, Chief Justice William, 124–
125, 127
Responsive democracy, 188–193. *See also*
Democracy
Responsive interpretation, 35–39, 41–50.
See also Constitutional interpretation;
Doctrinal interpretation; Historical
interpretation
Rex v. Woolston, 95
Reynolds v. United States, 90
Rhetorical hyperbole, 154–156
Ridicule, 129–131, 444
Roberts, Justice Owen, 24, 203–205,
207–208, 216
Roe v. Wade, 43, 341
Rorty, Richard, 182
Rosenbloom v. Metromedia, Inc., 165–
166
Rousseau, Jean–Jacques, 7, 184–185, 273
Rule, James, 86–87
Rule of law, 17, 30–32, 40–41, 65

Rules of deference and demeanor, 54–
56, 181–184

Sandel, Michael, 121, 180–182, 300
Scarman, Lord, 98–100, 103–105
Schauer, Frederick, 16, 184, 187
Schneider v. State, 202–204, 250
Schumpeter, Joseph, 6
Self–determination: autonomy and, 7,
184–188, 272–278, 282–286, 299, 305;
collective, 2, 7–8, 184–188, 272–278,
282–286, 312–323; and collectivist
theory, 268–289; and community,
7–8, 191–196, 300–302, 312–323; and
democracy, 6–8, 184–191, 272–278,
286–288, 299; versus heteronomy,
184–187, 273, 280, 286–288; identification and, 192, 273, 280, 286–288,
319–323; and individualism, 7, 184–
189, 278, 299; and legal rights, 3; legitimation and, 23, 273, 280, 286–
288, 319–323, 431; and
majoritarianism, 184–187, 272–274;
and management, 13–14, 272–278,
286–288; participation and, 192, 273,
280, 286–288, 319–323; public/private
distinction and, 188–189, 280–282,
299, 304–305. *See also* Democracy;
Public discourse
Self–government. *See* Self–determination
Selznick, Philip, 3, 4, 36, 46
Sidis v. F–R Publishing Corp., 78–81
Silencing, 315–323, 445
Simmel, Georg, 61, 175
Social domains: authority and, 12–13;
constitutional law and, 1–2, 15–18,
74–85, 164–177, 191–196, 239–255,
272–289, 329–331; First Amendment
doctrine and, 15–16, 184–196, 239–
255, 272–289; interdependence of, 2,
13–15, 174–178, 189–196, 286–288,
301; judicial justification and, 12–13;
legal construction of, 2, 15–18, 193–
196, 239–265, 286–288; and legal
constructions of the person, 10–12,
195–196, 288–302; and legal system,
2, 12–13, 138, 347
Social personality, 56–57, 132–133, 345

Southeastern Promotions, Ltd. v. Conrad, 214–215, 218, 220, 409
Speech/action distinction, 110–111, 144–148, 190–193, 310, 313, 368–369, 385–386, 444
Stare decisis, 17, 26–32, 38–41, 47
Starkie, Thomas, 75
Steele, Shelby, 308
Stephen, James Fitzjames, 362
Stewart, Justice Potter, 128, 215
Stone, Geoffrey, 16
Street v. New York, 170–171
Subjectivism, 113–134, 139, 157–159
Subordination, 110–111, 310, 315–323
Substantive due process, 9, 37, 188–190, 401
Sunstein, Cass, 269, 279, 283, 285

Talley v. California, 384–385
Taylor, Charles, 105, 106, 182, 273–274
Territories of the self: and civility rules, 60–64; and information preserves, 72–74
Thornhill v. Alabama, 169–170
Tinker v. Des Moines Independent Community School District, 219, 238–239, 242–244, 258–259, 326–327, 417
Tönnies, Ferdinand, 180
Total institutions, 128–129, 261–263
Town meeting, 256–257, 270–272, 274–276
Treatise on the Law of Slander, Libel, Scandalum Magnatum and False Rumours (Starkie), 75
Tussman, Joseph, 35

United States Postal Service v. Council of Greenburgh Civic Associations, 248–250, 253, 419
United States v. Eichman, 298, 440
United States v. Grace, 230–231
Universities: and public forum doctrine, 323–324; and racist speech, 291–292, 296–297, 323–329

Vassiliades v. Garfinckel's, Brooks Bros., 71–74
Verifiability, 157–159
Viewpoint discrimination, 113–114, 223, 231, 234–235, 260–261, 414–415
Vindication, 58–59, 73–74, 345
Voluntary public figures, 76–77
Voneye v. Turner, 71

Warranted deference, 259, 261–265
Warren, Samuel, 51, 57, 66, 73, 76, 166–167
Weber, Max, 12, 85
Westmoreland, General William, 391–392
West Virginia State Board of Education v. Barnette, 93–94
White, Justice Byron, 124–125, 222
Whitehouse, Mary, 98, 363
Whitman, Walt, 91
Widmar v. Vincent, 221–226, 228, 243–244
Williams, Patricia, 295
Wilson, William Julius, 308
Wisconsin v. Yoder, 92–93, 105
Wolin, Sheldon, 277
Wright, J. Skelly, 284–287